A NORTON CRITICAL EDITION

IBSEN'S
SELECTED PLAYS

AUTHORITATIVE TEXTS OF

PEER GYNT
A DOLL HOUSE
THE WILD DUCK
HEDDA GABLER
THE MASTER BUILDER

BACKGROUNDS
CRITICISM

Selected and Edited by

BRIAN JOHNSTON

CARNEGIE MELLON UNIVERSITY

W. W. NORTON & COMPANY

New York • London

W. W. Norton & Company has been independent since its founding in 1923, when William Warder and Mary D. Herter Norton first published lectures delivered at the People's Institute, the adult education division of New York City's Cooper Union. The Nortons soon expanded their program beyond the Institute, publishing books by celebrated academics from America and abroad. By mid-century, the two major pillars of Norton's publishing program—trade books and college texts—were firmly established. In the 1950s, the Norton family transferred control of the company to its employees, and today—with a staff of four hundred and a comparable number of trade, college, and professional titles published each year—W. W. Norton & Company stands as the largest and oldest publishing house owned wholly by its employees.

The text of this book is composed in Fairfield Medium
with the display set in Bernhard Modern.
Composition by PennSet, Inc.
Manufacturing by Maple Press
Book design by Antonina Krass.
Production manager: Ben Reynolds.

ISBN 978-0-393-92404-6 (pbk.)

W. W. Norton & Company, Inc., 500 Fifth Avenue, New York, N.Y. 10110
www.wwnorton.com

W. W. Norton & Company Ltd.
15 Carlisle Street, London W1D 3BS

8   9   0

To Edward Said,
for his example of intellectual
courage and honesty.

Contents

Acknowledgments

Any contemporary translation and interpretation of Ibsen owes a boundless, incalculable debt to innumerable predecessors, beginning with William Archer's first English translation of the *Collected Works*. The late Rolf Fjelde, both as translator and tireless advocate and as founder of The Ibsen Society of America, did most to establish Ibsen as a force in contemporary American scholarship and theater. James Walter McFarlane's *The Oxford Ibsen* edition, with its copious notes, source material, and early drafts of the plays, has been an especially useful resource. Other important influences over the years have cumulatively infiltrated my consciousness and are part of the unconscious 'plagiarism' accrued by all intellectual life.

Francis Pitt supplied invaluable help in accessing permissions for source material, while guilding me through the intricacies of the Internet. He offered valuble suggestions on the illustrations and compiled the "Ibsen on the Internet" section at the end of the Selected Bibliography.

I owe special thanks to the heroic staff of W. W. Norton and Company, especially Carol Bemis and Brian Baker, for bringing coherence to an often chaotic manuscript and for maintaining patience in the face of a succession of revisions.

Gratitude is due to my colleagues and students in the School of Drama, Carnegie Mellon University, for providing a supportive and stimulating environment for my work over the years.

Introduction

Henrik Ibsen's ascendancy to the front rank of European writers in the second half of the nineteenth century was achieved against stupendous odds. He was born in 1828, in Skien, in southern Norway—a small provincial town in a culturally remote outpost of Europe. As William Archer, his first major English translator, wrote: "His Dano-Norwegian language is spoken by some four and a half million people in all, and the number of foreigners who learn it is infinitesimal. The sheer force of his genius has broken this barrier of language."[1] At the age of fifteen, after the bankruptcy of his father, he left home (never to return) to be apprenticed to an apothecary in Grimstad, a small town on the seacoast. He left Grimstad for Christiania (now Oslo) six years later, in 1850, having written a number of verses (some in support of the revolutionary events of 1848) and a tragedy, *Catiline* (1850). Twenty-five years later, he remarked how the play prefigured much of his subsequent work with its "conflict between one's aims and one's abilities, between what man proposes and what is actually possible, constituting at once both the tragedy and comedy of mankind."[2] The play was published just before Ibsen left for Christiania; it was enthusiastically reviewed by a young critic and later friend of Ibsen, Paul Botten Hansen, and quite favorably noticed by a few others, but it failed to interest the public. It sold very few copies and remained unperformed.

Christiania (then a raw, newly emerging "city" of about 30,000) was the capital of a country that had no dramatic tradition. The theater in Norway at the time was dominated by Denmark; its plays were performed mostly by Danish companies and imported from the current European repertory. They included no examples of major drama. Ibsen's early dramatic criticism in Christiania continually deplored the dismal state of the theater and the public's lack of taste. He wrote a one-act play, *The Warrior's Barrow* (1850), that was accepted and produced by the Christiania Theater; edited a student paper; and wrote various journalistic pieces and reviews of plays.

1. *William Archer on Ibsen*, ed. Thomas Postlewait (Westport, Conn.: Greenwood Press, 1984), 55.
2. *Ibsen: Letters and Speeches*, ed. Evert Sprinchorn (New York: Hill and Wang, 1964), 12.

He also had ambitions to be a painter. He was later to abandon this plan, but we can see in his plays a very heightened sense of the visual aspects of drama: he uses the stage space like a canvas to create a thoroughly "composed" and powerful theatrical iconography. *The Warrior's Barrow*, for example, though it handles its huge historical dialectic—the conflict between paganism and Christianity—with considerable naïveté, nevertheless introduces a theatric device that will be of immense importance to the development not just of Ibsen's drama but of modern drama in general. The play, in fact, is named after this device—the onstage visual *symbol*— the Viking, masculine burial mound, recently strewn with flowers from a Christian, feminine hand. The flowers reveal the present at work upon the past represented by the tomb of the pagan warrior. This visual symbol encapsulates the pagan-Christian, masculine-feminine dialectic of the play; the contest between the distant past and the present continues all through Ibsen's work, making it his distinctive theme.

The stage object, however, not only *symbolizes* the conflict; it plays a decisive part in the *action* of the play. In his later plays (such as *A Doll House*) Ibsen will compose the entire stage set simultaneously as a vehicle of symbolic meaning ˙and as an active element of the drama, using meticulous stage directions, lighting, and props as ways of extending the metaphoric action. The set, in fact, will become a major "actor" in an Ibsen play, its props, lighting, and layout all reinforcing the action and extending the overall metaphor of the play. Visual imagery is as important to Ibsen's art as verbal imagery is to Shakespeare's.[3] It creates a "poetry of the theater" for those modern plays, following *Peer Gynt*, in which he abandoned the verse medium and created modern realist drama. The stage space is not just a setting or milieu, but a potent source of metaphors and an integral and active element of the plot. The dynamic interplay between the stage space and the characters who occupy it generates much of the dramatic tension of Ibsen's dramaturgy.

In 1851, Ibsen was engaged as playwright in residence for the newly created Norwegian Theater in Bergen, founded by an eccentric genius, the violinist Ole Bull, (founder of the colony of Oleanna in the United States). Much of Ibsen's artistic responsibility in Bergen consisted of staging what he termed "Scribe and Co's sugar-candy dramas"[4]—that is, well-made plays by, or after the model of, Eugene Scribe, a prolific French dramatist. It is still de-

3. One of the first commentators to detect the importance of this was Jennette Lee in *The Ibsen Secret: A Key to the Prose Dramas of Henrik Ibsen* (1907; reprint, Honolulu, Hawaii: University Press of the Pacific, 2001).
4. In a review of Karl Gutzkow's *Zopf und Schwert*, April 13, 1851. *The Oxford Ibsen* (London: Oxford University Press, 1961), 1:600–603.

bated to what extent the technically adroit but intellectually vapid formula of the "well-made play" influenced Ibsen's dramatic method. Whatever the case, Ibsen's involvement, early in his career, in the actual staging of plays gave him a firm grounding in the technical aspects of the theater.

The standing of the theater in the 1850s was at its lowest, in both Europe and the United States. In Britain, for example, the last new play of any significance to appear until the arrival of *A Doll House* in London in 1889 was Richard Brinsley Sheridan's *The School for Scandal* (1777). During one of the most prolific periods of English-speaking literature, which saw the full flowering of the Romantic movement in poetry and the arts and the rise of the realistic novel as a major literary genre, not a single drama of major significance appeared. It was the period, in fiction, of Austen, the Brontës, Dickens, George Eliot, Hawthorne, Melville, James, Wharton; in poetry, of Blake, Wordsworth, Coleridge, Byron, Shelley, Keats, Tennyson, Browning, Whitman. No other period has been at once so rich in literature and so barren in drama.

In France, a fine dramatic poet such as Alfred de Musset wrote only "closet drama"—intended only for reading—finding the theater unfit for work of any literary value. The French theater, controlled by a vigilant censorship determined to suppress any resurgence of the revolutionary sentiments of 1848, set the dramatic agenda for Europe. The dramatists developed popular, morally stereotypical melodramas in which, as on Broadway today, audiences were dazzled by spectacular stage effects and the violent exercise of conventional emotions. More refined tastes preferred technically adroit, well-made plays whose main themes were adultery and murder in the fashionable classes. Later came "thesis plays"—well-made plays taking up some theme of topical social morality for a thoroughly uncontroversial airing. In 1851, the thesis play *La Dame aux camélias* by Alexandre Dumas created public commotion for the sentimental treatment of its courtesan heroine. The official censor allowed the play to be performed because the scandal usefully distracted attention from the more serious political and financial problems of the government.

In Germany, Friedrich Hebbel (1813–1863) was the last of a line of great German dramatists beginning with Gotthold Ephraim Lessing (1729–1781), and including Johann Wolfgang von Goethe (1749–1832), Friedrich von Schiller (1759–1805), and Heinrich von Kleist (1777–1811). Their works, though, were primarily *literary* dramas with little impact upon the theater of the day. Ibsen's early work reveals influences from the German dramatists and their Danish followers. His first play, *Catiline*, owes a debt to Schiller's *The Robbers*; *Peer Gynt* could not have been written without the precedent of Goethe's *Faust*. By the time Ibsen came to the theater, however, there was no challenge to the flood of popular well-made plays from Paris that, in Bergen, he was obliged to stage.

The theater in Britain and the United States in the nineteenth century had fallen into social disrepute: it was a vehicle for melodrama and farce and a venue for dubious social assignations. No respectable family would venture into such an unsavory milieu—hence the rise of the novel for innocuous "family reading" for the benefit of the middle classes. A handful of Shakespeare's dramas continued to be performed, so drastically "adapted" to the needs of inappropriately elaborate staging and the vanity of actor-managers that Bernard Shaw, in the 1890s, protested that if Sir Henry Irving were to present himself on the stage in as mutilated a condition as he presented Shakespeare's text, a shriek of horror would go up from the entire audience. "In a true republic of art Sir Henry Irving would ere this have expiated his acting versions on the scaffold. He does not merely cut plays: he disembowels them," Shaw remarked of Irving's production of *Cymbeline*.[5]

Attempts at modern verse drama only produced escapist costume drama whose rhetoric was utterly remote from the realities of modern industrial-capitalist society. By the late nineteenth century the British theater struggled to emerge from this disreputable past. In the 1880s the middle classes began to be lured back to the Savoy Theater by the "wholesome" delights of Gilbert and Sullivan, and by theatrical fare to which a father could safely take his young daughter. Reassured that it would encounter nothing unseemly or alarming, the public returned, and in great numbers; the theater suddenly became a very lucrative business, making theater managers excessively cautious about what they deemed fit to offer.

Victorian society concealed a host of skeletons in the closets of its private and public life and maintained highly developed antennae for detecting "impropriety," in response to which it uttered what Henry James, in a review of *Hedda Gabler*, called "those cries of outraged purity which have so often and so pathetically resounded through the Anglo-Saxon world."[6] Theater audiences, from the stalls to the gallery, reflected the class divisions of the nation and there was great fear of alienating any one social group or of setting one class against another. The precautionary strategy of actor-managers was to present works in which the maximum dramatic excitement could be aroused with the minimum of intellectual risk: the formula for most popular drama and cinema today. In the nine-

5. George Bernard Shaw, *Our Theatres in the Nineties* (London: John Constable and Co., 1932), 2:197–98.
6. Henry James, "On the Occasion of *Hedda Gabler*" (1891), in *The Scenic Art* (New Brunswick, N.J.: Rutgers University Press, 1948), 245.

teenth century this meant melodramas and well-made plays plagia-
rized from Paris and bowdlerized in Britain. The huge expense of
mounting a production lavish enough to lure the public meant that
failure threatened financial ruin for all concerned. Oscar Wilde's
strategy of infiltrating subversive commentary on society in his otherwise conventional (and expensive) fashionable melodramas ended
with his own social disgrace and ruin—which only reinforced the
theater's alarm over even the mildest challenge to the status quo.
However, a cultural space was now emerging into which a dramatist independent of the London commercial scene and its moralizing censorship could enter.

Ibsen's volatile confrontation with the theater of his time is one
of the great ironies of cultural history. His identity as a dramatist
was the direct opposite of Wilde's; it seemed almost programmed to
repudiate, at every point, the theatrical medium he was intellectually to dominate. Although he was continually rejected and assailed
by the public, reduced to poverty, in exile, he doggedly worked upon
public hostility and the debased condition of the theater of his time
until he forged a modern drama for his own revolutionary artistic
purposes and vision. Even after his first major success, *Brand*
(1866), at the age of thirty-eight, he kept up his contentious stance
toward the public.

At a time when a playwright was hardly more than a hack sup-
plying "material" to be reshaped by the actor-manager, or an oppor-
tunist reworking approved theatrical formulas, Ibsen, like his
contemporary Richard Wagner in the opera, was determined the
medium should be remade to conform to his artistic demands. More
than Wagner, Ibsen put the integrity of his art above all temptation
to exploit a potentially very lucrative medium. Michael Meyer, in his
biography of Ibsen, estimates that even at the height of his fame, in
the ten years following *A Doll House* in which he created *Ghosts, An
Enemy of the People, The Wild Duck, Rosmersholm, The Lady from
the Sea,* and *Hedda Gabler,* Ibsen earned less from this total output
than a fashionable playwright would make in a single year.[7]

Ibsen's drama required rejecting the falsity of sentimentalized
artistic representations of modern reality; it is an act of total cultural demolition accompanied by an unsettling new idea of what
authentic human life, and art, might be. This meant reformulating
what theatrical art should be. Ibsen's advocates insisted his plays
needed a new kind of presentation, a new kind of acting, to do justice to their revolutionary form. In his critical writings, Bernard
Shaw insisted on the complete unsuitability of the old acting style
for the "New Drama"—a theme taken up by Ibsen's translator,

7. Michael Meyer, *Ibsen, A Biography* (New York: Doubleday, 1971), 472.

William Archer, and by Elizabeth Robins in *Ibsen and the Actress* (1928). The tremendous care with which, in London, the Ibsen texts were translated and prepared for performance, despite pitifully impoverished means and for runs often of no more than two or three days, was something entirely new. The great respect for the author's intentions, and the evolution of a critical tradition to introduce, champion, and interpret the plays in the face of an unremittingly hostile critical reception, constituted a collaborative discipline between scholars, interpreters, actors, and enthusiasts that stood in stark contrast to the cavalier indifference to the text shown by the traditional theater.

A minority public hungry for a theater into which it could take its intellect was evolving; in part this accounts for the astonishing success of Ibsen with the "thinking world" when, in the 1880s, his plays began to appear on the European stage. Ibsen offered a drama that was in tune with the leading ideas and artistic achievements of the time. His audience was made up of a highly critical, often rebellious intelligentsia variously at odds with the aesthetic, moral, political, and religious premises of conventional society. Ibsen's dramas addressed all these levels of cultural alienation. Henry James, Thomas Hardy, George Moore, Oscar Wilde, Bernard Shaw, and James Joyce were among the many who, with the progressive men and women of Europe and, later, the United States, took up the cause of Ibsen and the new independent theater movement. This minority theater, the cradle of serious modern drama, came into being in Berlin (the Freie Bühne, 1889) and London (the Independent Theater, 1891) specifically to perform Ibsen's *Ghosts*. In Paris, André Antoine's recently created *Théâtre Libre* performed *Ghosts* in 1890. George Moore, sitting in the audience, was so moved by the play that he became a founding member of a new Irish Literary Theater—later to become the Abbey Theater.

Drama now followed the other arts by splitting into mutually incompatible—and often hostile—mainstream and minority camps. Performing an Ibsen play was considered virtually an insurrectionary act (*Ghosts* was banned from public performance in England for twenty-three years), and Ibsen became the most vilified, championed, talked- and written-about individual in Europe. "It may be questioned," wrote James Joyce in his review of *When We Dead Awaken*, "whether any man has held so firm an empire over the thinking world in modern times."[8] Within an astonishingly short time the theater, through Ibsen, had shaken off its insignificance and disrepute to became a major, and highly controversial, force in modern culture.

8. James Joyce, "Ibsen's New Drama," *Fortnightly Review* 73 (April 1, 1900): 575–90.

The dominant middle class of the nineteenth century was as potentially tragic—or comic—as any in history. The modern world was a post-Darwinian, industrial-capitalist, pragmatist culture, uncertain of its identity, history, or destiny, and unwilling to acknowledge the sources and consequences of its materialist success. Most art and public discourse supplied a reassuring image of conventional values that the public gratefully consumed. Many thinkers, however, were deeply uneasy about the discrepancy between these flattering images and the grim realities that contradicted them. In response, a revolution in sensibility in all the arts took place, which in literature led to a radical rethinking of the (potentially tragic) human condition. Earlier tragic characters, from Sophocles' Ajax to Jean Racine's Phèdre, agonized over the threat to their *integrity*; the tragic dilemma of Romantic and post-Romantic characters can be stated as loss of *authenticity*: an existential doubt as to whether they have an identity to be true to. This dilemma is exemplified by Ibsen's Peer Gynt, who can ask:

> Was I ever myself? Where, whole and true?
> Myself, with God's seal stamped on my brow?

The terror of nonidentity and the quest for authenticity are the driving forces of Ibsen's drama. They bring Nora Helmer, of *A Doll House*, to realize she knows neither the world she lives in nor her own identity in it. Gregers Werle, of *The Wild Duck*, sees his mission as the rescue of the Ekdal family from a swamp of inauthenticity, presided over by his manipulative father and the dispenser of false identities ("life-lies"), Dr. Relling. The same quest fuels Hedda Gabler's simmering resentment of the role assigned her in the "absurd" world she finds closing around her, and it urges Halvard Solness, of *The Master Builder*, desperately to recover and replay one genuinely authentic, supremely self-willed action: his ascent and challenge to the "Creator." An Ibsen play is the uncovering of an abyss concealed beneath the reality we think we inhabit. It is not the airing of some problem to be put right. As early as 1907, Jennette Lee protested against this still prevalent, anodyne interpretation: "The conception of a problem play as one in which some problem of modern life is discussed by the characters and worked out in the plot is foreign to Ibsen, as to all great artists."[9]

A deep fissure ran through nineteenth-century culture. On the positive side, it was a time of political and intellectual emancipation. From Eastern Europe to Ireland, peoples struggled for independence from foreign rule. There were the stirrings of universal suffrage; the unparalleled advances of knowledge, prosperity, and

9. Lee, *The Ibsen Secret*, 9.

science; and, in the arts, a dynamism such as never had been seen before, creating a series of revolutions in form and subject matter. On the negative side, it was the age, also, of cynical colonial imperialism in the Middle East, Africa, and the Far East; of the dispossession and annihilation of the native inhabitants of North America; of the creation, in Europe, of huge cities with their hideous slums and an exploited proletariat living and working in inhuman conditions. Modern humanity was markedly more rapacious, destructive, and violent than the moral and religious pieties it proclaimed, especially in its literature and art. As the Old Man of the Dovrë tells Peer Gynt:

> You human creatures are all of a kind.
> In your speech it's all "spirit" that governs your deeds;
> But you count on your fists to take care of your needs.

Ibsen's aim was to liberate society's imagination by making it face up to a more adequate idea of itself. This emancipation from self-deceit meant exploring the active presence of the cultural past that lives on in us, making us what we are: those forces and powers that both drive our conflicts and set limits to our capacity for freedom. The past is always ambiguously present in Ibsen's modern plays: on the one hand, it is a power imprisoning our souls, encouraging the lethal atavisms that still plague us—the "ghosts" that Helene Alving, in *Ghosts*, sees as numerous as the grains of sand, making humanity fearful of the light. On the other hand, the past is the reservoir of neglected, forbidden, and banished forces that, if resurrected, could help liberate us from the tyranny of dead habits and thoughts.

For Ibsen, conflict is the healthy condition of the spirit, not the destructive disorder that so appalled the Shakespearean worldview. All that the Shakespearean drama considered positive—order, hierarchy, established tradition—now is seen as unnatural, intolerably constraining, standing in the way of self-determination. The result is that there will be a total change in all the main elements of drama: in dramatic scene, character, action, dialogue. The method of *A Doll House* can stand for all the plays. The *scene*—the pleasant, tastefully furnished Helmer home and its assured place in its community—will be exposed as a realm of unreality, of false consciousness. The social order that sustains the *character* of Torvald as a pillar of society and Nils Krogstad as a social outcast is based on a false idea of reality, one held by most in Ibsen's audience. When Torvald declares, "I literally feel sick when I'm around someone like [Krogstad]," he reveals that he is actually living off the moral as well as financial credit advanced by Krogstad, who performs the convenient role of moral villain by which Torvald can define himself as moral pillar. The separation of humanity into mutually exclusive categories is a common but lethal fiction. "A man shares the responsibilities and the guilt of the society to which he belongs," Ibsen wrote.[1] From the intricate web of human history in which we all are entangled, there is no innocent class, race, or gender.

Under the pressure of events (the *action*), the charming and reassuring Helmer home becomes, in the evolving consciousness of the main character, Nora, first suddenly fragile, something to be desperately defended, then an unbearable prison of inauthenticity from which she flees to search for her own identity and the nature of the world she inhabits. As she undergoes this evolution, the *dialogue* (her language's imagery and key terms—and that of the other characters) also evolves, discarding false concepts and evolving new ones. There is, for instance, the dialectical evolution of the meaning of the key term "wonderful" in the three acts: from material happiness (Act 1), to a romantic fiction of mutual heroism (Act 2), to, finally, a call for a new form of human existence (Act 3). The dialectic is irreversible; there can be no going back to a previous phase of consciousness: the Nora of Act 2 has journeyed irrevocably from the Nora of Act 1 and is evolving the equally irreversible consciousness of the Nora of Act 3. Torvald, too, at the end, no longer inhabits the same world, speaks the same language, or is the same person as in Act 1. Ibsen's theater brings to the Helmers, at Christmastime, the devastating gifts of truth and freedom that everyday life is designed to deny.

Dialectical evolution, in which situations are forced to reveal, and overcome, their inherent contradictions, is the pulse beat of the whole twelve-play Realist Cycle (see p. 142), driving its irreversible sequence of evolving forms from the first play, *Pillars of Society*, to the last, *When We Dead Awaken*. At first glance, no two plays could be more different than these in both subject and dramatic method. Viewed side by side in isolation, they seem to be written by radically different dramatists. But Ibsen insisted on "the mutual connections between the plays," and he added: "Only by grasping and comprehending my entire production as a continuous whole will the reader be able to conceive the precise impression I sought to convey in the individual parts of it. I therefore appeal to the reader that he not put any play aside . . . experiencing them intimately in the order in which I wrote them."[2] If we read the realist plays in order, we will see how *Pillars of Society* and *When We Dead Awaken* are linked in a single, evolutionary chain. This is the imaginative voyage Ibsen invites us to share with him.

---

1. *Letters of Henrik Ibsen*, ed. John Nilsen Laurvik and Mary Morison (New York: Duffield and Company, 1908), 334.
2. *Ibsen: Letters and Speeches*, 330.

Realism, in the nineteenth century, was an extension of the Romantic movement.[3] From Romanticism came the conviction that society and its conventions are forms of false consciousness, of alienation, that stand in the way of achieving our free and full humanity. The purpose of art is not to imitate this "bad" reality but to create an alternative artistic space where it might be possible to see to what extent our potential humanity has been disfigured, warped by history, and what forces might be summoned to restore to us a more adequate human identity. "Art reveals life to us as it should be," wrote Ibsen's son, Sigurd. "If the natural process that life is, for the most part, could ever be organized in such a way that existence should be recreated in the image of humanity, then art would be superfluous: for life itself would have become art."[4] Present life is a defective work of art, a disfigurement of the "image of humanity," which a true artist must seek to restore or re-create.

It is through his plots, working upon the material contained in the play's stories, that Ibsen sets in motion this process of the undoing of false reality. If Ibsen's plays are plot-driven, it is not in order to subject his stories to the thrilling artifices of the theater but because the plots are the dialectic in action, reshaping "bad" reality into a medium more responsive to the possibilities on which everyday reality has turned its back. In the cunning plotting of *A Doll House*, the "false" Nora of the opening action already is being re-created by the pressure of the uncanny coincidence of events, little by little, into the "true" Nora identity that is waiting for her, still as a project only, at the play's end. This is no implausible, sudden change of character: all through the play, one seismic shock after another undermines the reality of her world, as Nora futilely attempts to evade the insight that finally devastates her illusory identity.

Dialectical procedure in drama is as old as Aeschylus. The house of Atreus in the *Oresteia* undergoes its triple convulsion as the trilogy journeys painfully from a world of savage vendetta violence, through the god-directed and suffering avenger, Orestes, to the enlightened world of democratic justice. In *The Master Builder*, the dialectical three-act plot releases the hero, Solness, from his conventional condition of crippling self-reproach and self-torment and sets in motion the recovery of an alternative past and a new, fearful, and fatal liberation. In *The Wild Duck* and *Hedda Gabler* the corrosive action of the dialectic seems to end only in negation; in the cycle as a continuous whole, however, and for us as audience, these, too, are necessary stages of the cycle's evolution.

3. Cf. Charles Rosen and Henri Zerner, *Romanticism and Realism* (New York: W. W. Norton, 1984), *passim*.
4. Sigurd Ibsen, *Human Quintessence* 1911; reprint (Freeport, N.Y.: Books for Libraries Press, 1972), 93.

Ibsen spent all but the last few years of his major creative life in self-imposed exile, reimagining from a distance his Norwegian scene as a metaphoric space for his dramatic vision, a space in which archetypal forces invade the modern scene. Art, wrote Sigurd Ibsen, "gives liberty of action to forces and possibilities to which life does not grant the chance of coming into their rights."[5] The metaphoric space of the cycle extends from "the depths of the sea" (*The Wild Duck*) to the mountain heights and beyond of the last four plays. This landscape of seasons, light and darkness, sunrises and sunsets, storms and avalanches, undertows and cosmic rhythms is echoed as an internal landscape within the responsive characters. To be unresponsive to these natural forces, and to the historical past, means being trapped in the condition of one-dimensional humanity. A note to an early draft of *When We Dead Awaken* reads, "In this country it is only the mountains that give an echo, not the people."[6]

Even before it sought the séance or the psychoanalytic couch, the nineteenth-century middle class was deeply uneasy about itself; it was attacked from the right for its crass materialist values and tastes and from the left for its gross social injustices. This, however, made it an ideal fictional subject. Its tortuous complexities were good dramatic material; the proletariat has not been able to rival it in interest, however much it might surpass it in virtue. This guilt-ridden class, whose passing the cycle seems to envisage, also carried, if only unconsciously, a huge cargo of archetypal memory, the reproachful ghosts that erupt continually to the surface of the psyche and extend the scale of the modern drama.

The present translations are based on the edition *Henrik Ibsen: Samlede Værker* (København og Kristiania: Gyldendalske Boghandel Nordisk Forlag, 1906), vols. 2, 4, 5.

5. *Ibid.*, 92.
6. *The Oxford Ibsen*, 8:355.

THE TEXTS OF THE PLAYS

Peer Gynt (1867)

Peer Gynt is an extremely varied text, with shifts in meter and rhyme patterns. It has frequent changes of scene and alternating dimensions of reality: peasant realism, wild natural settings, supernatural realms of fantasy and fairy tale, cynical entrepreneurial opportunism, extravagant Arabian settings, an insane asylum in Cairo, and more. Sometimes, different locations of the play have different verse patterns. I have attempted an equivalent for this textural variety. Ibsen's play employs rhyme throughout. For the original audience, more familiar with Norwegian folklore traditions, the transitions from reality to folktale fantasy would not need any signaling. For a modern audience, more distanced from traditions of folklore and legend, I thought it helpful to keep the fantastic sequences in rhyme, in contrast to the blank verse of the rest, suggesting an area of the imagination located in Peer's childhood that continually erupts into his adult consciousness. Peer's mother, Åse, describes how she and Peer would console each other with this legendary past:

> . . . we'd retreat into fairy tales,
> You know, princes and trolls and all kinds of beasts . . . [32]

It is natural to think of these tales as persisting like an imaginative reservoir within Peer's mind—a recidivism that increasingly takes over. The shift into rhyme could alert the audience that these sequences are of a different order of experience than the real-life sequences. I let the rhymed passages first appear in Act 2, scene 4, in which Peer, "wild, distraught" after the encounter with the three herd girls, is about to enter his own unconscious in the troll sequence; he actually falls unconscious at the conclusion of a long speech in which, unlike his earlier daydreaming, he is unable to separate reality from fantasy. In later sections, when he struggles to combat this tendency to fantasy (for example, 3.1), I make his language slide in and out of rhyme, matching his vacillating condition.

The inmates of the Cairo madhouse at the conclusion to Act 4 have taken to an extreme and permanent condition Peer's intermittent driftings into unreality. The meter and rhyme scheme drastically change in this sequence; the speeches of Huhu, the Fellah, and Hussein each use a different meter, which suggests that each is hermetically sealed from the condition of the others. I have closely followed Ibsen's verse form here. The speeches need to be reeled off at a manic pitch, revealing speakers completely shut off from normal communication. The asylum

3

director, Begriffenfeldt, tells how the inmates have retreated entirely
into worlds of private fantasy:

> Here a man's himself with a vengeance;
> Himself, and not in the slightest way other—
> Each goes, as himself, full steam ahead.
> Each shuts himself inside a barrel of self . . .
> No one has tears for another's sorrow,
> No one has time for another's ideas,
> We are ourselves in thought and in feeling.
> Ourselves to ambition's uttermost edge. [98]

In Act 5, the sequence of Peer's homecoming gains its poetic density
from the continual intersection of realistic and fantastic sequences, as
if Peer no longer can distinguish fact from fiction. The repeated rever-
sion to rhymed fantasy should suggest an eerily abiding, menacing dimension that always threatens to overwhelm Peer's consciousness as it
did the asylum inmates.'

The play uses typical metaphors of Romantic poetry and drama: the
majestic natural settings, the outlaw or rebel-hero, the journey into the
grotesque, the faithful abandoned lover—all powerful elements of such
Romantic poets as Wordsworth, Byron, and Goethe. In *Peer Gynt*, however, these elements are employed and deflated at the same time as the
hero continually betrays the powerful Romantic values that challenge
him. The reader senses another text shadowing the play's disenchanted
text: a suppressed Romantic text struggling to get out. The most re-
sounding Romantic passage in the play, Peer's account of the reindeer
ride in Act 1, parodies Romantic nature-sublimity; yet at the same time
it introduces powerful metaphors and imagery that will be developed,
contrapuntally, throughout the play. That is, the imagery is doing *more*
work in the drama than the Romantic equivalent it is deflating. E. M.
Forster's justly famous essay "Ibsen the Romantic" (p. 546) describes
how the Romantic metaphors persisted all through Ibsen's work: "All
his life they kept returning to him, clothed in streams, trees, precipices,
and hallowing his characters while they recriminated."[1]

A major achievement of the play is the plausible use of supernatural
figures in a modern drama, the modern equivalent of the supernatural
forces in Greek and Elizabethan drama. Ibsen had the example of
Goethe's *Faust*, but his method is more successful in creating *theatrical*
presences possible for a drama of the modern stage. As serious spiritual
forces (the trolls, the Bøyg, the Strange Passenger, the Button-Molder
and the Lean One) they carry the chill of real terror, standing for our
deepest anxieties. To be recycled in the melting ladle is as desolate a
prospect as the eternity of infernal tortures was for Marlowe's Dr. Faus-
tus. In a post-Einstein cosmos Dante's *Inferno* may no longer terrorize;
our modern imaginations, nevertheless, have metaphysical apprehen-
sions as dismaying as anything the old systems threatened us with.

There is a (probably apocryphal) story that the philosopher Arthur

1. E. M. Forster, *Abinger Harvest* (London: Edward Arnold, 1940), p 85.

Schopenhauer, walking one night in a park, was stopped by a police-man who asked, "Who are you? What are you doing here?" The philosopher replied, "Ah, yes! *Those* are the questions!" Those *are* the questions over which Romantic protagonists agonized. *Peer Gynt* might take a disenchanted view of Romantic aspirations, but it is a thor-oughly Romantic work. In earlier drama, an Oedipus, Electra, Hamlet, Othello or Phèdre at least possessed a strong sense of a self ("Who are you?") and of a violated human order that needed to be expiated or set right ("What are you doing here?"). Even for Shakespeare's most doubt-ing hero, Hamlet, there was "a divinity that shapes our ends," a provi-dence in the fall of a sparrow. In death, Hamlet could ask Horatio to "report me and my cause aright / to the unsatisfied." In his last mo-ments Peer has neither self nor cause to be reported aright, only the failure to discover either self or cause. Ibsen's protagonists experience reality as unreal—as mysterious, threatening, enigmatically challeng-ing, as forcing upon them an unnerving isolation. One critic recently has described it as a "dramaturgy of fear."[2]

The idea that one's self and the world are both equally unknown en-tities, that the self is not a given but a *project*, only, to be "realized," au-thentically or otherwise, in an alien environment, removes all sense of abiding normality, any set of certainties against which the human drama can be played. Ibsen's drama is "existentialist" in the way Jean Paul Sartre described the existential condition:

> Not only is man what he conceives himself to be, but he is only what he wills himself to be after this first thrust towards existence. Man is nothing else but what he makes of himself. Such is the first principle of existentialism.[3]

The crisis that Peer confronts, that he may have no authentic identity at all, is the same that Nora Helmer, Hedda Gabler, and Halvard Sol-ness are brought to experience: of the self and the familiar world dis-solving into unreality.

In the quest myth (for example, in *Gilgamesh*, *The Odyssey*, the Oedi-pus story) the hero leaves home, travels extensively through the world performing heroic actions, meets monstrous and divine beings, de-scends to the underworld, and returns at last to his native home, often with some magic possession or knowledge that might redeem the wasteland his home has become. *Peer Gynt* follows this quest pattern as parody. He leaves home; is outcast; travels over a land and seas; journeys underground (the troll sequence); speaks with monstrous and phantasmal figures; encounters the Sphinx, like Oedipus; and returns, in old age, to a wasteland where his wife, like Odysseus's Penelope, is faithfully waiting. He returns, though, with no healing wisdom or power. His global journey betrays the redemptive purpose of the quest myth.

---

2. Michael Goldman, *Ibsen: The Dramaturgy of Fear* (New York: Columbia University Press, 1999).
3. J. P. Sartre, "Existentialism and Human Emotion," in *Literary and Philosophical Essays*, trans. Annette Michelson (London: Rider, 1955).

The "circuitous journey" of the quest myth, M. H. Abrams reminds us, was linked in Romantic poetry with the parable of the Prodigal Son, another pattern shadowing Ibsen's play:

> The Bible contained an apt, detailed and impressive figure of life as a circular rather than a linear journey, which had been uttered explicitly as a parable of Man's sin and redemption, and by the authoritative voice of Jesus himself. This was the story of the Prodigal Son (Luke 15:11–32) who collected his inheritance and "took his journey into a far country, and there wasted his substance with riotous living: then, remorseful, made his way back to his homeland and the house of his father, who joyously received him, clothed him in the best robe, a ring and shoes, and ordered the fatted calf that they might "eat, and be merry: For this my son was dead, and is alive again; he was lost, and is found."[4]

In Act 5 the play also takes on the aspect of a morality play, such as the medieval *Everyman*, in which the hero is summoned to discover some redeeming aspect of his life as he prepares for his death. The famous "Onion episode" of the disillusioned old man summoning layer after layer of his past for a recapitulation of former nonidentities anticipates Samuel Beckett's *Krapp's Last Tape*, in which a lonely old man plays back tapes recorded at previous disillusioning stages of his life.

Peer Gynt, however, is far from being a lugubrious allegory. What most impresses is the boundless energy and high spirits of its hero, who has the comic improvisational agility of a dropped cat always to land on its feet. Although Peer is not the lovable rogue some have claimed, he possesses what will be called in a later play, *Ghosts*, "joy of life" (*livsglede*)—a resourcefulness and energy that exults in living. This is what Solveig perceives at the Haegstad wedding feast at which she and Peer "change eyes" and enact a true marriage, in contrast to the socially approved but cynical marriage of Ingrid and Mads Moen.

The play honors as much as it deplores Peer's mental agility, which can superficially play at any role or take up any subject, and which is matched by an amazing physical agility. The number of physical actions given to Peer exceeds, perhaps, that of any other hero of drama. Peer runs; jumps; carries his mother through a stream; wrestles; rides a reindeer in space (in imagination where lie and physical agility combine); climbs mountains; carries off and has sex with a bride, three herd girls, a troll woman, and a Bedouin girl; rides various steeds; crosses a desert; fights with trolls and monkeys; is shipwrecked; swims; crawls on all fours; and, finally exhausted, collapses in Solveig's arms. The actions given him seem to make up the entire range of physical human ability.

Yet for all this mobility, Peer spiritually gets nowhere, as the play makes clear by showing a persistent pattern of *repetition*. The reindeer ride is a piece of fraudulent boasting on Peer's part, but it also is a variably recurring metaphor in the play. It is first described in that collision where

4. M. H. Abrams, *Natural Supernaturalism* (New York: W. W. Norton, 1971), p 165.

> . . . there below us, something flashed
> White, just like a reindeer's belly!
> Mother, it was our own reflection
> Hurtling up through the dark water
> To the mirror-surface of the lake
> As fast as we sped down to meet it! . . .
> Buck plunging down, buck hurtling upward
> Collide, horns tangling, in one instant;
> A burst of foam cascades over us. [12]

Not only does it introduce the image of Peer and his various "mounts"—from reindeer, to pig, to Arabian stallion, to upturned dinghy—here, in the mirror identities, above and below, hurtling toward each other, is a brilliant metaphor for an unresolved collision of conscious and unconscious forces that will be repeated all through the play. The Haegstad wedding feast, where Peer is attacked, is repeated in the troll underworld "wedding": the Woman in Green and her hideous offspring erupt from the underworld to invade the outlaw hut in which Peer and Solveig are to set up their home. In Act 4 the insane asylum is the extreme version of this mental division, where fantasies from the unconscious totally take over reality. In Act 5 the two areas, world and underworld, conscious and unconscious, are helplessly confused as Peer journeys through a landscape of his own disordered and disintegrating imagination. The pattern of repetition becomes more evident if the same actors play the wedding guests, the trolls, the monkeys, the asylum dwellers, and the funeral guests of 5; and if Ingrid, the Woman in Green, and Anitra are played by the same actress. Peer's "progress" through the world becomes a spiritual paralysis.

This is the condition the spirit is doomed to if it accepts the troll condition of "to yourself be enough" instead of the human "to yourself be true." Being true to yourself is to achieve your best potential self: "You shall become who you are"—a goal of modern liberation movements (and of every fitness class!). As the Button-Molder tells the uncomprehending Peer, "To be yourself means to slay yourself": to slay "that false self competently adjusted to our alienated social reality" (as R. D. Laing expressed it)[5] that prevents you from becoming who you are. Dialectical thinking is shadowed by the anxiety of unattained identity. "Say where's Peer Gynt been . . . with his destiny's mark on his brow . . . since he sprang new from God's thought!" [140], Peer finally cries out to Solveig; her answer insists he exists only as *potentiality*: an attainable identity preserved only within her faith, hope, and love.

In *Peer Gynt*, Ibsen created for modern drama an existential portrait of modern man: immensely resourceful yet without direction, unable to invest his material and intellectual world with compelling reasons for continuing. Ibsen's fellow Scandinavian, Søren Kierkegaard, described this modern condition:

> Our age reminds one of the dissolution of the Greek city-state:
> Everything goes on as usual and yet there is no longer anyone who

5. R. D. Laing, *The Politics of Experience* (New York: Pantheon Books), p 119.

Playbill for Théâtre de l'Oeuvre, 1896. Copyright © 2003 The Munch Museum/The Munch-Ellingsen Group/Artists Rights Society (ARS), NY.

believes in it. The invisible spiritual bond which gives it validity, no longer exists, and so the whole age is at once comic and tragic— tragic because it is perishing, comic because it goes on.[6]

Peer Gynt, whose hero is tragic because he is perishing, comic because he goes on, is Ibsen's last verse drama; it also, arguably, is the last major verse play. Ibsen himself predicted that the future of modern drama did not lie with verse, a prediction he more or less single-handedly brought about by creating for modern drama a "poetry of the theater" that has proved irresistible. Yet no more impressive a leave-taking of verse drama can be imagined than this prodigious *Peer Gynt*.

Peer Gynt†

Characters

ÅSE,[1] a farmer's widow
PEER GYNT,[2] her son
TWO WOMEN carrying sacks of grain
ASLAK, a blacksmith
WEDDING GUESTS, THE MASTER OF CEREMONIES, FIDDLERS, etc.
A NEW COUPLE from outside town
SOLVEIG and LITTLE HELGA, their daughters
THE FARMER at Haegstad
INGRID, his daughter
THE BRIDEGROOM and HIS PARENTS
THREE HERD GIRLS
A WOMAN DRESSED IN GREEN
THE OLD MAN OF DOVRE
A TROLL COURTIER, SEVERAL SIMILAR TROLLS
TROLL GIRLS and TROLL CHILDREN, A PAIR OF WITCHES
TROLL FIGURES, BROWNIES, NIXIES, GNOMES, etc.
AN UGLY TROLL-CHILD, A VOICE IN THE DARKNESS, BIRD CRIES
KARI, a peasant neighbor to ÅSE
MR. COTTON, M. BALLON, HERREN VON EBERKOPF and
TRUMPETERSTRÅLER, traveling gentlemen
A THIEF and A RECEIVER
ANITRA, daughter of a Bedouin chief
ARABS, FEMALE SLAVES, DANCING GIRLS, etc.
THE MEMNON STATUE (singing), THE SPHINX AT GEZA (mute)
BEGRIFFENFELDT, professor, Ph.D., director of the madhouse in
    Cairo

6. Søren Kierkegaard, *Either/Or* (New York: Doubleday Anchor), 2:19.
† Translated by Brian Johnston. Published for the first time in this Norton Critical Edition.
1. Pronounced "Aw-suh."
2. Pronounced "Pair Günt."

    HUHU, a language reformer from the coat of Malabar
    HUSSEIN, an Eastern Minister
    A FELLAH with a royal mummy
    SEVERAL MADMEN with their keepers
    A NORWEGIAN SKIPPER and his CREW, A STRANGE PASSENGER,
    A PASTOR, A FUNERAL PARTY, A PARISH OFFICER, A BUTTON-
        MOLDER, A LEAN PERSON.

[The action, which opens in the beginning of the nineteenth century and ends toward Ibsen's own time (1867), takes place in Gudbrandsdalen and the surrounding mountains, in Norway; on the coast of Morocco, in the Sahara; in a madhouse in Cairo; and returns to the Norwegian setting.]

Act One

SCENE ONE

A hillside with birch trees near Åse's farm. A river bubbles over the slope. On the other side is an old mill shed. It is a hot day in summer.
    Peer Gynt, a strongly built boy of twenty, comes down the pathway. Åse, his mother, is following him, angry and scolding.

ÅSE Peer, you're lying.
PEER   I'm *not* lying.
ÅSE Then let's hear you swear it's true.
PEER Why should I swear?
ÅSE   You see, you daren't!
   All you've said is a heap of rubbish.
PEER (*Halting.*) No, it's true—everything I told you.
ÅSE (*Confronts him.*) Aren't you ashamed? And to your own mother!
   First you go running off to the mountains,
   Chasing reindeer the whole month long,
   Just when I need you here at home;
   Then you come back, your clothes in shreds,
   Losing your gun and no game to show for it.
   And there you stand, acting the wide-eyed
   Innocent, expecting me to swallow
   Your pathetic pack of hunter's lies!
   Let's hear, then! Where'd you meet this buck?
PEER West of Gjendin.[3]
ÅSE (*Laughs scornfully.*) Oh yes, naturally.
PEER I waited there, crouching in the icy wind;

---

3. Pronounced "*Yendeen.*" An extremely precipitous mountain edge in Jotunheimen, Norway.

And then, hidden behind a clump of alders,
There he was!—pawing at the snow
Looking for moss—

ÅSE (*As before.*)   Yes, of course!

PEER I hold my breath, keep still, and listen—
Can hear the scraping of his hoof,
Just glimpse one antler jutting out.
I duck between the boulders. On my belly,
Snaking forward so as not to be seen,
I catch full sight of this splendid buck,
Sleek and fat, the kind of quarry
Your eyes seldom get to feast on.

ÅSE Oh yes, I bet!

PEER   Then bang! I fired.
Down the buck crumpled to the ground.
The moment he fell I was on his back.
I grab his left ear with one hand,
Ready to drive the blade of my knife
Behind his skull, right into his neck,
When hei!—the brute lets out a bellow
And in one bound is back on his feet.
He jerks his head. With one sharp blow,
Whams my knife and sheath out of reach,
Then pins me down right at the waist,
And using his horns like a pair of tongs,
Jams my legs in a vice and lifts me,
Then leaps away, flying full speed
Across the sheer height of the Gjendin ridge!

ÅSE (*Involuntary.*) Oh my God!

PEER   Have you ever
Seen the Gjendin Ridge? It stretches
Nearly four miles long—way, way up high.
There it runs, sharp as a knife-edge,
Over glaciers, landslides, jutting ledges
And precipices dropping sheer beneath.
On either side you see distant, deep
Pools of black water, in slumbering stillness,
More than a thousand yards below.
The pair of us raced across that ledge,
Cutting our way through the keen wind,
Launched on the wildest ride of my life!
As we sped on that frantic journey,
Suns seemed to flash between the peaks.
Brown backs of eagles veered and hovered
Below, in that dizzying stretch of space,

Halfway between us and the water,
Then dropped away like specks beneath us.
Ice floes down there cracked and shattered,
Yet their clamor never reached me.
All I sensed were shadows whirling,
Like manic dancers, circling, singing,
In a frantic mix of sights and sounds!

ÅSE (*Giddy.*) God preserve us!

PEER   All at once,
We pitched onto the ridge of a precipice.
Then, right into our faces, a ptarmigan flew
From its hiding place down at our feet,
Flapping, squawking up from the rocks
Making the buck veer wildly and leap
Out over the abyss, the pair of us plunging!
(*Åse sways and totters, gripping a tree-trunk. Peer continues.*)
Behind us, the black wall of the mountain;
Beneath us, dropped the bottomless chasm.
First, we fell into drifting fog-clouds,
Next, cleaved through a flock of gulls
That scattered wildly in all directions,
Filling the air with their angry screeching.
Down, down, we plunged precipitously,
Until, there below us, something flashed
White, just like a reindeer's belly!
Mother, it was our own reflection
Hurtling up through the dark water
To the mirror-surface of the lake
As fast as we sped down to meet it!

ÅSE (*Gasping for breath.*) Peer! For God's sake—tell me quickly—!

PEER Buck plunging down, buck hurtling upward
Collide, horns tangling, in one instant;
A burst of foam cascades over us.
And there we were, splashing and swimming
For hours, imagine! before we managed
Somehow, to struggle to the north shore.
The buck did the swimming; I hung on behind.
Then I came home . . .

ÅSE   And the buck, Peer?

PEER Oh, he's probably still back there—
(*Snapping his fingers, turns on his heels and continues.*)
If you find him, you're welcome to him!

ÅSE And your neck—tell me, it isn't broken?
Neither of your legs hurt, nor your spine?
I give praise and thanks to the good Lord,

For taking care of my dear boy.
You've torn your trousers, but that's nothing,
When I think what such a terrifying fall—
(*Suddenly stops, looks at him open-mouthed and with staring eyes,
unable to speak. Then she bursts out*)
Oh, you shameless little devil!
God in Heaven, what lies you tell!
All this drivel you've come out with—
Now I remember hearing most of it
When I was still a girl of twenty.
It was Gudmund Glesne it happened to,
Not you, you—
PEER   To me, as well as him.
   Such things can happen more than once.
ÅSE Oh yes, a lie can be refashioned,
   Stuck about with rags of ranting
   So it looks like something new,
   And no one sees the rotten carcass.
   That is all you've ever accomplished;
   Embroidering lurid and wild details,
   Like all that business with eagles' backs,
   And the rest of that fantastic nonsense;
   Mixing the familiar and the strange,
   Frightening me almost out of my wits,
   Until I scarcely could recognize
   Stuff I'd known since I was a child.
PEER If anyone else spoke to me like that,
   I'd grab him and beat him to a pulp!
ÅSE (*Weeping.*) Oh God, if only I could die,
   Just lie in peace in the dark earth!
   Prayers and tears don't seem to reach you.
   Peer, you are lost and always will be.
PEER Dearest, prettiest little mother!
   You're right in every word you say,
   Now, try to be nice and happy—
ÅSE   Hold your tongue!
   How could I be happy, even if I wanted to,
   With a great lout like you for a son?
   Don't I have cause to be bitter—
   A poor, helpless, struggling widow,
   Whose only reward is endless shame?
   (*Crying again.*)
   What's become of all the grandeur
   From your grandad's glory days?
   Where are all those bags of money

Left us by old Rasmus Gynt?
Your father sure gave them feet to scurry.
Scattering the cash as free as sand,
Buying up land in every parish,
And riding around in a gilded carriage.
What's become of all he wasted
On those lavish winter feasts,
Where guests hurled bottles and glasses
At the tapestries hanging on the walls?
PEER What's become of last year's snow?
ÅSE Shut up when your mother's speaking!
Look at this farmhouse! Every other
Window pane stuffed with filthy rags.
Hedges and fences wasted, broken,
Cattle exposed to the wind and weather,
Fields and meadows lying fallow,
And the bailiff calling every month—
PEER What's the point of all this whining?
You know how, when our luck looks bleakest,
It can spring to life as fresh as ever.
ÅSE Not where salt tears water the ground.
God in Heaven, you're a smart aleck,
Still as cocky and conceited
As on the day that pastor called;
The one that came from Copenhagen
And asked about your Christian name;
Flattering us that where he came from
Princes hadn't half your talents.
As a reward for *that* fine compliment,
Your father gave him a horse and sleigh!
Ah, yes! We were swells in those days!
Bishops, Captains, all the gentry
Hung their hats here, eating, drinking,
Stuffing themselves to bursting point.
You soon find out fair-weather friends, though!
The house became uncannily silent,
As empty as Jon Gynt's moneybags,
When he took to peddling on the highways.
(*Drying her eyes with her apron.*)
You've got a fine, strong body on you;
You ought to be a pillar of support
To your poor old helpless mother.
You should be working here on the farm,
Protecting what little you've inherited.
(*Crying again.*)
God knows what kind of help you've been,

Whenever I most needed you, you lout!
Loafing by the fireside raking ashes,
Or annoying the townsfolk, and frightening
All the girls at the barnyard dances,
Making me the laughingstock of the parish;
And brawling with the local bullies—

PEER (*Moving off.*) Stop pestering me!

ÅSE (*Following him.*) Are you going to deny
You were the chief cause of that commotion
That ruckus the other day at Lunde,
Where the lot of you scrapped like a pack of dogs?
And wasn't it you who broke the arm
Of Aslak the blacksmith, or at the least,
Dislocated one of his fingers?

PEER Who's been filling you with that garbage?

ÅSE (*Fiercely.*) The neighbor's wife heard all the yelling.

PEER (*Rubbing his elbow.*) Yes, but I was the one doing the
yelling.

ÅSE You?

PEER Yes, mother—me: I got the beating.

ÅSE What's that?

PEER Well, he's really tough.

ÅSE Who's tough?

PEER He is. Aslak, as I found out!

ÅSE Ecch! Ecch! Now I want to spit.
You mean you let that walking keg,
That drunken punk, that boozing lout,
That—bloated sponge bag—give you a pasting?
(*Weeping again.*)
I've put up with many humiliations,
But that a thing like this could happen to me—
That absolutely is the worst.
Even though he's a hefty fellow
Do you have to take a thrashing from him?

PEER What's the difference? If I beat or get beaten,
You're going to moan about it either way!
(*Laughing.*)
Take it easy, Ma—

ÅSE What's this? Were you lying
All over again?

PEER Yes, I was, just this one time
So, now you can go dry your eyes.
(*Clenching his fist.*)
See! With this powerful pair of tongs
I held the smith in my grip like a vice,
Then worked my fist like a sledgehammer—

ÅSE Oh, you brawling lout! The trouble you cause me
    Will bring me to an early grave!
PEER No, you're worth a lot more than that!
    Twenty thousand times more worth,
    Little, ugly, dearest mother!
    You can take my word for it; I promise,
    This whole district's going to honor you;
    Just wait until I get to do something—
    Something—that's going to be really tremendous.
ÅSE (*Snorting.*) You!
PEER   Who knows what I might come up with?
ÅSE If you could just come up with enough sense
    Now and then to do some necessary repairs
    To your own pants, that might be something.
PEER (*Exultantly.*) I'm going to king, emperor!
ÅSE Well, God help us, there goes the last
    Remnant of what's left of his mind!
PEER I will, though! Just you give me time!
ÅSE Given time, yes, you'll become a Prince
    As the saying goes, if I remember right.[4]
PEER You'll get to see it—
ÅSE   Hold your tongue!
    You're mad, both inside and out.
    All the same, it has to be said
    Something could have been made of you
    If you hadn't wasted all of your days
    Lost in a world of lies and fantasies.
    That Haegstad girl had her eye on you.
    You could have had her for the asking,
    If you'd seriously gone after her.
PEER You think so?
ÅSE   The old man hasn't the will
    To go against his daughter's wishes.
    He might be stubborn in his habits,
    But Ingrid gets her way in the end,
    And where she leads though the father grumbles,
    He always follows in her footsteps.
    (*Starts crying again.*)
    Oh, my Peer; that girl's worth plenty—
    All she'll inherit—just think of it!
    If only you'd set your mind to it,
    You'd be standing there, a splendid bridegroom;
    Not like you're standing here, a tramp.

---

4. *Ja, gi tid, så blir du prins, sies der,* "Given time, you'll be a prince, as they say."

PEER (*Briskly.*) Come on then, it's high time to get going.
ÅSE To where?
PEER   To Haegstad!
ÅSE   You're out of luck;
   That road to matrimony's closed off.
PEER How come?
ÅSE   Ah, I could cry out loud!
   "Where the carcass is, there the eagles gather."
PEER So?
ÅSE   All the time you were with your reindeer
   Riding over the hills and far away
   Mads Moen rode to the farm and got the girl.
PEER What! That antidote to love? Ingrid to *him*?
ÅSE Well, he's the one she chose to marry.
PEER Wait for me here, until I've harnessed
   The horse and wagon—
   (*Going.*)
ÅSE   You can spare the effort;
   The wedding's taking place tomorrow.
PEER What of it? I'll be there this evening.
ÅSE You idiot! Will you add to our miseries
   Making yourself a laughingstock again?
PEER Trust me, everything will go fine.
   (*Shouting and laughing.*)
   Let's get going, Ma! We'll leave the cart
   It'll take too long to bridle the mare.
   (*He lifts her into the air.*)
ÅSE Let me down!
PEER   Not on your life!
   I'm carrying you to the wedding feast.
   (*Wading into the stream.*)
ÅSE Help! The Good Lord Jesus save us!
   Peer! We'll drown.
PEER   I am destined
   For a more glorious death—
ÅSE   Oh, yes!
   You're definitely marked out for hanging.
   (*Pulling his hair.*)
   You great brute!
PEER   Now, keep still!
   My feet are sliding around on slime.
ÅSE Jackass!
PEER   That's right, only use your mouth;
   That way you won't do any harm.
   Ah! Now the ground's sloping up again.

ÅSE Don't you drop me!
PEER   Hei, giddyap!
  Let's play at being Peer and the buck;
  (*Jigging her up and down.*)
  I'll be the buck; you can be Peer.
ÅSE Oh, I'm going out of my mind!
PEER There! Now we're back on firm ground.
  (*Climbing the bank.*)
  So give the nice buck a grateful kiss
  For the lovely ride you've just enjoyed—
ÅSE (*Boxes his ear.*) That's all the thanks you're getting!
PEER   Ow!
  Now that was not a proper payment!
ÅSE Put me down!
PEER   First to the wedding feast!
  You speak up for me. You're clever enough.
  Talk to the old man on my behalf,
  Tell him Mads Moen's a total loss—
ÅSE Down!
PEER   Let him know what he'll be missing,
  What kind of bargain he'll get in Peer Gynt.
ÅSE Ooooh! You can bet your life I will!
  I'll paint a lovely character likeness.
  A truly lifelike rendering
  Of every one of your devil's pranks;
  That's what I'll show, depend on it.
PEER Oh?
ÅSE (*Kicking in rage.*) I won't give my tongue a minute's rest
  Until the old man sets his dogs on you,
  Treating you like the tramp you are!
PEER Hm! Then I'd better go alone.
ÅSE Ah! But I'll be following close after!
PEER Little mother, you don't have the strength.
ÅSE Is that so? I'm so furious
  I've the stamina for smashing stones!
  I could make a meal of flints!
  Put me down!
PEER   Only if you promise—
ÅSE Nothing! I'm going there with you
  To make sure they'll know just who you are!
PEER Is that so? Then it's best you wait here.
ÅSE Never! I'm going to the wedding feast.
PEER Oh no you're not!
ÅSE   How will you stop me?
PEER By setting you up here on the mill house roof.
  (*He puts her there. Åse screams.*)

Åse Take me down!

PEER   Only if you listen—

Åse Rubbish!

PEER   Now mother, I'm asking you—

Åse (*Throwing roof-turf at him.*) Get me down at once, Peer!

PEER If I could, I would; but I just daren't.
   (*Comes closer.*)
   Remember, now, try to sit still.
   Don't kick and wriggle your legs about,
   Or start dislodging and chucking the shingles.
   You could slip and begin a painful fall
   And even get nastily hurt.

Åse   You beast!

PEER Don't excite yourself!

Åse   You should have been
   Shot up the chimney like a changeling.[5]

PEER Now that's not nice, Ma!

Åse   Pah!

PEER   Just give me
   Your blessing on my perilous journey.
   Come, do it!

Åse   I'll give you a beating
   Even if you are a big lout!

PEER "Then fare you well, my mother dear"—
   Just keep patient, I won't be long.
   (*Starts to go but turns and lifts a warning finger to her.*)
   Remember now, don't get too excited!
   (*He goes.*)

Åse Peer! God help me, he's really going!
   Reindeer-rider! Rotten liar! Hei!
   Do you hear me? No, he's disappearing
   Over the fields.
                   (*Screams.*) Help! I'm dizzy.
   (*Two old women with sacks on their backs come down the path.*)

FIRST WOMAN Lord, who's screaming?

Åse   Here! It's me!

SECOND WOMAN Åse! Why, how you've come up!

Åse Not enough! This is just the start.
   Soon, God knows, I'll be in heaven.

FIRST WOMAN Pleasant journey!

Åse   Fetch a ladder;
   I've got to get down. That devil, Peer—

SECOND WOMAN That son of yours?

Åse   Now you can say,

5. In Norwegian folklore, changelings left in place of children stolen by elves can be made
   by magic to disappear up the chimney.

You've seen the kind of thing he does.

FIRST WOMAN We'll be witness.

ÅSE   Just help me down.
   I'm about to make my way to Haegstad.

SECOND WOMAN That's where he is?

FIRST WOMAN   You'll get your own back.
   The blacksmith's going to be one of the guests.

ÅSE Oh God help us! The poor boy,
   They'll kill him when they've done with him.

FIRST WOMAN They've been talking of doing it long enough.
   It's high time they did something about it.

SECOND WOMAN She seems to have taken leave of her senses.
   (*Calling out.*)
   Hi, Eivind, Anders! Come over here!

MAN'S VOICE What's going on?

SECOND WOMAN   Peer Gynt has stranded
   His mother up on the mill house roof.

SCENE TWO

*A small hill covered with bushes and heather. The main road runs be-
hind it; a fence lies between. Peer Gynt comes along a footpath, hurries up to the fence, stops, and looks over at the view before him.*

PEER Down there lies Haegstad. I could soon be there.
   (*Half climbs over the fence but then thinks about it.*)
   I wonder if Ingrid's sitting alone now.
   (*Shades his eyes as he looks down the hill.*)
   No. The guests are already swarming like midges.
   Hm. It's probably wisest I turn back home.
   (*He draws back his leg from the fence.*)
   They snigger and sneer behind your back,
   And that whispering can burn right through you.
   (*Steps away from the fence and starts plucking leaves from a bush.*)
   If I only had a drink to set me up;
   Or could be invisible as I walk among them;
   Or if I were a stranger. Best, a strong drink;
   That way, the bite of their laughter can't hurt.
   (*He looks round, startled, and then conceals himself among the
   bushes. Some Wedding Guests pass by on their way to the farm.*)

A MAN His dad was a drunk and his mother's a mess.

A WOMAN Yes, small wonder the boy's a basket case.
   (*They move off. Shortly after, Peer Gynt emerges, red with shame
   and staring after them.*)

PEER Was it me they were talking about?

(*With a half-hearted shrug.*)
                                        Well, let them talk!
All their talk's not going to kill me.
(*Throws himself down in the heather, lies for some time on his
back with his hands under his head and stares up at the sky.*)
What a peculiar cloud. It looks just like a horse.
There's a man on it too—and a saddle—a bridle—
And right behind an old witch on a broomstick.
(*Laughing quietly to himself.*)
It's Ma! She's screaming and scolding her loudest.
Hi there, Peer—you beast!
(*Gradually closing his eyes.*)
                            Yes, and now she's frightened.
Peer Gynt rides ahead of a great procession.
The horse's harness is silver, its shoes are gold,
While *he* wears gauntlets, a saber and scabbard.
His cloak hangs loosely, showing silk lining.
He has a shimmering train of lords and ladies,
But no one sits prouder than Peer on his horse,
Or gleams more finely in the bright sunshine.
By the roadside fence crowds throng eagerly,
Lifting their hats to gaze up in wonder.
Women are curtseying. All of them recognize
Emperor Peer and his thousand courtiers.
Casually, he flings coins of silver and gold
That scatter and glitter on the wayside.
The parish folk now are richer than lords.
Peer Gynt imperiously crosses the ocean
Where Engelland's[6] prince and Engelland's maidens
Are eagerly waiting on the seashore.
Engelland's nobles and Engelland's monarch
Stand to attention when Peer approaches.
Lifting his crown their Emperor speaks—
ASLAK THE SMITH (*To some others as they pass by the other side of the
    fence.*)
    Well, look here—it's that drunken pig, Peer—!
PEER (*Half rising.*) What, my lord—?
ASLAK (*Grinning over the fence.*) Come on now, get up, boy!
PEER What the devil! The blacksmith! What do you want?
ASLAK (*To the others.*) He's still reeling from the fight at Lunde.
PEER (*Leaping up.*) Just get going.
ASLAK   That's what I'm doing.
    But you—where have you been the last six weeks?

6. The old ballad-form of "England" that Peer would have learned as a child in fairy tales.
   The connotation of "angel-land" (engel-land) adds to the daydream's cloudy fantasizing.

Did you get spirited away by the trolls?
PEER What I've been doing is unbelievable.
ASLAK (*Winking to the others.*) Let's hear it, Peer!
PEER   It's not for you to hear.
ASLAK (*After a pause.*) Are you going to Haegstad?
PEER   No.
ASLAK   There was a time
They say, the girl had her sights on you.
PEER You filthy crow—!
ASLAK (*Backing off.*) Take it easy, Peer!
Though Ingrid's done with you, there's plenty left.
Think—the son of Jon Gynt! Come with us to the feast.
You'll find soft wenches and well-seasoned widows—
PEER To hell—
ASLAK There'll be someone there who won't mind having you.
So, good evening. I'll give the bride your greetings.
(*They go off laughing and whispering.*)
PEER (*Stares after them, shrugs and half turns away.*)
The Haegstad girl can marry whomever she likes
For all I care. I don't give a damn.
(*Looks himself over.*)
Trousers torn. Dirty and ragged.
If I just had something new to wear.
(*Stamps on the ground.*)
If only I had the skill of a butcher
To cut the mockery out of their hearts.
(*Looking suddenly about him.*)
What was that? Someone sniggering behind me?
Hm. I thought I heard—No it was nothing.
I'll go home to mother.
(*Begins to go up the hill, but stops again and listens to sounds from
the wedding feast.*)
                              They've started the dancing!
(*Staring and listening, starts moving down the hill, his palms rub-
bing his thighs.*)
The place is teeming with girls—seven, eight to a man!
Oh, death or disaster, I've got to join in.
But what about mother, stuck alone on the roof?
(*His eyes stray back to the farm. He leaps up, laughing.*)
Hei! Just listen how they're playing the halling[7]—
And that Guttorm's really great on the fiddle—
And then, that glittering flock of young girls—
Yes, death or disaster, I've got to join in!

---

7. A leaping folk dance, performed by young men to display acrobatic skill.

SCENE THREE

Courtyard at Haegstad. The farmhouse to the rear. Many Guests. Lively dancing going on on the grass. The Fiddler is sitting on a table. The Master of Ceremonies stands in the doorway. Kitchen Maids go back and forth between the buildings. Older People sit around here and there, talking.

A WOMAN (*Taking her place among a group sitting on a pile of logs.*)
   The bride? Oh yes, she's crying a bit.
   But you shouldn't pay any attention to that.
MASTER OF CEREMONIES (*To another group.*)
   Come on, friends, let's see you empty the jug.
A MAN Many thanks, but you're filling it up too fast.
A BOY (*To the fiddler, while he dances past with a girl on his arm.*)
   Hey there, Guttorm, don't spare the strings.
A GIRL Play so it carries right over the meadows.
GIRLS (*In a ring round a boy dancing.*) Look at him leaping!
A GIRL   He's got steel in his legs!
THE BOY (*Dancing.*) Out here, the roof's high and the walls wide
   apart.[8]
THE BRIDEGROOM (*Whimpering, approaching his father, who is engaged in conversation with a couple of other men, and pulling on his sleeve.*)
   She won't father, she's much too proud.
FATHER What is it she won't?
BRIDEGROOM   She's locked herself in.
FATHER Well, it's up to you to find the key.
BRIDEGROOM I don't know the way.
FATHER   You're a blockhead.
   (*Turning to the others again. The Bridegroom wanders across the yard.*)
A BOY (*Coming from behind the house.*) Girls! Now it's going to liven up!
   Peer Gynt's just come into the yard.
ASLAK (*Who has just appeared.*) Who invited him?
MASTER OF CEREMONIES (*Going to the house.*) Nobody I know.
ASLAK (*To the girls.*) If he speaks to you, you don't hear him!
A GIRL (*To the others.*) No, we'll act as though we don't even see him.
PEER (*Entering eagerly and excited, stops in front of the girls and rubs his hands.*)
   Who's the liveliest girl in this group?
A GIRL (*As he approaches.*) Not me.

8. Usually, the idea is for the dancer to try to kick the rafters; but as they are outside, the boy boasts that there's no limit to how high he kicks. (Based on William Archer's note to his translation of *Peer Gynt*.)

ANOTHER   Me neither.

A THIRD   Nor me, for sure.

PEER (*To a fourth.*) So you'll have to do, till someone better turns up.

THE GIRL (*Turning away.*) Don't have the time.

PEER (*To a fifth.*)   Well, then you!

THE GIRL   I'm going home.

PEER Tonight? Have you gone out of your mind?

ASLAK (*Shortly after, quietly.*) Look Peer, she's gone to dance with an old man.

PEER (*Turning sharply to an older man.*) Are there any free girls?

THE MAN   Find out for yourself.

(*Leaves him.*)

(*Peer Gynt is all at once crestfallen. He glances shyly and furtively at the crowd. They are all staring at him but none will speak. He goes up to other groups, but wherever he goes there is silence. When he edges away, they look after him, grinning.*)

PEER (*Softly.*) Needle-sharp glances, whispers and smiles.

They grate, like a saw blade under a file!

(*He slinks along the fence. Solveig, holding onto little Helga, comes into the yard with their Parents.*)

A MAN (*To another, standing closer to Peer.*)

Look, here are the newcomers.

THE OTHER   The ones from the west?

THE FIRST MAN Right! They're from Hedal.

THE OTHER   Yes, that's who they are.

PEER (*Steps in front of them as they approach, glances at Solveig, and asks the Father.*) May I dance with your daughter?

FATHER (*Quietly.*)   You may, but first

We need to go in and greet the family.

(*They go in.*)

MASTER OF CEREMONIES (*To Peer as he offers him a drink.*)

Since you're here, you might as well take a swig at the bottle.

PEER (*Staring fixedly after the newcomers.*)

Thanks, I'll be dancing. I don't have a thirst.

(*The Master of Ceremonies leaves him.*)

PEER (*Looks toward the house and laughs.*)

How lovely! Have you seen anything like it?

Gazing down at her shoes and her snow-white apron—!

And then holding onto her mother's skirt,

And carrying a prayer book wrapped in a kerchief—

I must see her again, whoever she is.

A BOY (*Coming out with some others.*) Peer, you're giving up dancing already?

PEER No.

THE BOY Then you're going the wrong way.
  (*Takes him by the shoulder to swing him around.*)
PEER Let go of me!
THE BOY   Are you scared of the blacksmith?
PEER Afraid? Me!
THE BOY That ruckus at Lunde must be fresh in your mind.
  (*The group goes off, laughing, to the dancing green.*)
SOLVEIG (*In the doorway.*) You must be the boy who wanted to dance?
PEER That's who I am. Can't you tell just by looking at me? (*Takes
  her by the hand.*)
  Come then!
SOLVEIG   But not too far, Mother said.
PEER Mother said! Mother said! Were you born yesterday?
SOLVEIG You're making fun of me—!
PEER   You're still just a child.
  Haven't you grown up?
SOLVEIG   I've just been confirmed.
PEER Tell me your name; it makes talking easier.
SOLVEIG My name's Solveig. What is your name?
PEER Peer Gynt.
SOLVEIG (*Withdrawing her hand.*) Oh, my God!
PEER   Why, what's wrong?
SOLVEIG It's my garter. It's come loose. I must . . . fix it.
  (*She leaves him.*)
BRIDEGROOM (*Tugging at his mother.*) Mother, she won't—!
MOTHER   Won't? What won't she?
BRIDEGROOM She just won't, mother!
MOTHER   What?
BRIDEGROOM   Unlock the door.
FATHER (*Quietly, furious.*) Ah, you're only fit to be tied in a stall.
MOTHER Don't scold him. The poor boy will work out all right.
  (*They move off.*)
A BOY (*Coming with a whole crowd of others from the dancing.*)
  Some brandy, Peer?
PEER   No.
BOY   Just a drop.
PEER (*Looking somberly at him.*)   You have some?
BOY Could just happen.
  (*Pulls a hip flask out of his pocket and drinks.*)
                    Wow! That warms the gullet! Well?
PEER Let's have a go. (*Drinks.*)
ANOTHER BOY   Now get a taste of mine.
PEER No!
THE BOY Oh, come on! Don't be a wimp!
  Take a swig, Peer.

PEER   Well, just a taste.
   (*Drinks again.*)
A GIRL (*Softly.*) Come on, let's get going!
PEER   Are you scared of me, girl?
A THIRD BOY Who's *not* scared of you!
A FOURTH   Over at Lunde,
   You showed us just what you could get up to.
PEER That's nothing to what I could do if I tried!
FIRST BOY (*Whispering.*) Now here it comes!
SEVERAL (*Forming a ring round him.*)   Tell us then, tell us!
   What can you do?
PEER   Tomorrow—!
THE CROWD   No, now, tonight!
A GIRL Can you do magic tricks, Peer?
PEER   I can call up the devil!
A MAN So could my grandma, before I was born.
PEER You're lying. What *I* can do, no one else can.
   One time, I conjured him into a nut.
   The nut was worm-eaten, you see.
SEVERAL (*Laughing.*)   Oh yes, naturally.
PEER He yelled and cursed and then tried to bribe me
   With all kinds of stuff—
ONE OF THE CROWD   But he had to go in?
PEER That's right! I blocked up the hole with a peg.
   Wow! You should have heard him grumbling and growling!
A GIRL Yes, imagine!
PEER   Like a hornet going frantic.
GIRL You still have him captive in the nut?
PEER   No.
   By now, the devil's flown on his way.
   It's because of him the blacksmith still hates me.
A BOY How's that?
PEER I went over to his workplace and asked him
   If he would crack open that nutshell—
   Which he promised to do. He set it on the anvil;
   But Aslak, as you know, is a bit heavy-handed;
   He's made only for hitting with a sledgehammer—
A VOICE FROM THE CROWD And did he smash the devil?
PEER   He struck like a man.
   But the devil beat him to it, shot up like a flame
   Right through the roof and exploding the walls.
SEVERAL And Aslak—?
PEER   Just stood there with his hands scorched.
   And since that day, we've never been friends.
   (*General laughter.*)

SOMEONE That's a good yarn.

ANOTHER   Could be one of his best.

PEER You think I'm making it up?

A MAN   Oh no,
   You're not guilty of that; I heard the bulk of it
   From my grandfather.

PEER Liar!   Liar! It happened to me!

THE MAN Like everything else.

PEER (*Flinging back his head.*) Hey, I can ride
   Clean through the air on the finest of horses!
   I can do such things—one day I'll show you.
   (*Another burst of laughter.*)

ONE OF THE GROUP Peer, ride through the air!

OTHERS   Yes, go on Peer!

PEER You don't have to beg me so earnestly.
   I'll ride like a hurricane over you all.
   This whole parish is going to fall at my feet.

AN OLDER MAN Now he's gone totally crazy.

ANOTHER   The idiot!

A THIRD Loudmouth!

FOURTH   Liar!

PEER (*Squaring up to them.*) You wait and see!

A MAN (*Half drunk.*) Yes, wait, till your shirt's torn off your back!

SEVERAL Then a good thrashing and two black eyes!
   (*The crowd breaks up, the older ones angrily, the younger laughing
   and jeering.*)

BRIDEGROOM (*Close to Peer.*) Peer, is it true you can ride through
   the air?

PEER (*Curtly.*) Anything, Mads! You had better believe it.

BRIDEGROOM Then maybe you've got the Invisible Cloak?

PEER The Hat, do you mean? Yes, I've got that.
   (*Turns away from him as Solveig goes across the yard leading Helga
   by the hand.*)

PEER (*Goes to them, his face lit with joy.*) Solveig! Oh it's so good
   that you've come!
   (*Seizing her by the wrist.*)
   Now let's swing you around, fast and free!

SOLVEIG Let me go!

PEER   Why should I?

SOLVEIG   You are so wild.

PEER So is the reindeer when summer's approaching.
   Come on, girl, don't be so shy!

SOLVEIG I daren't.

PEER   Why's that?

SOLVEIG   You've been drinking.

(*She goes back to Helga.*)

PEER If only I'd taken my knife blade and stabbed it
   Right through the heart of every one of them!

BRIDEGROOM (*Nudging him.*) Can you help me get into the
   bride?

PEER (*Absently.*) The bride—Where is *she*?

BRIDEGROOM   In the storehouse.

PEER   Oh yes?

BRIDEGROOM So please, Peer Gynt, won't you do what you can?

PEER You'll have to manage without my help.
   (*Struck by the thought, he says, softly but intensely.*)
   Ingrid—the storehouse!—(*Going to Solveig.*)
                               Have you given it some thought?
   (*Solveig tries to leave but he stands in her way.*)
   No, you're ashamed to. Because I look like a tramp.

SOLVEIG (*Quickly.*) No you don't; that isn't true.

PEER Oh, yes. And then I'm a bit drunk.
   I did that on purpose, because you'd hurt me.
   Come then!

SOLVEIG   I daren't, even if I wanted to.

PEER Who are you afraid of?

SOLVEIG   Mostly of Father.

PEER Your father? Yes, he's one of the pious;
   The silent, godly ones? Come on, answer!

SOLVEIG How shall I answer?

PEER   Your father's a saintly one?[9]
   You and your mother also? Come now,
   How do you answer?

SOLVEIG   Let me go in peace.

PEER No! (*Quietly, but in a menacing tone.*)
               I can change myself into a troll!
   I'll come to your bedside as midnight strikes.
   If you think you hear something that hisses and spits
   Don't calm yourself whispering, "It's only the cat!"
   It's me, come to drain your blood in a cup!
   As for your little sister, I'll gobble her up;
   Ah yes, you must know I'm a werewolf by night;
   I shall bite you all over the loins and the back—
   (*Relapses suddenly and begs her in anguish.*)
   Dance with me, Solveig!

SOLVEIG (*Regarding him darkly.*) That was hideous of you!
   (*Goes into the house.*)

---

9. Literally, "a reader." Maybe "an elder" is equivalent. Solveig's father probably belongs to
   the puritan sect of pietists that flourished in Norway.

BRIDEGROOM (*Wandering in again.*)
You'll get an ox if you agree to help me.
PEER   Come!
(*They go behind the house. At the same time a large crowd, most of whom are drunk, enters from the dancing place. Noise and confusion. Solveig, Helga, and their Parents appear in the doorway with some older people.*)
MASTER OF CEREMONIES Keep calm!
ASLAK (*Taking off his jacket.*) No, it's time at last to settle matters.
Peer Gynt or I will have to bite the dust.
SOME Let them scrap!
OTHERS   No, let them just argue.
ASLAK It's got to be a fight. This time, words aren't enough.
SOLVEIG'S FATHER Control yourself, man!
HELGA   Will they beat him up, Mother?
A BOY Let's just rile him for all his lies.
ANOTHER Throw him out of here!
A THIRD   Spit in his eye!
A FOURTH Are you backing off?
ASLAK (*Throwing his jacket to the ground.*) I'll murder the bastard!
SOLVEIG'S MOTHER (*To Solveig.*) You can see what they think of that lunatic.
ÅSE (*Arriving carrying a stick.*) Is my son here? Now he'll get a good thrashing.
I'll beat him within an inch of his life.
ASLAK (*Rolling up his shirtsleeves.*) His body needs a tougher stick than that.
SOME The smith's going to smash him!
OTHERS   Flay him!
ASLAK (*Spits on his hands and nods to Åse.*)   Slay him!
ÅSE What? Kill my Peer? Oh, just you go and try!
—Yes, I, Åse!—while we've still teeth and claws!—
Where is he? (*Calls across the yard.*) Peer!
BRIDEGROOM (*Running in.*) Oh, holy death and terror!
Father, Mother, come look—
FATHER What's the matter?
BRIDEGROOM Just imagine, Peer Gynt—!
ÅSE (*Shrieking.*)   Have you murdered him?
BRIDEGROOM No—Peer Gynt—look there up on the hillside—
CROWD With the bride!
ÅSE (*Lets the stick fall.*) The beast!
ASLAK (*Thunderstruck.*)   He's climbing the cliff face;
Oh my God, he's clambering like a goat.
BRIDEGROOM (*Wailing.*) Oh Mother! He's carrying her just like a pig.

ÅSE (*Shakes her fist at him.*) Go on then, fall and—
  (*Shrieks in fear.*)
                                     watch out for the danger!
INGRID'S FATHER (*Emerging bareheaded and white with rage.*)
  I'll have his life. This is bride-rape!
ÅSE God punish me forever if I let you harm him.

Act Two

SCENE ONE

A narrow trail high up in the mountains. It is early morning. Peer Gynt comes hastily and sullenly along the path. Ingrid, with still half of her bridal finery, tries to hold him back.[1]

PEER GYNT Get away from me!
INGRID (*Crying.*):   After this! Where can I go?
PEER The further you go, the better!
INGRID (*Wringing her hands.*) Oh, you cheat!
PEER   No point in whining—
  We'd best go different ways.
INGRID Sin, and sin again, binds us together.
PEER The devil's in all memories! The devil's in all women!
  Except for *one*—
INGRID   And who is that?
PEER   Not you.
INGRID So, who is she then?
PEER   Just go! Back where you came from.
  Go on! Back to your father!
INGRID   Dearest, sweetheart—
PEER   Keep quiet!
INGRID You can't possibly mean what you're saying.
PEER I can, and do.
INGRID   Make love to me—and then leave!
PEER What have you got to offer, tell me?
INGRID Haegstad farm—and more besides.
PEER Do you carry a prayer book in a handkerchief?
  Does your hair fall in a gold braid down your back?
  Do you glance down shyly at your apron?
  Do your fingers cling to your mother's skirt?
  Tell me!
INGRID   No, but—
PEER This spring were you newly confirmed?
INGRID No, Peer but—

---

1. The sequence of Act 2 will go from morning, through day, to evening and midnight, to the next morning.

PEER   Do you glance about you, shyly?
    Can you refuse me when I beg you?
INGRID Jesus! I think he's lost his mind—!
PEER Do you make each day I see you, holy? Tell me!
INGRID No, but—
PEER   Then what's all the rest?
    (*About to leave.*)
INGRID (*Standing in his path.*) You know this is something you can
    hang for,
    If you desert me.
PEER   Then so be it.
INGRID   You'll get property and honor
    If you take me—
PEER   I can't afford it.
INGRID (*Bursts into tears.*)   You talked me into it—!
PEER You were willing!
INGRID   I was desperate.
PEER   I'd been drinking.
INGRID (*Menacing.*) Yes, well now you're going to pay for it.
PEER So be it! I'm willing to pay the price.
INGRID Are you set on that?
PEER   Set like concrete.
INGRID Good. We'll soon see who's going to win.
    (*She goes down the hill.*)
PEER (*Silent a moment, then shouts after her.*) The devil's in all
    memories! The devil's in all women!
INGRID (*Turning her head and calling to him mockingly.*)
    Except for *one*—
PEER   Yes, except for one.
    (*They go their separate ways.*)

SCENE TWO

*By a mountain lake surrounded by swamp and moorland. A storm is
starting up. Åse, desperate, is calling and searching on all sides.
Solveig has difficulty keeping up with her. Her parents and Helga are
a few paces behind her.*

ÅSE All the elements are against us!
    The heavens, the lake, these hideous mountains!
    The sky sends down fog to confuse him!
    The lakes and bogs plot to destroy him!
    The mountains to bury him in an avalanche;
    And the people—they're the worst!—to kill him!
    By God, if I let them! I'll never abandon him!
    The poor fool! Letting the devil confuse him!

(*Turns to Solveig.*)
Oh, but it's maddening beyond belief!
He, who'd idle his time spinning fantasies—
Whose only real strength was in his jaw;
Who couldn't set about a decent day's work;
He—! I don't know whether to laugh or cry!
Still, we stuck together when the going was rough.
Because, you see, my husband—well, he drank,
And traipsed about the parish acting the fool,
Wasting and ruining all that we had.
And little Peer and I sat at home all the while.
All we could think of were ways to forget;
Because the misery was more than I could face,
Like finding yourself staring your fate in the eye.
It's a comfort, then, to shake troubles from you,
And find ways to keep black thoughts at bay.
Some take to brandy and others to fantasy.
And therefore—we'd retreat into fairy tales,
You know, princes and trolls and all kinds of beasts.
And bride-rapes as well. But who'd ever imagine
Those devil's stories would cling on inside him?
(*Terrified again.*)
Ah, what a shriek! It's a demon or monster.
Peer! Peer! It came from up on that hillside—!
(*She runs up a low hill and looks over the water. The others join her.*)

ÅSE Not a trace to be seen!
FATHER (*Quietly.*)   All the worse for him.
ÅSE (*Crying.*) Oh, my Peer! My own lost lamb!
FATHER (*Nodding gently.*) You can well say lost.
ÅSE   No, don't speak that way!
    He's so splendid. There's no one can match him.
FATHER You foolish woman!
ÅSE   Oh, yes. Oh, yes.
    Maybe I'm foolish, but the boy is fine.
FATHER (*All the time softly, his eyes gentle.*)
    His heart is hardened; his soul is lost.
ÅSE (*Fearfully.*) No, no. The Savior's not so cruel.
FATHER Do you think he can repent his burden of sin?
ÅSE (*Eagerly.*) No, but he can ride a buck through the air!
MOTHER Good Lord, are you mad?
FATHER   Woman, what are you saying?
ÅSE There's nothing on earth he can't perform.
    You'll see, if he only lives long enough.
FATHER Better for you if he swung on the gallows.
ÅSE (*Shrieks.*) In Jesus' name, no!

FATHER   In the hands of a hangman
His soul at last might turn to repentance.
ÅSE (*Confused.*) Oh, your talk is making me dizzy.
We must find him!
FATHER   To save his soul.
ÅSE   And his body!
If he's stuck in a swamp, we must drag him out;
If the trolls have snatched him, we must ring the bells.[2]
FATHER Hm! Here's a sheep's trail—
ÅSE   God will reward you
For helping me.
FATHER   It's a Christian duty.
ÅSE Then all those others are nothing but heathens!
There wasn't even one willing to join me.
FATHER They know him too well.
ÅSE   He was too far above them!
(*Wringing her hands.*)
Only think, just think—his life's in danger.
FATHER Here are tracks of a man.
ÅSE   Then let us follow.
FATHER Best divide forces around these meadows.
(*He and his wife go on ahead.*)
SOLVEIG (*To Åse.*) Tell me some more.
ÅSE (*Drying her eyes.*)   About my son?
SOLVEIG   Yes.
Everything!
ÅSE (*Smiling and tossing her head.*) Everything? You'll soon get
tired!
SOLVEIG You'd tire of telling, sooner than I of listening.

SCENE THREE

*Low, treeless heights close under the mountain moorlands; peaks in
the distance. It is late in the day and the shadows are lengthening.*

PEER (*Running at full speed and halting on the hillside.*)
I've got the whole parish hunting me down!
They're armed to the teeth with rifles and clubs.
And the old man of Haegstad is howling the loudest.
The word's got about Peer Gynt's on the loose.
This is much better than a brawl with the blacksmith.
This is life! Each sinew becomes tough like a bear's.
(*He leaps and strikes out at the air.*)
To crush, overthrow, stem the river's wild torrent.
Strike! Rip the fir tree out from its roots!

2. The sound of church bells was believed to render trolls powerless.

This is the real life! To rouse you and stir you!

Then to hell with all those feeble old lies!

THREE HERD GIRLS (*Running across the hillside, screaming and singing.*)

GIRLS Trond of the Valfjeld![3] Baard and Kaare[4]

Troll pack, will you sleep in our arms?[5]

PEER Who are you calling?

GIRLS   The trolls! The trolls!

FIRST GIRL Trond! Take me gently!

SECOND GIRL   Baard! Take me roughly.

THIRD GIRL In our hut our beds are waiting, empty.

FIRST GIRL Gentle is rough.

SECOND GIRL   And rough is gentle.

THIRD GIRL When our boys are missing we make do with trolls.

PEER Where are your boys, then?

ALL THREE (*Roaring with laughter.*) They can't come here!

FIRST GIRL Mine used to call me his sweetheart and darling

Now he's married a middle-aged widow.

SECOND GIRL Mine met a gypsy girl up in the north.

Now they're tramping the country roads.

THIRD GIRL Mine put our bastard brat to death.

Now his head grins from a stake on the ground.

ALL THREE Trond of the Valfjeld, Baard and Kaare,

Troll pack! Will you sleep in our arms?

PEER (*With a sudden leap, he stands among them.*)

I'm a three-headed troll[6] and a boy for three girls.

GIRLS You're up to the test?

PEER   You get to judge for yourselves.

FIRST GIRL Let's make for the hut!

SECOND GIRL   We've got mead.

PEER   Then let's drink it!

THIRD GIRL So our beds won't lie empty this Saturday night!

SECOND GIRL (*Kissing him.*) He sizzles and glows like white-hot steel.

THIRD GIRL Like a leaping trout from the darkest pool.[7]

PEER (*Dancing among them.*) Grief in the heart, thoughts running riot,

Eyes lit with laughter, tears choking the throat!

THE GIRLS (*Thumbing noses at the mountains, screaming and singing.*)

---

3. Pronounced "Vahl-fyell."
4. Pronounced "Bawd" and "Kaw-ruh."
5. Herd girls in Norway traditionally lived isolated in the pastures during the summer months. The girls and Peer have degenerated considerably from their sources in Asbjörnson's "Peer Gynt," in which the girls, menaced by the trolls, are chivalrously rescued by Peer and chastely sent home.
6. Trolls traditionally possessed multiple heads, sometimes as many as a dozen.
7. Leaping trout; *barneøyne*, "baby's eyes," is the archaic folk term for a trout.

Trond of the Valfjerd! Baard and Kaare!
Troll pack! Who'll get to sleep in our arms?
(*They dance across the meadow with Peer amongst them.*)

SCENE FOUR

In the Rondë mountains.[8] *Sunset. Gleaming snow tops all round.*

PEER (*Entering, wild, distraught.*)
    Palace on palace soaring!
    There stands the glittering gate!
    Stay! Just stay! It's vanishing
    Further and further away!
    High on the vane the weathercock
    Lifts his wings to take flight;
    All darkens into blue shadow,
    The mountains are locked in night.
    What are those trunks deep-rooted
    Growing from clefts in the rock?
    They're warriors, heron-footed!
    Now they are lost in the dark.
    I'm blinded by rainbow arrows,
    Piercing my eyes and brain.
    What's that ringing far in the distance?
    What's weighing my eyelids down?
    Ah, that pain in my forehead,
    It grips like a red-hot band!
    Who on earth was the devil
    Who tightened and clamped it round?
    (*Sinking down.*)
    Racing across Gjendin ridge;
    Tales and damnable lies!
    With Ingrid climbing the cliff face,
    Lost in a drunken haze.
    Hunting with hawks and falcons,
    Menaced by monsters and trolls
    Messing with crazy women—
    Lies and damnable tales!
    (*Staring upward a long time.*)
    See there—two brown eagles!
    And southward the wild geese fly;
    While all I do here is wallow
    Mired like a pig in its sty.
    (*Leaping up.*)

8. A magnificent mountain range.

Let me fly with you there! Bathing,
Cleansing in the cool breeze.
I'll climb first, then plunge, deeply,
In the font where my soul is baptized.
Then to skim over the meadows below
And fly up till my soul's pure as snow!
Sailing far and wide over the ocean
While Engelland's prince gapes below.
You young girls can stare your eyeful;
My journey must leave you behind.
It will do you no good waiting around—
Though I might just deign to descend.
But what's become of those eagles—?
They must have been snatched by the devil!—
Look! The shape of a roof's appearing!
Then eaves, and the jut of a gable!
It's rising in size out of nothing—
And the doorway is opening wide.
But of course! Now I can see it's
Grandfather's farm in its pride!
Gone are the rags from the windows.
Gone too, the broken-down fences.
From every glass pane light is gleaming,
In the hall the feasting commences.
The provost is tapping his wine glass
With the back of his knife where he sits;
Now the Captain hurls his bottle
Shattering the mirror to bits.
Why not squander, and let all go waste!
Don't fuss, Ma, there's plenty to spare!
All provided by wealthy Jon Gynt!
Then make merry and good-bye to care!
What's causing that tumult and clamor?
They're calling for Jon Gynt's son,
And the priest is proposing my health.
Go in Peer, for your place in the sun!
They ring out in loud acclamation:
"Peer Gynt, your greatness awaits you.
To that greatness at last you have come!"
(*He leaps forward but runs his nose against a rock, falls and lies motionless.*)[9]

9. The sequence that follows, through night, to midnight, to dawn, could be read as a journey through the unconscious, in which the Haegstad events are played out as a troll
nightmare. If the actors portraying Ingrid and the wedding guests also play the Woman
in Green and the trolls, this can become evident.

SCENE FIVE

A hillside, with tall, leafy trees sighing in the wind. The stars twinkle, while birds sing in the treetops. A woman in green[1] walks over the hill, with Peer following making amorous gestures.

WOMAN IN GREEN (*Stopping and turning around.*) Is it true?
PEER (*Drawing his finger across his throat.*) As true as my name's
    Peer—
  As true as you are a beautiful woman!
  Will you take me? We'll make a convivial pair.
  You'll never have to weave or spin.
  You'll get to eat until you're ready to burst.
  And I'll never, ever, pull your hair—
WOMAN IN GREEN Nor beat me, either?
PEER   Of course not—the very idea!
  We royalty don't go around beating women.
WOMAN IN GREEN *Are* you a prince?
PEER   Yes.
WOMAN IN GREEN   I'm the Dovrë King's daughter.
PEER Then, well met by starlight, princess of Dovrë!
WOMAN IN GREEN My father's palace lies deep in Rondë.
PEER I can claim my mother's is even grander.
WOMAN IN GREEN Do you know my father? His name's King Brosë.[2]
PEER Do you know my mother? She's called Queen Åse.
THE WOMAN IN GREEN When my father's angry, the mountains crack.
PEER If my mother scolds, they shift and break.
WOMAN IN GREEN My father can kick to the highest beams.
PEER My mother can ride through the wildest streams.
WOMAN IN GREEN Have you no other clothes than those rags there?
PEER Stick around till Sunday then see what I wear!
THE WOMAN IN GREEN I go everyday in gold threads and silks.
PEER They look to me more like straw and stalks.
WOMAN IN GREEN Ah, yes! That's one thing to keep in mind.
  The Rondë folk's ways are a peculiar kind.
  The things we own have a duplicate nature.
  If you come unprepared to my father's home,
  You're likely to misperceive every feature
  And think you stood in a hideous slum.
PEER Why, that's exactly the case with us;
  All our golden glories can look like dross.
  It could be you'd think each glittering pane
  Was stuffed with old rags to keep out the rain.

1. "Women in green" belonged to the realm beneath the earth.
2. Pronounced "Broh-suh."

Peer and the Woman in Green. "*Peer Gynt*: Peer and the Greenclad One [Act II]." Copyright © 2003 The Munch Museum/The Munch-Ellingsen Group/Artists Rights Society (ARS), NY.

WOMAN IN GREEN Black seems white, and ugliness fair.
PEER Big seems little, filth passes for pure.
WOMAN IN GREEN (*Casting her arms round his neck.*)
  Oh, Peer, I can see, we're made to belong!
PEER Like a leg for a trouser, or hair for a comb.
WOMAN IN GREEN (*Calling down the hillside.*)
  My wedding mount! Wedding mount! Come, bridal horse!
  (*A gigantic pig runs in, a rope's end for its bridle and an old sack
  for saddle. Peer Gynt swings himself onto its back and sets the
  woman in green in front of him.*)
PEER Heigh-ya! Rondë gate lies on our course.
  We'll race through it, won't we, my galloping steed?
WOMAN IN GREEN (*Amorously.*) Just now I was feeling such misery
    and need.
  It all goes to show you never can tell.
PEER (*Whips the pig, which goes trotting off.*)
  From the way a man rides, you know he's a swell.

SCENE SIX

The royal hall of the Old Man of the Dovrë trolls[3]. *Great assemblage
of troll courtiers, gnomes, goblins, troll people. The Old Man's children and nearest relatives are on either side of him. Peer Gynt stands
before him. A great tumult in the hall.*

TROLL COURTIERS Kill him! The son of a Christian dare
  Mess with the Old Man's favorite daughter!
TROLL CHILD Can I slice his finger in two?
ANOTHER TROLL CHILD   Can I drag him by the hair?
TROLL GIRL CHILD Hei, hei, let me bite his rear.
TROLL WITCH (*With ladle.*) He should be boiled into broth and stew.
ANOTHER TROLL WITCH (*With a carving knife.*)
  He should be stuck on a spit or browned in a pan.
OLD MAN Chill out! (*Beckons his advisers closely round him.*)
  Go easy on the bragging, if you can!
  Things have been going downhill these past few years.
  We no longer know if we can stay the course.
  Help could prove useful even from Man.
  This boy seems to me a fine specimen:
  No defects, well built, as far as I can tell.
  It must be conceded he's only one head,
  But that's my daughter's condition, as well.

---

3. His title is Old Man of Dovrë, not Dovrë King. That he has a "royal hall" or "king's hall"
(*kongshall*) and courtiers is only a symptom of the fraudulent pretensions already suggested by his daughter, the woman in green.

The craze for three-headed trolls is now dead.
Even two-headed trolls are a rare enough quantity;
And the heads on those are of fairly poor quality. (*To Peer.*)
So is it my daughter you're after marrying?

PEER And the kingdom that comes along with the daughter.

OLD MAN You get half while I'm in the land of the living.
As for the rest—you'll come into that later.

PEER Sounds reasonable to me.

OLD MAN   Now, just wait my boy.
You also have some pledges to give.
Break one of them and the contract's void,
And there's no way then you'll leave here alive.
For starters, you must promise never to care
For anything outside these precincts here.
You must shun the day and all sources of light.

PEER Make me a king, that's a clause I won't fight.

OLD MAN Next, we must test if you're clever or not.
(*Rises from his seat.*)

THE OLDEST TROLL COURTIER (*To Peer Gynt.*)
If you've a wisdom tooth, let's see if you can
Crack the shell of the riddle the Old Man will set.

OLD MAN What is the difference between Troll and Man?

PEER No difference at all as far as I can see.
Big trolls will roast you, the little ones scratch.
If we humans dared, we'd do as much.

OLD MAN Granted. In that, and more, we're inclined to agree.
However, morning is morning and night is night.
And one huge difference looms into sight.
And now you're to hear what that difference is:
Out there, beneath the expanse of blue
The edict stands: "To yourself be true!"
But in here, we trolls will have none of that stuff.
Our motto's, "Troll, to yourself be enough!"[4]

OLDEST TROLL COURTIER Can you plumb that abyss?

PEER   I have to confess—

OLD MAN "Enough!" my son; that word, whose dark power
Must be sealed on your coat of arms from this hour!

PEER (*Scratching behind his ear.*) Well—

OLD MAN   *Must be*, if you're to rule over us.

PEER What the hell—O.K! It could be worse!

---

4. A crucial text. To be true to oneself is to work to realize one's true human identity, as in the Pindaric injunction, "You shall become who you are!" That is, through self-determination a person can "slay" inadequate "selves" or identities, as the Button-Molder, in Act 5, will tell Peer, who will not understand. The troll motto, on the contrary, means to remain slothfully content with one's given and unrealized identity.

OLD MAN The next thing is to hold very dear
  The national customs we practice here.
  (*He beckons; two trolls with pigs' heads, white nightcaps, etc.,
  bring food and drink.*)
  Our cows give cakes, our bullocks, mead.
  Don't ask if they taste sour or sweet.
  The main thing is always to keep in mind,
  It's all homemade; all imports are banned.
PEER (*Pushing the offerings away.*) You can send that homemade
    drink to the devil.
  I'll never get used to this country style.
OLD MAN The bowl goes with it; it's gold—and be sure
  Who owns the bowl is my son-in-law.
PEER (*Reflecting.*) Well, it's written: "You must subdue your nature."
  And in time this drink might not taste so sour.
  Here goes! (*Drinks.*)
OLD MAN Now that was very wisely expressed.
  But you spit—?
PEER   Old ways aren't so easily suppressed.
OLD MAN Next you must cast off your Christian gear.
  There's a rule of the trolls that operates here:
  "All must derive from these mountain walls,
  Not the valleys"—except the silk bows on our tails.[5]
PEER (*Indignantly.*) I don't have a tail.
OLD MAN   Then you must get one.
  Steward, tie on him my Sunday-best one.
PEER Hell if you will! Are you taking me for a ride?
OLD MAN You don't court my daughter with a bare backside.
PEER Turn a man into a beast!
OLD MAN   You're way off the mark;
  I'm letting you see how troll courtships work.
  You'll get to wear a bright flame-colored bow;
  It's the highest of honors we trolls bestow.
PEER (*Reflecting.*) It's said that Man is only an atom
  And it's always wisest to follow the custom.
  So, tie away!
OLD MAN   You seem a reasonable fellow, at least.
OLDEST TROLL COURTIER Try swinging it freely and elegantly.
PEER Ha, is there anything more you want out of me?
  Is my Christian faith the next on your list?
OLD MAN No, don't let that thought disturb your rest.
  Faith is free, not a thing we control.
  It's by his deeds you can tell the troll.

5. Trolls were supposed to lose their tails when they married a Christian. Peer is willing to
reverse this and acquire a tail when he marries the troll girl.

Just keep to our ways and the fashions we wear,
And you're free to call "faith" what we tend to call "fear."
PEER You know, in spite of these many provisions
    You're more reasonable than I previously thought.
OLD MAN My son, we trolls are much better than report.
    (Another difference in troll and human conditions).
    "But now, the dull business of the day is o'er"—
    In other words, let's feast the ears and eyes.
    Strike up the Dovrë-harp's melodies!
    Dancing girls, hit the Dovrë dance floor!
    (*Music and dancing.*)
OLDEST TROLL COURTIER How do you like it?
PEER   Like it? Er—
OLD MAN   No need to be shy.
    What do you see?
PEER   A hideous monstrosity.
    A cow with a cloven hoof strumming on gut strings.
    A sow wiggling about and dancing in stockings.
OLDEST TROLL COURTIER Eat him!
OLD MAN   Remember, he's trapped in his human senses.
TROLL GIRLS Rip off his ears and tear out his eyes!
WOMAN IN GREEN (*Sobbing.*) Boo-hoo! Must we hear such
    calumnies
    When my sister and I perform our dances?
PEER Oh my! Was it you? Well, what is the harm
    In a joke at a party, with the friends you're among.
WOMAN IN GREEN You'll swear that's true?
PEER   There was inexpressible charm
    In both playing and dancing—or the cat get my tongue!
OLD MAN It's a curious thing, this human nature;
    It proves such a difficult thing to discard.
    In a battle with us it can get badly scarred,
    But it's amazing how quickly the wound gets better.
    My son-in-law seemed the most yielding of creatures,
    He willingly cast off his Christian breeches.
    He willingly drank our simple home ale
    And willingly wore, on request, a tail.
    So willing, in fact, to do all we bade him
    I honestly thought the stubborn old Adam
    Had at last been expelled and shown the front door.
    But here he comes back through the window once more!
    Well then, my son, there's nothing else for it:
    You've a human condition and we'd better cure it.
PEER What will you do?
OLD MAN   I'll scratch your left eye

Just a smidgeon, so you'll see properly askew;
Then all you observe will seem lovely and true.
And then this right window pane we'll just pull—
PEER Are you drunk?
OLD MAN (*Setting a large collection of instruments on the table.*)
                Here are the tools I'll apply.
You're to be blinkered, like a recalcitrant bull.
Then your new bride will seem most beautiful—
We must treat what's causing that optic distorting
That makes you see pigs and bell-cows cavorting.
PEER You must be deranged!
THE OLDEST TROLL COURTIER Hear our Great Man!
Whose words are wisdom: it's you are insane.
OLD MAN Consider how much self-torture and doubt
You'll free yourself from, year in and year out.
Only recall your eyes are the fountains
Of tears that can scald like lava fire.
PEER True enough; and as the Good Book maintains
If your eye offends, pluck it out entire.
But listen; when will my eyes return
To human sight?
OLD MAN   My friend, never again.
PEER Oh, really! In that case then—have a nice day!
OLD MAN Where do you think you're going?
PEER   I can find my own way.
OLD MAN Wait a moment! Getting in's not that hard,
But Dovrë gates don't open easily outward.
PEER You don't think of keeping me here by brute force?
OLD MAN Listen, try to be reasonable Prince Peer!
You are made for a troll; it was abundantly clear
From the start you signed up for the classic troll course.
You want to be a troll?
PEER   I don't deny it.
When a bride and a well-managed kingdom's on offer,
There are many small losses I'd be willing to suffer.
But in this world everything still has a limit.
I've gone along with having a tail, that's true.
But what the Steward tied on I can always undo.
I've cast off my pants; they were old and in tatters.
But I can wear them again, so that hardly matters.
And when the time comes I can unlearn at will
All these Dovrë habits you've tried to instill.
Say a cow is a girl? Yes, I'll take an oath;
An oath can always be swallowed again.
But *this*, to know you can never return

To a free human life, and a true human death,
To live like a troll for the rest of your days,
As a condition you are damned to remain in always—
It's true the text warns us, "If you make your bed"—
But that irrevocable act is something I dread.

OLD MAN I'm becoming quite angry, I swear by my crimes,
And when I am angry I do not play games.
You pale thing of daylight, do you know who I am?
Making free with my daughter, you miserable sham!

PEER You lie in your throat!

OLD MAN   And now you must marry.

PEER You dare to suggest—

OLD MAN   Are you going to deny
That you lusted after her? Is that what you claim?

PEER What if I did? Who the hell's going to mind?

OLD MAN You human creatures are all of a kind.
In your speech it's all "spirit" that governs your deeds;
But you count on your fists to take care of your needs.
So it's your opinion that lust's not that bad?
Only wait. You're soon to get proof that it is—

PEER You'll need better bait to hook me with lies.

WOMAN IN GREEN Peer, before the year's end, you'll be a dad.

PEER Open up, I am off!

OLD MAN   You'll be getting your brat
Wrapped in a goatskin.

PEER (*Wiping sweat from his forehead.*) Let me out of this nightmare!

OLD MAN Should he be sent to the palace?

PEER   Put him on welfare!

OLD MAN Very well, Prince Peer, if you really want that.
But one thing is certain: the die is cast.
And your offspring will thrive, you'd better not doubt.
These bastard troll brats grow extraordinarily fast.

PEER Old Man, it's best we sort this thing out;
Be reasonable, girl! Let's make a deal.
You should know I'm not a prince for real,
Nor rich any way you choose to measure.
In fact you're not getting much of a treasure.
(*Woman in green faints and is carried out by the troll maids.*)

OLD MAN (*Regards him contemptuously a moment and then speaks.*)
Crush him to pulp, children, there on the rocks.

YOUNG TROLLS Please, Pa, can we play owl and eagle tricks!
The wolf game! Gray mouse and the bright-eyed cat.

OLD MAN Yes, but be quick. I'm tired and angry. Good night.
(*He goes.*)

PEER (*Pursued by young trolls.*) Keep off, brats from hell!
YOUNG TROLLS   Gnomes, nixies, bite
   His back and buttocks.
PEER (*Trying to escape through a trap door.*) Ow!
YOUNG TROLLS   Block every exit.
TROLL COURTIER They love it, the youngsters!
PEER (*Fighting with a troll child who is biting his ear.*)
                                   Let go, little beast!
TROLL COURTIER (*Rapping him over the knuckles.*)
   That's not how a prince of the blood is addressed!
PEER There's a rathole—!
YOUNG TROLLS   Block it before he breaks loose!
PEER The old one was foul but the children are worse!
YOUNG TROLLS Flay him!
PEER   If I were only a mouse! (*Runs about.*)
YOUNG TROLLS (*Closing in on him.*) Pen him in! Pen him in!
PEER (*Sobbing.*) Or even a louse.
   (*He collapses.*)
YOUNG TROLLS   Now get his eyes.
PEER (*Buried under the trolls.*)   Help, mother, I'll die.
   (*Church bells ring in the distance.*)
YOUNG TROLLS Mountain bells! Blackfrock's herd's passing by![6]
   (*The trolls fly in confusion, shrieking. The Hall collapses; every-
   thing vanishes.*)

SCENE SEVEN

*Pitch darkness. Peer is heard slashing and flailing about him with a
huge branch.*

PEER Answer! Say who you are!
A VOICE IN THE DARK[7]   Myself!
PEER   Give way!
VOICE Go round about. You've room; you give way.
PEER (*Tries another place but pushes up against something.*) Who are
   you?
VOICE   Myself. Can you make that claim?
PEER I'll claim what I like! My sword can strike home
   So watch out! Now feel how my sword lands.
   Saul slew his hundreds; Peer slays his thousands.

---

6. "Blackfrock" means a priest, so the herd (of cows) is the congregation or "flock" of the parish.
7. This voice is theatrically more effective if it is sinisterly weak, wheezing, and asthmatic, not booming. The Bøyg, in folk legend, is an invisible gigantic troll. As it appears in "pitch darkness," here, it suggests the matrix of Peer's identity, like the Freudian id before the ego wills its energies into action.

(*Slashing and flailing.*)
Who are you?

VOICE   Myself.

PEER   Why not spare
   That stupid reply; it makes nothing clear.
   What are you?

VOICE   The Great Bøyg.

PEER   You don't say!
   If the riddle was black once, now it is gray.

VOICE   Go round about, Peer.

PEER Then through!
   (*Slashing and striking.*)
                  He's down!
   (*Tries to go forward but again is stopped.*)
                       What's this? You're still here?

THE VOICE The Bøyg, Peer Gynt! The sole, the unique!
   The Bøyg fights unhurt; the Bøyg's strong while weak.
   The Bøyg who is dead, yet the Bøyg who persists.

PEER This sword is bewitched; yet Peer still has his fists!
   (*Thrashing about.*)

VOICE That's right, trust in fists, trust in your strength.
   Hey, hey, Peer! You think you're winning at length?

PEER (*Trying again.*) Forward or back, it's just as far.
   Out or in, I'm trapped as before!
   There he is! *There!* Then round he will swing.
   I'm no sooner out then I'm back in the ring.
   Name yourself! Show yourself! Do you exist?

VOICE I'm the Bøyg.

PEER (*Groping about.*) Not dead. Not alive. Made of slime? Made of
      mist?
   No shape to you either! Like stumbling unawares
   Into a cave full of snarling half-awake bears.
   (*Screaming.*) Strike back at me then!

VOICE   The Bøyg isn't mad.

PEER Strike back!

VOICE   The Bøyg doesn't strike.

PEER   Fight, by God!

VOICE The Great Bøyg can defeat you without any fight.

PEER If there were only some goblin set on to draw blood
   Even a fierce troll babe still fresh from his nurse.
   Just something to battle, but here, there's a void.
   Are you *snoring?* Hi, Bøyg!

VOICE   What's the matter?

PEER   Use force!

VOICE The Bøyg overcomes when his touch is most light.

PEER (*Biting his own arms and hands.*)
　　Desperate teeth and claws, rip into my flesh!
　　Let me at least see my own life's blood jet!
　　(*The sound of the beating of great birds' wings can be heard.*)
BIRD CRIES Is he coming to us, Bøyg?
VOICE   Oh yes, bit by bit.
BIRD CRIES You sisters, out there! Fly in here and perch.
PEER If you want to save me, girl, there's no time to waste.
　　Don't fix your glance downward, timid and shy—
　　You prayer book! Now! Cast it right in his eye!
BIRD CRIES He's weakening!
VOICE   We've got him!
BIRD CRIES   Sisters, make haste.
PEER Even my life is a price paid too high,
　　To endure one hour of such agony.
　　(*Sinking down.*)
BIRD CRIES Bøyg, he's sinking. Seize him. Bind him!
　　(*Church bells and psalm-singing heard in the distance.*)

THE VOICE (*Shrinking to nothing as he says with a gasp.*)
　　He was too strong. There were women behind him.

SCENE EIGHT

*Sunrise. On the hillside outside Åse's mountain hut. The door is shut.
Everything is deserted and still. Peer Gynt lies sleeping against the
wall.*

PEER (*Wakes up, looking around him with dull and heavy eyes. He
　　spits.*)
　　What I wouldn't give for a pickled herring!
　　(*Spits again and at the same moment sees Helga who arrives with a
　　basket of food.*)
　　Hey, kid, so it's you. What do you want?
HELGA It's Solveig—
PEER (*Springing up.*) Where is she?
HELGA   Behind the hut.
SOLVEIG (*Concealed.*) If you come near me, I'll take off!
PEER (*Halting.*) Maybe you're scared I'll grab hold of you?
SOLVEIG Shame on you!
PEER You want to know where I was last night?
　　The Dovrë-boss's daughter clung to me like a leech.
SOLVEIG A good thing, then, that we rang the bells.
PEER Peer Gynt's not the fellow to get caught like that—
　　What do you say—?

HELGA (*In tears.*)   Oh, she's running away!
  (*Starts running after her.*)
  Wait!
PEER (*Grabbing her arm.*) See what I've got in my pocket!
  A silver button, eh, kid? This shall be yours—
  Only speak to her for my sake!
HELGA   Please, let me go!
PEER There it is!
HELGA   Let go. The food basket's there.
PEER God help you if you don't—
HELGA   You're frightening me!
PEER (*Gently, as he releases her.*) No, all I mean is—ask her not to
    forget me!
  (*Helga runs off.*)

Act Three

SCENE ONE

*Deep within a pine forest. Gray autumn weather. Snow is falling.
Peer Gynt, in his shirtsleeves, is felling timber.*

PEER (*Chopping at a huge fir tree with crooked branches.*)
  I can tell you're a fighter, tough Old Man!
  But it's not going to help—you're coming down.
  (*Chopping again.*)
  What if you've a coat of hard chain mail;
  I'll hack through it, though made of steel.
  Go on, shake your twisting arms at me!
  You're mad and want to hurt me. Naturally!
  But I'm going to make you fall to your knees—
  (*Breaking off in self-disgust.*)
  Lies! It's nothing more than an old tree.
  All lies! There's no man here in chain mail,
  Only a fir tree with a craggy bark.
  It's hard enough just chopping the tree;
  Mixing dreams with work makes it worse.
  I must put an end to this drifting off
  Into stupid daydreams while still awake.
  You're an outlaw, boy, chased into the forest!
  (*Chopping vigorously for a while.*)
  That's right, an outlaw! You've no mother now
  To bring your food to a well-laid table.
  You want to eat, boy? Then go hunt for your food.
  Fetch it raw from the forest and rivers.

Split your own kindling and make your own fire.
It's self-preservation, so work out a plan.
You want warm clothes? You must skin a deer!
To build a house you need to break stones.
And to raise that house means chopping trees,
Hauling logs on your back to the clearing.
(*The axe sinks down as Peer stares ahead.*)
The house will be splendid. A tower will rise
From a rooftop that soars way up to the skies.
And then I'll carve on the top of the gable
A mermaid shaped like a fish from the navel.
Weather vane and locks—they'll be shining brass!
The windows—glass so clear it gleams!
My house on the hill sends out dazzling beams
So that strangers gaze in awe when they pass—
(*Laughs bitterly.*)
Damnable lies! They're starting again.
You're an outlaw, boy.
(*Chopping fiercely.*)
                        A hut made out of bark
To keep out the weather, that's all you need.
(*Looks up at the tree.*)
So there he stands, tottering. Just a kick!
He'll soon be measuring his length in the dust.
And the saplings will shudder around him!
(*Starts lopping the branches from the trunk; for a moment he stoops and listens, his axe suspended.*)
There's someone after me! Is it you then,
Old Man from Haegstad? Sneaking around here!
(*Crouches behind a tree and peeps out.*)
A boy! And alone. He seems afraid.
He peers all around him. What's he hiding
Under his jacket? A sickle? He looks furtively about;
Now he's laying his hand on a tree stump—
What's he up to? Why is he leaning over like that—?
Acch! He's not chopping off his finger—!?
The whole finger, off! He's bleeding like a bull.
And now he runs off with his fist in a rag. (*Rises.*)
What courage the kid has! An irreplaceable finger!
Clean off! And no one made him do it!
Aha! Now I get it! It's the only way
Of getting out of military service.
That's it then! They want to send him to the war,
And the boy, of course, doesn't want to go.
But to chop off—? To lose, forever—?

It's what you could imagine, wish, *will* it even—
But to *do* it! No, I can never grasp that.
(*Shaking his head, he goes back to his work.*)

SCENE TWO

*A room in Åse's house, below. Everything is in disorder; chests lie
open, clothes are strewn about. A cat is lying on the bed. Åse and
Kari, a neighbor, are busy packing things and clearing up.*

ÅSE (*Hurrying to one side.*) Kari, listen!
KARI   What is it?
ÅSE (*Crossing to the other side.*)   Listen, now—!
   Where's that—? Where can I find—? Tell me where—?
   What is it I'm looking for? I'm so distracted!
   Where's the key to the chest?
KARI   In the keyhole.
ÅSE What's that rumbling?
KARI   The last wagon load
   Getting carried off to Haegstad.
ÅSE (*Weeping.*)   I'd be happy
   Carted off in my coffin along with the rest.
   Ah, what we must put up with in this life!
   Merciful God! They've emptied the house!
   What Haegstad left me, the bailiff took.
   Not even sparing the clothes on my back.
   It was shameful, giving such a cruel sentence.
   (*Sitting on the corner of the bed.*)
   Both the farm and the land now gone from the family!
   The old man was savage—but the law was worse!
   No one would help and no one showed mercy.
   Peer was away and I had no one to turn to.
KARI But you can stay in this house right to the end.
ÅSE Oh yes, me and the cat—eating charity bread.
KARI God help you, poor mother, Peer's cost you dear.
ÅSE Peer? I think you're losing your mind!
   After all, Ingrid got home all in one piece.
   It would have been more proper to have blamed the devil;
   He was the culprit, he and no one else.
   That monster tempted my unfortunate boy.
KARI Wouldn't it be best if we sent for the priest?
   It could be you are worse than you realize.
ÅSE For the priest? Yes, maybe that would be best;
   (*Gets up.*)
   No, God help me, I can't! I'm the boy's mother!

I must help; that's no more than what I should do.
To stand up for him when all the rest are against him.
At least they left him this jacket. I'll need to mend it.
Now if I could get away with keeping this fur rug—
Where are the stockings?

KARI *There*, in all that clutter.

ÅSE What's this I've found? It's the old casting ladle,
    Kari! What he played being Button-Molder with,
    Melting, shaping, setting the stamp on the button.
    One day, when we'd company, in came Peer
    And asked his father for a lump of tin.
    "You don't get tin," said Jon, "but royal coin;
    Real silver, to show you're the son of Jon Gynt!"
    God have mercy on him, but he was drunk
    And wouldn't notice if it were silver or tin.
    Here's the stockings. They've got hole after hole.
    They'll need darning.

KARI They look like they do.

ÅSE And when that's done, I must go to bed;
    I'm feeling so weary, so worn out and ill.
    (*Joyfully.*) Two woolen shirts, Kari! They didn't see them!

KARI You're right, they didn't.

ÅSE That's a piece of luck.
    One of them we can put to one side.
    Or else—why not just take both of them?
    The one he's got is so thin and worn.

KARI But, mother Åse, you know that's a sin!

ÅSE Maybe, but that's what the priest's there for.
    To forgive that—and all our other sins.

SCENE THREE

Outside a newly built hut in the forest. There are reindeer horns over the door. The snow has piled up high. It is dusk. Peer Gynt stands outside the doorway, fastening a large wooden bolt.

PEER (*Laughing intermittently.*) I must have a lock: a lock that can
    guard
    The door against trolls and men and women.
    I must have a lock: a lock to keep out
    All that malicious goblin tribe.
    They appear with the darkness, rattling, pounding;
    "Open up, Peer Gynt, we're as stealthy as thought.
    That's us rustling there under the bed, in the ashes,
    Dancing in the chimney like glowing dragons!

Hei-yo! Peer Gynt, do you think nails and planks
Can keep out torturing, demon thoughts?"
(*Solveig enters on skis across the clearing. She has a shawl over her
head and carries a bundle.*)

SOLVEIG God bless your work. Don't send me away.
I come as you bid me and so you must take me.

PEER Solveig! It can't be—but yet—yes it is!—
You're not afraid then to come out to me here?

SOLVEIG One message you sent me by little Helga;
Others were borne on the wind and the silence.
I heard you call in all your mother told me,
And that summons entered and grew in my dreams.
The nights were heavy, the days became empty,
Each strengthened the message calling me to you.
It made life down there seem to come to an end;
I could put no heart into laughter or tears,
Not knowing what you were thinking or feeling.
I knew only what I should—what I had—to do.

PEER But your father?

SOLVEIG   On all of God's wide earth
I've none I now call father or mother.
I've left them forever.

PEER   Solveig, so lovely—
That you should come to me!

SOLVEIG   Yes, to you only;
You must be all to me, both friend and comforter.
(*In tears.*) It was so hard, leaving my little sister—
Worse, though, was having to part from my father;
Even worse was leaving her who had borne me.
No, God forgive me—I can see that the worst
Was deciding to leave them all forever.

PEER You understand the sentence they passed last spring?
It takes my farm and my heritage from me.

SOLVEIG It was not for the sake of any heritage
That I cut myself off from all I hold dear.

PEER You know there's a bounty? Outside this forest
I'm the prey of anyone I chance to encounter.

SOLVEIG Coming over the snow, I would ask the way;
They asked, "Where are you going?" I answered, "Home."

PEER Then to hell with relying on nails and planks.
I don't need them now against demon thoughts.
If you dare to join my life as an outlaw,
I know a blessing will be on this house.
Solveig! Let me look at you. No, not too near!
Just to look at you, only. You are bright and pure.

Let me lift you. You're so delicate and light
If I carried you I could never grow tired.
I'll not stain you. I'll stretch my arms
To keep you at a distance, my lovely one.
Who could imagine I'd draw you to me—
You, love, I've longed for both day and night?
You see all this I've been building out here—?
It must all come down, now. It's mean and unworthy.
SOLVEIG Mean or splendid, it's all I ask for.
This bracing wind makes it easy to breathe.
Down there it was stifling, I gasped for free air.
That was partly why I had to leave the valley;
But up here, hearing the pine trees sighing,
There's song in the silence. Here I'm at home.
PEER And you're sure of this—that this is forever?
SOLVEIG The path I've taken can never lead back.
PEER You are mine then! Let me see you inside there.
Go in, while I fetch in pinewood for burning
To warm you and cast a soft light around you.
You shall sit at a hearth where no cold will touch you.
(*He opens the door; Solveig goes inside. He stands motionless for a moment, then laughs aloud joyfully, leaping into the air.*)
My princess! Now I've found her and won her!
Hei! A royal palace shall rise from the ground.
(*He takes up the axe and moves away; at the same moment an old-looking woman in a ragged green dress emerges from the forest. A hideous boy with a beer flask in his hand limps behind her, holding onto her skirt.*)
WOMAN Good evening, Peer Lightfoot.
PEER   What's that? Who's there?
WOMAN Old friends, Peer Gynt! My place is quite near.
So we're neighbors.
PEER   Is that so? I never knew.
WOMAN As you were building your hut, mine rose up too.
PEER (*About to leave.*) I'm afraid I'm in a hurry—
WOMAN   You always were;
But I tramped behind, boy, and tracked you down here.
PEER You've made a mistake—
WOMAN   I did once before!
When your promises equaled the oaths that you swore.
PEER I promised—? I don't know what the devil you mean.
WOMAN You've forgotten that night when the Dovrë Old Man,
My father—?
PEER   I've forgotten what never took place.
This stuff that you're claiming—when did we meet last?

WOMAN The last time we met was the time we met first.
   (*To the boy.*)
   Give your father a drink: he's developing a thirst.
PEER Father? Are you drunk? Are you trying to blame—
WOMAN Can't you recognize a pig by its hide?
   You've got eyes in your head. Can't you see how he's lame
   In his legs, just as you're crippled inside?
PEER Are you trying to tell me—
WOMAN   You're about to protest—?
PEER That gangling delinquent—!
WOMAN   He grew up fast.
PEER You troll mug, do you dare to impute—
WOMAN You know what, Peer—you're an ill-mannered brute.
   (*Crying.*) How can I help it if I'm not as alluring
   As when you tricked me on the hills with your lying?
   Last fall I gave birth while the devil held me down.
   So it's hardly a marvel how ugly I've grown.
   To see me as beautiful as I was before
   Just take that girl and show her the door.
   Drive her out of your mind and out from your thought
   And I promise you, love, I'll be rid of this snout!
PEER Get away from me, troll witch!
WOMAN   Just see if I do!
PEER You'll get this axe in your head—!
WOMAN   Try it—I dare you!
   Although you may beat me, I'll not go away,
   I'll keep coming back day after day,
   To pry the door open and peep at you both
   As you sit on the bench like a loving pair.
   You feel like some petting, there by the hearth?
   I'll creep in between you and ask for my share.
   We'll have you in turns, your sweetheart and I,
   Eat, drink and be merry; tomorrow we'll marry!
PEER You nightmare from hell!
WOMAN   Oh, I almost forgot;
   You light-footed rascal: you must bring up this brat!
   Now go to your dad, little spawn of the devil.
BOY (*Spitting at him.*) I'll hit you with the axe, just see if I will!
WOMAN (*Kissing the boy.*) What a head on his shoulders, the dear
   little pup!
   He'll be just like his dad the day he grows up.
PEER (*Stamping his foot.*) If only you were as far away—
WOMAN   As we are near.
PEER (*Clenches his fists.*) And all this—

WOMAN   For thoughts and desires, Peer.
  Yes, it is hard on you, boy.
PEER   Beyond measure
  For another! Solveig, my pure, dearest treasure!
WOMAN
  "How the innocent suffer!" said the devil, when thrashed
  By his mother the night his father got smashed.
  (*She trudges out with the boy, who throws the flask at Peer.*)
PEER (*After a long silence.*) Go round about, said the Bøyg; it seems
    now I must.
  My royal palace has crashed, shattered in pieces.
  And a wall's grown round her, who was so near.
  All's become hideous, my joy has turned gray.
  Go round about, boy! There's no possible path
  To lead me straight through this horror to her.
  Straight through? Perhaps I might find a way!
  Something about repentance, I vaguely recall,
  But what? What does it say? I don't have the book,
  And I've forgotten most of it. And there's no one at hand
  To put me on the right track, here in the forest.
  Repentance? Why, that could go on for years
  Before I win through. My life would be wasted.
  To rend to pieces what is radiant and pure,
  And then patch it again in fragments and cracks,
  Can be done with a fiddle, but not with a bell.
  Best not tread down what you want to grow green.
  But it's got to be a lie what the old witch said!
  All that foul business now is clear out of sight.
  Yes, clear out of sight, but not out of mind!
  Inside there, memories will still pursue me.
  Ingrid! And those three from the hillside!
  Will they also join in? With their greedy cackling,
  Demanding to be held close to me, like her?
  Or lifted gently in outstretched arms?
  Go round about, boy. Were your arm as long
  As the root of the fir or the tallest pine,
  I'd defile her by touching. I could never
  Set her down pure and unsullied again.
  I'll go round about, one way or another;
  If it leads to new life or to the heart of loss—
  I must get rid of this past and try to forget!
  (*Goes a few paces toward the hut, but stops again.*)
  To go in after this? So corrupted and foul?
  Go in with that troll-filth still clinging to me?

To speak yet keep silent; confess, yet conceal—?
(*Throwing his axe aside.*)
This evening's a sabbath.[1] To go to her now,
  In my state of sin, would be sacrilege.
SOLVEIG (*In the doorway.*) Are you coming in?
PEER (*Half aloud.*)   Round about!
SOLVEIG   What?
PEER   You must wait.
  It is dark out here and I've something heavy to carry.
SOLVEIG Wait. Let me help. We'll both share the load.
PEER No, stay where you are! I must carry it all.
SOLVEIG But not for too long love.
PEER   Be patient, my dear.
  Long or short, you must wait.
SOLVEIG   Yes, I'll wait.

SCENE FOUR

*Åse's hut. Evening. A wood fire is burning and lights up the room.
The cat is on a chair at the foot of the bed. Åse is lying in bed fumbling uneasily with the blanket.*

ÅSE Oh, dear Lord, will he never come?
  How cruelly long this endless waiting.
  There's no way I can send him a message,
  And I have so much to say to him.
  There is so little time to lose.
  So soon! Who could have guessed it!
  Oh, if only I could feel sure
  I haven't been too hard on him!
PEER (*Entering.*) Good evening!
ÅSE   Heaven bless you!
  Then you've come at last, dearest boy.
  But how could you risk coming here?
  You know there's a bounty on your head!
PEER My life—what's that to me?
  I just had to come to see you.
ÅSE Now Kari should feel ashamed
  And I can go in peace at last.
PEER Go at last? What are you saying?
  And where do you think you're going?
ÅSE Ah, Peer, the end is drawing near.
  There's only a short time left me.
PEER (*Writhing and crossing the room.*)

1. *Helgedagkveld*, "holy day's evening." This Sunday is also made holy by Solveig's arrival.

I ran away from one heavy burden
Thinking at least here I'd be free—!
Are your hands or your feet very cold?
ÅSE Yes, Peer. It will soon be over—
  When you see my eyes are glazing,
  Then close them very gently.
  And when you're ordering my coffin,
  Make sure, my dear, it is splendid.
  Oh no, I'm forgetting—
PEER   Hush, now!
  There's plenty of time for that.
ÅSE Yes, yes. (*Looks uneasily about the room.*)
              Here you can see what little
  They've left me. That's just like them.
PEER (*Flinching.*) That again!
  (*Harshly.*)   I know it's my fault!
  But why remind me of the fact?
ÅSE You! No, it was that damnable drink,
  That's where all the mischief came from!
  My dearest boy, you'd been drinking
  And couldn't know what you were doing.
  And then, you'd been riding that reindeer,
  So it's no wonder you were confused.
PEER Yes, yes, let's drop that subject.
  In fact, let's forget the whole business.
  We can keep everything depressing and sad
  For later—for some other day.
  (*Sitting on the corner of the bed.*)
  So now, mother, let's have a chat;
  But just about things here and there,
  And forget everything twisted and awkward
  And all that's painful and harsh.
  Say, now, isn't that our old cat,
  Still keeping alive then, mother?
ÅSE She's acting so strangely at night, now.
  You know what that's warning us of.
PEER (*Changing the subject.*) What's the news in the parish?
ÅSE (*Smiling.*) They say that somewhere around here
  Is a girl whose heart's set on the mountains—
PEER (*Hastily.*) Mads Moen, how do things stand with him?
ÅSE They say she's shut her ears
  To the words and pleas of her parents.
  You ought to go over and visit them
  Peer, you could be of help.
PEER How do things stand with the blacksmith?

ÅSE Don't bring up that filthy smith.
  I'd much rather tell you the name
  Of her, that young girl who you—
PEER No, now we'll just have a chat
  Only about things here and there.
  Let's drop whatever's uncomfortable,
  Everything painful and harsh.
  Are you thirsty? Should I fetch you a drink?
  Can you stretch out? This bed's a bit short—
  Let me see—Why, I think it's the same one
  I slept in when I was a boy!
  Do you remember how in the evenings,
  You'd come and sit at my bedside
  And tuck the blankets around me
  And sing old ballads and songs?
ÅSE Yes, remember we played at sleigh rides
  While your father was out on his travels.
  The blanket became the sleigh-apron,
  And the floor a fjord locked in ice.
PEER Yes, but the most splendid of all—
  Do you remember that, mother?
  Our pair of thoroughbred horses!
ÅSE Do you think I could ever forget—?
  It was Kari's cat that we borrowed;
  She sat on the log-bench here.
PEER To the castle west of the moon and
  The castle east of the sun,
  To Soria-Moria castle[2]
  The road ran both high and low!
  We searched out a stick in the closet
  And made it a whip for the horse.
ÅSE I sat proud in the driver's seat—
PEER So you did, and let the reins fall;
  You kept turning even as we traveled
  To ask if I was feeling cold.
  God bless you, you ugly old darling
  You were always a loving soul—!
  But why are you moaning?
ÅSE   My back hurts;
  The bed planks are pressing too hard.
PEER Stretch yourself; I will support you.
  See there! Now you are comfy.
ÅSE (*Uneasily.*) No, Peer, I should be moving!

2. Famous isles of the blessed in Arabic legend.

PEER Moving?

ÅSE   Yes, that's what I want.

PEER What nonsense! Just pull up the blanket.
  Let me sit on the bedside here.
  That's it; now we'll shorten the evening
  With ballads and songs like before.

ÅSE But bring the prayer book from the closet.
  I feel so uneasy in mind.

PEER In Soria-Moria castle
  There's a feast for the king and the prince.
  Just relax among the sleigh cushions—
  I'm driving you over the heath.

ÅSE But Peer, love, am I invited?

PEER You bet, Mother, both of us are.
  (*Throws a cord over the chair where the cat is sleeping, takes a
  stick in his hand and sits at the foot of the bed.*)
  Hei-yo! Get moving there, Blackie!
  Mother, you're not feeling cold?
  Ah yes, you know you're traveling
  When Granë's[3] setting the pace!

ÅSE Peer, dearest, what is that ringing—

PEER The glittering sleigh-bells, Mother!

ÅSE Yes, but—how hollow they're echoing!

PEER We're driving over a fjord.

ÅSE I'm frightened. What's making that roaring
  And that sighing, so savage and strange?

PEER That's the wind in the fir trees, Mother,
  Across the heath. Just keep still.

ÅSE Lights flicker and flash in the distance.
  Where does all that brightness come from?

PEER From the windows and doors of the castle.
  Can you hear all the dancing?

ÅSE   Yes.

PEER There outside, Saint Peter is standing,
  He's waiting to ask you inside.

ÅSE He's greeting me?

PEER   Oh yes, with honor,
  And pouring the sweetest wine.

ÅSE Wine! Will there be cakes also?

PEER You can bet! A whole tasty heapful.
  And the dean's wife—remember?—is serving
  Coffee, and the classiest treats!

---

3. Granë ("Grah-nuh") is a horse, famous in Norwegian lore, descended from Sleipnir, the
  horse of the god Odin. This repeats the riding motif that began with the first scene and
  continues throughout.

ÅSE O Lord! Will we two be meeting?
PEER Just as soon and as long as you like.
ÅSE Oh Peer, this is a grand banquet
  You're taking your poor mother to.
PEER (*Cracking his whip.*) Hup! Get a move on, Blackie!
ÅSE Peer, are you on the right road, love?
PEER (*Cracking the whip again.*) The way here is broad.
ÅSE   This journey
  Is making me tired and weak.
PEER I can see the castle rising,
  Now this journey will soon be done.
ÅSE I'll just lie back with my eyes closed,
  And trust in your driving, my son.
PEER Gee up, Granë, my faithful beauty!
  In the castle the crowd is immense.
  At the gateway they're swarming and bustling:
  Peer Gynt and his mother are here!
  What's that, Mister Saint Peter?
  You won't let my mother come in?
  I think you can search the world over
  And not find a more honest soul.
  Myself?—let's not bring up that subject!
  I can turn round and leave by the gate.
  If you treat me, well, thanks for the pleasure!
  If not, no hard feelings, I'll leave.
  I've told as many tall stories
  As the devil got up like a priest,
  And called my old mother a hen,
  For the way she would cackle and scold;
  But you'd better receive her with honor
  And welcome her to her new home.
  There'll not come anyone better,
  From the whole district around.
  O-ho! Who's here? God the Father!
  You're in for it now, Saint Peter!
  (*In a deep voice.*) "Enough of this red tape nonsense;
  Mother Åsë is free to come in."
  (*Laughing loudly as he turns round to her.*)
  Well, isn't that just what I told you?
  Now they're playing a different tune.
  (*Uneasily.*) Why do you look like your eyes are glazing?
  Mother, are you going out of your mind?
  (*Goes up to the head of the bed.*)
  Don't lie there staring so strangely—
  Say something; it's me, your son!

(*Cautiously feeling her forehead and hands; then throwing the
cord back on the chair, he says, quietly.*)
So that's it! You can rest now, Granë;
The journey has come to an end.
(*Closes her eyes as he bends over her.*)
Thank you, for our life together,
For beatings and kisses, both.
Now give me thanks in return.
(*Presses his cheek against her lips.*)
So there, that was thanks for the ride.

KARI (*Entering.*) What? Peer! So now that answers
Her deepest sorrow and need.
Lord, how soundly she's sleeping—
Or is she—

PEER   Hush! She's dead.
(*Kari cries by the body. Peer Gynt paces round the room, finally
stopping by the bed.*)

PEER See that she's decently buried.
I'll try getting away from here.

KARI You'll be going far?

PEER   To the sea.

KARI As far as that?

PEER   Yes, and still farther.

Act Four

SCENE ONE

*The southwest coast of Morocco. A grove of palm trees. A table is
spread for a meal beneath an awning covered with rush matting. Further back inland, hammocks are slung. Beyond the shore lies a steam
yacht with Norwegian and American flags. On the shore, a dinghy. It
is approaching sunset.*

*Peer Gynt, a handsome, middle-aged man in elegant traveling
clothes, with a gold lorgnette dangling on his chest, is the host
presiding at the table. Mr. Cotton, M. Ballon, Herr von Eberkopf
and Herr Trumpeterstråle[1] are seated at the table concluding the
meal.*

---

1. The names of the characters are all emblematic of their nations. Mr. Cotton represents
British-American materialism; M. Ballon, French bourgeois "culture" or "tone"; Herr
Eberkopf, "boar's head," is Prussian aggression; the Swede, Trumpeterstråle, "trumpet-
blast," is Scandinavian diplomacy, all bluster in the face of Prussian aggression. Peer,
with these associates, is the modern Hollow Man, as in T. S. Eliot's poem "The Hollow
Man" (1925).

PEER Drink, my friends. As man is made
   For enjoyment, then let him enjoy!
   For it's written: "What's lost is lost,
   What's gone is gone." What can I offer you?
TRUMPETERSTRÅLE You're a lavish host, brother Gynt!
PEER I share that honor with my bank,
   My cook and steward—
COTTON   Very well;
   A skoal to our company of four.
BALLON Monsieur, you have a *gout*, a *ton*[2]
   Which one so seldom finds these days
   Among men who live *en garçon*—
   A certain—how to express it—
VON EBERKOPF   An air,
   A tinge of spiritually free reflection
   And world-citizen-solidarity.[3]
   A sighting, through a rift in the clouds,
   Undimmed by gray conformity;
   A stamp of high enlightenment,
   An *Ur Natur*[4] grounded in life
   But realizing the dialectic summit.
   That, monsieur, was what you meant?
BALLON Yes, very possibly, though lacking in
   The style it would acquire in French.
VON EBERKOPF *Ei was!* That language is so stiff.
   But, for the ground of the phenomenon
   We're seeking—
PEER   It's already found.
   The answer is: I never married.
   Oh yes, gentlemen, it's perfectly clear
   What the cause is. What is a man?
   Himself! That in brief's my answer.
   He and what's *his* should be his care.
   Not possible when, like a poor pack camel
   He must bear another's burden and grief.
VON EBERKOPF But this in-and-for-yourself-condition[5]
   I guarantee, has cost some struggle—
PEER Oh yes, for sure. In earlier times.
   But I always came out of it with honor.
   One time I came very close
   To getting trapped against my will.

2. A taste, a tone. French in the original.
3. *Verdensborgerdomsforpaktning*; a glance at the German language's propensity for com-
   pound forms.
4. Basic/original nature. German in the original.
5. A form of the Hegelian term "in-and-for-itself"; an achieved identity.

I was a fiery, well-set-up fellow,
And the girl I fell for at the time
Turned out to be royalty—
BALLON Royalty?
PEER (*Casually.*) Of ancient stock.
   You know the—
TRUMPETERSTRÅLE (*Thumping the table.*) These lordly trolls!
PEER (*Shrugging his shoulders.*) Aristocratic fossils who set their
   pride
   In family blood above plebeian stock,
   To spare it from contamination.
COTTON Did the affair come to grief?
BALLON The family opposed the alliance?
PEER Quite the opposite.
BALLON   Ah!
PEER (*Circumspectly.*)   You should understand,
   Things arose—making it increasingly urgent
   To hold the wedding as soon as possible.
   But, quite frankly, the whole affair
   Was distasteful to me from first to last.
   I can be fastidious about certain matters,
   And prefer to be my own man completely.
   When my father-in-law-to-be hinted
   I ought to change my name and status,
   Submit to applying for noble rank,
   Mixed with other objectionable demands,
   I made a dignified withdrawal.
   I rejected his rude ultimatum,
   And broke it off with my young bride.
   (*Drumming on the table and looking self-righteous.*)
   Yes, there's a destiny that shapes our ends,
   A comfort we mere mortals can depend on.
BALLON And is that where the matter ended?
PEER No. Certain intrusive individuals
   Kicked up a fuss about the business.
   Worst were the junior family members.
   I fought a duel with seven of them.
   What a time that was—I'll never forget it—
   Although I came out of it in one piece.
   It cost blood; but that same blood
   Is testimony to my personal merit,
   And points very gratifyingly toward—
   As we said—the guiding role of destiny!
VON EBERKOPF You possess a perspective on life
   That enlists you in the ranks of thinkers.

For while the commonplace opinion
Sees only *its* piece of the panorama,
Never grasping more than a fragment,
You comprehend the grand totality.
You measure all things by one norm;
Focusing on each rule of living,
Till each and all spread out like rays
Of light from one philosophic center—
And yet you never graduated?
PEER No! Completely self-taught, an autodidact!
I've taken up nothing methodically.
But I've thought a lot and speculated,
And read about things here and there.
I started somewhat late in life.
You know what heavy going that can be,
Plowing up and down the pages,
Trying like hell to take it all in.
I've picked up my history in scraps,
Not having time to go into it more.
But still, you feel the need to fall back
On something for more serious times;
I've done some dabbling in religion.
My rule: books are there for you to use,
Not to take up too much of your time!
COTTON Good pragmatism!
PEER (*Lighting a cigar.*)   Dear friends;
When I consider how my life was spent—
What was I when I first ventured out west?
A pauper with completely empty hands,
Scrambling for food to keep himself alive;
Believe me, those were times that tried a man.
But "Life, my friends, is a very precious thing
And Death a downer," as someone, somewhere, says.
Well! Luck, you see, was favorable to me,
Old Fate itself being reasonably well-disposed.
Things went well, for I was adaptable.
And so my affairs kept getting better and better.
And in ten years I even acquired a title:
"The Croesus[6] of the Charleston traders."
From port to port my reputation followed,
And with it followed my fortune and my fleet.
COTTON What did you trade in?
PEER   Mostly, I dealt in

---

6. King of the ancient land of Lydia; he was famous for his wealth.

Negro slaves to Carolina
And pagan images to China.
BALLON *Fi donc!*[7]
TRUMPETERSTRÅLE Good heavens, brother Gynt!
PEER You find the enterprise teetering
   On the edge of the unacceptable?
   I, too, felt a tad queasy over it;
   However, a business once started, is darned
   Difficult to break off—devilishly complicated
   In an enterprise as vast as mine,
   Employing so many thousand workers.
   You just can't give the whole thing up at once.
   I've never liked that "at once." However,
   I've always felt the greatest veneration
   For what folk call the consequences;
   And that to overstep the bounds,
   Can make one's conscience a trifle tremulous.
   What's more, I wasn't getting any younger,
   My fiftieth birthday was closing in,
   With the gray hairs inexorably advancing.
   And though still in the best of health—
   I couldn't escape the painful thought
   The summons may come when one has it least in mind,
   And the ultimate jury will deliver its verdict,
   Announcing division of the sheep and goats.
   What, then, to do? Closing the whole trade
   With China was utterly unthinkable!
   I found the way out, though, and quickly opened
   A whole new business without changing location.
   The cargo of idols I exported in springtime
   Created a pressing need for priests each fall.
   I sent out missionaries with necessary provisions,
   Like Bibles, stockings, rice, and rum—
COTTON At a good profit?
PEER   That goes without saying.
   It worked! And *they* worked, tirelessly.
   Every idol image I sold, guaranteed
   They got a coolie to thoroughly baptize.
   So the effect, you can see, was neutralized.
   The missionary fields were never barren,
   Irrigated by a constant flood of idols,
   Which the good priests labored earnestly to stem.
COTTON But what about the African merchandise?

7. Expression of disgust (French).

PEER There too, I won a moral victory.
  I'd got to feeling the traffic was a bit dubious
  For someone, like me, of advancing years.
  (Who knows when you may be asked to exit?)
  Not to mention the thousand snares
  Set by the leagues of ethical do-gooders;
  Then on top of that, the Barbary pirates.
  Add to these, hazards of wind and weather—
  These combined to get me thinking: "Peer,
  Reef in your sails, and mend your way of life."
  So I bought some land down in the South
  And kept the last cargo of meat for myself,
  Which happened to be particularly prime.
  They thrived and grew so sleek and plump,
  It worked out just fine for all of us.
  Yes, I can claim, without exaggeration,
  I treated them like their own father,
  And that paid off in very nice returns.
  I built schools for them so that virtue
  Might be strictly and uniformly maintained
  And kept close watch that this high level
  Of the moral thermometer should never sink.
  Anyway, soon after, I sold the whole plantation,
  Got rid of the livestock, all the hide and hair.
  On the last day I passed round the grog.
  The men and women got drunk, the widows
  Got their supply of snuff, so I can truly say
  The motto's still valid: "He who does no evil
  Does good." My earlier errors are wiped away,
  And more than most folk I think I can claim
  My virtues and vices cancel out each other.
VON EBERKOPF (*Clinking glasses with him.*) How much it fortifies
    the spirit
  To hear a whole life-principle put into practice!
  Freed from the dark obscurity of theory,
  Unshaken by the clamor from outside.
PEER (*Who has been emptying his glass somewhat frequently.*)
  We northerners understand the obligation
  To carry our battles through! The key to life
  Is simple: to keep one's ears forever shut
  Against the urgings of the deadly serpent.
COTTON What serpent might that be, my friend?
PEER A little one, but really tricky, to tempt you
  To do that which never can be undone.
  (*Drinking again.*)

What the whole art of risk-taking boils down to
Is this: keeping your feet all the time free
To dodge the traps that are placed in your path.
To realize there will still be other days
To follow, when that day of battle's over.
To know there's always behind you, waiting,
A bridge for beating a quick retreat when needed.
This theory has kept me going and colored
My entire career. It was an inheritance
From the people of my childhood home.

BALLON You are Norwegian?

PEER   By birth, yes!
But a citizen of the world by inclination.
For the fortune I've come into I must thank
America. My fine, extensive library
I owe to Germany's new crop of scholars.
From France I'm indebted for my waistcoats,
My wit and elegance. From England,
An industrious streak and a nose for the main chance.
The Jew has taught me patience to wait. And Italy,
A sense of *dolce far niente*.
And when I was in a very tight situation,
I got out of the danger with Swedish steel.

TRUMPETERSTRÅLE (*Raising his glass.*) Yes, Swedish steel—!

VON EBERKOPF   To the wielder of that steel,
We first and foremost pay our heartfelt homage!
(*They clink glasses again and drink with Peer. The drink begins to
go to his head.*)

COTTON All very good. But what I'd like to know, sir,
Is, what do you intend doing with all your gold?

PEER (*Smiling.*) Hm. Intend doing? Eh?

ALL FOUR (*Approaching.*)   Yes, let's hear!

PEER Well, in the first place, to travel. That is why
I took you abroad in Gibraltar as companions.
I needed a choir of friends to dance around
The altar of my golden calf.

VON EBERKOPF   Most witty!

COTTON But you don't hoist sail for the joy of the journey.
You have to have a goal, that goes without saying.
And that goal is—?

PEER   To be Emperor.

ALL FOUR What?

PEER (*Nodding.*) Emperor!

ALL FOUR   Where?

PEER   Of the whole world.

BALLON But how, my friend—?
PEER   By the power of gold!
   The plan's in no way at all original;
   It's been the heart and soul of all my actions.
   As a boy I often dreamt of soaring
   On a white cloud across the seven seas,
   In royal robes and with a golden sword.
   But I'd fall to earth, floundering on all fours.
   The ambition, though, stayed as strong as ever.
   I think it's written, or maybe spoken,
   If you won the world but lost your *self*
   Your gain would be nothing more than a wreath
   Crowning a skull. Something like that.
   And those wise words are not just poetry.
VON EBERKOPF But what is it then, this Gyntian self?
PEER The world behind my rounded brow,
   Which determines "I am I" and am no other
   As certainly as God is not the Devil.
TRUMPETERSTRÅLE Ah, now I understand what you are after!
BALLON Sublime thinker!
VON EBERKOPF   Exalted poet!
PEER (*In rising excitement.*) The Gyntian *self*. It is the army
   Of wishes, appetites, and desires.
   The Gyntian Self, a tumultuous sea
   Of fancies, cravings, and demands:
   In short, all that's fermenting in my breast
   Ensuring that I, as I, therefore exist.
   But just as the Lord has need of common clay
   To mold a world where he will be the God,
   So I, likewise, have a need for gold,
   To fulfill my project of imperial power.
BALLON But you have gold!
PEER   Nowhere near enough.
   Maybe for a two-to-three day's imperial spree,
   As Emperor *à la* Lippe-Detmold,[8]
   But I must be MYSELF *en bloc*,
   Must be the Gynt of the whole earth,
   Sir Gynt entire from top to toe.
BALLON (*Ecstatic.*) Owning the world's supremest beauty!
VON EBERKOPF A century old Johannisberger wine!
TRUMPETERSTRÅLE And all the swords of Charles the Twelfth!
COTTON But first a lucrative opening
   For capital—

8. A tiny principality in Westphalia, the kind satirized in Georg Büchner's *Leonce and Lena* (1836).

PEER   It's found already!
  It's the reason why we're anchored here.
  Tonight our journey takes us northward.
  The newspapers that just arrived
  Inform me of some breaking news.
  (*Rises with his glass raised.*)
  It appears Fortune never fails to favor
  Those with the initiative to seize it—
ALL FOUR So? Then tell us—
PEER   There's rebellion in Greece.[9]
ALL FOUR (*Rising to their feet.*) What! The Greeks—?
PEER   Have risen up.
ALL FOUR Hurrah!
PEER   And Turkey has a problem.
BALLON To Greece! The path to glory's opened!
  I'll help them with the sword of France.
VON EBERKOPF I'll cheer them on—from the sidelines.
COTTON I, too—with arms deliveries.
TRUMPETERSTRÅLE Lead on! In Bender maybe I'll discover
  The famous spurs of Charles the Twelfth.[1]
BALLON (*Falling on Peer Gynt's neck.*)
  Forgive me, friend. Just for a while,
  I quite misjudged you!
VON EBERKOPF (*Grasping his hands.*) I, like an idiot,
  Nearly took you for a swine.
COTTON A little harsh. A fool, perhaps—
TRUMPETERSTRÅLE (*Makes to kiss him.*)
  I, brother, for a specimen
  Of the Yankee rabble's lowest scum—!
  Forgive me—
VON EBERKOPF We have all blundered—
PEER What are you talking about?
VON EBERKOPF   Now we can see
  Gathered in one the glorious Gyntian
  Army of wishes, appetites, and desires—!
BALLON (*In admiration.*) So this is being Monsieur Gynt!
VON EBERKOPF *This* is to be Gynt with honor!
PEER Will you please tell me—?
BALLON   Surely you understand?
PEER Hell if I do, or may I be hanged!

9. The Greeks rose up against Turkish occupation in 1827, finally gaining independence in
   1838.
1. A very obscure reference for non-Swedes. After his defeat at the hands of the Turks
   (1709), the Swedish king, Charles XII, in a rage, is reputed to have torn the clothes of
   the Sultan's messenger with his spurs on hearing that Turkey had made a pact with Russia.

BALLON Where is the problem? Aren't you sailing
  With your ship and money to help the Greeks?
PEER (*Contemptuously.*) No thanks! I play the power game.
  I'm lending my money to the Turks.
BALLON Impossible!
VON EBERKOPF   Witty, but of course, a joke!
PEER (*Pauses a while, leaning back in his chair and putting on an air
    of dignity.*)
  Gentlemen, listen, I think it best
  We part before the last remains
  Of friendship blow away like smoke.
  Risks are fine when you've little to lose.
  When the only share of earth you own
  Is little more than what your shadow covers,
  You're only ripe for cannon fodder.
  But when you're very well set up,
  As I am, then the stakes are higher.
  Travel to Greece! I'll gladly take you,
  Free of charge and armed to the teeth.
  The more you fan the flames of war,
  The better it turns out for me.
  Battle for freedom and for justice!
  Raise fury and hellfire against the Turks!
  And heroically end your days
  On the lance points of the Janissaries—
  But, for my part, please excuse me.
  (*Patting his pocket.*)
                              I have cash
  And am myself, Sir Peter Gynt.
  (*He puts up his sunshade and goes into the grove where the
  hammocks are hung.*)
TRUMPETERSTRÅLE A swine, after all!
BALLON   No sense of honor!
COTTON Honor? Well, be that as it may.
  But think of the enormous profits
  To be gotten if Greece gets its freedom.
BALLON I saw myself as a conquering hero
  Flanked by a bevy of Grecian girls!
TRUMPETERSTRÅLE My Swedish hands were itching to grasp
  Spur buckles of heroic fame!
VON EBERKOPF I saw my mighty Fatherland
  Spreading its culture *uber alles!*
COTTON Worse, though, is the loss of capital.
  Goddamit! It could make me weep!
  I saw myself owner of Olympus.

If that mountain's all it's cracked up to be,
It's got to have some veins of copper
Ready to be opened up at last.
And then there's that Castalian spring[2]
That's gotten itself much talked about;
Those waterfalls, one after the other,
Should generate a thousand horsepower—

TRUMPETERSTRÅLE Nevertheless, I'll go! My Swedish sword
Is worth far more than Yankee gold!

COTTON Maybe, but jammed tight in the fighting ranks,
We'd soon be drowned in waves of troops;
And where would the profit be in that?

BALLON Damnation! So close to Fortune's summit,
Only to stand beside its grave!

COTTON (*Shaking his fist at the yacht.*) Contained inside that long
black chest,
Is the gold he sweated from Negro slaves.

VON EBERKOPF A kingly thought! Quick! Get going!
We've got his empire by the throat!
Hurrah!

BALLON   What are you up to?

VON EBERKOPF   Seize power!
It won't be hard to bribe the crew.
On board then! I annex the yacht!

COTTON You—what—?

VON EBERKOPF   Grab all, in one fell swoop!
(*He goes to the dinghy.*)

COTTON Self-interest dictates that I
Must grab as well.
(*Follows.*)

TRUMPETERSTRÅLE   What a crook!

BALLON Abominable behavior—! but—*enfin!*
(*Following the others.*)

TRUMPETERSTRÅLE No choice is left me but to follow—
But I protest to all the world—!
(*Follows after.*)

SCENE TWO

*Another part of the coast. Moonlight with drifting clouds. The yacht
is going full steam ahead in the distance.*

(*Peer Gynt runs along the shore, now pinching himself awake, now
staring out to sea.*)

2. A spring sacred to Apollo and the Muses. Not on Mount Olympus (home of the gods),
however, but Mount Parnassus.

PEER A nightmare! A mirage! Soon I'll wake up!
  She's out at sea! Going full steam ahead!
  A mirage! I'm sleeping! I'm drunk and delirious.
  (*Clenching his hands.*)
  It can't be possible I'm going to die!
  (*Tearing his hair.*)
  A dream! I *will* it to be a dream!
  Horrifying! No doubt it's real, worse luck!
  My scumbags of friends—! Hear me, O Lord!
  Thou art righteous and wise—! O, judgment—!
  (*With upraised arms.*)
  It's *me*, Peer Gynt! Take notice, Lord!
  Take care of me, Father; or else I'm finished!
  Make them reverse the engine! Lower the dinghy!
  Stop the thieves! Confuse all the rigging!
  Hear me! Stop worrying about other people!
  The world can go its own way for a while!
  Oh God! He's not listening. Deaf as usual!
  That's just great! A God who's no help at all!
  (*Signaling to the sky.*)
  Psst! I've got rid of the slave-plantation!
  I've shipped flocks of missionaries over to Asia!
  Surely a good deed should count for something!
  Help me get aboard—!
  (*A jet of flame shoots into the air from the yacht, and a thick smoke
  envelops it. A hollow explosion follows. Peer Gynt gives out a cry
  and sinks into the sand. Soon after, the smoke clears and the
  ship sinks from sight.*)
PEER (*Pale and hushed.*) The sword of Justice!
  To the depths in a flash with man and mouse!
  O, lasting praise for this stroke of Fortune!
  (*With feeling.*) Fortune? No, here there was more than luck.
  It was ordained I live and they would perish.
  O, thanks and praise that you have protected me.
  Kept your care for me despite my sins.
  (*Draws a deep breath.*)
  What a wonderful sense of peace and comfort,
  Knowing one is singled out to be blessed.
  But in this desert! How to find food and drink?
  Something will turn up; He understands.
  Things could be much worse.
  (*Loudly and insinuatingly.*) *He* won't permit
  Me, his poor little sparrow, to perish!
  Be humble in spirit. Just leave things to Him.
  The Lord will provide, so don't be cast down!

(*Leaping with a shriek of terror.*)
Was that a lion growling in the brush?
(*His teeth chattering.*)
No, that was no lion.
(*Getting hold of himself.*)
A lion!! What an idea!
These beasts make sure they keep out of our way.
They know better than meddle with their superiors.
It's instinctual; for example, they feel how
It's dangerous to mess with elephants.
All the same—might be wise to find a tree!
Over there, acacias and palms are swaying;
If I climbed up there, I'd be sheltered and safe.
If I could just remember a couple of psalms.
(*He clambers up.*)
"Morning and evening are not alike." A text
That's frequently been searched and pondered.
(*Making himself comfortable.*)
How delightful to feel one's spirit uplifted.
Thinking nobly's better than knowing you're rich.
Just trust Him! He knows exactly what portion
Of the cup of affliction I can bear to drink.
He keeps a fatherly look out for my person.
(*Casts his eyes over the sea and whispers, sighing.*)
But economical—no, He's no idea of *that*!

SCENE THREE

Night. A Moroccan camp on the edge of the desert. Sentry fires with soldiers at rest.

A SLAVE (*Enters, tearing his hair.*) The Emperor's white charger is gone!
ANOTHER SLAVE (*Enters, tearing his clothes.*) The Emperor's sacred robes are stolen!
OFFICER (*Entering.*) A hundred lashes on the soles of the feet
For all who fail to catch the thief.

SCENE FOUR

Daybreak. A grove of trees with acacias and palms. Peer Gynt in a tree with a broken branch in his hand trying to fend off a swarm of monkeys.

PEER Appalling! A most disagreeable night!
(*Flailing about him.*)

Are you back again! This is god-damned hellish.
Now they're throwing fruit. Oh no, it's something else!
A disgusting beast, your Barbary ape!
It is written, "Keep awake, and fight."
But I'm darned if I can. I'm tired and wasted.
(*He is attacked again; losing his patience.*)
I must put a stop to these filthy attacks,
Maybe see if I can trap one of these devils,
Hang him and skin him and then get inside
His shaggy pelt, as best as I can,
So the others will think I am one of them.
What are we humans? No more than dust.
And it's always wise to follow the custom.
Another swarm! Crowding and pressing.
Get away! Shoo! They're going crazy!
Now if I only had a temporary tail,
Something to make me a bit more like a beast.
What now? Something's padding over my head. (*Looks up.*)
It's the Old Man, with his fists full of filth—!
(*Crouches down apprehensively and goes still for a moment. The
ape makes a gesture. Peer Gynt starts to coax and wheedle him as if
he were a dog.*)
Hey, are you there, my good old Bus!
Oh, he's a good beast, he wants to be friendly!
He wouldn't throw—! Oh no, 'course he wouldn't—!
It's me! Pip-pip! We're good friends, we are!
Ai-ai. Can you hear how I speak your language?
Bus and I, we're even related, we're family.[3]
Bus shall have sugar tomorrow—! The beast!!
The whole load pitched over me! Ugh, disgusting!—
Or is it perhaps food? The taste was—equivocal;
Where taste is concerned, it's habit that decides.
Who was that thinker who at one time said
You must spit and trust to the force of habit?
Now here come the youngsters!
(*Slashes and hitting out.*)
                                                It's totally wrong
That Man, by rights the lord of creation,
Should be reduced to—Ah, murder! Murder!
The old one was foul but the children are worse!

---

3. Charles Darwin's *Origin of Species* was published in 1859, eight years before *Peer Gynt*,
and translated into Norwegian, with an informed commentary, in the magazine *Bud-
stikken* in 1861. Ibsen seems to have equably accepted the theory, which so convulsed
his contemporaries.

Early morning. A stony region with a view over the desert. On the one side a ravine and a cave.

(*A thief and a receiver are hidden in the ravine with the Emperor's horse and robes. The horse, richly caparisoned, stands tied to a rock. Horsemen appear in the distance.*)

THE THIEF The lances' tongues
Are flickering, gleaming.
See, see!
THE RECEIVER I see my head
In the sand, blood streaming
Oh misery, misery!
THE THIEF (*Folding his arms.*) My father thieved;
His son now is thieving.
RECEIVER My father received;
His son's now receiving.
THE THIEF Bear your fate patiently;
Be what you're meant to be.
THE RECEIVER (*Listening.*) Footsteps approaching.
Run! Before it's too late!
THE THIEF The cavern is deep
And the Prophet is great!
(*They run off leaving the booty behind. The horsemen in the distance vanish.*)
PEER GYNT (*Enters, cutting a reed pipe.*)
What a delectable hour of the morning!
The dung beetle trundles his ball through the sand.
The snail creeps out of his little snail house.
Morning! As they say, it has gold in its mouth.
When you think about it, it's a wonderful power
That Nature bestows on the light of day!
You feel so secure, there's an increase of courage;
One's prepared, if need be, to take on a bull.
What a stillness all round! Ah yes, earthly joys!
I can't imagine how I neglected them earlier;
Spending your life walled up in a city
Enduring the clamorous mob at your door.
No, observe how the lizards are frisking about,
Snapping and thinking of nothing at all!
What innocence animals reveal in their lives!
Each, carrying out its Creator's agenda,
Preserving, intact, its own unique stamp,
Is itself—itself in combat or play;

Itself, as God shaped it on the first day.
(*Sets his lorgnette on his nose.*)
A Toad! At the center of a sandstone block!
In a sea of stone, just his head jutting out.
He sits there, gazing, as if through a window
At the wide world. To himself, he's enough—
(*Reflecting.*) Enough? Himself? Now where's that written?
I read it as a boy in one of the Great Books.
The family prayer book? Solomon's Proverbs?
It's dreadful; I notice that year by year
My memory for dates and places gets worse.
(*Seats himself in the shade.*)
Here's a cool spot to stretch one's legs.
And see—ferns! They seem like edible roots;
(*Tastes one.*) More suitable, perhaps, for the animal appetite,
But it *is* written: you must subdue your nature!
And somewhere else: pull down thy pride!
For whoso humbleth himself shall be exalted!
(*Uneasily.*) Exalted? Yes, that's got to happen to me!
It's intolerable to think of anything else.
Destiny will help me escape this place
And arrange it so I can start all over again.
This is just a trial; salvation comes after,
As long as the good Lord looks after my health.
(*He shakes off these thoughts, lights a cigar, stretches, and gazes out over the desert.*)
What an unbounded and measureless waste!
In the far distance an ostrich is strutting.
What is one to imagine was in God's mind,
Creating this vast, lifeless emptiness?
This, where all means of existence is lacking;
This burnt-out cinder, that profits no one;
This remnant of earth that forever lies barren;
This corpse that, since the world's creation,
Never returned so much as thanks to its Maker.
What's the point of it? Nature is wasteful.
Is that ocean, to the east, that shimmering stretch
Gleaming out there? No, it must be a mirage.
The ocean's to the west; it rises, behind me.
Dammed off from the desert by that ridge of dunes.
(*A thought flashes through him.*)
Dammed off? Then I could—! The ridge is low . . .
Dammed off! Then to break through—with a canal!
And a life-giving flood of water would rush
Through the canal and into the desert!

Before long, this entire, scorching graveyard
Would yield up a fresh and rippling sea.
Oases, like islands, would rise into sight,
With the green cliffs of Atlas on the north shore;
The sails of ships, like flocks of great birds,
Would skim the caravans' trek to the south.
Life-giving breezes would scatter the torpid
Miasma, and dew would descend from the clouds.
People would come and build town after town;
Meadows would merge with the swaying palms.
The land lying south behind the Sahara
Would become the coastline of a new culture.
Steam power would drive Timbuktoo's factories,
And Bornu would give way to colonization.
Scholars, researchers, would travel through Habès.[4]
In sleeping cars, to the Upper Nile regions.
On a luxuriant oasis, in the midst of this ocean,
I'll plant there settlers of the Nordic race.
A dalesman's blood is more or less royal;
And crossed with the Arab, would make the race perfect.
Surrounding a bay on the rising terrain,
I shall found Peeropolis, the capital city.
The old world is finished. Now is the time
For Gyntiana,[5] my new found land.
(*Leaps up.*) If I'd only the capital, the thing would be done.
A key of gold for the gates of the ocean!
A crusade against Death! That malicious miser
Must be made to open his sack of treasures.
Freedom's the battle cry in every land.
Like the ass in the ark[6] I'll cry to the world,
I'll be the baptizer of liberty's blessings
To those shores whose beauty still lies in bondage.
I must get to work! There's capital in East and West!
My kingdom—half my kingdom—for a horse![7]
(*The horse in the ravine whinnies.*)
A horse! And costume—! And jewels—and weapons!
(*Approaching.*) Impossible! But true! And how? I've read
Somewhere that faith is known to move mountains,
But nowhere that it can transport a horse—

4. Abyssinia.
5. The famous Norwegian violinist, Ole Bull, lost his entire life savings founding Oleana, a
colony in the United States. Earlier, Bull had been instrumental in securing Ibsen his
first theatrical position in the theater Bull founded in Bergen, Norway, in 1851.
6. A reference to an old conundrum: "What ass could bray so loud the entire world could
hear?" The ass in Noah's ark.
7. An echo of "A horse! A horse! My kingdom for a horse!" *Richard III*, 5.7.13.

Well? Here the horse stands, undeniably transported!
Ab esse ad posse[8] etcetera, etcetera.
(*Puts on the robes, then looks down at himself.*)
Sir Peter!—and now, as completely, the Turk!
Well, who can tell what the future will bring?
Gee up there Granë, my faithful beauty.
(*Climbs into the saddle.*)
Gold stirrups, too, for my feet to go in.
From the way a man rides, you know he's a swell!

SCENE SIX

The tent of an Arab sheik, standing by itself in an oasis. Peer Gynt, in his Eastern robes, is resting on cushions. He is drinking coffee and smoking from a long pipe while Anitra and a group of girls dance and sing for him.

THE CHORUS OF GIRLS The Prophet has come!
　The Prophet, the lord, the Omniscient One,
　Unto us, unto us, he has come,
　Over the sand, the magnificent One!
　The Prophet, the lord, the unfailing,
　Unto us, unto us, has he come,
　Over the desert's ocean, sailing!
　Rouse the flute and the drum,
　The Prophet, the Prophet has come!
ANITRA His stallion is as milky-white,
　As are the rivers of Paradise.
　Bend your knee, lower your gaze,
　His eyes are stars burning bright,
　None born of earth can bear
　The glare that streams from that fire.
　Through the desert he came.
　Gold and pearls sprang from his breast.
　Where he rode, his light blessed;
　Behind, all was gloom,
　Behind him, the drought and simoom.
　He, the glorious one, came!
　Through the desert he came,
　Putting on mortal form.
　Kaaba, Kaaba[9] stands empty;
　This truth the Prophet proclaims!

8. "From actuality to possibility" (Latin), an axiom in logic.
9. The cubical structure in the center of the courtyard of the Great Mosque in Mecca, containing the famous Black Stone; the holiest of Islamic shrines.

Peer Gynt: Anitra [Act IV]." Copyright © 2003 The Munch Museum/The Munch-Ellingsen Group/Artists Rights Society (ARS), NY.

CHORUS OF GIRLS Rouse the flute and the drum,
   The Prophet, the Prophet has come!
PEER I've read it in print—and the text is true—
   "No one's a Prophet in his own land."
   This setup here suits me much better
   Than life among the Charleston traders.
   Something was hollow about that business,
   A bit out of character, distinctly dubious.
   I never felt quite at home in that company,
   Not one of the fraternity, so to speak.
   Whatever was I doing in that *galère*?[1]
   Rooting around in the garbage of trade?
   No, when I think of it, I can't explain it!
   That's how things happened: it's all I can say.
   Being oneself on a basis of gold—
   That is to build your house on sand.
   You can get folk to grovel and creep in the dirt,
   For your watch, rings, and trinkets—things like that;
   They'll raise their hat to your diamond stickpin,
   But your ring and your pin are not your real person.
   A Prophet! Now there the position is clearer!
   A man can be sure on what foot he is standing.
   If you succeed, it's yourself that receives
   Ovations, and not your pounds, dollars, and francs.
   You *are* who you are, and no question about it.
   You owe nothing to chance or a throw of the dice,
   Nor to licenses, contracts, patents, or deeds.
   A Prophet! Yes! Just the vocation for me!
   And I slipped into the role so effortlessly,
   Simply by galloping over the desert,
   And encountering these children of nature en route!
   Their Prophet had come; the matter was clear.
   It wasn't as if I had tried to deceive them;
   Lies aren't the same as oracular answers,
   And in any case I can always retire.
   I'm in no way committed, so it's not compromising.
   The whole business is private and need go no further.
   I can leave as I came; my horse stands prepared;
   In brief, I'm in total control of the outcome.
ANITRA (*Approaching the tent door.*)
   Prophet and Master!
PEER   Yes, my young slave?
ANITRA Waiting outside are the sons of the desert;

1. Galley ship. The quotation is from a comedy by Molière.

They beg for the sight of your countenance.

PEER Stop! Tell them to wait at a distance.
  Say, a distance best suits men's prayers.
  Emphasize I allow no menfolk in here.
  Men, my child, are an untrustworthy lot.
  They can truly be called vile-tempered beasts.
  Anitra, you've no idea how often, without shame
  They have swind—, I mean they have sinned, my child.
  No, you can't know. Dance for me, women!
  The Prophet prefers to forget the sad past.

GIRLS (*Dancing.*) The Prophet is good! The Prophet is grieving
  For the evil the sons of the dust have been living.
  The Prophet is mild. For his mildness give praise.
  He shows sinners the path to Paradise.

PEER (*His eyes following Anitra as she is dancing.*)
  Her legs flash as quick as the beat of the drums.
  Hey! She's a succulent dish, that wench.
  Her build's a mite on the extravagant side,
  Not quite in accord with today's ideals.
  But what's beauty? Nothing more than convention,
  Like currency valid in one time and place.
  And the extravagant can seem very alluring.
  When you're fed with too much familiar menu,
  Conventional fare can fail to entice.
  Then one's taste starts to savor the ample or lean,
  Too tenderly young or toughened with age.
  Everything in between is insipid.
  Her feet, now—not scrupulously clean.
  Nor the arms, either—especially the one.
  But when you get down to it, that's not a detraction,
  It might even qualify as an enticement.
  Anitra, come listen!

ANITRA (*Approaching.*) Your slave has heard.

PEER Child, you attract me. The Prophet is moved.
  If you don't believe me I can give you the proof.
  I'll make you a Houri in Paradise.

ANITRA Impossible, lord!

PEER   What? You don't think I'm serious?
  Believe me I could not be more so.

ANITRA But I haven't a soul.[2]

PEER   Then you must acquire one.

ANITRA How, Lord?

---

2. Why Anitra thinks this is hard to explain. It is not part of Islamic tradition. Maybe it is
  to emphasize her ignorance.

PEER   Just let me work that out.
  I shall take up the mission of your education.
  No soul? Yes, maybe you're not too bright,
  As they say. I have observed it with sorrow.
  What of it? One can always find room for a soul.
  Come here, child! Let me measure your brainpan.
  There is room, there is room! It's just as I thought.
  True enough, it's unlikely you'll ever explore
  Very deeply. Your soul's never going to be large.
  But hell! That, too, can be all for the best.
  You'll get sufficient to not be ashamed—
ANITRA The Prophet is good—
PEER   You hesitate? Speak!
ANITRA But I'd much rather have—
PEER   Speak! Don't be afraid—
ANITRA I'm not so concerned about having a soul—
  I'd much rather have—
PEER   What?
ANITRA (*Pointing to his turban.*) That beautiful opal!
PEER (*Enchanted, handing her the jewel.*)
  Anitra! Natural daughter of Eve!
  I'm magnetically drawn to you, being a man,
  And as a certain famous author has written
  "Das Ewig-Weibliche ziehet uns an!"[3]

SCENE SEVEN

A moonlit night. A grove of palms outside Anitra's tent. Peer Gynt sits underneath a tree. His hair and beard are trimmed and he looks considerably younger.

PEER (*Strumming and singing.*)

> I locked away my Paradise
> Departing with the key,
> Borne southward on a northern breeze.
> Salt tears from fair women's eyes
> Forlornly fed the sea.
>
> Southward, southward, my keel ploughed
> Salt furrows in the waves.

---

3. Peer's revealing misquotation, fully intended by Ibsen. Goethe had written, more platonically, "the eternal feminine draws us upward" (*zieht uns hinan*). The misquotation makes the attraction merely sexual.

There, where the palm trees thickly crowd
Round golden sands, fronds swaying, bowed,
I set my ship ablaze.

I climbed aboard a desert ship;
On its four legs set sail.
It foamed beneath my lashing whip
I am a bird so swift, I skip
And sing on hill and dale.

Anitra, redolent of palms!
Rewarding he that knows you.
Angora goat cheese, though it charms,
Ranks less than thee, when in my arms.
Anitra, I enclose you.

(*He hangs the lute over his shoulder and moves closer in.*
Silence! Was the fair one listening?)
Attending, in rapture, to my song?
Is she peeping coyly through the curtain,
Discarding her veil—and other items?
Hush! There sounded a subtle explosion
Not unlike a cork leaping from a bottle.
Yet once again! And one more time!
Can these be the sighs of love, or singing?
No, a distinctly audible snoring!
Nonetheless, music! Anitra is sleeping.
Nightingale, suspend your clamor!
There's no telling the awful consequence
If you wake her with impertinent chirping.
Oh, forget it! As it is written, "Let it be!"
You are simply a natural-born singer.
And so am I, when you come down to it.
You, like me, melodiously snare
Tender, shrinking, beating hearts.
A night like this is made for singing.
Song is the sphere we both inhabit.
We sing, therefore we are, we two.
Peer Gynt and the nightingale unite.
And this girl's deep and tranquil slumber
Becomes my passion's highest bliss.
Lips ready on the glass's rim,
Not yet tasting—hesitating—
But there, my soul, she starts and stirs!
It's best she waken, after all.

ANITRA (*From the tent.*) Lord, did you call me in the night?
PEER Yes, indeed. The Prophet called.
  I was awakened by the noise
  Of cats emitting hunting cries.
ANITRA Not hunting noises, Lord and Master.
  They were up to something worse.
PEER And what could that be?
ANITRA   Don't make me answer!
PEER Speak!
ANITRA   Oh, I'm blushing—!
PEER (*Closing in.*)   Was it, maybe
  That which suddenly shot through me
  When I handed you my opal?
ANITRA (*Horrified.*) Can I compare thee, O Earth's treasure,
  With a horrible old tomcat!
PEER Child, as far as passion's concerned,
  The humble tomcat and the Prophet
  Can be said to come to the same thing.
ANITRA Master, sweet pleasantries and jesting
  Flow like honey from your lips.
PEER Little friend, like other girls, you judge
  Great men only by appearances.
  I'm full of hilarity deep down;
  Especially when it's tête-à-tête.
  It's my position forces me
  To go around with this somber expression.
  I'm so taken up with daily duties
  And tedious responsibilities,
  That often I seem to come across
  As a particularly lugubrious prophet.
  But all that's only on the surface.
  So to hell with that! Now we're together
  I am Peer—yes, that's who I am.
  Hey now, let's forget the Prophet;
  Now it's just me, so here I am!
  (*Seats himself under a tree, drawing her to him.*)
  Come, Anitra, we'll recline
  Beneath the green shade of this palm.
  I'll whisper to you, you will smile,
  Later, we'll reverse the roles.
  And, while I smile, your dewy lips
  Will whisper words of tender passion.
ANITRA (*Lying at his feet.*) All your speech is like a singing,
  Sweet, but beyond my comprehension.
  Tell me, Master, can your daughter

       Gain a soul by listening only?
PEER The soul, the spirit's light and wisdom,
   Will be yours in the fullness of time.
   When the East, with its rosy font,
   Prints in gold type: "Here is day!"
   Then, my child, we'll start instruction.
   You'll be sufficiently well educated.
   But in this night's enchanted stillness,
   It would be crazy to endeavor
   To set up for your schoolmaster,
   With a few unsorted scraps of learning.
   And when all's said and done the soul
   Is not the main thing after all.
   It's the heart that really matters.
ANITRA Speak, O Lord! When you discourse,
   Gleams of light, like opals, greet me.
PEER Too much cleverness is folly;
   Cowardice grows to cruelty.
   Truth, when taken to excess,
   Is wisdom's script set in reverse.
   Yes, my child, I would be lying
   Like a dog if I didn't confess,
   There are souls who walk our earth
   Too overfed with facts to see.
   I have met just such a fellow,
   A pearl among the usual swine;
   And even this man lost his way
   Mistaking sound for solid sense.[4]
   You see the sands round this oasis?
   With but a wave now of my turban,
   I could force the mighty ocean
   To inundate the entire expanse.
   But I would be a total blockhead
   To slave away at seas and lands.
   What do you think is the point of life?
ANITRA Teach me!
PEER   It is to float
   With dry feet down the stream of time,
   Whole and entirely as oneself.
   Only full manhood gives me compass
   To be myself, my little sweetheart.
   Aging eagles molt their feathers;
   Ancient limbs begin to totter;

4. This mysterious reference has been linked to the hero of Ibsen's previous play, *Brand*, who is the absolute antithesis of Peer Gynt.

Teeth desert decrepit beauty;
In dotage, misers' fists grow feeble;
And all of them get withered souls.
Youth! Glorious Youth! I'll be master;
Like a great Sultan, fierce and strong;
Not on the banks of Gyntiana,
Under trellises and palm trees;
But rooted in the fresh green bower
Of a young girl's virgin thoughts.
Do you see now, little darling,
Why I wove my magic round you.
Chose your heart as my sweet vassal,
Establishing, as one might phrase it,
There, my being's Caliphate.
I'll be master of your longings.
A potentate in passion's realm!
You shall belong to me alone;
I will be your jealous keeper,
Guarding his gold and precious jewels.
The day we part, our life is over.
Yours, at least; so please take note.
All of you, each nerve and fiber,
Without the will for yes or no,
Shall be consumed by me alone.
All your lovely midnight tresses,
All the charms that I could name,
Will be like Babylonian gardens,
Luring your Sultan to his couch.
So it turns out—all things considered—
It's just as well your head is empty.
A person saddled with a soul-life
Gets too preoccupied with self.
And listen, while we're on that subject,
If you like it, you'll be getting
A ring to go around your ankle.
It's the best thing for both of us
I can deputize for your soul.
And for the rest—the status quo.

(*Anitra snores.*)

What? She sleeps! Did all my wisdom
Unregarded glide right by her?
No, on the contrary, my speech's
Power conveyed her into dreams

Where love-talk floats her on its streams.
(*Rises and places jewels on her lap.*)
Here are jewels. More will follow.
Sleep! In sleep you set the golden
Crown upon your emperor's brow.
Peer's personality has triumphed,
Which he celebrates this night!

SCENE EIGHT

A caravan route with the oasis in the distance. Peer Gynt on his white horse gallops across the desert. He is clasping Anitra before him on the saddlebow.

ANITRA Let go! I'll bite.
PEER   You little spitfire!
ANITRA What are you trying?
PEER   Trying? Playing hawk and dove!
   Carrying you off! Let's fool around!
ANITRA You should be ashamed. An old prophet like—!
PEER   Old!
   This Prophet's not old, you dumb little goose.
   Do you think this looks like a sign of age?
ANITRA Give over! I want to go home!
PEER   You're a tease!
   Go home! Imagine! To father-in-law!
   Oh, very nice! No, we are two naughty birds
   Escaped from the cage. We can never again
   Come into his sight. In any case, child,
   The rule is, never stay long in one place;
   Too much familiarity can breed contempt!
   When you set yourself up in the prophetic line,
   Best a brief appearance—then gone like a song.
   I could see it was time to terminate my visit.
   These sons of the desert are fickle at heart,
   And the prayers and incense were petering out.
ANITRA But *are* you a prophet?
PEER   I am your emperor.
   (*Tries to kiss her.*)
   My, aren't you the bold little woodpecker!
ANITRA Give me that ring, there on your finger.
PEER Anitra, you can have the whole of this trash.
ANITRA Your words are music. How sweet they sound!
PEER What a blessing to know you're loved so completely.
   I'll dismount! Be your slave and lead your horse!

(*Handing her the riding whip as he dismounts.*)
There now, my rosebud, my beautiful flower.
I'll trudge before you through this hot sand,
And a lethal sunstroke will be my reward.
I'm young, Anitra, and don't you forget it.
So don't be surprised at my crazy behavior;
It's the privilege of youth to be playing the fool;
And if you were just a little bit brighter
You would quickly conclude—my sleek little tulip[5]—
That your lover is playful—*ergo* he is young!
ANITRA Yes, you're young—do you have any more rings?
PEER Aren't I young! Here, grab! I can leap like a stag.
If there were any vine leaves I'd fashion a crown.
Yes, young all the way! Hey! I'm going to dance!
(*Dancing and singing.*)

> I'm your happy little rooster;
> Peck me, pretty little pullet.
> Hey, I'm dancing. Watch me do it!
> I'm your happy little rooster.

ANITRA You're sweating, my Prophet; I'm worried you'll melt.
Take that bag from your waist. I can carry it for you.
PEER Now that is most thoughtful! Yes, take it for keeps.
Unburdened of gold, hearts in love become free!
(*Dancing and singing again.*)

> Young Peer is such a crazy guy,
> He doesn't know where his feet should go.
> Who cares, says Peer, it's what I do!
> Young Peer is such a crazy guy!

ANITRA What a treat to see the Prophet dancing!
PEER Let up on the prophet stuff. Let's change clothes!
Come on! Take them off!
ANITRA   Your caftan's too long;
Your belt is too wide and your stockings too tight.
PEER *Eh, bien!* (*Kneels.*) Then inflict some painful blow.
It's sweet for the loving heart to suffer.
Listen, when we get home to my castle—
ANITRA In your paradise? How long must we ride?
PEER Oh, a thousand miles.
ANITRA   Too far!

5. Peer calls her his "oleander," most likely because the Norwegian word *nerium* is needed for rhyme in the original. "Tulip" seems a more accessible endearment.

PEER   But listen—
  You'll be getting that soul I promised you.
ANITRA Thanks! I can get along without the soul.
  But you asked for a painful blow—
PEER   I did.
  Searing, but brief. Lasting two or three days.
ANITRA Anitra obeys the Prophet! Goodbye—!
  (*She gives him a sharp rap over the knuckles and dashes off back across the desert.*)
PEER (*Standing as if thunderstruck for a long time.*) Well, I'll be——

SCENE NINE

The same place. An hour later. Peer Gynt, now sober and thoughtful, is stripping off his Turkish costume, piece by piece. Finally, he takes out his little traveling cap from his coat pocket and stands once again in European dress.

PEER (*As he is casting his turban from him.*)
  There lies the Turk, and here stand I!
  These heathenish ways are no use to me.
  It's just as well it was nothing but costume,
  And not, as they say, bred in the bone.
  Whatever was I doing in that galley?
  Really, it's best to live the Christian life,
  And set aside all that peacock strutting;
  Base one's life on morality and law;
  Be and act, so when your time comes,
  You get a funeral oration over your coffin.
  (*Walks a few steps.*)
  That baggage! I admit she was just on the verge
  Of making me lose my head completely.
  If I turn into a troll, I'll never make out
  What got me so bewitched and stupid.
  Well, what's done is done. If the joke had been carried
  Just a step further, I would have looked idiotic.
  My mistake! But there's this consolation:
  The error was caused by the false situation;
  Not anything crucial to my own character.
  It was all due to that prophetic vocation;
  It lacked the spice of genuine action,
  And tempted me into a bad lapse of taste.
  You get poor returns from playing the prophet!
  The role needs a certain spiritual fog.
  It's a game in which you give up the trump

As soon as you start to act like a man.
Up to now, I did what the occasion demanded
Just by paying attention to that little goose.
But, all the same— (*Bursts out laughing.*)
                              What on earth was I thinking,
Trying to put back the clock by dancing;
Holding back the tide by prancing and twirling,
Strumming the lute, ogling and sighing,
Then getting plucked at last like a rooster?
I guess you can call it prophetic frenzy.
Yes, plucked! Whew! Not a feather remaining.
Well, not quite: I've still got cash in reserve.
Some in America, some in my pockets;
I'm not yet in the position of begging.
Maybe this middle condition's the best.
I'm no longer burdened with servants and horses,
No luggage or coaches to bother about.
In short, in control of my own situation!
What path shall I choose? Many lie open.
Choosing right, separates wise men from fools.
My career as a capitalist's now a closed chapter.
The Don Juan role was a losing game.
Unlike the crab, I've no urge to go backward.
"Forward or back, it's just as far.
Out or in, I'm trapped as before!"
I've read that in some inspirational text.
I must try something new, more elevating;
Something that's worth the time and the money.
Why not write a candid account of my life?
To serve as a guide and encourage imitation?
Or, wait a bit—! I've got time on my hands;
Why not set up as a travelling scholar,
Salvaging the past devoured by Time.
Yes! That'll just suit me down to the ground!
I read a few legends back in the old days,
And dabbled in all kinds of knowledge since then.
I'll follow the course of the human race,
Float like a feather on the stream of history.
Bring it to life again, as in a dream.
See heroes battle for truth and glory
(As onlooker, of course, from a safe distance),
See thinkers perish and martyrs bleed,
See empires rise and then fall into dust.
See world epochs grow from minutest seeds;
In short, I'll skim off the cream of history.

I must set about getting a volume of Becker,[6]
And proceed chronologically as far as I can.
I admit, my grounding's not very thorough,
And the inner workings of history are puzzling.
So what! The more far out you begin,
The more original will be the result!
How uplifting it is to set up a goal
And drive straight through it, like flint or steel!
(*Quietly moved.*)
To shut off all ties in every direction,
All bonds that link you to friends and home,
To cast to the winds all your worldly riches,
Even bid the joys of love goodbye—
All this, in pursuit of the mystery of truth!
(*Wipes a tear from his eye.*)
That is the mark of the true man of science.
I can't express how happy it makes me,
Solving the riddle of my whole life's quest.
The main thing's to stick to it through thick and thin!
I can be excused for feeling some pride,
Some sense of what being Peer Gynt means:
Alias, the Emperor of the Human Condition!
I'll master the whole Past, make it my province
Without engaging the world of the living.
This present time's not worth the sole of a shoe.
Today's generation lacks guts and conviction.
Its spirit can't soar, its actions are feeble.
(*Shrugging his shoulders.*)
As for women—well, they're a pitiful bunch!
(*He goes.*)

SCENE TEN

*A summer's day, far up in the north. A hut in the forest. An open door
with a large wooden bolt. Reindeer horns over the door. A flock of
goats by the wall of the hut. A middle-age woman, fair-haired and attractive, is sitting and spinning outside in the sunshine.*

THE WOMAN (*Glancing down the path and singing.*)
    Winter may pass, one more spring yet appear,
    A new summer arrive, then a new year;
    But one day you'll return; I know that you will
    And I will be waiting here, loving you still.
    (*She calls to the goats and goes back to singing and spinning.*)

6. Becker's *World History* was published in Scandinavia about the time of the play.

God strengthen your journey by sea and by land;
God give you joy if before Him you stand.
When your long journey ends, you'll find me still here,
Or above, if that be our meeting, my dear.

SCENE ELEVEN

In Egypt. Daybreak. Memnon's statue upright, in the sand. Peer Gynt enters and looks around him for a while.

PEER This seems the right spot to start my wanderings.
    So, I'll transform myself into an Egyptian;
    An Egyptian, though, founded on the Gyntian ego.
    Then I'll take in Assyria on the way.
    Best not start *right* at the world's creation;
    That could only lead the way to disaster.
    I'll go round about with Bible history,
    Just focus on tracking its secular traces.
    Exploring the subject right down to its seams,
    As they say, is not part of my plan.
    (*He sits on a stone.*)
    I'll rest here a while, and wait patiently
    Until the statue's ready to sing its matins.
    After breakfast, I'll climb the pyramid
    And, time permitting, explore its interior.
    After that, it's down land to the Red Sea;
    Perhaps I can find King Potiphar's grave.
    Next, Orientalism! I'll look in on Babylon,
    For the famous hanging gardens and whores,
    And other such high spots of the culture.
    Then, with one bound, to the walls of Troy.
    From Troy there's a direct route leading
    Across to glorious, ancient Athens—
    I'll go to the exact spot and, stone by stone,
    Inspect the pass Leonidas defended.
    I'll become familiar with the better philosophers,
    Find the prison where Socrates met his martyrdom—
    Ah no, I forgot, there's a war going on!
    So Hellenism must be put to one side.
    (*Looks at his watch.*)
    It's really absurd just how long it's taking
    For the sun to rise. My time is precious.
    Well then, back to Troy; that's where I left off.
    (*He gets up and listens.*)
    Whatever's that weird whispering I'm hearing?
    (*The sun rises.*)

MEMNON'S STATUE (*Singing.*)

> From the demigod's ashes rise, youth renewing,
> Birds ever singing.
> Zeus, the all-seeing,
> Made struggle their being.
> Wise owl, why keep
> My birds to their sleep?
> You must try to untie
> This song's riddle, or die![7]

PEER Remarkable! I really think there came
  A sound from that statue. Music of the Past.[8]
  I heard the stone accents rising and falling.
  I will write this down for scholars to mull over.
  (*Writing in his notebook.*)
  "The statue sang. I distinctly heard the sound.
  But couldn't make out what it was singing.
  The whole thing's obviously a hallucination.
  Otherwise, observed nothing notable today."

SCENE TWELVE

Near the village of Gizeh. The great Sphinx carved out of the rock. In the distance, Cairo's spires and minarets can be seen. Peer Gynt enters; he examines the Sphinx attentively, now through his lorgnette, now through his cupped hand.

PEER Now, where in the world have we met before?
  There's something I remember like this monster!
  Because I know I've met it! In the north or south?
  A person, maybe? If that's the case, who?
  That Memnon character, it came to me later,
  Was like the Old Man of the Dovrë,
  The way he sat there, stiff and unyielding,
  His bottom squatting on a stump of pillars.
  But this peculiar hybrid animal,
  This enigma who's at once lion and woman,
  Emerges from the dark abyss of memory;

7. Memnon, a legendary king of Ethiopia, was the son of the dawn goddess, Eos, and the mortal Tithonus. He was killed in battle by Achilles and made immortal by Zeus. He became the object of an oracular cult; his statue was reputed to sing when touched by the rays of the dawning sun. Zeus transformed the ashes of his funeral pyre into two flocks of birds that annually rose and fought each other. Memnon thus represents the capacity for confrontation and heroic struggle (dialectic) evaded by Peer.
8. *Fortidsmusik.* A glance at the contentious "Music of the Future" (*Zukunftsmusik*) by Ibsen's great contemporary, Richard Wagner.

Or is it fairy tale? Is he a real memory,
Or a legend? Ah, yes, now I recall him.
It's the Bøyg, of course, whose skull I thumped!
Or, maybe, dreamt I did—for I lay in a fever.
(*Comes closer.*)
Definitely the same eyes, the selfsame lips—
Not quite as sluggish, a bit more cunning.
But, in all essentials, still identical.
So that's it then, Bøyg! You look like a lion
When seen from behind and met in broad daylight.
Still good at riddles? Let's put it to the test.
Will you give the same answer you gave me last time?
(*Calls out to the Sphinx.*)
Hey, Bøyg, who are you?
A VOICE (*Behind the Sphinx.*) *Ach, Sphinx, wer bist du?*
PEER What's this? Echo answers in German! Remarkable!
VOICE *Wer bist du?*
PEER   It speaks the language fluently.
   This observation is new—and it's my own!
   (*Writing in his notebook.*)
   "Echo in German. Dialect, Berlin.
   (*Begriffenfeldt emerges from behind the Sphinx.*)
BEGRIFFENFELDT A human being!
PEER   So that's who was talking!
   (*Making another note.*)
   "Later, came to another conclusion."
BEGRIFFENFELDT (*Showing many signs of uncontrolled excitement.*)
   Mein Herr—excuse me—! *Eine lebensfrage*[9]—!
   What brings you here on precisely this day?
PEER Visiting. Greeting a friend of my youth.
BEGRIFFENFELDT Who? The Sphinx—?
PEER (*Nodding.*) Yes, I knew him in the old days.
BEGRIFFENFELDT Staggering! And this, after such a night!
   My head is pounding! It's close to bursting!
   You know him, man? Speak! Answer! Can you say
   What he is?
PEER   What he is? Oh yes I can, easily;
   He is—*himself.*
BEGRIFFENFELDT (*With a leap.*) Ach! The riddle of life flashes
   Its answer across my gaze. You are absolutely certain
   He is himself?
PEER   Yes, at least that's what he says.
BEGRIFFENFELDT Himself! The hour of revolution's at hand.

9. "A vital question."

(Takes off his hat.) Your name, *mein Herr?*

PEER   I was christened Peer Gynt.

BEGRIFFENFELDT *(In silent awe.)* Peer Gynt! Allegorical! The One
    awaited—

    Peer Gynt? That signifies, the Unknown One—

    The Appointed, whose arrival was foretold to me.

PEER Is that so! And so you came here to meet—?

BEGRIFFENFELDT Peer Gynt! Profound! Enigmatic! Incisive!

    Each word constitutes an abyss of meaning.

    What are you?

PEER *(Modestly.)* I have always striven to be

    Myself. The rest you can find on my passport.

BEGRIFFENFELDT Again! That deep, mysterious word.

    (Seizes him by the wrist.)

    To Cairo! Illumination's Emperor is found!

PEER Emperor?

BEGRIFFENFELDT Follow!

PEER   Am I really known—?

BEGRIFFENFELDT *(As he drags him along.)*

    Enlightenment's Emperor, grounded in Self!

SCENE THIRTEEN

*Cairo. A large courtyard, surrounded by high walls and buildings.
Barred windows; iron cages. Three keepers in the courtyard. A fourth
enters.*

THE NEWCOMER Schafman, tell me: where's the Director?

A KEEPER He drove out this morning long before dawn.

FIRST KEEPER I think something's happened to unsettle him,

    Because last night—

ANOTHER Sh! Be quiet; he's there at the door.

    *(Begriffenfeldt leads in Peer Gynt, locks the gate and puts the key
    in his pocket.)*

PEER Truly, this is a most wonderfully erudite man;

    Almost every word he speaks goes right over my head.

    (Looking about him.)

    So this, then, is the Scholars' Club?

BEGRIFFENFELDT Yes, here's where you'll find the whole gaggle of
    scribblers.

    The fifty-plus-twenty[1] Interpreters' Circle.

    Newly augmented by one hundred and sixty.

---

1. Ibsen uses the circumlocutory *halvfjersinnstyve.* The reference is to the Septuagint, the
Greek version of the Old Testament reputedly translated by seventy Jewish scholars under Ptolemy II.

(*Calls to the Keepers.*)
Mikkel, Schlingelberg, Schafman, Fuchs—
Get into the cages at once!
THE KEEPERS We!
BEGRIFFENFELDT Who else? Get in, get in!
When the world is spinning, we must spin along with it.
(*Forcing them into a cage.*)
He has arrived this day, the mighty Peer.
The rest you can guess; I will say no more.
(*Locks the door and throws the key into a well.*)
PEER But, my dear doctor . . . dear director—
BEGRIFFENFELDT Neither of those! They applied before—
Herr Peer, are you discreet? I must ease my mind—
PEER (*Increasingly uneasy.*) What is it?
BEGRIFFENFELDT Promise me you'll keep calm.
PEER I'll try my best—
BEGRIFFENFELDT (*Draws him into a corner and whispers.*) Absolute
Reason
Dropped dead last night at eleven o'clock.
PEER God help us—!
BEGRIFFENFELDT   Yes, it is extremely deplorable.
And in my position it's twice as intolerable.
Because this institution, up to that moment
Had been known as a madhouse.
PEER   A madhouse!
BEGRIFFENFELDT But no longer, you understand!
PEER (*Pale, hushed.*) I understand now what this place is.
And the man is mad and no one knows it!
(*Trying to move away.*)
BEGRIFFENFELDT (*Following him.*) However, I hope you follow my
meaning.
When I pronounced him dead, that was not quite accurate.
He's beside himself. Jumped right out of his skin.
Just like my compatriot Munchausen's fox.[2]
PEER Excuse me a moment—
BEGRIFFENFELDT (*Holding him.*)
No, it was more like an eel—
Not a fox. With a nail through his eye
He was fixed, writhing on the wall.
PEER   Is there any rescue!
BEGRIFFENFELDT Just a slit in his neck and then whiii-sh!—out of
his skin.
PEER Demented! Completely lost his senses!

---

2. Baron von Munchausen (1720–1797), a teller of tall stories. In one, he reached inside a fox's throat down to the tail and pulled it inside out.

BEGRIFFENFELDT Now it's become quite clear and can't be concealed—
This from-himself-going must have a dire consequence!
A total revolution by land and by sea!
Those folk we called insane up to now,
As a result became sane at eleven o'clock,
Conforming to Reason in its current phase.
And so, if you look at the matter correctly,
It follows, at this aforementioned hour,
All the so-called intellectuals began to rave.

PEER You mentioned the hour: my time is limited—

BEGRIFFENFELDT Your time? That happens to jog my memory!
(*Opens a door and calls out.*)
Come out now! What was foretold has arrived!!
Reason is dead. So long live Peer Gynt!

PEER No, my dear sir—
(*The Lunatics come, one by one, into the courtyard.*)

BEGRIFFENFELDT Good morning! Step forward
And greet emancipation's dawn!
Your Emperor's arrived!

PEER Emperor?

BEGRIFFENFELDT Exactly!

PEER The honor's so great, it's really too much—!

BEGRIFFENFELDT Ach! Don't let false modesty deter you,
At a time like this.

PEER Just give me time to consider—!
No, I'm not worthy—I'm totally dumbfounded.

BEGRIFFENFELDT A man who has fathomed the Sphinx's meaning?
Who is himself?

PEER Yes, that's just the point.
I am myself in every part of my being.
But here, as far as I understand, the whole point
With one's self, so to speak, is to be out of it.

BEGRIFFENFELDT Out of it? No, there you're strangely mistaken!
Here a man's himself with a vengeance;
Himself, and not in the slightest way other—
Each goes, as himself, full steam ahead.
Each shuts himself inside a barrel of self,
And in self-fermenting, he dives to the bottom—
Is hermetically sealed with the bung of self,
And seasons the staves in self's own well.
No one has tears for another's sorrow,
No one has time for another's ideas,
We are ourselves in thought and in feeling.
Ourselves to ambition's uttermost edge.

Clearly, if an emperor's to sit on our throne,
It follows, inarguably, you are the man.
PEER If the devil would only—
BEGRIFFENFELDT   Now don't get depressed;
Everything in life is new to begin with.
"One's self?" Here, I'll show you an example;
I'll pick out the first one that comes along.
(*To a gloomy figure.*)
Good day, Huhu! How's it going, old fellow?
Still hanging around looking miserable as sin?
HUHU Why shouldn't I when generations[3]
Of my race die *sans* interpretation? (*To Peer Gynt.*)
You're a stranger. Do you wish to hear?
PEER (*Bowing.*) Yes, By all means!
HUHU   Then lend an ear.
In far distant eastern lands,
Stretch the Malabaric strands.
The Portuguese and Dutchmen spread
Cultural influence with their trade.
Fused with this there swarms a mass
Of purest Malabari race.
These have mixed the language and
Now they lord it in the land.
But in times far in the past
The orang-outan ruled the roost.
He was the forest's autocrat
Free to snarl and rage and fight.
Free as nature's hand had shaped,
As such he bared his teeth and gaped
And shrieked though none could understand
The monarch of this uncouth land.
But then the foreign yoke descended;
The primal tongue lay undefended.
Four centuries of night unfurled
Over the entire simian world.
You know a night of that duration
Cruelly blights a population.
With the forest sounds replaced,
Primeval grunts and howls all ceased.
If our thoughts are to be heard,
We must reform the spoken word.
Harsh restraints affect all sides,

---

3. The meter changes abruptly in the original. Huhu has long been interpreted as a satire on Norwegian language reformers who tried to purge Norwegian of its non-native elements. But Huhu can stand for any cranky, tunnel-visioned reformer.

Portuguese and Dutch, besides
Half-caste races. Malabari
Suffer the same quandary.
I have battled hard and long
For the cause of our true tongue.
Revivifying its cadaver
Proving our right to shriek and slaver.
Worked to show that shrieks belong
To the folk-domain of song.
Scant have my efforts been respected.
You understand why I'm dejected.
Thanks for lending me an ear.
If you can help I wish to hear.

PEER It's written: if wolves are on the prowl
When you're around, it's best to howl.
(*Aloud.*) Friend, if my memory is sound
In Morocco can be found
Orang-outans whose lives have long
Been deprived of bards or song.
Their language sounded Malabaric.
Pure, uninfluenced, barbaric.
Why not, like many émigrés,
Advance the interests of their race?

HUHU Thanks for paying me attention.
I'll set out in that direction.
(*With a grand gesture.*)
East! You disowned your poet's fate.
Out West, orang-outans await!
(*He leaves.*)

BEGRIFFENFELDT Well, was he not himself? I certainly think so.
His feeling was all for himself and for nothing else.
He's himself in all that he expresses—
Himself because he's beside himself.
Come here! I'll show you another one
Who since last night also conforms to Reason.
(*To a Fellah who carries a mummy on his back.*)
King Apis, how goes it, O mighty lord?

FELLAH (*Wildly to Peer.*) Am I King Apis?

PEER (*Hiding behind the doctor.*)   I regret to say
I'm not familiar with the situation.
But I would hazard, to judge from your tone—

FELLAH Now you are lying, too.

BEGRIFFENFELDT Your Highness needs to explain
Just how the matter stands.

FELLAH   Then I shall relate.

(*Turning to Peer.*)
You see him I bear on my shoulders?[4]
His name was King Apis, so it is said;
Though now known as a mummy,
And worse, he's completely dead.
      He built the massive pyramids
And carved out the mighty Sphinx;
He fought, as our Herr Doktor would put it,
On the Turk's side, both *rechts und links.*[5]
      And therefore the ancient Egyptians
Worshiped him as a god
And set him up in their temples,
Where, in bull's shape, he stood.
      But *I'm* this same King Apis,
I claim it's as clear as the day—
And if this is all beyond you,
You'll soon comprehend what I say.
      King Apis, one day, was out hunting,
And got off his horse out of need,
And took himself off unattended,
Onto land that my grandfather had.
      Now, the meadow manured by King Apis,
Has long nourished me with its corn;
And if further proof were looked for,
Well, I have invisible horns.
      But here's what's completely appalling,
No one accepts my dominion.
By birth I'm King Apis of Egypt,
But a peasant in common opinion.
      So commend me a course of action;
Be candid in what you relate.
What solution from me is needed
To become King Apis the Great?
PEER Your Highness should build more pyramids
And carve out a greater Sphinx
And fight, as the good Doctor tells you
On the Turks' side, both *rechts und links.*
FELLAH Oh, that is so easy to utter!
I'm a peasant! A mere hungry louse!
I've enough to do keeping my dwelling
Unravaged by rat or by mouse.
      Quick man, find something better,
Great but safe, to put me on track

4. The verse rhythm and rhyme scheme changes similarly from Huhu's in the original.
5. Right and left; German in the original.

To achieve a status identical
With King Apis here on my back.

PEER What if your Highness should hang himself
And subsequently, in the earth's bed,
In the natural confines of a coffin,
Keep yourself regally dead?

FELLAH It's what I'll do! My life for a halter!
Onto the gallows I'll climb!
I'll feel some change to begin with,
But that will smooth over in time.
(*He goes off to get ready to hang himself.*)

BEGRIFFENFELDT Now there was a personality for you, Herr Peer—
A man of method—

PEER   Yes, yes, I can see—
But he's really going to hang himself! God help us!
I'm going to be sick. My head's in a whirl!

BEGRIFFENFELDT A stage of transition; it won't last long.

PEER Transition? To what? Excuse me, I have to be going—

BEGRIFFENFELDT (*Restraining him.*) Are you mad?

PEER   Not just yet—Mad? God forbid!
(*Uproar. Hussein, a political minister,*[6] *forces his way through a mob.*)

HUSSEIN I am informed an emperor has arrived today. (*To Peer Gynt.*)
Is it you?

PEER (*Desperately.*) It seems to be turning out that way.[7]

HUSSEIN Good. You must have dispatches needing an answer?

PEER (*Tearing his hair.*) Why not? The worse the better, I think.

HUSSEIN Would you honor me by dipping me in the ink?
(*Bowing deeply.*) I'm a pen.

PEER (*Bowing even lower.*)   And I'm meant
To be a piece of crumpled, imperial parchment.

HUSSEIN My history, sir, I'll quickly explain.
Though I'm called a sandbox, I'm really a pen.

PEER My history, Sir Pen, can be quickly described.
I'm a piece of paper on which nothing's inscribed.

HUSSEIN What I'm worthy of, none can yet understand,
So I'm merely misused for sprinkling sand.

PEER I was a woman's precious silver-clasped book.
Mad or sane? Just something a printer mistook!

HUSSEIN Imagine the frustration of spending my life

---

6. As with Trumpeterstråle, this is a satire on what Ibsen thought was the pusillanimous stance of the Swedes in the Dano-Prussian war. Count Manderström, the foreign minister, prided himself on his epistolary style in diplomacy, however ineffective in reality.
7. Rhyme scheme and meter change in the original.

As a pen, and never meet up with a knife!
PEER (*Leaping high.*) Imagine being a reindeer, to leap from a
    height,
    And falling, find no ground for your feet!
HUSSEIN A knife! Cut and slit me this instant, I'm blunt!
    The world falls to ruin if I lose my sharp point.
PEER It's a shame that the world like all things self-made
    Was thought by the Lord exceedingly good.
BEGRIFFENFELDT Here's a knife!
HUSSEIN (*Seizing it.*)   Ah, now the ink will flow from the
    gash!
    What rapture to slit oneself.
    (*He cuts his throat.*)
BEGRIFFENFELDT (*Moving to one side.*) Try not to splash.
PEER (*His terror increasing.*) Hold on to him!
HUSSEIN   Hold on to me! That is the word!
    Hold the pen to the paper and press it down hard.
    (*Falls.*) I'm worn out. The postscript. Write it at once:
    His whole life was a pen writing other men's sense.
PEER (*Dizzily.*) What shall I—What am I—, O Great One, hold fast!
    I'm whatever you will, a Turk, sinner, defector,
    A hill troll—; but help me; something has burst—!
    (*Crying out.*) Your name—? I can't recall—! Now I am lost!
    O come to my aid—you, the madman's protector.
    (*He sinks down unconscious.*)
BEGRIFFENFELDT (*Carrying a wreath of straw, he gives a bound and
    sits astride Peer.*)
    Ha! See him enthroned in filth and mire
    Beside himself! Now crown him here!
    (*Presses the wreath on Peer Gynt's head and shouts.*)
    Long life to Self-hood's Emperor!
SCHAFMAN (*In the cage.*) *Es lebe hoch der grosse Peer!*[8]

Act Five

SCENE ONE

*On board a ship in the North Sea off the Norwegian coast. Sunset.
Stormy weather. Peer Gynt, a vigorous old man with ice-gray hair
and beard, is standing on the poop. He is dressed partly in seaman's
clothes, in a pea jacket and high boots. His clothes are somewhat the
worse for wear; he himself is weather-beaten and his expression
harder. The Captain is standing beside the Helmsman at the wheel.
The crew is forward.*

8. Long live Peer the Great! German in the original.

PEER (*Leaning on the rail and gazing toward the land.*)
  There's Hallingskarv—look!—in his winter coat,
  Showing off in the evening sunset!
  And Jøkel[1] his brother, just to one side of him;
  I see he still wears his green jacket of ice.
  There's the Folgefonn,[2] as lovely as ever,
  Like a virgin lying under pure white linen.
  You two old men, don't step out of line!
  Stay where you are; you're just lumps of granite!
CAPTAIN (*Shouting forward.*) Two hands to the wheel! **Hoist the**
  lantern!
PEER It's blowing up rough.
CAPTAIN   There'll be a storm tonight.
PEER Can you get a view of the Rondë from here?
CAPTAIN No chance. It lies way back of the snowfields.
PEER Or the Blåhø?[3]
CAPTAIN   No, but from up in the rigging
  You can glimpse Galdhøpiggen[4] in the distance.
PEER Where is Hårteigen?[5]
CAPTAIN (*Pointing.*)   About over there.
PEER Ah yes.
CAPTAIN You know these parts, it seems.
PEER When I left the country, I sailed this way.
  The dregs, as they say, hang round longest.
  (*Spits and gazes at the coast.*)
  You see where the clefts and crags show blue,
  Where the valley blackens like a trench or ditch,
  And below there, skirting the open fjords—
  There's where people choose to live;
  (*He looks at the captain.*)
  In this part of the country they build far apart.
CAPTAIN Yes, the houses are few and far between.
PEER Shall we get ashore before daybreak?
CAPTAIN We could make it
  If the weather tonight isn't too filthy.
PEER Clouds are thickening westward
CAPTAIN   That they are!
PEER   Wait!
  Remind me—when we settle accounts,
  I've a mind, as they say, to do a good turn

---

1. Hallingskarv and Jøkel ("YOOR-kul") are mountains.
2. Folgefonn ("FOHL-guh-fun") is a glacier.
3. Pronounced "BLAW-hu."
4. Pronounced "GAL-doh-PIG-un."
5. Pronounced "Haw-TAY-gun."

For the crew—
CAPTAIN   Thanks!
PEER   It won't be much.
  I dug for gold in my time but lost what I made.
  Fate and I—well, we fell out with each other.
  You know what I've got stowed on board.
  That's the lot—all the rest went to the devil.
CAPTAIN It's more than enough to give you some weight
  With your people at home.
PEER   I don't have a family.
  There'll be no one waiting for the rich old rogue;
  Well, at least it spares you scenes on the dock!
CAPTAIN Here comes the storm.
PEER   So then, don't forget—
  If any of the men are really in need
  I won't stint when it comes to the money.
CAPTAIN That's handsome! Most have a hard life.
  They've all got wives and children at home.
  What they get for pay doesn't go very far;
  So when they can come back with a bit extra,
  It makes for a reunion they won't soon forget.
PEER What's that you say? They've wives and family?
  They're married?
CAPTAIN   Married? Yes, every last one of them.
  But the one most desperately in need is the Cook.
  Black hunger's set up home in his house.
PEER Married. Back home they've got someone waiting?
  Someone overjoyed when they return? Yes?
CAPTAIN   Well, yes,
  In the manner of poor folk.
PEER   So they come home one evening;
  What follows?
CAPTAIN I imagine the wife sets about trying to find
  Something good for a treat—
PEER   And a lamp on the table?
CAPTAIN Could even be two. And a drink to celebrate.
PEER They sit there all snugly? A fire in the hearth?
  Youngsters around them? The room full of chatter?
  When they're talking no one can wait to the end,
  So much happiness fills them—?
CAPTAIN   Maybe like that.
  So it's all the more splendid you promised
  To add a bit more.
PEER (Thumping the rail.) I'm damned if I will!
  Do you think I'm mad? That I'd actually fork out,

At random, money for other men's brats?
I've sweated enough to build up my pile!
There's no one waiting for old Peer Gynt.
CAPTAIN Yes, yes, please yourself. Your money's your own.
PEER Darn right it is! Mine, and nobody else's.
We'll settle accounts when we drop anchor!
Just my cabin passage from Panama here.
Some brandy all round for the crew. Nothing more.
If I give any more, Captain, break my jaw.
CAPTAIN All you'll get from me is a receipt, not a fight.
But excuse me, we've got a storm on our hands.
(*He goes across the deck. It is becoming dark. Lights are lit in the cabin. The waves get rougher. Fog and dense clouds.*)
PEER To have an eager flock of children waiting,
Living in their hearts, waiting their return—
Knowing thoughts of others follow them.
There's no one in the world thinking of me.
Lights lit in welcome? I'll put out those lights!
I'll think of a way. Yes! I'll get them all drunk!
Not one of those devils will walk ashore sober;
They'll return to their families drunk out of their minds,
Curses and rioting, fists slammed on the table.
Those at home will be terrified out of their wits!
The wives will scream and run out of the house
Clutching their children. That's *their* reunion!
(*The ship lurches violently. He staggers and nearly loses his balance.*)
Whoa! That was a severe roll of the waves!
The sea's working as if paid overtime—
It's still its old self in these northern waters—
The cross-sea's as wild and angry as ever!
(*He listens.*)
Was that screaming I heard?
WATCH (*Forward.*)   Wreck to leeward!
CAPTAIN (*Amidships. Giving orders.*) Helm hard to starboard! Close
    to the wind!
HELMSMAN Are there men on the wreck?
WATCH   I can make out just three.
PEER Lower a boat!
CAPTAIN   She'd fill almost at once.
(*Goes forward.*)
PEER You can't think about that now!
(*To some of the crew.*)
                              You are men, you must save them!
What the devil does it matter getting drenched doing it—

BO'SUN It just can't be done, with the sea like this.
PEER They're yelling again! Look, the wind is dropping—
    Cook, will you risk it? Quick! I'll pay you—
COOK Not if you paid me twenty pounds sterling.
PEER You dogs! You cowards! Are you forgetting
    These are men with wives and children at home
    Sitting and waiting?
BO'SUN   Well, patience is good for them.
CAPTAIN Keep clear of those breakers!
HELMSMAN   The wreck's gone under!
PEER All silent of a sudden?
HELMSMAN   If they were married, like you said,
    The world's just hatched three new widows.
    (*The storm increases. Peer Gynt moves away aft.*)
PEER There's no faith to be found in men any more!
    No Christianity as it's preached and written.
    Good deeds are rare and prayers even fewer,
    And scant respect for the power of the Almighty.
    In a storm like tonight, the Lord sends a warning.
    These brutes really ought to consider their danger
    (You shouldn't risk playing with elephants).
    Yet here they're openly courting His anger!
    I'm not guilty! The sacrifice was offered;
    I can claim I stood there with money in hand.
    But what do I get out of it? As the saying goes,
    "A clear conscience makes for a soft pillow."
    Well, that may hold when you're on dry land,
    But it's not worth a pinch of snuff here on board,
    Where an upright man might go down with the crew.
    You can't be yourself when you are at sea;
    You must follow the crowd from the deck to the hold;
    If nemesis strikes for the Cook or the Bo'sun,
    You find yourself sinking with the rest of the flock.
    Your personal merits just shoved to one side—
    Much like a sausage in a slaughterhouse.
    My error is, I've been too pious by half,
    And I got few thanks for taking that stand.
    If I were younger, I'd probably change tactics
    And try at throwing my weight around.
    There's still time left! They'll learn in the parish
    Peer's sailed back over the sea in triumph!
    I'll win back the farm by hook or by crook—
    I'll build it again so it looks like a palace.
    And I won't let anyone into the hall!
    They'll stand at the gateway, twisting their caps;

Begging, beseeching; they can do that for free—
But none of them gets a cent of my money.
Since I've been bruised by the hard knocks of fate,
I'll see if I can't make some other folk suffer.

THE STRANGE PASSENGER (*Standing in the darkness at Peer Gynt's side and greeting him amiably.*)
Good evening!

PEER Good evening! What—? Who are you?

PASSENGER Your fellow passenger—at your service.

PEER Really? I thought I was the only one.

PASSENGER A wrong impression, which can now be discarded.

PEER But it's very strange that until this evening
We've never met—

PASSENGER   I don't go out in daytime.

PEER You're sick, perhaps? You're as white as a sheet.

PASSENGER Thank you, no—I find myself uncommonly fit.

PEER The storm's getting worse.

PASSENGER   Yes, what a blessing!

PEER A blessing?

PASSENGER   Waves reaching as high as houses.
Ah, it positively makes your mouth water!
Think of the wrecks that will go down this night,
And think of the corpses floating ashore.

PEER Lord save us!

PASSENGER   Have you seen someone strangled,
Or hanged—or drowned?

PEER   No! This is outrageous—!

PASSENGER Their corpses laugh. But the laughter is forced.
The majority have bitten through their tongues.

PEER Get away from me—!

PASSENGER   Just one question!
If, for example, we run onto the rocks
And go down in darkness—

PEER   You think there's a danger?

PASSENGER I don't really know how I should answer.
But suppose I floated and you sank to the bottom—

PEER That's absurd!

PASSENGER   A possibility, nevertheless.
And when a man has one foot in the grave,
He weakens—is inclined to make bequests—

PEER (*Putting his hand in his pocket.*) Oh, it's money!

PASSENGER No, but if you'd oblige me
By making me a gift of your esteemed cadaver—?

PEER Now you go too far!

PASSENGER   Just your corpse, you understand!
  It's for my scientific research.
PEER   Go away!
PASSENGER But consider, friend, you'll get the best of the bargain.
  I intend opening you up to the light of day.
  I'm especially researching the source of dreams.
  I'll make a critical probe of arteries and nerves.
PEER Get away from me!
PASSENGER   My dear sir—it's only a corpse!
PEER Blasphemous man! You're encouraging the storm!
  Isn't it enough already, with the wind and the rain,
  A raging sea and any number of omens
  Suggesting our lives are about to be cut short—!
  You act as if to make sure it happens!
PASSENGER You're clearly not in the mood for negotiation,
  But time, as you know, brings about many changes—
  (*With a friendly bow.*)
  We'll be meeting when we go down, if not sooner;
  Perhaps, then, you'll be in a much better humor.
  (*He goes into the cabin.*)
PEER Sinister fellows, these men of science!
  It's all this freethinking—
  (*To the bo'sun as he is passing.*)
                  A word with you, friend.
  That passenger. What kind of lunatic is he?
BO'SUN As far as I know, you're the only one on board.
PEER No others! This gets worse and worse.
  (*To the ship's boy, who is coming out of the cabin.*)
  Who went through the cabin door just now?
BOY   The ship's dog, sir!
WATCH (*Calling.*) Land close ahead!
PEER   My trunk! My cases!
  All my baggage on deck!
BO'SUN   We've other things to do.
PEER It was all nonsense, Captain! Just kidding—a joke!
  Of course I'll be sure to look after the Cook.
CAPTAIN The jib's blown away!
HELMSMAN   There goes the foresail!
BO'SUN (*Yelling from forward.*) Breakers under the bow!
CAPTAIN   She's breaking up!
  (*The ship strikes. Noise and confusion.*)

SCENE TWO

Close under the cliffs, among rocks and breakers. The ship goes down. A dinghy with two men can be glimpsed through the mist. A wave breaks over it, and it fills and turns over. There is a shriek and then silence for a while. Soon after, the boat reappears floating keel up. Peer Gynt bobs up to the surface beside it.

PEER Help! Send a boat from land! I'm drowning!
   Have mercy dear God—like the Good Book says!
COOK (*Bobbing up on the other side.*)
   O please, Lord God, for my children's sake!
   Be merciful! Let me get to the land.
   (*Clinging to the keel.*)
PEER Let go!
COOK   Leggo!
PEER   I'll hit you!
COOK   I'll hit back!
PEER I'll punch you and kick you into a pulp.
   Let go. This boat won't carry two.
COOK I know that. Give up!
PEER   You give up!
COOK   Oh, yes?
   (*They fight; one of the Cook's hands is disabled. He clings on tightly with the other.*)
PEER Let go that hand!
COOK   O, be good, spare me!
   Think of my small children waiting for me!
PEER I need life more than you do.
   I haven't got any children yet.
COOK Let go! You've lived. I am still young!
PEER Quick; don't waste time. Sink—you're weighing us down.
COOK Be merciful! Let go, in the name of God.
   There's no one to mourn or grieve for you.
   (*Shrieks and lets go.*)
   I'm drowning!
PEER (*Grabbing him.*) I've got hold of your hair.
   So be quick about it and say the Lord's Prayer.
COOK I can't remember—it's all going dark.
PEER Say the important bits only.
COOK Give us this day—!
PEER   Skip that bit, Cook;
   Just get to the essentials, that's safe enough.
COOK Give us this day—

PEER   The same old song!
  It's easy to tell you were once a Cook.
COOK (*Sinking.*) Give us this day our—
  (*He goes under.*)
PEER   Amen, boy.
  You remained yourself up to the last gasp.
  (*He swings himself up onto the keel.*)
  Well, as they say, where there's life, there's hope!
PASSENGER (*Grabbing the boat.*) Good morning.
PEER   Huh?
PASSENGER   I heard the shouting.
  How pleasant meeting up with you again!
  Well? So you see, didn't my prediction prove true?
PEER Let go, let go! There's hardly enough room for one.
PASSENGER I'm swimming with my left leg—
  And floating, with my fingertips
  Just lightly resting, here on the hull.
  But now, apropos your corpse—
PEER   Shut up!
PASSENGER Because the rest of you is totally worthless—
PEER Hold your tongue!
PASSENGER   Just as you like.
  (*Silence.*)
PEER Now what?
PASSENGER   I'm keeping quiet.
PEER   Devil's tricks!
  What are you up to?
PASSENGER   Waiting.
PEER (*Tearing his hair.*)   I'm going mad!
  What are you?
PASSENGER (*Nodding.*) Friendly.
PEER   What else? Speak!
PASSENGER What do you think? Do you know anyone else
  Who's like me?
PEER   I know the devil—!
PASSENGER (*Quietly.*) Is it his way to light a lantern
  Leading you through night's passage of fear?
PEER So that's it! What it comes down to is,
  You claim to be a messenger of light?
PASSENGER Friend—have you *ever*, say, twice a year,
  Searched into the abyss of dread?[6]

---

6. *Angst* means dread or terror, in the Kierkegårdian sense of devastation of the soul.

peer Everyone's afraid when danger threatens—
   But the words you use are filled with menace.
passenger Well, have you even once in your life
   Known the victory that only comes with dread?
peer If you've arrived to open some portentous door
   For me, it was stupid not to do it before.
   It doesn't make sense to go choosing a time
   Just when the sea's about to swallow us up.
passenger Do you think the victory would be more authentic
   Sitting by the fireside all snug and cozy?
peer Maybe not; but your talk was ludicrous.
   You think that's an effective way to enlighten?
passenger Where I come from the comedic voice
   Is rated as high as the tragic style.
peer Everything in its place; what suits a publican
   As the text has it, would sink a bishop.
passenger Ordinary folks, on the road to the grave,
   Don't wear the cothurni of tragedy.[7]
peer Get away from me, you horror. Go, man, go!
   I don't want to die. I'll get to the shore!
passenger As far as *that's* concerned, you needn't panic.
   You just don't die in the middle of Act Five.
   (*He glides away.*)
peer There! I got it out of him at last;
   He was just a moralizing critic!

SCENE THREE

*A churchyard in a high-lying mountain parish. A funeral. A priest
and parishioners. The last verse of a psalm is being sung. Peer Gynt is
passing by on the road.*

peer (*At the gate.*) Here's a man going the way of all flesh;
   Praise be to God it isn't me.
   (*He enters the churchyard.*)
the priest (*Speaking at the graveside.*)
   And now, when the soul is summoned to its doom,[8]
   And the mortal dust lies here, an empty shell—
   Now, my dear friends, it's time to speak a word
   About this dead man's pilgrimage on earth.
      He was not rich in wealth or understanding;
   His voice was weak, his bearing quite unmanly;
   He spoke his thoughts uncertainly and shyly,

---

7. Ibsen writes *koturner* (cothurni).
8. The meter changes to iambic pentameter for this speech in the original.

Scarcely the master back in his own house!
He'd come to church like someone pleading
Permission to sit among his fellow men.
　He came, as you all know, from Gudbrandsdal,
Settling here when he was still a boy—
You all remember how to the very end,
He concealed his right hand in his pocket.
　That right hand in his pocket was the feature
That stamped his image in our minds—
Together with his awkwardness, his shy,
Reticent manner every time he entered.
　But though he chose to live his life obliquely
And therefore seemed a stranger in our midst,
You all know what he tried so hard to hide:
The hand he covered had only four fingers.
　I well recall a morning, years ago.
Recruiting sessions were under way at Lundë.
Wartime, it was; on everybody's lips,
The country's peril, and what lay ahead.
　I stood there watching. At the table sat
The Captain with recruiting clerk and sergeants.
Each boy in turn was measured carefully;
Name written down to be enrolled a soldier.
The room was crowded; outside you could hear
The sound of young throats laughing in the courtyard.
　A name was shouted. A new boy shuffled forward,
Looking as pale as snow upon a glacier.
Told to come closer, he ventured to the table,
His right hand bandaged in a piece of cloth.
He gasped and swallowed, struggling for words
But couldn't manage, though the Captain urged him.
And then, at last, fire burning though his cheeks,
His tongue now halting, now spilling out the words,
He mumbled something about a scythe that slipped
And sliced his finger off, both skin and bone.
　All at once the room fell deathly silent.
Men exchanged glances, tightening their mouths;
They stoned the boy with eyes filled with contempt.
He felt the hailstorm but he didn't see it.
The Captain then stood up, elderly, gray,
Spat, pointed to the door and rasped, "Get out!"
　And the boy went. On both sides men shrank back,
Making him run the gauntlet of their glances—
He reached the doorway; then he flew from sight.
Up, up he ran—up across fields and hills,

Up through the woods, clambering over rocks
To where he had his home among the mountains.
     Six months then passed and he was here again,
Bringing his mother, child, and bride-to-be.
He leased some land high up on the hillside,
Where waste ground merges into the parish of Lom.
As soon as he was able to, he married
And built a house and broke the stubborn earth.
He prospered, as many a rescued patch of ground
Bore witness, with its waving ranks of gold.
In church he kept his hand tight in his pocket,
But back at home I'm certain those nine fingers
Performed as much, at least, as any ten.
One spring, the floods washed everything away.
     They got away with their lives. Ruined, penniless,
He set himself to clear the land once more,
And by the fall, smoke was again seen rising
From a new-built and better-sheltered homestead.
Sheltered? From flooding, yes; not from the glacier;
Two years later it all lay under snow!
Yet long before the winter snowdrifts came
His homestead reemerged for a third time.
     He raised three sons, three fine and sturdy boys,
Who needed school, though the school was far away.
Their only passage was a perilous climb
Through narrow passes over headlong cliffs.
What could he do? The eldest was made to climb
As best he could, and where the track dropped sheer
The father roped himself to the boy for safety,
Carrying the others on his arm and back.
     Year after year he labored. They grew up.
Now, all his sacrifice would be repaid!
But three sons, thriving in the New World, forgot
Their Norwegian father and those hard school journeys.
     His vision was limited; he couldn't see.
Beyond the horizon of his little world,
Words that could rouse the hearts of other men,
To him, were only sounds without a meaning.
"Humanity," "the fatherland," "enlightenment,"
Were hidden from his mind as in a mist.
     Yes, he was humble, as men rate, very humble;
And from that first tribunal day, he bore
Its judgment like a brand burning his cheeks;
He kept that maimed hand hidden in his pocket.
An offender against his country's law? Yes, true!

But there's one thing that shines above the law,
As sure as the white tent of Glittertind[9]
Shows peaks of cloud soaring high above.
An indifferent patriot, maybe. For church and state,
He was a barren tree. But on those heights
In the small circle where he made his calling,
There he was great because he was himself.
He kept true to the note that he was born with,
His frugal life a music on muted strings.
So peace be with you, silent warrior.
That fought and fell in the peasant's little war.
    We will not probe his heart and inward being—
That is no job for us but for his Maker—
But I will dare at least the right to claim
It is no cripple now confronts his God.
(*The mourners separate and leave. Peer Gynt, alone, remains.*)
PEER Now *that's* what I call Christianity!
Nothing to make you feel uncomfortable.
The theme—to be unshakably oneself—
The central thread of this priest's argument,
Is by its nature admirably uplifting.
(*Looks down into the grave.*)
Was this maybe the boy who severed his finger,
That day when I was felling trees in the forest?
Who can tell? If I were not standing here,
At the edge of this kindred spirit's grave,
I might think it was *I* was down there sleeping,
Dreaming I listened to my life being praised.
It's a most commendable Christian custom,
This casting of a retrospective glance
Benevolently, over the life of the deceased.
I'd have nothing against receiving judgment
From this eminently worthy priest.
But hell! I think there's still time left to me
Before the gravedigger gets me as his guest.
As the Scripture tells us, "What's best is best,"
And, in the same vein, "To each day its own sorrow."
And "Don't pay for your funeral in advance."
    Ah yes! The Church! Always the true consoler!
I've really failed to appreciate it before.
But now I clearly see what good it does.
To hear, as it were, from the horse's mouth,
That even as you sow, thus shall you reap!

9. A high peak in Norway.

You must be yourself, and for yourself, entirely,
And endeavor your utmost in great things and small.
If Fate's against you, at least you have the honor
Of knowing your life and your ethics correspond.
Now homeward! Though the path is steep and narrow
And Fate has it in for me right to the end,
Old Peer Gynt still trudges on his way,
Poor but virtuous, as he's always been.

SCENE FOUR

A hillside beside a dried riverbed. A dilapidated mill by the riverbed.[1] *The
ground is torn up and all around is waste. Higher up, a large farmhouse.*

*An auction is being held in front of the farmhouse, and many
guests are gathered. There is much drinking and noise. Peer Gynt is
sitting on a rubbish heap beside the mill.*

PEER Forward or back, it's just as far.
  Out or in, I'm trapped as before.
  Time corrodes, the rivers run dry.
  Go around, said the Bøyg, and so must I.
A MAN IN MOURNING Now there's only the garbage left.
  (*Catches sight of Peer Gynt.*)
  Are there strangers here, too? God be with you, friend!
PEER Well met! You're lively here today.
  Is it a christening party or a wedding feast?
MAN IN MOURNING I'd prefer to call it a housewarming—
  The bride's lying in a bed of worms.
PEER And the worms are squabbling for scraps and rags?
MAN IN MOURNING The last verse of a song that's reached its end.
PEER All songs end in the same way.
  And all are ancient; I knew them as a boy.
A YOUTH OF TWENTY (*With a casting ladle.*)
  Hey, take a look at this neat thing I bought.
  Peer Gynt used it to make silver buttons.
ANOTHER Look at mine! A moneybag for a couple of cents.
A THIRD Is that all? This peddler's pack cost only five.
PEER Peer Gynt? Who's he?
MAN IN MOURNING   All I know is, he was
  Brother-in-law to the corpse and Aslak the Smith.

1. It might help the reader to realize that this funeral setting is either Ingrid's farm,
Haegstad, or Peer's old farm, punitively acquired by the Haegstad estate (as the scene
description and the Gyntian memorabilia would suggest). The funeral is for Ingrid; the
Man in Mourning is Aslak, the Man in Gray is Mads Moen. It seems Aslak married Ingrid, who was numerously unfaithful. The scene lets us see that Peer's future with Ingrid
would have been bleak. This whole scene shows the squalid degradation of the world of
Act 1.

A MAN IN GRAY You're forgetting me! Are you mad or drunk?

MAN IN MOURNING You're forgetting the Haegstad storehouse door![2]

MAN IN GRAY Granted! But you weren't so particular yourself.

MAN IN MOURNING As long as she doesn't screw around with Death!

MAN IN GRAY Come, brother-in-law: a drink for kinship's sake!

MAN IN MOURNING To hell with your kinship; you're drunk already.

MAN IN GRAY That's crap! Blood isn't as thin as all that.
  Always remember we're kin to Peer Gynt.
  (*Takes off with him.*)

PEER (*Softly.*) One meets old acquaintances!

A BOY (*Shouting after the man in mourning.*) My dead mother
  Will get on your case if you get too drunk.

PEER (*Rising.*) The old farmer's wisdom doesn't apply here:
  "The deeper you dig, the sweeter it smells."

A BOY (*With a bear skin.*) Look, the Dovrë Cat. Well, only the pelt.
  It's how he chased off the trolls on Christmas Eve.[3]

ANOTHER (*With a reindeer's skull.*) Here's the wonderful reindeer
    that carried
  Peer Gynt on its back over the Gjendin ridge.

A THIRD (*With a hammer, calling to the man in mourning.*)
  Hey there, Aslak, recognize this sledgehammer?
  Didn't you use it that day the devil split the wall?

A FOURTH (*Empty handed.*) Mads Moen! Here's the invisible cloak
  Used by Peer and Ingrid to fly through the air.

PEER Bring some brandy, lads! I'm feeling my age.
  I'll hold my own junkyard auction here.

A BOY What are you selling?

PEER   I've got a palace
  Up in the Rondë; it's solidly built.

A BOY I'll bid a button!

PEER   At least make it a pint.
  To bid any less would be a crime.

ANOTHER He's a playful old guy!
  (*The bystanders gather round Peer.*)

PEER (*Shouts.*)   Granë, my horse,
  Who bids?

ONE OF THE CROWD Where is he now?

PEER   Far off in the west,
  Where the sun sets, boys! And how he can fly!
  As fast—as fast as Peer Gynt could lie.

VOICES What else have you got?

---

2. This would confirm that the present scene is not Haegstad, but Peer's old farm.
3. A reference to an episode in the folk legend of Peer Gynt, in which Peer, by pretending a tame bear was his pet cat, terrified the trolls.

PEER   Both gold and junk.
   They were bought with a shipwreck; I'll sell at a loss.
A BOY Put them up!
PEER From a dream, a silver-clasped book!
   You can have it for a hook and an eye.
THE BOY To hell with dreams!
PEER   My Empire, then!
   I'll throw it to the crowd. You can scrap for it.
THE BOY Does it include a crown?
PEER   Of the finest straw.
   It will suit whoever puts it on first.
   Wait! There's more yet. A rotten egg.
   A madman's gray hair! A prophet's beard.
   You get all these if you can show me a sign
   On a hillside that says: "Here is your path."
THE BAILIFF (*Who has just arrived.*)
   I'd say, from the way you've been acting,
   Your path's more likely to lead straight to jail.
PEER (*Hat in hand.*) Very likely. But tell me, who's this Peer Gynt?
BAILIFF What nonsense—
PEER   If you don't mind, I'd like to know—
BAILIFF It's said he was an incorrigible fantasist.
PEER Fantasist—?[4]
BAILIFF Yes—anything that was glamorous or great
   He'd fantasize that he had done it.
   But excuse me, friend, I've got work to do.
   (*Leaves.*)
PEER And where is he now, this remarkable man?
OLDER MAN He went overseas to some foreign country
   And got into trouble, as you might imagine—
   It's been a long time now since he was hanged.
PEER Hanged? Well, well! It's what I imagined.
   The late Peer Gynt was himself to the end.
   (*Bows.*) Good-bye! And many thanks for today's chat!
   (*Goes a few steps, but stops again.*)
   Wait; you bright boys and pretty girls—
   Shall I tell a story as a kind of bonus?
SEVERAL If you know any.
PEER   No problem at all.
   (*He comes nearer; his face takes on an enigmatic expression.*)
   In San Francisco, once, I was digging for gold.
   The town was full of jugglers, entertainers.
   One man could play the fiddle with his toes;

4. *Dikter* in original, which means poet, but it also has the negative connotation of dreamer, fantasist, which obviously applies in this exchange.

Another danced a fandango on his knees;
A third, I was told, kept on making verses,
While a hole was being bored into his skull.
The devil, one day, visited this gathering,
Wanting to try his luck like anyone else.
His gig was this: to totally convince you
He could grunt like a bona fide pig.
Though no one recognized him, his personality
Attracted a full house, so hopes ran high.
He stepped forward in an ample cape;
"Man muss sich drapieren,"[5] as the Germans say.
But under the cape—which nobody knew—
He had managed to smuggle an actual pig.
And so began the great presentation.
The devil would pinch and the pig would sing out.
The whole show claimed to be a fantasia
On porcine existence, in bondage and free.
The grand finale was a slaughterhouse squeal,
Whereupon the artist bowed low and retired.
The act was debated fiercely by the critics,
And the performance itself both panned and praised.
Some found the vocal skill mediocre,
Others thought the death shriek too calculated.
But all could agree on one thing: the *grunt*!
Here, the presentation badly exaggerated!
That's what the devil got for being so dumb,
And overestimating the level of his public.
(*He bows and exits. A puzzled silence falls over the gathering.*)

SCENE FIVE

*The Eve of Pentecost. In the depths of the forest. Farther back, in a
cleared space, a hut with reindeer horns over the porch. Peer Gynt on
his hands and knees looking for wild onions in the undergrowth.*

PEER One stage of the journey! What's the next one?
　　Try everything first, then choose the best.
　　That's what I've done—starting with Caesar,
　　Then straight down the ladder to Nebuchadnezzar.[6]
　　So I went through Bible history, after all!

---

5. In the original, "one must cover/clothe oneself." This whole fable is adapted from a story
　by Phaedrus, *Scurra et Rusticus*, in which a clown wins a prize for uttering realistic
　porcine grunts, over a rival whose grunts were created by a real, concealed pig. The mes-
　sage is that the public is a poor judge of truth in art—something Ibsen's long career of
　failure with his Norwegian public probably confirmed for him.
6. King of Babylon (605–562 B.C.E.), conqueror and destroyer of Jerusalem who in his
　madness was reduced to the animalistic condition of eating grass.

The old boy's gone back to his mother again.
After all, it's written, from the earth thou comest!
The main thing in life is to fill up your belly.
But fill it with onions? That's quite a comedown!
I'd better be cunning and set out some snares.
Here is a brook, so I won't go thirsty.
And I still rank first among all the animals.
When it comes time to die—as no doubt it will—
I'll crawl under some fallen tree;
Like a bear I'll build a cover of leaves
And scratch on the tree bark in large capitals:
"Here lies Peer Gynt, a decent enough man,
Emperor over all the other animals."
Emperor?
(*Laughing to himself.*)
            You prophetic old fool!
You're no emperor—you're an onion.
Therefore, I'll peel you, my good friend, Peer,
And pleading and whining won't help a bit!
(*He takes up an onion, stripping one layer after another.*)
There lies the outermost, tattered layer;
It's the shipwrecked man on the overturned boat.
Here's the passenger-layer, shabby and thin—
But still retaining a tang of Peer Gynt.
Next layer down, there's the gold-mining ego.
Its juice is all gone—if it ever had any.
This rough layer next, with the toughened hide,
Is the fur trader from Hudson's Bay.
The one under that looks like a crown—no thanks!
Let's chuck it away without any comment.
Here's the archaeologist, brief but sturdy;
And here comes the Prophet, fresh and juicy,
But stinking, according to Scripture, of lies,
Enough to bring tears to an honest man's eyes.
Now comes a section rolled softly together;
It's the fine gentleman living in luxury.
The next seems rotten; it's all lined with streaks;
Do those black streaks stand for slave or priest?
(*Pulling off several layers at once.*)
What an incredible number of layers are left.
When will the core emerge into light?
(*Pulls the whole onion to pieces.*)
God knows if it will. Right down to the center
It's nothing but layers, getting smaller and smaller.

Nature's a joker!
(*He casts away the rest.*)
                    To hell with brooding.
Replaying old thoughts can make you stumble.
Though where that's concerned, I can laugh at the danger—
I'm already planted firmly on all fours!
(*Scratching his head.*)
It's a strange business, this whole enterprise;
What we call Life plays with loaded dice.[7]
You try to hold it, it slips through your fingers,
And you're holding something else—or nothing.
(*He approaches the vicinity of the hut, catches sight of it and gives a start.*)
This hut? On the moor—! Ha!
(*Rubbing his eyes.*)   It's exactly
As if, in the past, I've known this building.
A reindeer's skull jutting out from the gable—!
A mermaid shaped like a fish from the navel—!
Lies! There's no mermaid! Only nails and planks—
Locks against the malicious goblin tribe—!
SOLVEIG (*Singing inside the house.*)

> Now all's made ready for Pentecost.[8]
> My dearest boy, so far away,
> Come home at last.
> If your burden's great,
> Take time to rest.
> I shall wait,
> As I pledged from the first.

PEER GYNT (*Rises quietly, deathly pale.*)
One who remembered—and one who forgot.
One who squandered and one who stayed true!
O, grief! A life that was never lived!
O, dread—here's where my empire stood!
(*He runs away on the path into the forest.*)

---

7. *Med en rev bak øre*, "with a fox behind the ear"; a traditional expression for duplicity.
8. Pentecost celebrates the descent of the spirit from God to humanity, and from this point on, the play reveals this happening to Peer, despite his obstinate resistance. Solveig, then, is the magnetlike force drawing Peer up to her, as the ghosts of his past crowd about him.

SCENE SIX

Night. A barren heath with pine trees. A forest fire has ravaged the area and there are charred tree trunks for miles around. White trails of mist move here and there across the ground. Peer Gynt is hurrying over the moor.

PEER Ashes, fog, dust, blown in the wind—
   There's enough here to build upon!
   Stench and rottenness within;
   Outside, a whited sepulchre.
   Fantasies, dreams, and stillborn learning
   Make up my pyramid's foundation;
   Upon that base I built my life work,
   Raising a stairway stepped with lies.
   "Despise the truth, evade remorse"
   Proclaims the banner on its rooftop,
   Swelling the doomsday trumpet with
   Petrus Gyntus Caesar fecit![9]
   (*He laughs.*) What was that sound, like children weeping?
   They weep, but still it's more like singing.
   Here at my feet are thread balls, rolling—!
   (*Kicking at them.*) Get lost! You're cluttering my path.
TUMBLEWEEDS (*Along the ground.*)
   We are thoughts
   You should have thought us.
   Legs to run with
   You should have brought us.
PEER To *one* already I brought life
   He's proved a bungled, crooked oaf.
TUMBLEWEEDS We should have soared high
   As a vibrant choir
   We skirt the ground,
   As tumbleweeds now.
PEER Tumbleweed louts! Is this how we meet,
   So you can snare your father's feet?
WITHERED LEAVES (*Flying before the wind.*)
   We are each watchword
   You should have spoken.
   By sleeping, you erred;
   Our power is broken.
   The worm's bored through us
   Down to the root.

9. Thus did Peer Gynt, Caesar! Latin in the original.

No wreaths come to us
Bearing fruit.
PEER Not entirely fruitless was your birth.
At least you can manure the earth.
A SIGHING IN THE AIR
We are songs
Never brought forth;
A thousand times
Smothered at birth.
We've lain in wait
At the core of your heart;
Now poison's brought
Death to your throat.
PEER Poison yourselves, you foolish voices!
Did I ever have time for making verses?
DEWDROPS (*Dripping from the leaves.*)
We are tears
You never let fall.
Wounds of ice-spears
We were ready to heal.
Now the spear pierces
Deep to the bone;
The flesh has closed,
And our power is gone.
PEER Thanks: In the Rondë valley I had to wail,
And for my pains, ended up with a tail.
BROKEN STRAWS
We are deeds,
You should have performed.
By injurious doubt
Crushed and deformed.
On Judgment Day
We'll arrive as a host.
Then hear what we say,
And discover the cost!
PEER Weasel reasoning! Can you give
Bad marks for what's *negative*?
ÅSE'S VOICE (*Very distant.*)
Whoa! Drive more slow,
Ecch! The sleigh's upset
And rolls in the snow;
I'm cold now, and wet.
You drove like a madman;
Is the castle in view?
With that whip from the closet

The devil's tricked you.

PEER A poor fellow had better clear out at once
If he's expected to carry the devil's sins.
They'd flatten you till you're dead as a stone;
You've enough to bear with sins of your own.

SCENE SEVEN

(*Another part of the heath.*)

PEER (*Sings.*)
A sexton! A sexton! Where are your hounds?
From your bell-loud mouths let the hymns sound.
Circle your hats with a mourning band.
I'll be following soon; I've corpses in hand.
(*The button-molder, with a tool box and a huge casting ladle, enters from a side path.*)

BUTTON-MOLDER Well met, old fellow!
PEER   Good evening, my friend!
BUTTON-MOLDER The man's in a hurry. Where are you bound?
PEER To a funeral.
BUTTON-MOLDER   That's so? I don't see all that clear;
So excuse me—is your name, by any chance, Peer?
PEER Peer Gynt, as they say.
BUTTON-MOLDER   Well, that's luck all right!
It's precisely Peer Gynt I'm to fetch tonight.
PEER Is that so? What do you want?
BUTTON-MOLDER   As you can tell
I'm a button-molder. And you go in my ladle.
PEER What will I do in there?
BUTTON-MOLDER   You'll be melted down.
PEER Melted?
BUTTON-MOLDER Here, you see: ready, empty, and clean!
Your grave is dug and your coffin ordered.
On your body the worms will be very well fed.
But my orders are clear: Don't delay! So I call,
On my Master's behalf, to fetch your soul.
PEER Impossible! Like this, without being warned—?
BUTTON-MOLDER It's a custom, where births and wakes are
concerned,
To discreetly appoint the day of the feast.
With no warning at all for the principal guest.
PEER Right! I'm confused—my blood's running colder—
You are—

BUTTON-MOLDER As you heard, the button-molder.
PEER I get it! Like the favorite child, Death is given
   Many names. So, in *there* I'm to be driven
   To harbor? This method seems somewhat remiss.
   I'm sure I deserve better treatment that this.
   I am not so bad as you seem to believe—
   In fact I've done a lot of good in my life—
   In crime, I'm hardly more than a beginner,
   I'm definitely not your grand-scale sinner.
BUTTON-MOLDER But that is precisely the crux, my man!
   You are hardly a sinner on a grandiose plan.
   From tortures and pangs you go scot-free;
   So the casting ladle's your destiny.
PEER Ladle or sulfur pit—one thing is clear,
   Bitter or mild, they're both of them beer.[1]
   Get behind me, Satan!
BUTTON-MOLDER   You are not so coarse
   As to think I trot on the hoof of a horse?
PEER Whether a horse's hoof or a fox's paw,[2]
   Be off! Take more care who you're looking for.
BUTTON-MOLDER My friend, you're under a misapprehension.
   We're both in a hurry, so please pay attention.
   Let me make clear your current position.
   You are, as I have from your own admission,
   Not what you might call deeply mired in sin,
   In fact, barely middling—
PEER   Ah, now you begin
   To talk common sense—
BUTTON-MOLDER   Wait just a bit.
   To label you virtuous would be stretching it—
PEER I would never profess any such status.
BUTTON-MOLDER An indefinable state; as they say, "more or less."
   A sinner of really magnificent style
   Can't be found, these days, for many a mile.
   It demands much more than mere dabbling in mire.
   Real sin means you give yourself to it entire.
PEER Granted; it's very true, all that you say.
   One must pitch in with fury the berserker[3] way.
BUTTON-MOLDER You, however, sinned as lightly as you could.
PEER Just surface sins, friend! A mere splash of mud.
BUTTON-MOLDER We begin to agree. The sulfurous pit
   Is not the place for mere dabblers in dirt.

1. "Home brewed or foreign," in the original. "Bitter or mild" might be a good substitute.
2. Both attributes of the devil in disguise.
3. Legendary Viking warriors who fought in a state of frenzy.

PEER Then it follows, my friend, I can go as I came.

BUTTON-MOLDER No; it follows that melting's the name of the game.

PEER What new set of rules have you put on the record
   Here at home, while I was traveling abroad?

BUTTON-MOLDER The custom's as old as the Serpent's creation;
   Its aim is promotion of good conservation.
   You know the craft—how it sometimes occurs
   A casting turns out to have too many flaws.
   For example: a button comes out defaced.
   What would you do?

PEER   Throw it out, of course.

BUTTON-MOLDER Ah, yes; Jon Gynt was well known for waste
   So long as he thought he had a full purse.
   But the Master, you see, is an economist,
   (And so, as wealth goes, very well placed.)
   His method's to throw away nothing as refuse
   That, as raw material, might be put to good use.
   You were intended as a button, glistening
   On the world's vest, but the loop was missing.
   So, you're assigned to go into the Reject Chest
   To be merged and melted along with the rest.

PEER You don't intend dumping me into a stew
   With any Tom, Dick, and Harry to make something new?

BUTTON-MOLDER Yes, that's just what I mean; you can be sure!
   It's happened to many and will happen to more.
   It's done with old coins: they're sent to the mint,
   Whenever their image has become indistinct.

PEER But this is being horrendously miserly;
   My dear, good friend, please let me go free.
   A worn-down coin, an eyeless button—
   What's that to a man in your Master's position?

BUTTON-MOLDER While you still possess any spirit at all
   You'll always have value, at least as scrap metal.

PEER No, I say, no! I'll fight to the last breath.
   Anything, sooner than this kind of death!

BUTTON-MOLDER But what else can we do? Be reasonable.
   Heaven requires stuff more ethereal.

PEER I'm easily pleased! I don't aim so high;
   But no atom of self am I willing to let die.
   Set up Judgment Day in the old-fashioned style—
   Let the One with the Hoof take me in for a while.
   A hundred years, say, if that strikes you as fair.
   It's something I'm sure I could manage to bear.
   The torment's reputed to be mainly moral
   So it's unlikely it's all that intolerable.

"It's a transition (it's written) one has to endure,"
Said the fox, waiting to be skinned. "Nothing more!
One just waits for the hour of deliverance,
And hopes for a happier circumstance."
But this other idea: to become a mere cell,
In some mass of superfluous material—
This meltdown to ladle-annihilation—!
My innermost soul rises up in revulsion!

BUTTON-MOLDER But, my dear Peer Gynt, there's no need to get
So worked up over a small thing like that!
You've not been yourself any time at all,
So why does a clean disappearance appall?

PEER Not been myself! I could laugh myself hoarse!
Peer Gynt's been somebody else, of course?
No, Button-Molder! You judge without seeing.
If you could look into my innermost being,
You'd find only Peer, and no one but Peer;
Essence of Peer-self; nothing else there!

BUTTON-MOLDER That can't be right. My instructions are clear:
"You must summon Peer Gynt," it's written down here.
"Into the ladle with him. He's been ever at odds
With his life's true purpose; he's damaged goods!"

PEER What rubbish! It's some other Gynt they mean.
Does it really say Peer? Not Rasmus, or Jon?

BUTTON-MOLDER It's been many a day since I melted *them*.
So better come quietly and not waste my time.

PEER I'll be damned if I will! What a mess there'd be
If it turned out, tomorrow, it was not meant for me!
You'd better take care man, whatever you do.
Think of the consequence that would ensue!

BUTTON-MOLDER I have it in writing—

PEER   Just give me more time—

BUTTON-MOLDER What good would that do?

PEER   I'll prove my claim.
I've been myself the whole of my life—
As that's the question still needing proof.

BUTTON-MOLDER You'll get proof? But how?

PEER   Witnesses to attest—

BUTTON-MOLDER I'm afraid the Master will not be impressed.

PEER Impossible! However, to each day its sorrow!
Dear sir, just loan me myself till tomorrow!
I'll be back here soon. One is only born once.
You get much attached to the self you are given.
Come, are we agreed?

BUTTON-MOLDER   Well, just this one chance;

But only until the next crossroads then.
(*Peer Gynt runs off.*)

SCENE EIGHT

Farther up on the moor. Peer Gynt enters at full speed.

PEER Time is money, the Good Book says.
  If only I knew where the crossroads are.
  They could be near, or they could be far.
  The earth burns under me like red-hot iron.
  A witness! A witness! Where could I find one?
  It's unimaginable here in the forest.
  The world's a fine mess. What has it come to,
  When a man's got to prove the rights he's born with?
  (*A crooked old man, with a staff in his hand and a bag over his shoulder, trudges in front of him.*)
OLD MAN (*Coming to a halt.*) Kind sir, spare a coin for a homeless
  old man!
PEER Sorry—not carrying spare change with me.
OLD MAN Prince Peer! Oh my! Fancy meeting again!
PEER Who are you?
OLD MAN   You forget the Old Man of Rondë?
PEER You are never—!
OLD MAN The Old Man of the Dovrë, I swear!
PEER The Old Man . . . of the Dovrë. . . . Really! . . . For sure!
OLD MAN Ah, but since then, I've fallen on evil days.
PEER Ruined?
OLD MAN   Lost everything except the bare shelf.
  Now I'm trudging the highways, starved as a wolf.
PEER Hurrah! Such witnesses don't grown on trees!
OLD MAN The prince has gotten quite gray since we met.
PEER Dear Father-in-law, time tears life to tatters.
  But don't let us rake over private matters—
  Above all, not the family spats we regret.
  I was a wild man then—
OLD MAN   Ah yes, ah yes!—
  The prince was young and it's what youth does.
  But the prince was wise to turn down his bride.
  He spared himself embarrassment and shame.
  For since then she really has gone to the bad—
PEER Is that so?
OLD MAN   She's made a complete mess of her life.
  She and Trond have set up as man and wife!
PEER Which Trond?

OLD MAN   Of the Valfjeld.
PEER   Aha! With him!
  One of those I stole the three herd girls from.
OLD MAN But my grandson's turned out to be brawny and tough.
  With raucous offspring all over the land.
PEER Well, best spare the news till we find time enough.
  Just now I have other things on my mind.
  I find myself in a most dire situation—
  I'm in need of a character reference.
  Which is something a father-in-law could dispense.
  I might find the means to some welcome libation! . . .
OLD MAN Can I really be of service to the prince?
  In return, would you give *me* a reference?
PEER Gladly. I *am* rather short on money supplies.
  And I'm finding the need to economize.
  Let's explain what I want. Can you call to mind
  That night I came seeking your daughter's hand?
OLD MAN Of course, my prince.
PEER   Less of the "prince," by the way!
  Anyhow, you attempted to warp and control
  My sight with a little work on my eye
  To change me from Peer Gynt into a troll.
  What did I do? I vehemently opposed it
  And swore I would stand on my own two feet.
  I sacrificed love, and power and glory,
  To live and die my true self. End of story!
  That's what I want you to swear in the courts.
OLD MAN The devil I can!
PEER   What kind of garbage is this?
OLD MAN Now he wants me to add a lie to my faults?
  He surely remembers he put on troll breeches,
  And tasted the mead—
PEER   but not all the rest.
  And I firmly refused the ultimate test.
  That's how you judge for better or worse;
  The gist of a poem's found in the last verse.
OLD MAN But the ending, Peer, was just the contrary.
PEER What do you mean?
OLD MAN   When you left Rondë country
  You'd inscribed the troll-motto deep in your heart.
PEER What motto?
OLD MAN   The great Word, setting apart—
PEER The Word?
OLD MAN   —that sets apart man, segregating him off
  From troll-folk: "Troll, to thyself be enough!"

PEER (*Recoils a step.*) Enough!

OLD MAN   From that day since, you strained each sinew
    To set up this lifestyle, and from then on continue.

PEER I! Peer Gynt!

OLD MAN (*Weeping.*) There's ingratitude revealed!
    He lives by troll values then wants them concealed!
    I taught you that word; you took it in hand.
    It raised you and made you a wealthy man.
    Now you return and don't want to declare
    That I, and the motto, made what you are!

PEER *Enough!* I'm a hill-troll? An egoist?
    This has got to be garbage! You're joking, I trust?

OLD MAN (*Pulling out a bundle of old newspapers.*)
    I daresay you think we don't get the news.
    Wait; here see printed in red and black.
    The Blocksberg Post covering your course.
    The Hekle Mountain Times followed your track
    Since you left here, to the day you came back.
    You want to read them, Peer? Do you need proof?
    There's an article here by "Stallionhoof"—
    Look—"Troll Nationalism's Semiotic,"
    Where the author points out how it's quite idiotic
    To emphasize features like tail and horn;
    Just graft that one word, and your hill-troll is born!
    "Our *Enough*," he concludes, "is *intrinsically* troll."
    And you're the example he likes to extol.

PEER A hill-troll? I?

OLD MAN   The case is quite clear.

PEER Then it's the same as if I'd never left here?
    I could have stayed in the Rondë sitting at ease.
    And spared the expense of innumerable shoes.
    Peer Gynt, a troll?—It's absurd, a bad joke!
    Goodbye! Here—! Just enough for a smoke!

OLD MAN No, kind Prince Peer!

PEER   Get away! You're a fool,
    Or in second childhood. Find a hospital!

OLD MAN Just what my present wandering seeks.
    But my grandson's brood have populated
    The whole land, and me they've relegated
    To folklore! Saying I exist only in books!
    One's kin give the unkindest cut of all,
    They say, and it's what I've had to discover.
    Think! Only to exist under a book cover!

PEER There are many to whom that fate will befall.

OLD MAN And we never set up any pension or dole!

No mutual funds and no poor relief.
Rondë rejected these, down to the last troll.
PEER Yes, thanks to that damned "To yourself be *enough!*"
OLD MAN Oh, the prince can't complain about that word.
And if, somehow, he could just find a way—
PEER My man, I'm afraid you must have misheard;
As I stand, I'm totally cleaned out—every way!
OLD MAN That can't be possible! Is the prince broke?
PEER Completely. My princely ego's in hock.
And it's all the fault of you trollish devils.
Proving bad company's the worst of all evils.
OLD MAN So, down flaps my hope from its high perch position.
Farewell! Back to town! That's the way I must trudge!
PEER What will you do there?
OLD MAN   Go for an audition.[4]
They're looking for national types for the stage.
PEER Good luck on your journey! Greet them from me.
I might follow your example, if I ever get free.
I'll write a black farce—even act in it one day—
And its title? "Sic transit gloria mundi."[5]
(*He runs off along the road. The old man calls after him.*)

SCENE NINE

At a crossroads.

PEER You're in trouble, Peer, even worse than before.
That trollish "enough" has really caught up with you.
The ship's wrecked. I must cling to whatever drifts by.
Anything but merging into drifting flotsam.
BUTTON-MOLDER (*At the crossroads.*)
Well, Peer Gynt, have you found your witness?
PEER The crossroads already? That came round fast!
BUTTON-MOLDER I can read in your face—it's like a signpost—
What the facts are; they're not easy to miss.
PEER I got tired of the search. One can soon go astray.
BUTTON-MOLDER Right! And what would it all lead to, anyway?
PEER True enough—in the forest, and at this time of night.
BUTTON-MOLDER There's an old tramp passing. Shall we ask him to
wait?
PEER No, let him go, friend. He's drunk, you can see!
BUTTON-MOLDER But maybe he can—
PEER   No. Let him go on his way!

4. Literally, "go to be an actor."
5. Thus passes the glory of the world (Latin).

BUTTON-MOLDER So! Shall we begin?
PEER   A question—just one:
  What does this "being oneself" really mean?
BUTTON-MOLDER A curious question to hear from a man
  Who so recently—
PEER   Please be brief and have done.
BUTTON-MOLDER "To be oneself is to slay oneself."[6]
  On you this explanation's probably lost.
  So let's say: it's to reveal in each part of your life
  The Master's intention at whatever the cost.
PEER But what if a poor man is left in the dark,
  What his Master meant?
BUTTON-MOLDER   He must intuit it right.
PEER But intuitions are often so wide of the mark;
  They can send a man crashing down in midflight.
BUTTON-MOLDER That's for sure, Peer; errors of intuition
  Lead to "Him with the Hoof" and lasting perdition.
PEER The affair seems devilishly complex to me.
  Look, I no longer claim being myself. I can see,
  It is not going to be easy when put to the test.
  Let's assume *that* part of my petition's lost.
  But quite recently, wandering alone on the moor,
  The shoe of my conscience pinched, and I saw
  More clearly, and said to myself, "You're a sinner!"
BUTTON-MOLDER Let's not go back to square one like a beginner—!
PEER Not at all. I mean, as a sinner, I was a giant one.
  Not only in deed, but in word and intention.
  Overseas, I lived a life of debauchery.
BUTTON-MOLDER Could be. But can it be found in some registry?
PEER Just give me the chance. I'll search out a priest,
  Confess, have him vouch for it, then back with the list.
BUTTON-MOLDER Yes, if you bring that, it could help your case;
  Then you might be spared this casting device.
  But my orders, Peer—
PEER   That file's obsolete;
  Its details go back to an earlier state—
  A time when my life was corrupt and effete,
  And I played the Prophet and trusted in fate.
  So, do I get to try?
BUTTON-MOLDER   But—!
PEER   Come on, be nice.
  There can't be all that much to do in this place.
  The air in this district's so bracing and sweet

6. The idea is that in order to be one's authentic self, one has to slay inauthentic identities
   (selves) that prevent self-determination.

It stretches the lives out considerably.
Remember what the local parson wrote:
"It's seldom anyone dies in this valley."
BUTTON-MOLDER The next crossroads, then; beyond, you shan't
    pass.
PEER I'll get hold of a priest, if I must grab him by force!
    (*He runs off.*)

SCENE TEN

(*A heather-covered hillside. The path winds upward over the ridge.*)

PEER "*This* could come in useful in lots of ways,"
    As Espen[7] said, finding the magpie wing.
    Who'd have thought my record of sins
    Would get me out of danger on this last night?
    Well, it is an extremely delicate situation,
    This jumping from the frying pan into the fire;
    But we can take heart from the well-known proverb
    That tells us, where there's life there's hope.
    (*A lean person in a cassock tucked up high and with a fowling net over his shoulders comes hurrying across the slope.*)
    What's this? A priest with a fowling net.
    Yay! I really am Fortune's pet!
    Good evening, Pastor. This pathway's foul—
THE LEAN ONE Yes, but what wouldn't one do for a soul?
PEER Ah, someone bound for heaven—?
THE LEAN ONE   Nope!
    He'll be taking the other direction, I hope.
PEER Pastor, may I join you for a bit of the way?
THE LEAN ONE Of course. Always glad of company.
PEER I've a load on my mind—
THE LEAN ONE   *Heraus!*[8] Go on!
PEER You see here before you a decent man.
    I've strictly observed our country's laws.
    I have never been jailed for any cause;
    But there are times a man can stray and miss
    His footing—
THE LEAN ONE   It happens to the best of us.
PEER These trifles, you see—
THE LEAN ONE   Only trifles?

7. Espen Askeladd found a magpie wing, which led to a series of adventures leading to his gaining a kingdom and a princess—a story both paralleled and parodied (on the troll and human level) in *Peer Gynt*.
8. Out with it! (German).

PEER   Yes, on
  Occasion; but never a major transgression.
THE LEAN ONE Then in that case, good fellow, leave me in peace.
  I'm not the person you seem to surmise.
  You're checking my fingers. What do you think of them?
PEER A most remarkably developed nail-system.
THE LEAN ONE And now? You're giving my feet quite a stare.
PEER (*Pointing.*) Is that hoof natural?[9]
THE LEAN ONE   So I like to declare.
PEER I would have taken an oath you were a priest.
  But now I've the honor—well, best is sure best.
  When the front door's open, don't use the back way.
  If you're meeting the king—no need of the lackey.
THE LEAN ONE Shake hands. You seem without prejudice.
  Well, my dear sir, how can I be of service?
  Now, you mustn't ask me for power or money.
  I can't supply them, not if you were to hang me.
  You've no notion how business has gone downhill.
  The market provides no turnover at all;
  No movement in souls, except now and then
  A stray one—
PEER   Such a reformation in men?
THE LEAN ONE On the contrary; they're debased from the cradle.
  Why, most of them end up in the casting ladle.
PEER The ladle, ah yes! I have heard it mentioned.
  In fact, in coming to you, it was my intention—
THE LEAN ONE Go on!
PEER   To see, if it wouldn't be too rude,
  To ask if I might get—
THE LEAN ONE   A hangout, or pad?
PEER You've guessed my request before it was made.
  You just said your business has gone down the tube.
  So maybe you won't be over particular—
THE LEAN ONE But my dear—
PEER   My needs don't extend very far.
  As for a salary, I wouldn't really require it;
  Just an atmosphere as pleasant as conditions permit.
THE LEAN ONE A warm room?
PEER   Not *too* warm. And then
  Permission, at will, to exit again—
  The right, as they say, of opting out
  Should a better situation come about.

---

9. In Norwegian folklore, the devil has one hoof.

THE LEAN ONE My good friend, I'm most sincerely distressed—
  But you've no idea how many similar petitions
  People keep sending, begging just these conditions,
  When their earthly exertions are reaching their last.
PEER But when my past comes back in successive waves,
  I find I am eminently ripe for admittance.
THE LEAN ONE Only trifles, you said.
PEER   In a certain sense.
  However, I recollect I once trafficked in slaves.
THE LEAN ONE There are those who put wills and minds in chains;
  But they couldn't get in for all their pains.
PEER I've exported idolatrous figures to China.
THE LEAN ONE All second-rate stuff. We need something finer.
  There are folk exporting more hideous figures
  In their sermons and arts and literatures.
  Who still aren't admitted—
PEER   Wait, there's more yet.
  You must know, I once set up as a prophet.
THE LEAN ONE In foreign lands? Humbug! Most in clairvoyance
  Get the casting ladle, to their great annoyance!
  If you've nothing better to back up your claim,
  I can't house you! I can't tell you how sorry I am.
PEER Wait a bit! In a shipwreck—as I clung to a keel—
  ("A drowning man grabs at a straw," says some book—
  And it's also said, "Your first duty's to feel
  For yourself") Here goes! I halfway murdered a cook!
THE LEAN ONE I'd be just as impressed if you'd *halfway* managed
  To get a kitchen girl another way damaged.
  Why bother me with this halfway stuff?
  With due respect, do you imagine we squander
  Costly fuel, in times like these we live under,
  For a few peccadilloes, some prankish fluff?
  Don't get mad; it's not you, it's your sins I disparage—
  Forgive me using such straightforward language.
  But, my friend, just get this out of your mind;
  Consider the ladle your destiny.
  What would you gain from lodging with me?
  Think of it! I see you're the sensible kind.
  You'd keep your memory, that is a given—
  Excursions through *your* memory-land
  Would provide, for both your heart and your mind,
  What the Swedes call "only feeble bad fun."
  You'd have nothing for grief or for jubilation,
  No cause for despair or for celebration,

Nothing to chill or to heat your blood,[1]
Just endless trivia on which to brood.
PEER It's written: it's never easy to know
What's pinching your foot when you don't wear a shoe.
THE LEAN ONE That's true; I have—thanks to you-know-who!—
No occasion for more than a single shoe.
But it's fortunate we brought up this footwear theme;
It reminds me how I must be hurrying on.
I'm fetching a roast—a fat, juicy one,
I can't stand here gossiping, wasting my time.
PEER And dare one inquire on what diet of sin
This man has been gorging?
THE LEAN ONE   It seems he's been
Assiduously himself, by day and night—
Just the quality we seek in a candidate.
PEER Himself? Do those folks belong to *your* sphere?
THE LEAN ONE It depends. At least we keep open the door.
Remember, there are two ways you can be
Yourself: like a coat has a right side and wrong one.
In Paris they've managed recently
To make portraits with the help of the sun.
Either they can develop one way to give
The image, or what's called a negative,
Where light and shadow are seen in reverse.
To the uninformed eye it can look hideous.
But the likeness is in there, without any doubt;
All that you need is to bring it out.
If, then, a soul has conducted its life
Imaging itself in a negative way,
They don't just throw the whole plate away.
Instead, quite simply, it's handed to me.
I take it in hand for further treatment
And work to effect its development.
I scald it, plunge it, burn it, rinse
With sulfur and similar ingredients,
Until the image it was meant to give
Emerges and is called a positive.
But for a man like you, all half smudged out,
The sulfur-potash process won't work out.
PEER So, I must come to you first as black as a crow
To emerge white as a dove![2] Is it permitted to know
The name of this negative counterfeit

1. "You are neither cold nor hot. I wish you were one or the other, but since you are neither, but only lukewarm, I will spit you out of my mouth" Revelation 7.14–15.
2. *Rype* is a grouse or ptarmigan. Crow and dove are better antitheses in English.

Who's now to be worked to a positive state?
THE LEAN ONE It says Peter Gynt.
PEER   Peter Gynt? Ah yes!
   This Mr. Gynt's himself?
THE LEAN ONE   It's what he swears.
PEER Well, he's a man to be trusted, this Mr. Gynt fellow.
THE LEAN ONE You know him, maybe?
PEER   Oh yes! Well, just so-so.
   One knows so many.
THE LEAN ONE   My time's not cheap—
   Where did you see him last?
PEER   Down at the Cape.
THE LEAN ONE *Di buona speranza?*[3]
PEER   The same. I believe,
   However, he's already preparing to leave.
THE LEAN ONE Then I'd better scoot down there as quick as I can.
   It just might be possible to catch him in time.
   That Cape of Good Hope I really can't stand.
   Norwegian missionaries[4] have made it their home.
   (*He hurries off southward.*)
PEER The stupid dog! He's scampering away already,
   With his tongue lolling out! He had it coming!
   I like making fools of asses like him,
   Who put on an act and look down on us.
   He's not got so much to be bragging about;
   And he'll not get fat in his present job.
   He'll soon come a cropper, for all his tricks!
   But I can't say *I'm* so firm in the saddle,
   Blacklisted by all the being-yourself crowd.
   (*A shooting star is seen. He nods after it.*)
   Greetings from Peer Gynt, brother shooting star!
   Flash, then fade, and sink into the void.
   (*He clutches himself as if in terror and goes deeper into the mists.
   He pauses, then cries out.*)
   Is there no one, no one, in all creation—
   No one in the abyss, no one in heaven—!
   (*He comes forward again, throws his hat on the ground, and tears
   his hair. Gradually, a stillness descends upon him.*)
   So unspeakably poor, then, a soul can go
   Through the gray mist back to nothingness.
   You beautiful earth, do not be appalled
   If I trod your surface to no purpose at all.
   You beautiful sun, you've lavished in vain

3. Of Good Hope.
4. Missionaries from Stavanger.

Your blessing of light on an empty hut.
There was no one inside to greet or warm—
The owner, they say, was never at home.
Beautiful sun and beautiful earth,
Why did you lavish your light on my mother?
The spirit's a miser, but nature's prolific.
Life's *too* great a price to pay for one's birth.
I'll climb to the top of some high peak
And look a last time on the rising sun,
Stare, till I'm tired, at the promised land,
Then wait as the snows pile over me;
There they may write: "No one lies here."
Then afterward—? Let things take their course!

CHURCHGOERS (*Singing on the forest path.*)
      Blessed dawn
      When tongues that sang God's praise
      Speared the earth like flames of steel.
      Now from earth to God reborne
      Are songs his heirs raise
      Praising his will.[5]

PEER (*Crouching in fear.*) Don't look there! It's all desert and waste.
I fear I was dead before I died.
(*He tries to slink away among the bushes but comes upon a crossroads.*)

BUTTON-MOLDER Good morning Peer Gynt. Where's your record of sins?

PEER Don't you think I've been whistling and shouting
For all I'm worth?

BUTTON-MOLDER And you met no one at all?

PEER None but a traveling photographer.

BUTTON-MOLDER So, time has run out.

PEER   Everything's run out.
The owl smells its prey. Can you hear it hooting?

BUTTON-MOLDER That's the matins bell ringing.

PEER   What is that gleaming?

BUTTON-MOLDER Only light from a hut.

PEER   And that sound like sighing—?

BUTTON-MOLDER Just a woman singing.

PEER   Yes, there!—There's where I'll find
My record of sins!

BUTTON-MOLDER (*Seizing hold of him.*) Set your house in order![6]
(*They have emerged from the wood and are standing near the hut.*)

PEER Set my house in order? It is there! Leave me!

5. "Unless a man is born from above, he cannot see the kingdom of God" John 3.3–4.
6. Isaiah 38.1.

Get going! If your ladle were as huge as a coffin,
I tell you, it's too small for me and my sins.
BUTTON-MOLDER Until the third crossroad, Peer, but *then*—!
(*Turns aside and goes.*)
PEER (*Approaching the hut.*) Forward or back, it's just as far.
Out or in, I'm trapped as before. (*Stops.*)
No!—Like a wild, unending lament,
I hear, "Go in, go home, return."
(*Takes a few steps, but stops again.*)
Go round about, said the Bøyg!
(*Hears singing in the hut.*)   No! This time,
Straight through, however narrow the path!
(*He runs toward the house. At the same moment, Solveig appears
in the doorway, dressed for church and with her psalm book
wrapped in a kerchief. She has a staff in her hand. She stands up-
right and gentle.*)
PEER (*Throwing himself down on the threshold.*)
If you're to condemn this sinner, speak out now!
SOLVEIG He is here! He is here! Praise be to God!
(*She gropes for him.*)
PEER Cry out how sinfully I have offended!
SOLVEIG You've sinned in nothing, my only boy!
(*She gropes again and finds him.*)
BUTTON-MOLDER (*Behind the hut.*) The list, Peer Gynt!
PEER Cry out my guilt!
SOLVEIG (*Sitting beside him.*) You've made my life a beautiful song.
Bless you, that you've come home at last.
Blessëd this meeting at Pentecost.
PEER Then I'm lost!
SOLVEIG There is one who leads the way.
PEER Lost, unless you can solve a riddle!
SOLVEIG Name it.
PEER Name it? All right—here it is!
Say where's Peer Gynt been since we last met.
SOLVEIG Been?
PEER With his destiny's mark on his brow:
Been, since he sprang new from God's thought!
Can you tell me that? If not, I go home—
Below, to the land of mist and shadows.
SOLVEIG (*Smiling.*) Oh, that riddle's easy.
PEER Then tell what you know!
Was I ever myself? Where, whole and true?
Myself, with God's seal stamped on my brow?
SOLVEIG In my faith, in my hope, and in my love.

PEER (*Stepping back*) What are you saying? These are riddling
   words!
   The child born in that thought—you are its mother?
SOLVEIG   I am, I am! But who is his father?
   He who forgives when the mother implores.
PEER (*A ray of light breaks over him and he cries.*)
   My mother; my wife; purest of women!—
   Oh hide me, hide me, within.[7]
   (*He clings to her and hides his face in her lap. Long silence. The
   sun rises.*)
SOLVEIG (*Softly singing.*)
         Sleep my dear, my darling boy!
         I will comfort and watch over you—

         The boy has sat on his mother's knee;
         The two have played the lifelong day.

         The boy has slept on his mother's breast
         The lifelong day. God make him blessed.

         The boy has lain near my heart's core
         The lifelong day. He is weary and sore.

         Sleep my dear, my dearest boy!
         I will comfort and watch over you.

BUTTON-MOLDER (*Behind the hut.*)
   We'll meet at the next crossroads, Peer.
   Then we shall see—I'll say no more.
SOLVEIG (*Singing louder in the increasing daylight.*)
   I will comfort and watch over you;
   Sleep and dream, my dearest boy!

END OF THE PLAY

7. John 3.7.

The Realist Cycle

Ibsen described his realist plays as a cycle. Explaining the subtitle "Epilogue" to *When We Dead Awaken*, he commented, "the play forms an epilogue to the series of plays that began with *A Doll House* and which now ends with *When We Dead Awaken*. It completes the Cycle and makes an entity of it."[1] Of *When We Dead Awaken* he wrote, "the series which ends with the epilogue really began with *The Master Builder*."[2] If the last four plays thus form a distinct group within the cycle, it is reasonable to consider this as a structural principle for the cycle as an "entity." Study of the twelve plays suggests three groups, each forming a distinct unit. (Plays include in this volume are in bold print.)

Pillars of Society
A Doll House
Ghosts
An Enemy of the People

The Wild Duck
Rosmersholm
The Lady from the Sea
Hedda Gabler

The Master Builder
Little Eyolf
John Gabriel Borkman
When We Dead Awaken

1. Maurice Valency, *The Flower and the Castle: Introduction to Modern Drama* (New York: Macmillan, 1963), 234. This attribution reports Ibsen saying that the cycle began with *A Doll House*, but *Pillars of Society* clearly inaugurates the "entity" of twelve modern plays. Cf. Brian Johnston, *The Ibsen Cycle* (Boston: Twayne Publishers, 1975), passim.
2. *Letters of Henrik Ibsen*, trans. John Nilsen Laurvik and Mary Morison (New York: Duffield, 1908), 455.

A Doll House (1879)

The time of action is Christmas, the death of the old year and the birth of the new. In Norway, this seasonal feast retains the pagan name of *jul* (Old Norwegian *jöl*)—familiar to us as *Yule*. The two couples in the play experience this turning point of the year in radically different ways. Torvald's and Nora's names have pagan associations—*Torvald* is from the god *Thor*; *Nora*, a diminutive of *Eleonora*, is a variant of the Greek *Helen*—and the two characters emphasize the pagan aspects of the season: the yule tree, gifts, the tarantella dance, feasting, an emphasis on joy and aesthetic, emphasizing a pleasure in *this* world and its values. Kristine Linde and Nils Krogstad, by contrast, are the world's insulted and injured. Kristine's life of sacrifice for others and Krogstad's of guilt, sin, and painful expiation recall the Christian alternative. Their names—*Krist*-ine (*Christ*-ine) and *Krog*-stad (from *krok(g)et*, "crooked, sly")—evoke the Christian dualism of savior and satanic menace. The satanic figure appears in various guises throughout Ibsen's Realist Cycle as a necessary negative rather than an evil force, deriving, in part, from Goethe's Mephistopheles in *Faust*. Engstrand in *Ghosts*, Relling in *The Wild Duck*, and Judge Brack in *Hedda Gabler* are other instances. In the last act of *A Doll House*, the two worlds are vertically juxtaposed: the "pagan" couple are heard dancing in a room *above* just before their world is about to be smashed up, while the "Christian" couple, *below*, emerge from sorrow and separation to forgiveness and reunion.

The critic Jan Kott noted, how the action of Torvald and Nora seems to reenact a well-known Greek play about marriage—Euripides' *Alcestis*, in which a wife "dies" to save her husband, as Nora figuratively dies in Act 2 when she decides on suicide.[1] The death imagery includes Nora's death by drowning, and then, with the tarantella dance, death from the poison of the tarantula. Her final, ironic death as a wife to Torvald, in Act 3, is shadowed by Dr. Rank's almost simultaneous retreat into death. Nora's final rebellion against the social order represented by Torvald takes on the aspect of another Greek heroine, Antigone.

The stage set is an active participant in the drama, lightening and darkening at appropriate moments, with its props (the tree, the fancy dress, the letters) and sounds, on and off stage. The three doors create

1. Jan Kott, *The Theater of Essence* (Evanston, Ill. Northwestern University Press, 1984), 32–33.

the decisive locations of the action. In the rear wall, the door on the left leads to Torvald's study and is opened and closed only when he chooses. It represents security, authority, and patriarchal power, like the door leading to the inner chamber of a prince in neoclassical drama. Entrances and exits through that door carry decisive weight. Torvald's invisible presence, even, is godlike. When Krogstad enters, it is to receive his dismissal from the bank. Rank must try to keep Torvald in that room while Nora has her desperate conference with Krogstad in Act 2. Whenever Torvald emerges from this door, until the last act, it is always on his own terms, to direct and control events.

The door to the right in the rear wall leads to the outside world. Damaged people come through this door: Kristine, Rank, Krogstad, all of whom have been variously hurt by the world outside the doll house. The door lets in the terrifying Krogstad, and in the last act his letter to Torvald waits in the locked mailbox on the door. This door, then, represents the menacing reality of the outside world, its power to hurt. As a door opening onto danger and conflict, however, it represents an invitation to grow up, to stop being a doll, as both Nora and Torvald have become; and to confront a social world that has inflicted harm on Krogstad and has constrained Kristine and whose opinions Torvald himself fears. From this outside world Dr. Rank also introduces the dimension of tragic consequences built into human existence. Outside, too, is the natural world of harsh winter weather through which, Nora observes, it took Kristine courage to make her sea-voyage.

There is a third door, in the right wall—the door to the nursery and bedroom and the shared private life of Torvald and Nora, which, we discover, is a world of sexual fantasy, of Nora performing childlike roles (squirrel, lark, etc.) to keep Torvald infatuated with her and assured of his dominance in the doll home. In this unreal world the Helmer children are not being prepared for reality. In the course of the action the areas signified by the three doors will drastically change. The door to Torvald's study, in a kind of emasculation, will lose all authority and power. The menacing door to the outside world will become the door of liberation from the doll home, which has become an unbearable constriction to the newly awakening Nora. Most devastating of all, the third realm of gender playacting will collapse like a house of cards.

Each act in the play is organized around a specific crisis, bringing about an *anagnorisis* (perception/recognition) and a *peripeteia* (reversal/overturning). Each crisis involves the key word *vidunderlig*, "wonderful," which has a very different meaning in each act, so that each earlier meaning of the word is progressively deconstructed and replaced. Other words go through a less emphatic dialectical, deconstructive process, including *vejlede*, "guide," *plikter*, "duties," *sorgelig*, "sorrowful," *sorgløs*, "sorrow-free" or "carefree," but *vidunderlig* is the crucial doll house word.

In Act 1, the "wonderful" means the good life in material, social, and domestic terms. It is the new job Torvald will get at the bank with an increased income. For Nora, it is the end of the old hard times of economizing and debts. Torvald will no longer have to work at home; Nora need not trouble herself with housework. When Nora utters the word three times, the doorbell rings, bringing onto the stage Kristine Linde, immediately followed by Dr. Rank, characters representing a harsher reality that will undermine the young couple's idea of the good life as material happiness and their own innocent right to it. The next time Nora uses the word "wonderful" in this act, in her conversation with Kristine Linde (together with the triple iteration of the word "carefree/sorrow-free"—*sorgløs*), the doorbell rings again, bringing onto the stage Nils Krogstad, who more drastically will dispel the mirage of the good life in material terms. Ibsen's stage is an occult space where even uttering certain words can prove dangerous.

Nora's use of *sorgløs* is worth noting. She believes she and Torvald are about to enter a life free of sorrow "[because] my troubles are over. Oh, God, it's so lovely to think of, Kristine! Carefree! To be carefree, completely carefree." To be *sorgløs* implies a nontragic idea of life. In her dialogue with Dr. Rank, she treats the "most sorrowful" (*sorgeligste*) aspect of his impending death with playful incomprehension. To grow up out of the doll house way of life, one must be able to take in the *sorgelig* perspective of tragedy; this is all the more true for an adequate *theater* that Ibsen is training his public to embrace. When Ibsen confronted that public with the tragic dimension more grimly in his next play, *Ghosts*, it vehemently objected and the play caused an international scandal.

In Act 2 of *A Doll House*, *vidunderlig* is again repeated three times:

> NORA A wonderful thing is about to happen.
> MRS. LINDE Wonderful?
> NORA Yes, a wonderful thing. But also terrible, Kristine, and it just can't happen, not for all the world.

This time, however, it means something utterly different—even "terrible/fearful" (*forfærdeligt*), a thing that must not happen, not for all the world. In this scene, the Christmas tree is stripped of decorations; the gifts and presents—the emblems of material happiness—have disappeared. The dialogue of all the characters shifts from social to psychological themes. Torvald tells Nora how he has the inner strength to take on whatever Krogstad may threaten; Dr. Rank, as the stage darkens, reveals the depth of his love for Nora; Krogstad and Nora, in a mood of probing intimacy, sadly acknowledge their mutual inability to commit suicide. Overcoming this fear, Nora anticipates the *vidunderlig* as a "terrible" inner heroism in which, to prevent Torvald from taking the blame for her crime, she will at last find courage for suicide. In this state of inner turmoil she dances the tarantella, a dance those bitten by the tarantula were believed to dance until they died or until they expelled the poison from their blood. This new *vidunderlig* is the antithesis of the materialist term of Act 1. That it also is an illusion, Nora must learn in Act 3, when the word, finally in its superlative form, will be thrice repeated at the end of the play.

In Act 3, the play evolves beyond materialist and psychological terms to a philosophical dimension. One couple will be united; the other will separate. Kristine and Krogstad agree to rescue their own "ship-wrecked" (*skibbruden*) lives through a marriage free of illusions. As they move from desolation to joy, we hear Nora and Torvald dancing the tarantella above. The music suddenly stops, and Krogstad hastily leaves. The Helmers descend, Nora in her fancy-dress costume with a black shawl, Torvald in an elegant evening suit with a black domino. The emphasis on night, darkness, and black ushers in the tragic (*sorgelig*) events to follow.

Torvald's shock over the revelations in Krogstad's first letter is severe. He is in the hands of a blackmailer who can do what he likes with him. Furthermore, his pure doll wife is a criminal. Nora had three days to absorb the shock through three peripeties and anagnoreses. Torvald has less than three minutes. His collapse reveals to Nora the fantasy world she had inhabited. She realizes that she knows neither reality nor herself, and she certainly does not know Torvald. She has lived an in-authentic doll existence, bearing three children to a stranger. The marriage could only be regained if the "most wonderful" (*vidunderligste*) thing were to happen. In its superlative form the term is again sounded three times. As the last word in the play, it is uttered by Torvald, as the door slams.

A Doll House†

Characters

TORVALD HELMER, a lawyer
NORA, his wife
DR. RANK
MRS. LINDE
NILS KROGSTAD, a bank clerk
THE HELMERS' THREE SMALL CHILDREN
ANNE-MARIE, their nurse
HELENE, a maid
A DELIVERY BOY

Act One

A comfortable, tasteful, but not expensively furnished room. A door to the right in the back wall leads out to the hall; another door to the left leads in to Helmer's study. Between these doors is a piano. In the middle of the left wall, a door, and farther back, a window. Near the window a round table with armchairs and a small sofa. In the right wall, upstage, a door and, on this same side nearer the foreground, a porcelain stove with a pair of

† Translated by Rick Davis and Brian Johnston.

*armchairs and a rocking chair. Between the stove and the door, a
little table. Engravings on the walls. An étagère with porcelain
figures and other small art objects; a small bookcase with books
in rich bindings. Carpet on the floor; the fire burns in the stove.
A winter's day.*

(*A bell rings in the hallway; soon after, we hear the door being
opened. Nora, cheerfully humming, enters the room; she is dressed
in outdoor clothes and carries a great number of packages, which
she sets down on the table, right. She lets the door to the hall stand
open and we see a Porter carrying a Christmas tree and a basket,
which he hands to the Maid, who had opened the door for them.*)

NORA Be sure you hide the tree, Helene. We can't let the children
see it before it's decorated tonight. (*To the Porter as she takes
out her purse.*) How much—? Oh yes, I know, half a krone—
here's one—no, keep the change.
(*The Porter thanks her and leaves. Nora closes the door. She
continues laughing softly to herself while she takes off her outdoor clothes. She takes a bag of macaroons from her pocket and
eats a couple; then she walks cautiously and listens outside her
husband's door.*)
He's home, all right.
(*Humming again, she goes over to the table, right.*)

HELMER (*From within the study.*) Do I hear a skylark singing out
there?

NORA (*Busy opening some packages.*) Yes, you do.

HELMER Is there by any chance a squirrel rummaging around?

NORA Yes!

HELMER When did the squirrel get home?

NORA Just this second. (*She puts the bag of macaroons in her pocket
and wipes her mouth.*) Come out here, Torvald, and look at
what I've bought.

HELMER Can't be disturbed! (*After a moment, he opens the door and
looks in, his pen in his hand.*) Did you say bought? All that?
Has the little spendthrift been out wasting money again?

NORA Oh, Torvald—this year we really ought to let ourselves go a
little bit. It's the first Christmas we haven't had to watch our
money.

HELMER But we still can't go around wasting it, you know.

NORA Yes, Torvald, now we can afford to waste a little bit here and
there. Isn't that right? Just a teeny little bit. Now that you've
got such a big salary and we've got heaps and heaps of money
coming in?

HELMER Yes, after New Year's. And then it's three whole months
before the first paycheck.

A DOLL HOUSE

NORA Fuff! We can borrow till then.

HELMER Nora! (*Goes over to her and takes her playfully by the ear.*) Is that dizzy little head of yours spinning around again? Suppose I borrowed a thousand today, and you wasted it all on Christmas, and then on New Year's Eve I got hit in the head by a falling brick and lay there—

NORA (*Covering his mouth.*) Ugh! Don't say awful things like that!

HELMER Well, suppose it happened—what then?

NORA If anything that awful happened, some silly loan would be the least of my worries.

HELMER What about the people I'd borrowed from?

NORA Them? Who cares about them! They're only strangers.

HELMER Nora, Nora, you are such a woman! Seriously, Nora, you know what I think about these things. No debts! Never borrow! Some freedom's lost, and because of that some beauty too, from a home that's built on borrowing and debt. The two of us have managed to hold out bravely until now; and we'll stay the course for the little time remaining.

NORA (*Goes over to the stove.*) All right, Torvald, whatever you want.

HELMER (*Following.*) Now, now; the little songbird mustn't droop its wings. Right? Is the squirrel standing there sulking? (*Taking out his wallet.*) Nora, guess what I have?

NORA (*Turning quickly.*) Money!

HELMER There, see? (*Handing her some bills.*) For Heaven's sake, I know how much a house goes through at Christmastime.

NORA (*Counting.*) Ten—twenty—thirty—forty—Oh, thank you, thank you, Torvald. This will help me no end.

HELMER It had certainly better.

NORA Yes, yes, I'll make sure it does. But come here so I can show you what I've bought. And so cheap! Look—new clothes for Ivar, also a sword. Here's a horse and trumpet for Bob. And for Emmy, a doll and a doll bed. They're pretty plain, but she'll just tear them to pieces anyway before you know it. And here's some dress material and some handkerchiefs for the maids— even though old Anne-Marie really deserves a little more.

HELMER And what's in that package there?

NORA (*With a cry.*) No, Torvald! Not till tonight!

HELMER Aha! But tell me, you little spendthrift, what did you think of for yourself?

NORA For me? Oh, I don't need anything.

HELMER You most certainly do. Tell me what you'd like most of all— within reason.

NORA Oh, I really don't know. Yes—listen, Torvald—

HELMER Well?

NORA (*Fumbling with his button; not looking at him.*) If you want to give me something, you could—you could—

HELMER Well, say it.

NORA (*Quickly.*) You could give me money, Torvald. Only what you can spare; then one of these days I could buy something with it.

HELMER No, but Nora—

NORA Yes, do it, Torvald, darling. I'm begging you. And I'll hang the money in pretty gilt paper on the tree. Wouldn't that be lovely?

HELMER What do we call those little birds that are always spending their money?

NORA Spendthrifts—yes, I know, I know. But let's do what I say, Torvald; then I'll have time to think about what I really need. That's pretty practical, isn't it?

HELMER (*Smiling.*) Absolutely—if you could only hold on to the money I give you, and if you actually bought something for yourself with it. But it will go for the house, for a lot of things we don't need, and I'll just have to shell out again.

NORA Oh, Torvald—

HELMER Can't be denied, my dear little Nora. (*Puts his arm around her waist.*) Spendthrifts are sweet; but they go through an awful lot of money. It's unbelievable how expensive it is to keep a spendthrift.

NORA Oh, fuff—how can you say that? I save absolutely everything I can.

HELMER (*Laughing.*) Yes, that's true—everything you *can*. But the trouble is, you *can't*.

NORA (*Humming and smiling with quiet complacency.*) Hmm. You just can't imagine what kinds of expenses larks and squirrels have, Torvald.

HELMER You are a strange little one. Just like your father was. You'll try anything you can think of to get hold of some money; but the moment you get some, it slips through your fingers. You never know what you've done with it. But you are what you are. It's in your blood—these things are hereditary, Nora.

NORA I wish I'd inherited a lot of Papa's qualities.

HELMER Well I don't want you to be anything but what you are: my sweet little songbird. But listen—I'm getting the distinct impression—you've got a sort of a—what can I call it—a kind of a guilty look today.

NORA I do?

HELMER You certainly do. Look me straight in the eye.

NORA (*Looking at him.*) Well?

HELMER (*Wagging his finger.*) Our sweet tooth wouldn't have been running wild in town today, would it?

NORA No, what makes you think that?

HELMER You're sure that sweet tooth didn't make a little stop at the bakery?

NORA No, Torvald, I swear—

HELMER Didn't nibble a little candy?

NORA No, absolutely not.

HELMER Not even munched on a macaroon or two?

NORA No, Torvald, honestly, I promise—

HELMER Now, now—of course I'm only joking.

NORA (*Going to the table, right.*) I'd never dream of going against you.

HELMER No, I know that. And after all, you've given me your word. (*Goes to her.*) Well, you keep your little Christmas secrets to yourself, then, my dearest Nora. I guess everything will be revealed this evening when we light the tree.

NORA Did you remember to invite Doctor Rank?

HELMER No—there's no need; it's taken for granted. But I'll ask him again when he stops in this morning. I've ordered the very best wine. Nora, you can't imagine how excited I am about tonight.

NORA Me too! And the children are just going to love it!

HELMER Ah, it's so marvelous to have a secure position and a comfortable income. Isn't it fun just to think about that?

NORA Oh, it's wonderful!

HELMER Do you remember last Christmas? Three whole weeks beforehand, you locked yourself up every evening, till way past midnight, making flowers for the Christmas tree, and all the other little surprises you had for us. Uch—I've never been so bored in my whole life.

NORA I wasn't bored at all.

HELMER (*Smiling.*) But it didn't amount to much after all, Nora.

NORA Oh, are you going to tease me with that again? I couldn't help it that the cat came in and tore everything to bits.

HELMER No, that's right, you couldn't, my poor little Nora. You worked so hard to make us happy, that's the main thing. But it's good that those hard times are behind us.

NORA Yes, it's really wonderful.

HELMER Now I don't have to sit here all alone boring myself, and you don't have to torture your precious eyes and your delicate little fingers—

NORA (*Clapping her hands.*) No, is that true, Torvald, I really don't have to? How wonderful to hear that! (*Takes his arm.*) Now I'll tell you what I thought we should do—as soon as Christmas is over—(*The doorbell rings.*) Oh, that doorbell. (*Tidying up the room.*) That means a visitor—what a bore!

HELMER I'm not at home to visitors, remember that.

MAID (*In the doorway.*) Madam, there's a strange lady here to see you.

NORA Show her in.

MAID (*To Helmer.*) And the Doctor arrived at the same time.

HELMER He went straight to my study?

MAID Yes, sir, he did.

(*Helmer goes into his room. The Maid shows Mrs. Linde, dressed in traveling clothes, into the room and closes the door after her.*)

MRS. LINDE (*Timidly and somewhat hesitantly.*) Good day, Nora.

NORA (*Uncertainly.*) Good day—

MRS. LINDE You don't recognize me.

NORA No; I don't know—I think—(*Bursting out.*) Kristine! Is it really you?

MRS. LINDE Yes, it is.

NORA Kristine! How could I not recognize you? But then how could I—? (*Quieter.*) You've changed, Kristine.

MRS. LINDE Yes, I expect I have. In nine—ten—long years—

NORA Is it that long? Yes, that's right. Oh, the last eight years have been happy ones, believe me. And now you've come to town as well. Made the long trip in winter. That was brave.

MRS. LINDE I just got here this morning on the steamer.

NORA To enjoy yourself at Christmas, of course. That's a lovely idea! Yes, enjoy ourselves—we will certainly do that. But take off your coat. You're not too cold? (*Helps her.*) That's it; now let's settle down and be cozy here by the stove. No, take the armchair there. I'll sit here in the rocking chair. (*Gripping her hands.*) Yes, now you look more like yourself again; it was just those first few moments—you have gotten a bit paler, Kristine—and maybe a little thinner.

MRS. LINDE And much, much older, Nora.

NORA Well, maybe a little older, a tiny little bit; but not too much. (*Drawing back, suddenly serious.*) Oh, I can't believe how thoughtless I am, sitting here chattering—Kristine, can you forgive me?

MRS. LINDE What do you mean, Nora?

NORA (*Quietly.*) Poor Kristine, you're a widow.

MRS. LINDE Yes, for three years now.

NORA I knew it of course, I read it in the paper. Oh, Kristine, you have to believe me, I was always going to write you at the time, but I kept putting it off, and things kept getting in the way.

MRS. LINDE Nora, dear, I understood completely.

NORA No, it was horrible of me. You poor thing, it must have been so hard for you—and he didn't leave you anything to live on?

MRS. LINDE No.

NORA And no children?

MRS. LINDE No.

NORA So, nothing at all.

MRS. LINDE No—not even a sense of grief to hold on to.

NORA (*Looking at her in disbelief.*) Kristine, how is that possible?

MRS. LINDE (*Smiles sadly, stroking Nora's hair.*) Ah, sometimes it happens that way, Nora.

NORA So completely alone. That must be terribly sad for you. I have three lovely children—you can't see them right now, they're out with Anne-Marie. But now you have to tell me everything.

MRS. LINDE No, no, I'd rather hear about you.

NORA No, you have to go first. Today I'm not going to be selfish. Today I'm only going to think about you. But I have to tell you *one* thing. Did you hear about the great luck we just had?

MRS. LINDE No, what is it?

NORA My husband has been made manager of the Bank.

MRS. LINDE Your husband? That is lucky!

NORA Isn't it? The law is such a chancy business, especially when you won't take the ugly cases. Torvald would never do that, of course, and I agree with him completely. So you can imagine how happy we are! He starts at the Bank right after New Year's, and then he'll be getting a huge salary and lots of commissions. From now on we'll be able to live quite differently—we can actually do what we want. Oh, Kristine, I feel so light and happy! Isn't it lovely to have lots of money, and not have to worry about anything?

MRS. LINDE It's lovely just to have enough.

NORA No, not just enough, but lots and lots of money!

MRS. LINDE (*Smiling.*) Nora, Nora, haven't you gotten over that yet? You were such a spendthrift in school.

NORA (*Laughing softly.*) Yes, Torvald still says the same thing. (*Wagging her finger.*) But "Nora, Nora" hasn't been as wild as you all think. We haven't exactly been in a position where I could waste any money. We've both had to work.

MRS. LINDE You too?

NORA Yes, odd jobs—sewing, embroidery, work like that—(*Casually.*) and also other things. You know Torvald left the government when we got married; he saw he'd never be promoted, and he needed to earn more money than before. In that first year he worked himself to the bone, always looking for extra income, day and night. But he couldn't keep it up, and he got deathly sick. The doctor said he absolutely had to move south.

MRS. LINDE Didn't you stay a whole year in Italy?

NORA That's right. It wasn't that easy to get away, as you can imagine. Ivar had just been born. But we had to go, there was no question about it. Ah, it was a wonderful trip, and it saved Torvald's life. But it was incredibly expensive.

MRS. LINDE   I believe you.

NORA   Four thousand, eight hundred kroner. That's a lot of money.

MRS. LINDE   It's just lucky you had it when the emergency came up.

NORA   Well, I can tell you, we had to get it from Papa.

MRS. LINDE   So that's how. That was about the time your father died, I think.

NORA   Yes, Kristine, it was right then. Just think, I couldn't go and be with him. I stayed right here and waited every day for little Ivar to come into the world. And I had my poor, sick Torvald to take care of. Dear, sweet Papa! I never saw him again, Kristine. That was the saddest time in my whole marriage.

MRS. LINDE   I know how much he meant to you. But then you left for Italy?

NORA   Yes, we had the money then, and the doctors insisted. So we left in a month.

MRS. LINDE   And your husband came back completely cured?

NORA   Right as rain!

MRS. LINDE   But—the doctor—?

NORA   What do you mean?

MRS. LINDE   I thought the maid said the man who came in with me was a doctor.

NORA   Yes, Doctor Rank. He's not here on a house call, he's our best friend—he comes by at least once a day. No, Torvald hasn't been sick a day since then. And the children are strong and sound and so am I. (*Jumping up and clapping her hands.*) Oh God, oh God, Kristine, it's so wonderful to live and be happy! But I'm being hateful here, only talking about myself. (*Sits on a stool close by Kristine and lays her arms on her knees.*) Please don't be mad at me! Tell me something—is it really true that you didn't love your husband? So why did you marry him?

MRS. LINDE   My mother was still alive, but she was bedridden and couldn't take care of herself; and I also had to look after my two younger brothers. I couldn't justify refusing his offer.

NORA   No, no, you were right. He was rich at the time, wasn't he?

MRS. LINDE   He was pretty well-off, I think. But the business wasn't very solid, Nora: when he died it all went to pieces, nothing was left.

NORA   And then—?

MRS. LINDE   Well, I had to do what I could for myself—a little shop, a few students, whatever else I could find. These last three years have been like one long workday without a break. But now it's over, Nora. My poor mother doesn't need me anymore, she's gone. And the boys are working now, they're on their own.

NORA You must feel such relief—

MRS. LINDE No, not at all. Only inexpressibly empty. Nothing more to live for. (*Stands uneasily.*) So I couldn't stand it any longer out in that little backwater. It's got to be easier here to find something to do, something to keep my mind working. If only I could be lucky enough to find a steady job, some office work—

NORA But Kristine, that's so exhausting, and you're tired enough to begin with. You'd be better off if you could get away to a spa for a while.

MRS. LINDE (*Going over to window.*) I don't have a papa to send me on a trip, Nora.

NORA (*Getting up.*) Oh, don't be mad at me!

MRS. LINDE Nora, dear, don't you be mad at me. That's the worst thing about this situation of mine; it leaves you with so much bitterness. You've got nothing to work for, but you still have to watch out for every opportunity. You have to live, so you become selfish. When you told me your news, I was more excited for my own sake than yours.

NORA Why? Oh, I see—you mean maybe Torvald can do something for you.

MRS. LINDE That's exactly what I was thinking.

NORA And so he will, Kristine! Leave it to me—I'll suggest it so beautifully, so beautifully—find something charming that he'll really appreciate. Oh, I can't wait to help you.

MRS. LINDE You're so kind, Nora, to take such an interest in me— doubly kind, since you don't know much about life's hardships yourself.

NORA I—? Don't know much—?

MRS. LINDE (*Smiling.*) Well, good Lord, a little sewing and things like that—you're such a child, Nora.

NORA (*Tosses her head, walks across the room.*) You shouldn't be so sure about that.

MRS. LINDE Oh?

NORA You're like everyone else. You all think I'm not capable of anything serious—

MRS. LINDE Now, now—

NORA That I've never been put to the test in the cold, hard world.

MRS. LINDE Nora, you've just been telling me all about your troubles.

NORA Fuff! Trifles! (*Quietly.*) I haven't told you the big thing.

MRS. LINDE What big thing? What do you mean?

NORA You look down on me an awful lot, Kristine, but you really shouldn't. You're proud that you've worked so hard for your mother all these years.

MRS. LINDE I don't look down on anyone. But it's true that I'm proud—and happy—that I was given the chance to ease my mother's sorrow in her last days.

NORA And when you think about what you've done for your brothers, you're proud of that as well.

MRS. LINDE I think I'm entitled to that.

NORA So do I. But now you'll hear, Kristine. I also have something to be proud and happy about.

MRS. LINDE I don't doubt it. But how do you mean?

NORA Let's talk quietly. What if Torvald heard? He mustn't, not for anything in the world. Nobody can find out about this, nobody but you.

MRS. LINDE What is it?

NORA Come over here. (*Pulls her down on the sofa beside her.*) Now then: here's what I have to be proud and happy about. I saved Torvald's life.

MRS. LINDE Saved—? How did you save—?

NORA I told you about the trip to Italy. Torvald would never have survived if he hadn't gone down there—

MRS. LINDE Yes, well, your father gave you all the money you needed—

NORA (*Smiling.*) Yes, that's what Torvald and everyone else believe, but—

MRS. LINDE But—?

NORA Papa never gave anything. I got the money myself.

MRS. LINDE You? That was a lot of money.

NORA Four thousand, eight hundred kroner. What do you say to that?

MRS. LINDE But Nora, how was that possible? Did you win the lottery?

NORA (*Disdainfully.*) The lottery. (*Snorting.*) What kind of art would *that* have taken?

MRS. LINDE Then where did you get it from?

NORA (*Humming and smiling secretively.*) Hmm; tra la la la la!

MRS. LINDE Because you certainly couldn't have borrowed it.

NORA Oh? Why not?

MRS. LINDE No, a wife can't get a loan without her husband's permission.

NORA (*Tossing her head.*) Well, but a wife with a head for business, a wife who knows how to be a little clever—

MRS. LINDE Nora, I just don't understand—

NORA And you don't need to. Nobody said anything about *borrowing* the money. Maybe I got it some other way. (*Throwing her-*

self back on the sofa.) Maybe I got it from one of my admirers. When you're as alluring as I am—

MRS. LINDE You're crazy.

NORA I've got you really curious now, haven't I?

MRS. LINDE Listen to me, Nora: you haven't done anything foolish, have you?

NORA (*Sitting up again.*) Is it foolish to save your husband's life?

MRS. LINDE I think it's foolish that without his knowledge you—

NORA But that's just it—he mustn't know anything! Good Lord, can't you see that? He can never know how bad off he was. The doctors came to *me* to say his life was in jeopardy—that only a trip south could save him. At first I tried to coax him into it—I told him how lovely it would be to take a trip abroad like other young wives—then I begged and cried—I said he should be kind and indulge a woman in my condition—and I hinted that he could easily take out a loan. That really set him off, Kristine. He told me I was being frivolous, and that it was his duty as a husband not to indulge my every whim and caprice—I think that's what he called them. Well, well, I thought, saved you must be and saved you shall be—and that's when I came up with my plan.

MRS. LINDE Didn't your husband ever find out that the money wasn't your father's?

NORA Never. Papa died right after that. I thought about letting him in on it and asking him not to say anything. But with him lying there so sick—and finally it wasn't necessary.

MRS. LINDE And you've never confided in your husband?

NORA No, for heaven's sake, how can you even imagine that? He's so strict about those things. And besides, Torvald's a man—he'd be so humiliated if he knew he owed me anything. It could even spoil our relationship; it would be the end of our beautiful, happy home.

MRS. LINDE So you'll never tell him?

NORA (*Reflectively, half-smiling.*) Yes, maybe someday; years from now, when I can't count on my looks anymore. Don't laugh! I mean when Torvald's not as attracted to me as he is now—when my dancing and dressing-up and reciting for him don't interest him any more. Then it'll be good to have something to fall back on. (*Breaking off.*) Dumb, dumb, dumb! That'll never happen. So what do you think of my big secret, Kristine? I can do things after all, can't I? But as you can imagine, it's been a big worry for me. It hasn't been that easy to make the payments on time. So I had to save a little, here and there, whenever I could. I couldn't really take anything out of the housekeeping budget, because Torvald has to live in a certain style. And I couldn't scrimp on the children's clothes; I used up whatever I got for them—the angels!

MRS. LINDE Poor Nora! So it came out of your allowance?

NORA Yes, of course. But then it was mostly my problem. Whenever Torvald gave me money for new clothes or whatever, I'd only use half; I always bought the simplest, cheapest things. I'm lucky that everything looks good on me, so Torvald never noticed. But it made me sad sometimes, Kristine—because it's so nice to dress up now and then, isn't it?

MRS. LINDE Yes it is.

NORA But I found other ways to make some money too. Last winter I was lucky enough to get a big copying job to do. So I shut myself in and wrote every evening till late at night. Ah, I'd get so tired, so tired—but it was also great fun, sitting and working and earning money like that. Almost like being a man.

MRS. LINDE How much have you managed to pay off like that?

NORA Well, I can't really say exactly. This kind of account is very hard to keep track of. I only know that I've paid back everything I can scrape together. A lot of times I didn't know which way to turn. (*Smiling.*) I'd sit here and imagine that a rich old man had fallen in love with me.

MRS. LINDE What? Which man?

NORA Oh, come on! And that he'd just died and when they read his will, there it was in big letters: "My entire fortune is to be paid in cash, immediately, to the delightful Mrs. Nora Helmer."

MRS. LINDE But Nora, who is he?

NORA Good Lord, don't you get it? There never was any such person; it was just something I'd sit here and dream about when I couldn't think of any other way to get the money. But now it doesn't matter, the old bore can go back where he came from; I don't need him or his will, because my troubles are over. Oh, God, it's so lovely to think of, Kristine! Carefree! To be carefree, completely carefree! To run around and play with the children; to make everything in the house warm and beautiful, just the way Torvald likes it! Then maybe we can travel a little. Maybe I'll get down to the ocean again. Oh yes, it is so wonderful to live and be happy!

(*The bell rings in the hallway.*)

MRS. LINDE (*Rising.*) The bell—maybe I should go.

NORA No, stay here. It won't be for me. It's probably for Torvald.

MAID (*From the hall doorway.*) Excuse me, ma'am. There's a gentleman here to speak with the lawyer.

NORA With the Bank Manager, you mean.

MAID Yes, with the Bank Manager. But I didn't know if—since the Doctor's in there—

NORA Who is the gentleman?

KROGSTAD (*From the doorway.*) It's me, Mrs. Helmer.
    (*Mrs. Linde starts, checks herself, and turns toward the window.*)

NORA (*A step towards him, tense, in a low voice.*) You? What is it?
    What do you want to talk to my husband about?

KROGSTAD Bank matters—more or less. I have a minor position on
    the bank staff, and I hear your husband is our new chief.

NORA And so it's—

KROGSTAD Just dry business, Mrs. Helmer. Absolutely nothing else.

NORA Then would you please be good enough to step into his
    study?
    (*She nods indifferently and shuts the hallway door; then she goes
    and tends the stove.*)

MRS. LINDE Nora—who was that man?

NORA That was a lawyer named Krogstad.

MRS. LINDE So it really was him.

NORA Do you know that man?

MRS. LINDE I used to know him—a long time ago. He was a law
    clerk for a while up in our area.

NORA Yes, that's right, he was.

MRS. LINDE He certainly has changed.

NORA He had a very unhappy marriage.

MRS. LINDE And now he's a widower?

NORA With several children. There we go, now it's burning. (*She
    closes the stove door and moves the rocking chair a little to the
    side.*)

MRS. LINDE He's got himself involved in all kinds of businesses,
    they say.

NORA Oh yes? Probably; I really wouldn't know. But let's not think
    about business—it's so boring!
    (*Doctor Rank comes out from Helmer's study.*)

RANK (*Still in the doorway.*) No, no, Torvald: I don't want to be in
    the way; I'd just as soon go talk to your wife for a while. (*Clos-
    ing the door and noticing Mrs. Linde.*) I'm sorry—I'm in the
    way here too.

NORA You certainly are not. (*Introducing him.*) Doctor Rank, Mrs.
    Linde.

RANK Aha! That's an oft-mentioned name in this house. I think I
    passed you on the stairs when I arrived.

MRS. LINDE Yes, I don't handle stairs very well.

RANK Aha—are you having some kind of trouble?

MRS. LINDE Probably just overwork.

RANK Nothing more? So you've probably come to town to catch
    your breath in the holiday parties.

MRS. LINDE I'm looking for a job.

RANK Is that the prescription for overwork?

MRS. LINDE One has to live, Doctor.

RANK Yes, there's general agreement on that point.

NORA Oh, come on now, Doctor Rank, you want to live as much as anyone.

RANK Yes, I really do. Wretched as I am, I really want to stretch my torment to the limit. All my patients feel the same way. And it's the same with the morally diseased—right now there's a terminal moral case in there with Helmer—

MRS. LINDE (*Quietly.*) Ah—!

NORA Who's that?

RANK Oh, just a certain lawyer Krogstad, no one you'd know anything about. His character, my ladies, is rotten right down to the roots—but even he began making speeches—as if it were self-evident—that he had to *live*.

NORA Oh? What did he want to talk to Torvald about?

RANK I don't know for sure. All I heard was something about the bank.

NORA I didn't know Krog—that this lawyer Krogstad had anything to do with the bank.

RANK Yes, he's got some kind of position down there. (*To Mrs. Linde.*) I don't know if you have, in your part of the country, any of these moral detectives, these investigators who go around sniffing out moral corruption and then get their victims into a safe place where they can keep them under constant surveillance—it's a lucrative business these days. The healthy ones get left out in the cold—no room for them!

MRS. LINDE And yet it's the sick ones who need to be brought inside.

RANK (*Shrugs his shoulders.*) There you have it. That's the philosophy that's turning our whole world into a hospital.

(*Nora, lost in thought, breaks into quiet laughter, clapping her hands.*)

RANK Why do you laugh? Do you really know what the world is?

NORA What do I care about the boring old world? I was laughing at something else—something terribly funny. Tell me, Doctor Rank, all those people who work at the bank—are they all under Torvald now?

RANK Is *that* what's so terribly funny to you?

NORA (*Smiling and humming.*) Never mild! Never mind! (*Walking around the room.*) Yes, it is extremely amusing that we—that Torvald has so much influence over so many people. (*Takes a bag from her pocket.*) Doctor Rank, how about a little macaroon?

RANK Aha! Macaroons! I thought they were illegal here.

NORA Yes, but Kristine gave me these—

MRS. LINDE What? I—?

NORA Now, now, now, don't worry. How could you know that Torvald made a law against them? You see, he's afraid they'll rot
my teeth. But, fuff—just this once—don't you agree, Doctor
Rank? There you are! (*She pops a macaroon into his mouth.*)
You too, Kristine. And I'll have one too, just a little one—or
two at the most. (*Walking around again.*) Yes, now I am really
tremendously happy. There's just one last thing in the world I
have a tremendous desire to do.

RANK Oh? What's that?

NORA I have this tremendous desire to say something so that Torvald can hear it.

RANK So why can't you say it?

NORA No, I don't dare. It's too horrible.

MRS. LINDE Horrible?

RANK Well, then, maybe you'd better not. But with us—can't you?
What do you want to say so Torvald can hear?

NORA I have a tremendous desire to say: To hell with everything!

RANK Are you crazy?

MRS. LINDE For heaven' sake, Nora.

RANK Say it—here he is.

NORA (*Hiding the macaroons.*) Shh, shh, shh!
     (*Helmer enters from his study, hat in hand and overcoat on his
     arm.*)

NORA Well, my dear, are you through with him?

HELMER Yes, he just left.

NORA Let me introduce you—this is Kristine, who's just come to
town.

HELMER Kristine? I'm sorry, but I don't know—

NORA Mrs. Linde, Torvald dear, Mrs. Kristine Linde.

HELMER Oh, I see. A childhood friend?

MRS. LINDE Yes, we knew each other back then.

NORA And just think, she made the long trip here just to talk to
you.

MRS. LINDE Well, actually, I didn't—

NORA Kristine, you see, is extremely good at office work, and so
she's tremendously eager to place herself under the direction
of a capable man so that she can learn even more than she—

HELMER Very sensible, Mrs. Linde.

NORA So that when she heard you'd been made bank manager—
there was a bulletin about it in all the papers—she started out
as fast as she could, and—it's true, isn't it, Torvald? You could
do something for Kristine for my sake, yes?

HELMER It's not completely out of the question. You are, I suppose, a widow?

MRS. LINDE Yes.

HELMER And you have experience in office work?

MRS. LINDE Yes, quite a bit.

HELMER Well then, it's entirely possible that I can offer you a position—

NORA (*Clapping her hands.*) You see, you see!

HELMER You appeared at a lucky moment, Mrs. Linde.

MRS. LINDE How can I thank you—

HELMER Not at all necessary. (*Puts on overcoat.*) But today I'll have to ask you to excuse me—

RANK Wait—I'll go with you.

(*Rank gets his fur coat from the hall and warms it at the stove.*)

NORA Don't be out long, Torvald my dear.

HELMER Just an hour, no more.

NORA Are you leaving too, Kristine?

MRS. LINDE (*Putting on her outdoor things.*) Yes, now I've got to find myself a room.

HELMER Then maybe we can all walk together for a while.

NORA (*Helping her.*) It's so boring that we don't have space here, but it's just impossible for us to—

MRS. LINDE Don't even think of it! Goodbye, Nora, and thank you for everything.

NORA Goodbye for now. But I'll see you again this evening. You too, Doctor Rank. What? If you feel well? Of course you will! Wrap yourself up nice and warm.

(*They all go out together into the hall. Children's voices are heard on the stairs.*)

NORA There they are! There they are!

(*She runs to open the front door. Anne-Marie, their nanny, enters with the children.*)

NORA Come in, come in! (*Bends down and kisses them.*) Oh, you sweet little darlings! Look at them, Kristine, aren't they lovely!

RANK No loitering out here in the draft!

HELMER Let's go, Mrs. Linde; this place is unbearable now for anyone but mothers.

(*Doctor Rank, Helmer, Mrs. Linde go down the stairs. The nurse-maid goes into the living room with the children. Nora goes in also, after shutting the door to the hallway.*)

NORA You look so clean and healthy! Your cheeks are all red! Like apples and roses. (*The children chatter away to her throughout the following.*) Was it fun? That's great. Really? You pulled both Emmy and Bob on the sled? My goodness, both of them together! You're a clever boy, Ivar. Here, let me hold her for a little while, Anne-Marie. My sweet little doll-baby! (*Takes the smallest child from Anne-Marie and dances with her.*) Yes, yes, Mommy will dance with Bob too. What? A snowball fight? Oh, I wish I was there with you! No, don't bother, I'll undress them myself, Anne-Marie. Yes, let me do it, it's so much fun. Go in for a while—you look frozen. There's warm coffee for you on the stove. (*Anne-Marie goes into the room on the left. Nora takes off the children's outdoor clothes and throws them around while the children all talk at the same time.*) Is that so? A great big dog came running after you? But it didn't bite? No, dogs never bite lovely little doll-babies. Stop peeking into the packages, Ivar! What is it? Oh, wouldn't you like to know? No, it's something awful! Well? Do you want to play? What'll we play? Hide-and-seek. Yes, let's play hide-and-seek. Bob, you hide first. Me? All right, I'll hide first.

(*She and the children play, laughing and shouting, in the living room and the adjoining room to the right. At last Nora hides under the table; the children come storming in, searching, not finding her; then, hearing her muffled laughter, rush to the table, lift the tablecloth, and discover her. A storm of delight. Meanwhile, there has been a knocking at the front door; no one has noticed it. Now the door half opens, and Krogstad appears. He waits a little while the game continues.*)

KROGSTAD I beg your pardon, Mrs. Helmer.

NORA (*Turns, with a stifled cry, half jumps up.*) Ah! What do you want?

KROGSTAD Excuse me. The front door was open—somebody must have forgotten to shut it.

NORA (*Rising.*) My husband's not here, Mr. Krogstad.

KROGSTAD I know that.

NORA Well—what do you want?

KROGSTAD A word with you.

NORA With—? (*To the children, quietly.*) Go in with Anne-Marie. No, the strange man won't hurt Mama. When he's gone we can play some more. (*She leads the children in to the room on the left and closes the door after them. Now, tense and nervous.*) You want to speak with me?

KROGSTAD Yes, I do.

NORA Today—? But it's not the first of the month yet—

KROGSTAD No, it's Christmas Eve. It's up to you how much Christmas cheer you'll have.

NORA What do you want? Today I can't possibly—

KROGSTAD We won't talk about that right now. It's something else. I suppose you have a moment?

NORA Well, yes; all right—though—

KROGSTAD Good. I was sitting over at Olsen's Restaurant and I saw your husband going down the street—

NORA Oh yes.

KROGSTAD With a lady.

NORA So?

KROGSTAD I wonder if you'll allow me to ask if that lady was Mrs. Linde?

NORA Yes.

KROGSTAD Just arrived in town?

NORA Yes, today.

KROGSTAD She's a good friend of yours?

NORA Yes, she is. But I can't see—

KROGSTAD I also knew her at one time.

NORA I'm aware of that.

KROGSTAD Really? That's what I thought. Well, then, let me get right to the point: Is Mrs. Linde getting a job at the bank?

NORA Why do you think you can cross-examine me, Mr. Krogstad? You, who's just one of my husband's employees? But since you ask, you might as well know: yes, Mrs. Linde got a job. And I arranged it all for her, Mr. Krogstad. Now you know.

KROGSTAD As I thought.

NORA (*Pacing the floor.*) Oh, I should hope that one always has a little bit of influence. Just because one is a woman, it doesn't follow that—when one is in an inferior position, Mr. Krogstad, one ought to be very careful with somebody who—

KROGSTAD Who has influence?

NORA Exactly.

KROGSTAD (*Changing tone.*) Mrs. Helmer, would you be good enough to use your influence on my behalf?

NORA What? What do you mean?

KROGSTAD Would you be kind enough to make sure that I keep my inferior position at the bank?

NORA What do you mean? Who's trying to take it away from you?

KROGSTAD Oh, you don't have to play the innocent with me. I understand perfectly well that your friend doesn't want to run the risk of seeing me again; and now I also understand who to thank for being let go.

NORA But I promise you—

KROGSTAD Yes, yes, yes. But here's the point: there's still time, and I'd advise you to use your influence to prevent it.

NORA But, Mr. Krogstad, I have no influence at all.

KROGSTAD No? I thought a minute ago you said—

NORA I didn't mean it that way. What makes you think I've got any sort of influence over my husband in things like that?

KROGSTAD Oh, I've known your husband since we were students together—and I don't believe our Bank Manager has any more willpower than any other married man.

NORA You talk like that about my husband and I'll show you the door.

KROGSTAD The lady has courage.

NORA I'm not afraid of you any more. Soon after New Year's I'll be done with the whole business.

KROGSTAD Now listen to me, Mrs. Helmer. If it becomes necessary, I'll fight to the death for my little job at the bank.

NORA Yes, it looks that way.

KROGSTAD And not just for the money—that's the least of my concerns. It's something else—well, all right—you know, of course, like everyone else, that some years ago I was guilty of an indiscretion.

NORA I think I heard something about it.

KROGSTAD The case never came to trial, but even so every door was closed to me. So I had to go into the sort of business you're familiar with. I had to find something—and I think I can say that I've been far from the worst in that line of work. But now I want to put all of it behind me. My sons are growing up. For their sake I want to win back as much respect as I can in the community. That position in the bank was the first rung in the ladder for me. Now your husband wants to kick me right back off the ladder and into the mud again.

NORA But for God's sake, Mr. Krogstad, it's just not in my power to help you.

KROGSTAD That's because you don't have the will to do it—but I can force you to.

NORA You wouldn't tell my husband that I owe you money?

KROGSTAD Hmm—what if I did?

NORA That would be shameful. (*Choking with tears.*) That secret—my pride and my joy—if he learned about it in such a horrible way—learned it from you—. You'd put me through such an incredibly unpleasant scene—

KROGSTAD Only unpleasant?

NORA (*Vehemently.*) Just try it! It'll only be worse for you. Because then my husband will really get to see what kind of man you are, and you'll have no chance of keeping your job.

KROGSTAD I asked you if all you were afraid of was this unpleasant scene here at home?

NORA If my husband finds out about it, of course he'll pay you off immediately, and we'd have nothing more to do with you.

KROGSTAD (*A step nearer.*) Listen, Mrs. Helmer: either you've got a terrible memory or a very shaky grasp of business. Let me get a few facts straight for you.

NORA How do you mean?

KROGSTAD When your husband was sick, you came to me for four thousand, eight hundred kroner.

NORA I didn't know where else to go.

KROGSTAD I promised to get it for you—

NORA And you did.

KROGSTAD I promised to get it for you on certain conditions. At the time you were so wrapped up in your husband's illness that I suppose you didn't think through all the details. Maybe I'd better remind you of them. Now: I promised to get you the money based on a note that I drafted.

NORA Yes, which I signed.

KROGSTAD Very good. But below your signature I added some lines to the effect that your father would guarantee the loan. Your father was to sign there.

NORA Was to—? He signed it.

KROGSTAD I left out the date. Your father was supposed to date his own signature. Do you remember that?

NORA Yes, I think so—

KROGSTAD Then I handed the note over to you so you could mail it to your father. Isn't that the case?

NORA Yes.

KROGSTAD And of course you did that right away—because only about five, six days later, you brought me the note, with your father's signature. And then you got your money.

NORA Well? Haven't I been meeting my payments?

KROGSTAD Yes, more or less. But to return to the question: that was a difficult time for you, wasn't it, Mrs. Helmer?

NORA Yes, it was.

KROGSTAD Your father was very ill, I believe.

NORA He was very near the end.

KROGSTAD He died soon after that?

NORA Yes.

KROGSTAD Tell me, Mrs. Helmer, do you by any chance recall the date of your father's death? Which day of the month, I mean.

NORA Papa died on the twenty-ninth of September.

KROGSTAD Quite correct; I've already confirmed that. That brings us to an oddity that I simply cannot account for.

NORA What kind of oddity? I don't understand—

KROGSTAD Here's the oddity, Mrs. Helmer: your father countersigned the note three days after his death.

NORA How? I don't understand—

KROGSTAD Your father died on the twenty-ninth of September. But look at this. Here your father has dated his signature "October 2nd." Isn't that odd, Mrs. Helmer? (*Nora is silent.*) Can you explain it to me? (*Nora remains silent.*) Here's another remarkable thing: the date "October 2nd" and the year are not written in your father's hand, but in a hand that I ought to know. Now, that could be explained; your father forgot to date his signature, and someone else did it for him, somewhat carelessly, before anyone knew of his death. Nothing wrong with that. Everything hinges on the signature. And that *is* genuine, isn't it, Mrs. Helmer? It really was your father himself who signed his name there?

NORA (*After a short silence, throws back her head and looks firmly at him.*) No, it wasn't. *I* signed Papa's name.

KROGSTAD Listen, Mrs. Helmer—do you understand that this is a dangerous confession?

NORA Why? You'll get your money soon enough.

KROGSTAD Can I ask you—why didn't you send the note to your father?

NORA Impossible. Papa was so sick. If I had asked him for his signature, I'd have had to tell him what the money was for. I just couldn't tell him, in his condition, that my husband was dying. It was just impossible.

KROGSTAD Then it would have been better for you to give up the trip.

NORA No, impossible again. That trip was to save my husband's life. I couldn't give that up.

KROGSTAD But didn't it occur to you that you were committing a fraud against me?

NORA I couldn't worry about that. I certainly wasn't concerned about you. I could hardly stand you, making up all those cold conditions when you knew perfectly well how much danger my husband was in.

KROGSTAD Mrs. Helmer, you obviously don't have any idea what you've implicated yourself in. But let me tell you this: what I once did was nothing more, and nothing worse, and it destroyed me.

NORA You? Are you trying to get me to believe that you risked everything to save your wife?

KROGSTAD Laws don't much care about motives.

NORA Then they must be very bad laws.

KROGSTAD Bad or not, if I produce this paper in court, you'll be judged by those laws.

NORA I don't believe it. Doesn't a daughter have the right to spare her dying father from worry and anxiety? Shouldn't a wife have the right to save her husband's life? I don't know the law very well, but I'm sure it must say somewhere in there that these things are legal. You must be a very bad lawyer, Mr. Krogstad.

KROGSTAD Maybe so. But business—this kind of business we're in—don't you think I know something about that? Good. Do what you want. But hear this: if I get thrown down a second time, you're coming with me. (*He bows and goes out through the hall door.*)

NORA (*Stands for a moment, reflecting, then tosses her head.*) Nonsense! He's trying to frighten me! I'm not all that naïve. (*Starts gathering up the children's clothes, but soon stops.*) But—? No, impossible. I did it out of love.

CHILDREN (*In the doorway, left.*) Mama, the strange man's going down the street.

NORA Yes, I know. But don't mention the strange man to anyone. You hear? Not even Papa.

CHILDREN No, Mama. Now can we play again?

NORA No, no. Not now.

CHILDREN But Mama, you promised.

NORA Yes, but right now I can't. Go inside; I've got too much to do. Go in, go in, my dear, sweet little ones. (*She herds them carefully into the room and closes the door after them. She sits on the sofa, takes up her embroidery, makes some stitches, but soon stops.*) Helene! Let me have the tree in here. (*Goes to the table at left and opens a drawer, pauses again.*) No, that's completely impossible!

MAID (*With the spruce tree.*) Where should I put it, Ma'am?

NORA There—in the middle of the floor.

MAID Anything else?

NORA No, thank you. I have what I need.

(*The Maid, having set the tree down, goes out.*)

NORA (*Busy decorating the tree.*) Candles here, flowers here—that horrible man! Talk, talk, talk. Nothing's going to happen. The Christmas tree will be just lovely. I'll do anything you want me to, Torvald—I'll sing for you, dance for you—

(*Helmer, with a packet of papers under his arm, comes in through the hall.*)

NORA Ah! Back already?

HELMER Yes. Has someone been here?

NORA Here? No.

HELMER That's strange. I just saw Krogstad going out the door.

NORA Really? Oh, of course. Krogstad was here for a moment.

HELMER Nora, I can see it in your eyes, he's been here asking you to put in a good word for him.

NORA Yes.

HELMER And you were going to pretend it was your own idea. You'd pretend he'd never been here. Did he ask you to do that as well?

NORA Yes, Torvald, but—

HELMER Nora, Nora, you could go along with that? Do business with that sort of person, and make promises to him? And then, on top of it all, tell me a lie!

NORA A lie?

HELMER Didn't you tell me no one had been here? (*Wagging his finger.*) My little songbird mustn't ever do a thing like that again. A songbird needs a clean beak to chirp with. No false notes. (*Takes her by the waist.*) Isn't that the way it should be? Yes, of course it is. So let's not talk about it any more. (*Sits by the stove.*) Ah, it's so snug and cozy here.

NORA (*Working on the tree; after a short pause.*) Torvald!

HELMER Yes?

NORA I'm terribly excited about the Stenborg's party the day after tomorrow.

HELMER And I'm terribly curious to see what you'll surprise me with.

NORA Oh, that stupid nonsense!

HELMER What?

NORA I can't find anything I like; everything seems so pointless, so idiotic.

HELMER Is that what little Nora thinks?

NORA (*Behind his chair, her arms on its back.*) Are you very busy, Torvald?

HELMER Well—

NORA What are those papers?

HELMER Bank business.

NORA Already?

HELMER I've convinced the retiring manager to give me full authority to make changes in personnel and procedure. I'll have to use Christmas week for that. I want everything in order for the New Year.

NORA So that's why this poor Krogstad—

HELMER Hm.

NORA (*Still leaning on the back of his chair, stroking the hair on his neck.*) If you weren't so busy, I would ask you for a terribly big favor.

HELMER Let's hear it. What can it be?

NORA No one has your good taste. I really want to look my best at the costume party. Torvald, couldn't you take over from me and advise me what to wear and how to design my costume?

HELMER So our little rebel's ready for a cease-fire?

NORA Yes, Torvald. I can't get anywhere without your help.

HELMER All right. I'll think about it. We'll come up with something.

NORA How sweet of you! (*Goes over to the Christmas tree; pause.*) These red flowers are so pretty—But tell me, was what that Krogstad did really such a crime?

HELMER He forged people's names. Do you know what that means?

NORA Maybe he did it out of need.

HELMER Yes, or thoughtlessness, like so many others. And I wouldn't condemn a man categorically because of one isolated incident.

NORA No, you wouldn't, would you, Torvald?

HELMER Men can often redeem themselves by openly confessing their guilt and accepting their punishment.

NORA Punishment?

HELMER But Krogstad didn't do that. He got himself off the hook with tricks and loopholes. That's what's corrupted him.

NORA Do you think that would—?

HELMER Imagine what life is like for a man like that: he has to lie and dissemble and cheat everyone he meets—has to wear a mask in front of his nearest and dearest—yes, even his wife and children. And the children—that's the most terrible part of it.

NORA Why?

HELMER Because an atmosphere so filled with lies brings pestilence and disease into every corner of a home. Every breath the children take carries the infection.

NORA (*Closer behind him.*) Are you sure about that?

HELMER Ah, my dear, I'm a lawyer—I've seen it often enough. Almost everyone who turns bad as a youth has had a compulsive liar for a mother.

NORA Why just—a mother?

HELMER Usually you can trace it to the mother, but fathers have the same effect; it's something every lawyer knows. And yet this Krogstad has been living at home, poisoning his children with lies and deceit; that's why I call him morally corrupt. And that's why my sweet little Nora must promise me not to plead his case. Your hand on that. Now, now, what's this? Give me your hand. There. That's settled. And let me tell you, it would be impossible for me to work with him; I literally feel sick when I'm around someone like that.

NORA (*Withdraws her hand and goes over to the other side of the Christmas tree.*) It's so hot in here! And I've got so much to pull together!

HELMER (*Rising and gathering his papers.*) Yes, I've got to try to get through some of these before dinner. I'll also give some thought to your costume. And I might also be thinking about something to hang on the tree in gilt paper—. (*Lays his hand on her head.*) Oh, my sweet little songbird. (*He goes into his room and closes the door.*)

NORA (*Softly, after a silence.*) No, no! It's not true. It's impossible. It just can't be possible.

ANNE-MARIE (*In doorway, left.*) The children are asking if they can come in to Mama.

NORA No, no, no, don't let them in here with me! You stay with them, Anne-Marie.

ANNE-MARIE Very well, Ma'am.

NORA (*Pale with terror.*) Harm my children—! Poison my home? (*Short pause; she tosses her head.*) It's not true. It could never be true!

Act Two

The same room in the corner by the piano stands the Christmas tree, stripped, bedraggled, with its candle-stumps all burned down. Nora's outdoor clothing lies on the sofa.

(*Nora, alone, walks restlessly around the room. Finally she stands by the sofa and picks up her coat.*)

NORA (*Dropping the coat again.*) Somebody's coming! (*Goes to the door, listens.*) No, nobody there. Naturally—nobody's coming on Christmas Day—or tomorrow either. But maybe— (*She opens the door and looks out.*) No, nothing in the mailbox— perfectly empty: (*Comes forward.*) Oh, nonsense! Of course he wasn't serious about it. Nothing like that could happen. After all, I have three small children.

(*Anne-Marie, carrying a large carton, comes in from the room on the left.*)

ANNE-MARIE Well, I finally found the box of masquerade costumes.

NORA Thanks. Put it on the table.

ANNE-MARIE (*Does so.*) But it's a terrible mess.

NORA Ah, I wish I could rip them into a million pieces.

ANNE-MARIE Lord bless us—they can be fixed up again. Just have a little patience.

NORA Yes, I'll go and get Mrs. Linde to help.

ANNE-MARIE You're not going out again now? In this horrible weather? Mrs. Nora will catch cold—get sick.

NORA Worse things could happen. How are the children?

ANNE-MARIE The poor little things are playing with their Christmas presents, but—

NORA Are they always asking for me?

ANNE-MARIE They're so used to having their Mama with them.

NORA Yes, Anne-Marie, but I can't be with them as much as before.

ANNE-MARIE Well, little children get used to anything.

NORA Do you think so? Do you think they'd forget their mama if she were really gone?

ANNE-MARIE Lord help us—gone?

NORA Listen—tell me, Anne-Marie—I've wondered about this a lot—how could you ever, in your heart of hearts, stand to give your child away to strangers?

ANNE-MARIE But I just had to when I became little Nora's wet nurse.

NORA Yes, but how could you actually do it?

ANNE-MARIE When I could get such a good place? A poor girl in trouble has to jump at a chance like that. Because that slick good-for-nothing wouldn't do anything for me.

NORA But your daughter's completely forgotten you.

ANNE-MARIE Oh no, not really. She wrote to me when she was confirmed, and when she got married.

NORA (*Clasps her around the neck.*) Dear old Anne-Marie—you were a good mother for me when I was little.

ANNE-MARIE Poor little Nora, with me as her only mother.

NORA And if my little ones didn't have a mother, I know that you— stupid, stupid, stupid! (*Opening the carton.*) Go to them. Right now I have to—tomorrow you'll see how beautiful I look.

ANNE-MARIE Yes, Mrs. Nora will be the most beautiful woman at the party.

(*Anne-Marie goes into the room on the left.*)

NORA (*Begins to unpack the box, but soon throws the whole thing aside.*) Ah, if I had the nerve to go out. If only nobody would come. If only nothing happened here at home in the meantime. Stupid talk; nobody's coming. Just don't think. I have to brush out this muff. Beautiful gloves, beautiful gloves. Get it out, get it out! One, two, three, four, five, six, (*Screams.*) Oh, here they come. (*Goes toward the door, but stops, irresolute. Mrs. Linde comes in from the hall where she has removed her outdoor clothes.*) So it's you, Kristine. No one else out there? I'm glad you're here.

MRS. LINDE I heard you were asking for me.

NORA Yes, I happened to be passing by. I need your help with something. Come sit with me by the sofa. Look at this. There's going to be a costume party tomorrow over at Consul Stenborg's, and Torvald wants me to go as a Neapolitan fisher girl and dance the tarantella—I learned it in Capri.

MRS. LINDE Well, well—you're giving a real performance?

NORA Yes, Torvald says I should. Look—here's my costume. Torvald had it made for me down there. But it's all torn now and I just don't know—

MRS. LINDE We'll get that fixed up in no time; the trimmings are just coming loose here and there, that's all. Needle and thread? There, now we have what we need.

NORA This is so nice of you.

MRS. LINDE (*Sewing.*) So you're going in disguise tomorrow. Nora? You know what? I'll come by for a minute and look at you when you're all dressed up. You know I've completely forgotten to thank you for the lovely evening yesterday.

NORA (*Gets up and crosses the floor.*) Oh, I don't think it was as nice yesterday as it usually is. You should have gotten here a little earlier, Kristine. Torvald really knows how to make a home charming and elegant.

MRS. LINDE So do you, just as much, I'd say. You're not your father's daughter for nothing. Tell me—is Doctor Rank always so depressed?

NORA No, yesterday he was particularly low. But he's got a very serious illness—tuberculosis of the spine, poor man. You know his father was a disgusting creature who kept mistresses and things like that—that's how poor Doctor Rank got to be so sickly.

MRS. LINDE (*Dropping her sewing to her lap.*) Nora, my dear, how do you know about these things?

NORA (*Walking around.*) Fuff. When you've had three children you end up meeting some women who know a little about medicine, and they tell you a few things.

MRS. LINDE (*Sewing again, short silence.*) Does Doctor Rank come to the house every day?

NORA Every single day. He's Torvald's best friend ever since they were children, and he's my good friend too. Doctor Rank sort of belongs to the house.

MRS. LINDE But tell me this—is he honest? I mean, doesn't he like to tell people what they want to hear?

NORA No, not at all. What makes you think that?

MRS. LINDE When you introduced us yesterday he said he'd heard my name here so often—but then I noticed that your husband didn't have any idea who I was. So how could Doctor Rank—

NORA That's right, Kristine. Torvald is so unbelievably devoted to me—he says he wants me all to himself. When we were first married he'd get jealous if I so much as mentioned any of my old friends from back home. So, of course, I stopped. But with Doctor Rank I can talk about all those things, because he enjoys hearing about them.

MRS. LINDE Listen to me, Nora: in many ways you're still a child.

I'm quite a bit older than you and I have a little more experience. Let me tell you something: you should put an end to all this with Doctor Rank.

NORA What should I put an end to?

MRS. LINDE All of it, I think. Yesterday you said something about a rich admirer who was going to give you money—

NORA Yes, but unfortunately he doesn't exist. So what?

MRS. LINDE Is Doctor Rank rich?

NORA Yes.

MRS. LINDE No one to care for?

NORA No, no one—but—?

MRS. LINDE And he comes by every day?

NORA Yes, that's what I told you.

MRS. LINDE How can such a cultivated man be so obvious?

NORA I really don't understand you.

MRS. LINDE Don't play games, Nora. Don't you think I know who lent you the money?

NORA Are you out of your mind? How can you even think that? A good friend of ours, who comes over here every single day! That would have been horrible!

MRS. LINDE So it really wasn't him?

NORA No, I promise you. I would never have thought of that—anyway, he didn't have any money to lend back then—he inherited it all later.

MRS. LINDE Well, that was just as well for you, I think.

NORA No, I would never have thought of asking Doctor Rank. Even though I'm sure that if I did—

MRS. LINDE But of course you wouldn't.

NORA No, of course not. I can't imagine how it would be necessary. On the other hand, I'm sure that if I even mentioned it to him—

MRS. LINDE Behind your husband's back?

NORA I've got to get out of this other thing—that's also behind his back. I've really got to get out of that.

MRS. LINDE Yes, that's what I said yesterday. But—

NORA (*Walking up and down.*) A man can deal with these things so much better than a woman—

MRS. LINDE Your own husband can, yes.

NORA Nonsense. (*Stopping.*) When you pay back everything you owe you get your note back.

MRS. LINDE That's right.

NORA And you can tear it up in a hundred thousand pieces and burn it—that disgusting piece of paper!

MRS. LINDE (*Looking straight at her, putting the sewing down, rising slowly.*) Nora—you're hiding something from me.

NORA Can you see that?

MRS. LINDE Something's happened since yesterday morning. Nora, what is it?

NORA (*Going to her.*) Kristine! (*Listens.*) Ssh! Torvald's home. Look—go in there with the children for a while. Torvald can't stand to see people sewing. Let Anne-Marie help you.

MRS. LINDE (*Gathering some of her things.*) Yes, all right, but I'm not leaving before we talk all this through. (*She goes into the room at left; at the same time, Helmer comes in from the hall.*)

NORA (*Goes to meet him.*) Oh, I've been waiting for you, Torvald my dear.

HELMER Was that the dressmaker?

NORA No, it's Kristine; she's helping me with my costume. You know, I think I'm going to outdo myself this time.

HELMER Yes, that was a pretty good idea I had, wasn't it?

NORA Brilliant. But wasn't it also nice of me to agree to it?

HELMER (*Taking her under the chin.*) Nice of you? Agreeing with your husband? All right, you crazy thing, I know you didn't mean it that way. But I don't want to disturb you; I suppose you'll want to try it on.

NORA Will you be working?

HELMER Yes. (*Shows her a bundle of papers.*) See. I've been down to the bank— (*He is about to go into his study.*)

NORA Torvald.

HELMER Yes.

NORA If your little squirrel were to beg you ever so nicely for something—?

HELMER Well?

NORA Would you do it?

HELMER First, of course, I'd need to know what it is.

NORA The squirrel would romp around and do tricks if you'd be sweet and say yes.

HELMER Come on, what is it?

NORA The lark would sing high and low in every room—

HELMER So what, she does that anyway.

NORA I'd pretend I was a fairy child and dance for you in the moonlight, Torvald.

HELMER Nora, I hope this isn't that same business from this morning.

NORA (*Coming closer.*) Yes, Torvald, please, I beg you!

HELMER You really have the nerve to drag that up again.

NORA Yes, yes, you've got to do what I say; you've got to let Krogstad keep his job in the bank.

HELMER But Nora, I'm giving his job to Mrs. Linde.

NORA That's very sweet of you; but can't you get rid of another clerk, someone besides Krogstad?

HELMER I can't believe how stubborn you're being! Just because you went ahead and made a foolish promise to speak up for him, now I'm supposed to—

NORA That's not why, Torvald. It's for your own sake. That man writes articles for some horrible newspapers; you've said so yourself. He can do you an awful lot of harm. I'm scared to death of him—

HELMER Aha—I understand. You're frightened of the old memories.

NORA What do you mean by that?

HELMER You're thinking about your father.

NORA That's right. Remember how those horrible people wrote about Papa in the papers and slandered him so terribly. I believe they'd have gotten him fired if the government hadn't sent you up there to investigate and if you hadn't been so kind and fair to him.

HELMER My little Nora, there is a considerable difference between your father and me. Your father's public life was not exactly beyond reproach—but mine is. And that's how I plan to keep it for as long as I hold my position.

NORA Oh, you can never tell what spiteful people might do. It could be so nice and quiet and happy in our home—so peaceful and carefree—you and me and the children, Torvald—

HELMER And precisely by continuing to plead for him like this you're making it impossible for me to keep him on. It's already known around the bank that I'm letting Krogstad go. What if the rumor got around that the new bank manager was letting himself be overruled by his wife—

NORA Yes, so what?

HELMER Oh, of course—as long as our little rebel here gets her way—I should make myself look silly in front of my whole staff—make people think I can be influenced by all kinds of outside pressures—you can bet that would come back to haunt me soon enough. Besides—there's one thing that makes it impossible to have Krogstad in the bank as long as I'm the manager.

NORA What's that?

HELMER I might be able to overlook his moral failings if I had to—

NORA Yes, Torvald, isn't that right?

HELMER And I hear he's quite good at his job too. But he was a boyhood friend of mine—one of those stupid friendships you get into without thinking, and end up regretting later in life. I might just as well tell you—we're on a first-name basis. And that tactless idiot makes no secret of it in front of people. The opposite, in fact—he thinks it entitles him to take a familiar tone with me, so he's always coming out with "Hey, Torvald—Torvald, can I talk to you, Torvald—" and I can tell you I find it excruciating. He'll make my life at the bank completely intolerable.

NORA Torvald, you can't be serious.

HELMER Oh? Why not?

NORA No, because these are such petty things.

HELMER What are you saying? Petty? Do you think I'm petty?

NORA Not at all, Torvald, and that's just the reason—

HELMER All right; you call me petty, I might as well be just that. Petty! Very well! Now we'll put a stop to all of this. (*Goes to the door and calls.*) Helene!

NORA What are you doing?

HELMER (*Searching through his papers.*) A decision. (*The Maid enters.*) See this letter? Find a messenger right away and have him deliver it. Quickly. The address is on the envelope. There—here's some money.

MAID Yes sir. (*She leaves with the letter.*)

HELMER (*Tidying up his papers.*) So that's that, my little Miss Stubborn.

NORA (*Breathless.*) Torvald, what was that letter?

HELMER Krogstad's notice.

NORA Get it back, Torvald! There's still time. Oh, Torvald, get it back! Do it for my sake—for your own sake—for the children's sake! Listen, Torvald, do it! You don't realize what can happen to all of us.

HELMER Too late.

NORA Yes, too late.

HELMER Nora, I forgive you for being nervous about this, even though you're really insulting me. Yes, you are. Isn't it insulting to think that *I* would be afraid of what some hack journalist might do for revenge? But I forgive you, all the same, because it shows so beautifully how much you love me. That's how it should be, my own darling Nora. Come what may! When things get tough, I've got the courage—and the strength, you can believe it. I'm the kind of man who can take it all on himself.

NORA (*Terrified.*) What do you mean by that?

HELMER The whole thing, like I said.

NORA (*Resolutely.*) You'll never have to do that, never.

HELMER Good—so we'll share it, Nora, as man and wife. That's the way it should be. (*Fondling her.*) Happy now? Well, well, well—enough of those frightened dove's eyes. It's nothing but empty fantasy. Now you should run through your tarantella and try the tambourine. I won't hear a thing in the office, so you can make all the noise you want. (*Turning in the doorway.*) And when Rank comes, tell him where he can find me. (*He nods to her, goes to his study with his papers, and closes the door behind him.*)

NORA (*Distracted with fear, standing as though glued to the spot, whispering.*) He's really going to do it. He will do it. He'll do it in spite of everything—No, never, never in this world! Anything but that—escape! A way out—(*The bell rings in the hall.*) Doctor Rank! Anything but that! Whatever else happens!

(*She brushes her hands over her face, pulls herself together and goes to open the door in the hall. Doctor Rank is standing outside hanging up his fur coat. During the following, it begins to grow dark.*)

NORA Doctor Rank, I recognized your ring. But you can't see Torvald quite yet; I think he's busy.

RANK And you?

NORA (*While he comes into the room and she closes the door after him.*) Oh, as you know perfectly well, I always have an hour to spare for you.

RANK Thanks. I shall make use of it as long as I can.

NORA What do you mean? As long as you can?

RANK Yes, does that worry you?

NORA Well, it's such a strange way to talk. Is anything going to happen?

RANK Something that I've been expecting for a long time. But I didn't think it would come so soon.

NORA (*Gripping his arm.*) What have you found out? Doctor Rank, you have to tell me!

RANK (*Sitting by the stove.*) It's all over. There's no point in lying to myself.

NORA (*Breathing easier.*) Is it you—?

RANK Who else? I'm the worst of all my patients, Mrs. Helmer. Over the last few days I've done a general audit of my internal account. Bankrupt. Within a month I'll probably be rotting in the churchyard.

NORA Oh, really. What a horrible thing to say.

RANK It *is* a horrible thing. But the worst of it all is the horror beforehand. There's one more examination to go; when I've done that I'll know when the disintegration will begin. There is something I want to ask you. Helmer is so sensitive; he can't stand to be around anything ugly. I won't let him come to my sickroom.

NORA Oh, but Doctor Rank—

RANK I won't allow him in there. Under any circumstances. I'll lock the door to him. As soon as I'm absolutely certain of the worst, I'll send you my card with a black cross on it; then you'll know that it's begun.

NORA No, you are completely unreasonable today. And I especially wanted you to be in a really good mood.

RANK When I hold death in my hands? And to suffer like this for someone else's guilt? Is there any justice in that? In every family—every single one—somehow this inexorable retribution is taking its course.

NORA (*Stopping her ears.*) La la la la la! Cheer up! Cheer up!

RANK Yes, finally even I can only laugh at the whole thing. My poor, innocent back has to pay for my father's career as a lascivious lieutenant.

NORA (*By the table to the left.*) Was he that addicted to asparagus and *pâté de foie gras*?

RANK Yes, and truffles.

NORA Truffles, yes. And also oysters, I believe.

RANK Yes, oysters, oysters, of course.

NORA And port and champagne too. It's so sad that all these delicious things have to go and attack our bones.

RANK Especially when they attack the unfortunate bones that never got the slightest pleasure from them.

NORA Ah, yes—that's the greatest sadness of all.

RANK (*Looks searchingly at her.*) Hmm—

NORA (*Shortly after.*) Why did you smile?

RANK No, no—you laughed.

NORA No, you smiled, Doctor Rank!

RANK (*Getting up.*) You're an even bigger flirt than I thought!

NORA I'm full of crazy ideas today.

RANK So it seems.

NORA (*With both hands on his shoulders.*) Dear, dear Doctor Rank: for Torvald and me, you simply will not die.

RANK Oh, you'll soon get over that loss. Those who go away are soon forgotten.

NORA (*Looking anxiously at him.*) Do you think so?

RANK You make new relationships, and then—

NORA Who makes new relationships?

RANK Both you and Helmer will, after I'm gone. You're well on your way already, I'd say. What was that Mrs. Linde doing here last night?

NORA Come on now—you're not telling me you're jealous of poor Kristine?

RANK Yes I am. She'll be my successor here in this house. When my time is up, I'll bet that woman will—

NORA Ssh—don't talk so loud—she's in there.

RANK Again today! There, you see?

NORA She's just fixing my costume. Good Lord, you're unreasonable today. (*Sits on the sofa.*) Now be nice, Doctor Rank. Tomorrow you'll see how beautifully I'll dance—and you can imagine I'm doing it just for you—yes, for Torvald too, of course. (*Takes various things out of a carton.*) Doctor Rank, sit here. I want to show you something.

RANK (*Sitting.*) What is it?

NORA Look here. Look!

RANK Silk stockings.

NORA Flesh-colored. Lovely, aren't they? It's so dark in here now, but in the morning—no, no, no, only the feet. Oh, well, you might as well go ahead and look higher up.

RANK Hmm.

NORA What's this critical stare? Don't you think they'll fit?

RANK I couldn't possibly have an accurate opinion on that.

NORA (*Glancing at him for a moment.*) Shame on you. (*Hits him lightly on the ear with the stockings.*) That's what you get. (*Puts them away again.*)

RANK And what other splendors do I get to see?

NORA Not a thing—you're being bad. (*She hums a little and rummages through her things.*)

RANK (*After a short pause.*) When I'm sitting here like this, so close to you, I can't imagine—I can't begin to comprehend—what would have become of me if I had never found my way to this house.

NORA (*Smiling.*) Yes, I believe you really enjoy being here with us.

RANK (*Quietly, looking ahead.*) And to have to leave it all behind—

NORA Nonsense, you're not leaving us behind.

RANK (*As before.*) And to think that nothing remains after you're gone—no little gesture of gratitude—hardly even a passing regret—just a vacant place that the first person who comes along can fill.

NORA And what if I were to ask you now for—? No—

RANK For what?

NORA For a great proof of your friendship.

RANK Yes, yes?

NORA I mean a tremendously big favor—

RANK Would you really let me be so happy, just this once?

NORA You have no idea what it is.

RANK All right—so tell me.

NORA No, Doctor Rank, I can't. It's too big, too unreasonable. It's advice, and help, and a great service too.

RANK So much the better. I can't imagine what you mean. But keep talking. Don't you have confidence in me?

NORA Yes, in you before anyone else. You're my best and truest
      friend, you know that. That's why I can tell you. All right, Doc-
      tor Rank: there's something you've got to help me prevent. You
      know how intensely, how indescribably deeply Torvald loves
      me—he'd give his life for my sake without a moment's thought.
RANK (*Bending toward her.*) Nora—do you think he's the only one?
NORA (*With a slight start.*) Who—?
RANK Who would gladly give his life for you?
NORA (*Heavily.*) I see.
RANK I promised myself that you'd know before the end. I'll never
      find a better chance than this. Yes, Nora, now you know. And
      you also know that you can trust me like nobody else.
NORA (*Rises and speaks, evenly and calmly.*) Let me through.
RANK (*Makes way for her, but remains seated.*) Nora—
NORA (*In the hall doorway.*) Helene, bring in the lamp. (*She goes
      over to the stove.*) Ah, dear Doctor Rank, that was really awful
      of you.
RANK (*Rising.*) That I've loved you just as much as anyone? Was
      that awful?
NORA No, but that you felt you had to tell me. That was just not
      necessary.
RANK What do you mean? You mean that you knew—?
      (*The Maid enters with the lamp, sets it on the table, and goes
      out again.*)
RANK Nora—Mrs. Helmer—I'm asking you. Did you know?
NORA Oh, how do I know what I knew or didn't know? I can't say.
      How could you be so clumsy, Doctor Rank! When everything
      was so nice.
RANK Well, in any case now you know that I'm at your service with
      body and soul. So please go on.
NORA (*Looking at him.*) After this?
RANK Please, please tell me what it is.
NORA Now I can't tell you anything.
RANK Yes, yes. Don't torment me like this. Let me do whatever is
      humanly possible for you.
NORA You can't do anything for me now. In fact, I really don't need
      any help. You'll see—it was just my imagination. It really is. Of
      course! (*Sits in the rocking chair, looks at him, smiling.*) Well,
      you are a piece of work, Doctor Rank. Don't you think you
      should be a little ashamed, now that the lamp is here?
RANK No, not really. But maybe I'd better go—for good?
NORA No, you certainly will not do that. Of course you'll keep com-
      ing here just like before. You know perfectly well that Torvald
      can't do without you.
RANK Yes, but what about you?

NORA Oh, I always enjoy your visits very much.

RANK That's exactly what set me off on the wrong track. You're an enigma to me. I've often felt you'd almost rather be with me than with Helmer.

NORA Well, you see, there are the people you love the most, and the people you'd almost rather be with.

RANK Ah yes, you're on to something there.

NORA When I was at home, of course I loved Papa the most. But I always had the most fun sneaking into the maids' rooms, because they never tried to teach me anything and they always had so much fun talking to each other.

RANK Ah—so *they're* the ones that I've replaced.

NORA (*Jumping up and going to him.*) Oh, dear Doctor Rank, I didn't mean that at all. But you can see that with Torvald it's a lot like it was with Papa—

(*The Maid enters from the hall.*)

MAID Ma'am. (*Whispers and hands Nora a card.*)

NORA (*Glancing at the card.*) Ah! (*Puts it in her pocket.*)

RANK Something wrong?

NORA No, no, not at all. It's just—it's about my new costume.

RANK How could that be? Your costume's in there.

NORA Oh, yes—that one. But this is a different one, I ordered it— Torvald can't find out—

RANK Aha—there's our great secret.

NORA That's right. Go on in to him. He's working in the inner room. Keep him there as long as—

RANK Don't worry—he won't get by me. (*He goes into Helmer's study.*)

NORA (*To the Maid.*) And he's waiting in the kitchen?

MAID Yes, he came up the back stairs.

NORA Did you tell him somebody was here?

MAID I did, but that didn't help.

NORA He won't go away?

MAID No, he won't leave until he's talked to you.

NORA Let him come in then; but quietly. Helene, not a word of this to anyone; it's a surprise for my husband.

MAID Oh, yes, I understand. (*She goes out.*)

NORA This terrible thing is really happening. It's coming no matter what. No, no, no. It can't happen. It must not happen.

(*She goes and bolts Helmer's door. The Maid opens the hall door for Krogstad and closes it after him. He's dressed in traveling clothes, a fur coat, overshoes, and a fur cap.*)

NORA (*Goes toward him.*) Talk quietly—my husband's home.

KROGSTAD I don't care.

NORA What do you want from me?

KROGSTAD Some answers.

NORA Quick, then. What?

KROGSTAD You know, of course, I got my notice.

NORA I couldn't stop it, Mr. Krogstad. I fought for you as hard as I
could, but it was no use.

KROGSTAD Does your husband really love you so little? He knows
what I can do to you, and he still dares—

NORA How can you imagine he knows about it?

KROGSTAD No, I didn't think he did. It's not like my fine Torvald
Helmer to show that kind of strength.

NORA Mr. Krogstad, I demand respect for my husband.

KROGSTAD Good Lord, of course, all due respect. But since the lady
has kept all this so carefully hidden, might I ask if you've also
come to understand a little better than yesterday what you've
actually done?

NORA Better than you could ever teach me.

KROGSTAD Yes, I'm such a terrible lawyer—

NORA What do you want with me?

KROGSTAD Just to see how things are with you, Mrs. Helmer. I
couldn't stop thinking about you all day. A cashier, a hack journalist, a—well, a man like me also has a little of what is commonly called heart, you know.

NORA Then show it. Think of my little children.

KROGSTAD Have you or your husband given any thought to mine?
But that's not the issue right now. I just wanted to tell you that
you don't need to take this business too seriously. For the time
being I'm not taking any action.

NORA Oh, that's true, I was sure of it.

KROGSTAD The whole thing can be settled amicably. No one else
needs to know about it, just the three of us.

NORA My husband can never find out.

KROGSTAD How can you stop that? Can you pay off the balance?

NORA No, not right now.

KROGSTAD Maybe you can find a way to raise the money in a few
days?

NORA No way that I'd use.

KROGSTAD Well, it wouldn't do you any good anyway. Even if you
were standing there with a pile of cash in your hands you still
wouldn't get your note back.

NORA Tell me what you're going to do with it.

KROGSTAD Just keep it—just hold it in my custody. No one else
needs to know anything about it. So if you happen to be thinking of some desperate remedy—

NORA Which I am.

KROGSTAD If you're thinking of running away from home—

NORA Which I am.

KROGSTAD Or something worse—

NORA How did you know?

KROGSTAD Then give it up right now.

NORA How could you know I was thinking of *that*?

KROGSTAD Most of us think of *that* to begin with. I thought about it too—but I didn't have the courage.

NORA (*Lifelessly.*) I don't either.

KROGSTAD (*Relieved.*) That's true?

NORA I don't have it; I don't have it.

KROGSTAD It'd be pretty silly anyway. As soon as the first big storm blows over—I have here in my pocket a letter to your husband—

NORA Which tells everything?

KROGSTAD As nicely as possible.

NORA (*Quickly.*) He must never get that letter. Tear it up. I'll get the money somehow.

KROGSTAD Excuse me, Mrs. Helmer, but I think I just told you—

NORA I'm not talking about what I owe you. Just let me know how much you demand from my husband and I'll get you the money.

KROGSTAD I'm not demanding any money from your husband.

NORA So what then?

KROGSTAD I'll tell you. I want to get back on my feet, Mrs. Helmer; I want to move up. And your husband is going to help me. For the last year and a half I haven't gone near anything disreputable—all the time fighting to make ends meet—but I was happy to work my way up, step by step. Now I'm being driven out again and I'm not in a very forgiving mood, I'm ready to climb, I tell you. I'll get back in the bank, and in a higher position than before. Your husband will set me up.

NORA He'll never do that!

KROGSTAD He'll do it. I know him; he won't even dare to argue. And once I'm in there with him, you'll see how it goes. In a year I'll be the manager's right-hand man. Nils Krogstad will be running that bank, not Torvald Helmer.

NORA You'll never live to see that.

KROGSTAD You think you might—

NORA Now I have the courage.

KROGSTAD Forget it—a pampered, spoiled woman like you?

NORA You'll see—you'll see.

KROGSTAD Under the ice, maybe? Down in the freezing black water? Floating up in the spring, ugly, unrecognizable, your hair falling out—

NORA You don't frighten me.

KROGSTAD You don't frighten me either. People don't do such things, Mrs. Helmer. Besides, what would be the point? I'd have him in my pocket just the same.

NORA After—? Even when I'm no longer—?

KROGSTAD Are you forgetting? In that case I'll be in charge of your reputation. (*Nora stares speechless at him.*) Well, I've warned you. Don't do anything stupid. When Helmer gets my letter, I'll wait for a word from him. Just keep in mind that it's your husband who has forced me back onto these old roads of mine. I'll never forgive him for that. Goodbye, Mrs. Helmer. (*He goes out through the hallway.*)

NORA (*Goes to the hall door, opens it a fraction, and listens.*) Gone. He didn't leave the letter. No, no, no, that would be impossible! (*Opening the door farther.*) What? He's waiting outside. Not going downstairs. Changing his mind? Maybe he'll—?

(*A letter drops into the mailbox; then Krogstad's footsteps are heard receding as he walks downstairs. Nora, with a stifled cry, runs across the room to the sofa table; short pause.*)

NORA In the mailbox. (*Creeps cautiously to the hall door.*) Lying there. Torvald, Torvald—no saving us now!

(*Mrs. Linde enters with the costume from the room at the left.*)

MRS. LINDE Well, I think that's it for the repairs. Should we try it—

NORA (*In a low, hoarse voice.*) Kristine, come here.

MRS. LINDE (*Throws the dress onto the sofa.*) What's the matter—you're upset!

NORA Come here. See that letter? There—see it, through the window in the mailbox?

MRS. LINDE Yes, I see it.

NORA It's from Krogstad.

MRS. LINDE Nora—Krogstad's the one who lent you the money!

NORA Yes. And now Torvald will know everything.

MRS. LINDE Believe me, Nora, that's best for both of you.

NORA There's more to it. I forged a signature.

MRS. LINDE Oh for heaven's sake—

NORA I'm just telling you this, Kristine, so that you can be my witness.

MRS. LINDE What do you mean, witness? How can I—?

NORA If I were to lose my mind—that could easily happen—

MRS. LINDE Nora!

NORA Or if anything else happened to me, if I couldn't be here—

MRS. LINDE Nora, you're beside yourself!

NORA And if someone wanted to try to take the whole thing onto himself, all the blame, you see—

MRS. LINDE Yes, but how can you think—

NORA You've got to swear it isn't true, Kristine. I'm in my perfect mind; I understand exactly what I'm saying; and I'm telling you: no one else knew about it. I did it all alone. Remember that.

MRS. LINDE I will. But I don't understand any of it.

NORA How could you understand? A wonderful thing is about to happen.

MRS. LINDE Wonderful?

NORA Yes, a wonderful thing. But also terrible, Kristine, and it just can't happen, not for all the world.

MRS. LINDE I'm going to talk to Krogstad right away.

NORA Don't: he'll only hurt you some way.

MRS. LINDE Once upon a time he'd have gladly done anything for me.

NORA Him?

MRS. LINDE Where does he live?

NORA How should I know? Wait—(*Searches her pocket.*) Here's his card. But what about the letter, the letter—?

HELMER (*In his study, knocking on the door.*) Nora!

NORA (*Screams in panic.*) What is it? What do you want?

HELMER Now, don't be frightened. We're not coming in. The door's locked; are you trying on your costume?

NORA Yes, I'm trying it on. I'm going to be so beautiful, Torvald.

MRS. LINDE (*Having read the card.*) He lives right around the corner.

NORA Yes, but that's no help. We're lost. The letter's in the box.

MRS. LINDE Your husband has the key?

NORA Always.

MRS. LINDE Krogstad will have to ask for his letter back unopened—he'll have to find some excuse—

NORA But this is the time when Torvald usually—

MRS. LINDE Stall him. Go in there and stay with him. I'll get back as fast as I can. (*She goes out hurriedly through the hall door. Nora goes to Helmer's door and opens it, looking in.*)

NORA Torvald!

HELMER Well—can I finally come back into my own living room? Come on, Rank, now we'll get to see— (*In the doorway.*) But—?

NORA What, Torvald my dear?

HELMER Rank had me all set for a great dress parade.

RANK (*In the doorway.*) That's what I was expecting, but I guess I was wrong.

NORA No one gets to bask in my full glory until tomorrow.

HELMER But Nora, you look so tired. Have you been practicing too hard?

NORA No, I haven't practiced at all yet.

HELMER You know it's essential—

NORA Absolutely essential. But I can't possibly do it without your help; I've forgotten everything.

HELMER We'll get it back quick enough.

NORA Yes, take care of me right to the end, Torvald. Do you promise? Ah, I'm so nervous. That big party—you have to give up everything for me tonight. Not one bit of business, don't even go near your work. All right, Torvald. Promise?

HELMER I promise. Tonight I'll be completely at your service—you helpless little thing. Hmm—just one item to take care of first—(*Goes toward the hall door.*)

NORA What do you want out there?

HELMER Just seeing if there's any mail.

NORA No, no, Torvald, don't do that!

HELMER What now?

NORA Torvald, please, there's nothing there.

HELMER Just let me have a look. (*About to go; Nora, at the piano, plays the opening notes of the tarantella. Helmer stops at the door.*)

NORA I can't dance tomorrow if I don't rehearse with you.

HELMER (*Going to her.*) Nora, are you really so frightened of it?

NORA Tremendously frightened. Let's rehearse right now; there's still time before dinner. Oh, Torvald, sit down and play for me. Show me how it goes; direct me, like you always do.

HELMER I'd be glad to, if you want.

(*Nora snatches the tambourine out of the box, and also a long, multicolored shawl which she drapes around herself; then she springs forward and calls out.*)

NORA Play for me! Now I'll dance!

(*Helmer plays and Nora dances; Doctor Rank stands behind Helmer and watches.*)

HELMER (*Playing.*) Slower, slower—

NORA I can't help it.

HELMER Not so violent, Nora!

NORA That's how it has to be.

HELMER (*Stopping.*) No, no—that's not it at all.

NORA (*Laughing, swinging the tambourine.*) What did I tell you?

RANK Let me play for her.

HELMER (*Getting up.*) Yes, good idea. That way I can be a better teacher.

(*Rank sits at the piano and plays. Nora dances with increasing wildness. Helmer has placed himself by the stove, continually directing dancing instructions to her; she seems not to hear him;*)

*her hair loosens and falls over her shoulders; she doesn't notice,
but keeps on dancing. Mrs. Linde enters.*)

MRS. LINDE (*As though spellbound in the doorway.*) Ah—!

NORA (*Still dancing.*) See, Kristine, what fun!

HELMER But Nora, you're dancing as if your life were at stake.

NORA It is, it is!

HELMER Rank, stop. This is absolute madness. Stop it!
    (*Rank stops playing and Nora suddenly comes to a halt.*)

HELMER (*Goes to her.*) I would never have believed this—you've
    forgotten everything I taught you.

NORA (*Throwing down the tambourine.*) As you can see.

HELMER Some extra work's in order here.

NORA Yes, you see how important it is. You've got to keep teaching
    me right up to the last minute. Promise, Torvald?

HELMER Depend on it.

NORA You can't even think—today or tomorrow—about anything
    but me—don't open any letters, don't even touch the mail-
    box—

HELMER Ah—you're still afraid of that man.

NORA Yes, yes, that too.

HELMER Nora, I can see it in your face, there's a letter from him
    out there.

NORA I don't know. I think there is. But you can't read things like
    that now; there can't be anything horrible between us till all
    this is over.

RANK (*Softly to Helmer.*) You shouldn't go against her.

HELMER The child will have its way. But tomorrow night—after
    you've danced—

NORA Then you're free.

MAID (*In the doorway, right.*) Ma'am, dinner's on the table.

NORA We'll have champagne, Helene.

MAID Very good, ma'am. (*Goes out.*)

HELMER Hey, hey—a whole banquet?

NORA Yes—a champagne supper right through till dawn! (*Calling
    out.*) And some macaroons, Helene—lots of them—just this
    once.

HELMER (*Taking her hands.*) There, there, there—not so wild, not
    so scared—be my little skylark again.

NORA Oh, yes, I certainly will. But go to dinner—you too, Doctor
    Rank. Kristine, I need you to help me with my hair.

RANK (*Softly as they go.*) There wouldn't be anything—anything on
    the way?

HELMER No, my friend, not a thing; nothing more than these silly
    fears I've been telling you about. (*They go out, right.*)

NORA Well?

MRS. LINDE Gone to the country.

NORA I saw it in your face.

MRS. LINDE He gets back tomorrow night. I left him a note.

NORA You shouldn't have done that. You can't stop it now. Behind it all there's this great joy—waiting for a wonderful thing to happen.

MRS. LINDE What are you waiting for?

NORA You can't understand that. Go in with them—I'll be there in a minute.

(*Mrs. Linde goes into the dining room. Nora stands for a moment as if to compose herself; then she looks at her watch.*)

NORA Five. Seven hours to midnight. Then twenty-four hours to the next midnight. Then the tarantella will be done. Twenty-four plus seven—thirty-one hours to live.

HELMER (*In the doorway, right.*) What happened to the skylark?

NORA (*Going to him with open arms.*) Here's your skylark!

Act Three

Same room. The sofa-table, with chairs around it, has been moved to the middle of the room. A lamp is burning on the table. The door to the hall stands open. Dance music can be heard from the apartment above.

(*Mrs. Linde is sitting by the table, desultorily turning the pages of the book; she attempts to read but seems unable to fix her attention. Once or twice she listens, tensely, for a sound at the door.*)

MRS. LINDE Not here yet. And it's now or never. If he'd only—(*Listens again.*) Ah—there he is. (*She goes out into the hall and cautiously opens the outer door; quiet footsteps are heard on the stairs. She whispers.*) Come in. Nobody's here.

KROGSTAD (*In the doorway.*) I found a note from you at home. What does it mean?

MRS. LINDE I had to talk to you.

KROGSTAD Oh yes? And it had to be here, in this house?

MRS. LINDE My place is impossible—there's no private entrance to my room. Come in; we're all alone. The maid's asleep and the Helmers are at a party upstairs.

KROGSTAD (*Comes into the room.*) Well, well, well—so the Helmers are dancing tonight. How about that?

MRS. LINDE Why shouldn't they?

KROGSTAD True enough—why shouldn't they.

MRS. LINDE Well, Krogstad, let's talk.

KROGSTAD Do the two of us have anything more to talk about?

MRS. LINDE We have a lot to talk about.

KROGSTAD I wouldn't have thought so.

MRS. LINDE No, because you've never really understood me.

KROGSTAD What was there to understand, more than the usual thing? A heartless woman sends a man packing as soon as she gets a better offer.

MRS. LINDE Do you think I'm that heartless? Do you think it was easy for me to break up with you?

KROGSTAD Wasn't it?

MRS LINDE Krogstad, did you really think that?

KROGSTAD Then how could you have written to me that way?

MRS. LINDE I couldn't do anything else. If I had to make the break, it was my duty to try to stamp out whatever feelings you had for me.

KROGSTAD (*Clenching his hands.*) So that was it! And this—all this for money's sake!

MRS. LINDE Don't forget that I had a helpless mother and two little brothers. We couldn't wait for you, Krogstad; your prospects were so cloudy then.

KROGSTAD Maybe. But you had no right to abandon me for somebody else's sake.

MRS. LINDE Yes—I don't know. I've asked myself over and over if I had any right to do that.

KROGSTAD (*More quietly.*) When I lost you I felt the ground dissolve under my feet. Look at me: I'm a man adrift on a wreck.

MRS. LINDE Help could be close by.

KROGSTAD It was—until you appeared and blocked the way.

MRS. LINDE I didn't know, Krogstad. I only learned today that I'm replacing you at the bank.

KROGSTAD Since you say so, I believe it. But now you know—so won't you pull out?

MRS. LINDE No, because that wouldn't do you the least bit of good.

KROGSTAD Oh, who cares? I'd do it anyway.

MRS. LINDE I've learned to act rationally. Life and bitter necessity have taught me that.

KROGSTAD And life has taught me not to believe in empty phrases.

MRS. LINDE Then life has taught you a very rational lesson. But you do believe in deeds, don't you?

KROGSTAD What do you mean?

MRS. LINDE You said that you were like a man adrift, standing on a wreck.

KROGSTAD I said that with good reason.

MRS. LINDE Well I'm a woman adrift; I'm hanging on to a wreck as well.

KROGSTAD That was your choice.

MRS. LINDE There was no other choice at the time.

KROGSTAD So?

MRS. LINDE Krogstad, what if these two shipwrecks could reach across to one another?

KROGSTAD What are you saying?

MRS. LINDE Two on one raft stand a better chance than each one alone.

KROGSTAD Kristine!

MRS. LINDE Why do you suppose I came to town?

KROGSTAD Were you really thinking about me?

MRS. LINDE For me to go on living, I need to work. All my life, as long as I can remember, I've worked—it's given me my only real joy. But now I'm completely alone in the world, completely empty and desolate. Working for yourself—well, there's no joy in that. Krogstad: give me someone and something to work for.

KROGSTAD I don't believe all this. This is just some hysterical feminine urge for self-sacrifice.

MRS. LINDE Have you ever known me to be hysterical?

KROGSTAD Can you really mean all this? Do you know about my past—the whole story?

MRS. LINDE Yes.

KROGSTAD And you know what people think of me here?

MRS. LINDE You hinted just now that you thought you could have been a different person with me.

KROGSTAD I know that for sure.

MRS. LINDE Couldn't it still happen?

KROGSTAD Kristine—you're serious about this? Yes, you are. I can see it in you. Do you have the courage as well?

MRS. LINDE I need someone to be a mother to, and your children need a mother. The two of us need each other. Krogstad, I have faith in you, in what's there deep down in your heart. I could risk anything together with you.

KROGSTAD (*Seizing her hands.*) Thank you, Kristine, thank you— now I know I can bring myself up in people's eyes—ah, I forgot—

MRS. LINDE (*Listening.*) The tarantella! Go, go, go!

KROGSTAD What's going on?

MRS. LINDE Do you hear the music up there? When it's over, they'll be down.

KROGSTAD All right, I'll go. It's all pointless. Of course you don't know what I've done with the Helmers.

MRS. LINDE Yes, Krogstad, I know all about it.

KROGSTAD And you still have the courage to—

MRS. LINDE I know very well how far despair can drive a man like you.

KROGSTAD If I could only undo what I've done!

MRS. LINDE That's easy. Your letter's still in the mailbox.

KROGSTAD Are you sure?

MRS. LINDE Absolutely. But—

KROGSTAD (*Looks searchingly at her.*) Is that what this is all about? Would you save your friend at any price? Tell me honestly, tell me straight—is that it?

MRS. LINDE Krogstad: when you've sold yourself *once* for someone else's sake, you don't do it a second time.

KROGSTAD I'll demand my letter back.

MRS. LINDE No, no.

KROGSTAD Yes, of course I will. I'll stay here until Helmer comes down; I'll tell him to give me back my letter—that it's only about my dismissal—that he shouldn't read it.

MRS. LINDE No, Krogstad. Don't take back your letter.

KROGSTAD But wasn't that exactly why you got me over here?

MRS. LINDE Yes, in the first panic. But in the twenty-four hours between then and now, I've seen some incredible things in this house. Helmer has to learn everything; this awful secret has to come to light; those two have to come to a clear understanding—they can't go on with all this hiding, all these lies.

KROGSTAD Well, if you're willing to take the risk—. But there's one thing I can do right away.

MRS. LINDE (*Listening.*) Hurry! Go, go! The dance is over. We're not safe another second!

KROGSTAD I'll wait for you downstairs.

MRS. LINDE Yes, do that. You'll have to see me home.

KROGSTAD This incredible happiness—I've never felt anything like it!

(*He goes out by the front door; the door between the living room and the hall stays open.*)

MRS. LINDE (*Tidies the room a little and gets her outer garments ready.*) What a change! What a change! People to work for, to live for—a home to make. That's something worth doing. If only they'd come soon. (*Listens.*) Ah—there they are. Get dressed.

(*Helmer's and Nora's voices are heard outside; a key is turned and Helmer leads Nora almost forcibly into the hall. She is wearing the Italian costume with a large black shawl over it; he is in evening dress with an open black domino over it.*)

NORA (*Still in the doorway, resisting.*) No, no, no, not in there! I'm going up again. I don't want to leave so early!

HELMER But Nora, my dearest—

NORA Oh, I beg you, I implore you, from the bottom of my heart Torvald—just one more hour!

HELMER Not another minute, Nora, my sweet. You know we had an agreement. Come on now, into the drawing room; you're catching cold out here. (*He leads her gently into the drawing room against her resistance.*)

MRS. LINDE Good evening.

NORA Kristine!

HELMER Well, Mrs. Linde—here so late?

MRS. LINDE Yes, forgive me. I really wanted to see Nora in her costume.

NORA So you've been sitting here waiting for me?

MRS. LINDE Yes, I didn't get here in time—you'd all gone upstairs. And I just thought I couldn't leave without seeing you.

HELMER (*Taking off Nora's shawl.*) Well, get a good look at her. I think she's worth looking at. Isn't she lovely, Mrs. Linde?

MRS. LINDE Yes, I have to say—

HELMER Isn't she incredibly lovely? That was the general consensus at the party, too—but also incredibly stubborn, the sweet thing. What to do about that? Would you believe it, I almost had to use force to get her down here.

NORA Ah, Torvald, you're going to regret that you didn't let me have my way just a half-hour more.

HELMER Hear that, Mrs. Linde? She danced her tarantella to thunderous applause—well-deserved applause, too—even though there was something a little too naturalistic about the whole thing—I mean, something that went beyond the strict requirements of art. But so what? The main thing is, she was a success—a tremendous success. Should I let her stay around after that? Spoil the effect? No, thank you! I took my lovely Capri girl—my capricious little Capri girl, I could say—on my arm; made a quick trip around the ballroom—a curtsy to all sides—and as they say in novels, the lovely apparition vanished. Exits are tremendously important, Mrs. Linde—they should always be effective; but that's what I can't get Nora to see. Uch, it's hot in here. (*Throws his domino on a chair and opens the door to his room.*) What? it's dark—oh, yes, of course—excuse me— (*Goes in and lights candles.*)

NORA (*Whispering quickly and breathlessly.*) Well?

MRS. LINDE (*Quietly.*) I talked to him.

NORA And—?

MRS. LINDE Nora, you have to tell your husband everything.

NORA (*Dully.*) I knew it.

MRS. LINDE You've got nothing to worry about from Krogstad—but you have to speak out.

NORA I won't do it.

MRS. LINDE Then the letter will.

NORA Thank you, Kristine. Now I know what I have to do. Sssh!—

HELMER (*Coming in again.*) Now, Mrs. Linde—have you had a chance to admire her?

MRS. LINDE Yes, and now I'll say good night.

HELMER So soon? Is this yours, this knitting?

MRS. LINDE (*Taking it.*) Oh yes.

HELMER So you also knit.

MRS. HELMER Yes.

HELMER Know what? You should embroider instead.

MRS. HELMER Really? Why?

HELMER Much prettier. Want to see? You hold the embroidery like this with your left hand, and guide the needle with your right—like this—lightly, in and out, in a sweeping curve—right?

MRS. LINDE I suppose so—

HELMER Now knitting, on the other hand—so ugly to watch—see here, the arms jammed together, the needles going up and down—there's something Chinese about it. Ah—that was a tremendous champagne up there.

MRS. LINDE Well, Nora, good night! And no more stubbornness!

HELMER Well said, Mrs. Linde!

MRS. LINDE Good night, Mr. Helmer.

HELMER (*Following her to the door.*) Good night, good night. I hope you're all right getting home. I would, of course—but you don't have far to go. Good night, good night. (*She leaves; he closes the door after her and comes in again.*) Well, well. We finally got her out the door. What an incredible bore that woman is.

NORA Aren't you tired, Torvald?

HELMER No, not a bit.

NORA Not sleepy at all?

HELMER Absolutely not—in fact, I'm exhilarated! You, on the other hand, are looking very tired and sleepy.

NORA Yes, I'm tired. I'll got to sleep soon.

HELMER See, see! I was right! It was time to go home.

NORA Oh, everything you do is right.

HELMER (*Kisses her on the brow.*) Now my little lark is talking like a real person. Say—did you notice how lively Rank was tonight?

NORA Was he? I didn't get to talk to him.

HELMER I barely did myself, but I haven't seen him in such a good mood in a long time. (*Looks at Nora a while, then comes closer to her.*) Hmm—my God, it's glorious to be back in our own home again, completely alone with you—you enchanting young woman!

NORA Don't look at me like that, Torvald!

HELMER Shouldn't I look at my most precious possession? All this magnificence, and it's mine, mine alone, completely and utterly mine!

NORA You shouldn't talk this way to me tonight.

HELMER (*Following her.*) The tarantella's still in your blood. I understand. And that makes me want you even more. Listen! Now the guests are beginning to leave. (*More softly.*) Nora— soon the whole house will be silent.

NORA I hope so.

HELMER Yes, my own darling Nora, that's right. Ah—do you know why, whenever I'm out at a party with you—do you know why I barely speak to you, why I keep my distance, hardly even shoot you a stolen glance? Do you know why I do that? Because I'm imagining you're my secret lover, my young, secret sweetheart, and that no one in the room guesses there's anything going on between us.

NORA Oh yes, yes, yes—I know you're always thinking of me.

HELMER And when it's time to go, and I place the shawl over your smooth young shoulders, around this wonderful curve of your neck—then I pretend you're my young bride, that we've come straight from the wedding, that I'm bringing you home for the first time, alone with you for the first time, completely alone with you, you young, trembling, delicious—ah, I've done nothing but long for you all night! When I saw you doing the tarantella—like a huntress, luring us all to your trap—my blood started to boil. I couldn't stand it any longer. That's why I got you down here so early—

NORA Get away, Torvald! Please get away from me. I don't want all this.

HELMER What are you saying? Still playing the lark with me, Nora? You want, you don't want? Aren't I your husband?

(*There's a noise outside.*)

NORA (*Startled.*) Did you hear that?

HELMER (*Going to the door.*) Who's there?

RANK (*Outside.*) Just me. May I come in for a moment?

HELMER (*Softly, irritated.*) What can he possibly want now? (*Aloud.*) Just a second. (*Goes to the door and opens it.*) I'm so glad you didn't pass us by on your way out.

RANK I thought I heard voices, and I really wanted to stop in. (*Looking around.*) Oh, yes—the old haunts. What a warm little nest you've got here.

HELMER Speaking of which, you were having a pretty warm time upstairs—almost hot, I'd say.

RANK Absolutely. And why not? You have to get the most out of life—everything you can, anyway, for as long as you can. That was excellent wine.

HELMER And the champagne!

RANK You thought so too? My thirst for it was amazing—even to me.

NORA Torvald also had his share of champagne tonight.

RANK Oh yes?

NORA Yes, and that makes him so entertaining.

RANK And why shouldn't you enjoy an evening like this after a productive day?

HELMER Productive? I can't exactly say that for myself.

RANK (*Slaps him on the back.*) Ah, but you see, I can!

NORA Doctor Rank, it sounds like you've done some medical research today.

RANK That's right.

HELMER Oh come on—here's little Nora talking about medical research!

NORA And may I congratulate you on the results?

RANK Yes indeed.

NORA Were they good?

RANK The best kind—for doctor and patient alike—certainty.

NORA (*Quickly, inquisitively.*) Certainty.

RANK Absolute certainty. So haven't I earned a festive night out?

NORA Yes, Doctor Rank, you have.

HELMER I'm all for that—as long as the morning after's not too bad.

RANK Well, you never get something for nothing in this world.

NORA Doctor Rank, do you like masquerade balls?

RANK Oh yes—especially when the disguises are good and strange—

NORA So tell me. At the next one, how should the two of us appear?

HELMER You little noodlehead! You're already on to the next one?

RANK The two of us? I can tell you that: you'll go as Charmed Life—

HELMER All right, but what's the costume for that?

RANK Your wife can go just as she always is.

HELMER Well said. Now have you decided on something for yourself?

RANK Yes, Helmer, my mind's made up.

HELMER Well?

RANK At the next masquerade, I will be—invisible.

HELMER That's pretty funny.

RANK   I hear there's a hat—a huge, black hat—called the Hat of Invisibility. You put it on, and no one on earth can see you.

HELMER   (*Stifling a grin.*) Oh, yes, of course.

RANK   But I've forgotten what I really came for. Helmer, how about a cigar—a dark Havana.

HELMER   With pleasure. (*Holds out the case to him.*)

RANK   Thanks. (*Takes one and cuts the tip.*)

NORA   Let me give you a light.

RANK   Thank you. (*She holds the match as he lights the cigar.*) Now, good-bye.

HELMER   Old friend—good-bye, good-bye.

NORA   Sleep well, Doctor.

RANK   Thank you for that wish.

NORA   Now wish me the same.

RANK   Wish you?—All right, if you want—sleep well. And thanks for the light. (*He exits, nodding to both of them.*)

HELMER   (*Quietly.*) He's drunk.

NORA   (*Vaguely.*) Maybe.

(*Helmer takes his keys from his pocket and goes out into the hall.*)

NORA   What are you doing, Torvald?

HELMER   I've got to empty the mailbox—it's so full, there's no room for the morning papers.

NORA   Are you working tonight?

HELMER   You know I'm not. What's this? Someone's been fiddling with the lock.

NORA   The lock?

HELMER   Yes, definitely. Who could it be? I can't believe the maids—? Wait, here's a broken hairpin—Nora, this is yours—

NORA   (*Quickly.*) Then it must be the children.

HELMER   Well you've really got to break them of that. Hmm—there we go, finally got it open. (*Takes out the contents and shouts into the kitchen.*) Helene? Helene—put out the hall lamp. (*He comes back into the room and shuts the door. He holds the letters in his hand.*) Look—see how it piled up? (*Sorts through them.*) What's this?

NORA   (*By the window.*) The letter! No, no, Torvald!

HELMER   Two cards, from Rank.

NORA   From Doctor Rank?

HELMER   (*Looking at them.*) Doctor Rank, Physician and Surgeon. They were on top. He must have dropped them in as he left.

NORA   Is there anything on them?

HELMER   There's a black cross over the name. Look. That's gruesome. It's like he's announcing his own death.

NORA   That's exactly what he's doing.

HELMER What? Did he tell you anything?

NORA Yes. He said that when these cards arrived, it meant he's say-ing good-bye to us. Now he'll shut himself in and die.

HELMER My poor friend. Of course I knew I wouldn't have him for long. But so soon—and now he's hiding himself away like a wounded animal.

NORA If it has to happen, it's best to let it happen quietly. Isn't that right, Torvald?

HELMER (*Pacing up and down.*) He'd grown to be a part of us. I don't think I can imagine myself without him. His loneliness—his suffering was like a cloudy background to our sunlit happi-ness. Well, maybe it's best this way—at least for him. (*Stands still.*) And maybe for us too, Nora. Now we only have each other. (*Puts his arms around her.*) Ah, you—my darling wife. I don't think I'll ever be able to hold you close enough. You know, Nora—so many times I've wished that you were in some terrible danger, so I could risk my life, my blood, everything, everything for you.

NORA (*Tears herself free and says firmly and resolutely.*) Read your mail now, Torvald.

HELMER No, not tonight. Tonight I want to be with you—

NORA With your friend's death on your mind?

HELMER You're right. We're both a little shaken by this. This ugli-ness has come between us—thoughts of death and decay. We have to try to get rid of them; until then, we go our separate ways.

NORA (*Her arms around his neck.*) Torvald—good night! Good night!

HELMER (*Kissing her forehead.*) Good night, little songbird. Sleep well, Nora. Now I'll read the mail. (*He goes in with the letters, shuts the door behind him.*)

(*Nora, with wild eyes, fumbles around, seizes Helmer's domino, wraps it around herself, and whispers quickly, hoarsely, spasmod-ically.*)

NORA Never see him again—never, never, never. (*Throws the shawl over her head.*) Never see the children again either—not even the children—never, never—the icy black water—the bot-tomless—that—if only it weren't all over—now he has it, he's reading it now—no, no, not yet. Torvald, good-bye, children, good-bye—

(*She starts to go into the hall; at the same moment Helmer flings open his door and stands there, an open letter in his hand.*)

HELMER Nora!

NORA (*Screams.*) Ahh—!

HELMER What is this? Do you know what's in this letter?

NORA Yes. Yes I know. Let me go. Let me out!

HELMER (*Holding her back.*) Where are you going?

NORA (*Trying to break loose.*) Don't try to save me, Torvald!

HELMER (*Staggers back.*) It's true?! What he said is the truth? Horrible! No—it's impossible—this can't be true.

NORA It is true. I have loved you more than anything in the world.

HELMER Don't start with your silly excuses.

NORA (*Taking a step toward him.*) Torvald!

HELMER You miserable—what have you done?

NORA Let me go. You won't have to take the blame for me. You're not going to take it on yourself.

HELMER No more playacting! (*Locking the hall door.*) You'll stay right here and explain yourself. Do you understand what you've done? Answer me! Do you understand?

NORA (*Looking fixedly at him, her face hardening.*) Yes. Now I'm beginning to understand everything.

HELMER (*Pacing up and down.*) Ah!—what a rude awakening for me! For eight years—my pride and joy, a hypocrite, a liar,—even worse, a criminal! There's so much ugliness at the bottom of all this—indescribable ugliness! Uccch! (*Nora remains silent, looking fixedly at him.*) I should have seen it coming. Every one of your father's disgusting values—quiet!—every disgusting value is coming out in you. No religion, no morals, no sense of duty—this is my punishment for being so easy on him up there. I did it for your sake; and you repay me like this!

NORA Yes, like this.

HELMER You've destroyed my happiness. My whole future—thrown away! It's horrible when you think about it. I'm totally at the mercy of some amoral animal who can do whatever he wants with me—demand anything he wants, order me around, command me however he pleases, and I can't so much as squeak in protest. And this is how I'll go down, right to the bottom, all for the sake of some frivolous woman.

NORA When I'm gone from this world, then you'll be free.

HELMER Stop playacting! You sound like your father—he always had one of those phrases on the tip of his tongue. How would it help me if you were gone from this world, as you put it? Not in the least. He can still reveal everything, and if he does I'd be suspected of being an accomplice to your crimes! People might think I was behind it all, that it was my idea! And I have you to thank for all this—after I've carried you along, taken you and led you by the hand ever since we were married. Do you understand what you have done to me?

NORA (*Coldly and calmly.*) Yes.

HELMER I can't grasp this—it's just unbelievable to me. But we have to try to set things right. Take off that shawl. I said take it off! I've got to find some way to appease him—this thing has to be covered up, whatever it costs. As for you and me, things will seem just like before. For public consumption only, of course. You'll stay in the house, that's understood. But I can't trust you to bring up the children. Oh God—to have to say that to the one I—even now—well, that's over. After today there's no happiness, only holding the wreckage together, the scraps and shards— (*The doorbell rings. Helmer starts.*) What's that? It's so late! Is this it? Is he going to—? Nora, hide yourself! Say you're sick. (*Nora stands motionless. Helmer goes and opens the hall door.*)

MAID (*Half-dressed in the hall doorway.*) A letter for Mrs. Helmer.

HELMER Give it here. (*Takes the letter and closes the door.*) Yes, it's from him. You're not getting it. I'll read it myself.

NORA Read it.

HELMER (*By the lamp.*) I hardly dare. It could be the end for both of us. I've got to know. (*Tears open the letter; scans a few lines; looks at an enclosed paper and gives a cry of joy.*) Nora! (*Nora looks enquiringly at him.*) Nora! No, let me read it again—yes, yes, it's true. I'm saved! Nora, I'm saved!

NORA And I?

HELMER You too, of course. We're both saved, both of us. See? He sent you back your note—he writes that he's sorry and ashamed—that a happy change in his life—oh, what does it matter what he writes? We're saved, Nora! Now no one can hurt you. Oh, Nora, Nora—no: first, let's get all this ugliness out of here. Let me see. (*Glances at the note for a moment.*) No, I won't look at it. It'll be nothing more than a dream I had. (*He tears both letters in pieces and throws them both into the stove, watching them burn.*) So, nothing left. He wrote that ever since Christmas Eve—God, these must have been three terrible days for you, Nora.

NORA I have fought a hard battle these last three days.

HELMER And suffered, not seeing any way out but—no, we won't think about this ugly thing any more. We'll just rejoice and keep telling ourselves "it's over—it's all over." Do you hear me, Nora? It seems like you haven't quite got it yet—it's over! What's this about, this cold stare? Ah, poor little Nora, I understand—you can't bring yourself to believe I've forgiven you. But I have, Nora, I swear. I've forgiven everything. I know perfectly well that you did all this out of love for me.

NORA That's true.

HELMER You've loved me like a wife should love her husband. You just couldn't judge how to do it. But do you think that makes me love you any the less, because you couldn't manage by yourself? No, no—just lean on me. I'll counsel you, I'll direct you. I wouldn't be much of a man if this female helplessness didn't make you doubly attractive to me. Forget what I said in those first few terrible moments, when I thought I was going to lose everything. I've forgiven you, Nora—I swear, I've forgiven you.

NORA Thank you for your forgiveness. (*She goes out through the door on the right.*)

HELMER No, stay—(*Looking in.*) What are you doing?

NORA Taking off my costume.

HELMER (*By the open door.*) Yes, do that. Try to calm down, collect your thoughts, my little, shivering songbird. If you need protection, I have broad wings to shelter you with. (*Walks around near the door.*) Oh, Nora—our home is so snug, so cozy. This is your nest, where I can keep you like a dove that I've snatched, unharmed, from the falcon's claws; I'll bring peace and rest to your beating heart. Little by little it will happen, Nora, believe me. Tomorrow, this will all seem different to you; and soon everything will be back to normal. I won't need to keep saying I forgive you—you'll feel it, you'll know it's true. How could you ever think I could bring myself to disown you, or even punish you? You don't know how a man's heart works, Nora. There's something indescribably sweet and satisfying for a man in knowing he's forgiven his wife—forgiven her from the bottom of his heart. It's as if he possesses her doubly now—as if she were born into the world all over again—and she becomes, in a way, his wife and his child at the same time. And that's what you'll be for me from now on, you little, helpless, confused creature. Don't be frightened of anything—just open your heart to me and I'll be both your conscience and your will. What's this—? You've changed your dress?

NORA Yes, Torvald, I've changed my dress.

HELMER But why now, so late?

NORA I'm not sleeping tonight.

HELMER But Nora, dear—

NORA (*Looking at her watch.*) It's not all that late. Sit down, Torvald. We have a great deal to talk about together. (*She sits at one end of the table.*)

HELMER Nora—what's going on? That hard expression—

NORA Sit down. This will take time. I have a lot to say to you.

HELMER (*Sits at table directly opposite her.*) You're worrying me, Nora. I don't understand you.

NORA No, that's just it. You don't understand me. And I have never

understood you—not until tonight. No—no interruptions. You
have to hear me out. We're settling accounts, Torvald.

HELMER What do you mean by that?

NORA (*After a short silence.*) Doesn't *one* thing strike you about the
way we're sitting here?

HELMER What might that be?

NORA We've been married for eight years. Doesn't it strike you that
this is the first time that the two of us—you and I, man and
wife—have ever talked seriously?

HELMER Well—"seriously"—what does that mean?

NORA In eight whole years—no, longer—right from the moment we
met, we haven't exchanged one serious word on one serious
subject.

HELMER Should I constantly be involving you in problems you
couldn't possibly help me solve?

NORA I'm not talking about problems. I'm saying that we've never
sat down together and seriously tried to get to the bottom of
anything.

HELMER But Nora, dearest—would you have wanted that?

NORA Yes, of course, that's just it. You've never understood me. A
great wrong has been done me, Torvald. First by Papa, then by
you.

HELMER What! By us—who've loved you more than anyone in the
world.

NORA (*Shaking her head.*) You've never loved me. You just thought
it was a lot of fun to be in love with me.

HELMER Nora, how can you say that?

NORA It's a fact, Torvald. When I was at home with Papa, he told
me all his opinions; so of course I had the same opinions. And
if I had any others, I kept them hidden, because he wouldn't
have liked that. He called me his doll-child, and he played with
me like I played with my dolls. Then I came to your house—

HELMER What kind of way is that to describe our marriage?

NORA (*Undisturbed.*) I mean, I went from Papa's hands into yours.
You set up everything according to your taste; so of course I
had the same taste, or I pretended to, I'm not really sure. I
think it was half-and-half, one as much as the other. Now that
I look back on it, I can see that I've lived like a beggar in this
house, from hand to mouth; I've lived by doing tricks for you,
Torvald. But that's how you wanted it. You and Papa have committed a great sin against me. It's your fault that I've become
what I am.

HELMER Nora—this is unreasonable, and it's ungrateful! Haven't
you been happy here?

NORA　No, never. I thought so, but I never really was.

HELMER　Not—not happy!

NORA　No, just having fun. You've always been very nice to me. But our home has never been anything but a playpen. I've been your doll-wife here, just like I was Papa's doll-child at home. And my children, in turn, have been my dolls. It was fun when you came and played with me, just like they had fun when I played with them. That's what our marriage has been, Torvald.

HELMER　There's some truth in this—as exaggerated and hysterical as it is. But from now on, things will be different. Playtime is over: now the teaching begins.

NORA　Who gets this teaching? Me or the children?

HELMER　Both you and the children, my dearest Nora.

NORA　Ah, Torvald: you're not the man to teach me how to be a good wife to you.

HELMER　You can say that!

NORA　And me—how can I possibly teach the children?

HELMER　Nora!

NORA　Didn't you say that yourself, not too long ago? You didn't dare trust them to me?

HELMER　In the heat of the moment! How can you take that seriously?

NORA　Yes, but you spoke the truth. I'm not equal to the task. There's another task I have to get through first. I have to try to teach myself. And you can't help me there. I've got to do it alone. And so I'm leaving you.

HELMER　(*Springing up.*) What did you say?

NORA　If I'm going to find out anything about myself—about everything out there—I have to stand completely on my own. That's why I can't stay with you any longer.

HELMER　Nora, Nora!

NORA　I'll leave right away. Kristine can put me up for tonight—

HELMER　You're out of your mind! I won't allow it—I forbid you!

NORA　It's no use forbidding me anything any more. I'll take what's mine with me. I won't take anything from you, now or later.

HELMER　What kind of madness is this?

NORA　Tomorrow I'm going home—back to my old hometown, I mean. It'll be easier for me to find something to do up there.

HELMER　You blind, inexperienced creature!

NORA　I have to try to get some experience, Torvald.

HELMER　Abandon your home, your husband, your children! Do you have any idea what people will say?

NORA　I can't worry about that. I only know what I have to do.

HELMER　It's grotesque! You're turning your back on your most sacred duties!

NORA What do you think those are—my most sacred duties?

HELMER I have to tell you? Aren't they to your husband and children?

NORA I have other duties, equally sacred.

HELMER No, you don't! Like what?

NORA Duties to myself.

HELMER You're a wife and mother, first and foremost.

NORA I don't believe that any more. I believe that, first and foremost, I'm a human being—just as much as you—or at least I should try to become one. I'm aware that most people agree with you, Torvald, and that your opinion is backed up by plenty of books. But I can't be satisfied any more with what most people say, or what's written in the books. Now I've got to think these things through myself, and understand them.

HELMER What don't you understand about your place in your own home? Don't you have an infallible teacher for questions like this? Don't you have your religion?

NORA Oh, Torvald, I really don't know what religion is.

HELMER What are you saying?

NORA I only know what Pastor Hansen said when I was confirmed. He told me that religion was this and that and the other thing. When I get away from here, when I'm alone, I'll look into that subject too. I'll see if what Pastor Hansen said is true—or at least, if it's true for me.

HELMER These things just aren't right for a young woman to be saying. If religion can't get through to you, let me try your conscience. You do have some moral feeling? Or—answer me—maybe not?

NORA Well, Torvald, it's not easy to answer that. I really don't know. I'm actually quite confused about these things. I only know that my ideas are totally different from yours. I find out that the law is not what I thought it was—but I can't get it into my head that the law is right. A woman has no right to spare her dying father's feelings, or save her husband's life! I just can't believe these things.

HELMER You're talking like a child. You don't understand the society you live in.

NORA No, I don't. But now I'm going to find out for myself. I've got to figure out who's right—the world or me.

HELMER You're ill, Nora—you have a fever. I almost think you're out of your mind.

NORA I've never been so clear—and so certain—about so many things as I am tonight.

HELMER You're clear and certain that you'll desert your husband and children?

NORA   Yes, I will.

HELMER   There's only one explanation left.

NORA   What is it?

HELMER   You no longer love me.

NORA   No. That's precisely it.

HELMER   Nora!—you can say that!

NORA   Oh, it hurts so much, Torvald. Because you've always been so kind to me. But I can't help it. I don't love you any more.

HELMER   (*Struggling to control himself.*) Are you also clear and certain about that?

NORA   Yes, absolutely clear and certain. That's why I can't live here any more.

HELMER   Can you tell me how I lost your love?

NORA   Yes, I can. It was this evening, when the wonderful thing didn't happen—then I saw that you weren't the man I thought you were.

HELMER   Say more—I'm not following this.

NORA   I've waited so patiently for ten years now—good Lord. I know that these wonderful things don't come along every day. Then this disaster broke over me, and I was absolutely certain: now the wonderful thing is coming. While Krogstad's letter was lying out there, I never imagined you'd give in to his terms, even for a minute. I was so certain you'd say to him: tell your story to the whole world! And when that was done—

HELMER   Yes, then what? When I'd given my wife up to shame and disgrace—!

NORA   When that was done, I was completely certain that you would step forward and take everything on yourself—you'd say "I am the guilty one."

HELMER   Nora!

NORA   You're thinking that I'd never accept such a sacrifice from you? No, of course I wouldn't. But what good would my protests be over yours? *That* was the wonderful thing I was hoping for, and in terror of. And to prevent it, I was willing to end my life.

HELMER   I'd work for you night and day, Nora—gladly—suffer and sacrifice for your sake. But no one gives up his honor even for the one he loves.

NORA   That's exactly what millions of women have done.

HELMER   Oh—! You're thinking and talking like an ignorant child.

NORA   Maybe. But you don't think—or talk—like the man I could choose to be with. When your big fright was over—not the danger I was in, but what might happen to you—when that threat was past, then it was like nothing happened to you. I was just what I was before, your little songbird, your doll, and you'd have to take care of it twice as hard as before, since it was so frail and fragile. In that moment, Torvald, it dawned on me that I'd been living with a stranger—that I'd borne three children with him—. Aah—I can't stand the thought of it! I could tear myself to pieces.

HELMER (*Heavily.*) I see. I see. A gulf has really opened up between us. But Nora, can't we fill it in somehow?

NORA The way I am now, I'm no wife for you.

HELMER I can transform myself—I have the strength for it.

NORA Maybe—if your doll is taken away from you.

HELMER To live without—without you! Nora, I can't bear the thought of it!

NORA All the more reason it has to happen. (*Having gone in to the right, she returns with her outdoor clothes and a little traveling bag, which she sets on a chair by the table.*)

HELMER Nora, Nora, not now! Wait until tomorrow.

NORA (*Puts on her coat.*) I can't spend the night in a strange man's house.

HELMER Can't we live here like brother and sister?

NORA (*Tying her hat.*) You know very well how long that would last. (*Throws her shawl around her.*) Good-bye, Torvald. I won't see the children. They're in better hands than mine, that much I know. The way I am now, I can't do anything for them.

HELMER But some day, Nora—some day—?

NORA How do I know? I have no idea what will become of me.

HELMER But you're my wife, right now and always, no matter what becomes of you.

NORA Listen, Torvald; when a wife deserts her husband's house, as I'm doing now, I've heard that the law frees him from any responsibility to her. And anyway, I'm freeing you. From everything. Complete freedom on both sides. See, here's your ring. Give me mine.

HELMER Even that.

NORA Even that.

HELMER Here it is.

NORA So. Well, now it's finished. I'm putting the keys here. As far as the household goes, the maids know all about it—better than I do. Tomorrow, after I'm gone, Kristine will come and pack the things I brought from home. I'll have them sent.

HELMER All finished, all over! Nora—will you never think about me after this?

NORA Of course I'll think about you often—and the children, and the house—.

HELMER Could I write to you, Nora?

NORA No, never. You can't do that.

HELMER But I'll have to send you—

NORA Nothing; nothing.

HELMER —help you, if you need—

NORA No. I'm telling you, I accept nothing from strangers.

HELMER Nora—can't I ever be anything more than a stranger to you?

NORA (*Taking her traveling bag.*) Oh, Torvald—not unless the most wonderful thing of all were to happen—

HELMER Name it—what is this most wonderful thing?

NORA It's—both you and I would have to transform ourselves to the point that—oh, Torvald, I don't know if I believe in it any more—

HELMER But I will. Name it! Transform ourselves to the point that—

NORA That our living together could become a marriage. Good-bye. (*She goes through the hall door.*)

HELMER (*Sinking down into a chair by the door and burying his face in his hands.*) Empty. She's not here. (*A hope flares up in him.*) The most wonderful thing of all—?

(*From below, the sound of a door slamming shut.*)

END OF PLAY

The Wild Duck (1884)

The plot is the substantially realistic story of the intrusion by Gregers Werle into the world of the Ekdal family, which he believes needs rescuing from his father's malign power. Believing truth will make Hjalmar Ekdal free, Gregers comes into conflict with Dr. Relling, who lives in an apartment below the Ekdals and whose opposite mission is to generate "life-lies" to help fallen humanity reconcile itself with its alienated condition. However, the truth Gregers brings proves destructive, and the play, for all its considerable comedy, ends as a domestic tragedy. George Bernard Shaw commented, in 1897,

> Where shall I find an epithet magnificent enough for The Wild Duck! To sit there getting deeper and deeper into the Ekdal home, and getting deeper and deeper into your own life all the time, until you forget you are in a theatre; to look with horror and pity at a profound tragedy, shaking with laughter all the time at an irresistible comedy; to go out, not from a diversion, but from an experience deeper than real life ever brings to most men, or often brings to any man.[1]

The Wild Duck is a superb example of the tragicomic genre in the modern realist style. However, the play can be viewed from another, archetypal perspective that does not violate but metaphorically expands the realistic and domestic story. This play of the "insulted and injured" is unique in the cycle (see p. 142) for focusing on an impoverished and humble family, with their strange menagerie in the background. It is infused with a visual and verbal imagery taken from the Christ story. The text continually resonates with Christian phrases and iconography. Gregers tells Hedvig, "I can tell by looking at you it's not fulfilled" (*fuldbragt*), echoing Jesus' words on the cross. Hjalmar talks of "when the fullness of time has come," which recalls Galatians 4: "when the fullness of time was come, God sent forth his Son, made of a woman, made under the law, to redeem them that were under the law." The disgraced Ekdal family are "under the law" that has convicted old Ekdal and acquitted old Werle. Though Hjalmar appropriates this phrase to his own condition, the self-appointed version of the messianic "Son" is Gregers Werle, son of the reigning power of the play, Haakon Werle; Gregers believes his mission is to save the Ekdals and his destiny is al-

1. George Bernard Shaw, "The Triumph of Ibsen," *Our Theatres in the Nineties* (London: Constable and Company, 1932), 3:138.

207

ways to be "the thirteenth at table," as if at a perpetual Last Supper. When, in Act 4, he reveals the devastating truth to Hjalmar, he expects to see "a transfiguring light shining from both husband and wife," with the husband forgiving "one who has gone astray, then raising her up" in love. Hjalmar, however, talks of the "bitter cup I've just drained," like Jesus in Gethsemane. Hjalmar, the Sancho Panza to Gregers' Don Quixote, hilariously attempts to play the redemptive role Gregers incongruously thrusts upon him. (Ibsen's friend and first biographer, Henrik Jæger, first pointed out the likeness between Don Quixote and Gregers Werle.)

Gregers talks of the "Cross" he has to bear and mysteriously predicts his own early death. In fact, from the opening scene on, the play verbally and visually intertwines the realistic with the archetypal Christian story. If we tell the plot again, foregrounding the archetypal story (as the play subtly does not), it would go as follows: A son descends into the world with a mission to redeem a fallen humanity suffering under the law that empowered his father. He finds he must combat a deceiver (Relling) who lives *below* with a "demonisk" (demonic) companion, manufacturing "life-lies" to keep humanity reconciled to its fallen condition. The redeemer and the deceiver, who once quarreled before on high (Høydal means High Valley), now join battle again over the fallen Ekdals. After the self-sacrificial death of Hedvig, they resume their seemingly endless quarrel.

By now, we will detect a (far from solemn) version of the huge Christian narrative, infiltrated into the small domestic story. The greatness of the play lies in the fact that the archetypal dimension does not compromise or inflate the realistic and domestic drama but seems more an ironic, subliminal shadowing of that drama, taking nothing away from its affective quality. The success of this daring but demure method is revealed in the fact that in performance the Christian parallel is rarely consciously recognized.

The Wild Duck†

Characters

HAAKON WERLE, wholesale merchant and mill owner
GREGERS WERLE, his son
OLD EKDAL
HJALMAR EKDAL, his son
GINA EKDAL, Hjalmar's wife
HEDVIG, their daughter, aged fourteen
MRS. SØRBY, housekeeper for the elder Werle
RELLING, a doctor
MOLVIK, former divinity student
GRÅBERG, a bookkeeper

† Translated by Brian Johnston.

PETTERSEN, a manservant
JENSEN, a hired waiter
A FAT MAN
A BALD-HEADED MAN
A NEARSIGHTED MAN
SIX OTHER MEN, guests at Werle's
OTHER HIRED SERVANTS

Act One

*Merchant Werle's house. An expensively and comfortably fur-
nished study with bookcases and upholstered furniture, a desk
with papers and documents in the middle of the room. Soft
lights with green shades, so that the room's lighting is subdued.
Open folding doors in the background with drawn curtains.
Through them can be seen a large and elegant room, brightly
lit with lamps and a candelabra. In the study, right front, a
tapestry-covered door leads to offices. Front left a stove with coals
glowing in it, and further back a double door to the dining
room.*

*Mr. Werle's servant, Pettersen, in livery, and the hired waiter,
Jensen, in black, are setting things in order in the study. In the
larger room to the rear two or three other hired waiters, arranging things and lighting more candles. From within the dining
room can be heard the buzz of conversation and the laughter of
many voices. A knife is heard tapping a wineglass and silence en-
sues. A toast is proposed; cheers, and the buzz of conversation re-
sumes.*

PETTERSEN (*Lights a lamp on the stove and sets a shade on it.*) Just
   listen to them, Jensen. Now the old man's on his feet giving a
   toast to Mrs. Sørby.
JENSEN (*Moving an armchair forward.*) So maybe it's true what they
   say—that there's something between them?
PETTERSEN Devil knows.
JENSEN He's sure been a bit of a goat in his day.
PETTERSEN Could be he has.
JENSEN They say he's really giving this dinner for his son.
PETTERSEN Yes, his son came home yesterday.
JENSEN It's the first I knew old Werle had a son.
PETTERSEN Oh yes, he's got a son. But he's always kept himself way
   up there at the Høydal works. He's never once been to town all
   the years I've served in this house.
A HIRED WAITER (*In the doorway of the other room.*) Hey, Pettersen,
   here's an old fellow who—
PETTERSEN (*Grumbling.*) Who the devil would come at this time.

(*Old Ekdal appears in the room from the right. He is dressed in a shabby greatcoat with a high collar. He has soiled gloves, a stick, and a fur hat in his hand and under his arm a parcel wrapped in brown packing paper. Wears a red-brown, soiled wig and has a little grey moustache.*)

PETTERSEN (*Going toward him.*) Christ! What are *you* doing here?

EKDAL (*In the doorway.*) Absolutely must get into the office, Pettersen.

PETTERSEN The office has been closed for the past hour, so—

EKDAL So I heard at the gate, old man. But Gråberg's still in there. Do me a favor, Pettersen, and let me slip in this way. (*Points to the tapestry door.*) I've been that way before.

PETTERSEN Well, if you really must get in. (*Opens the door.*) But make sure you use the right way going out. We've got company.

EKDAL I know that. Thanks, Pettersen, old man! Good old friend. Thanks. (*He mutters to himself.*) Idiot! (*He goes into the office. Pettersen shuts the door after him.*)

JENSEN One of the office staff?

PETTERSEN No, just someone they give some copying to do at home when they need it. But he's been a fine enough fellow in his day, old Ekdal.

JENSEN He looked like he might have been.

PETTERSEN Yes, just think, at one time he was a lieutenant.

JENSEN I'll be damned—him a lieutenant!

PETTERSEN As God's my witness, he was. But then he went into the forestry business, or something like that. It's said he once played a really dirty trick on Mr. Werle. The two of them were then partners in the Høydal works, you see. Yes, I know him very well, old Ekdal. Many's the time we've drunk a glass of brandy and a bottle of beer together at Madam Erikson's.

JENSEN He can't have much to treat drinks with.

PETTERSEN Good Lord, Jensen, I'm the one that does the treating. It's my opinion we ought to have some respect for folks who've come down in the world.

JENSEN He went bankrupt, then?

PETTERSEN No, much worse than that. He was sentenced to hard labor.

JENSEN Hard labor!

PETTERSEN Or perhaps it was the penitentiary—(*Listens.*) Shh, now they're leaving the table.

(*The doors to the dining room are opened from the inside by a couple of servants. Mrs. Sørby, in conversation with two gentlemen, comes out. Soon after the rest of the party follows, among them, Mr. Werle. Last come Hjalmar Ekdal and Gregers Werle.*)

MRS. SØRBY (*In passing, to the servant.*) Pettersen, have coffee served in the music room, please.

PETTERSEN Very good, Mrs. Sørby.

(*She and the two gentlemen go into the drawing room and from there out to the right. Pettersen and the hired waiter Jensen leave the same way.*)

A FAT GUEST (*To a balding guest.*) Phew—that dinner took some effort getting through!

BALDING GUEST Oh, with a little good will, it's amazing what you can manage in three hours.

FAT GUEST Yes, but afterwards, my dear fellow, afterwards!

A THIRD GUEST I hear mocha and maraschino are to be served in the music room.

FAT GUEST Splendid! Then perhaps Mrs. Sørby will be playing something for us.

BALDING GUEST (*In a low voice.*) So long as she doesn't try playing something *on* us.

FAT GUEST Oh, I hardly think so. Berta won't throw over her old friends. (*Laughing, they go into the drawing room.*)

WERLE (*Quietly, troubled.*) I don't think anybody noticed, Gregers.

GREGERS (*Looking at him.*) What?

WERLE Then you didn't notice, either?

GREGERS What should I have noticed?

WERLE We were thirteen at table.

GREGERS Really. We were thirteen at table?

WERLE (*With a glance at Hjalmar Ekdal.*) As a rule, we prefer to be twelve. (*To the others.*) If you would be so good, gentlemen!

HJALMAR (*Who has overheard the conversation.*) You shouldn't have sent me that invitation, Gregers.

GREGERS What! The party's supposed to be in my honor—and I can't invite my best—my only friend?

HJALMAR I don't think your father's very pleased about it. Usually, I never come to this house.

GREGERS So I've heard. But I just had to see you and speak with you. Because soon I'll be leaving again. So! We two old school comrades—we've certainly drifted far apart from each other. Not seen each other the last sixteen or seventeen years.

HJALMAR It's been that long?

GREGERS Yes, it's been that long. Well then, how have you been? You look all right—even got a little stouter.

HJALMAR Hm. I wouldn't quite call it stout. No doubt I seem a bit burlier than I once did.

GREGERS Yes, you do. Your outer self doesn't seem to have changed for the worse.

HJALMAR (*In a gloomy voice.*) But the inner self, Gregers! Believe me, there's a different story. You know how terribly everything collapsed for me and my family since we last saw each other.

GREGERS (*More gently.*) How are things with your father just now?

HJALMAR Ah, my friend, don't let's talk about it. My poor, unhappy father lives with me, of course. He has no one else in the whole world to turn to. But it crushes me to have to talk about all this, you know. Tell me, instead, how you're doing up at the works.

GREGERS Beautifully alone—that's what I've been, with plenty of opportunity to think over so many things. Come over here. Let's make ourselves comfortable. (*He sits in an armchair by the stove and draws Hjalmar down into another beside him.*)

HJALMAR (*Sentimentally.*) But thank you all the same, Gregers, for inviting me to your father's table. Now I can see you no longer have anything against me.

GREGERS (*Surprised.*) How could you think I had anything against you?

HJALMAR You definitely had in those first years.

GREGERS What first years?

HJALMAR When the great misfortune struck. And it was only natural you should have. It was only by a hair that your own father missed being dragged into—all that horrible business.

GREGERS And that's why I should have something against you? Whoever gave you that idea?

HJALMAR I know you did, Gregers; your father himself told me.

GREGERS (*Startled.*) My father! So that's it. Hm. Is that the reason you never let me hear from you—not even a single word?

HJALMAR Yes.

GREGERS Not even when you decided to become a photographer?

HJALMAR Your father said there was no point in writing you about anything.

GREGERS (*Distantly.*) Well, well, maybe he was right in that—. But tell me now, Hjalmar, are you more or less content with your situation?

HJALMAR (*With a light sigh.*) Oh yes, I suppose I am. I can't honestly say otherwise. At first, you understand, it was all a bit strange for me. It was a completely changed situation I found myself in. But then, everything else had completely changed, too. The great catastrophe with my father—the shame and disgrace, Gregers.

GREGERS (*Moved.*) I know, I know.

HJALMAR I couldn't think of going on with my studies—there wasn't a penny left. On the contrary, there were debts. Mostly to your father, I think—

GREGERS Hm.

HJALMAR So I thought it best to make a clean break—to drop all my old connections and ties. It was your father especially who advised me to do that. And as he was being so helpful to me—

GREGERS He was?

HJALMAR Yes, surely you must know that? How else could I have got the money to study photography and to set up the studio business? It's expensive, let me tell you.

GREGERS Father paid for all that?

HJALMAR Yes, Gregers, didn't you know? I understood him to say he'd written and told you.

GREGERS Not a word that it was *him*. He must have forgotten to. We've only exchanged business letters. So then it was *Father*—!

HJALMAR Yes, it certainly was. He never wanted anyone to know, but it was him. He also made it possible for me to get married. But maybe—you don't know about that, either?

GREGERS No, I certainly didn't. (*Grasping Hjalmar's arm.*) But, my dear Hjalmar, I can't tell you how glad I am about all this—and a bit ashamed, too. Maybe I've done my father an injustice—in certain things. Because you see, this shows he has a good heart. And also some kind of conscience—

HJALMAR Conscience?

GREGERS Yes, yes—or whatever you want to call it. No, I really can't tell you how glad I am to hear all this about my father. So—you're married, Hjalmar. That's more than I'm likely to be. I hope you enjoy being a married man?

HJALMAR Oh yes, I really do. She's as capable and fine a wife as any man could wish. And she's not entirely without culture.

GREGERS (*Somewhat surprised.*) No, I shouldn't think so.

HJALMAR For life itself's an education, you see. Her daily contact with me—and then there's a couple of very gifted friends who often visit us. I assure you, you wouldn't recognize Gina now.

GREGERS Gina?

HJALMAR Yes, Gregers, don't you remember her name's Gina?

GREGERS Whose name is Gina? I haven't the least idea who—

HJALMAR But don't you remember she was in service here at one time?

GREGERS (*Looking at him.*) Is it Gina Hansen—?

HJALMAR Yes, of course it's Gina Hansen.

GREGERS —who kept house for us the last year of my mother's illness?

HJALMAR Of course it is. But, my dear Gregers, I know very well your father wrote you I'd got married.

GREGERS (*Who has got up from his chair.*) Yes, so he did, but not that it was—(*Paces the floor.*) Yes, wait a bit—maybe after all—

now I think of it. But father always writes me such short letters. (*Sits on the arm of the chair.*) Listen, tell me, Hjalmar—
this is intriguing—how did you come to meet Gina—your wife,
that is?

HJALMAR Well, it all happened quite simply. Gina didn't stay long
here in this house. There was so much trouble here at that
time: your mother's illness—Gina couldn't stand all that. So
she quit and left. That was the year before your mother died—
or maybe it was the same year.

GREGERS It was the same year. I was up at the works at the time.
But what happened after?

HJALMAR Well, so Gina went to live with her mother, Mrs. Hansen,
a very practical and hardworking woman, who ran a little
restaurant. She also had a room to rent, a really nice and comfortable room.

GREGERS Which you, perhaps, were fortunate enough to snap up?

HJALMAR Quite. As a matter of fact it was your father told me about
it. And it was *there*, you see, where I really got to know Gina.

GREGERS And then followed the engagement?

HJALMAR Yes. Young people so easily get to be fond of each other.
Hm—

GREGERS (*Rises and walks around.*) Tell me—when you got engaged—was it then my father got you to—I mean—was it then
that you became interested in photography?

HJALMAR That's right. Because I was eager to do something and
settle down, the sooner the better. And then both your father
and I decided that photography suited me best. And Gina
thought so, too. Oh yes, that was another reason: It so happened that Gina had taken up retouching.

GREGERS So it all miraculously fitted together.

HJALMAR (*Pleased, rises.*) Yes, didn't it! Didn't it all just fit together
wonderfully?

GREGERS I must admit it did. In fact, Father's been a kind of Providence to you.

HJALMAR (*Moved.*) He didn't desert his old friend's son in his hour
of need. He's got a heart, you see.

MRS. SØRBY (*Enters arm in arm with Mr. Werle.*) Not another word,
my dear Werle. No more staying in there, staring at all those
lights. They're not good for you.

WERLE (*Letting go of her arm and passing his hand in front of his
eyes.*) I'm inclined to think you're right.
(*Pettersen and the hired waiter enter with trays.*)

MRS. SØRBY (*To the guests in the other room.*) If you please, gentlemen, anybody who wants a glass of punch must bring himself
in here.

FAT GENTLEMAN (*Coming over to Mrs. Sørby.*) Good Lord, Mrs. Sørby, is it true you've rescinded our precious freedom to smoke?

MRS. SØRBY Yes, my dear chamberlain, here in Mr. Werle's private domain, it's forbidden.

THIN-HAIRED GENTLEMAN When did you introduce these severe restrictions into our cigar regulations, Mrs. Sørby?

MRS. SØRBY After the previous dinner party, Chamberlain; when certain persons present allowed themselves to overstep the limit.

THIN-HAIRED MAN And it isn't permitted to go just a tiny bit over the limit? Not even the slightest little step?

MRS. SØRBY Not under any circumstances, Chamberlain Balle.
(*Most of the guests have gathered in Werle's study. The waiters hand round glasses of punch.*)

WERLE (*To Hjalmar standing by a table.*) What's that you're studying, Ekdal?

HJALMAR It's just an album, Mr. Werle.

THIN-HAIRED GENTLEMAN (*Who is drifting about.*) Aha, photographs! Just in your line, eh?

FAT GENTLEMAN (*In an armchair.*) Haven't you brought any of your own?

HJALMAR No, I haven't.

FAT GENTLEMAN You should have done. It's so good for the digestion to sit looking at pictures.

THIN-HAIRED GENTLEMAN And contributes a mite to the general entertainment, you know.

NEARSIGHTED GENTLEMAN And all contributions are gratefully accepted.

MRS. SØRBY Our good chamberlains mean if you're invited for the evening, you should sing for your supper, Mr. Ekdal.

FAT GENTLEMAN In a house where the food's so good, that's a sheer pleasure.

THIN-HAIRED GENTLEMAN Good Lord, if it involved a struggle for existence, then—

MRS. SØRBY How right you are!
(*They continue laughing and joking.*)

GREGERS (*Softly.*) You should join in, Hjalmar.

HJALMAR (*Writhing.*) What can I talk about?

THIN-HAIRED GENTLEMAN You agree, Werle, Tokay may be considered a relatively healthy wine for the stomach?

WERLE (*By the stove.*) I dare vouch for the Tokay you had today, at any rate. It was from one of the very best years. But then, I expect you noticed that yourself.

FAT GENTLEMAN Yes, it had a remarkably delicate bouquet.

HJALMAR (*Hesitantly.*) Is there some difference between the years, then?

FAT GENTLEMAN (*Laughing.*) That's a good one!

WERLE (*Smiling.*) There's no point putting a noble wine in front of you.

THIN-HAIRED GENTLEMAN It's the same with Tokay wine as with photographs, Mr. Ekdal. There must be sunshine. Isn't that so?

HJALMAR Yes, light is essential.

MRS. SØRBY And it's no different with court chamberlains: They, too, want a place in the sun, or so they say.

THIN-HAIRED GENTLEMAN Ouch! That sarcasm's seen long service.

NEARSIGHTED GENTLEMAN The lady's putting on a show.

FAT GENTLEMAN —*and* it's at our expense. (*Admonishing.*) Berta! Berta!

MRS. SØRBY But it's really true that vintages can be tremendously different. The oldest are the finest.

NEARSIGHTED GENTLEMAN You count me among the old ones?

MRS. SØRBY Oh, far from it.

THIN-HAIRED GENTLEMAN There, you see! But what about me, dear Mrs. Sørby—?

FAT GENTLEMAN Yes, and me! What vintages do you count us among?

MRS. SØRBY I count you among the sweet vintages, gentlemen.
(*She sips her glass of punch; the chamberlains laugh and flirt with her.*)

WERLE Mrs. Sørby always finds a way out when she wants to. Refill your glasses, gentlemen! Pettersen, see to it—! Gregers, I think we might take a glass together. (*Gregers does not move.*) Won't you join us, Ekdal? I missed the chance to toast you at dinner.
(*Gråberg, the bookkeeper, looks in through the tapestry door.*)

GRÅBERG Excuse me, Mr. Werle, but I can't get out.

WERLE What, are you locked in again?

GRÅBERG Yes, and Flakstad's left with the keys.

WERLE All right. You'd better come through here then.

GRÅBERG But there's someone else—

WERLE Well, come on, come on, both of you.
(*Gråberg and Old Ekdal enter from the office.*)

WERLE (*Involuntarily.*) Oh, no.
(*The laughter and chatter of the guests die away. Hjalmar gives a start at the sight of his father, puts down his glass and turns away toward the stove.*)

EKDAL (*Not looking up but making quick bows to both sides as he crosses and mumbles.*) Beg pardon. Came the wrong way. Door was locked . . . door was locked. Do beg your pardon. (*He and Gråberg go out back right.*)

WERLE (*Between his teeth.*) That damned Gråberg.

GREGERS (*With open mouth, staring at Hjalmar.*) But surely that was never—

FAT GENTLEMAN What's going on? Who was that?

GREGERS Nothing. Just the bookkeeper and someone else.

NEARSIGHTED GENTLEMAN (*To Hjalmar.*) Do *you* know the man?

HJALMAR I don't know. I didn't really notice—

FAT GENTLEMAN (*Getting up.*) What the devil's going on? (*He joins the others, who are talking in subdued voices.*)

MRS. SØRBY (*Whispering to the servant.*) Slip him something out there. Something really good.

PETTERSEN (*Nodding.*) I'll see to it. (*Goes out.*)

GREGERS (*Shaken, in a low voice to Hjalmar.*) So it really was him!

HJALMAR Yes.

GREGERS And yet you stood here and denied you knew him.

HJALMAR (*Whispering vehemently.*) But how *could* I—?

GREGERS —acknowledge your own father?

HJALMAR (*Bitterly.*) Oh, if you were in my place, then—
(*The conversation between the guests, which has been conducted in low voices, now gives way to a loud and forced conviviality.*)

THIN-HAIRED GENTLEMAN (*Adopting a friendly manner, approaches Hjalmar and Gregers.*) Aha, standing here, are we, brushing up memories of old student days? Eh? Not smoking, Ekdal? Do you want a light? Ah, no, that's right, we're not permitted—

HJALMAR Thanks, but I'd rather not—

FAT GENTLEMAN Don't you have some nice piece of poetry to recite to us, Mr. Ekdal? You used to do that so beautifully once.

HJALMAR I'm sorry, but I can't remember any.

FAT GENTLEMAN Oh, what a pity. Well, what shall we find to do now, Balle? (*Both men cross and go into the drawing room.*)

HJALMAR (*Dejectedly.*) Gregers, I'm leaving! When a man has felt the bludgeoning of fate, you know—. Say good-bye to your father for me.

GREGERS Yes, yes. You're going straight home?

HJALMAR Yes. Why do you ask?

GREGERS I might call on you later on.

HJALMAR No, you mustn't do that. Not my house. My home's a sad place, Gregers—especially after a brilliant banquet like this. We can always meet some place in town.

MRS. SØRBY (*Approaching, in a low voice.*) Are you leaving, Mr. Ekdal?

HJALMAR Yes.

MRS. SØRBY Give my regards to Gina.

HJALMAR Thanks.

MRS. SØRBY And tell her I'll be up to see her one of these days.

HJALMAR Thank you. (*To Gregers.*) Stay here. I'd rather disappear unnoticed. (*He crosses the room, then into the other room and out to the right.*)

MRS. SØRBY (*To the servant who has come back.*) Did you give the old man something?

PETTERSEN I did. I slipped him a bottle of brandy.

MRS. SØRBY Oh, you could have found him something better.

PETTERSEN Not at all, Mrs. Sørby. Brandy's the best thing he knows.

FAT GENTLEMAN (*In the doorway with a sheet of music in his hand.*) Why don't we play something together, Mrs. Sørby.

THE GUESTS Bravo! Bravo!

(*She and all the others cross the room and go out right. Gregers remains, standing by the stove. Werle is searching for something on the desk and seems to wish Gregers to leave. When he doesn't, Werle goes toward the doorway.*)

GREGERS Father, won't you stay a moment.

WERLE (*Stopping.*) What is it?

GREGERS I need to have a word with you.

WERLE Can't it wait till we're alone?

GREGERS No, it can't. Because it's likely we may never be alone again.

WERLE (*Approaching.*) What's that supposed to mean?

(*During the following, piano music can be heard distinctly from the music room.*)

GREGERS How could people here let that family fall so pitiably low?

WERLE I presume you mean the Ekdals.

GREGERS Yes, I mean the Ekdals. Lieutenant Ekdal was once so close to you.

WERLE Yes, unfortunately, altogether *too* close to me. I was made to pay for that for many years. It's him I can thank for the stain on my good name and reputation.

GREGERS (*Quietly.*) Was *he* in fact the only one who was guilty?

WERLE Who else, do you think?

GREGERS You were in on that big timber sale together—

WERLE But wasn't it Ekdal who drew up the survey map of the area—that disastrously false map? He's the one who illegally felled the timber on state land. And it was he who was responsible for the whole operation up there. I'd no idea what Lieutenant Ekdal was doing.

GREGERS Lieutenant Ekdal most likely had no idea himself what he was doing.

WERLE That might be so. But the outcome was that he was found guilty and I was acquitted.

GREGERS Yes, I'm well aware there was no evidence.

WERLE When you're acquitted, you're acquitted. Why do you rake up those hideous old details of what turned my hair grey years before its time? Is this the sort of thing you've been brooding over all these years up there? Down here in town, I can assure you, Gregers, the whole story's quite forgotten—as far as I'm concerned, anyway.

GREGERS But what about the unhappy Ekdal family?

WERLE What do you expect I should have done for them? When Ekdal was set free again, he was a broken man, completely past saving. In this world there are people who dive to the bottom after getting only a couple of slugs in them and never rise again to the surface. You can take my word for it, Gregers, I've stretched myself for them just as far as I could—short of leaving myself open to all kinds of gossip and suspicion.

GREGERS Suspicion—? Yes, I suppose so.

WERLE I've given Ekdal copying work to do for the office, and I pay him far more than his work is worth—

GREGERS (*Not looking at him.*) Hm. I don't doubt that.

WERLE What are you laughing at. Don't you think it's true what I'm saying? Granted, there's nothing in my books to show it. I don't keep records of expenses like that.

GREGERS (*Smiling coldly.*) No, there are certain expenses best not accounted for.

WERLE (*Startled.*) What do you mean by *that*?

GREGERS (*Summoning his courage.*) Have you kept records of what it cost you to enable Hjalmar Ekdal to learn photography?

WERLE No. Why should I record that?

GREGERS I've just found out it was you who paid for it. I've also found out it was you who made it possible for him to set himself up.

WERLE There! And you call that not doing anything for the Ekdals. I can assure you, those people have caused me quite enough expense.

GREGERS Have you recorded any of those expenses?

WERLE Why do you ask about that?

GREGERS I have my reasons. Listen, tell me—that time you took such a warm interest in your old friend's son—wasn't that just when he was about to get married?

WERLE How the devil—after so many years how can I—?

GREGERS At the time you wrote me a short letter—a business letter, naturally. And in a postscript, very briefly, you wrote that Hjalmar Ekdal had got married to a Miss Hansen.

WERLE Yes, that's quite right. That was her name.

GREGERS But what you didn't write was that this Miss Hansen was Gina Hansen, our former housekeeper.

WERLE (*Laughs scornfully, but uneasily.*) Well no, because I didn't think you were particularly interested in our former house-keeper.

GREGERS I wasn't. But, (*Lowering his voice.*) there was someone else in the house greatly interested in her.

WERLE What do you mean by that? (*Flaring up.*) You're not refer-ring to me.

GREGERS (*Quietly, but firmly.*) Yes, I'm referring to you.

WERLE And you dare to—! You have the insolence to—! How can he, that ungrateful photographer—how dare he come up with such an accusation.

GREGERS Hjalmar never said a word about this. I doubt he has even the slightest suspicion.

WERLE Then where did you get it from? Who could have said such a thing?

GREGERS My poor unhappy mother said it. The last time I saw her.

WERLE Your mother! Shouldn't I have guessed as much! You and she—you always stuck together. She was the one who turned you against me from the beginning.

GREGERS No. It was watching all she suffered and endured—until she broke down and collapsed so pitiably.

WERLE Oh, she didn't have to suffer and endure so much. No more than plenty of others have to. But there's no getting along with sickly, neurotic people. That's something I found out to my cost . . . So you go around nursing those same suspicions, rak-ing up all kinds of old rumors and slanders against your own father. Listen here, Gregers, I really think at your age you could be doing something more useful.

GREGERS Yes, maybe now it's time.

WERLE And then perhaps you'll take a brighter view of things than now. How does it help you, sitting up at the works year in and year out, slaving away like a simple desk clerk, not accepting a cent above the standard wage? It's simply stupid of you.

GREGERS If only I could be so sure about that.

WERLE I understand you all right. You want to be independent, not owe me anything. Well, now's the chance to become indepen-dent—your own master in everything.

GREGERS Really? In what way?

WERLE When I wrote it was essential you come into town at once—hm—

GREGERS Yes, what do you actually want with me? I've been waiting the whole day to find out.

WERLE To propose that you join me as partner in the firm.

GREGERS Me? In your firm? As a partner?

WERLE Yes. We wouldn't always have to be together. You'd manage the business down here in town, and I could transfer up to the works.

GREGERS You would?

WERLE Yes. You see, I'm no longer as fit for work as I used to be. I need to take care of my eyes. They're beginning to get a bit weak.

GREGERS They always have been.

WERLE Not like now. And besides—circumstances might make it advisable for me to live up there—at least for a time.

GREGERS I'd not thought of anything like this.

WERLE Listen, Gregers. There are so many things on which we think differently. But we're father and son just the same. I think we should be able to come to some kind of understanding with each other.

GREGERS To all appearances, do you mean?

WERLE Well, at least that would be something. Think it over, Gregers. Don't you think it could be arranged? Eh?

GREGERS (*Looking at him coldly.*) There's something behind this.

WERLE How do you mean?

GREGERS Something you want to use me for.

WERLE When we're as close as we are, one will always have use for the other.

GREGERS Yes, so they say.

WERLE I'd like to have you home with me for a while. I'm a lonely man, Gregers—have always felt lonely my whole life through. But above all, now, when I am beginning to get old. I need somebody about me.

GREGERS You've got Mrs. Sørby.

WERLE Yes, so I have. And she, you could say, has become practically indispensable. She's bright, easygoing and livens up the house. And that's something I need badly.

GREGERS Well then, you've everything you could wish for.

WERLE But I'm worried it won't last. In the eyes of the world a woman in that situation can easily be seen in a false light. And, I might add, it doesn't help the man very much, either.

GREGERS Oh, when a man gives the kind of dinner parties you do, he can allow himself a few risks.

WERLE But what about *her*, Gregers? I'm afraid she'll not put up with it much longer. And even if she did, out of devotion to me, even if she ignored all the gossip and slander and suchlike—? Don't you think, Gregers, you with your strong sense of justice—

GREGERS (*Interrupting.*) Just tell me in brief—are you thinking of marrying her?

WERLE And if I was thinking of that? What then?

GREGERS Just what I'm asking. What then?

WERLE Would you be so thoroughly against it?

GREGERS Absolutely not. In no way.

WERLE I didn't know if perhaps out of respect for your mother's memory—

GREGERS I'm not neurotic.

WERLE Well, whether you are or not, you've taken a great weight off my mind. It's a tremendous relief to know I can count on your support in this matter.

GREGERS (*Looking at him steadily.*) Now I understand what you want to use me for.

WERLE Use you for? What kind of talk is that?

GREGERS Let's not be so particular in our choice of words—not when it's just the two of us, at least. (*Short laugh.*) So that's it! That's the reason! Damnation! I must be seen in person here in town. For the sake of Mrs. Sørby, a charade of family life's to be arranged in this house. A tableau of Father and Son! *That's* definitely something new!

WERLE How dare you take that tone with me!

GREGERS When has there ever been any family life here? Not as long as I can remember. But suddenly there's a pressing need for a little touch of that. It will certainly create a fine impression when it's reported that the son, on the wings of piety, has flown home for his elderly father's wedding feast. What then becomes of all the rumors of what the poor dead wife had to suffer and endure? Not a trace. Her son's wiped them all away.

WERLE Gregers, I don't think there's a man in all the world you hate as much as me.

GREGERS (*Quietly.*) I've seen you too close up.

WERLE You've seen me with your mother's eyes. (*Slightly lowering his voice.*) But you should remember those eyes were—not always clear-sighted.

GREGERS (*Trembling.*) I know what you're driving at. But who's to blame for Mother's unfortunate weakness? It was you, and all those—! The last of them was this housekeeper Hjalmar Ekdal was made to take on when you no longer—Ecch!

WERLE (*Shrugs his shoulders.*) Word for word as if I were listening to your mother.

GREGERS (*Taking no notice of him.*) And there he's sitting now, with his great, trusting, childlike mind, surrounded by deceit—living under the same roof with a creature like that, unaware what he calls his home is built upon a lie. (*Comes a step closer.*) When I look back upon your whole career, it's as if I were looking over a battlefield with shattered human lives strewn all across it.

WERLE I almost believe the gulf between us is too wide.

GREGERS (*Bowing, controlled.*) So I've observed. I'll take my hat and go.

WERLE Go? Out of the house?

GREGERS Yes. Because now I see a mission I can live for.

WERLE What kind of mission might that be?

GREGERS You'd only laugh if you heard it.

WERLE A lonely man doesn't laugh that easily, Gregers.

GREGERS (*Pointing to the rear.*) Look, Father, the chamberlains are playing blindman's bluff with Mrs. Sørby. Good night—and good-bye.
(*He exits through the back, right. Laughter and banter can be heard from the party, which comes into view in the drawing room.*)

WERLE (*Muttering scornfully after Gregers.*) Ha! Poor wretch—and he says he's not neurotic!

Act Two

Hjalmar Ekdal's studio. The room, which is quite large, is seen to be an attic. To the right is a pitched roof with a large skylight half-covered by a blue curtain. At the rear, in the right corner, is the entrance door; downstage, on the same side, a door to the living room. In the wall to the left there also are two doors and between these an iron stove. In the rear wall there's a wide double door that can be pulled to both sides. The studio is frugally but pleasantly furnished and arranged. Between the doors on the right a little away from the wall is a sofa with a table and some chairs. On the table a burning lamp with a shade, near the stove an old armchair. Various pieces of photographic equipment and instruments here and there about the room. Against the back wall, near the sliding doors, is a bookcase with some books, boxes and bottles of chemicals, different kinds of instruments, and other objects. Photographs and other small objects like brushes, paper, and suchlike, lying on the table.

Gina Ekdal is sitting on a chair by the table, sewing. Hedvig sits on the sofa with her hands shading her eyes, her thumbs in her ears, reading a book.

GINA (*Glances at her a couple of times, as if secretly anxious.*) Hedvig! (*Hedvig does not hear.*) (*Louder.*) Hedvig!

HEDVIG (*Removes her hands from her face and looks up.*) Yes, Mother?

GINA Hedvig, dear, you mustn't sit reading any longer.

HEDVIG Oh, but Mother, can't I read a little bit more? Just a little.

GINA No, no. You must put the book down now. Your father doesn't like it. He never reads in the evening himself.

HEDVIG (*Closing the book.*) No, but then Father isn't all that keen on reading, is he?

GINA (*Setting the sewing aside and taking up a pencil and a small notebook from the table.*) Can you remember how much we paid for the butter today?

HEDVIG It was one kroner and sixty-five.

GINA That's right. (*Makes a note.*) It's amazing how much butter we go through in this house. Then there was the sausage and the cheese—let me see— (*Makes a note.*) and then the ham— hm—(*Adding up.*) so that altogether—

HEDVIG And then there's the beer.

GINA Yes, that's right. (*Makes a note.*) It all mounts up. But it can't be helped.

HEDVIG But then we didn't need to cook dinner today since Father went out.

GINA Yes, that was lucky. And I took in eight kroner fifty for the photographs.

HEDVIG Really! As much as that?

GINA Eight kroner fifty exactly.
    (*Silence. Gina takes up her sewing. Hedvig takes a pencil and paper and starts to draw something, with her left hand shielding her eyes.*)

HEDVIG Isn't it lovely to think of Father at Mr. Werle's big dinner party?

GINA You can't really say he's at Mr. Werle's. It was his son who actually sent him the invitation. (*Soon after.*) We don't have anything to do with Mr. Werle.

HEDVIG I'm so excited waiting for him to come home. He promised he'd ask Mrs. Sørby to get something nice for me.

GINA Yes, there's lots of fine things in *that* house, I can tell you.

HEDVIG (*Still drawing.*) I'm starting to feel a bit hungry.
    (*Old Ekdal, carrying a bundle of papers under his arm, and another packet in his coat pocket, comes in through the entrance door.*)

GINA How late you're home today, Grandfather!

EKDAL They'd locked up the office. Had to wait in Gråberg's room. And then I had to go through—hm.

HEDVIG Did they give you something new to copy, Grandfather?

EKDAL This whole packet. Just look.

GINA That's very nice.

HEDVIG And there's another in your pocket.

EKDAL What's that? Nonsense, that's nothing. (*Puts his walking stick in the corner.*) There's work, Gina, for a long time, here.

(*Opens one of the rear sliding doors a little to one side.*) Shh! (*Peeps a moment into the room and then carefully shuts the door closed again.*) Hee, hee! There they are, all asleep. And she's settled in the basket herself. Hee, hee!

HEDVIG Are you sure she won't be cold in that basket, Grandfather?

EKDAL Whatever makes you think that? Cold? In all that straw? (*Crosses to the rear door, left.*) Are there any matches around?

GINA The matches are on the dresser.

(*Ekdal goes into his room.*)

HEDVIG It's lovely they've given Grandfather all that copying to do.

GINA Yes, poor old fellow. Now he can earn himself a little pocket money.

HEDVIG And then he won't be sitting all morning in that awful Mrs. Erickson's.

GINA Yes, there's that as well.

(*Short silence.*)

HEDVIG Do you think they're still sitting down to dinner?

GINA Lord knows. They could be.

HEDVIG Imagine all the lovely food Father will be eating! I'm sure he's going to be in such a good mood when he comes home. Don't you think so, Mother?

GINA Oh, yes. Just think if we could tell him we'd been able to let the room, as well.

HEDVIG But that won't be necessary tonight.

GINA But it would be nice, all the same. And it's not doing any good standing empty.

HEDVIG No, I mean it's not necessary because Father will be feeling good, anyway. It's best we have news about the room for another time.

GINA (*Looking across at her.*) Are you happy when you have something good to tell your father when he comes home evenings?

HEDVIG Yes, because then it makes everything more cheerful.

GINA (*Thinks this over.*) Yes, there's something in that.

(*Old Ekdal re-enters, making for the the door farthest left.*)

GINA (*Turning round halfway in her chair.*) Do you want something from the kitchen, Grandfather?

EKDAL That's right. But stay in your chair. (*Goes out.*)

GINA He's not messing about with that fire, I hope. (*Waits a moment.*) Hedvig, go see what he's up to.

(*Ekdal re-enters with a mug of steaming water.*)

HEDVIG Are you getting hot water, Grandfather?

EKDAL Yes, that's right. I need it for something. I've got to do some writing and the ink's as clotted as porridge—hm.

GINA But Grandfather, shouldn't you have supper first? It's all set out.

EKDAL No need to bother with supper, Gina. I'm terribly busy, you
know. And I don't want anyone coming into my room. No
one—hm. (*He goes into his room; Gina and Hedvig look at each
other.*)

GINA (*Softly.*) Where do you think he got the money from?

HEDVIG Perhaps from Gråberg.

GINA No way. Gråberg always sends the money to me.

HEDVIG Then he must have got a bottle on credit.

GINA Grandfather? Poor thing, who would give him anything on
credit?

(*Hjalmar in an overcoat and grey felt hat, enters right.*)

GINA (*Putting down her sewing and getting up.*) Really, Ekdal,
you're back already?

HEDVIG (*Jumping up at the same time.*) Fancy coming home so
soon!

HJALMAR (*Puts his hat down.*) Most of the others were leaving.

HEDVIG So early?

HJALMAR Well, it was a dinner party, you see. (*Starts taking off his
overcoat.*)

GINA Let me help you.

HEDVIG Me too.

(*They take off his overcoat. Gina hangs it up on the rear wall.*)

HEDVIG Were there many there, Father?

HJALMAR No, not many. There were about twelve—fourteen of us
at table.

GINA And you got to talk with all of them?

HJALMAR Oh yes, a little. Though it was Gregers, of course, who
took up most of my time.

GINA Is he still as ugly as ever?

HJALMAR Well, he's not all that good-looking. Has the old man
come back yet?

HEDVIG Yes, Grandfather's in his room writing.

HJALMAR Did he say anything?

GINA No, what should he have said?

HJALMAR Didn't he say anything about—? I believe I heard something about him going to see Gråberg. I'll go in and see him for
a moment.

GINA No, no, it's best not to.

HJALMAR Why's that? Did he say he didn't want to see me?

GINA He won't want to see *anyone* this evening.

HEDVIG (*Making signals.*) Hm. Hm.

GINA (*Not noticing.*) He's been out here and got himself some hot
water.

HJALMAR Ah, so he's sitting and—

GINA That's what he's up to.

HJALMAR Dear Lord, my poor old white-haired father—! Well, at least
let him go on sitting there taking whatever pleasure's left him.
(*Old Ekdal, in a dressing gown and with an empty tobacco pipe,
enters from his room.*)

EKDAL So you're back! I thought it was you I heard talking.

HJALMAR Yes, I just came in.

EKDAL You didn't see me, by any chance?

HJALMAR No. But they said you'd gone through. So I thought I'd
follow you home.

EKDAL Hm. That was decent of you, Hjalmar. Who were they, all
those people?

HJALMAR Oh, there were all sorts. There was Chamberlain Flor
and Chamberlain Balle and Chamberlain Kaspersen and then
Chamberlain so-and-so—oh, I don't know.

EKDAL (*Nodding.*) Do you hear *that*, Gina. He's been mixing only
with chamberlains.

GINA Yes, it's pretty high-class in that house now.

HEDVIG Did the chamberlains sing, father? Or recite anything?

HJALMAR No, they only chattered away. They wanted *me* to recite
something for *them*. But they couldn't get me to do it.

EKDAL They couldn't get you to?

GINA But really, you could have done it for them.

HJALMAR No. One shouldn't be at everyone's beck and call all the
time. (*Pacing up and down.*) That's not *my* way, anyhow.

EKDAL No, no. That's not Hjalmar's way.

HJALMAR I can't see why *I* alone should take care of the entertainment when I happen to go out for an evening every now and
then. Let the others make an effort. These fellows go from one
feast to another, eating and drinking day and night. Let them
be obliged to do something for all the good food they get.

GINA But you didn't tell them that?

HJALMAR (*Humming.*) Hm—mm—mm. They got to hear some
things like that.

EKDAL And that straight to the chamberlains' faces!

HJALMAR It can't be denied. (*Casually.*) After, we had a little dispute
over Tokay.

EKDAL Tokay, was it? Now that's a fine wine.

HJALMAR (*Stops.*) It *can* be fine. But, I must point out, not all years
are equally fine. It depends on how much sunshine the grapes
have had.

GINA No! Is there anything you don't know, Ekdal?

EKDAL And they started arguing about that?

HJALMAR They tried to. But then they were given to understand it
was the same with chamberlains. With them not all vintages
were equally fine either—they were told.

GINA No! The things you come up with!

EKDAL Heh, heh! So they got that on their plates?

HJALMAR Right between the eyes, that's how they got it.

EKDAL Hear that, Gina. The chamberlains got it right between the eyes.

GINA No! Imagine, right between the eyes.

HJALMAR Yes, but I wouldn't want all this talked about. One doesn't repeat such things. The whole thing passed in a very amiable spirit. They were all pleasant, decent people. Why should I try to hurt them? No.

EKDAL But right between the eyes—

HEDVIG (*Ingratiatingly.*) How lovely to see you in evening clothes. You look so fine in them, Father!

HJALMAR Yes, don't you think so? And this one really fits me remarkably well. You'd think it had been tailor-made for me. A little tight under the arms, perhaps. Help me, Hedvig. (*Taking off the tailcoat.*) I'd rather wear my jacket instead. Where have you put the jacket, Gina?

GINA Here it is. (*Brings the jacket and helps him into it.*)

HJALMAR There. Don't forget that Molvik gets the coat back first thing in the morning.

GINA (*Puts it away.*) That'll be taken care of.

HJALMAR (*Stretching.*) Ah, that makes it more like home. This more casual and comfortable outfit much better suits my whole temperament. Don't you agree, Hedvig?

HEDVIG Yes, Father.

HJALMAR And when I pull my tie out in two flowing ends—look! What?

HEDVIG Oh yes. And it goes so well with your moustache and your thick, curly hair.

HJALMAR I wouldn't exactly call it curly. Rather, I'd say "wavy."

HEDVIG Yes, for they're such thick curls.

HJALMAR Waves, actually.

HEDVIG (*After a pause, tugging at his coat.*) Father!

HJALMAR What is it now?

HEDVIG Oh, you know what it is.

HJALMAR No, I don't know, really.

HEDVIG (*Laughing and crying.*) Yes you do, Father. You mustn't tease me any longer.

HJALMAR But what *is* it?

HEDVIG (*Shaking him.*) Don't be silly. Bring them out. You know— all those good things you promised me.

HJALMAR No! To think I should go and forget!

HEDVIG No, you're just making fun of me, Father! Oh, that's mean of you! Where have you put them?

HJALMAR No, honestly. I just didn't remember. But wait a bit! I've got something else for you, Hedvig.
(*Goes across and searches in his overcoat pockets.*)

HEDVIG (*Jumping and clapping her hands.*) Oh, Mother, Mother!

GINA You see, if you just give him time, then—.

HJALMAR (*With a paper.*) See, here it is.

HEDVIG That there? It's only a piece of paper.

HJALMAR It's the list of all the dishes, Hedvig. The complete menu. Here it's written: "Menu." That means the list of dishes.

HEDVIG Don't you have anything else?

HJALMAR No, I forgot all the rest, I tell you. But you can take my word for it: It's not much fun eating all those fancy foods. Go and sit at the table and read out the list and I'll describe how the dishes tasted. Here you are, Hedvig.

HEDVIG (*Swallowing her tears.*) Thanks. (*She sits down, but without reading. Gina signals to her and Hjalmar notices.*)

HJALMAR (*Pacing up and down.*) It's incredible the number of things the breadwinner of a family has to think about, and if he forgets just the least little thing—straightaway he is greeted with sour looks. But—he gets used to *that* as well. (*Standing by the stove next to his father.*) Have you looked in there this evening, Father?

EKDAL Yes, I sure have. She's gone into her basket.

HJALMAR No! Gone into her basket! She's beginning to get used to it.

EKDAL That's right. It's what I said would happen. But now, you see, there's still a few little things to—

HJALMAR Some improvements, you mean.

EKDAL But they've got to be done, you know.

HJALMAR Yes, let's talk a bit about those improvements, Father. Come and sit over here on the sofa.

EKDAL Very well. Hm, I think I'll just fill my pipe first. Might have to clean it, too. Hm. (*He goes into his room.*)

GINA (*Smiling to Hjalmar.*) Clean his pipe, eh!

HJALMAR Ah well, Gina, just let him—poor, shipwrecked old fellow. Yes, those improvements—it's best we start on them tomorrow.

GINA Tomorrow you'll not have time, Ekdal.

HEDVIG (*Interrupting.*) Yes he will, Mother.

GINA Because remember those prints have to be retouched. They've been asking after them so many times.

HJALMAR Oh yes! So it's the prints again! They'll be ready all right. Any new orders as well?

GINA No, I'm afraid. I've just those two portrait sittings, you know.

HJALMAR Nothing else! Well, of course, if you're not willing to make an effort—

GINA What more can I do? I'm putting ads into the papers as much as we can afford, I reckon.

HJALMAR Oh yes, the papers, the papers. You see what good *that* does. And I suppose there's been no one to look at the room, either?

GINA No, not yet.

HJALMAR What else can you expect! If someone doesn't make the effort—. We really have to pull ourselves together, Gina!

HEDVIG (*Going over to him.*) Shall I bring you your flute, Father?

HJALMAR No. No flute. I've no need of any pleasures in this world. (*Pacing about.*) Yes, I'll really be working tomorrow, don't worry. I'll work as long as my strength holds out.

GINA But Ekdal, dear, I didn't mean it like that.

HEDVIG Shall I get you a bottle of beer, Father?

HJALMAR No, certainly not. I'm not in need of any— (*Stops.*) Beer? Was it beer you said?

HEDVIG (*Brightly.*) Yes, Father, lovely, cool beer.

HJALMAR Well—if you absolutely must, you might just bring in a bottle.

GINA Yes, do that. Then it'll be nice and cozy.
    (*Hedvig runs toward the kitchen door.*)

HJALMAR (*By the stove, stops her, looks at her, takes her head in his hands, and presses her to him.*) Hedvig! Hedvig!

HEDVIG (*Happy, in tears.*) Oh, you're a dear, kind father.

HJALMAR No, don't call me that. There I sat, taking my fill at the rich man's table, gorging myself on the sumptuous dishes—! And I couldn't even—

GINA (*Sitting by the table.*) Don't be silly, Ekdal.

HJALMAR It's true! But you mustn't think badly of me. You know I love you, just the same.

HEDVIG (*Throws her arms round him.*) And we love you ever so much too, Father!

HJALMAR And if I should be unreasonable every now and again, then, dear God—remember I'm a man battered by a sea of troubles. Ah well! (*Drying his eyes.*) No beer at such a moment. Bring me my flute. (*Hedvig runs to the bookcase and fetches it.*)

HJALMAR Thanks! That's it. With flute in hand and with you two beside me—ah!
    (*Hedvig sits by the table with Gina. Hjalmar walks up and down, forcefully rendering a Bohemian folk dance, but in a slow, elegiac tempo and with emotional emphasis.*)

HJALMAR (*Breaking off the melody, reaches out his left hand to Gina, saying with much feeling.*) What if it's modest and humble here in this house, Gina. It's still home. And so I say: It's good to be here.

(*He starts playing again. Soon after, there is a knock on the door.*)

GINA (*Getting up.*) Shh, Ekdal—I think someone's at the door. (*She goes to open the front door.*)

GREGERS (*Out in the hall.*) Excuse me—

GINA (*Stepping back.*) Oh no!

GREGERS —is this where Mr. Ekdal the photographer lives?

GINA Yes, it is.

HJALMAR (*Going to the door.*) Gregers! Is that you? Well, come on in.

GREGERS (*Entering.*) I told you I'd drop in on you, didn't I?

HJALMAR But this evening—? Did you leave the party?

GREGERS I left the party and my home. Good evening, Mrs. Ekdal. I don't know if you recognize me?

GINA Oh yes, It's not hard to recognize young Mr. Werle.

GREGERS No, I resemble my mother, and you would certainly remember her.

HJALMAR You've left the house, you said?

GREGERS Yes, I've moved into a hotel.

HJALMAR Is that so? Well, since you're here, take off your coat and sit down.

GREGERS Thanks. (*Takes off his overcoat. He is now dressed in a simple, grey suit cut in countryside style.*)

HJALMAR Here, on the sofa. Make yourself comfortable.
(*Gregers sits on the sofa, Hjalmar on a chair next to the table.*)

GREGERS (*Looking about him.*) So this is where you keep yourself, Hjalmar. You live here, too.

HJALMAR This is the studio, as you can see—

GINA But it's much roomier, so we'd rather sit out here.

HJALMAR We had a better place before. But this apartment has one great advantage—there's so much splendid extra space—

GINA And we've got a room on the other side of the hall we can rent out.

GREGERS (*To Hjalmar.*) I see—so you take in lodgers as well.

HJALMAR No, not just now. It's not as easily done as that. One has to make an effort. (*To Hedvig.*) But what about the beer?
(*Hedvig nods and goes into the kitchen.*)

GREGERS So that's your daughter?

HJALMAR Yes, that's Hedvig.

GREGERS And she's your only child?

HJALMAR She's the only one, yes. She's our greatest joy in the world and— (*Lowers his voice.*) also our deepest sorrow, Gregers.

GREGERS What do you mean?

HJALMAR It's true. Because in all likelihood she's in danger of losing her sight.

GREGERS Going blind?

HJALMAR Yes. So far there's only been the first signs, and it could be all right for some time yet. But the doctor has warned us. It'll happen inevitably.

GREGERS But this is a dreadful misfortune. How did she get like that?

HJALMAR (*Sighing.*) Heredity, apparently.

GREGERS (*Startled.*) Heredity?

GINA Ekdal's mother also had weak eyesight.

HJALMAR Yes, so Father says. I can't remember her myself.

GREGERS Poor child. How does she take it?

HJALMAR Oh, as you can imagine, we can't bring ourselves to tell her. She's no idea of her danger. Happy and carefree, singing like a little bird, she's fluttering into life's eternal night. (*Overcome.*) Oh, it's all so crushingly hard on me, Gregers.
(*Hedvig brings a tray with beer and glasses and sets them on the table.*)

HJALMAR (*Stroking her head.*) Thank you, Hedvig.
(*Hedvig puts her arms round his neck and whispers in his ear.*)

HJALMAR No. No sandwiches just now. (*Looking across.*) Unless Gregers would like some?

GREGERS (*Declining.*) No, no thanks.

HJALMAR (*Continuing dolefully.*) Well, set a few down in here, just the same. If you have a crust, that would do fine. And make sure there's plenty of butter on it.
(*Hedvig nods happily and goes into the kitchen again.*)

GREGERS (*Following her with his eyes.*) She seems strong and healthy otherwise, I think.

GINA Yes, thank God, there's nothing else wrong with her.

GREGERS She'll grow to look like you in time, Mrs. Ekdal. How old must she be, now?

GINA Hedvig's almost exactly fourteen. It's her birthday the day after tomorrow.

GREGERS She's quite big for her age.

GINA Yes, she shot up this last year.

GREGERS Seeing the young grow up, you realize how old you are yourself. How long is it you've been married?

GINA We've been married—let's see, nearly fifteen years.

GREGERS No, imagine. Is it as long as that?

GINA (*Becomes alerted and looks at him.*) Yes, it's as long as that all right.

HJALMAR Yes, that's what it is. Fifteen years, short of a few months. (*Changing the subject.*) They must have been long years for you up there in the works, Gregers.

GREGERS They were long while I lived them. But now, looking back, I hardly know where all the time went.
(*Old Ekdal comes out of his room, without his pipe, but with his old-fashioned officer's cap on his head. His walk is a little unsteady.*)

EKDAL Let's see, Hjalmar, now we can sit down and talk about that—hm. What was it now?

HJALMAR (*Going up to him.*) Father, there's someone here. Gregers Werle—I don't know if you remember him.

EKDAL (*Looking at Gregers, who has got up.*) Werle? Is that the son? What does he want with me?

HJALMAR Nothing. It's me he's come to see.

EKDAL Ah! Then there's nothing the matter?

HJALMAR No, really there's not.

EKDAL (*Swinging his arms.*) Not that I care, you know. I'm not afraid, but—

GREGERS (*Goes up to him.*) I just want to bring you greetings from your old hunting grounds, Lieutenant Ekdal.

EKDAL Hunting grounds?

GREGERS Yes, up there round the Høydal works.

EKDAL Ah yes, up there. I was well known up there, once.

GREGERS In those days you were a great hunter.

EKDAL That I was, yes. It's true. You're looking at my uniform. I don't need anyone's permission to wear it in the house. So long as I don't go out into the street with it on—
(*Hedvig brings a tray of sandwiches, which she sets on the table.*)

HJALMAR Sit down now, Father, and have a glass of beer. Help yourself, Gregers.
(*Ekdal mutters and stumbles over to the sofa. Gregers sits on the chair closest to him. Hjalmar is on the other side of Gregers. Gina sits a little away from the table, sewing. Hedvig stands by her father.*)

GREGERS Do you remember, Lieutenant Ekdal, when Hjalmar and I used to go up and visit you in the summers and at Christmas?

EKDAL Did you? No, no, no, I can't say I remember that. But I *can* say I've been a first-rate hunter. Shot bears, too. As many as nine.

GREGERS (*Looks sympathetically at him.*) And now you don't hunt anymore?

EKDAL Oh, I wouldn't say that, lad. I do my hunting every now and then. Of course, not in the old way. Because the forests, you see—the forests, the forests—! (*Drinks.*) Everything's fine with the forest up there?

GREGERS Not as healthy as in your day. They've cut into it a lot.

EKDAL Cut into it? (*Softly as if scared.*) That's a dangerous business.
It brings trouble. The forests take their revenge.

HJALMAR (*Filling his glass.*) Here we are: just a little more, Father.

GREGERS How can a man like you—someone who belongs to the
world outdoors—live in the middle of a stuffy town, inside
these four walls?

EKDAL (*Laugh briefly and glances at Hjalmar.*) Oh, it's not so bad
here. Not bad at all.

GREGERS But all those things your mind grew up with. The feel
of the cool wind, the free life in the forests and mountains,
among the animals and birds—

EKDAL (*Smiling.*) Hjalmar, shall we show him?

HJALMAR (*Quickly, a little embarrassed.*) Oh no, no Father. Not tonight.

GREGERS What does he want to show me?

HJALMAR It's only something that—that you can see another time.

GREGERS (*Continuing to the old man.*) This is what I had in mind,
Lieutenant Ekdal: you ought to come with me up to the
Works, because I'll be leaving very soon. You can just as easily
get copying work up there. And there's nothing in the world
down here to give you much pleasure, or much sense of life.

EKDAL (*Staring astonished at him.*) Nothing in the world to—!

GREGERS Of course, you have Hjalmar. But he's got his own family.
And a man like you, who's always felt drawn to what is wild
and free, is—

EKDAL (*Strikes the table.*) Hjalmar, now he's got to see it!

HJALMAR But Father, is it worth it just now? It's so dark—

EKDAL Nonsense. There's the moonlight. (*Gets up.*) He's got to see
it, I tell you. Let me pass. Come and help me, Hjalmar.

HEDVIG Yes, let's do it, Father!

HJALMAR (*Getting up.*) Oh, very well.

GREGERS (*To Gina.*) What is it?

GINA You mustn't expect anything so very special.

(*Ekdal and Hjalmar have gone to the rear wall and each slides
one of the double doors aside, Hedvig helping old Ekdal. Gregers
remains standing by the sofa. Gina sits unconcerned and sewing.
Through the door opening can be seen a large, long, irregularly
shaped loft with recesses and a pair of freestanding stove pipes.
Bright moonlight falls through skylights on some parts of the
room while others remain in deep shadow.*)

EKDAL (*To Gregers.*) Come right over here.

GREGERS (*Walks over to him.*) Just what is it?

EKDAL Take a look and see. Hm.

HJALMAR (*Rather embarrassed.*) All this belongs to Father, you
understand.

GREGERS (*At the doorway, looking into the loft.*) So you keep poultry, Lieutenant Ekdal.

EKDAL I should think we *do* keep poultry. They've flown up to roost just now. You'll need to see the poultry by daylight.

HEDVIG And then there's—

EKDAL Shh, shh. Don't say anything just yet.

GREGERS And you keep pigeons, too, I see.

EKDAL Ah, yes. You could certainly say we keep pigeons! They've got their nesting boxes up there under the rafters. Because pigeons like to roost high up, you know.

HJALMAR Some are not just ordinary pigeons.

EKDAL Ordinary! No, you can be sure of that! We have tumblers. And a pair of pouters, as well. But come over here. Can you see that hutch over there by the wall?

GREGERS Yes. What do you use that for?

EKDAL That's where the rabbits lie at night, young fellow.

GREGERS No! So you've got rabbits, as well?

EKDAL Yes, you can be sure as hell we've got rabbits. He's asking if we've got rabbits, do you hear, Hjalmar? Hm. But now comes the real thing, just wait. Here it is! Move away, Hedvig. Now come and stand here, just so, and then look down there. Can you see a basket with straw in it?

GREGERS Yes. And I can see a bird lying in it.

EKDAL Hm—"a bird"—

GREGERS Isn't it a duck?

EKDAL (*Offended.*) Yes, of course it's a duck.

HJALMAR But what kind of duck, do you suppose?

HEDVIG It's not just any ordinary duck—

EKDAL Shh!

GREGERS And it isn't a turkish duck, either.

EKDAL No, Mr.—Werle. That's no turkish duck. It's a wild duck.

GREGERS No, is it really? A *wild* duck?

EKDAL Yes, that's what it is. The "bird," as you called it, it's a wild duck. It's our wild duck, young fellow.

HEDVIG My wild duck. It belongs to me.

GREGERS And it can live up here in the attic? And thrive here?

EKDAL Well, you see, she's got a trough of water to splash about in.

HJALMAR Fresh water every other day.

GINA (*Turning to Hjalmar.*) Ekdal, dear, it's getting freezing in here.

EKDAL Hm. Let's close it then. It's better not to disturb them when they're resting for the night, anyway. Give us a hand, Hedvig. (*Hjalmar and Hedvig slide the loft doors shut.*)

EKDAL You can get a proper look at her another time. (*Sits in the armchair by the stove.*) Yes, wild ducks—they're really very remarkable, let me tell you.

GREGERS But how did you manage to catch it, Lieutenant Ekdal?

EKDAL Didn't catch it, myself. There's a certain man here in town we can thank for that.

GREGERS (*Starting slightly.*) That man would never be my father, would he?

EKDAL That's it, precisely. Your father's who it was. Hm.

HJALMAR It's odd you should guess that, Gregers.

GREGERS Well, you told me earlier how you owed so much to my father, so I thought that—

GINA But we didn't get the duck from Mr. Werle himself—

EKDAL It's Håkon Werle we can thank for her just the same, Gina. (*To Gregers.*) He was out in his boat, you see. And then he shot at her. But his eyesight is not so good now, your father's. Hm. So she was only winged.

GREGERS I see. She got a couple of slugs in her.

EKDAL Right, she caught two or three.

HEDVIG She caught them under the wing and couldn't fly.

GREGERS So she dived right down to the bottom, is that it?

EKDAL (*Sleepily, his voice thick.*) You can bet on it. Always do, wild ducks. Dive right to the bottom, deep as they can, young fellow. Bite fast into the weeds and waste—all the devil's mess down there. And they never come up again.

GREGERS But, Lieutenant Ekdal, your wild duck *did* come up again.

EKDAL He had such an extraordinarily clever dog, your father. And that dog—it dived right down and fetched her up again.

GREGERS (*Turning to Hjalmar.*) And then you brought her here?

HJALMAR Not straightaway. First she went to your father's house. But she didn't thrive there, so Pettersen was given orders to do away with her.

EKDAL (*Half asleep.*) Hm. Pettersen, that idiot—

HJALMAR (*More quietly.*) That's the way we got her, you see. For Father knew Pettersen slightly, and when he heard all this about the wild duck he set about getting her for himself.

GREGERS So she's thriving wonderfully well, here in the attic?

HJALMAR Yes, incredibly well. She's even become plump. She's been so long in there she's forgotten her natural, wild life. And that's the main thing, of course.

GREGERS You're surely right there, Hjalmar. Just never let her catch a glimpse of the sea or sky—. But I ought not stay longer, for I believe your father's asleep.

HJALMAR Oh, don't go for that reason—

GREGERS But, by the way—you said you had a room to let—a spare room.

HJALMAR That's right, why? You know someone perhaps—?

GREGERS Could *I* have the room?

HJALMAR You?

GINA No, not *you*, Mr. Werle—

GREGERS May I have the room? I could move in first thing tomorrow.

HJALMAR Yes, with the greatest of pleasure—

GINA But Mr. Werle, it's just not the sort of room for you.

HJALMAR Gina, how can you say that?

GINA Well, because it isn't big enough or light enough, and—

GREGERS I'm not so particular about that, Mrs. Ekdal.

HJALMAR I think it's quite a pleasant room, and not so badly furnished, either.

GINA But think of those two who live down below.

GREGERS Which two are they?

GINA Well, there's the one who's been a private tutor—

HJALMAR That's Molvik, who was at university—

GINA —and then there's a doctor called Relling.

GREGERS Relling? I know him slightly. He practiced up at Høydal for a while.

GINA They're a really wild pair, the two of them. Out living it up night after night. And when they get back, late, they're not always so—

GREGERS One soon gets used to these things. Let's hope it will be the same with me as it is with the wild duck—

GINA Hm. I think you ought to sleep on it first, just the same.

GREGERS You don't seem very keen on having me in the house, Mrs. Ekdal.

GINA Lord, whatever makes you think that?

HJALMAR Yes, Gina, you're behaving very strangely. (*To Gregers.*) But tell me, are you thinking of staying in town for a while?

GREGERS (*Putting on his overcoat.*) Yes, now I'm thinking of staying.

HJALMAR But not at home with your father? What do you intend doing with yourself?

GREGERS Ah, if only I knew *that*, Hjalmar, then maybe I could put up with life better. But if you once have to carry the cross of being called Gregers—"Gregers" and then "Werle" on top of that! Have you ever heard anything so revolting?

HJALMAR But I don't think that at all.

GREGERS Ugh! I'd like to spit on a fellow with a name like that. But once you've carried the cross of being Gregers Werle in this world the way I have—

HJALMAR (*Laughing.*) Ha-ha! If you weren't Gregers Werle, what would you like to be?

GREGERS If I could choose, I'd like best to be a clever dog.

GINA A dog!

HEDVIG (*Involuntarily.*) Oh, no!

GREGERS Yes, an extraordinarily clever dog. One that goes to the
bottom after wild ducks when they dive and bite fast to all the
weeds and waste down in the mud.

HJALMAR You know what, Gregers—I don't understand a single
word of this.

GREGERS Ah well, there's probably not much meaning in it, anyway. So, tomorrow morning, early then—I'll be moving in. (*To
Gina.*) You'll find I'll give you no trouble: I do everything for
myself. (*To Hjalmar.*) We'll talk about the rest tomorrow. Good
night, Mrs. Ekdal. (*Nodding to Hedvig.*) Good night!

GINA Good night, Mr. Werle.

HEDVIG Good night.

HJALMAR (*Who has lit a candle.*) Wait a moment. I'll light your way.
It's bound to be dark on the stairs.

(*Gregers and Hjalmar go out through the entrance door.*)

GINA (*Staring ahead, her sewing on her lap.*) Wasn't that a queer
thing to say—that he wanted to be a dog.

HEDVIG I'll tell you something, Mother. I believe he meant something quite different by that.

GINA What on earth could *that* be?

HEDVIG I don't know: But it was as if he meant something different
than what he was saying—the whole time.

GINA You think so? Well it *was* strange.

HJALMAR (*Returning.*) The lamp was still burning. (*Extinguishes the
candle and sets it down.*) Ah, at last a man can get a bite to eat.
(*Starts eating the bread and butter.*) There, you see, Gina—if
one just makes the effort, then—

GINA How "make the effort?"

HJALMAR Well, it was lucky just the same that at last we got the
room rented. And just imagine, to a man like Gregers Werle, a
dear old friend.

GINA Oh, I'm not sure what to say, myself.

HEDVIG Ah, Mother, you'll see! It will be lovely.

HJALMAR You really are very peculiar, Gina. Before, you were so eager to get the room rented. And now you don't like it.

GINA True, Ekdal, if only it could have been someone else. What
do you think Mr. Werle will say?

HJALMAR Old Werle? It's none of his business.

GINA But you can be sure there's some bad blood between them
again, seeing the young one's left the house. You know well
enough what it's like between those two.

HJALMAR Maybe you're right, but—

GINA And perhaps Mr. Werle will think that you're behind it, this
time.

HJALMAR Let him think what he likes. Mr. Werle has done a good deal for me, God knows. I admit it. But that doesn't mean I'm to be beholden to him for all eternity.

GINA But Ekdal, dear. It could work out badly for Grandfather. Perhaps he'll lose the little money he gets working for Grå-berg.

HJALMAR I was on the point of saying, a good thing too. Isn't it humiliating for a man like me to see his grey-haired father treated as an outcast. But now the fullness of time will come, I believe. (*Takes another sandwich.*) As truly as I've a mission in life, so I shall fulfill it.

HEDVIG Oh yes, Father. Do it!

GINA Shh. Careful you don't wake him.

HJALMAR (*More softly.*) I shall fulfill it, I tell you. A day will come at last when—and that's why it's so good we rented the room, because now I'm more independently situated. A man's got to be that when he has a mission in life. (*Over by the armchair, greatly affected.*) Poor, old, white-haired Father. Trust in your Hjalmar. He has broad shoulders—strong shoulders, at any rate. A great day will come when you'll wake up and—(*To Gina.*) Don't you believe it?

GINA (*Getting up.*) Yes, of course I do. But let's first see about getting him to bed.

HJALMAR Yes, let's do that.

(*Carefully, they lift the old man.*)

Act Three

Hjalmar Ekdal's studio. It is morning; the daylight is falling through the great windows in the sloping roof. The curtain is drawn back.

Hjalmar is sitting by the table engaged in retouching a photograph. Several other photographs lie before him. Soon after, Gina enters through the hall door in her hat and coat, a basket with a lid over her arm.

HJALMAR Back already, Gina?

GINA Yes, I'll have to be quick about it. (*Places the basket on a chair and takes off her hat and coat.*)

HJALMAR Did you look in on Gregers?

GINA O-oh yes, I sure did! And a fine sight it is in there. He's certainly made it cozy for himself as soon as he moved in.

HJALMAR He has?

GINA Yes. He wanted to do everything for himself, he said. So he decides to light the stove, and naturally turns down the

damper so that the whole room's filled with smoke. Uff. There
was such a stink, just like—

HJALMAR Oh, no!

GINA Oh, yes! But now comes the best part. Because then he wants
to put it out and so he empties his washbasin into the stove—
and now the whole floor's the most awful mess.

HJALMAR How tiresome.

GINA I got the janitor's wife to clean up after him, the pig. But it
won't be fit to enter again till this afternoon.

HJALMAR What's he done with himself since?

GINA He's going out for a while, he said.

HJALMAR I looked in on him for a moment, just after you left.

GINA So I heard. You've gone and asked him up for lunch.

HJALMAR Just a little snack, you understand. It's his first day; we
can't really not ask him. You've always got something in the
house.

GINA I'll see what I can find.

HJALMAR Don't let it be too stingy. Relling and Molvik are coming
up here too, I believe. I just met Relling on the stairs, you see,
so I had to—

GINA What, we're going to have that pair as well?

HJALMAR Good Lord! A couple more or less won't make much difference.

EKDAL (*Opens his door and looks in.*) Listen, Hjalmar. (*Notices
Gina.*) Um, Ah.

GINA Something you want, Grandfather?

EKDAL No, no. It doesn't matter. Hm! (*Goes back in.*)

GINA (*Picking up basket.*) Keep an eye on him, so he doesn't go out.

HJALMAR Yes, yes, I'll do that. Listen, Gina, a little herring salad
would be a good idea. Relling and Molvik were out on a bender
last night.

GINA Just as long as they don't get in the way before—

HJALMAR They won't do that. Just take your time.

GINA Yes, all right. And then meantime you can work a bit more.

HJALMAR I'm sitting here working. I'm working as hard as I can!

GINA Then you'll have *that* off your hands, you see. (*Goes to the
kitchen with her basket. Hjalmar sits for a while working on the
photographs with a brush, clearly disliking the work.*)

EKDAL (*Peers in, looks around the studio and says quietly.*) You busy,
Hjalmar?

HJALMAR Yes, I'm sitting here, wrestling with these pictures—

EKDAL Well, well, God help us, if you're as busy as all that, then—
Hm. (*He goes in again; the door remains open.*)

HJALMAR (*Continuing a while in silence. Then he lays down the
brush and goes over to the door.*) Are you busy, Father?

EKDAL (*Grumbling from within.*) Well, since you're so busy, I'm busy too. Hm!

HJALMAR Very well. (*Goes back to his work.*)

EKDAL (*Soon after, appears in the doorway again.*) Hm. Look, Hjalmar, I'm not really as busy as all that.

HJALMAR I thought you were sitting in there, copying.

EKDAL What the hell, can't he—can't that Gråberg—wait a day or two? No one's life depends on it.

HJALMAR No, and you're nobody's slave, either.

EKDAL And then there's that other thing in there—

HJALMAR Yes, that's just it. Do you want to go in? Shall I open it for you?

EKDAL Wouldn't really be a bad idea.

HJALMAR (*Getting up.*) For then you'll have *that* off your hands.

EKDAL That's right. Then it'll be ready for tomorrow. Because it *is* tomorrow, isn't it? Hm!

HJALMAR Tomorrow it is.

(*Hjalmar and Ekdal each slides his half-door open. The morning sun shines through the skylights. Some pigeons fly back and forth, others are cooing from the rafters. Hens cackle now and then farther within the loft.*)

HJALMAR Now you can go ahead, Father.

EKDAL (*Going inside.*) Aren't you coming in?

HJALMAR Yes, you know what—I rather think— (*Sees Gina in the kitchen doorway.*) Me? No, I haven't time—I've got to work. But, now with our contraption— (*He pulls a cord, and inside the door a curtain descends. The lower part consists of a strip of old sailcloth; the rest, above, a piece of fishing net, stretched taut. The floor of the loft is thus no longer visible.*)

HJALMAR (*Returning to the table.*) There! Now perhaps I can sit in peace for a while.

GINA Must he be in there rampaging around again?

HJALMAR Perhaps you'd think it better if he slipped off to Madam Erickson's! (*Sitting.*) Is there anything you want? You were going to say—

GINA I was only going to ask if you think we can set the table in here.

HJALMAR Yes, for I don't suppose there are any appointments this early?

GINA No. Just those two sweethearts who want to be taken together.

HJALMAR Damn! Why can't they be taken another day!

GINA Now, Ekdal dear, I've booked them after lunch, when you'll be sleeping.

HJALMAR Ah, that's fine then. Yes, let's eat in here.

GINA All right. But there's no need to hurry laying the table. You can still use it for a while yet.

HJALMAR I would have thought you could see I'm using the table as much as I can.

GINA And then you'll be free later, you see. (*Returns to the kitchen.*) (*Brief pause.*)

EKDAL (*In the loft door, behind the net.*) Hjalmar!

HJALMAR Well?

EKDAL I'm afraid we're going to have to move the water trough after all.

HJALMAR Yes, that's what I've been saying all along.

EKDAL Hm—hm—hm. (*Disappears behind the door again. Hjalmar continues working a little, glancing at the loft. He half rises. Hedvig enters from the kitchen. Hjalmar hastily sits down again.*)

HJALMAR What is it you want?

HEDVIG I just wanted to be with you, Father.

HJALMAR (*After a pause.*) I think you're here snooping around. Are you spying, perhaps?

HEDVIG No, really I'm not.

HJALMAR What's your mother now up to out there?

HEDVIG Oh, Mother's halfway through the herring salad. (*Goes over to the table.*) Isn't there any little thing I could help you with, Father?

HJALMAR No, no. It's best I do all this alone—as long as my strength holds out. No need for you, Hedvig, as long as your father keeps his health.

HEDVIG Please, Father! You mustn't say such horrid things. (*She wanders around a while, stops by the door opening and looks into the loft.*)

HJALMAR What's he up to in there?

HEDVIG Seems like a new path to the water trough.

HJALMAR There's no way in this world he can manage that by himself. And I'm condemned to sit here!

HEDVIG (*Going to him.*) Give me the brush, Father. I can do it.

HJALMAR Nonsense. You'll only ruin your eyes.

HEDVIG Of course I won't. Give me the brush.

HJALMAR (*Getting up.*) All right. It'll only be for a minute or two.

HEDVIG Huh! What does that matter? (*Takes the brush.*) There we go! (*Sits down.*) Here's one I can work on.

HJALMAR Just don't ruin your eyes, do you hear! I'll not take any responsibility. You must take the responsibility yourself. I'm warning you.

HEDVIG (*Retouching.*) Yes, yes. I will.

HJALMAR You're such a clever girl, Hedvig. Just a couple of minutes, you understand. (*He slips past the edge of the curtain into the loft. Hedvig sits at her work. Hjalmar and Ekdal can be heard arguing inside.*)

HJALMAR (*Appearing behind the net.*) Hedvig, hand me those pliers off the shelf. And the chisel, too. (*Turns back to the loft.*) Now you'll see, Father. Just give me the chance to show you what I mean!

(*Hedvig has fetched the tools from the shelf and hands them in to him.*)

HJALMAR Thanks. Yes, it's just as well I came, you know.

(*He goes from the door opening; hammering and talking are heard inside. Hedvig stands and watches them. Soon after, there is a knock on the entrance door. She does not hear it. Gregers Werle, bareheaded and without an overcoat, stands near the door.*)

GREGERS Hm—!

HEDVIG (*Turns and goes to him.*) Good morning. Please, come in.

GREGERS Thanks. (*Looks over at the loft.*) Sounds like you've got workmen in the house.

HEDVIG No, it's only Father and Grandfather. I'll go tell them.

GREGERS No, no, don't do that. I'd rather wait a little. (*Sits on the sofa.*)

HEDVIG It's such a mess, here— (*Starts clearing away the photographs.*)

GREGERS No, leave them. Are those photographs waiting to be finished?

HEDVIG Yes, they're some I'm helping Father with.

GREGERS Don't let me disturb you at all.

HEDVIG Oh, no. (*She settles the things around her again and settles down to work. Gregers watches her in silence.*)

GREGERS Did the wild duck sleep well last night?

HEDVIG Yes, thank you. I'm sure she did.

GREGERS (*Turning toward the loft.*) By daylight it looks quite different than yesterday in the moonlight.

HEDVIG Yes, it changes all the time. In the morning it's different from in the afternoon. And when it rains it's quite different from when it's fine.

GREGERS So you've noticed that, have you?

HEDVIG Yes, you can't help seeing.

GREGERS Do you also like being in there with the wild duck?

HEDVIG Yes, when there's a chance, then—

GREGERS But of course you don't have much spare time. You're going to school, aren't you?

HEDVIG No, not any more. Father's afraid I'll ruin my eyes.

GREGERS So he gives you lessons himself.

HEDVIG Father's promised me he'll give me lessons. But he's not had time to, so far.

GREGERS But isn't there anyone else who can help you a little?

HEDVIG Yes, there's Mr. Molvik. But he's not always quite, well, properly—

GREGERS He's often drunk?

HEDVIG He certainly is.

GREGERS So then you've got time for all sorts of things. And in there, it's really like a world of its own, I imagine?

HEDVIG Completely of its own. And then there are so many strange things.

GREGERS Such as?

HEDVIG Well, there are big cupboards with books in them. And in many of the books there are pictures.

GREGERS Aha!

HEDVIG And then there's an old cabinet with drawers and compartments in it, and a big clock with figures which are supposed to come out. But the clock doesn't go any longer.

GREGERS So time has come to a stop in there—where the wild duck lives.

HEDVIG Yes. And then there are old paint boxes and things like that. And all the books.

GREGERS And do your read these books?

HEDVIG Oh yes, when I can. But most of them are in English, which I don't understand. But I do look at the pictures. There's one very big book called *Harrison's History of London*. It must be a hundred years old and it has a tremendous number of pictures in it. In the front there's a picture of Death with an hourglass and a girl. I think it's horrible. But then there're all the other pictures with churches and castles and streets and big ships sailing on the sea.

GREGERS But tell me, where did you get all these treasures from?

HEDVIG Well, once an old sea captain used to live here and he brought them home. They called him "The flying Dutchman" —which is strange, because he wasn't a Dutchman at all.

GREGERS He wasn't?

HEDVIG No. And then he went away for good. And so all these things just stayed here after him.

GREGERS Listen, tell me now. When you're sitting in there looking at the pictures, don't you ever wish to get away and see the great big real world for yourself?

HEDVIG Oh no! I want to stay at home always and help Father and Mother.

GREGERS Retouching photographs?

HEDVIG No, not only that. Most of all I'd like to learn to engrave pictures, like those in the English books.

GREGERS Hm. What does your father say to that?

HEDVIG I don't think Father would like it. He's so funny about such things. Just think, he said I should learn basket weaving and wickerwork! But I really don't think that can amount to much.

GREGERS No, I don't think so either.

HEDVIG But Father was right when he said if I'd learned basket-weaving, I could have made the new basket for the wild duck.

GREGERS You could have done, yes. And you're the one most concerned.

HEDVIG Yes, because it's my wild duck.

GREGERS Yes, it really is.

HEDVIG Because it belongs to me. But Father and Grandfather can borrow it any time they like.

GREGERS Really? What do they do with it?

HEDVIG They take care of it and build things for it—that sort of thing.

GREGERS I can see why. The wild duck's quite the aristocrat in there.

HEDVIG Yes, she is. For she's a real wild bird. And it's so sad for her. She has no one to keep her company, poor thing.

GREGERS No family, like the rabbits.

HEDVIG No. There's lots of hens and they've been together since they were chicks. But she's been completely cut off from all her companions. And then there's all this mystery about the wild duck. No one knows her, or where she comes from, either.

GREGERS And then she's been to the depths of the sea.

HEDVIG (Glances quickly at him, suppresses a smile and asks.) Why do you say "the depths of the sea"?

GREGERS What should I have said?

HEDVIG You could have said, "the seabed" or "the floor of the sea."

GREGERS But can't I just as well say the "depths of the sea?"

HEDVIG Yes, but for me it's so strange to hear anyone else say "the depths of the sea."

GREGERS Why is that? Come, tell me why.

HEDVIG No, I can't. Because it's so stupid.

GREGERS It isn't at all. Tell me then, why did you smile?

HEDVIG It's because if at any time I suddenly—all at once—find myself remembering what's in there—then I always think that the whole room and everything in it's called "the depths of the sea." But that's so stupid.

GREGERS You shouldn't say that.

HEDVIG Yes, because it's only an attic.

GREGERS (*Looking intently at her.*) Are you so sure of that?

HEDVIG (*Astonished.*) That it's an attic?

GREGERS Yes. Are you so sure of that?

> (*Hedvig, in silence, looks at him with open mouth. Gina enters from the kitchen with things for the table.*)

GREGERS (*Getting up.*) I'm afraid I've come too early.

GINA Well, you've got to be somewhere. Anyway, everything's nearly ready.

> (*Hedvig clears up. She and Gina lay the table during the following. Gregers sits in an armchair and leafs through an album.*)

GREGERS I gather you can do retouching, Mrs. Ekdal.

GINA (*With a side glance.*) Oh yes, I can do that.

GREGERS That was really very lucky.

GINA Why lucky?

GREGERS Since Ekdal became a photographer, I mean.

HEDVIG Mother can take photographs, too.

GINA Oh, yes. I even managed to learn *that* art.

GREGERS So maybe it's you who runs the business?

GINA Yes, when Ekdal can't spare time himself—

GREGERS He's so taken up with his father, I imagine.

GINA Yes. And then, it's no job for a man like Ekdal going about taking pictures of just any old riffraff.

GREGERS That's what I think, too. But now that he's taken up that line of work—

GINA Mr. Werle, you must understand that Ekdal is not one of your ordinary photographers.

GREGERS Well, perhaps not. But— (*A shot is fired inside the loft.*)

GREGERS (*Jumps up.*) What's that?

GINA Uff! Now they're shooting again.

GREGERS They shoot as well?

HEDVIG They go out hunting.

GREGERS What on earth—! (*Goes to the loft door.*) Are you hunting, Hjalmar?

HJALMAR (*Behind the net.*) So you're here? I'd no idea. I was so involved— (*To Hedvig.*) And you never told us! (*Comes into the studio.*)

GREGERS You go shooting in the loft?

HJALMAR (*Showing a double-barreled pistol.*) Oh, only with this.

GINA Yes. You and Grandfather will go and have an accident one day with that piston.

HJALMAR (*Irritably.*) I think I've already told you this firearm is called a pistol.

GINA That doesn't make it any better, as far as I can see.

GREGERS So you've also become a hunter, Hjalmar?

HJALMAR Just a little rabbit hunting once in a while. It's mostly for Father's sake, you know.

GINA Men are really so peculiar. They always need something to diverse themselves with.

HJALMAR (*Angrily.*) Yes, that's right. We always need something to divert ourselves with.

GINA Well, that's exactly what I said.

HJALMAR Oh, well! (*To Gregers.*) So, as you can see, we're really lucky that the loft is so placed that no one hears us when we're shooting. (*Puts the pistol on the shelf.*) Don't touch the pistol, Hedvig! One of the barrels is loaded. Remember that.

GREGERS (*Looking through the net.*) You've got a shotgun, too, I see.

HJALMAR That's Father's old shotgun. You can't shoot with it any more; there's something wrong with the lock. But it's quite nice to have it, just the same: We can take it to pieces and clean it once in a while and grease it with bone marrow and put it together again. Of course, it's mostly Father who fiddles around with such things.

HEDVIG (*Going to Gregers.*) Now you can really see the wild duck.

GREGERS I'm looking at it. She's trailing a little in one wing, I think.

HJALMAR Well, that's hardly surprising. That's where she was shot.

GREGERS And she's dragging a little on one foot. Isn't that right?

HJALMAR Perhaps just a little bit.

HEDVIG You see it was in the foot the dog bit her.

HJALMAR But she's hale and healthy otherwise. And that's really remarkable for one that's had a charge of shot in her body and who's been held in the jaws of a dog—

GREGERS (*With a glance at Hedvig.*) And has been in the depths of the sea—for so long.

HEDVIG (*Smiling.*) Yes.

GINA That blessed wild duck! There's been more than enough crucifying over her.

HJALMAR Hm! Will lunch soon be ready?

GINA Any minute now. Hedvig, you must come and help me now. (*Gina and Hedvig go into the kitchen.*)

HJALMAR (*Half aloud.*) It's best not to stand there watching Father. He doesn't like it. (*Gregers moves away from the loft doorway.*) And I'd better close up now, for the others are coming. (*Waving his hands to chase the birds back.*) Shoo! Shoo! Off you go! (*Lifting the curtain and pulling the doors shut.*) This gadget is my own invention. It's really great fun having something like this to take care of and to repair when it gets broken. In any case, it's absolutely essential, you see, because Gina doesn't like having rabbits and hens in the studio.

GREGERS Of course not. And it's your wife who has the managing of it.

HJALMAR I leave the running of the routine matters to her, because then I can retire to the living room and give my mind to the really important things.

GREGERS What things are these, Hjalmar?

HJALMAR I'm surprised you haven't asked about that before. Or maybe you haven't heard about the invention?

GREGERS Invention? No.

HJALMAR Really? You haven't? Ah well, up there in the forests and wilderness—

GREGERS So you've come up with an invention!

HJALMAR Not exactly completed it yet, but I'm working on it. You can well imagine that when I decided to dedicate myself to photography, it wasn't merely to set about taking pictures of a collection of local nonentities.

GREGERS No, no. Your wife said the same thing just now.

HJALMAR I swore if I devoted my powers to this calling, I would raise it to a level where it would become at the same time both an art and a science. And so I decided to create this remarkable invention.

GREGERS What's the nature of this invention? What's its function?

HJALMAR Ah, my dear Gregers, you mustn't ask for details just yet. It takes time, you see. And you mustn't think it's vanity that's driving me. I'm certainly not working for my own sake. No, I have a life's mission that I see before me night and day.

GREGERS What life's mission?

HJALMAR Do you forget the silver-haired old man?

GREGERS Your poor father, yes. But what can you actually do for him?

HJALMAR I can resurrect his self-respect—by restoring the Ekdal name to honor and dignity again.

GREGERS So that's your life's mission?

HJALMAR Yes, I will rescue that shipwrecked man. For shipwrecked was what he was when the storm broke over him. When that terrible inquiry was held, he was no longer himself. That pistol over there, Gregers, the one we use to shoot rabbits with, *that* has played a role in the dreadful Ekdal tragedy.

GREGERS The pistol! How?

HJALMAR When the judgement was pronounced and he was about to go to prison, he held that pistol in his hand.

GREGERS He did—!

HJALMAR Yes, but he didn't dare. He was a coward. So destroyed and broken in spirit he'd become by then! Can you imagine it? He, a military man, who had shot nine bears and who was descended from two lieutenant colonels—one after the other, of course—. Can you imagine it, Gregers?

GREGERS Yes, I can imagine it very well.

HJALMAR I can't. That pistol featured once again in our family history. When he was clad in the grey uniform of a convict and sat under lock and key—ah, that was a terrible time for me, I can tell you. I had the blinds drawn down on both windows. When I peeped out the sun was shining just as usual. I couldn't understand that. I saw people walking in the street, laughing and chatting about trivial things. I couldn't understand it. I thought the whole of existence should have come to a stop as if under an eclipse.

GREGERS That's how I felt when my mother died.

HJALMAR In such an hour Hjalmar Ekdal put the pistol to his own breast.

GREGERS You also thought of—

HJALMAR Yes.

GREGERS But you didn't shoot?

HJALMAR No. At the decisive moment I won a victory over myself. I chose to live. But, you must know, it takes courage to choose life on those terms.

GREGERS Well, that depends on how you look at it.

HJALMAR Yes, no doubt about it. And it was all for the best. Because soon I'll finish my invention and then, Doctor Relling believes, as well as I do, that Father will be allowed to wear his uniform again. I'll demand it as my only reward.

GREGERS So it's about the uniform he's so—

HJALMAR Yes, that's what he most yearns for and dreams of. You can't imagine how my heart bleeds for him. Every time we hold a little family celebration—like Gina and my wedding anniversary—then the old fellow comes in, dressed in the uniform from his happier days. But there need only be a knock on the door—because he daren't show himself in front of strangers—and then he scuttles off to his room again as fast as his old legs can carry him. A spectacle like that, Gregers, can break a son's heart.

GREGERS How soon, roughly, do you think the invention will be ready?

HJALMAR Good Lord! You mustn't ask me about details like time. An invention's not something one has complete control over. A great part of it is inspiration, intuition, and it's almost impossible to tell in advance when that will happen.

GREGERS But it *is* making progress?

HJALMAR Certainly it's making progress. I wrestle with the invention every day. It obsesses me. Every afternoon, after I've eaten, I shut myself in the living room where I can concentrate in peace. But I mustn't be rushed, that will do no good. Relling says the same thing.

GREGERS And you don't think all these distractions in the loft draw you away from your work and scatter your concentration?

HJALMAR No, no. On the contrary. You mustn't say such things. I can't be always and eternally brooding on the same, exhausting problem. I need to have something on the side to occupy the waiting periods between. Inspiration, intuition, you see, when it comes, it comes of its own accord.

GREGERS My dear Hjalmar, I almost believe you have something of the wild duck in you.

HJALMAR The wild duck? How do you mean?

GREGERS You have dived down to the sea bed and bitten into the weeds there.

HJALMAR I take it you're talking about the almost fatal shot that wounded Father in the wing—and me too.

GREGERS Not primarily. I wouldn't say you're wounded, but you've ended up in a poisoned swamp, Hjalmar. You've picked up an insidious disease and so you've gone down to die in the dark.

HJALMAR Me? Die in the dark! Now see here, Gregers, you really must stop that kind of talk.

GREGERS Not to worry. I'm going to see that you rise up again. Because I now have a purpose in life, you see. I found that out yesterday.

HJALMAR That might be the case, but you'll kindly leave me out of it. I can assure you that—apart from a quite understandable melancholy—I find myself as content as any man could wish.

GREGERS That's also due to the poison.

HJALMAR My dear Gregers, no more of this talk of disease and poison. I'm not at all used to this kind of conversation. In my house we never talk about unpleasant things.

GREGERS No, I can easily believe that.

HJALMAR Because it doesn't do me any good. And here there's no swamp gas, as you call it. In the humble photographer's home, I know well enough the roof might be low—and my means only modest. But I am an inventor, my friend, and I'm also the family breadwinner. This raises me above my petty circumstances. Ah! Here they come with the lunch.

(*Gina and Hedvig bring in bottles of beer, a brandy decanter, glasses, and other things for the lunch. At the same time Relling and Molvik enter from the hallway. Both are without hat or overcoat. Molvik is dressed in black.*)

GINA (*Setting the things on the table.*) Well, you two know the right time to come.

RELLING Molvik got the idea he could smell herring salad, and so there was no stopping him. Good morning for the second time, Ekdal.

HJALMAR Gregers, may I introduce you to Mr. Molvik, and Doctor —but you know Relling, don't you?

GREGERS Yes, slightly.

RELLING Ah, it's Werle junior. Yes, we two have had our skirmishes up at the Høydal Works. You've just moved in?

GREGERS I moved in this morning.

RELLING Well Molvik and I live down below, so if you're in need of doctor or priest you don't have far to go.

GREGERS Thanks, it could happen. Yesterday we were thirteen at table.

HJALMAR Oh, don't bring up that unpleasant subject again!

RELLING No need to worry, Ekdal. It won't affect you.

HJALMAR I hope not, for my family's sake. But let's sit down and eat, drink, and be merry.

GREGERS Shouldn't we wait for your father?

HJALMAR No, he'll have his in his room later. Let's start.

(*The men sit down at the table and begin eating and drinking. Gina and Hedvig go in and out, waiting on them.*)

RELLING Molvik was properly plastered last night, Mrs. Ekdal.

GINA What? Last night again?

RELLING Didn't you hear when I brought him home in the night?

GINA No, I can't say I did.

RELLING That was lucky. Because last night Molvik was pretty foul.

GINA Is that true, Mr. Molvik?

MOLVIK Let us draw a veil over last night's proceedings. Such things bear absolutely no relation to my better self.

RELLING (*To Gregers.*) It just comes over him like an irresistible impulse and then I have to go out on the town with him. Because Mr. Molvik is demonic, you see.

GREGERS Demonic?

RELLING No doubt about it: Molvik is demonic.

GREGERS Hm.

RELLING And demonic natures are not designed to keep to a straight path through life. They have to stray off course every once in a while. Well, are you still sticking it out at those black and ugly works?

GREGERS I've stuck it out till now.

RELLING And were you able to collect on any of those claims you went around presenting?

GREGERS Claims? (*Understands him.*) Oh, that!

HJALMAR Were you a debt collector, Gregers?

GREGERS It's nonsense.

RELLING But that's just what he was. He'd go around all the workmen's cottages presenting something he called "the claim of idealism."

GREGERS I was young in those days.

RELLING That's right, you were very young. And this "claim of idealism"—you never got it honored all the time I was up there.

GREGERS Nor later, either.

RELLING I imagine because you've got wise enough to mark down the price.

GREGERS Never when I stand facing a genuine human being.

HJALMAR Well, that sounds only reasonable. Some butter, Gina.

RELLING And a slice of pork for Molvik.

MOLVIK Ugh, no pork!

(*There is a knock on the attic door.*)

HJALMAR Open up, Hedvig. Father wants to come out.

(*Hedvig goes across and opens the door a little. Old Ekdal enters with a fresh rabbit skin. She closes the door behind him.*)

EKDAL Good morning, gentlemen. Had good hunting today. Shot a big one.

HJALMAR And you skinned it before I could join you.

EKDAL Salted it, too. It's fine, tender meat, rabbit meat. And sweet, too. Tastes like sugar. Enjoy your meal, gentlemen! (*Goes into his room.*)

MOLVIK (*Getting up.*) Excuse me . . . I can't . . . I have to go downstairs right away . . .

RELLING Drink some soda water, man!

MOLVIK (*Hurrying.*) Ugh! Ugh! (*Dashes through the entrance door.*)

RELLING (*To Hjalmar.*) Let's drink a toast to the old huntsman.

HJALMAR (*Clinking a glass with him.*) Yes, to the sportsman on the brink of the grave.

RELLING To the grey-haired . . . (*Drinks.*) But tell me, has he got grey hair or white?

HJALMAR It's really somewhere in between. As a matter of fact, there isn't that much hair left on his head anymore.

RELLING No matter, a wig will also get you through the world. Yes, basically you're a lucky man, Ekdal. You've got your great life's mission to struggle for.

HJALMAR And I do struggle, let me tell you.

RELLING And then you have your clever wife, padding around in her slippers, wiggling her hips and coddling and caring for you.

HJALMAR Yes, Gina— (*Nodding to her.*) you're a good companion to have on life's journey.

GINA Oh, don't sit there atomizing me.

RELLING Then what about your Hedvig, Ekdal?

HJALMAR (*Moved.*) The child, yes! The child first of all. Hedvig, come here to me. (*Stroking her hair.*) What day is it tomorrow?

HEDVIG (*Shaking him.*) Oh, no. Don't talk about it, Father.

HJALMAR It pierces my heart like a knife when I think how inadequate it will be. Just a small party there in the loft.

HEDVIG But that will be just lovely.

RELLING And just wait till the wonderful invention comes into the world, Hedvig!

HJALMAR Ah, yes! Then you'll see! Hedvig, I've decided to secure your future. You shall be well off for as long as you live. I shall insist upon something for you, something or other. It will be the humble inventor's only reward.

HEDVIG (*Whispers, her arms round his neck.*) Oh, you're a dear, good father.

RELLING (*To Gregers.*) Well, don't you think it's pleasant for a change to sit at a well-laid table in a happy family circle?

HJALMAR Yes, these hours at the table are something I really treasure.

GREGERS For my part, I can't thrive in swamp air.

RELLING Swamp air?

HJALMAR Oh, don't start all that again.

GINA God knows there are no swamp smells here, Mr. Werle. For I air out the whole place every day.

GREGERS (*Leaving the table.*) The stench I have in mind can't be aired out so easily.

HJALMAR Stench!

GINA Yes, what do you think of that, Ekdal!

RELLING Excuse me! Couldn't you have brought the stench from the mines up there?

GREGERS Yes, it would be like you to call what I bring into this house a stench.

RELLING (*Going up to him.*) Listen here, Mr. Werle, I've a strong suspicion you're still carrying that "claim of idealism" in your back pocket.

GREGERS I carry it in my heart.

RELLING Where the devil you carry it, you'd be well-advised not to try cashing in on it here—so long as I'm around.

GREGERS And if I should do just that?

RELLING Then you'll end up headfirst down the stairs. Now you know.

HJALMAR (*Getting up.*) No, Relling, not that—

GREGERS Yes, just try throwing me out—

GINA (*Stepping between them.*) You can't do that, Relling. But I must say, Mr. Werle, after you made such a mess with your stove you shouldn't come to me talking of stenches.

(*There's a knock on the door.*)

HEDVIG Mother, someone's knocking.

HJALMAR Just fine! The whole world's coming to our door.

GINA Let me see to it. (*She goes and opens the door, starts, shudders and starts back.*) Uff! No!

(*Håkon Werle, in a fur coat, steps into the room.*)

WERLE Do excuse me, but I gather my son's living in this house.

GINA (*Gulping agreement.*) Yes.

HJALMAR (*Approaching.*) Would Mr. Werle do me the honor of—

WERLE Thanks. I merely wish to speak with my son.

GREGERS Yes, what is it. I'm standing here.

WERLE I wish to speak with you in your room.

GREGERS In my room? Very well— (*About to go.*)

GINA No, God knows it's not in a fit state for—

WERLE Well, out in the hallway, then. I want to talk in private.

HJALMAR You can talk here, Mr. Werle. Come into the living room, Relling.

(*Hjalmar and Relling go off right. Gina takes Hedvig into the kitchen.*)

GREGERS (*After a short pause.*) So, now we can talk in private.

WERLE You let fall certain remarks last night . . . And since you've now installed yourself with the Ekdals I have to conclude you've something or other in mind against me.

GREGERS What I have in mind is to open Hjalmar Ekdal's eyes. He shall see his situation for what it is—that's all.

WERLE Is this the mission in life you spoke about yesterday?

GREGERS Yes. You've left me no other.

WERLE Is it I who've warped your mind, Gregers?

GREGERS You've warped my entire life. I'm not thinking of what you did to Mother—. But it's you I can thank that I go through life pursued and tormented by a guilty conscience.

WERLE Aha. So it's your conscience that's the problem.

GREGERS I should have stood up to you that time the trap was laid for Lieutenant Ekdal. I should have warned him, for I had a suspicion what was going to happen.

WERLE Yes, that's when you should have spoken out.

GREGERS I didn't dare. So cowardly and frightened as I was. I was inexpressibly afraid of you—both at that time and long after.

WERLE That fear is over now, it would seem.

GREGERS It is, fortunately. Whatever wrongs have been done against Old Ekdal, both by me and by—others, can never be put right. But I can free Hjalmar from the lies and deceptions that threaten to destroy him.

WERLE And you think the outcome of that would be good?

GREGERS I'm certain of it.

WERLE You believe our photographer Ekdal's the kind of man who'd thank you for such a charitable act?

GREGERS Yes. He's that kind of man.

WERLE Hm. Well, we'll see.

GREGERS In any case, if I'm to go on living, I must find a cure for my sick conscience.

WERLE It will never be healthy. Your conscience has been sickly since your childhood. It's an inheritance from your mother— the only legacy she left you.

GREGERS (*With a scornful half-smile.*) You've still not got over what you felt—that time you discovered she'd not be bringing the fortune you counted on?

WERLE Don't let's stray into irrelevant matters. Are you still set on leading Ekdal onto what you think is the right path?

GREGERS Yes, I'm still set on that.

WERLE Then I could have spared myself this visit. For I take it there's no point now in asking if you'll move back home?

GREGERS No.

WERLE And you won't come into the business either.

GREGERS No.

WERLE Very well. But now I'm about to marry again, the estate will be divided between us.

GREGERS (*Quickly.*) No. I don't want that.

WERLE You don't want it?

GREGERS No, I daren't. For the sake of my conscience.

WERLE (*After a pause.*) Will you be going up to the works again?

GREGERS No. I regard myself as released from your service.

WERLE Then what will you do instead?

GREGERS Just fulfill my life's mission. Nothing else.

WERLE And after that? What will you live on?

GREGERS I've saved something out of my salary.

WERLE That's not going to last long!

GREGERS I think it will last out my time.

WERLE What do you mean by that?

GREGERS I'm answering no more questions.

WERLE Then good-bye, Gregers.

GREGERS Good-bye. (*Werle leaves.*)

HJALMAR (*Peeping in.*) Has he gone?

GREGERS Yes.

(*Hjalmar and Relling come in. Gina and Hedvig enter from the kitchen.*)

RELLING There's a lunch gone down the drain.

GREGERS Get your things, Hjalmar. You and I must go for a long walk.

HJALMAR Gladly. What did your father want? Was it anything to do with me?

GREGERS Just come. We must have a little talk. I'll go get my coat. (*Goes out by the hall door.*)

GINA You shouldn't go out with him, Hjalmar.

RELLING No, don't do it. Stay where you are.

HJALMAR (*Putting on his hat and overcoat.*) Why ever not? When my childhood friend feels the need to open his heart to me in private—!

RELLING But—the devil take him—don't you see the fellow's insane, deranged, out of his mind!

GINA Yes, just listen to that. His mother sometimes used to have those kinds of physical ruptions.

HJALMAR Then he'll be needing even more a friend's watchful eye. (*To Gina.*) Make sure dinner's ready in good time. Good-bye for now. (*He leaves through the hall door.*)

RELLING It's a great misfortune that fellow didn't fall straight to hell down one of the Høydal mine shafts.

GINA Jesus! Why do you say that?

RELLING (*Muttering.*) Oh, I've got my own good reasons.

GINA Do you think young Mr. Werle's really mad?

RELLING No, unfortunately. No madder than most people. But there's a sickness in his system, just the same.

GINA What's ailing him then?

RELLING I'll tell you, Mrs. Ekdal. He's suffering from a case of virulent rectitude.

GINA Virulent rectitude?

HEDVIG Is that a kind of disease?

RELLING Oh, yes! It's a national disease. But it breaks out only sporadically. (*Nods to Gina.*) Thanks for lunch. (*He leaves by the hall door.*)

GINA (*Pacing the floor uneasily.*) Ugh, that Gregers Werle. He's always been a queer fish.

HEDVIG (*Stands by the table and looks probingly at her.*) I think this is all very strange.

Act Four

Hjalmar Ekdal's studio. A photograph has recently been taken; a camera covered by a cloth, a tripod, a couple of chairs, a console, and other such things are set out in the middle of the room. Late afternoon light. The sun about to set. Later, it begins to get dark. Gina is standing by the open door with a small container and a wet photographic plate in her hand, speaking to someone outside.

GINA Yes, quite definitely. When I make a promise, I always keep it. The first dozen will be ready on Monday. Good-bye, good-bye. (*Footsteps heard going downstairs. Gina closes the door, puts the plate in the container and puts it in the covered camera.*)

HEDVIG (*Entering from the kitchen.*) Have they gone now?

GINA (*Tidying up.*) Yes, thank God. I got rid of them at last.

HEDVIG Do you know why Father hasn't come home yet?

GINA Are you sure he's not down at Relling's?

HEDVIG No, he isn't. I just went down the back stairs to ask.

GINA And there's his dinner standing and getting cold.

HEDVIG Yes, imagine! Father always makes sure he's on time for dinner.

GINA Oh, he'll be home soon, you'll see.

HEDVIG Yes, if only he'd come. It's all becoming so strange here.

GINA (*Calling out.*) There he is!

(*Hjalmar enters through the hall door.*)

HEDVIG (*Running to him.*) Father! We've been waiting for you so long!

GINA (*Glancing across.*) You've been gone a long time, Ekdal.

HJALMAR (*Not looking at her.*) A long time, yes. (*He takes off his overcoat, Gina and Hedvig helping him. He waves them off.*)

GINA Perhaps you had something to eat with Werle?

HJALMAR (*Hanging up his coat.*) No.

GINA (*Going to the kitchen.*) Then I'll bring your dinner in.

HJALMAR Don't bother about dinner. I'm not eating just now.

HEDVIG (*Coming closer.*) Aren't you feeling well, Father?

HJALMAR Well? Yes, tolerably well. We had a very exhausting walk, Gregers and I.

GINA You shouldn't have, Ekdal. You're not used to it.

HJALMAR Hm. There's a lot of things a man's got to get used to in this world. (*Paces up and down.*) Has anyone been here while I was out?

GINA Only the two sweethearts.

HJALMAR No new orders?

GINA No. Not today.

HEDVIG You'll see, Father, there'll be more tomorrow.

HJALMAR There'd better be. Because tomorrow I intend getting down to work in real earnest.

HEDVIG Tomorrow! Don't you remember what day it is tomorrow?

HJALMAR Oh yes, that's true——. Well, the day after tomorrow, then. From now on, I'm going to do everything myself.

GINA But what good will that do, Ekdal? It will only make your life miserable. I can manage the photography, and you can go on with your invention.

HEDVIG And then there's the wild duck, Father—and all the hens and the rabbits.

HJALMAR Don't talk to me about that nonsense! From tomorrow on
I'll never set foot in that loft again.

HEDVIG But Father, you promised me there'd be a party—

HJALMAR Hm. That's true. Well then, from the day after tomorrow.
That damned wild duck, I'd really like to wring its neck!

HEDVIG (*Crying out.*) The wild duck!

GINA Well, I've never heard the like!

HEDVIG (*Shaking him.*) But Father, it's *my* wild duck!

HJALMAR And that's why I won't do it. I haven't the heart to—
haven't the heart for your sake, Hedvig. But deep down I feel I
should do it. I ought not tolerate under my roof any creature
that's been in that man's hands.

GINA Good Lord, just because grandfather got it from that awful
Pettersen—

HJALMAR (*Pacing about.*) There are certain demands—. What shall I
call those demands? Let us say—ideal demands—certain claims
that a man can't set aside without doing damage to his soul.

HEDVIG (*Going to him.*) But think, the wild duck—the poor wild
duck!

HJALMAR You heard me say, I'll spare it—for your sake. No harm
shall come to a hair of its—well, as I said, I'll spare it. Because
there are far more important matters to deal with. But you
ought to go outside for a while, Hedvig, like you usually do. It's
just dark enough for you.

HEDVIG No, I don't feel like going out now.

HJALMAR Yes, you must. It seems to me you're blinking your eyes a
lot. It's not good for you, all these fumes in here. The air is
stale under this roof.

HEDVIG All right. I'll run down the kitchen stairs and walk around
for a little while. My coat and hat—? Oh, they're in my room.
Father, you mustn't do anything bad to the wild duck while I'm
out.

HJALMAR Not a feather shall be ruffled on its head. (*Hugging her.*)
You and I, Hedvig—we two—! Now, run along, dear.

(*Hedvig nods to her parents and goes out through the kitchen.*)

HJALMAR (*Walking about without looking up.*) Gina.

GINA Yes?

HJALMAR From tomorrow on—or, rather, from the day after tomorrow—I would like to keep the household accounts myself.

GINA You want to keep the household accounts as well?

HJALMAR Yes. Or at any rate keep an eye on what comes in.

GINA God knows, that won't take up much time.

HJALMAR I wouldn't be so sure. It seems to me you make the money
go a remarkably long way. (*Stops and looks at her.*) How do you
explain that?

GINA It's because I and Hedvig don't need very much.

HJALMAR Is it true Father's very generously paid for the copying work he does for Mr. Werle?

GINA I don't know if it's so generous. I don't know the rate for such work.

HJALMAR Well, what does he get, altogether? Tell me!

GINA It varies. It comes to roughly what he costs us, and then a little pocket money.

HJALMAR What he costs us! You've never told me this before!

GINA No. I couldn't bring myself to. You were so happy believing he got everything from you.

HJALMAR Instead, Father gets it from Mr. Werle!

GINA Well, Mr. Werle's got enough to spare.

HJALMAR I'd like to have the lamp lit.

GINA (*Lighting lamp.*) And we don't know that it is Mr. Werle himself. It could just as well be Gråberg—

HJALMAR Why come up with this smoke screen about Gråberg?

GINA I don't know. I simply thought—

HJALMAR Hm.

GINA It wasn't me got Grandfather the copying. It was Berta, that time she became housekeeper.

HJALMAR It seems to me your voice is shaking.

GINA (*Putting the shade on the lamp.*) Is it?

HJALMAR And your hands are trembling. Or am I wrong?

GINA (*Firmly.*) Say it straight out, Ekdal. What is it he's gone and said about me?

HJALMAR Is it true—can it be true, that—that there was some kind of relationship between you and Mr. Werle when you were in service in his house?

GINA It isn't true. Not at that time, never. He was always after me, that's a fact. And his wife thought there was something in it. All the hocus-pocus and hubbub she raised! And she ranted and she raved at me, that's what she did—and so I quit service.

HJALMAR But then afterwards?

GINA And so I went back home. And Mother—she wasn't as straight as you thought, Ekdal. She went on at me all the time telling me I should do this and I should do that—now Mr. Werle was a widower.

HJALMAR All right! And then?

GINA Yes, it's best you know. He wouldn't let up till he got what he wanted.

HJALMAR (*Clasping his hands together.*) And this is my child's mother! How could you hide such a thing from me?

GINA Yes, it was wrong of me. I should have told you about it long ago.

HJALMAR You should have told me right from the beginning. I
would have known then what kind of woman you were.

GINA But would you have married me, all the same?

HJALMAR How can you imagine I would?

GINA No. And that's why I daren't say anything at the time. Because I'd come to care for you so much, as you know. And I
couldn't go and make my life completely miserable—

HJALMAR (*Walking about.*) And this is my Hedvig's mother! To think
everything here that meets my eyes— (*Kicks a chair.*) —my entire home—I owe to someone you'd already favored! To that
lecherous Werle!

GINA Do you regret the fourteen–fifteen years we've lived together?

HJALMAR (*Stands and faces her.*) You tell *me* whether you haven't—
every day, every hour—regretted this web of deception you've
spun like a spider around me. Answer me that! Haven't you
truly gone around here writhing with shame and remorse?

GINA Ah, Ekdal dear, I've had more than enough to think about,
what with the house and all the day-to-day problems—

HJALMAR You've never cast a searching glance back over your past?

GINA No. God knows, I'd all but about forgotten that old affair.

HJALMAR To think! Such dull, unfeeling calm! There's something
outrageous about it. To think of it—! Not one pang of remorse!

GINA Tell me now, Ekdal, what would have become of you if you
hadn't found a wife like me?

HJALMAR Like you—!

GINA Yes, for I've always been more practical and enterprising than
you. Well, that's understandable—I'm also a couple of years older.

HJALMAR What would have become of me?

GINA Because you were in all kinds of bad ways that time you first
met me. You really can't deny that.

HJALMAR So you call that being in bad ways. Ah, how little you
understand a man sunk in sorrow and despair—particularly a
man with my fiery temperament.

GINA Well, well, that may be. And I'm not approaching you for it,
either, because you turned out to be a good husband once you
got yourself a house and home. And now we've made it so
comfortable and cozy. Both Hedvig and I could soon start
spending a little on ourselves—on food and clothes.

HJALMAR In a swamp of deceit, yes.

GINA Uff! That horrible creature—making his tracks through our
house!

HJALMAR I believed our home was a good place to be in. All a delusion! Where shall I find the resilience I need now to urge my
invention into the world of reality? Maybe it will die with me,
and your past, Gina, will have killed it.

GINA (*Near to tears.*) No, you mustn't say such things like that, Ekdal. To me, who only wanted to do what's best for you as long as I lived!

HJALMAR What, I ask, has become of the breadwinner's dream? When I lay in there on the sofa pondering the invention, I often suspected it would drain away the last of my strength. Many's the time I felt that the day I held the patent in my hand—that day would be my—day of departure. It was my dream you'd stay on here as the late inventor's prosperous widow.

GINA (*Drying her tears.*) No, Hjalmar, you mustn't talk like that. The Lord forbid I should live to see the day I remain behind a widow.

HJALMAR Oh, either way it's the same. It's all over now, anyway. Everything!

(*Gregers cautiously opens the door and looks in.*)

GREGERS May I come in?

HJALMAR Yes, do.

GREGERS (*Advancing with a radiant, joyful expression, reaching his hands to them.*) Now, you two dear people—! (*He looks from one to the other and whispers to Hjalmar.*) Isn't it done yet?

HJALMAR (*Loudly.*) It's done.

GREGERS It is?

HJALMAR I have lived the bitterest hour of my life.

GREGERS But the most elevating too, I think.

HJALMAR Well, it's off our hands for the time being.

GINA God forgive you, Mr. Werle.

GREGERS (*Greatly astonished.*) But I don't understand this.

HJALMAR What don't you understand?

GREGERS After so great a reckoning—one on which a whole new way of life can be based—a way of life together in truth, void of all deceit—

HJALMAR Yes, I know all that; I know all that.

GREGERS I was expecting for certain when I came in through that door, I'd be greeted with a transfiguring light shining from both husband and wife. Instead I see nothing but this somber, heavy, gloomy—

GINA Very well, then. (*Takes off lampshade.*)

GREGERS You don't want to understand me, Mrs. Ekdal. Well, well. For you, there'll need to be time. But with you, Hjalmar? You must feel you've been initiated into a higher purpose by this great confrontation.

HJALMAR Yes, naturally—I do. That's to say, in a manner of speaking.

GREGERS For nothing in the world can compare with finding forgiveness for one who has gone astray, then raising her up to you in love.

HJALMAR Do you think a man can easily recover from a bitter cup like I've just drained?

GREGERS No, for an ordinary man that might be true. But a man like you—.

HJALMAR Yes, Good Lord, I know all about that. But you mustn't hound me, Gregers. It'll take time, you know.

GREGERS You've much of the wild duck in you, Hjalmar.

(*Relling has come in through the entrance door.*)

RELLING What's this? Is the wild duck in flight again?

HJALMAR Yes, the wounded victim of Mr. Werle's hunting.

RELLING Mr. Werle's—? Is it him you're talking about?

HJALMAR Of him and—us, as well.

RELLING (*Half-aloud to Gregers.*) The devil take you!

HJALMAR What's that you're saying?

RELLING I'm expressing the heartfelt wish that this quacksalver would take himself off home. If he remains here, he's just the man to ruin both of you.

GREGERS These two won't be ruined, Mr. Relling. Of Hjalmar, I need not speak. We know him. But she also, undoubtedly, has deep within her something of true value, something one can have faith in.

GINA (*Close to tears.*) Then you should have let me stay as I was.

RELLING (*To Gregers.*) Would it be impertinent to inquire what it is you want in this house?

GREGERS I want to establish a true marriage.

RELLING So you don't think the Ekdals' marriage is good enough as it is?

GREGERS It's no doubt as good as most marriages, unfortunately. But it's never been a true marriage.

HJALMAR You've never had an eye for the claim of idealism, Relling.

RELLING Rubbish, my boy! Excuse me, Mr. Werle; how many—just a rough guess—how many true marriages have you seen in your life?

GREGERS I think I've seen scarcely one.

RELLING Neither have I.

GREGERS But I've seen countless marriages of the opposite kind. And I've had the occasion of seeing, close-up, what such a marriage can destroy in two people.

HJALMAR The whole moral foundation of a man can crumble under his feet. That's what's so terrible.

RELLING Well, I've never actually been married, so I wouldn't want to judge such things. But I do know this; the child is part of the marriage, too. You should leave the child in peace.

HJALMAR Ah, Hedvig! My poor Hedvig!

RELLING Yes, would you please keep Hedvig out of all this. You two are grown-up people. You can, in God's name, botch and bungle your relationship, if that's what you want. But you'd better be careful with Hedvig. If not, you might bring some disaster on her.

HJALMAR Disaster!

RELLING Yes, or she could bring the disaster on herself—and on others as well.

GINA But how can you know that, Relling?

HJALMAR There's no immediate danger to her eyes?

RELLING This has nothing to do with her eyes. But Hedvig's at a difficult age. She could come up with all kinds of craziness.

GINA Yes, now I think of it, that's what she's doing already. She's a scary habit of playing around with the fire in the kitchen. She calls it playing "house on fire." I'm often afraid she'll really set the house on fire.

RELLING There, you see. I knew it.

GREGERS (*To Relling.*) But how do you explain such a thing?

RELLING (*Sullenly.*) Her voice is changing, man.

HJALMAR As long as the child has me—! As long as my head's above the ground—

(*There's a knock on the door.*)

GINA Hush, Ekdal. Someone's in the hall. (*Calls.*) Come in!

(*Mrs. Sørby, in outdoor clothes, enters.*)

MRS. SØRBY Good evening!

GINA (*Going toward her.*) No! Is it you, Berta!

MRS. SØRBY Yes, it's me. But maybe I come at an awkward time?

HJALMAR Not at all. A messenger from that house—

MRS. SØRBY (*To Gina.*) Frankly speaking, I'd hoped I wouldn't find your menfolk home at this time, so I ran over here to have a few words and say good-bye.

GINA Really! Are you going away?

MRS. SØRBY Yes, early tomorrow. Up to Høydal. Mr. Werle left this afternoon. (*Casually to Gregers.*) He sends you his regards.

GINA Just fancy—!

HJALMAR So Mr. Werle's gone away? And now you're following him?

MRS. SØRBY Yes. What do you say to that, Ekdal?

HJALMAR Watch out, is what I say.

GREGERS I should explain. My father is marrying Mrs. Sørby.

HJALMAR He's marrying her!

GINA Oh, Berta! So, at last!

RELLING (*A tremor in his voice.*) This surely can't be true!

MRS. SØRBY Yes, my dear Relling, it's definitely true.

RELLING You want to marry again?

MRS. SØRBY Yes, that's how it is. Werle's got a special license, and so we're celebrating the wedding quietly up at the works.

GREGERS Then, like a good stepson, I must wish you all happiness.

MRS. SØRBY Thank you, if you mean what you say. And I do hope it will bring happiness both for Werle and for me.

RELLING You've good reason to hope. Mr. Werle never gets drunk— as far as *I* know. And he's not given to beating his wives either, as the late horse-doctor did.

MRS. SØRBY Oh, let Sørby rest in peace. There were many good sides to him as well.

RELLING Mr. Werle has even better sides to him, I imagine.

MRS. SØRBY Well, at least he hasn't wasted what's best in him. The man who does that must take the consequences.

RELLING Tonight I'm going out with Molvik.

MRS. SØRBY You mustn't do that, Relling. Don't do it—for my sake.

RELLING There's nothing else to do. (*To Hjalmar.*) Would you like to come along?

GINA No, thanks. Ekdal doesn't go out on those kinds of dipsipations.

HJALMAR (*Annoyed, half-aloud.*) Oh do be quiet!

RELLING Good-bye, Mrs.—Werle. (*Leaves through the entrance door.*)

GREGERS (*To Mrs. Sørby.*) You and Dr. Relling know each other quite well it seems.

MRS. SØRBY We've known each other for many years. At one time it was even possible something might have come of it.

GREGERS It was a good thing for you it didn't.

MRS. SØRBY Yes, you might well say that. But I'm always on guard against acting on impulse. And a woman shouldn't just throw herself away, either.

GREGERS Aren't you the slightest bit afraid I might let my father know of this old friendship?

MRS. SØRBY You can be sure I've told him myself.

GREGERS Really?

MRS. SØRBY Your father knows every smallest detail that anyone could honestly say about me. I've told him everything about that kind of thing. It was the first thing I did when he let me know what he had in mind.

GREGERS You're more than uncommonly candid, I think.

MRS. SØRBY I've always been candid. For us women, it's the best thing to be.

HJALMAR What do you say to that, Gina?

GINA Oh, we women are different from one another. Some are one way and some another.

MRS. SØRBY Well, Gina, I believe it's wisest to behave as I've done.

And Werle, for his part, hasn't kept anything secret from me either. You see, that's really what brought us together. Now he can sit and talk with me as openly as a child. He never had the opportunity for that before. With his fine health and zest for life, he spent all his youth and the best years of his manhood hearing nothing else but sermons on his sins. And many times these sermons were directed at mostly imaginary sins—at least as far as I could see.

GINA That's true enough, what you say.

GREGERS If you ladies intend embarking on that topic, it's best I leave.

MRS. SØRBY In that case, you may just as well stay. I won't say another word. But I wanted you to understand I've done nothing in any way devious or underhanded. Maybe you think I've come into a great deal of good luck; and in a way, that's true. All the same, I believe I'm getting no more than I'm giving. In no way will I ever let him down. I'll be able to help him and look after him as no one else can, now he'll soon become helpless.

HJALMAR He'll become helpless?

GREGERS (*To Mrs. Sørby.*) All right, all right, don't talk about that here.

MRS. SØRBY There's no point in hiding it any longer, no matter how much one would like to. He's going blind.

HJALMAR (*Stunned.*) He's going blind too?

GINA There's so many are.

MRS. SØRBY And you can imagine what that will be like for a businessman. Well, I will try to use my eyes for him as best I can. But I can't stay any longer. I'm so terribly busy just now. Ah, yes, there was something I was to tell you, Mr. Ekdal. If there is anything Mr. Werle can do for you, all you have to do is get in touch with Gråberg.

GREGERS That is an offer Hjalmar Ekdal will certainly decline.

MRS. SØRBY Well, well. I don't believe that in the past he ever—

GINA Yes, Berta. Ekdal no longer needs to take anything from Mr. Werle.

HJALMAR (*Slowly and with emphasis.*) Will you give my regards to your intended husband and tell him that at the earliest opportunity I intend calling on bookkeeper Gråberg—

GREGERS What! You want to do that!

HJALMAR —calling on bookkeeper Gråberg, I say, and demanding an account of the full sum I owe his employer. I will pay this debt of honor—ha-ha—that it should be called a debt of honor! But enough of that. I shall pay it all, with five percent interest.

GINA But Ekdal dear, God knows we don't have the money for that.

HJALMAR Will you tell your future husband that I am working inde-
fatigably on my invention. Will you tell him that what sustains
my spiritual strength throughout these exhausting exertions is
the desire to be freed of a painful burden of debt. That's why I
work on the invention. The entire proceeds will be devoted to
freeing me from your future husband's pecuniary favors.

MRS. SØRBY Something or other has definitely happened in this
house.

HJALMAR Yes, it has.

MRS. SØRBY Well, good-bye then. I still had something I wanted to
talk to you about, Gina, but that can wait until another time.
Good-bye.
(*Hjalmar and Gregers bow silently; Gina follows Mrs. Sørby to
the door.*)

HJALMAR Not over the threshold, Gina! (*Mrs. Sørby leaves. Gina
closes the door after her.*) There, Gregers. Now I've got that
heavy debt off my hands.

GREGERS You soon will have, anyway.

HJALMAR I believe my attitude may be called correct.

GREGERS You're the man I always held you to be.

HJALMAR In certain circumstances it is impossible to disregard the
claim of the ideal. As family breadwinner I'll suffer anguish
and agony over it. For believe me, it's really no joke for a man
of limited means to pay off a debt of many years standing; a
debt, one might say, over which the dust of oblivion had settled. But that makes no difference. My human dignity demands its rights.

GREGERS (*Laying his hands upon his shoulders.*) Dear Hjalmar—
wasn't it good I came?

HJALMAR Yes.

GREGERS And that you came to a clear understanding of your situation—wasn't that good?

HJALMAR (*A little impatiently.*) Yes, certainly it's good. But there's
just one thing that offends my sense of justice.

GREGERS What might that be?

HJALMAR It's just that—well, I don't know if I should speak so
frankly about your father.

GREGERS Have no scruples on my account.

HJALMAR Well then. To my mind, you see, there's something offen-
sive in the thought that now the true marriage will be founded
not by me but by him.

GREGERS No, how can you say such a thing.

HJALMAR But it's really true. Your father and Mrs. Sørby are entering a marriage founded on total confidence, on complete and

unconditional openness on both sides. Nothing swept under the carpet or hidden from each other. They've announced, you could say, a mutual forgiveness of sins.

GREGERS Well, well, what of it?

HJALMAR Yes, but *there* it's all been achieved. And just *this* was the great difficulty you said had to be overcome in order to found a true marriage.

GREGERS But that's in a completely different way, Hjalmar. You're surely not going to compare yourself or her with those two— you understand what I mean.

HJALMAR But I can't help thinking there's something that hurts and outrages my sense of what's right. It looks exactly as if there was no justice at all guiding the world.

GINA Oh no, Ekdal, you really shouldn't say things like that.

GREGERS Hm. Don't let's get into *that* question.

HJALMAR But then, on the other hand, it's as if I can see distinctly the controlling hand of destiny after all. He's going blind.

GINA Maybe that's not so certain.

HJALMAR There's no doubt about it. At least we ought not doubt it: for in just that circumstance lies righteous retribution. In his time he blinded the eyes of a trusting human being—

GREGERS Unfortunately, he's blinded many.

HJALMAR And now arrives the inexorable, the unutterable, and demands in turn the old man's eyes.

GINA Oh, no! How can you say something as horrible as that! I'm really frightened.

HJALMAR It helps to immerse oneself in the night side of existence once in a while.

(*Hedvig, in hat and coat, enters through the hall door, happy and out of breath.*)

GINA Back again already?

HEDVIG Yes, I didn't feel like walking any farther. And that was a good thing; because I just met somebody at the door.

HJALMAR That would have been Mrs. Sørby.

HEDVIG Yes.

HJALMAR (*Pacing the floor.*) I hope you've seen her for the last time. (*Silence. Hedvig looks timidly from one to another, trying to gauge their mood.*)

HEDVIG (*Moves toward Hjalmar ingratiatingly.*) Father.

HJALMAR Well—what is it, Hedvig?

HEDVIG Mrs. Sørby had something for me.

HJALMAR (*Stopping.*) For you?

HEDVIG Yes, it's something for tomorrow.

GINA Berta has always given you a little something for your birthday.

HJALMAR What is it?

HEDVIG No, you mustn't know what it is yet, for Mother is to give it to me in bed tomorrow morning.

HJALMAR Oh, all these secrets I'm being kept out of!

HEDVIG (*Hurriedly.*) No, you can see it if you want to. It's a big letter. (*Takes the letter from her coat pocket.*)

HJALMAR A letter, too?

HEDVIG Yes, it's just the letter. The rest will come later. But think—a letter! I've never had a letter before. And then it has "Miss" written on it. (*Reading.*) "Miss Hedvig Ekdal." Just think—that's me.

HJALMAR Let me see the letter.

HEDVIG (*Handing it to him.*) There, you see.

HJALMAR It's Mr. Werle's handwriting.

GINA Are you sure of that, Ekdal?

HJALMAR See for yourself.

GINA How would I would know about that?

HJALMAR Hedvig, may I open the letter and read it?

HEDVIG Yes, of course you may, if you want to.

GINA No, not this evening Ekdal. It's meant to be for tomorrow.

HEDVIG (*Quietly.*) Oh, let him read it! It's sure to be something good—then Father will be happy. And everything will be pleasant again.

HJALMAR Then I may open it?

HEDVIG Please do, Father. It'll be lovely to find out what it is.

HJALMAR Good. (*Opens the envelope, takes out a piece of paper, reads through it and seems bewildered.*) What *is* this—?

GINA What does it say?

HEDVIG Oh yes, Father, tell us!

HJALMAR Quiet! (*Reads the letter once more. He has gone pale but speaks with control.*) It's a deed of gift, Hedvig.

HEDVIG Just imagine! What do I get?

HJALMAR Read for yourself.

(*Hedvig goes over to the lamp and reads it for a moment.*)

HJALMAR (*Half-aloud, clenching his fists.*) The eyes! The eyes—and then that letter!

HEDVIG (*Interrupts her reading.*) Yes, but it looks to me as if it's Grandfather who's getting it.

HJALMAR (*Taking the letter from her.*) You, Gina. Can you understand this?

GINA I haven't any idea what it is. Just tell me.

HJALMAR Mr. Werle writes to Hedvig that her old grandfather doesn't have to trouble himself with copying work anymore but that he can draw one hundred kroner a month from the office.

GREGERS Aha!

HEDVIG A hundred kroner, Mother! I read that.

GINA That's very good for Grandfather.

HJALMAR —a hundred kroner for as long as he needs it. That means, of course, until he passes on.

GINA So then he's provided for, poor old man.

HJALMAR But there's more to follow. You didn't read far enough, Hedvig. Afterwards, this gift goes over to you.

HEDVIG To me! All of it?

HJALMAR You're assured the same amount for the rest of your life, he writes. Do you hear, Gina?

GINA Yes, I heard all right.

HEDVIG Imagine—all the money I'll be getting. (*Shaking him.*) Father, Father—aren't you glad—?

HJALMAR (*Detaching himself from her.*) Glad! (*Paces about.*) Oh, what vistas—what perspectives open before me. Hedvig—it's her he remembers so generously!

GINA Yes, because it's Hedvig who has a birthday—

HEDVIG And you'll get the money in any case, Father! You know I'll give all the money to you and Mother.

HJALMAR To your mother, yes! That's just it.

GREGERS Hjalmar, this is a trap being set for you.

HJALMAR You believe this is yet another trap?

GREGERS When he was here this morning he told me: "Hjalmar Ekdal isn't the man you imagine him to be."

HJALMAR Not the man—!

GREGERS "You'll get to see," he said.

HJALMAR Get to see me bought off with money—!

HEDVIG But Mother, what's this all about?

GINA Go and take off your coat.

(*Hedvig, close to tears, goes out through the kitchen door.*)

GREGERS Yes, Hjalmar—now you can show if he's right—him or me.

HJALMAR (*Tears the letter in two and places both pieces on the table, saying.*) Here's my answer.

GREGERS I knew it.

HJALMAR (*Goes to Gina, who stands by the stove, and speaks in a low voice.*) Let's have no more secrets. If the relationship between him and you was completely over when you—came to fall in love with me, as you put it—why did he arrange it so we could get married?

GINA He probably thought he could come here when he liked.

HJALMAR Only *that*? Wasn't he afraid of a certain possibility?

GINA I don't know what you mean.

HJALMAR I would like to know whether—your child has the right to live under my roof.

GINA (*Drawing herself up, her eyes flashing.*) And you can ask *that!*

HJALMAR You shall answer me this: Does Hedvig belong to me or to—? Well!

GINA (*Looking at him with cold defiance.*) I don't know.

HJALMAR (*His voice trembling.*) You don't know!

GINA How could I know? A woman like me—

HJALMAR (*Quietly, as he turns from her.*) Then I've nothing more to do in this house.

GREGERS Think about this, Hjalmar!

HJALMAR (*Putting on his overcoat.*) For a man like me, there's nothing more to think about.

GREGERS But there is, inexpressibly much to think about. You three must stay together if you're going to reach a state of forgiving self-sacrifice.

HJALMAR I don't want to. Never, never! My hat! (*Takes his hat.*) My home lies in ruins around me. (*Bursts into tears.*) Gregers, I have no child!

HEDVIG (*Who has opened the kitchen door.*) What are you saying? (*She goes to him.*) Father, Father!

GINA There, there!

HJALMAR Don't come near me, Hedvig! Get away from me. I can't bear to look at you. Ah, the eyes—! Good-bye. (*Makes for the door.*)

HEDVIG (*Hanging on to him and crying loudly.*) No, oh no! Don't leave me!

GINA (*Shouts.*) Look at the child, Ekdal! Look at the child!

HJALMAR I won't! I can't! I must get out—away from all this! (*He tears himself free from Hedvig and leaves.*)

HEDVIG (*With despair in her eyes.*) He's leaving us, Mother! He's leaving us! He'll never come back!

GINA Don't cry, Hedvig. Father will come back.

HEDVIG (*Throwing herself, sobbing, on the sofa.*) No, no, he'll never come home to us again!

GREGERS You must believe that I meant everything for the best, Mrs. Ekdal.

GINA I almost believe you, but God forgive you just the same.

HEDVIG (*Lying on the sofa.*) I think I shall die from all this! What have I done to him? Mother, you must bring him home again!

GINA Yes, yes. Just calm down. I'll go out and look for him. (*Puts on her overcoat.*) Perhaps he's gone to Relling's. But you musn't lie there, crying. Promise me that?

HEDVIG (*Crying convulsively.*) Yes, I'll stop. As long as Father comes home.

GREGERS (*To Gina as she leaves.*) Wouldn't it be better if you let him fight his painful battle to the end?

GINA Oh, he can do that later. First of all we have to calm down the child. (*She goes out through the hall door.*)

HEDVIG (*Sitting up and drying her tears.*) You have to tell me what is happening. Why doesn't Father want to know me anymore?

GREGERS You mustn't ask about that until you are big and grown up.

HEDVIG (*Sobbing.*) But I can't go around being so horribly unhappy until I'm big and grown up. I think I know what it is. Maybe I'm not really Father's child.

GREGERS (*Uneasily.*) How could that be?

HEDVIG Mother could have found me. And maybe Father's just found out. I've read about such things.

GREGERS Well, but even if—

HEDVIG Yes, I think he could love me as much just the same. Even more. The wild duck was sent to us as a present, but all the same I love her ever so much.

GREGERS (*Diverting her.*) Yes, the wild duck, that's right! Let us talk a bit about the wild duck, Hedvig.

HEDVIG The poor wild duck. He said he couldn't stand the sight of her, either. Just imagine, he wanted to wring its neck!

GREGERS Oh, he'd never do that.

HEDVIG No, but he said he would. And I think it was horrible of Father to say that. For I say a prayer for the wild duck every night, and ask that she be protected from death and everything that's evil.

GREGERS (*Looking at her.*) Do you usually say prayers at night?

HEDVIG Oh, yes.

GREGERS Who taught you to?

HEDVIG I taught myself. Because one time Father was very sick and had leeches on his neck, and he said he was being gripped in the jaws of death.

GREGERS Really?

HEDVIG So I said a prayer for him when I went to bed. And I've gone on doing it ever since.

GREGERS And now you pray for the wild duck as well?

HEDVIG I thought it best to put in the wild duck because she was so sickly at first.

GREGERS Do you say morning prayers as well?

HEDVIG No, I don't do that at all.

GREGERS Why don't you say morning prayers as well?

HEDVIG In the morning it's light so that there's nothing to be afraid of any more.

GREGERS And the wild duck that you love so deeply, your father wanted to wring its neck.

HEDVIG No, he said it would be best for him if he did but that he'd spare it for my sake. And that was very nice of Father.

GREGERS (*Coming closer.*) But what if you, of your own free will, sacrificed the wild duck for his sake?

HEDVIG (*Getting up.*) The wild duck!

GREGERS If you were willing to sacrifice for him the best thing you possess in the whole world.

HEDVIG Do you believe that would help?

GREGERS Try it, Hedvig.

HEDVIG (*Quietly, her eyes shining.*) Yes, I *will* try it.

GREGERS Do you think you have the right strength of mind for it?

HEDVIG I'll ask Grandfather to shoot the wild duck for me.

GREGERS Yes, do that. But not a word to your mother about this.

HEDVIG Why not?

GREGERS She doesn't understand us.

HEDVIG The wild duck? I'll try it tomorrow morning.

  (*Gina enters through the hall door.*)

HEDVIG (*Going to her.*) Did you find him, Mother?

GINA No, but I heard he went down to Relling and went out with him.

GREGERS Are you sure of that?

GINA Yes, the janitor's wife said so. Molvik went with them as well, she said.

GREGERS At such a time, when his soul so desperately needs to struggle in solitude—!

GINA (*Taking off her overcoat.*) Yes, men are complicated, that's for sure. God knows where Relling has dragged them off to! I flew over to Madam Erikson, but they weren't there.

HEDVIG (*Fighting back her tears.*) What if he never comes home again!

GREGERS He'll come home again. I'll just send word to him in the morning, and then you'll see in what way he comes back. Sleep well and trust in me, Hedvig. Good night. (*He leaves through the entrance door.*)

HEDVIG (*Throwing herself, sobbing on Gina's neck.*) Mother, Mother!

GINA (*Patting her on the back and sighing.*) Ah, yes. Relling was right. This is what happens when crazy people turn up presenting their claim of the idol.

Act Five

Hjalmar Ekdal's studio. A cold grey morning light. Wet snow lies on the big panes of the skylight. Gina, wearing an apron and carrying a broom and dust cloth, enters from the kitchen and goes toward the living room. At the same time Hedvig comes in quickly from the hall.

GINA (*Stopping.*) Any news?

HEDVIG You know, Mother, I'm almost sure he's down at Relling's.

GINA There, you see!

HEDVIG Because the janitor's wife said Relling had two other people with him when he came in last night.

GINA That's just what I thought.

HEDVIG But that's no good if he won't come up here.

GINA Well, at least I can go down and talk with him.

(*Old Ekdal in a dressing gown and smoking a pipe, appears in the doorway of his room.*)

EKDAL Say, Hjalmar—. Isn't Hjalmar home?

GINA No, he just went out.

EKDAL So early? And in a snowstorm like this? Well, well, it doesn't matter. I can make the morning inspection by myself. (*He slides the loft door to one side. Hedvig helps him. He goes in and she closes the door after him.*)

HEDVIG (*Half-aloud.*) Mother, imagine when poor Grandpa finds out Father's leaving us.

GINA Nonsense! Grandfather mustn't find out anything about it. It's a godsend he wasn't home yesterday during all that hullabaloo.

HEDVIG Yes, but— (*Gregers enters through the hall doorway.*)

GREGERS Well? Any news of him yet?

GINA He's staying downstairs with Relling, so they say.

GREGERS With Relling! Has he actually been out with those two?

GINA That's what he did.

GREGERS When he so desperately needed to find the solitude to gather himself together—

GINA Yes, you might well say that.

(*Relling comes in from the hallway.*)

HEDVIG (*Going to him.*) Is Father with you?

GINA (*At the same time.*) Is he there?

RELLING He certainly is.

HEDVIG And you didn't tell us!

RELLING Yes, I am a bea . . . east. But first I had that other bea . . . east to deal with—the demonic one, I mean. And after that, I slept so heavily that—

GINA What did Ekdal have to say today?

RELLING Not a single word.

GREGERS No, no. I can well understand that.

GINA What's he doing with himself, then?

RELLING He's lying on the sofa, snoring.

GINA Really? Yes, Ekdal's a great one for snoring.

HEDVIG He's sleeping? Then he can sleep?

RELLING Yes, he's managing to pretty well.

GREGERS It's understandable. After the conflict in his soul that
  must have shattered him—

GINA And then he's not used to being out of doors late at night.

HEDVIG Perhaps it's best, Mother, that he get some sleep.

GINA I think so, too. So it's just as well we don't disturb him
  too early. Thank you, Relling. Now I must first get the house
  cleaned and tidied up, and then—. Come and help me, Hedvig. (*Gina and Hedvig go into the living room.*)

GREGERS (*Turning to Relling.*) Can you account for the spiritual
  upheaval now going on in Hjalmar Ekdal?

RELLING For myself, I've not detected any sign of spiritual upheaval
  in him.

GREGERS What! At such a turning point, when his whole life has
  gained a new foundation—? How can you imagine a personality like Hjalmar—?

RELLING Personality—him! If at any time he had a tendency to that
  abnormal state you call personality, it was torn out of him, root
  and branch, while he was still a boy—I can assure you.

GREGERS That would be very strange—considering the loving care
  with which he was brought up.

RELLING By those two neurotic, hysterical maiden aunts, you
  mean?

GREGERS Let me tell you, they were women who never abandoned
  the claims of idealism—ah yes, now you're going to laugh at
  that, I suppose.

RELLING No, I'm not in the mood. Besides, I know what I'm talking
  about. For he's spouted a great quantity of gush on those "twin
  soul mothers" of his. But I don't think he's got much to thank
  them for. Ekdal's misfortune is that in his circle he's always
  been held as a shining light—

GREGERS And *isn't* he, perhaps? Deep down, I mean?

RELLING I've never noticed anything of the kind. His father
  thought so—but what does that signify? The old lieutenant's
  been a simpleton all his life.

GREGERS All his life he's been a man with the soul of a child: That's
  what you can't comprehend.

RELLING Have it your way! But when our dear sweet Hjalmar became a student of sorts, straight away he was counted a great
  light of the future among his comrades. And besides, he was
  very handsome, pink and white—just like young girls want
  their fellows to be. With his sentimental disposition, something appealing in his voice, and knowing how to declaim very
  prettily other people's verses and ideas—

GREGERS (*Angrily.*) Is it Hjalmar Ekdal you're talking about like
  that?

RELLING Yes, with your permission, it is. For that's what he looks like inside, this idol you're grovelling before.

GREGERS I wouldn't have thought I was as completely blind as that.

RELLING Oh, yes. You're not far from it. Because you see, you're a sick man—you as well.

GREGERS You're right there.

RELLING Yes. You're suffering from a complicated condition. First, there's this virulent righteousness-fever, and then, what's worse, you're continually in a delirious state of adoration. You always need something to admire outside yourself.

GREGERS Yes, I certainly need to look for it outside myself.

RELLING But you're preposterously wrong about the great miraculous presences you imagine you see and hear around you. Once again, you've turned up at a laborer's cottage with your claim of the ideal, but there's no one here can pay up.

GREGERS If your idea of Hjalmar's no better than that, how can you find any pleasure continuing in his company?

RELLING Good Lord, I'm supposed to be a doctor of sorts, I'm ashamed to say. So I must at least look after the poor sick folk I share the house with.

GREGERS Really! Is Hjalmar Ekdal sick as well?

RELLING People are sick just about everywhere, unfortunately.

GREGERS And what cure do you prescribe for Hjalmar?

RELLING The usual one. I try to keep the life-lie going within him.

GREGERS Life-lie? I didn't quite catch—?

RELLING That's right, I said the life-lie. Because the life-lie is the vitalizing principle, you see.

GREGERS Might I ask what kind of life-lie Hjalmar is injected with?

RELLING No way. I don't divulge professional secrets to quack-salvers. You'd then be in a position to mess him up even more for me. But the method's effective. I've applied it to Molvik as well. Him I made "demonic." *That* is the treatment I use to keep him going.

GREGERS Then he isn't demonic?

RELLING What the devil does it mean, to be demonic? That was just some nonsense I thought up to let him go on living. If I hadn't, the poor, harmless swine would have broken down in self-contempt and despair many years ago. Then there's the old lieutenant! But he actually found his own cure himself.

GREGERS Lieutenant Ekdal? What was that?

RELLING Well, just think of the way the old bear-hunter can go into that dark attic hunting his rabbits. There's not a happier sportsman in the world than the old man, romping around among all that rubbish. For him, the four or five Christmas trees he's collected are the entire, vast, living forest of Høydal.

The cock and hens are the great birds in the treetops. And the rabbits hopping across the loft floor—they're the bears he tussles with: he, the virile hunter of the wild open spaces!

GREGERS Yes, poor old Lieutenant Ekdal. He's certainly had to give up his youthful ideals.

RELLING While I think of it, Mr. Werle junior—don't use that foreign word, "ideals." We've a perfectly good Norwegian word: "lies."

GREGERS Meaning the two things are related?

RELLING Yes, about the same as typhus and typhoid fever.

GREGERS Dr. Relling, I'll not give up until I have rescued Hjalmar from your clutches.

RELLING All the worse for him. Take the life-lie away from your average person and you take happiness away at the same time. (*To Hedvig who enters from the living room.*) Well, little wild duck mother, now I'm going downstairs to see if your father is still lying there pondering on his remarkable invention. (*Goes out through the entrance door.*)

GREGERS (*Approaching Hedvig.*) I can see by looking at you that it's not fulfilled.

HEDVIG What isn't? Oh, with the wild duck. No.

GREGERS Your resolve broke down when it came to action, I suppose.

HEDVIG No, it wasn't *that* exactly. But when I woke up this morning and remembered what we'd been talking about, it all seemed so strange.

GREGERS Strange?

HEDVIG Yes, I don't know—. Last night, at the time, I thought there was something so beautiful about the idea; but after I'd slept, and thought about it again, I didn't think so much of it.

GREGERS No, you can't have grown up here and not have been damaged in some way.

HEDVIG I don't care about that. So long as Father comes back up here, then—

GREGERS Ah, if only you had your eyes opened to what really makes life worth living—if you had the true, joyful, and brave spirit of sacrifice, then you'd see how he'd come back to you. But I still believe in you, Hedvig. (*He leaves through the hall door. Hedvig wanders about the room; she is about to go to the kitchen when there is a knocking from behind the loft door. Hedvig goes over and opens the door a little. Old Ekdal comes out. She shuts the door again.*)

EKDAL Hm. There's not much fun making the morning tour alone, you know.

HEDVIG Don't you want to go hunting, Grandfather?

EKDAL It's not hunting weather today. It's so dark you can hardly see in front of you.

HEDVIG Don't you ever want to shoot anything except rabbits?

EKDAL Maybe you don't think rabbits are good enough, eh?

HEDVIG Yes, but the wild duck, then?

EKDAL Oho! Are you scared I'll shoot the wild duck? I'd never do that. Never in all this world.

HEDVIG No, I suppose you couldn't. It must be difficult to shoot wild ducks.

EKDAL I couldn't? I should just think I could!

HEDVIG How would you go about it, Grandfather—I mean, not my wild duck, but with others?

EKDAL You have to shoot them in the breast, you understand—that's the surest way. And you have to shoot *against* the feathers, you see, not *with* the feathers.

HEDVIG Then they die, Grandfather?

EKDAL They die all right—if you shoot correctly. Well, I must go in and clean myself up. Hm. You understand—Hm. (*He goes into his room.*)

(*Hedvig waits a little, glances toward the living-room door, goes over to the bookcase, stretching on tiptoe, and takes down the double-barreled pistol from the shelf and looks at it. Gina, with broom and dust cloth, enters from the living room. Hedvig quickly puts back the pistol.*)

GINA Don't stand there playing with your father's things, Hedvig.

HEDVIG (*Moving from the bookcase.*) I just wanted to tidy up a little.

GINA Go into the kitchen instead and see if the coffee's still hot. I want to take a tray with me when I go down to him.

(*Hedvig goes out. Gina begins to dust and clean in the studio. After a while, the hall door is opened hesitantly, and Hjalmar looks in. He's wearing his overcoat, but without a hat, and is unwashed and with uncombed hair. His eyes are listless and dull.*)

GINA (*Stands with the broom in her hand and looks at him.*) Oh, Ekdal—you're back after all?

HJALMAR (*Steps into the room and answers in a dull voice.*) I come—only to remove myself at the same time.

GINA Yes, yes. I suppose so. But Good Lord, what a mess you look.

HJALMAR A mess?

GINA And look at your good winter coat! Well, that's seen its last days.

HEDVIG (*In the kitchen doorway.*) Mother, shouldn't I—? (*Sees Hjalmar and cries out loudly and joyfully, running toward him.*) Oh, Father, Father!

HJALMAR (*Turns aside and waves her away.*) Go away, go away! (*To Gina.*) Get her away from me, do you hear!

GINA (*Quietly.*) Go into the living room, Hedvig.

(*Hedvig goes silently into the living room.*)

HJALMAR (*Busy, pulling out the table drawer.*) I must have my books with me. Where are my books?

GINA What books?

HJALMAR My scientific works, naturally—the technical journals I use for my invention.

GINA (*Looking in the bookcase.*) These here, that don't have any covers?

HJALMAR Of course, they're the ones.

GINA (*Putting a stack onto the table.*) Shall I get Hedvig to cut the pages for you?[1]

HJALMAR I don't need anyone cutting pages for me.
(*Short silence.*)

GINA Then you're really set on leaving us, Ekdal?

HJALMAR (*Rummaging through the books.*) I would have thought that spoke for itself.

GINA Oh, well.

HJALMAR (*Vehemently.*) For I certainly can't go around here having my heart pierced every hour of the day.

GINA God forgive you for believing something so wicked of me.

HJALMAR Prove to me—!

GINA Seems to me it's you should do the proving.

HJALMAR After a past like yours? There are certain claims—ideal claims I'm tempted to call them—

GINA But what about Grandfather? What will happen to him, poor old thing?

HJALMAR I know my duty. The helpless old man will come with me. I will go into town and make the arrangements—. Hm. (*Hesitantly.*) Has anyone found my hat on the stairs?

GINA No. Have you lost your hat?

HJALMAR Naturally, I had it on when I came back last night. There's no doubt about that. But today I can't find it.

GINA Lord, where did you go with those two drunken rowdies?

HJALMAR Don't question me about unimportant things. Do you think I'm in the mood to remember details?

GINA As long as you haven't caught a cold, Hjalmar. (*Goes into the kitchen.*)

HJALMAR (*Talking to himself, half aloud, and bitterly as he empties the table drawer.*) You're a scoundrel, Relling!—A villain, that's what you are! Ah, you fiendish tempter! If only I could get someone to get rid of you on the quiet. (*He sets some old letters to one side and discovers the torn piece of paper from the day before. He picks it up and looks at the pieces, quickly putting them down as Gina enters.*)

GINA (*Setting a laden coffee tray on the table.*) Here's a drop of

---

1. Books once were published with pages requiring cutting before reading. Ibsen is telling us that Hjalmar has not read his "research material."

something hot if you fancy it. There's also some bread and butter and a little salt meat.

HJALMAR (*Glances at the tray.*) Salt meat? Never under this roof! It's
true I've had no solid nourishment for over twenty-four hours,
but what does that matter! My notes! The autobiography I
started! Where can I find my diary and my important papers?
(*He opens the living-room door but steps back.*) She's there as
well!

GINA Good Lord, the child's got to be somewhere.

HJALMAR Get out. (*He makes way as Hedvig, terrified, comes into the
studio.*)

HJALMAR (*His hand on the door handle, says to Gina.*) In the last
moments I spend in my former home I wish to be spared the
presence of intruders—(*Goes into the living room.*)

HEDVIG (*Goes toward her mother and asks in a low and trembling
voice.*) Does he mean me?

GINA Stay in the kitchen, Hedvig. Or no—go into your own room
instead. (*Speaking to Hjalmar as she goes into him.*) Wait a little, Ekdal. Don't mess up the bureau like that. I know where
everything is.

HEDVIG (*Stands awhile immobile, frightened, and confused, biting
her lips to keep from crying. She clenches her hands convulsively together and says softly.*) The wild duck! (*She steals across
the room and takes the pistol from the shelf, opens the loft door
and closes it after her. Hjalmar and Gina start arguing in the living room.*)

HJALMAR (*Entering with some notebooks and old, loose papers.*) Oh,
what use will that traveling bag be! There are a thousand
things I will have to take away with me.

GINA (*Following with the traveling bag.*) Why not leave all the other
things for the time being and just take a shirt and a pair of un-
derpants.

HJALMAR Puh! It's exhausting—all these preparations—! (*Takes off
his overcoat and throws it on the sofa.*)

GINA And the coffee's standing there getting cold.

HJALMAR Hm. (*Drinks a mouthful involuntarily, and then another.*)

GINA (*Dusts the back of the chairs.*) The worst problem will be finding another attic big enough for the rabbits.

HJALMAR What! I'm supposed to haul the rabbits along with me as
well?

GINA Well, Grandfather can't do without his rabbits, you know.

HJALMAR Father will just have to get used to it. There are higher
things in life than rabbits which I will have to renounce.

GINA (*Dusting the bookcase.*) Shall I pack the flute in the traveling
bag?

HJALMAR No. Not the flute. But give me the pistol!

GINA You want to take the piston with you?

HJALMAR Yes, my loaded pistol.

GINA (*Looking for it.*) It's gone. He must have taken it in with him.

HJALMAR Is he in the attic?

GINA Of course he's in the attic.

HJALMAR Hm. Poor lonely old fellow. (*He takes a piece of bread and butter, eats it, and drinks the rest of the coffee.*)

GINA If we hadn't let the room, you could have moved in there.

HJALMAR So I should be living under the same roof—! Never—! Never!

GINA But couldn't you settle down in the living room for a day or two? You could have it all to yourself.

HJALMAR Never within these walls!

GINA Well then, below with Relling and Molvik?

HJALMAR Don't mention the names of those creatures. It's enough to make me lose my appetite just thinking about them. Oh no, I must go out into the storm and the blizzard—go from house to house, seeking shelter for my father and me.

GINA But you don't have a hat, Ekdal! You've lost your hat.

HJALMAR Ah, those two animals, they're capable of every vice. A hat must be obtained! (*He takes another piece of bread and butter.*) Arrangements have to be made! Because I'm in no mind to put my life in danger as well. (*Searching for something on the tray.*)

GINA What are you looking for?

HJALMAR Butter.

GINA Butter will be here right away. (*She goes into the kitchen.*)

HJALMAR (*Calling after her.*) Don't bother. I can just as well eat dry bread.

GINA (*Bringing in a dish of butter.*) There we are. They say it's freshly churned. (*She pours him another cup of coffee. He sits down on the sofa, spreads more butter on his bread, and eats and drinks a while in silence.*)

HJALMAR Could I, without being pestered by anyone—by anyone at all—put up in the living room for a day or two?

GINA Yes, of course you could, if you wanted to.

HJALMAR Because I can't see how I can possibly move all Father's things in such short time.

GINA And there's another thing—you've first got to tell him you don't want to live with us anymore.

HJALMAR (*Pushes the cup away.*) Yes, that too. I shall have to cut my way through all these complicated matters. I need time to plan—and breathing space. I can't bear the whole burden in a single day.

GINA No, especially with the horrible weather outside.

HJALMAR (*Moves Mr. Werle's letter.*) I see this paper is still lying around.

GINA Yes, I haven't touched it.

HJALMAR Not that this paper concerns me—

GINA Well, I'm certainly not going to do anything with it.

HJALMAR Just the same, there's no point in letting it get lost in all the shambles; it easily could in the confusion when I leave.

GINA I'll take care of it, Ekdal.

HJALMAR The deed of gift belongs first of all to Father. He's the one must decide what to do with it.

GINA (*Sighing.*) Yes, poor old Grandfather.

HJALMAR Just to be sure—where can I find some paste?

GINA (*Goes to the bookcase.*) Here's the paste pot.

HJALMAR And a brush.

GINA Here's the brush, too. (*Brings them to him.*)

HJALMAR (*Picking up a pair of scissors.*) Just needs a strip of paper on the back—. (*Cutting and pasting.*) It's not for me to lay hands on someone else's property—least of all that of a destitute old man. Nor that of—another person either. There, then. Let it lie there for a while. And when it's dry—take it away. I don't want to set eyes on that document again. Ever!
(*Gregers Werle enters from the hall.*)

GREGERS (*Somewhat surprised.*) What—you sitting here, Hjalmar?

HJALMAR (*Quickly getting up.*) I sank down from exhaustion.

GREGERS You've eaten breakfast, I see.

HJALMAR The body makes its demands upon us sometimes.

GREGERS What have you decided to do?

HJALMAR For a man like me, there can only be one path to take. I'm in the process of gathering together my most important items. But it takes time, you have to realize.

GINA (*A little impatiently.*) Shall I get the room ready for you or do I pack the bag?

HJALMAR (*After an embarrassed glance at Gregers.*) Pack—and get the room ready.

GINA (*Taking the bag.*) Very well. I'll put in the shirt and the other things. (*Goes into the living room and closes the door after her.*)

GREGERS (*After a short silence.*) I never thought this is how it would end. Do you really have to leave house and home?

HJALMAR (*Pacing uneasily about.*) Well, what would you have me do? I'm not made to deal with unhappiness, Gregers. I must have things nice and secure and peaceful around me.

GREGERS But can't you still have that? Just try! In my opinion, you've now got a firm foundation to build on—to make a new start. And remember you've got your invention to live for.

HJALMAR Oh, don't talk about the invention. Its prospects are still very distant.

GREGERS Really?

HJALMAR Well, for God's sake, what would you actually have me invent? Other people have invented almost everything already. It gets more difficult every day.

GREGERS And yet you've put so much work into it.

HJALMAR It was that unspeakable Relling who got me to do it.

GREGERS Relling?

HJALMAR Yes, it was he who first made me see my potential for making some remarkable discovery or other in photography.

GREGERS So—it was Relling!

HJALMAR I have been so deeply happy over this project. Not so much for the invention itself, but because Hedvig believed in it—believed with all the strength and fervor a child's soul can muster. Well, that's to say, like a fool I went around imagining she believed in it.

GREGERS Can you actually believe Hedvig would deceive you?

HJALMAR I can believe anything now. It's Hedvig that stands in my way. She'll be there always blotting the sun from my life.

GREGERS Hedvig! Is it Hedvig you mean? How could she do a thing like that?

HJALMAR (*Without answering.*) How inexpressibly I loved that child. I can't describe how happy I felt each time I came home to my simple rooms and she rushed to meet me with her sweet, straining little eyes. What a gullible fool I was! I loved her beyond words—and I dreamed and deluded myself in my imagination that she loved me as inexpressibly in return.

GREGERS You're saying it was just your imagination?

HJALMAR How can I tell? I can't get anything out of Gina. She completely lacks any sense of the ideal aspects of the problem. But with you I feel the need to open myself up, Gregers. I have this dreadful doubt—that perhaps Hedvig has never really and truly loved me.

GREGERS You might possibly soon get proof of that. (*Listening.*) What's that? I think I heard the wild duck cry out.

HJALMAR The wild duck's quacking. Father's in the loft.

GREGERS Is he? (*His face lights up.*) I tell you, you may soon have proof that your poor misunderstood Hedvig loves you!

HJALMAR What proof can she give me! I daren't believe in any assurance from that quarter.

GREGERS Hedvig knows nothing at all of deceit.

HJALMAR Oh, Gregers, *that* is precisely what I can't be sure of. Who knows how many times Gina and this Mrs. Sørby have sat here, whispering and gossiping? And Hedvig knows how to use her ears. Perhaps the deed of gift wasn't so unexpected after all. I believe I noticed something of the sort at the time.

GREGERS What's this spirit that's entered you?

HJALMAR I've had my eyes opened. Just you wait—you'll see the deed of gift is just the beginning. Mrs. Sørby always had a great liking for Hedvig, and now she has the power to do whatever she wants with the child. They can take her away from me any time they like.

GREGERS No way in the world would Hedvig leave you.

HJALMAR Don't be so sure of that. What if they stood there, beckoning her with full hands—? And I, who have loved her so inexpressibly—whose greatest joy was to take her gently by the hand and lead her as one leads a child frightened of the dark through a great, empty room—! Now I feel with gnawing certainty that the poor photographer up in his attic never meant all that much to her. She's only been cunning enough to be on a good footing with him until the right time came.

GREGERS You don't believe a word of this yourself, Hjalmar.

HJALMAR The dreadful thing is precisely that I don't know what I should believe—and I shall never know. Can you really doubt it must be like I say? Ha-ha, you rely too much on the claims of ideals, my dear Gregers! As soon as the others come, with their overflowing hands, calling to the child: "Leave him; there's a new life waiting for you with us—"

GREGERS (*Hurriedly.*) Yes, what then, do you think?

HJALMAR If I then asked her, "Hedvig, are you willing to renounce that life for me?" (*Laughs scornfully.*) Oh yes, thank you! You'd soon hear what answer I'd get!

(*A pistol shot is heard inside the loft.*)

GREGERS (*Loudly, in joy.*) Hjalmar!

HJALMAR What the—! Now he has to go hunting!

GINA (*Entering.*) Uff, Ekdal, I do believe Grandfather is firing away in the loft all by himself.

HJALMAR I'll have a look—

GREGERS (*Excitedly, stirred.*) Wait a moment! Do you know what that was?

HJALMAR Of course I know.

GREGERS No, you don't know. But *I* know. That was the proof!

HJALMAR What proof?

GREGERS That was the child's sacrifice. She's got your father to shoot the wild duck.

HJALMAR Shoot the wild duck!

GINA No! Just imagine—!

HJALMAR Whatever for?

GREGERS She wanted to sacrifice the most precious thing she possessed in all the world. For then she believed you would have to love her again.

HJALMAR (*Tenderly, moved.*) Oh, that child!

GINA The things she thinks of!

GREGERS All she wanted was your love again, Hjalmar. She didn't believe she could live without it.

GINA (*Fighting back her tears.*) There, you see, Ekdal!

HJALMAR Gina, where is she?

GINA (*Sniffing.*) Poor thing, she's sitting out there in the kitchen, I suppose.

HJALMAR (*Goes over and opens the kitchen door, calling.*) Hedvig— come! Come here to me! (*Looks around.*) No, she's not in here.

GINA Then she'll be in her own little room.

HJALMAR (*Offstage.*) No, she's not here either. (*Entering.*) She must have gone out.

GINA Well, you didn't want her anywhere in the house.

HJALMAR Oh, if only she would come home soon—so I can really tell her. Now everything will be all right, Gregers. For now I believe we can truly begin life over again.

GREGERS (*Quietly.*) I knew it. Redemption would come through the child.

(*Old Ekdal appears in the door to his room. He is in full dress uniform and is busy trying to buckle on his saber.*)

HJALMAR (*Astonished.*) Father! You *there*!

GINA Were you shooting in your room?

EKDAL (*Indignantly approaching.*) So, you go hunting by yourself do you, Hjalmar?

HJALMAR (*Tensely, bewildered.*) Then it wasn't you, shooting in the loft?

EKDAL I, shooting? Hm.

GREGERS (*Calling out to Hjalmar.*) She's shot the wild duck herself!

HJALMAR What *is* all this! (*Rushes to the loft door, tears it open, looks in, and loudly screams.*) Hedvig!

GINA (*Running to the door.*) Jesus, what is it?

HJALMAR (*Going in.*) She's lying on the floor!

GREGERS Hedvig! On the floor!

GINA (*At the same time.*) Hedvig! (*Goes into the loft.*) No, no, no.

EKDAL Ha-ha. So she also goes shooting?

(*Hjalmar, Gina, and Gregers carry Hedvig into the studio. In her*

*right hand, which is hanging down, a pistol is firmly gripped by
her fingers.*)

HJALMAR (*Distraught.*) The pistol went off. She's shot herself. Call
for help! Help!

GINA (*Runs into the hall and calls down.*) Relling! Relling! Doctor
Relling! Come up here as fast as you can!

(*Hjalmar and Gregers lay Hedvig down on the sofa.*)

EKDAL (*Quietly.*) The forest's revenge.

HJALMAR (*On his knees beside her.*) Now she's coming to. Now she's
coming to—Yes, yes, yes.

GINA (*Who has come in again.*) Where did she shoot herself? I
can't see anything.

(*Relling enters rapidly, and right after him, Molvik. The latter is
without waistcoat, collar, or tie. His coat is open.*)

RELLING What's going on here?

GINA They say Hedvig's shot herself.

RELLING Shot herself! (*He pushes the table aside and begins examining her.*)

HJALMAR It can't really be serious? Eh, Relling? She's hardly bleeding at all. It can't really be serious?

RELLING How did it happen?

HJALMAR Oh, how would I know—?

GINA She wanted to shoot the wild duck.

RELLING The wild duck?

HJALMAR The pistol must have gone off.

RELLING Hm. Indeed.

EKDAL The forest's revenge. But I'm not afraid, all the same. (*Goes
into the loft and closes the door after him.*)

HJALMAR Well, Relling, why don't you say something?

RELLING The bullet went into the breast.

HJALMAR Yes, but she's coming to!

RELLING Surely you can see Hedvig's not alive.

GINA (*Bursting into tears.*) Oh, my child, my child!

GREGERS (*Hoarsely.*) In the depths of the sea—.

HJALMAR (*Jumping up.*) Yes, yes, she *must* live! Oh, for God's sake,
Relling, only for a moment—just long enough for me to tell
her how inexpressibly I always loved her.

RELLING The shot reached the heart. Internal hemorrhage. She
died instantly.

HJALMAR And I drove her from me like some animal! And she crept
in terror into the loft and died out of love for me. (*Sobbing.*)
Never to make up for it again! Never to tell her—! (*Clenching
his hands and crying upward.*) Ah, you up there—! If you *are*
there! Why did you do this to me!

GINA Hush, hush, you mustn't say such awful things. We didn't have the right to keep her, I suppose.

MOLVIK The child is not dead. It sleepeth.

RELLING Rubbish!

HJALMAR (*Becomes quiet, goes over to the sofa and looks with folded arms at Hedvig.*) She's lying so rigid and silent.

RELLING (*Trying to loosen the pistol.*) It's held so tight, so tight.

GINA No, no, Relling, don't break her fingers. Let the piston stay.

HJALMAR She shall take it with her.

GINA Yes, let her. But the child shouldn't be lying paraded out here. She shall go into her own little room, she shall. Help me with her, Ekdal.

(*Hjalmar and Gina carry Hedvig between them.*)

HJALMAR (*As they carry her out.*) Oh, Gina, Gina, can you bear this!

GINA We shall have to help each other. For now we share her equally, you know.

MOLVIK (*Stretching out his arms and muttering.*) Praised be the Lord! Dust to dust, dust to dust.

RELLING (*Whispering.*) Hold your tongue, man! You're drunk!

(*Hjalmar and Gina carry the body through the kitchen door. Relling closes the door after them. Molvik sneaks out into the hall.*)

RELLING (*Goes up to Gregers, saying*) No one shall ever convince me this was an accident.

GREGERS (*Who has stood horror-stricken, twitching convulsively.*) No one can say how this dreadful thing happened.

RELLING There were powder burns on the bodice of her dress. She must have pressed the pistol against her breast and fired.

GREGERS Hedvig didn't die in vain. You saw how sorrow released all the nobility in him?

RELLING Most people are noble when they stand grieving by a corpse. But how long do you think this transfiguration will last?

GREGERS It will last and grow the rest of his life!

RELLING Before the year is out little Hedvig will be nothing more to him than a theme for pretty declamations.

GREGERS You dare say that about Hjalmar Ekdal!

RELLING We'll talk about this again before the first grass has withered on her grave. Then you'll hear him gushing forth about "the father's heart from which the child was torn all too soon"; then watch him wallowing in self-admiration and self-pity. Wait and see!

GREGERS If *you* are right and *I* am wrong, then this life on earth is not worth living.

RELLING Oh, life could be quite bearable, all the same, if only we

were rid of the blessed moral bailiffs who badger us poor folk
with their claims of idealism.

GREGERS *(Staring straight ahead of him.)* In that case I'm glad my
destiny is what it is.

RELLING May I ask—what *is* your destiny?

GREGERS *(Preparing to leave.)* To be thirteenth at table.

RELLING The devil it is.

END OF PLAY

Hedda Gabler (1890)

Hedda Gabler is a good example of Ibsen's ability to create "infinite riches in a little room." The predominant form of drama in Ibsen's day was the Scribean "well-made play" whose method was to transfer dramatic interest from potentially controversial *ideas* to innocuous *things*—a glass of water, a poisoned drink, a concealed letter—and in this way to create maximum theatrical excitement with minimum intellectual risk. It was drama written under censorship. Ibsen's genius was to see that *things* in the theater could be made into subversive vehicles of *ideas*. Things are what they are perceived to be, and "ideology" changes the world and the things in it. A cup or bowl (or a glass of water) is just that; but if a character such as Melville in Friedrich Schiller's *Mary Stuart* suddenly reveals he is secretly a priest and can take a cup of wine and convert it into a chalice of the blood of Christ, and so offer Mary the last sacrament, the idea has radically changed the thing. This stage event roused controversy when performed in Schiller's Protestant Germany at the Weimar Hoftheater in 1800.

Two crossed sticks mean nothing to a non-Christian; to a Christian they evoke the crucifixion, the Roman Empire, Palestine, and so on. To a Marxist they might mean institutionalized superstition, intellectual bondage. Thus they would have radically different symbolic functions in a Christian or a Marxian drama. *Ideas* drastically change and symbolically enrich *things*. A "drama of ideas" is likely to be a drama of significant things charged with dramatic meaning. A drama of limited ideas, such as Eugene Scribe's *A Glass of Water*, is a drama of utilitarian things introduced merely to facilitate the plot.

Hedda Gabler is the apotheosis of the well-made play, transforming the Scribean method into Ibsen's own subversive art. The action unfolds in an intensely charged environment in which things, objects, wait to disclose their latent power and their significance in the total meaning of the play. The stage set itself, as in *The Wild Duck*, sets up a key division between foreground and inner rooms. The progress of this set, from morning light to the final night scene of the darkened stage and its black-clad inhabitants, amplifies an action that opens on intimations of birth and new life (Hedda's pregnancy, Løvborg's new book) and closes on multiple mourning: the deaths of aunt Rina, Løvborg, Løvborg and Thea's "child" (the manuscript), Hedda and her unborn child. Ibsen has demurely engineered within a fashionable drawing room a carnage of Shakespearean magnitude.

Within this fateful stage set, objects undergo "epiphanies" in which they release their power. The bouquets, the piano, Tesman's slippers, the aunt's hat, the photograph album, the fateful drink, the manuscript and its "resurrection" by Tesman and Thea, the stove, Hedda's pistols, her father's portrait—all these are employed with more than the technical skill of the well-made-play and with a metaphoric richness far beyond scope of Scribean drama.

Hedda Gabler, with *A Doll House*, is the most performed (Ibsen) play in the United States and too frequently is seen as a "star vehicle." Ibsen, however, insisted on the importance of the whole ensemble. To an actress who objected to being given the role of Berte, Ibsen insisted, in effect, that there were no minor roles in the play: "Jörgen Tesman, his old aunts, and the faithful serving maid Berte together form a picture of complete unity. They think alike; they share the same memories and have the same outlook on life. To Hedda they appear like a strange and hostile power, aimed at her very being."[1]

In fact, the important division in the play might be seen as between two groups rather than between individuals. Tesman, the aunts, Berte, Thea Elvsted, and Judge Brack make up one group. The other is made up of Hedda, Løvborg, the courtesan Diana, and General Gabler whose portrait dominates the scene. This division into two groups seems to reflect the Christian-pagan dichotomy in the Western mind that runs all through Ibsen's drama, at least from *The Warrior's Barrow* (1850). Many critics have seen the close resemblance of the play to the earlier *The Vikings at Helgeland* (1858), with its overt pagan-Christian conflict. Awareness of this dimension should prevent anyone reading *Hedda Gabler* as if it were a case study of a single individual. Hedda is the crucible in which the conflicting forces of the play explosively meet.

Hedda Gabler†

Characters

GEORGE TESMAN, research fellow in cultural history
HEDDA TESMAN, his wife
MISS JULIANE TESMAN, his aunt
MRS. ELVSTED
JUDGE BRACK
EILERT LØVBORG
BERTE, the maid to the Tesmans

The action takes place in the fashionable west side of Christiania, Norway's capital.

---

1. *Ibsen, Letters and Speeches*, ed. Evert Sprinchorn (New York: Hill and Wang, 1964).
† Translated by Rick Davis and Brian Johnston.

Act One

A large, pleasantly and tastefully furnished drawing room, decorated in somber tones. In the rear wall is a wide doorway with the curtains pulled back. This doorway leads into a smaller room decorated in the same style. In the right wall of the drawing room is a folding door leading into the hall. In the opposite wall, a glass door, also with its curtains pulled back. Outside, through the windows, part of a covered veranda can be seen, along with trees in their autumn colors. In the foreground, an oval table surrounded by chairs. Downstage, near the right wall, is a broad, dark porcelain stove, a high-backed armchair, a footstool with cushions and two stools. Up in the right-hand corner, a corner-sofa and a small round table. Downstage, on the left side, a little distance from the wall, a sofa. Beyond the glass door, a piano. On both sides of the upstage doorway stand shelves displaying terra cotta and majolica objects. By the back wall of the inner room, a sofa, a table and a couple of chairs can be seen. Above the sofa hangs the portrait of a handsome elderly man in a general's uniform. Above the table, a hanging lamp with an opalescent glass shade. There are many flowers arranged in vases and glasses all around the drawing room. More flowers lie on the tables. The floors of both rooms are covered with thick rugs.

Morning light. The sun shines in through the glass door.

(Miss Julie Tesman, with hat and parasol, comes in from the hall, followed by Berta, who carries a bouquet wrapped in paper. Miss Tesman is a kindly, seemingly good-natured lady of about sixty-five, neatly but simply dressed in a grey visiting outfit. Berta is a housemaid, getting on in years, with a homely and somewhat rustic appearance.)

MISS TESMAN *(Stops just inside the doorway, listens, and speaks softly.)* Well—I believe they're just now getting up!

BERTA *(Also softly.)* That's what I said, Miss. Just think—the steamer got in so late last night, and then—Lord, the young mistress wanted so much unpacked before she could settle down.

MISS TESMAN Well, well. Let them have a good night's sleep at least. But—they'll have some fresh morning air when they come down. *(She crosses to the glass door and throws it wide open.)*

BERTA *(By the table, perplexed, holding the bouquet.)* Hmm. Bless me if I can find a spot for these. I think I'd better put them down here, Miss. (*Puts the bouquet down on the front of the piano.*)

MISS TESMAN So, Berta dear, now you have a new mistress. As God's my witness, giving you up was a heavy blow.

BERTA And me, Miss—what can I say? I've been in yours and Miss Rina's service for so many blessed years—

MISS TESMAN We must bear it patiently, Berta. Truly, there's no other way. You know George has to have you in the house with him—he simply has to. You've looked after him since he was a little boy.

BERTA Yes, but Miss—I keep worrying about her, lying there at home—so completely helpless, poor thing. And that new girl! She'll never learn how to take care of sick people.

MISS TESMAN Oh, I'll teach her how soon enough. And I'll be doing most of the work myself, you know. Don't you worry about my sister, Berta dear.

BERTA Yes, but there's something else, Miss. I'm so afraid I won't satisfy the new mistress—

MISS TESMAN Ffft—Good Lord—there might be a thing or two at first—

BERTA Because she's so particular about things—

MISS TESMAN Well, what do you expect? General Gabler's daughter—the way she lived in the general's day! Do you remember how she would go out riding with her father? In that long black outfit, with the feather in her hat?

BERTA Oh, yes—I remember that all right. But I never thought she'd make a match with our Mr. Tesman.

MISS TESMAN Neither did I. But—while I'm thinking about it, don't call George "Mister Tesman" any more. Now it's "Doctor Tesman."

BERTA Yes—that's what the young mistress said as soon as they came in last night. So it's true?

MISS TESMAN Yes, it's really true. Think of it, Berta—they've made him a doctor. While he was away, you understand. I didn't know a thing about it, until he told me himself, down at the pier.

BERTA Well, he's so smart he could be anything he wanted to be. But I never thought he'd take up curing people too!

MISS TESMAN No, no, no. He's not that kind of doctor. (*Nods significantly.*) As far as that goes, you might have to start calling him something even grander soon.

BERTA Oh no! What could that be?

MISS TESMAN (*Smiling.*) Hmm—wouldn't you like to know? (*Emotionally.*) Oh, dear God . . . if our sainted Joseph could look up from his grave and see what's become of his little boy. (*She looks around.*) But, Berta—what's this now? Why have you taken all the slipcovers off the furniture?

BERTA The mistress told me to. She said she can't stand covers on chairs.

MISS TESMAN But are they going to use this for their everyday living room?

BERTA Yes, they will. At least she will. He—the doctor—he didn't say anything.

(*George Tesman enters, humming, from the right of the inner room, carrying an open, empty suitcase. He is a youthful-looking man of thirty-three, of medium height, with an open, round, and cheerful face, blond hair and beard. He wears glasses and is dressed in comfortable, somewhat disheveled clothes.*)

MISS TESMAN Good morning, good morning, George!

TESMAN Aunt Julie! Dear Aunt Julie! (*Goes over and shakes her hand.*) All the way here—so early in the day! Hm!

MISS TESMAN Yes, you know me—I just had to peek in on you a little.

TESMAN And after a short night's sleep at that!

MISS TESMAN Oh, that's nothing at all to me.

TESMAN So—you got home all right from the pier, hm?

MISS TESMAN Yes, as it turned out, thanks be to God. The Judge was kind enough to see me right to the door.

TESMAN We felt so bad that we couldn't take you in the carriage— but you saw how many trunks and boxes Hedda had to bring.

MISS TESMAN Yes, it was amazing.

BERTA (*To Tesman.*) Perhaps I should go in and ask the mistress if there's anything I can help her with.

TESMAN No, thank you, Berta. You don't have to do that. If she needs you, she'll ring—that's what she said.

BERTA (*Going out to right.*) Very well.

TESMAN Ah—but—Berta—take this suitcase with you.

BERTA (*Takes the case.*) I'll put it in the attic.

TESMAN Just imagine, Auntie. I'd stuffed that whole suitcase with notes—just notes! The things I managed to collect in those archives—really incredible! Ancient, remarkable things that no one had any inkling of.

MISS TESMAN Ah yes—you certainly haven't wasted any time on your honeymoon.

TESMAN Yes—I can really say that's true. But, Auntie, take off your hat—Here, let's see. Let me undo that ribbon, hm?

MISS TESMAN (*While he does so.*) Ah, dear God—this is just what it was like when you were home with us.

TESMAN (*Examining the hat as he holds it.*) My, my—isn't this a fine, elegant hat you've got for yourself.

MISS TESMAN I bought it for Hedda's sake.

TESMAN For Hedda's—hm?

MISS TESMAN Yes, so Hedda won't feel ashamed of me if we go out for a walk together.

TESMAN (*Patting her cheek.*) You think of everything, Auntie Julie, don't you? (*Putting her hat on a chair by the table.*) And now— let's just settle down here on the sofa until Hedda comes. (*They sit. She puts her parasol down near the sofa.*)

MISS TESMAN (*Takes both his hands and gazes at him.*) What a blessing to have you here, bright as day, right before my eyes again, George. Sainted Joseph's own boy!

TESMAN For me too. To see you again, Aunt Julie—who've been both father and mother to me.

MISS TESMAN Yes, I know you'll always have a soft spot for your old aunts.

TESMAN But no improvement at all with Rina, hm?

MISS TESMAN Oh dear no—and none to be expected, poor thing. She lies there just as she has all these years. But I pray that Our Lord lets me keep her just a little longer. Otherwise I don't know what I'd do with my life, George. Especially now, you know—when I don't have you to take care of any more.

TESMAN (*Patting her on the back.*) There. There. There.

MISS TESMAN Oh—just to think that you've become a married man, George. And that you're the one who carried off Hedda Gabler! Beautiful Hedda Gabler. Imagine—with all her suitors.

TESMAN (*Hums a little and smiles complacently.*) Yes, I believe I have quite a few friends in town who envy me, hm?

MISS TESMAN And then—you got to take such a long honeymoon— more than five—almost six months . . .

TESMAN Yes, but it was also part of my research, you know. All those archives I had to wade through—and all the books I had to read!

MISS TESMAN I suppose you're right. (*Confidentially and more quietly.*) But listen, George—isn't there something—something extra you want to tell me?

TESMAN About the trip?

MISS TESMAN Yes.

TESMAN No—I can't think of anything I didn't mention in my letters. I was given my doctorate—but I told you that yesterday.

MISS TESMAN So you did. But I mean—whether you might have any—any kind of—prospects—?

TESMAN Prospects?

MISS TESMAN   Good Lord, George—I'm your old aunt.

TESMAN   Well of course I have prospects.

MISS TESMAN   Aha!

TESMAN   I have excellent prospects of becoming a professor one of these days. But Aunt Julie dear, you already know that.

MISS TESMAN   (*With a little laugh.*) You're right, I do. (*Changing the subject.*) But about your trip. It must have cost a lot.

TESMAN   Well, thank God, that huge fellowship paid for a good part of it.

MISS TESMAN   But how did you make it last for the both of you?

TESMAN   That's the tricky part, isn't it?

MISS TESMAN   And on top of that, when you're travelling with a lady! That's always going to cost you more, or so I've heard.

TESMAN   You're right—it was a bit more costly. But Hedda just had to have that trip, Auntie. She really had to. There was no choice.

MISS TESMAN   Well, I suppose not. These days a honeymoon trip is essential, it seems. But now tell me—have you had a good look around the house?

TESMAN   Absolutely! I've been up since dawn.

MISS TESMAN   And what do you think about all of it?

TESMAN   It's splendid! Only I can't think of what we'll do with those two empty rooms between the back parlor and Hedda's bedroom.

MISS TESMAN   (*Lightly laughing.*) My dear George—when the time comes, you'll think of what to do with them.

TESMAN   Oh, of course—as I add to my library, hm?

MISS TESMAN   That's right, my boy—of course I was thinking about your library.

TESMAN   Most of all I'm just so happy for Hedda. Before we got engaged she'd always say how she couldn't imagine living anywhere but here—in Prime Minister Falk's house.

MISS TESMAN   Yes—imagine. And then it came up for sale just after you left for your trip.

TESMAN   Aunt Julie, we really had luck on our side, hm?

MISS TESMAN   But the expense, George. This will all be costly for you.

TESMAN   (*Looks at her disconcertedly.*) Yes. It might be. It might be, Auntie.

MISS TESMAN   Ah, God only knows.

TESMAN   How much, do you think? Approximately. Hm?

MISS TESMAN   I can't possibly tell before all the bills are in.

TESMAN   Luckily Judge Brack lined up favorable terms for me—he wrote as much to Hedda.

MISS TESMAN That's right—don't you ever worry about that, my boy. All this furniture, and the carpets? I put up the security for it.

TESMAN Security? You? Dear Auntie Julie, what kind of security could you give?

MISS TESMAN I took out a mortgage on our annuity.

TESMAN What? On your—and Aunt Rina's annuity!

MISS TESMAN I couldn't think of any other way.

TESMAN (*Standing in front of her.*) Have you gone completely out of your mind, Auntie? That annuity is all you and Aunt Rina have to live on.

MISS TESMAN Now, now, take it easy. It's just a formality, you understand. Judge Brack said so. He was good enough to arrange it all for me. Just a formality, he said.

TESMAN That could very well be, but all the same . . .

MISS TESMAN You'll be earning your own living now, after all. And, good Lord, so what if we do have to open the purse a little, spend a little bit at first? That would only make us happy.

TESMAN Auntie . . . you never get tired of sacrificing yourself for me.

MISS TESMAN (*Rises and lays her hands on his shoulders.*) What joy do I have in the world, my dearest boy, other than smoothing out the path for you? You, without a father or mother to take care of you . . . but we've reached our destination, my dear. Maybe things looked black from time to time. But, praise God, George, you've come out on top!

TESMAN Yes, it's really amazing how everything has gone according to plan.

MISS TESMAN And those who were against you—those who would have blocked your way—they're at the bottom of the pit. They've fallen, George. And the most dangerous one, he fell the farthest. Now he just lies there where he fell, the poor sinner.

TESMAN Have you heard anything about Eilert—since I went away, I mean?

MISS TESMAN Nothing, except they say he published a new book.

TESMAN What? Eilert Løvborg? Just recently, hm?

MISS TESMAN That's what they say. God only knows how there could be anything to it. But when *your* book comes out—now that will be something else again, won't it, George? What's it going to be about?

TESMAN It will deal with the Domestic Craftsmanship Practices of Medieval Brabant.

MISS TESMAN Just think—you can write about that kind of thing too.

TESMAN However, it might be quite a while before that book is ready. I've got all these incredible collections that have to be put in order first.

MISS TESMAN Ordering and collecting—you're certainly good at that. You're not the son of sainted Joseph for nothing.

TESMAN And I'm so eager to get going. Especially now that I've got my own snug house and home to work in.

MISS TESMAN And most of all, now that you've got her—your heart's desire, dear, dear George!

TESMAN (*Embracing her.*) Yes, Auntie Julie! Hedda . . . that's the most beautiful thing of all! (*Looking toward the doorway.*) I think that's her, hm?

(*Hedda comes in from the left side of the inner room. She is a lady of twenty-nine. Her face and figure are aristocratic and elegant. Her complexion is pale. Her eyes are steel-grey, cold and clear. Her hair is an attractive medium brown but not particularly full. She is wearing a tasteful, somewhat loose-fitting morning gown.*)

MISS TESMAN (*Going to meet Hedda.*) Good morning, Hedda, my dear. Good morning.

HEDDA (*Extending her hand.*) Good morning, Miss Tesman, my dear. You're here so early. How nice of you.

MISS TESMAN (*Looking somewhat embarrassed.*) Well now, how did the young mistress sleep in her new home?

HEDDA Fine thanks. Well enough.

TESMAN (*Laughing.*) Well enough! That's a good one, Hedda. You were sleeping like a log when I got up.

HEDDA Yes, lucky for me. But of course you have to get used to anything new, Miss Tesman. A little at a time. (*Looks toward the window.*) Uch! Look at that. The maid opened the door. I'm drowning in all this sunlight.

MISS TESMAN (*Going to the door.*) Well then, let's close it.

HEDDA No, no, don't do that. Tesman my dear, just close the curtains. That gives a gentler light.

TESMAN (*By the door.*) All right, all right. Now then, Hedda. You've got both fresh air and sunlight.

HEDDA Yes, fresh air. That's what I need with all these flowers all over the place. But Miss Tesman, won't you sit down?

MISS TESMAN No, but thank you. Now that I know everything's all right here, I've got to see about getting home again. Home to that poor dear who's lying there in pain.

TESMAN Be sure to give her my respects, won't you? And tell her I'll stop by and look in on her later today.

MISS TESMAN Yes, yes I'll certainly do that. But would you believe it, George? (*She rustles around in the pocket of her skirt.*) I almost forgot. Here, I brought something for you.

TESMAN And what might that be, Auntie, hm?

MISS TESMAN (*Brings out a flat package wrapped in newspaper and hands it to him.*) Here you are, my dear boy.

TESMAN (*Opening it.*) Oh my Lord. You kept them for me, Aunt Julie. Hedda, isn't this touching, hm?

HEDDA Well, what is it?

TESMAN My old house slippers. My slippers.

HEDDA Oh yes, I remember how often you talked about them on our trip.

TESMAN Yes, well, I really missed them. (*Goes over to her.*) Now you can see them for yourself, Hedda.

HEDDA (*Moves over to the stove.*) Oh, no thanks, I don't really care to.

TESMAN (*Following after her.*) Just think, Aunt Rina lying there embroidering for me, sick as she was. Oh, you couldn't possibly believe how many memories are tangled up in these slippers.

HEDDA (*By the table.*) Not for me.

MISS TESMAN Hedda's quite right about that, George.

TESMAN Yes, but now that she's in the family I thought—

HEDDA That maid won't last, Tesman.

MISS TESMAN Berta—?

TESMAN What makes you say that, hm?

HEDDA (*Pointing.*) Look, she's left her old hat lying there on that chair.

TESMAN (*Terrified, dropping the slippers on the floor.*) Hedda—!

HEDDA What if someone came in and saw that.

TESMAN But Hedda—that's Aunt Julie's hat.

HEDDA Really?

MISS TESMAN (*Taking the hat.*) Yes, it really is. And for that matter it's not so old either, my dear little Hedda.

HEDDA Oh, I really didn't get a good look at it, Miss Tesman.

MISS TESMAN (*Tying the hat on her head.*) Actually I've never worn it before today—and the good Lord knows that's true.

TESMAN And an elegant hat it is too. Really magnificent.

MISS TESMAN (*She looks around.*) Oh that's as may be, George. My parasol? Ah, here it is. (*She takes it.*) That's mine too. (*She mutters.*) Not Berta's.

TESMAN A new hat and a new parasol. Just think, Hedda.

HEDDA Very charming, very attractive.

TESMAN That's true, hm? But Auntie, take a good look at Hedda before you go. Look at how charming and attractive she is.

MISS TESMAN Oh my dear, that's nothing new. Hedda's been lovely all her life. (*She nods and goes across to the right.*)

TESMAN (*Following her.*) Yes, but have you noticed how she's blossomed, how well she's filled out on our trip?

HEDDA Oh, leave it alone!

MISS TESMAN (*Stops and turns.*) Filled out?

TESMAN Yes, Aunt Julie. You can't see it so well right now in that gown—but I, who have a little better opportunity to—

HEDDA (*By the glass door impatiently.*) Oh you don't have the opportunity for anything.

TESMAN It was that mountain air down in the Tyrol.

HEDDA (*Curtly interrupting.*) I'm the same as when I left.

TESMAN You keep saying that. But it's true, isn't it Auntie?

MISS TESMAN (*Folding her hands and gazing at Hedda.*) Lovely . . . lovely . . . lovely. That's Hedda. (*She goes over to her and with both her hands takes her head, bends it down, kisses her hair.*) God bless and keep Hedda Tesman for George's sake.

HEDDA (*Gently freeing herself.*) Ah—! Let me out!

MISS TESMAN (*With quiet emotion.*) I'll come look in on you two every single day.

TESMAN Yes, Auntie, do that, won't you, hm?

MISS TESMAN Good-bye, good-bye.

  (*She goes out through the hall door. Tesman follows her out. The door remains half open. Tesman is heard repeating his greetings to Aunt Rina and his thanks for the slippers. While this is happening, Hedda walks around the room raising her arms and clenching her fists as if in a rage. Then she draws the curtains back from the door, stands there and looks out. After a short time, Tesman comes in and closes the door behind him.*)

TESMAN (*Picking up the slippers from the floor.*) What are you looking at, Hedda?

HEDDA (*Calm and controlled again.*) Just the leaves. So yellow and so withered.

TESMAN (*Wrapping up the slippers and placing them on the table.*) Yes, well—we're into September now.

HEDDA (*Once more uneasy.*) Yes—It's already—already September.

TESMAN Didn't you think Aunt Julie was acting strange just now, almost formal? What do you suppose got into her?

HEDDA I really don't know her. Isn't that the way she usually is?

TESMAN No, not like today.

HEDDA (*Leaving the glass door.*) Do you think she was upset by the hat business?

TESMAN Not really. Maybe a little, for just a moment—

HEDDA But where did she get her manners, flinging her hat around any way she likes here in the drawing room. People just don't act that way.

TESMAN Well, I'm sure she won't do it again.

HEDDA Anyway, I'll smooth everything over with her soon enough.

TESMAN Yes, Hedda, if you would do that.

HEDDA When you visit them later today, invite her here for the evening.

TESMAN Yes, that's just what I'll do. And there's one more thing you can do that would really make her happy.

HEDDA Well?

TESMAN If you just bring yourself to call her Aunt Julie, for my sake, Hedda, hm?

HEDDA Tesman, for God's sake, don't ask me to do that. I've told you that before. I'll try to call her Aunt once in a while and that's enough.

TESMAN Oh well, I just thought that now that you're part of the family . . .

HEDDA Hmm. I don't know— (*She crosses upstage to the doorway.*)

TESMAN (*After a pause.*) Is something the matter, Hedda?

HEDDA I was just looking at my old piano. It really doesn't go with these other things.

TESMAN As soon as my salary starts coming in, we'll see about trading it in for a new one.

HEDDA Oh, no, don't trade it in. I could never let it go. We'll leave it in the back room instead. And then we'll get a new one to put in here. I mean, as soon as we get the chance.

TESMAN (*A little dejectedly.*) Yes, I suppose we could do that.

HEDDA (*Taking the bouquet from the piano.*) These flowers weren't here when we got in last night.

TESMAN I suppose Aunt Julie brought them.

HEDDA (*Looks into the bouquet.*) Here's a card. (*Takes it out and reads.*) "Will call again later today." Guess who it's from.

TESMAN Who is it, hm?

HEDDA It says Mrs. Elvsted.

TESMAN Really. Mrs. Elvsted. She used to be Miss Rysing.

HEDDA Yes, that's the one. She had all that irritating hair she'd always be fussing with. An old flame of yours, I've heard.

TESMAN (*Laughs.*) Oh, not for long and before I knew you, Hedda. And she's here in town. How about that.

HEDDA Strange that she should come visiting us. I hardly know her except from school.

TESMAN Yes, and of course I haven't seen her since—well God knows how long. How could she stand it holed up out there so far from everything, hm?

HEDDA (*Reflects a moment and then suddenly speaks.*) Just a minute, Tesman. Doesn't he live out that way, Eilert Løvborg, I mean?

TESMAN Yes, right up in that area.

(*Berta comes in from the hallway.*)

BERTA Ma'am, she's back again. The lady who came by with the flowers an hour ago. (*Pointing.*) Those you've got in your hand, Ma'am.

HEDDA Is she then? Please ask her to come in.

(*Berta opens the door for Mrs. Elvsted and then leaves. Mrs. Elvsted is slender with soft, pretty features. Her eyes are light blue, large, round and slightly protruding. Her expression is one of alarm and question. Her hair is remarkably light, almost a white gold and exceptionally rich and full. She is a couple of years younger than Hedda. Her costume is a dark visiting dress, tasteful but not of the latest fashion.*)

HEDDA (*Goes to meet her in a friendly manner.*) Hello my dear Mrs. Elvsted. So delightful to see you again.

MRS. ELVSTED (*Nervous, trying to control herself.*) Yes, it's been so long since we've seen each other.

TESMAN (*Shakes her hand.*) And we could say the same, hm?

HEDDA Thank you for the lovely flowers.

MRS. ELVSTED I would have come yesterday right away but I heard you were on a trip—

TESMAN So you've just come into town, hm?

MRS. ELVSTED Yesterday around noon. I was absolutely desperate when I heard you weren't home.

HEDDA Desperate, why?

TESMAN My dear Miss Rysing—I mean Mrs. Elvsted.

HEDDA There isn't some sort of trouble—?

MRS. ELVSTED Yes there is—and I don't know another living soul to turn to here in town.

HEDDA (*Sets the flowers down on the table.*) All right then, let's sit down here on the sofa.

MRS. ELVSTED Oh no, I'm too upset to sit down.

HEDDA No you're not. Come over here. (*She draws Mrs. Elvsted to the sofa and sits beside her.*)

TESMAN Well, and now Mrs.—

HEDDA Did something happen up at your place?

MRS. ELVSTED Yes—That's it—well, not exactly—Oh, I don't want you to misunderstand me—

HEDDA Well then the best thing is just to tell it straight out, Mrs. Elvsted—

TESMAN That's why you came here, hm?

MRS. ELVSTED Yes, of course. So I'd better tell you, if you don't already know, that Eilert Løvborg is in town.

HEDDA Løvborg?

TESMAN Eilert Løvborg's back again? Just think, Hedda.

HEDDA Good Lord, Tesman, I can hear.

MRS. ELVSTED He's been back now for about a week. The whole week alone here where he can fall in with all kinds of bad company. This town's a dangerous place for him.

HEDDA But my dear Mrs. Elvsted, how does this involve you?

MRS. ELVSTED (*With a scared expression, speaking quickly.*) He was the children's tutor.

HEDDA Your children?

MRS. ELVSTED My husband's. I don't have any.

HEDDA The stepchildren then?

MRS. ELVSTED Yes.

TESMAN (*Somewhat awkwardly.*) But was he sufficiently—I don't know how to say this—sufficiently regular in his habits to be trusted with that kind of job, hm?

MRS. ELVSTED For the past two years no one could say anything against him.

TESMAN Really, nothing. Just think, Hedda.

HEDDA I hear.

MRS. ELVSTED Nothing at all I assure you. Not in any way. But even so, now that I know he's here in the city alone and with money in his pocket I'm deathly afraid for him.

TESMAN But why isn't he up there with you and your husband, hm?

MRS. ELVSTED When the book came out he was too excited to stay up there with us.

TESMAN Yes, that's right. Aunt Julie said he'd come out with a new book.

MRS. ELVSTED Yes, a major new book on the progress of civilization—in its entirely I mean. That was two weeks ago. And it's been selling wonderfully. Everyone's reading it. It's created a huge sensation—

TESMAN All that, really? Must be something he had lying around from his better days.

MRS. ELVSTED From before, you mean?

TESMAN Yes.

MRS. ELVSTED No, he wrote the whole thing while he was up there living with us. Just in the last year.

TESMAN That's wonderful to hear, Hedda. Just think!

MRS. ELVSTED Yes, if only it continues.

HEDDA Have you met him here in town?

MRS. ELVSTED No, not yet. I had a terrible time hunting down his address but this morning I finally found it.

HEDDA (*Looks searchingly.*) I can't help thinking this is a little odd on your husband's part.

MRS. ELVSTED (*Starts nervously.*) My husband—What?

HEDDA That he'd send you to town on this errand. That he didn't come himself to look for his friend.

MRS. ELVSTED Oh no, no, no. My husband doesn't have time for that. And anyway I had to do some shopping too.

HEDDA (*Smiling slightly.*) Oh well, that's different then.

MRS. ELVSTED (*Gets up quickly, ill at ease.*) And now I beg you, Mr. Tesman, please be kind to Eilert Løvborg if he comes here—and I'm sure he will. You were such good friends in the old days. You have interests in common. The same area of research, as far as I can tell.

TESMAN Yes, that used to be the case anyway.

MRS. ELVSTED Yes, that's why I'm asking you—from the bottom of my heart to be sure to—that you'll—that you'll keep a watchful eye on him. Oh, Mr. Tesman, will you do that—will you promise me that?

TESMAN Yes, with all my heart, Mrs. Rysing.

HEDDA Elvsted.

TESMAN I'll do anything in my power for Eilert. You can be sure of it.

MRS. ELVSTED Oh, that is so kind of you. (*She presses his hands.*) Many, many thanks. (*Frightened.*) Because my husband thinks so highly of him.

HEDDA (*Rising.*) You should write to him, Tesman. He might not come to you on his own.

TESMAN Yes, that's the way to do it, Hedda, hm?

HEDDA And the sooner the better. Right now, I think.

MRS. ELVSTED (*Beseechingly.*) Yes, if you only could.

TESMAN I'll write to him this moment. Do you have his address, Mrs. Elvsted?

MRS. ELVSTED Yes. (*She takes a small slip of paper from her pocket and hands it to him.*) Here it is.

TESMAN Good, good. I'll go write him— (*Looks around just a minute.*) —Where are my slippers? Ah, here they are. (*Takes the packet and is about to leave.*)

HEDDA Make sure your note is very friendly—nice and long too.

TESMAN Yes, you can count on me.

MRS. ELVSTED But please don't say a word about my asking you to do it.

TESMAN Oh, that goes without saying.

(*Tesman leaves to the right through the rear room.*)

HEDDA (*Goes over to Mrs. Elvsted, smiles and speaks softly.*) There, now we've killed two birds with one stone.

MRS. ELVSTED What do you mean?

HEDDA Didn't you see that I wanted him out of the way?

MRS. ELVSTED Yes, to write the letter—

HEDDA So I could talk to you alone.

MRS. ELVSTED (*Confused.*) About this thing?

HEDDA Yes, exactly, about this thing.

MRS. ELVSTED (*Apprehensively.*) But there's nothing more to it, Mrs. Tesman, really there isn't.

HEDDA Ah, but there is indeed. There's a great deal more. I can see that much. Come here, let's sit down together. Have a real heart-to-heart talk. (*She forces Mrs. Elvsted into the armchair by the stove and sits down herself on one of the small stools.*)

MRS. ELVSTED (*Nervously looking at her watch.*) Mrs. Tesman, I was just thinking of leaving.

HEDDA Now you can't be in such a hurry, can you? Talk to me a little bit about how things are at home.

MRS. ELVSTED Oh, that's the last thing I want to talk about.

HEDDA But to me? Good Lord, we went to the same school.

MRS. ELVSTED Yes, but you were one class ahead of me. Oh, I was so afraid of you then.

HEDDA Afraid of me?

MRS. ELVSTED Horribly afraid. Whenever we'd meet on the stairs you always used to pull my hair.

HEDDA No, did I do that?

MRS. ELVSTED Yes, you did—and once you said you'd burn it off.

HEDDA Oh, just silly talk, you know.

MRS. ELVSTED Yes, but I was so stupid in those days, and anyway since then we've gotten to be so distant from each other. Our circles have just been totally different.

HEDDA Well let's see if we can get closer again. Listen now, I know we were good friends in school. We used to call each other by our first names.

MRS. ELVSTED No, no, I think you're mistaken.

HEDDA I certainly am not. I remember it perfectly and so we have to be perfectly open with each other just like in the old days. (*Moves the stool closer.*) There now. (*Kisses her cheek.*) Now you must call me Hedda.

MRS. ELVSTED (*Pressing and patting her hands.*) Oh, you're being so friendly to me. I'm just not used to that.

HEDDA There, there, there. I'll stop being so formal with you and I'll call you my dear Thora.

MRS. ELVSTED My name is Thea.

HEDDA That's right, of course, I meant Thea. (*Looks at her compassionately.*) So you're not used to friendship, Thea, in your own home?

MRS. ELVSTED If I only had a home, but I don't. I've never had one.

HEDDA (*Glances at her.*) I suspected it might be something like that.

MRS. ELVSTED (*Staring helplessly before her.*) Yes, yes, yes.

HEDDA I can't exactly remember now, but didn't you go up to Sheriff Elvsted's as a housekeeper?

MRS. ELVSTED Actually I was supposed to be a governess but his wife—at that time—she was an invalid, mostly bedridden, so I had to take care of the house too.

HEDDA So in the end you became mistress of your own house.

MRS. ELVSTED (*Heavily.*) Yes, that's what I became.

HEDDA Let me see. How long has that been?

MRS. ELVSTED Since I was married?

HEDDA Yes.

MRS. ELVSTED Five years now.

HEDDA That's right, it must be about that.

MRS. ELVSTED Oh these five years—! Or the last two or three anyway—! Ah, Mrs. Tesman, if you could just imagine.

HEDDA (*Slaps her lightly on the hand.*) Mrs. Tesman; really, Thea.

MRS. ELVSTED No, no, of course, I'll try to remember. Anyway, Hedda, if you could only imagine.

HEDDA (*Casually.*) It seems to me that Eilert Løvborg's been living up there for about three years, hasn't he?

MRS. ELVSTED (*Looks uncertainly at her.*) Eilert Løvborg? Yes, that's about right.

HEDDA Did you know him from before—from here in town?

MRS. ELVSTED Hardly at all. I mean his name of course.

HEDDA But up there he'd come to visit you at the house?

MRS. ELVSTED Yes, every day. He'd read to the children. I couldn't manage everything myself, you see.

HEDDA No, of course not. And what about your husband? His work must take him out of the house quite a bit.

MRS. ELVSTED Yes, as you might imagine. He's the sheriff so he has to go traveling around the whole district.

HEDDA (*Leaning against the arm of the chair.*) Thea, my poor sweet Thea—You've got to tell me everything just the way it is.

MRS. ELVSTED All right, but you've got to ask the questions.

HEDDA So, Thea, what's your husband really like? I mean, you know, to be with? Is he good to you?

MRS. ELVSTED (*Evasively.*) He thinks he does everything for the best.

HEDDA I just think he's a little too old for you. He's twenty years older, isn't he?

MRS. ELVSTED (*Irritatedly.*) There's that too. There's a lot of things. I just can't stand being with him. We don't have a single thought in common, not a single thing in the world, he and I.

HEDDA But doesn't he care for you at all in his own way?

MRS. ELVSTED I can't tell what he feels. I think I'm just useful to him, and it doesn't cost very much to keep me. I'm very inexpensive.

HEDDA That's a mistake.

MRS. ELVSTED (*Shaking her head.*) Can't be any other way, not with him. He only cares about himself and maybe about the children a little.

HEDDA And also for Eilert Løvborg, Thea.

MRS. ELVSTED (*Stares at her.*) For Eilert Løvborg? Why do you think that?

HEDDA Well, my dear, he sent you all the way into town to look for him. (*Smiling almost imperceptibly.*) And besides, you said so yourself, to Tesman.

MRS. ELVSTED (*With a nervous shudder.*) Oh yes, I suppose I did. No, I'd better just tell you the whole thing. It's bound to come to light sooner or later anyway.

HEDDA But my dear Thea.

MRS. ELVSTED All right, short and sweet. My husband doesn't know that I'm gone.

HEDDA What, your husband doesn't know?

MRS. ELVSTED Of course not. Anyway he's not at home. He was out traveling. I just couldn't stand it any longer, Hedda, it was impossible. I would have been so completely alone up there.

HEDDA Well, then what?

MRS. ELVSTED Then I packed some of my things, just the necessities, all in secret, and I left the house.

HEDDA Just like that?

MRS. ELVSTED Yes, and I took the train to town.

HEDDA Oh, my good, dear Thea. You dared to do that!

MRS. ELVSTED (*Gets up and walks across the floor.*) Well, what else could I do?

HEDDA What do you think your husband will say when you go home again?

MRS. ELVSTED (*By the table looking at her.*) Up there, to him?

HEDDA Of course, of course.

MRS. ELVSTED I'm never going back up there.

HEDDA (*Gets up and goes closer to her.*) So you've really done it? You've really run away from everything?

MRS. ELVSTED Yes, I couldn't think of anything else to do.

HEDDA But you did it—so openly.

MRS. ELVSTED Oh, you can't keep something like that a secret anyway.

HEDDA Well, what do you think people will say about you, Thea?

MRS. ELVSTED They'll say whatever they want, God knows. (*She sits tired and depressed on the sofa.*) But I only did what I had to do.

HEDDA (*After a brief pause.*) So what will you do with yourself now?

MRS. ELVSTED I don't know yet. All I know is that I've got to live here where Eilert Løvborg lives if I'm going to live at all.

HEDDA (*Moves a chair closer from the table, sits beside her and strokes her hands.*) Thea, my dear, how did it come about, this—bond between you and Eilert Løvborg?

MRS. ELVSTED Oh, it just happened, little by little. I started to have a kind of power over him.

HEDDA Really?

MRS. ELVSTED He gave up his old ways—and not because I begged him to. I never dared do that. But he started to notice that those kinds of things upset me, so he gave them up.

HEDDA (*Concealing an involuntary, derisive smile.*) So you rehabilitated him, as they say. You, little Thea.

MRS. ELVSTED That's what he said, anyway. And for his part he's made a real human being out of me. Taught me to think, to understand all sorts of things.

HEDDA So he read to you too, did he?

MRS. ELVSTED No, not exactly, but he talked to me. Talked without stopping about all sorts of great things. And then there was that wonderful time when I shared in his work, when I helped him.

HEDDA You got to do that?

MRS. ELVSTED Yes. Whenever he wrote anything, we had to agree on it first.

HEDDA Like two good comrades.

MRS. ELVSTED (*Eagerly.*) Yes, comrades. Imagine, Hedda, that's what he called it too. I should feel so happy, but I can't yet because I don't know how long it will last.

HEDDA Are you that unsure of him?

MRS. ELVSTED (*Dejectedly.*) There's the shadow of a woman between Eilert Løvborg and me.

HEDDA (*Stares intently at her.*) Who could that be?

MRS. ELVSTED I don't know. Someone from his past. Someone he's never really been able to forget.

HEDDA What has he told you about all this?

MRS. ELVSTED He's only talked about it once and very vaguely.

HEDDA Yes, what did he say?

MRS. ELVSTED He said that when they broke up she was going to shoot him with a pistol.

HEDDA (*Calm and controlled.*) That's nonsense, people just don't act that way here.

MRS. ELVSTED No they don't—so I think it's got to be that red-haired singer that he once—

HEDDA Yes, that could well be.

MRS. ELVSTED Because I remember they used to say about her that she went around with loaded pistols.

HEDDA Well, then it's her, of course.

MRS. ELVSTED (*Wringing her hands.*) Yes, but Hedda, just think, I hear this singer is in town again. Oh, I'm so afraid.

HEDDA (*Glancing toward the back room.*) Shh, here comes Tesman. (*She gets up and whispers.*) Now, Thea, all of this is strictly between you and me.

MRS. ELVSTED (*Jumping up.*) Oh yes, yes, for God's sake!
(*George Tesman, a letter in his hand, comes in from the right side of the inner room.*)

TESMAN There now, the epistle is prepared.

HEDDA Well done—but Mrs. Elvsted's got to leave now, I think. Just a minute, I'll follow you as far as the garden gate.

TESMAN Hedda dear, do you think Berta could see to this?

HEDDA (*Takes the letter.*) I'll instruct her.
(*Berta comes in from the hall.*)

BERTA Judge Brack is here. Says he'd like to pay his respects.

HEDDA Yes, ask the Judge to be so good as to come in, and then— listen here now—Put this letter in the mailbox.

BERTA (*Takes the letter.*) Yes, ma'am.
(*She opens the door for Judge Brack and then goes out. Judge Brack is forty-five years old, short, well built and moves easily. He has a round face and an aristocratic profile. His short hair is still almost black. His eyes are lively and ironic. He has thick eyebrows and a thick moustache, trimmed square at the ends. He is wearing outdoor clothing, elegant, but a little too young in style. He has a monocle in one eye. Now and then he lets it drop.*)

BRACK (*Bows with his hat in his hand.*) Does one dare to call so early?

HEDDA One does dare.

TESMAN (*Shakes his hand.*) You're welcome any time. Judge Brack, Mrs. Rysing. (*Hedda sighs.*)

BRACK (*Bows.*) Aha, delighted.

HEDDA (*Looks at him laughing.*) Nice to see you by daylight for a change, Judge.

BRACK Do I look different?

HEDDA Yes, younger.

BRACK You're too kind.

TESMAN Well, how about Hedda, hm? Doesn't she look fine? Hasn't she filled out?

HEDDA Stop it now. You should be thanking Judge Brack for all of his hard work—

BRACK Nonsense. It was my pleasure.

HEDDA There's a loyal soul. But here's my friend burning to get away. Excuse me, Judge, I'll be right back.
(*Mutual good-byes. Mrs. Elvsted and Hedda leave by the hall door.*)

BRACK Well, now, your wife's satisfied, more or less?

TESMAN Oh yes, we can't thank you enough. I gather there might be a little more rearrangement here and there and one or two things still missing. A couple of small things yet to be procured.

BRACK Is that so?

TESMAN But nothing for you to worry about. Hedda said that she'd look for everything herself. Let's sit down.

BRACK Thanks. Just for a minute. (*Sits by the table.*) Now, my dear Tesman, there's something we need to talk about.

TESMAN Oh yes, ah, I understand. (*Sits down.*) Time for a new topic. Time for the serious part of the celebration, hm?

BRACK Oh, I wouldn't worry too much about the finances just yet— although I must tell you that it would have been better if we'd managed things a little more frugally.

TESMAN But there was no way to do that. You know Hedda, Judge, you know her well. I couldn't possibly ask her to live in a middle-class house.

BRACK No, that's precisely the problem.

TESMAN And luckily it can't be too long before I get my appointment.

BRACK Well, you know, these things often drag on and on.

TESMAN Have you heard anything further, hm?

BRACK Nothing certain. (*Changing the subject.*) But there is one thing. I've got a piece of news for you.

TESMAN Well?

BRACK Your old friend Eilert Løvborg's back in town.

TESMAN I already know.

BRACK Oh, how did you find out?

TESMAN She told me, that lady who just left with Hedda.

BRACK Oh, I see. I didn't quite get her name.

TESMAN Mrs. Elvsted.

BRACK Ah yes, the sheriff's wife. Yes, he's been staying up there with them.

TESMAN And I'm so glad to hear that he's become a responsible person again.

BRACK Yes, one is given to understand that.

TESMAN And he's come out with a new book, hm?

BRACK He has indeed.

TESMAN And it's caused quite a sensation.

BRACK It's caused an extraordinary sensation.

TESMAN Just think, isn't that wonderful to hear. With all his remarkable talents, I was absolutely certain he was down for good.

BRACK That was certainly the general opinion.

TESMAN But I can't imagine what he'll do with himself now. What will he live on, hm?

(*During these last words, Hedda has entered from the hallway.*)

HEDDA (*To Brack, laughing a little scornfully.*) Tesman is constantly going around worrying about what to live on.

TESMAN My Lord, we're talking about Eilert Løvborg, dear.

HEDDA (*Looking quickly at him.*) Oh yes? (*Sits down in the armchair by the stove and asks casually.*) What's the matter with him?

TESMAN Well, he must have spent his inheritance a long time ago, and he can't really write a new book every year, hm? So I was just asking what was going to become of him.

BRACK Perhaps I can enlighten you on that score.

TESMAN Oh?

BRACK You might remember that he has some relatives with more than a little influence.

TESMAN Unfortunately they've pretty much washed their hands of him.

BRACK In the old days they thought of him as the family's great shining hope.

TESMAN Yes, in the old days, possibly, but he took care of that himself.

HEDDA Who knows? (*Smiles slightly.*) Up at the Elvsteds' he's been the target of a reclamation project.

BRACK And there's this new book.

TESMAN Well, God willing, they'll help him out some way or another. I've just written to him, Hedda, asking him to come over this evening.

BRACK But my dear Tesman, you're coming to my stag party this evening. You promised me on the pier last night.

HEDDA Had you forgotten, Tesman?

TESMAN Yes, to be perfectly honest, I had.

BRACK For that matter, you can be sure he won't come.

TESMAN Why do you say that, hm?

BRACK (*Somewhat hesitantly getting up and leaning his hands on the back of his chair.*) My dear Tesman, you too, Mrs. Tesman, in good conscience I can't let you go on living in ignorance of something like this.

TESMAN Something about Eilert, hm?

BRACK About both of you.

TESMAN My dear Judge, tell me what it is.

BRACK You ought to prepare yourself for the fact that your appointment might not come through as quickly as you expect.

TESMAN (*Jumps up in alarm.*) Has something held it up?

BRACK The appointment might just possibly be subject to a competition.

TESMAN A competition! Just think of that, Hedda!

HEDDA (*Leans further back in her chair.*) Ah yes—yes.

TESMAN But who on earth would it—surely not with—?

BRACK Yes, precisely, with Eilert Løvborg.

TESMAN (*Clasping his hands together.*) No, no, this is absolutely unthinkable, absolutely unthinkable, hm?

BRACK Hmm—well, we might just have to learn to get used to it.

TESMAN No, but Judge Brack, that would be incredibly inconsiderate. (*Waving his arms.*) Because—well—just look, I'm a married man. We went and got married on this very prospect, Hedda and I. Went and got ourselves heavily into debt. Borrowed money from Aunt Julie too. I mean, good Lord, I was as much as promised the position, hm?

BRACK Now, now, you'll almost certainly get it but first there'll have to be a contest.

HEDDA (*Motionless in the armchair.*) Just think, Tesman, it will be a sort of match.

TESMAN But Hedda, my dear, how can you be so calm about this?

HEDDA Oh I'm not, not at all. I can't wait for the final score.

BRACK In any case, Mrs. Tesman, it's a good thing that you know how matters stand. I mean, before you embark on any more of these little purchases I hear you're threatening to make.

HEDDA What's that got to do with this?

BRACK Well, well, that's another matter. Good-bye. (*To Tesman.*) I'll come by for you when I take my afternoon walk.

TESMAN Oh yes, yes, forgive me—I don't know if I'm coming or going.

HEDDA (*Reclining, stretching out her hand.*) Good-bye, Judge, and do come again.

BRACK Many thanks. Good-bye, good-bye.

TESMAN (*Following him to the door.*) Good-bye, Judge. You'll have to excuse me.

(*Judge Brack goes out through the hallway door.*)

TESMAN (*Pacing about the floor.*) We should never let ourselves get lost in a wonderland, Hedda, hm?

HEDDA (*Looking at him and smiling.*) Do you do that?

TESMAN Yes, well, it can't be denied. It was like living in wonderland to go and get married and set up housekeeping on nothing more than prospects.

HEDDA You may be right about that.

TESMAN Well, at least we have our home, Hedda, our wonderful home. The home both of us dreamt about, that both of us craved, I could almost say, hm?

HEDDA (*Rises slowly and wearily.*) The agreement was that we would live in society, that we would entertain.

TESMAN Yes, good Lord, I was so looking forward to that. Just think, to see you as a hostess in our own circle. Hm. Well, well, well, for the time being at least we'll just have to make do with each other, Hedda. We'll have Aunt Julie here now and then. Oh you, you should have such a completely different—

HEDDA To begin with, I suppose I can't have the liveried footmen.

TESMAN Ah no, unfortunately not. No footmen. We can't even think about that right now.

HEDDA And the horse!

TESMAN (*Horrified.*) The horse.

HEDDA I suppose I mustn't think about that any more.

TESMAN No, God help us, you can see that for yourself.

HEDDA (*Walking across the floor.*) Well, at least I've got one thing to amuse myself with.

TESMAN (*Beaming with pleasure.*) Ah, thank God for that, and what is that, Hedda?

HEDDA (*In the center doorway looking at him with veiled scorn.*) My pistols, George.

TESMAN (*Alarmed.*) Pistols?

HEDDA (*With cold eyes.*) General Gabler's pistols.
(*She goes through the inner room and out to the left.*)

TESMAN (*Running to the center doorway and shouting after her.*) No, for the love of God, Hedda, dearest, don't touch those dangerous things. For my sake, Hedda, hm?

Act Two

The Tesmans' rooms as in the first act except that the piano has been moved out and an elegant little writing table with a bookshelf has been put in its place. Next to the sofa a smaller table has been placed. Most of the bouquets have been removed. Mrs. Elvsted's bouquet stands on the larger table in the foreground. It is afternoon.

(*Hedda, dressed to receive visitors, is alone in the room. She stands by the open glass door loading a pistol. The matching pistol lies in an open pistol case on the writing table.*)

HEDDA (*Looking down into the garden and calling.*) Hello again, Judge.

BRACK (*Is heard some distance below.*) Likewise, Mrs. Tesman.

HEDDA (*Raises the pistol and aims.*) Now, Judge Brack, I am going to shoot you.

BRACK (*Shouting from below.*) No, no, no. Don't stand there aiming at me like that.

HEDDA That's what you get for coming up the back way. (*She shoots.*)

BRACK Are you out of your mind?

HEDDA Oh, good Lord, did I hit you?

BRACK (*Still outside.*) Stop this nonsense.

HEDDA Then come on in, Judge.

(*Judge Brack, dressed for a bachelor party, comes in through the glass doors. He carries a light overcoat over his arm.*)

BRACK In the devil's name, are you still playing this game? What were you shooting at?

HEDDA Oh, I just stand here and shoot at the sky.

BRACK (*Gently taking the pistol out of her hands.*) With your permission, ma'am? (*Looks at it.*) Ah, this one. I know it well. (*Looks around.*) And where do we keep the case? I see, here it is. (*Puts the pistol inside and shuts the case.*) All right, we're through with these little games for today.

HEDDA Then what in God's name am I to do with myself?

BRACK No visitors?

HEDDA (*Closes the glass door.*) Not a single one. Our circle is still in the country.

BRACK Tesman's not home either, I suppose.

HEDDA (*At the writing table, locks the pistol case in the drawer.*) No, as soon as he finished eating he was off to the aunts. He wasn't expecting you so early.

BRACK Hmm, I never thought of that. Stupid of me.

HEDDA (*Turns her head, looks at him.*) Why stupid?

BRACK Then I would have come a little earlier.

HEDDA (*Going across the floor.*) Then you wouldn't have found anyone here at all. I've been in my dressing room since lunch.

BRACK Isn't there even one little crack in the door wide enough for a negotiation?

HEDDA Now that's something you forgot to provide for.

BRACK That was also stupid of me.

HEDDA So we'll just have to flop down here and wait. Tesman won't be home any time soon.

BRACK Well, well, Lord knows I can be patient.

(*Hedda sits in the corner of the sofa. Brack lays his overcoat over the back of the nearest chair and sits down, keeps his hat in his hand. Short silence. They look at each other.*)

HEDDA So?

BRACK (*In the same tone.*) So?

HEDDA I asked first.

BRACK (*Leaning a little forward.*) Yes, why don't we allow ourselves a cozy little chat, Mrs. Hedda.

HEDDA (*Leaning further back in the sofa.*) Doesn't it feel like an eternity since we last talked together? A few words last night and this morning, but I don't count them.

BRACK Like this, between ourselves, just the two of us?

HEDDA Well, yes, more or less.

BRACK I wished you were back home every single day.

HEDDA The whole time I was wishing the same thing.

BRACK You, really, Mrs. Hedda? Here I thought you were having a wonderful time on your trip.

HEDDA Oh yes, you can just imagine.

BRACK But that's what Tesman always wrote.

HEDDA Yes, him! He thinks it's the greatest thing in the world to go scratching around in libraries. He loves sitting and copying out old parchments or whatever they are.

BRACK (*Somewhat maliciously.*) Well, that's his calling in the world, at least in part.

HEDDA Yes, so it is, and no doubt it's—but for me, oh dear Judge, I've been so desperately bored.

BRACK (*Sympathetically.*) Do you really mean that? You're serious?

HEDDA Yes, you can imagine it for yourself. Six whole months never meeting with a soul who knew the slightest thing about our circle. No one we could talk with about our kinds of things.

BRACK Ah no, I'd agree with you there. That would be a loss.

HEDDA Then what was most unbearable of all.

BRACK Yes?

HEDDA To be together forever and always—with one and the same person.

BRACK (*Nodding agreement.*) Early and late, yes, night and day, every waking and sleeping hour.

HEDDA That's it, forever and always.

BRACK Yes, all right, but with our excellent Tesman I would have imagined that you might—

HEDDA Tesman is—a specialist, dear Judge.

BRACK Undeniably.

HEDDA And specialists aren't so much fun to travel with. Not for the long run anyway.

BRACK Not even the specialist that one loves?

HEDDA Uch, don't use that syrupy word.

BRACK (*Startled.*) Mrs. Hedda.

HEDDA (*Half laughing, half bitterly.*) Well, give it a try for yourself. Hearing about the history of civilization every hour of the day.

BRACK Forever and always.

HEDDA Yes, yes, yes. And then his particular interest, domestic crafts in the Middle Ages. Uch, the most revolting thing of all.

BRACK (*Looks at her curiously.*) But, tell me now, I don't quite understand how—hmmm.

HEDDA That we're together? George Tesman and I, you mean?

BRACK Well, yes. That's a good way of putting it.

HEDDA Good Lord, do you think it's so remarkable?

BRACK I think—yes and no, Mrs. Hedda.

HEDDA I'd danced myself out, dear Judge. My time was up. (*Shudders slightly.*) Uch, no, I'm not going to say that or even think it.

BRACK You certainly have no reason to think it.

HEDDA Ah, reasons— (*Looks watchfully at him.*) And George Tesman? Well, he'd certainly be called a most acceptable man in every way.

BRACK Acceptable and solid, God knows.

HEDDA And I can't find anything about him that's actually ridiculous, can you?

BRACK Ridiculous? No—I wouldn't quite say that.

HEDDA Hmm. Well, he's a very diligent archivist anyway. Some day he might do something interesting with all of it. Who knows.

BRACK (*Looking at her uncertainly.*) I thought you believed, like everyone else, that he'd turn out to be a great man.

HEDDA (*With a weary expression.*) Yes, I did. And then when he went around constantly begging with all his strength, begging for permission to let him take care of me, well, I didn't see why I shouldn't take him up on it.

BRACK Ah well, from that point of view . . .

HEDDA It was a great deal more than any of my other admirers were offering.

BRACK (*Laughing.*) Well, of course I can't answer for all the others, but as far as I'm concerned you know very well that I've always maintained a certain respect for the marriage bond, that is, in an abstract kind of way, Mrs. Hedda.

HEDDA (*Playfully.*) Oh, I never had any hopes for you.

BRACK All I ask is an intimate circle of good friends, friends I can be of service to in any way necessary. Places where I am allowed to come and go as a trusted friend.

HEDDA Of the man of the house, you mean.

BRACK (*Bowing.*) No, to be honest, of the lady. Of the man as well, you understand, because you know that kind of—how should I put this—that kind of triangular arrangement is really a magnificent convenience for everyone concerned.

HEDDA Yes, you can't imagine how many times I longed for a third person on that trip. Ach, huddled together alone in a railway compartment.

BRACK Fortunately, the wedding trip is over now.

HEDDA (*Shaking her head.*) Oh no, it's a very long trip. It's nowhere near over. I've only come to a little stopover on the line.

BRACK Then you should jump out, stretch your legs a little, Mrs. Hedda.

HEDDA I'd never jump out.

BRACK Really?

HEDDA No, because there's always someone at the stop who—

BRACK (*Laughing.*) Who's looking at your legs, you mean?

HEDDA Yes, exactly.

BRACK Yes, but for heaven's sake.

HEDDA (*With a disdainful gesture.*) I don't hold with that sort of thing. I'd rather remain sitting, just like I am now, a couple alone. On a train.

BRACK But what if a third man climbed into the compartment with the couple?

HEDDA Ah yes. Now that's quite different.

BRACK An understanding friend, a proven friend—

HEDDA Who can be entertaining on all kinds of topics—

BRACK And not a specialist in any way!

HEDDA (*With an audible sigh.*) Yes, that would be a relief.

BRACK (*Hears the front door open and glances toward it.*) The triangle is complete.

HEDDA (*Half audibly.*) And there goes the train.

(*George Tesman in a gray walking suit and with a soft felt hat comes in from the hallway. He is carrying a large stack of unbound books under his arm and in his pockets.*)

TESMAN (*Goes to the table by the corner sofa.*) Phew—hot work lugging all these here. (*Puts the books down.*) Would you believe I'm actually sweating, Hedda? And you're already here, Judge, hm. Berta didn't mention anything about that.

BRACK (*Getting up.*) I came up through the garden.

HEDDA What are all those books you've got there?

TESMAN (*Stands leafing through them.*) All the new works by my fellow specialists. I've absolutely got to have them.

HEDDA By your fellow specialists.

BRACK Ah, the specialists, Mrs. Tesman. (*Brack and Hedda exchange a knowing smile.*)

HEDDA You need even more of these specialized works?

TESMAN Oh, yes, my dear Hedda, you can never have too many of these. You have to keep up with what's being written and published.

HEDDA Yes, you certainly must do that.

TESMAN (*Searches among the books.*) And look here, I've got Eilert Løvborg's new book too. (*Holds it out.*) Maybe you'd like to look at it, Hedda, hm?

HEDDA No thanks—or maybe later.

TESMAN I skimmed it a little on the way.

HEDDA And what's your opinion as a specialist?

TESMAN I think the argument's remarkably thorough. He never wrote like this before. (*Collects the books together.*) Now I've got to get all these inside. Oh, it's going to be such fun to cut the pages. Then I'll go and change. (*To Brack.*) We don't have to leave right away, hm?

BRACK No, not at all. No hurry at all.

TESMAN Good, I'll take my time then. (*Leaves with the books but stands in the doorway and turns.*) Oh, Hedda, by the way, Aunt Julie won't be coming over this evening.

HEDDA Really? Because of that hat business?

TESMAN Not at all. How could you think that of Aunt Julie? No, it's just that Aunt Rina is very ill.

HEDDA She always is.

TESMAN Yes, but today she's gotten quite a bit worse.

HEDDA Well, then it's only right that the other one should stay at home with her. I'll just have to make the best of it.

TESMAN My dear, you just can't believe how glad Aunt Julie was, in spite of everything, at how healthy and rounded out you looked after the trip.

HEDDA (*Half audibly getting up.*) Oh, these eternal aunts.

TESMAN Hm?

HEDDA (*Goes over to the glass door.*) Nothing.

TESMAN Oh, all right. (*He goes out through the rear room and to the right.*)

BRACK What were you saying about a hat?

HEDDA Oh, just a little run-in with Miss Tesman this morning. She'd put her hat down there on that chair (*Looks at him smiling.*) and I pretended I thought it was the maid's.

BRACK (*Shaking his head.*) My dear Mrs. Hedda, how could you do such a thing to that harmless old lady.

HEDDA (*Nervously walking across the floor.*) Oh, you know—these things just come over me like that and I can't resist them. (*Flings herself into the armchair by the stove.*) I can't explain it, even to myself.

BRACK (*Behind the armchair.*) You're not really happy—that's the heart of it.

HEDDA (*Staring in front of her.*) And why should I be happy? Maybe you can tell me.

BRACK Yes. Among other things, be happy you've got the home that you've always longed for.

HEDDA (*Looks up at him and laughs.*) You also believe that myth?

BRACK There's nothing to it?

HEDDA Yes, heavens, there's something to it.

BRACK So?

HEDDA And here's what it is. I used George Tesman to walk me home from parties last summer.

BRACK Yes, regrettably I had to go another way.

HEDDA Oh yes, you certainly were going a different way last summer.

BRACK (*Laughs.*) Shame on you, Mrs. Hedda. So you and Tesman . . .

HEDDA So we walked past here one evening and Tesman, the poor thing, was twisting and turning in his agony because he didn't have the slightest idea what to talk about and I felt sorry that such a learned man—

BRACK (*Smiling skeptically.*) You did . . .

HEDDA Yes, if you will, I did, and so just to help him out of his torment I said, without really thinking about it, that this was the house I would love to live in.

BRACK That was all?

HEDDA For that evening.

BRACK But afterward?

HEDDA Yes, dear Judge, my thoughtlessness has had its consequences.

BRACK Unfortunately, our thoughtlessness often does, Mrs. Hedda.

HEDDA Thanks, I'm sure. But it so happens that George Tesman and I found our common ground in this passion for Prime Minister Falk's villa. And after that it all followed. The engagement, the marriage, the honeymoon and everything else. Yes, yes, Judge, I almost said: you make your bed, you have to lie in it.

BRACK That's priceless. Essentially what you're telling me is you didn't care about any of this here.

HEDDA God knows I didn't.

BRACK What about now, now that we've made it into a lovely home for you?

HEDDA Ach, I feel an air of lavender and dried roses in every room—or maybe Aunt Julie brought that in with her.

BRACK (*Laughing.*) No, I think that's probably a relic of the eminent prime minister's late wife.

HEDDA Yes, that's it, there's something deathly about it. It reminds me of a corsage the day after the ball. (*Folds her hands at the back of her neck, leans back in her chair and gazes at him.*) Oh, my dear Judge, you can't imagine how I'm going to bore myself out here.

BRACK What if life suddenly should offer you some purpose or other, something to live for? What about that, Mrs. Hedda?

HEDDA A purpose? Something really tempting for me?

BRACK Preferably something like that, of course.

HEDDA God knows what sort of purpose that would be. I often wonder if— (*Breaks off.*) No, that wouldn't work out either.

BRACK Who knows. Let me hear.

HEDDA If I could get Tesman to go into politics, I mean.

BRACK (*Laughing.*) Tesman? No, you have to see that politics, anything like that, is not for him. Not in his line at all.

HEDDA No, I can see that. But what if I could get him to try just the same?

BRACK Yes, but why should he do that if he's not up to it? Why would you want him to?

HEDDA Because I'm bored, do you hear me? (*After a pause.*) So you don't think there's any way that Tesman could become a cabinet minister?

BRACK Hmm, you see my dear Mrs. Hedda, that requires a certain amount of wealth in the first place.

HEDDA (*Rises impatiently.*) Yes, that's it, this shabby little world I've ended up in. (*Crosses the floor.*) That's what makes life so contemptible, so completely ridiculous. That's just what it is.

BRACK I think the problem's somewhere else.

HEDDA Where's that?

BRACK You've never had to live through anything that really shakes you up.

HEDDA Anything serious, you mean.

BRACK Yes, you could call it that. Perhaps now, though, it's on its way.

HEDDA (*Tosses her head.*) You mean that competition for that stupid professorship? That's Tesman's business. I'm not going to waste a single thought on it.

BRACK No, forget about that. But when you find yourself facing what one calls in elegant language a profound and solemn calling— (*Smiling.*) a new calling, my dear little Mrs. Hedda.

HEDDA (*Angry.*) Quiet. You'll never see anything like that.

BRACK (*Gently.*) We'll talk about it again in a year's time, at the very latest.

HEDDA (*Curtly.*) I don't have any talent for that, Judge. I don't want anything to do with that kind of calling.

BRACK Why shouldn't you, like most other women, have an innate talent for a vocation that—

HEDDA (*Over by the glass door.*) Oh, please be quiet. I often think I
  only have one talent, one talent in the world.
BRACK (*Approaching.*) And what is that may I ask?
HEDDA (*Standing, staring out.*) Boring the life right out of me. Now
  you know. (*Turns, glances toward the inner room and laughs.*)
  Perfect timing; here comes the professor.
BRACK (*Warning softly.*) Now, now, now, Mrs. Hedda.
  (*George Tesman, in evening dress, carrying his gloves and hat,
  comes in from the right of the rear room.*)
TESMAN Hedda, no message from Eilert Løvborg?
HEDDA No.
BRACK Do you really think he'll come?
TESMAN Yes, I'm almost certain he will. What you told us this
  morning was just idle gossip.
BRACK Oh?
TESMAN Yes, at least Aunt Julie said she couldn't possibly believe
  that he would stand in my way anymore. Just think.
BRACK So, then everything's all right.
TESMAN (*Puts his hat with his gloves inside on a chair to the right.*)
  Yes, but I'd like to wait for him as long as I can.
BRACK We have plenty of time. No one's coming to my place until
  seven or even half past.
TESMAN Meanwhile, we can keep Hedda company and see what
  happens, hm?
HEDDA (*Sets Brack's overcoat and hat on the corner sofa.*) At the very
  worst, Mr. Løvborg can stay here with me.
BRACK (*Offering to take his things.*) At the worst, Mrs. Tesman,
  what do you mean?
HEDDA If he won't go out with you and Tesman.
TESMAN (*Looking at her uncertainly.*) But, Hedda dear, do you think
  that would be quite right, him staying here with you? Remem-
  ber, Aunt Julie can't come.
HEDDA No, but Mrs. Elvsted will be coming and the three of us can
  have a cup of tea together.
TESMAN Yes, that's all right then.
BRACK (*Smiling.*) And I might add, that would be the best plan for
  him.
HEDDA Why so?
BRACK Good Lord, Mrs. Tesman, you've had enough to say about
  my little bachelor parties in the past. Don't you agree they
  should be open only to men of the highest principle?
HEDDA That's just what Mr. Løvborg is now, a reclaimed sinner.
  (*Berta comes in from the hall doorway.*)
BERTA Madam, there's a gentleman who wishes to—

HEDDA Yes, please, show him in.

TESMAN (*Softly.*) It's got to be him. Just think.

(*Eilert Løvborg enters from the hallway. He is slim and lean, the same age as Tesman, but he looks older and somewhat haggard. His hair and beard are dark brown. His face is longish, pale, with patches of red over the cheekbones. He is dressed in an elegant suit, black, quite new, dark gloves and top hat. He stops just inside the doorway and bows hastily. He seems somewhat embarrassed.*)

TESMAN (*Goes to him and shakes his hands.*) Oh my dear Eilert, we meet again at long last.

LØVBORG (*Speaks in a low voice.*) Thanks for the letter, George. (*Approaches Hedda.*) May I shake your hand also, Mrs. Tesman?

HEDDA (*Takes his hand.*) Welcome, Mr. Løvborg. (*With a gesture.*) I don't know if you two gentlemen—

LØVBORG (*Bowing.*) Judge Brack, I believe.

BRACK (*Similarly.*) Indeed. It's been quite a few years—

TESMAN (*To Løvborg, his hands on his shoulders.*) And now Eilert, make yourself completely at home. Right, Hedda? I hear you're going to settle down here in town, hm?

LØVBORG Yes, I will.

TESMAN Well, that's only sensible. Listen, I got your new book. I haven't really had time to read it yet.

LØVBORG You can save yourself the trouble.

TESMAN What do you mean?

LØVBORG There's not much to it.

TESMAN How can you say that?

BRACK But everyone's been praising it so highly.

LØVBORG Exactly as I intended—so I wrote the sort of book that everyone can agree with.

BRACK Very clever.

TESMAN Yes, but my dear Eilert.

LØVBORG Because I want to reestablish my position, begin again.

TESMAN (*A little downcast.*) Yes, I suppose you'd want to, hm.

LØVBORG (*Smiling, putting down his hat and pulling a package wrapped in paper from his coat pocket.*) But when this comes out, George Tesman—this is what you should read. It's the real thing. I've put my whole self into it.

TESMAN Oh yes? What's it about?

LØVBORG It's the sequel.

TESMAN Sequel to what?

LØVBORG To my book.

TESMAN The new one?

LØVBORG Of course.

TESMAN But my dear Eilert, that one takes us right to the present day.

LØVBORG So it does—and this one takes us into the future.

TESMAN The future. Good Lord! We don't know anything about that.

LØVBORG No, we don't—but there are still one or two things to say about it, just the same. (*Opens the package.*) Here, you'll see.

TESMAN That's not your handwriting, is it?

LØVBORG I dictated it. (*Turns the pages.*) It's written in two sections. The first is about the cultural forces which will shape the future, and this other section (*Turning the pages.*) is about the future course of civilization.

TESMAN Extraordinary. It would never occur to me to write about something like that.

HEDDA (*By the glass door, drumming on the pane.*) Hmm, no, no.

LØVBORG (*Puts the papers back in the packet and sets it on the table.*) I brought it along because I thought I might read some of it to you tonight.

TESMAN Ah, that was very kind of you, Eilert, but this evening (*Looks at Brack.*) I'm not sure it can be arranged—

LØVBORG Some other time then, there's no hurry.

BRACK I should tell you, Mr. Løvborg, we're having a little party at my place this evening, mostly for Tesman, you understand—

LØVBORG (*Looking for his hat.*) Aha, well then I'll—

BRACK No, listen, why don't you join us?

LØVBORG (*Briefly but firmly.*) No, that I can't do, but many thanks just the same.

BRACK Oh come now, you certainly can do that. We'll be a small, select circle and I guarantee we'll be "lively," as Mrs. Hed— Mrs. Tesman would say.

LØVBORG No doubt, but even so—

BRACK And then you could bring your manuscript along and read it to Tesman at my place. I've got plenty of rooms.

TESMAN Think about that, Eilert. You could do that, hm?

HEDDA (*Intervening.*) Now, my dear, Mr. Løvborg simply doesn't want to. I'm quite sure Mr. Løvborg would rather settle down here and have supper with me.

LØVBORG (*Staring at her.*) With you, Mrs. Tesman?

HEDDA And with Mrs. Elvsted.

LØVBORG Ah— (*Casually.*) I saw her this morning very briefly.

HEDDA Oh did you? Well, she's coming here; so you might almost say it's essential that you stay here, Mr. Løvborg. Otherwise she'll have no one to see her home.

LØVBORG That's true. Yes, Mrs. Tesman, many thanks. I'll stay.

HEDDA I'll go and have a word with the maid.

(*She goes over to the hall door and rings. Berta enters. Hedda speaks quietly to her and points toward the rear room. Berta nods and goes out again.*)

TESMAN (*At the same time to Løvborg.*) Listen, Eilert, your lecture—Is it about this new subject? About the future?

LØVBORG Yes.

TESMAN Because I heard down at the bookstore that you'd be giving a lecture series here this fall.

LØVBORG I plan to. Please don't hold it against me.

TESMAN No, God forbid, but—?

LØVBORG I can easily see how this might make things awkward.

TESMAN (*Dejectedly.*) Oh, for my part, I can't expect you to—

LØVBORG But I'll wait until you get your appointment.

TESMAN You will? Yes but—yes but—you won't be competing then?

LØVBORG No. I only want to conquer you in the marketplace of ideas.

TESMAN But, good Lord, Aunt Julie was right after all. Oh yes, yes, I was quite sure of it. Hedda, imagine, my dear—Eilert Løvborg won't stand in our way.

HEDDA (*Curtly.*) Our way? Leave me out of it.

(*She goes up toward the rear room where Berta is placing a tray with decanters and glasses on the table. Hedda nods approvingly, comes forward again. Berta goes out.*)

TESMAN (*Meanwhile.*) So, Judge Brack, what do you say about all this?

BRACK Well now, I say that honor and victory, hmm—they have a powerful appeal—

TESMAN Yes, yes, I suppose they do but all the same—

HEDDA (*Looking at Tesman with a cold smile.*) You look like you've been struck by lightning.

TESMAN Yes, that's about it—or something like that, I think—

BRACK That was quite a thunderstorm that passed over us, Mrs. Tesman.

HEDDA (*Pointing toward the rear room.*) Won't you gentlemen go in there and have a glass of punch?

BRACK (*Looking at his watch.*) For the road? Yes, not a bad idea.

TESMAN Wonderful, Hedda, wonderful! And I'm in such a fantastic mood now.

HEDDA You too, Mr. Løvborg, if you please.

LØVBORG (*Dismissively.*) No, thank you, not for me.

BRACK Good Lord, cold punch isn't exactly poison, you know.

LØVBORG Maybe not for everybody.

HEDDA Then I'll keep Mr. Løvborg company in the meantime.

TESMAN Yes, yes, Hedda dear, you do that.

(*Tesman and Brack go into the rear room, sit down and drink*

*punch, smoking cigarettes and talking animatedly during the
following. Eilert Løvborg remains standing by the stove and
Hedda goes to the writing table.*)

HEDDA (*In a slightly raised voice.*) Now, if you like, I'll show you
some photographs. Tesman and I—we took a trip to the Tyrol
on the way home.

(*She comes over with an album and lays it on the table by the
sofa, seating herself in the farthest corner. Eilert Løvborg comes
closer, stooping and looking at her. Then he takes a chair and
sits on her left side with his back to the rear room.*)

HEDDA (*Opening the album.*) Do you see these mountains, Mr.
Løvborg? That's the Ortler group. Tesman's written a little cap-
tion. Here. "The Ortler group near Meran."

LØVBORG (*Who has not taken his eyes off her from the beginning,
says softly and slowly.*) Hedda Gabler.

HEDDA (*Glances quickly at him.*) Shh, now.

LØVBORG (*Repeating softly.*) Hedda Gabler.

HEDDA (*Staring at the album.*) Yes, so I was once, when we knew
each other.

LØVBORG And from now—for the rest of my life—do I have to
teach myself never to say Hedda Gabler?

HEDDA (*Turning the pages.*) Yes, you have to. And I think you'd better start practicing now. The sooner the better, I'd say.

LØVBORG (*In a resentful voice.*) Hedda Gabler married—and then—
with George Tesman.

HEDDA That's how it goes.

LØVBORG Ah, Hedda, Hedda—how could you have thrown yourself
away like that?

HEDDA (*Looks sharply at him.*) What? Now stop that.

LØVBORG Stop what, what do you mean?

HEDDA Calling me Hedda and—[1]

(*Tesman comes in and goes toward the sofa.*)

HEDDA (*Hears him approaching and says casually.*) And this one
here, Mr. Løvborg, this was taken from the Ampezzo Valley.
Would you just look at these mountain peaks. (*Looks warmly
up at Tesman.*) George, dear, what were these extraordinary
mountains called?

TESMAN Let me see. Ah, yes, those are the Dolomites.

HEDDA Of course. Those, Mr. Løvborg, are the Dolomites.

TESMAN Hedda, dear, I just wanted to ask you if we should bring
some punch in here, for you at least.

HEDDA Yes, thank you my dear. And a few pastries perhaps.

---

1. This line is interpolated in an attempt to suggest the difference between the informal *du*
(thee or thy) and the formal *de* (you) in the Norwegian text. Løvborg has just addressed
Hedda in the informal manner and she is warning him not to.

TESMAN Any cigarettes?

HEDDA No.

TESMAN Good.

> (*He goes into the rear room and off to the right. Brack remains sitting, from time to time keeping his eye on Hedda and Løvborg.*)

LØVBORG (*Quietly, as before.*) Then answer me, Hedda—how could you go and do such a thing?

HEDDA (*Apparently absorbed in the album.*) If you keep talking to me that way, I just won't speak to you.

LØVBORG Not even when we're alone together?

HEDDA No. You can think whatever you want but you can't talk about it.

LØVBORG Ah, I see. It offends your love for George Tesman.

HEDDA (*Glances at him and smiles.*) Love? Don't be absurd.

LØVBORG Not love then either?

HEDDA But even so—nothing unfaithful. I will not allow it.

LØVBORG Answer me just one thing—

HEDDA Shh.

> (*Tesman, with a tray, enters from the rear room.*)

TESMAN Here we are, here come the treats. (*He places the tray on the table.*)

HEDDA Why are you serving us yourself?

TESMAN (*Filling the glasses.*) I have such a good time waiting on you, Hedda.

HEDDA But now you've gone and poured two drinks and Mr. Løvborg definitely does not want—

TESMAN No, but Mrs. Elvsted's coming soon.

HEDDA Yes, that's right, Mrs. Elvsted.

TESMAN Did you forget about her?

HEDDA We were just sitting here so completely wrapped up in these. (*Shows him a picture.*) Do you remember this little village?

TESMAN Yes, that's the one below the Brenner Pass. We spent the night there—

HEDDA —and ran into all those lively summer visitors.

TESMAN Ah yes, that was it. Imagine—if you could have been with us, Eilert, just think. (*He goes in again and sits with Brack.*)

LØVBORG Just answer me one thing—

HEDDA Yes?

LØVBORG In our relationship—wasn't there any love there either? No trace? Not a glimmer of love in any of it?

HEDDA I wonder if there really was. For me it was like we were two good comrades, two really good, faithful friends. (*Smiling.*) I remember you were particularly frank and open.

LØVBORG That's how you wanted it.

HEDDA When I look back on it, there was something really beautiful—something fascinating, something brave about this secret comradeship, this secret intimacy that no living soul had any idea about.

LØVBORG Yes, Hedda, that's true isn't it? That was it. When I'd come to your father's in the afternoon—and the General would sit in the window reading his newspaper with his back toward the room—

HEDDA And us on the corner sofa.

LØVBORG Always with the same illustrated magazine in front of us.

HEDDA Instead of an album, yes.

LØVBORG Yes, Hedda—and when I made all those confessions to you—telling you things about myself that no one else knew in those days. Sat there and told you how I'd lost whole days and nights in drunken frenzy, frenzy that would last for days on end. Ah, Hedda—what kind of power was in you that drew these confessions out of me?

HEDDA You think it was a power in me?

LØVBORG Yes. I can't account for it in any other way. And you'd ask me all those ambiguous leading questions—

HEDDA Which you understood implicitly—

LØVBORG How did you sit there and question me so fearlessly?

HEDDA Ambiguously?

LØVBORG Yes, but fearlessly all the same. Questioning me about—About things like that.

HEDDA And how could you answer them, Mr. Løvborg?

LØVBORG Yes, yes. That's just what I don't understand anymore. But now tell me, Hedda, wasn't it love underneath it all? Wasn't that part of it? You wanted to purify me, to cleanse me—when I'd seek you out to make my confessions. Wasn't that it?

HEDDA No, no, not exactly.

LØVBORG Then what drove you?

HEDDA Do you find it so hard to explain that a young girl—when it becomes possible—in secret—

LØVBORG Yes?

HEDDA That she wants a glimpse of a world that—

LØVBORG That—

HEDDA That is not permitted to her.

LØVBORG So that was it.

HEDDA That too, that too—I almost believe it.

LØVBORG Comrades in a quest for life. So why couldn't it go on?

HEDDA That was your own fault.

LØVBORG You broke it off.

HEDDA Yes, when it looked like reality threatened to spoil the situation. Shame on you, Eilert Løvborg, how could you do violence
to your comrade in arms?

LØVBORG (*Clenching his hands together.*) Well, why didn't you do it
for real? Why didn't you shoot me dead right then and there
like you threatened to?

HEDDA Oh, I'm much too afraid of scandal.

LØVBORG Yes, Hedda, underneath it all, you're a coward.

HEDDA A terrible coward. (*Changes her tone.*) Lucky for you. And
now you've got plenty of consolation up there at the Elvsteds'.

LØVBORG I know what Thea's confided to you.

HEDDA And no doubt you've confided to her about us.

LØVBORG Not one word. She's too stupid to understand things like
this.

HEDDA Stupid?

LØVBORG In things like this she's stupid.

HEDDA And I'm a coward. (*Leans closer to him without looking him
in the eyes and says softly.*) Now I'll confide something to you.

LØVBORG (*In suspense.*) What?

HEDDA My not daring to shoot you—

LØVBORG Yes?!

HEDDA —that wasn't my worst cowardice that evening.

LØVBORG (*Stares at her a moment, understands and whispers passionately.*) Ah, Hedda Gabler, now I see the hidden reason why
we're such comrades. This craving for life in you—

HEDDA (*Quietly, with a sharp glance at him.*) Watch out, don't believe anything of the sort.

(*It starts to get dark. The hall door is opened by Berta.*)

HEDDA (*Clapping the album shut and crying out with a smile.*) Ah,
finally. Thea, darling, do come in.

(*Mrs. Elvsted enters from the hall. She is in evening dress. The
door is closed after her.*)

HEDDA (*On the sofa, stretching out her arms.*) Thea, my sweet, you
can't imagine how I've been expecting you.

(*Mrs. Elvsted, in passing, exchanges a greeting with the gentlemen in the inner room, crosses to the table, shakes Hedda's
hand. Eilert Løvborg has risen. He and Mrs. Elvsted greet each
other with a single nod.*)

MRS. ELVSTED Perhaps I should go in and have a word with your
husband.

HEDDA Not at all. Let them sit there. They'll be on their way soon.

MRS. ELVSTED They're leaving?

HEDDA Yes, they're going out on a little binge.

MRS. ELVSTED (*Quickly to Løvborg.*) You're not?

LØVBORG No.

HEDDA Mr. Løvborg . . . he'll stay here with us.

MRS. ELVSTED (*Takes a chair and sits down beside him.*) It's so nice to be here.

HEDDA No, you don't, little Thea, not there. Come right over here next to me. I want to be in the middle between you.

MRS. ELVSTED All right, whatever you like. (*She goes around the table and sits on the sofa to the right of Hedda. Løvborg takes his chair again.*)

LØVBORG (*After a brief pause, to Hedda.*) Isn't she lovely to look at?

HEDDA (*Gently stroking her hair.*) Only to look at?

LØVBORG Yes. We're true comrades, the two of us. We trust each other completely and that's why we can sit here and talk so openly and boldly together.

HEDDA With no ambiguity, Mr. Løvborg.

LØVBORG Well—

MRS. ELVSTED (*Softly, clinging to Hedda.*) Oh, Hedda, I'm so lucky. Just think, he says I've inspired him too.

HEDDA (*Regards her with a smile.*) No, dear, does he say that?

LØVBORG And she has the courage to take action, Mrs. Tesman.

MRS. ELVSTED Oh God, me, courage?

LØVBORG Tremendous courage when it comes to comradeship.

HEDDA Yes, courage—yes! That's the crucial thing.

LØVBORG Why is that, do you suppose?

HEDDA Because then—maybe—life has a chance to be lived. (*Suddenly changing her tone.*) But now, my dearest Thea. Why don't you treat yourself to a nice cold glass of punch?

MRS. ELVSTED No thank you, I never drink anything like that.

HEDDA Then for you, Mr. Løvborg.

LØVBORG No thank you, not for me either.

MRS. ELVSTED No, not for him either.

HEDDA (*Looking steadily at him.*) But if I insisted.

LØVBORG Doesn't matter.

HEDDA (*Laughing.*) Then I have absolutely no power over you? Ah, poor me.

LØVBORG Not in that area.

HEDDA But seriously now, I really think you should, for your own sake.

MRS. ELVSTED No, Hedda—

LØVBORG Why is that?

HEDDA Or to be more precise, for others' sakes.

LØVBORG Oh?

HEDDA Because otherwise people might get the idea that you don't, deep down inside, feel really bold, really sure of yourself.

LØVBORG Oh, from now on people can think whatever they like.

MRS. ELVSTED Yes, that's right, isn't it.

HEDDA I saw it so clearly with Judge Brack a few minutes ago.

LØVBORG What did you see?

HEDDA That condescending little smile when you didn't dare join them at the table.

LØVBORG Didn't dare? I'd just rather stay here and talk with you, of course.

MRS. ELVSTED That's only reasonable, Hedda.

HEDDA How was the Judge supposed to know that? I saw how he smiled and shot a glance at Tesman when you didn't dare join them in their silly little party.

LØVBORG Didn't dare. You're saying I don't dare.

HEDDA Oh, I'm not. But that's how Judge Brack sees it.

LØVBORG Well let him.

HEDDA So you won't join them?

LØVBORG I'm staying here with you and Thea.

MRS. ELVSTED Yes, Hedda, you can be sure he is.

HEDDA (*Smiling and nodding approvingly to Løvborg.*) What a strong foundation you've got. Principles to last a lifetime. That's what a man ought to have. (*Turns to Mrs. Elvsted.*) See now, wasn't that what I told you when you came here this morning in such a panic—

LØVBORG (*Startled.*) Panic?

MRS. ELVSTED (*Terrified.*) Hedda, Hedda, no.

HEDDA Just see for yourself. No reason at all to come running here in mortal terror. (*Changing her tone.*) There, now all three of us can be quite jolly.

LØVBORG (*Shocked.*) What does this mean, Mrs. Tesman?

MRS. ELVSTED Oh God, oh God, Hedda. What are you doing? What are you saying?

HEDDA Keep calm now. That disgusting Judge is sitting there watching you.

LØVBORG In mortal terror on my account?

MRS. ELVSTED (*Quietly wailing.*) Oh, Hedda—

LØVBORG (*Looks at her steadily for a moment; his face is drawn.*) So that, then, was how my brave, bold comrade trusted me.

MRS. ELVSTED (*Pleading.*) Oh, my dearest friend, listen to me—

LØVBORG (*Takes one of the glasses of punch, raises it and says in a low, hoarse voice.*) Your health, Thea. (*Empties the glass, takes another.*)

MRS. ELVSTED (*Softly.*) Oh Hedda, Hedda—how could you want this to happen?

HEDDA Want it? I want this? Are you mad?

LØVBORG And your health too, Mrs. Tesman. Thanks for the truth. Long may it live. (*He drinks and goes to refill the glass.*)

HEDDA (*Placing her hand on his arm.*) That's enough for now. Remember, you're going to the party.

MRS. ELVSTED No, no, no.

HEDDA Shh. They're watching us.

LØVBORG (*Putting down the glass.*) Thea, be honest with me now.

MRS. ELVSTED Yes.

LØVBORG Was your husband told that you came here to look for me?

MRS. ELVSTED (*Wringing her hands.*) Oh, Hedda, listen to what he's asking me!

LØVBORG Did he arrange for you to come to town to spy on me? Maybe he put you up to it himself. Aha, that's it. He needed me back in the office again. Or did he just miss me at the card table?

MRS. ELVSTED (*Softly moaning.*) Oh, Løvborg, Løvborg—

LØVBORG (*Grabs a glass intending to fill it.*) Skøal to the old Sheriff too.

HEDDA (*Preventing him.*) No more now. Remember, you're going out to read to Tesman.

LØVBORG (*Calmly putting down his glass.*) Thea, that was stupid of me. What I did just now. Taking it like that I mean. Don't be angry with me, my dear, dear comrade. You'll see. Both of you and everyone else will see that even though I once was fallen— now I've raised myself up again, with your help, Thea.

MRS. ELVSTED (*Radiant with joy.*) Oh God be praised.
      (*Meanwhile Brack has been looking at his watch. He and Tesman get up and come into the drawing room.*)

BRACK (*Taking his hat and overcoat.*) Well, Mrs. Tesman, our time is up.

HEDDA Yes, it must be.

LØVBORG (*Rising.*) Mine too.

MRS. ELVSTED (*Quietly pleading.*) Løvborg, don't do it.

HEDDA (*Pinching her arm.*) They can hear you.

MRS. ELVSTED (*Crying out faintly.*) Ow.

LØVBORG (*To Brack.*) You were kind enough to ask me along.

BRACK So you're coming after all.

LØVBORG Yes, thanks.

BRACK I'm delighted.

LØVBORG (*Putting the manuscript packet in his pocket and saying to Tesman.*) I'd really like you to look at one or two things before I send it off.

TESMAN Just think, that will be splendid. But, Hedda dear, how will you get Mrs. Elvsted home?

HEDDA Oh, there's always a way out.

LØVBORG (*Looking at the ladies.*) Mrs. Elvsted? Well, of course, I'll come back for her. (*Coming closer.*) Around ten o'clock, Mrs. Tesman, will that do?

HEDDA Yes, that will be fine.

TESMAN Well, everything's all right then; but don't expect me that early, Hedda.

HEDDA No dear, you stay just as long—as long as you like.

MRS. ELVSTED (*With suppressed anxiety.*) Mr. Løvborg—I'll stay here until you come.

LØVBORG (*His hat in his hand.*) That's understood.

BRACK All aboard then, the party train's pulling out. Gentlemen, I trust it will be a lively trip, as a certain lovely lady suggested.

HEDDA Ah yes, if only that lovely lady could be there—invisible, of course.

BRACK Why invisible?

HEDDA To hear a little of your liveliness, Judge, uncensored.

BRACK (*Laughing.*) Not recommended for the lovely lady.

TESMAN (*Also laughing.*) You really are the limit, Hedda. Think of it.

BRACK Well, well, my ladies. Good night. Good night.

LØVBORG (*Bowing as he leaves.*) Until ten o'clock, then.

(*Brack, Løvborg and Tesman leave through the hall door. At the same time Berta comes in from the rear room with a lighted lamp which she places on the drawing room table, going out the way she came in.*)

MRS. ELVSTED (*Has gotten up and wanders uneasily about the room.*) Oh, Hedda, where is all this going?

HEDDA Ten o'clock—then he'll appear. I see him before me with vine leaves in his hair, burning bright and bold.

MRS. ELVSTED Yes, if only it could be like that.

HEDDA And then you'll see—then he'll have power over himself again. Then he'll be a free man for the rest of his days.

MRS. ELVSTED Oh God yes—if only he'd come back just the way you see him.

HEDDA He'll come back just that way and no other. (*Gets up and comes closer.*) You can doubt him as much as you like. I believe in him. And so we'll see—

MRS. ELVSTED There's something behind this, something else you're trying to do.

HEDDA Yes, there is. Just once in my life I want to help shape someone's destiny.

MRS. ELVSTED Don't you do that already?

HEDDA I don't and I never have.

MRS. ELVSTED Not even your husband?

HEDDA Oh yes, that was a real bargain. Oh, if you could only understand how destitute I am while you get to be so rich. (*She passionately throws her arms around her.*) I think I'll burn your hair off after all.

MRS. ELVSTED Let me go, let me go. I'm afraid of you.

BERTA (*In the doorway.*) Tea is ready in the dining room, Madam.

HEDDA Good. We're on our way.

MRS. ELVSTED No, no, no! I'd rather go home alone! Right now!

HEDDA Nonsense! First you're going to have some tea, you little bubblehead, and then—at ten o'clock—Eilert Løvborg—with vine leaves in his hair! (*She pulls Mrs. Elvsted toward the doorway almost by force.*)

Act Three

The room at the Tesmans'. The curtains are drawn across the center doorway and also across the glass door. The lamp covered with a shade burns low on the table. In the stove, with its door standing open, there has been a fire that is almost burned out.

(*Mrs. Elvsted, wrapped in a large shawl and with her feet on a footstool, sits sunk back in an armchair. Hedda, fully dressed, lies sleeping on the sofa with a rug over her.*)

MRS. ELVSTED (*After a pause suddenly straightens herself in the chair and listens intently. Then she sinks back wearily and moans softly.*) Still not back . . . Oh God, oh God . . . Still not back.
(*Berta enters tiptoeing carefully through the hall doorway; she has a letter in her hand.*)

MRS. ELVSTED Ah—did someone come?

BERTA Yes, a girl came by just now with this letter.

MRS. ELVSTED (*Quickly stretching out her hand.*) A letter? Let me have it.

BERTA No ma'am, it's for the doctor.

MRS. ELVSTED Oh.

BERTA It was Miss Tesman's maid who brought it. I'll put it on the table here.

MRS. ELVSTED Yes, do that.

BERTA (*Puts down the letter.*) I'd better put out the lamp; it's starting to smoke.

MRS. ELVSTED Yes, put it out. It'll be light soon anyway.

BERTA (*Putting out the light.*) Oh, ma'am, it's already light.

MRS. ELVSTED So, morning and still not back—!

BERTA Oh, dear Lord—I knew all along it would go like this.

MRS. ELVSTED You knew?

BERTA Yes, when I saw a certain person was back in town. And then when he went off with them—oh we'd heard plenty about that gentleman.

MRS. ELVSTED   Don't speak so loud, you'll wake your mistress.

BERTA   (*Looks over to the sofa and sighs.*) No, dear Lord—let her sleep, poor thing. Shouldn't I build the stove up a little more?

MRS. ELVSTED   Not for me, thanks.

BERTA   Well, well then. (*She goes out quietly through the hall doorway.*)

HEDDA   (*Awakened by the closing door, looks up.*) What's that?

MRS. ELVSTED   Only the maid.

HEDDA   (*Looking around.*) In here—! Oh, now I remember. (*Straightens up, stretches sitting on the sofa and rubs her eyes.*) What time is it, Thea?

MRS. ELVSTED   (*Looks at her watch.*) It's after seven.

HEDDA   What time did Tesman get in?

MRS. ELVSTED   He hasn't.

HEDDA   Still?

MRS. ELVSTED   (*Getting up.*) No one's come back.

HEDDA   And we sat here waiting and watching until almost four.

MRS. ELVSTED   (*Wringing her hands.*) Waiting for him!

HEDDA   (*Yawning and speaking with her hand over her mouth.*) Oh yes—we could have saved ourselves the trouble.

MRS. ELVSTED   Did you finally manage to sleep?

HEDDA   Yes, I think I slept quite well. Did you?

MRS. ELVSTED   Not a wink. I couldn't, Hedda. It was just impossible for me.

HEDDA   (*Gets up and goes over to her.*) Now, now, now. There's nothing to worry about. I know perfectly well how it all turned out.

MRS. ELVSTED   Yes, what do you think? Can you tell me?

HEDDA   Well, of course they dragged it out dreadfully up at Judge Brack's.

MRS. ELVSTED   Oh God yes—that must be true. But all the same—

HEDDA   And then you see, Tesman didn't want to come home and create a fuss by ringing the bell in the middle of the night. (*Laughing.*) He probably didn't want to show himself either right after a wild party like that.

MRS. ELVSTED   For goodness sake—where would he have gone?

HEDDA   Well, naturally, he went over to his aunts' and laid himself down to sleep there. They still have his old room standing ready for him.

MRS. ELVSTED   No, he's not with them. A letter just came for him from Miss Tesman. It's over there.

HEDDA   Oh? (*Looks at the inscription.*) Yes, that's Aunt Julie's hand all right. So then, he's still over at Judge Brack's and Eilert

Løvborg—he's sitting—reading aloud with vine leaves in his hair.

MRS. ELVSTED Oh, Hedda, you don't even believe what you're saying.

HEDDA You are such a little noodlehead, Thea.

MRS. ELVSTED Yes, unfortunately I probably am.

HEDDA And you look like you're dead on your feet.

MRS. ELVSTED Yes, I am. Dead on my feet.

HEDDA And so now you're going to do what I tell you. You'll go into my room and lie down on my bed.

MRS. ELVSTED Oh no, no—I couldn't get to sleep anyway.

HEDDA Yes, you certainly will.

MRS. ELVSTED But your husband's bound to be home any time now and I've got to find out right away—

HEDDA I'll tell you as soon as he comes.

MRS. ELVSTED Promise me that, Hedda?

HEDDA Yes, that you can count on. Now just go in and sleep for a while.

MRS. ELVSTED Thanks. At least I'll give it a try. (*She goes in through the back room.*)

(*Hedda goes over to the glass door and draws back the curtains. Full daylight floods the room. She then takes a small hand mirror from the writing table, looks in it and arranges her hair. Then she goes to the hall door and presses the bell. Soon after Berta enters the doorway.*)

BERTA Did Madam want something?

HEDDA Yes, build up the stove a little bit. I'm freezing in here.

BERTA Lord, in no time at all it'll be warm in here. (*She rakes the embers and puts a log inside. She stands and listens.*) There's the front doorbell, Madam.

HEDDA So, go answer it. I'll take care of the stove myself.

BERTA It'll be burning soon enough. (*She goes out through the hall door.*)

(*Hedda kneels on the footstool and puts more logs into the stove. After a brief moment, George Tesman comes in from the hall. He looks weary and rather serious. He creeps on tiptoes toward the doorway and is about to slip through the curtains.*)

HEDDA (*By the stove, without looking up.*) Good morning.

TESMAN (*Turning around.*) Hedda. (*Comes nearer.*) What in the world—Up so early, hm?

HEDDA Yes, up quite early today.

TESMAN And here I was so sure you'd still be in bed. Just think, Hedda.

HEDDA Not so loud. Mrs. Elvsted's lying down in my room.

TESMAN Has Mrs. Elvsted been here all night?

HEDDA Yes. No one came to pick her up.

TESMAN No, no, they couldn't have.

HEDDA (*Shuts the door of the stove and gets up.*) So, did you have a jolly time at the Judge's?

TESMAN Were you worried about me?

HEDDA No, that would never occur to me. I asked if you had a good time.

TESMAN Yes, I really did, for once, in a manner of speaking— Mostly in the beginning, I'd say. We'd arrived an hour early. How about that? And Brack had so much to get ready. But then Eilert read to me.

HEDDA (*Sits at the right of the table.*) So, tell me.

TESMAN Hedda, you can't imagine what this new work will be like. It's one of the most brilliant things ever written, no doubt about it. Think of that.

HEDDA Yes, yes, but that's not what I'm interested in.

TESMAN But I have to confess something, Hedda. After he read— something horrible came over me.

HEDDA Something horrible?

TESMAN I sat there envying Eilert for being able to write like that. Think of it, Hedda.

HEDDA Yes, yes, I'm thinking.

TESMAN And then, that whole time, knowing that he—even with all the incredible powers at his command—is still beyond redemption.

HEDDA You mean he's got more of life's courage in him than the others?

TESMAN No, for heaven sakes—he just has no control over his pleasures.

HEDDA And what happened then—at the end?

TESMAN Well, Hedda, I guess you'd have to say it was a bacchanal.

HEDDA Did he have vine leaves in his hair?

TESMAN Vine leaves? No, I didn't see anything like that. But he did make a long wild speech for the woman who had inspired him in his work. Yes—that's how he put it.

HEDDA Did he name her?

TESMAN No, he didn't, but I can only guess that it must be Mrs. Elvsted. Wouldn't you say?

HEDDA Hmm—where did you leave him?

TESMAN On the way back. Most of our group broke up at the same time and Brack came along with us to get a little fresh air. And you see, we agreed to follow Eilert home because—well—he was so far gone.

HEDDA He must have been.

TESMAN But here's the strangest part, Hedda! Or maybe I should say the saddest. I'm almost ashamed for Eilert's sake—to tell you—

HEDDA So?

TESMAN There we were walking along, you see, and I happened to drop back a bit, just for a couple of minutes, you understand.

HEDDA Yes, yes, good Lord but—

TESMAN And then when I was hurrying to catch up—can you guess what I found in the gutter, hm?

HEDDA How can I possibly guess?

TESMAN Don't ever tell a soul, Hedda. Do you hear? Promise me that for Eilert's sake. (*Pulls a package out of his coat pocket.*) Just think—this is what I found.

HEDDA That's the package he had with him here yesterday, isn't it?

TESMAN That's it. His precious, irreplaceable manuscript—all of it. And he's lost it—without even noticing it. Oh just think, Hedda—the pity of it—

HEDDA Well, why didn't you give it back to him right away?

TESMAN Oh, I didn't dare do that—The condition he was in—

HEDDA You didn't tell any of the others that you found it either?

TESMAN Absolutely not. I couldn't, you see, for Eilert's sake.

HEDDA So nobody knows you have Eilert's manuscript? Nobody at all?

TESMAN No. And they mustn't find out either.

HEDDA What did you talk to him about later?

TESMAN I didn't get a chance to talk to him any more. We got to the city limits, and he and a couple of the others went a different direction. Just think—

HEDDA Aha, they must have followed him home then.

TESMAN Yes, I suppose so. Brack also went his way.

HEDDA And, in the meantime, what became of the bacchanal?

TESMAN Well, I and some of the others followed one of the revelers up to his place and had morning coffee with him—or maybe we should call it morning-after coffee, hm? Now, I'll rest a bit—and as soon as I think Eilert has managed to sleep it off, poor man, then I've got to go over to him with this.

HEDDA (*Reaching out for the envelope.*) No, don't give it back. Not yet, I mean. Let me read it first.

TESMAN Oh no.

HEDDA Oh, for God's sake.

TESMAN I don't dare do that.

HEDDA You don't dare?

TESMAN No, you can imagine how completely desperate he'll be when he wakes up and realizes he can't find the manuscript. He's got no copy of it. He said so himself.

HEDDA (*Looks searchingly at him.*) Couldn't it be written again?

TESMAN No, I don't believe that could ever be done because the inspiration—you see—

HEDDA Yes, yes—That's the thing, isn't it? (*Casually.*) But, oh yes—there's a letter here for you.

TESMAN No, think of that.

HEDDA (*Hands it to him.*) It came early this morning.

TESMAN From Aunt Julie, Hedda. What can it be? (*Puts the manuscript on the other stool, opens the letter and jumps up.*) Oh Hedda—poor Aunt Rina's almost breathing her last.

HEDDA It's only what's expected.

TESMAN And if I want to see her one more time, I've got to hurry. I'll charge over there right away.

HEDDA (*Suppressing a smile.*) You'll charge?

TESMAN Oh, Hedda dearest—if you could just bring yourself to follow me. Just think.

HEDDA (*Rises and says wearily and dismissively.*) No, no. Don't ask me to do anything like that. I won't look at sickness and death. Let me stay free from everything ugly.

TESMAN Oh, good Lord, then— (*Darting around.*) My hat—? My overcoat—? Ah, in the hall—Oh, I hope I'm not too late, Hedda, hm?

HEDDA Then charge right over—

(*Berta appears in the hallway.*)

BERTA Judge Brack is outside.

HEDDA Ask him to come in.

TESMAN At a time like this! No, I can't possibly deal with him now.

HEDDA But I can. (*To Berta.*) Ask the Judge in.

(*Berta goes out.*)

HEDDA (*In a whisper.*) The package, Tesman. (*She snatches it off the stool.*)

TESMAN Yes, give it to me.

HEDDA No, I'll hide it until you get back.

(*She goes over to the writing table and sticks the package in the bookcase. Tesman stands flustered, and can't get his gloves on. Brack enters through the hall doorway.*)

HEDDA (*Nodding to him.*) Well, you're an early bird.

BRACK Yes, wouldn't you say. (*To Tesman.*) You're going out?

TESMAN Yes, I've got to go over to my aunt's. Just think, the poor dear is dying.

BRACK Good Lord, is she really? Then don't let me hold you up for even a moment, at a time like this—

TESMAN Yes, I really must run—Good-bye. Good-bye. (*He hurries through the hall doorway.*)

HEDDA (*Approaches.*) So, things were livelier than usual at your place last night, Judge.

BRACK Oh yes, so much so that I haven't even been able to change clothes, Mrs. Hedda.

HEDDA You too.

BRACK As you see. But, what has Tesman been telling you about last night's adventures?

HEDDA Oh, just some boring things. He went someplace to drink coffee.

BRACK I've already looked into the coffee party. Eilert Løvborg wasn't part of that group, I presume.

HEDDA No, they followed him home before that.

BRACK Tesman too?

HEDDA No, but a couple of others, he said.

BRACK (*Smiles.*) George Tesman is a very naïve soul, Mrs. Hedda.

HEDDA God knows, he is. But is there something more behind this?

BRACK I'd have to say so.

HEDDA Well then, Judge, let's be seated. Then you can speak freely. (*She sits to the left side of the table, Brack at the long side near her.*) Well, then—

BRACK I had certain reasons for keeping track of my guests—or, more precisely, some of my guests' movements last night.

HEDDA For example, Eilert Løvborg?

BRACK Yes, indeed.

HEDDA Now I'm hungry for more.

BRACK Do you know where he and a couple of the others spent the rest of the night, Mrs. Hedda?

HEDDA Why don't you tell me, if it can be told.

BRACK Oh, it's certainly worth the telling. It appears that they found their way into a particularly animated soirée.

HEDDA A lively one?

BRACK The liveliest.

HEDDA Tell me more, Judge.

BRACK Løvborg had received an invitation earlier—I knew all about that. But he declined because, as you know, he's made himself into a new man.

HEDDA Up at the Elvsteds', yes. But he went just the same?

BRACK Well, you see, Mrs. Hedda—unfortunately, the spirit really seized him at my place last evening.

HEDDA Yes, I hear he was quite inspired.

BRACK Inspired to a rather powerful degree. And so, he started to reconsider, I assume, because we men, alas, are not always so true to our principles as we ought to be.

HEDDA Present company excepted, Judge Brack. So, Løvborg—?

BRACK Short and sweet—He ended up at the salon of a certain Miss Diana.

HEDDA Miss Diana?

BRACK Yes, it was Miss Diana's soirée for a select circle of ladies and their admirers.

HEDDA Is she a redhead?

BRACK Exactly.

HEDDA A sort of a—singer?

BRACK Oh, yes—She's also that. And a mighty huntress—of men, Mrs. Hedda. You must have heard of her. Eilert Løvborg was one of her most strenuous admirers—in his better days.

HEDDA And how did all this end?

BRACK Apparently less amicably than it began. Miss Diana, after giving him the warmest of welcomes, soon turned to assault and battery.

HEDDA Against Løvborg?

BRACK Oh, yes. He accused her, or one of her ladies, of robbing him. He insisted that his pocketbook was missing, along with some other things. In short, he seems to have created a dreadful spectacle.

HEDDA And what did that lead to?

BRACK A regular brawl between both the men and the women. Luckily the police finally got there.

HEDDA The police too?

BRACK Yes. It's going to be quite a costly little romp for Eilert Løvborg. What a madman.

HEDDA Well!

BRACK Apparently, he resisted arrest. It seems he struck one of the officers on the ear, and ripped his uniform to shreds, so he had to go to the police station.

HEDDA How do you know all this?

BRACK From the police themselves.

HEDDA (*Gazing before her.*) So, that's how it ended? He had no vine leaves in his hair.

BRACK Vine leaves, Mrs. Hedda?

HEDDA (*Changing her tone.*) Tell me now, Judge, why do you go around snooping and spying on Eilert Løvborg?

BRACK For starters, I'm not a completely disinterested party—especially if the hearing uncovers the fact that he came straight from my place.

HEDDA There's going to be a hearing?

BRACK You can count on it. Be that as it may, however—My real concern was my duty as a friend of the house to inform you and Tesman of Løvborg's nocturnal adventures.

HEDDA Why, Judge Brack?

BRACK Well, I have an active suspicion that he'll try to use you as a kind of screen.

HEDDA Oh! What makes you think that?

BRACK Good God—we're not that blind, Mrs. Hedda. Wait and see. This Mrs. Elvsted—she won't be in such a hurry to leave town again.

HEDDA If there's anything going on between those two, there's plenty of places they can meet.

BRACK Not one single home. Every respectable house will be closed to Eilert Løvborg from now on.

HEDDA And mine should be too—Is that what you're saying?

BRACK Yes. I have to admit it would be more than painful for me if this man secured a foothold here. If this—utterly superfluous—and intrusive individual—were to force himself into—

HEDDA Into the triangle?

BRACK Precisely! It would leave me without a home.

HEDDA (Looks smilingly at him.) I see—The one cock of the walk— That's your goal.

BRACK (Slowly nodding and dropping his voice.) Yes, that's my goal. And it's a goal that I'll fight for—with every means at my disposal.

HEDDA (Her smile fading.) You're really a dangerous man, aren't you—when push comes to shove.

BRACK You think so?

HEDDA Yes, I'm starting to. And that's all right—just as long as you don't have any kind of hold on me.

BRACK (Laughing ambiguously.) Yes, Mrs. Hedda—you might be right about that. Of course, then, who knows whether I might not find some way or other—

HEDDA Now listen, Judge Brack! That sounds like you're threatening me.

BRACK (Gets up.) Oh, far from it. A triangle, you see—is best fortified by free defenders.

HEDDA I think so too.

BRACK Well, I've had my say so I should be getting back. Good-bye, Mrs. Hedda. (He goes toward the glass doors.)

HEDDA Out through the garden?

BRACK Yes, it's shorter for me.

HEDDA And then, it's also the back way.

BRACK That's true. I have nothing against back ways. Sometimes they can be very piquant.

HEDDA When there's sharpshooting.

BRACK (In the doorway, laughing at her.) Oh, no—you never shoot your tame cocks.

HEDDA (Also laughing.) Oh, no, especially when there's only one—

(*Laughing and nodding they take their farewells. He leaves. She closes the door after him. Hedda stands for a while, serious, looking out. Then she goes and peers through the curtains in the back wall. She goes to the writing table, takes Løvborg's package from the bookcase, and is about to leaf through it. Berta's voice, raised in indignation, is heard out in the hall. Hedda turns and listens. She quickly locks the package in the drawer and sets the key on the writing table. Eilert Løvborg, wearing his overcoat and carrying his hat, bursts through the hall doorway. He looks somewhat confused and excited.*)

LØVBORG (*Turned toward the hallway.*) And I'm telling you, I've got to go in! And that's that! (*He closes the door, sees Hedda, controls himself immediately, and bows.*)

HEDDA (*By the writing table.*) Well, Mr. Løvborg, it's pretty late to be calling for Thea.

LØVBORG Or a little early to be calling on you. I apologize.

HEDDA How do you know that she's still here?

LØVBORG I went to where she was staying. They told me she'd been out all night.

HEDDA (*Goes to the table.*) Did you notice anything special when they told you that?

LØVBORG (*Looks inquiringly at her.*) Notice anything?

HEDDA I mean—did they seem to have any thought on the subject—one way or the other?

LØVBORG (*Suddenly understanding.*) Oh, of course, it's true. I'm dragging her down with me. Still, I didn't notice anything. Tesman isn't up yet, I suppose?

HEDDA No, I don't think so.

LØVBORG When did he get home?

HEDDA Very late.

LØVBORG Did he tell you anything?

HEDDA Yes. I heard Judge Brack's was very lively.

LØVBORG Nothing else?

HEDDA No, I don't think so. I was terribly tired, though—
     (*Mrs. Elvsted comes in through the curtains at the back.*)

MRS. ELVSTED (*Runs toward him.*) Oh, Løvborg—at last!

LØVBORG Yes, at last, and too late.

MRS. ELVSTED (*Looking anxiously at him.*) What's too late?

LØVBORG Everything's too late. I'm finished.

MRS. ELVSTED Oh no, no—Don't say that!

LØVBORG You'll say it too, when you've heard—

MRS. ELVSTED I won't listen—

HEDDA Shall I leave you two alone?

LØVBORG No, stay—You too, I beg you.

MRS. ELVSTED But I won't listen to anything you tell me.

LØVBORG I don't want to talk about last night.

MRS. ELVSTED What is it, then?

LØVBORG We've got to go our separate ways.

MRS. ELVSTED Separate!

HEDDA (*Involuntarily.*) I knew it!

LØVBORG Because I have no more use for you, Thea.

MRS. ELVSTED You can stand there and say that! No more use for me! Can't I help you now, like I did before? Won't we go on working together?

LØVBORG I don't plan to work any more.

MRS. ELVSTED (*Desperately.*) Then what do I have to live for?

LØVBORG Just try to live your life as if you'd never known me.

MRS. ELVSTED I can't do that.

LØVBORG Try, Thea. Try, if you can. Go back home.

MRS. ELVSTED (*Defiantly.*) Where you are, that's where I want to be. I won't let myself be just driven off like this. I want to stay at your side—be with you when the book comes out.

HEDDA (*Half aloud, tensely.*) Ah, the book—Yes.

LØVBORG (*Looking at her.*) Mine and Thea's, because that's what it is.

MRS. ELVSTED Yes, that's what I feel it is. That's why I have a right to be with you when it comes out. I want to see you covered in honor and glory again, and the joy. I want to share that with you too.

LØVBORG Thea—our book's never coming out.

HEDDA Ah!

MRS. ELVSTED Never coming out?

LØVBORG It can't ever come out.

MRS. ELVSTED (*In anxious foreboding.*) Løvborg, what have you done with the manuscript?

HEDDA (*Looking intently at him.*) Yes, the manuscript—?

MRS. ELVSTED What have you—?

LØVBORG Oh, Thea, don't ask me that.

MRS. ELVSTED Yes, yes, I've got to know. I have the right to know.

LØVBORG The manuscript—all right then, the manuscript—I've ripped it up into a thousand pieces.

MRS. ELVSTED (*Screams.*) Oh no, no!

HEDDA (*Involuntarily.*) But that's just not—!

LØVBORG (*Looking at her.*) Not true, you think?

HEDDA (*Controls herself.*) All right then. Of course it is, if you say so. It sounds so ridiculous.

LØVBORG But it's true, just the same.

MRS. ELVSTED (*Wringing her hands.*) Oh God—oh God, Hedda. Torn his own work to pieces.

LØVBORG I've torn my own life to pieces. I might as well tear up my life's work too—

MRS. ELVSTED And you did that last night!

LØVBORG Yes. Do you hear me? A thousand pieces. Scattered them all over the fjord. Way out where there's pure salt water. Let them drift in it. Drift with the current in the wind. Then, after a while, they'll sink. Deeper and deeper. Like me, Thea.

MRS. ELVSTED You know, Løvborg, all this with the book—? For the rest of my life, it will be just like you'd killed a little child.

LØVBORG You're right. Like murdering a child.

MRS. ELVSTED But then, how could you—! That child was partly mine, too.

HEDDA (*Almost inaudibly.*) Ah, the child—

MRS. ELVSTED (*Sighs heavily.*) So it's finished? All right, Hedda, now I'm going.

HEDDA You're not going back?

MRS. ELVSTED Oh, I don't know what I'm going to do. I can't see anything out in front of me. (*She goes out through the hall doorway.*)

HEDDA (*Standing a while, waiting.*) Don't you want to see her home, Mr. Løvborg?

LØVBORG Through the streets? So that people can get a good look at us together?

HEDDA I don't know what else happened to you last night but if it's so completely beyond redemption—

LØVBORG It won't stop there. I know that much. And I can't bring myself to live that kind of life again either. Not again. Once I had the courage to live life to the fullest, to break every rule. But she's taken that out of me.

HEDDA (*Staring straight ahead.*) That sweet little fool has gotten hold of a human destiny. (*Looks at him.*) And you're so heartless to her.

LØVBORG Don't call it heartless.

HEDDA To go and destroy the thing that has filled her soul for this whole long, long time. You don't call that heartless?

LØVBORG I can tell you the truth, Hedda.

HEDDA The truth?

LØVBORG First, promise me—Give me your word that Thea will never find out what I'm about to confide to you.

HEDDA You have my word.

LØVBORG Good. Then I'll tell you—What I stood here and described—It wasn't true.

HEDDA About the manuscript?

LØVBORG Yes. I haven't ripped it up. I didn't throw it in the fjord, either.

HEDDA No, well—so—Where is it?

LØVBORG I've destroyed it just the same. Utterly and completely, Hedda!

HEDDA I don't understand any of this.

LØVBORG Thea said that what I'd done seemed to her like murdering a child.

HEDDA Yes, she did.

LØVBORG But killing his child—that's not the worst thing a father can do to it.

HEDDA Not the worst?

LØVBORG No. And the worst—that is what I wanted to spare Thea from hearing.

HEDDA And what is the worst?

LØVBORG Imagine, Hedda, a man—in the very early hours of the morning—after a wild night of debauchery, came home to the mother of his child and said, "Listen—I've been here and there to this place and that place, and I had our child with me in this place and that place. And the child got away from me. Just got away. The devil knows whose hands it's fallen into, who's got a hold of it."

HEDDA Well—when you get right down to it—it's only a book—

LØVBORG All of Thea's soul was in that book.

HEDDA Yes, I can see that.

LØVBORG And so, you must also see that there's no future for her and me.

HEDDA So, what will your road be now?

LØVBORG None. Only to see to it that I put an end to it all. The sooner the better.

HEDDA (*Comes a step closer.*) Eilert Løvborg—Listen to me now— Can you see to it that—that when you do it, you bathe it in beauty?

LØVBORG In beauty? (*Smiles.*) With vine leaves in my hair, as you used to imagine?

HEDDA Ah, no. No vine leaves—I don't believe in them any longer. But in beauty, yes! For once! Good-bye. You've got to go now. And don't come here any more.

LØVBORG Good-bye, Mrs. Tesman. And give my regards to George Tesman. (*He is about to leave.*)

HEDDA No, wait! Take a souvenir to remember me by.
(*She goes over to the writing table, opens the drawer and the pistol case. She returns to Løvborg with one of the pistols.*)

LØVBORG (*Looks at her.*) That's the souvenir?

HEDDA (*Nodding slowly.*) Do you recognize it? It was aimed at you once.

LØVBORG You should have used it then.

HEDDA Here, you use it now.

LØVBORG (*Puts the pistol in his breast pocket.*) Thanks.

HEDDA In beauty, Eilert Løvborg. Promise me that.

LØVBORG Good-bye, Hedda Gabler. (*He goes out the hall doorway.*)
(*Hedda listens a moment at the door. Afterward, she goes to the
writing table and takes out the package with the manuscript,
looks inside the wrapper, pulls some of the pages half out and
looks at them. She then takes it all over to the armchair by the
stove and sits down. She has the package in her lap. Soon after
she opens the stove door and then opens the package.*)

HEDDA (*Throws one of the sheets into the fire and whispers to herself.*) Now, I'm burning your child, Thea—You with your curly
hair. (*Throws a few more sheets into the fire.*) Your child and
Eilert Løvborg's. (*Throws in the rest.*) Now I'm burning—burning the child.

Act Four

*The same room at the Tesmans'. It is evening. The drawing room
is in darkness. The rear room is lit with a hanging lamp over the
table. The curtains are drawn across the glass door.*

(*Hedda, dressed in black, wanders up and down in the darkened
room. Then she goes into the rear room, and over to the left side.
Some chords are heard from the piano. Then she emerges again,
and goes into the drawing room. Berta comes in from the right of
the rear room, with a lighted lamp, which she places on the
table in front of the sofa, in the salon. Her eyes show signs of crying, and she has black ribbons on her cap. She goes quietly and
carefully to the right. Hedda goes over to the glass door, draws
the curtains aside a little, and stares out into the darkness. Soon
after, Miss Tesman enters from the hallway dressed in black with
a hat and a veil. Hedda goes over to her and shakes her hand.*)

MISS TESMAN Yes, here I am, Hedda—in mourning black. My poor
sister's struggle is over at last.

HEDDA As you can see, I've already heard. Tesman sent me a note.

MISS TESMAN Yes, he promised he would but I thought I should
bring the news myself. This news of death into this house of
life.

HEDDA That was very kind of you.

MISS TESMAN Ah, Rina shouldn't have left us right now. Hedda's
house is no place for sorrow at a time like this.

HEDDA (*Changing the subject.*) She died peacefully, Miss Tesman?

MISS TESMAN Yes, so gently—Such a peaceful release. And she was
happy beyond words that she got to see George once more and

could say a proper good-bye to him. Is it possible he's not home yet?

HEDDA No. He wrote saying I shouldn't expect him too early. But, please sit down.

MISS TESMAN No, thank you, my dear—blessed Hedda. I'd like to, but I have so little time. She'll be dressed and arranged the best that I can. She'll look really splendid when she goes to her grave.

HEDDA Can I help you with anything?

MISS TESMAN Oh, don't even think about it. These kinds of things aren't for Hedda Tesman's hands or her thoughts either. Not at this time. No, no.

HEDDA Ah—thoughts—Now they're not so easy to master—

MISS TESMAN (*Continuing.*) Yes, dear God, that's how this world goes. Over at my house we'll be sewing a linen shroud for Aunt Rina, and here there will be sewing too, but of a whole different kind, praise God.

(*George Tesman enters through a hall door.*)

HEDDA Well, it's good you're finally here.

TESMAN You here, Aunt Julie, with Hedda. Just think.

MISS TESMAN I was just about to go, my dear boy. Well. Did you manage to finish everything you promised to?

TESMAN No, I'm afraid I've forgotten half of it. I have to run over there tomorrow again. Today my brain is just so confused. I can't keep hold of two thoughts in a row.

MISS TESMAN George, my dear, you mustn't take it like that.

TESMAN Oh? How should I take it, do you think?

MISS TESMAN You must be joyful in your sorrow. You must be glad for what has happened, just as I am.

TESMAN Ah, yes. You're thinking of Aunt Rina.

HEDDA You'll be lonely now, Miss Tesman.

MISS TESMAN For the first few days, yes. But that won't last long, I hope. Our sainted Rina's little room won't stand empty. That much I know.

TESMAN Really? Who'll be moving in there, hm?

MISS TESMAN Oh, there's always some poor invalid or other who needs care and attention, unfortunately.

HEDDA You'd really take on a cross like that again?

MISS TESMAN Cross? God forgive you child. It's not a cross for me.

HEDDA But a complete stranger—

MISS TESMAN It's easy to make friends with sick people. And I so badly need someone to live for. Well, God be praised and thanked—there'll be a thing or two to keep an old aunt busy here in this house soon enough.

HEDDA Oh, please don't think about us.

TESMAN   Yes. The three of us could be quite cozy here if only—

HEDDA   If only—?

TESMAN   (*Uneasily.*) Oh, it's nothing. Everything'll be fine. Let's hope, hm?

MISS TESMAN   Well, well, you two have plenty to talk about, I'm sure. (*Smiling.*) And Hedda may have something to tell you, George. Now it's home to Rina. (*Turning in the doorway.*) Dear Lord, isn't it strange to think about. Now Rina's both with me and our sainted Joseph.

TESMAN   Yes, just think, Aunt Julie, hm?

(*Miss Tesman leaves through the hall door.*)

HEDDA   (*Follows Tesman with cold, searching eyes.*) I think all this has hit you harder than your aunt.

TESMAN   Oh, it's not just this death. It's Eilert I'm worried about.

HEDDA   (*Quickly.*) Any news?

TESMAN   I wanted to run to him this afternoon and tell him that his manuscript was safe—in good hands.

HEDDA   Oh? Did you find him?

TESMAN   No, he wasn't home. But later I met Mrs. Elvsted, and she told me he'd been here early this morning.

HEDDA   Yes, just after you left.

TESMAN   And apparently he said that he'd ripped the manuscript up into a thousand pieces, hm?

HEDDA   That's what he said.

TESMAN   But, good God, he must have been absolutely crazy. So you didn't dare give it back to him, Hedda?

HEDDA   No, he didn't get it back.

TESMAN   But, you told him we had it?

HEDDA   No. (*Quickly.*) Did you tell Mrs. Elvsted?

TESMAN   No, I didn't want to. But you should have told him. What would happen if in his desperation he went and did something to himself? Let me have the manuscript, Hedda. I'll run it over to him right away. Where did you put it?

HEDDA   (*Cold and impassively leaning on the armchair.*) I don't have it any more.

TESMAN   Don't have it! What in the world do you mean?

HEDDA   I burned it up—every page.

TESMAN   (*Leaps up in terror.*) Burned? Burned? Eilert's manuscript!

HEDDA   Don't shout like that. The maid will hear you.

TESMAN   Burned! But good God—! No, no, no—That's absolutely impossible.

HEDDA   Yes, but all the same it's true.

TESMAN   Do you have any idea what you've done, Hedda? That's—that's criminal appropriation of lost property. Think about that. Yes, just ask Judge Brack, then you'll see.

HEDDA Then it's probably wise for you not to talk about it, isn't it? To the Judge or anyone else.

TESMAN How could you have gone and done something so appalling? What came over you? Answer me that, Hedda, hm?

HEDDA (*Suppressing an almost imperceptible smile.*) I did it for your sake, George.

TESMAN My sake?

HEDDA Remember you came home this morning and talked about how he had read to you?

TESMAN Yes, yes.

HEDDA You confessed that you envied him.

TESMAN Good God, I didn't mean it literally.

HEDDA Nevertheless, I couldn't stand the idea that someone would overshadow you.

TESMAN (*Exclaiming between doubt and joy.*) Hedda—Oh, is this true?—What you're saying?—Yes, but. Yes, but. I never noticed that you loved me this way before. Think of that!

HEDDA Well, you need to know—that at a time like this— (*Violently breaking off.*) No, no—go and ask your Aunt Julie. She'll provide all the details.

TESMAN Oh, I almost think I understand you, Hedda. (*Clasps his hands together.*) No, good God—Can it be, hm?

HEDDA Don't shout like that. The maid can hear you.

TESMAN (*Laughing in extraordinary joy.*) The maid! Oh, Hedda, you are priceless. The maid—why it's—why it's Berta. I'll go tell Berta myself.

HEDDA (*Clenching her hands as if frantic.*) Oh, I'm dying—Dying of all this.

TESMAN All what, Hedda, what?

HEDDA (*Coldly controlled again.*) All this—absurdity—George.

TESMAN Absurdity? I'm so incredibly happy. Even so, maybe I shouldn't say anything to Berta.

HEDDA Oh yes, go ahead. Why not?

TESMAN No, no. Not right now. But Aunt Julie, yes, absolutely. And then, you're calling me George. Just think. Oh, Aunt Julie will be so happy—so happy.

HEDDA When she hears I've burned Eilert Løvborg's manuscript for your sake?

TESMAN No, no, you're right. All this with the manuscript. No. Of course, nobody can find out about that. But, Hedda—you're burning for me—Aunt Julie really must share in that. But I wonder—all this—I wonder if it's typical with young wives, hm?

HEDDA You'd better ask Aunt Julie about that too.

TESMAN Oh yes, I certainly will when I get the chance. (*Looking uneasy and thoughtful again.*) No, but, oh no, the manuscript. Good Lord, it's awful to think about poor Eilert, just the same. (*Mrs. Elvsted, dressed as for her first visit with hat and coat, enters through the hall door.*)

MRS. ELVSTED (*Greets them hurriedly and speaks in agitation.*) Oh, Hedda, don't be offended that I've come back again.

HEDDA What happened to you, Thea?

TESMAN Something about Eilert Løvborg?

MRS. ELVSTED Oh yes, I'm terrified that he's had an accident.

HEDDA (*Grips her arm.*) Ah, do you think so?

TESMAN Good Lord, where did you get that idea, Mrs. Elvsted?

MRS. ELVSTED I heard them talking at the boarding house—just as I came in. There are the most incredible rumors about him going around town today.

TESMAN Oh yes, imagine, I heard them too. And still I can swear he went straight home to sleep. Just think.

HEDDA So—What were they saying at the boarding house?

MRS. ELVSTED Oh, I couldn't get any details, either because they didn't know or—or they saw me and stopped talking. And I didn't dare ask.

TESMAN (*Uneasily pacing the floor.*) Let's just hope—you misunderstood.

MRS. ELVSTED No, I'm sure they were talking about him. Then I heard them say something about the hospital—

TESMAN Hospital?

HEDDA No—That's impossible.

MRS. ELVSTED I'm deathly afraid for him, so I went up to his lodgings and asked about him there.

HEDDA You dared to do that?

MRS. ELVSTED What else should I have done? I couldn't stand the uncertainty any longer.

TESMAN You didn't find him there either, hm?

MRS. ELVSTED No. And the people there didn't know anything at all. They said he hadn't been home since yesterday afternoon.

TESMAN Yesterday? How could they say that?

MRS. ELVSTED It could only mean one thing—Something terrible's happened to him.

TESMAN You know, Hedda—What if I were to go into town and ask around at different places—?

HEDDA No! You stay out of this.

(*Judge Brack, carrying his hat, enters through the hall door, which Berta opens and closes after him. He looks serious and bows in silence.*)

TESMAN Oh, here you are, Judge, hm?

BRACK Yes, it was essential for me to see you this evening.

TESMAN I see you got the message from Aunt Julie.

BRACK Yes, that too.

TESMAN Isn't it sad, hm?

BRACK Well, my dear Tesman, that depends on how you look at it.

TESMAN (*Looks at him uneasily.*) Has anything else happened?

BRACK Yes, it has.

HEDDA (*Tensely.*) Something sad, Judge Brack?

BRACK Once again, it depends on how you look at it, Mrs. Tesman.

MRS. ELVSTED (*In an uncontrollable outburst.*) It's Eilert Løvborg.

BRACK (*Looks briefly at her.*) How did you guess, Mrs. Elvsted? Do you already know something—?

MRS. ELVSTED (*Confused.*) No, no, I don't know anything but—

TESMAN Well, for God's sake, tell us what it is.

BRACK (*Shrugging his shoulders.*) Well then—I'm sorry to tell you—that Eilert Løvborg has been taken to the hospital. He is dying.

MRS. ELVSTED (*Crying out.*) Oh God, oh God.

TESMAN Dying?

HEDDA (*Involuntarily.*) So quickly—?

MRS. ELVSTED (*Wailing.*) And we were quarrelling when we parted, Hedda.

HEDDA (*Whispers.*) Now, Thea—Thea.

MRS. ELVSTED (*Not noticing her.*) I'm going to him. I've got to see him alive.

BRACK It would do you no good, Mrs. Elvsted. No visitors are allowed.

MRS. ELVSTED At least tell me what happened. What—?

TESMAN Yes, because he certainly wouldn't have tried to—hm?

HEDDA Yes, I'm sure that's what he did.

TESMAN Hedda. How can you—

BRACK (*Who is watching her all the time.*) Unfortunately, Mrs. Tesman, you've guessed right.

MRS. ELVSTED Oh, how awful.

TESMAN To himself, too. Think of it.

HEDDA Shot himself!

BRACK Right again, Mrs. Tesman.

MRS. ELVSTED (*Tries to compose herself.*) When did this happen, Mr. Brack?

BRACK Just this afternoon, between three and four.

TESMAN Oh, my God—Where did he do it, hm?

BRACK (*Slightly uncertain.*) Where? Oh, I suppose at his lodgings.

MRS. ELVSTED No, that can't be. I was there between six and seven.

BRACK Well then, some other place. I don't know precisely. All I know is that he was found—he'd shot himself—in the chest.

MRS. ELVSTED Oh, how awful to think that he should die like that.

HEDDA (*To Brack.*) In the chest?

BRACK Yes, like I said.

HEDDA Not through the temple?

BRACK The chest, Mrs. Tesman.

HEDDA Well, well. The chest is also good.

BRACK What was that, Mrs. Tesman?

HEDDA (*Evasively.*) Oh, nothing—nothing.

TESMAN And the wound is fatal, hm?

BRACK The wound is absolutely fatal. In fact, it's probably already over.

MRS. ELVSTED Yes, yes, I can feel it. It's over. It's all over. Oh, Hedda—!

TESMAN Tell me, how did you find out about all this?

BRACK (*Curtly.*) From a police officer. One I spoke with.

HEDDA (*Raising her voice.*) Finally—an action.

TESMAN God help us, Hedda, what are you saying?

HEDDA I'm saying that here, in this—there is beauty.

BRACK Uhm, Mrs. Tesman.

TESMAN Beauty! No, don't even think it.

MRS. ELVSTED Oh, Hedda. How can you talk about beauty?

HEDDA Eilert Løvborg has come to terms with himself. He's had the courage to do what had to be done.

MRS. ELVSTED No, don't ever believe it was anything like that. What he did, he did in a moment of madness.

TESMAN It was desperation.

MRS. ELVSTED Yes, madness. Just like when he tore his book in pieces.

BRACK (*Startled.*) The book. You mean his manuscript? Did he tear it up?

MRS. ELVSTED Yes, last night.

TESMAN (*Whispering softly.*) Oh, Hedda, we'll never get out from under all this.

BRACK Hmm, that's very odd.

TESMAN (*Pacing the floor.*) To think that Eilert Løvborg should leave the world this way. And then not to leave behind the work that would have made his name immortal.

MRS. ELVSTED Oh, what if it could be put together again.

TESMAN Yes—just think—what if it could? I don't know what I wouldn't give—

MRS. ELVSTED Maybe it can, Mr. Tesman.

TESMAN What do you mean?

MRS. ELVSTED (*Searching in the pocket of her skirt.*) See this? I saved all the notes he dictated from.

HEDDA (*A step closer.*) Ah.

TESMAN You saved them, Mrs. Elvsted, hm?

MRS. ELVSTED Yes, they're all here. I brought them with me when

I came to town, and here they've been. Tucked away in my pocket—

TESMAN Oh, let me see them.

MRS. ELVSTED (*Gives him a bundle of small papers.*) But they're all mixed up, completely out of order.

TESMAN Just think. What if we could sort them out. Perhaps if the two of us helped each other.

MRS. ELVSTED Oh yes. Let's at least give it a try—

TESMAN It will happen. It must happen. I'll give my whole life to this.

HEDDA You, George, your life?

TESMAN Yes, or, anyway, all the time I have. Every spare minute. My own research will just have to be put aside. Hedda—you understand, don't you, hm? I owe this to Eilert's memory.

HEDDA Maybe so.

TESMAN Now, my dear Mrs. Elvsted, let's pull ourselves together. God knows there's no point brooding about what's happened. We've got to try to find some peace of mind so that—

MRS. ELVSTED Yes, yes, Mr. Tesman. I'll do my best.

TESMAN Well. So, come along then. We've got to get started on these notes right away. Where should we sit? Here? No. In the back room. Excuse us, Judge. Come with me, Mrs. Elvsted.

MRS. ELVSTED Oh God—if only it can be done.

(*Tesman and Mrs. Elvsted go into the rear room. She takes her hat and coat off. Both sit at the table under the hanging lamp and immerse themselves in eager examination of the papers. Hedda goes across to the stove and sits in the armchair. Soon after, Brack goes over to her.*)

HEDDA (*Softly.*) Ah, Judge—This act of Eilert Løvborg's—there's a sense of liberation in it.

BRACK Liberation, Mrs. Hedda? Yes, I guess it's a liberation for him, all right.

HEDDA I mean, for me. It's a liberation for me to know that in this world an act of such courage, done in full, free will, is possible. Something bathed in a bright shaft of sudden beauty.

BRACK (*Smiles.*) Hmm—Dear Mrs. Hedda—

HEDDA Oh, I know what you're going to say, because you're a kind of specialist too, after all, just like—Ah well.

BRACK (*Looking steadily at her.*) Eilert Løvborg meant more to you than you might admit—even to yourself. Or am I wrong?

HEDDA I don't answer questions like that. All I know is that Eilert Løvborg had the courage to live life his own way, and now—his last great act—bathed in beauty. He—had the will to break away from the banquet of life—so soon.

BRACK It pains me, Mrs. Hedda—but I'm forced to shatter this pretty illusion of yours.

HEDDA Illusion?

BRACK Which would have been taken away from you soon enough.

HEDDA And what's that?

BRACK He didn't shoot himself—so freely.

HEDDA Not freely?

BRACK No. This whole Eilert Løvborg business didn't come off exactly the way I described it.

HEDDA (*In suspense.*) Are you hiding something? What is it?

BRACK I employed a few euphemisms for poor Mrs. Elvsted's sake.

HEDDA Such as—?

BRACK First, of course, he's already dead.

HEDDA At the hospital?

BRACK Yes. And without regaining consciousness.

HEDDA What else?

BRACK The incident took place somewhere other than his room.

HEDDA That's insignificant.

BRACK Not completely. I have to tell you—Eilert Løvborg was found shot in—Miss Diana's boudoir.

HEDDA (*About to jump up but sinks back again.*) That's impossible, Judge. He can't have gone there again today.

BRACK He was there this afternoon. He came to demand the return of something that he said they'd taken from him. He talked crazily about a lost child.

HEDDA Ah, so that's why—

BRACK I thought maybe he was referring to his manuscript but I hear he'd already destroyed that himself so I guess it was his pocketbook.

HEDDA Possibly. So—that's where he was found.

BRACK Right there, with a discharged pistol in his coat pocket, and a fatal bullet wound.

HEDDA In the chest, yes?

BRACK No—lower down.

HEDDA (*Looks up at him with an expression of revulsion.*) That too! Oh absurdity—! It hangs like a curse over everything I so much as touch.

BRACK There's still one more thing, Mrs. Hedda. Also in the ugly category.

HEDDA And what is that?

BRACK The pistol he had with him—

HEDDA (*Breathless.*) Well, what about it?

BRACK He must have stolen it.

HEDDA (*Jumping up.*) Stolen? That's not true. He didn't.

BRACK There's no other explanation possible. He must have stolen it—Shh.

(*Tesman and Mrs. Elvsted have gotten up from the table in the rear room and come into the living room.*)

TESMAN (*With papers in both hands.*) Hedda, my dear—I can hardly see anything in there under that lamp. Just think—

HEDDA I'm thinking.

TESMAN Do you think you might let us sit a while at your desk, hm?

HEDDA Oh, gladly. (*Quickly.*) No, wait. Let me just clean it up a bit first.

TESMAN Oh, not necessary, Hedda. There's plenty of room.

HEDDA No, no, I'll just straighten it up, I'm telling you. I'll just move these things here under the piano for a while.

(*She has pulled an object covered with sheet music out of the bookcase. She adds a few more sheets and carries the whole pile out to the left of the rear room. Tesman puts the papers on the desk and brings over the lamp from the corner table. He and Mrs. Elvsted sit and continue their work.*)

HEDDA Well, Thea, my sweet. Are things moving along with the memorial?

MRS. ELVSTED (*Looks up at her dejectedly.*) Oh, God—It's going to be so difficult to find the order in all of this.

TESMAN But it must be done. There's simply no other choice. And finding the order in other people's papers—that's precisely what I'm meant for.

(*Hedda goes over to the stove and sits on one of the stools. Brack stands over her, leaning over the armchair.*)

HEDDA (*Whispers.*) What were you saying about the pistol?

BRACK (*Softly.*) That he must have stolen it.

HEDDA Why stolen exactly?

BRACK Because there shouldn't be any other way to explain it, Mrs. Hedda.

HEDDA I see.

BRACK (*Looks briefly at her.*) Eilert Løvborg was here this morning, am I correct?

HEDDA Yes.

BRACK Were you alone with him?

HEDDA Yes, for a while.

BRACK You didn't leave the room at all while he was here?

HEDDA No.

BRACK Think again. Weren't you out of the room, even for one moment?

HEDDA Yes. Perhaps. Just for a moment—out in the hallway.

BRACK And where was your pistol case at that time?

HEDDA I put it under the—

BRACK Well, Mrs. Hedda—

HEDDA It was over there on the writing table.

BRACK Have you looked since then to see if both pistols are there?

HEDDA No.

BRACK It's not necessary. I saw the pistol Løvborg had, and I recognized it immediately from yesterday, and from before as well.

HEDDA Have you got it?

BRACK No, the police have it.

HEDDA What will the police do with that pistol?

BRACK Try to track down its owner.

HEDDA Do you think they can do that?

BRACK (*Bends over her and whispers.*) No, Hedda Gabler, not as long as I keep quiet.

HEDDA (*Looking fearfully at him.*) And what if you don't keep quiet—then what?

BRACK Then the way out is to claim that the pistol was stolen.

HEDDA I'd rather die.

BRACK (*Smiling.*) People make those threats but they don't act on them.

HEDDA (*Without answering.*) So—let's say the pistol is not stolen and the owner is found out? What happens then?

BRACK Well, Hedda—then there'll be a scandal.

HEDDA A scandal?

BRACK Oh, yes, a scandal. Just what you're so desperately afraid of. You'd have to appear in court, naturally. You and Miss Diana. She'd have to detail how it all occurred. Whether it was an accident or a homicide. Was he trying to draw the pistol to threaten her? Is that when the gun went off? Did she snatch it out of his hands to shoot him, and then put the pistol back in his pocket? That would be thoroughly in character for her. She's a feisty little thing, that Miss Diana.

HEDDA But all this ugliness has got nothing to do with me.

BRACK No. But you would have to answer one question. Why did you give the pistol to Eilert Løvborg? And what conclusions would people draw from the fact that you gave it to him?

HEDDA (*Lowers her head.*) That's true. I didn't think of that.

BRACK Well. Fortunately you have nothing to worry about as long as I keep quiet.

HEDDA (*Looking up at him.*) So I'm in your power now, Judge. You have a hold over me from now on.

BRACK (*Whispering more softly.*) Dearest Hedda—Believe me—I won't abuse my position.

HEDDA But in your power. Totally subject to your demands—And your will. Not free. Not free at all. (*She gets up silently.*) No, that's one thought I just can't stand. Never!

BRACK (*Looks mockingly at her.*) One can usually learn to live with the inevitable.

HEDDA (*Returning his look.*) Maybe so. (*She goes over to the writing table, suppressing an involuntary smile and imitating Tesman's intonation.*) Well, George, this is going to work out, hm?

TESMAN Oh, Lord knows, dear. Anyway, at this rate, it's going to be months of work.

HEDDA (*As before.*) No, just think. (*Runs her fingers lightly through Mrs. Elvsted's hair.*) Doesn't it seem strange, Thea. Here you are, sitting together with Tesman—just like you used to sit with Eilert Løvborg.

MRS. ELVSTED Oh, God, if only I could inspire your husband too.

HEDDA Oh, that will come—in time.

TESMAN Yes, you know what, Hedda—I really think I'm beginning to feel something like that. But why don't you go over and sit with Judge Brack some more.

HEDDA Can't you two find any use for me here?

TESMAN No, nothing in the world. (*Turning his head.*) From now on, my dear Judge, you'll have to be kind enough to keep Hedda company.

BRACK (*With a glance at Hedda.*) That will be an infinite pleasure for me.

HEDDA Thanks, but I'm tired tonight. I'll go in there and lie down on the sofa for a while.

TESMAN Yes, do that, Hedda, hm?
(*Hedda goes into the rear room and draws the curtains after her. Short pause. Suddenly she is heard to play a wild dance melody on the piano.*)

MRS. ELVSTED (*Jumping up from her chair.*) Oh—what's that?

TESMAN (*Running to the doorway.*) Oh, Hedda, my dear—Don't play dance music tonight. Just think of poor Aunt Rina and of Eilert Løvborg too.

HEDDA (*Putting her head out from between the curtains.*) And Aunt Julie and all the rest of them too. From now on I shall be quiet. (*She closes the curtains again.*)

TESMAN (*At the writing table.*) This can't be making her very happy—Seeing us at this melancholy work. You know what, Mrs. Elvsted—You're going to move in with Aunt Julie. Then I can come over in the evening, and we can sit and work there, hm?

MRS. ELVSTED Yes, maybe that would be the best—

HEDDA (*From the rear room.*) I can hear you perfectly well, Tesman. So, how am I supposed to get through the evenings out here?

TESMAN (*Leafing through the papers.*) Oh, I'm sure Judge Brack will be good enough to call on you.

BRACK (*In the armchair, shouts merrily.*) I'd be delighted, Mrs. Tesman. Every evening. Oh, we're going to have some good times together, the two of us.

HEDDA (*Loudly and clearly.*) Yes, that's what you're hoping for, isn't it, Judge? You, the one and only cock of the walk—

(*A shot is heard within. Tesman, Mrs. Elvsted and Brack all jump to their feet.*)

TESMAN Oh, she's playing around with those pistols again.

(*He pulls the curtains aside and runs in. Mrs. Elvsted follows. Hedda is stretched out lifeless on the sofa. Confusion and cries. Berta comes running in from the right.*)

(*Shrieking to Brack.*) Shot herself! Shot herself in the temple! Just think!

BRACK (*Half prostrate in the armchair.*) But God have mercy—People just don't act that way!

END OF PLAY

The Master Builder (1892)

The Master Builder was the first play Ibsen wrote after returning to Norway from his twenty-seven years of self-exile. To Moritz Prozor, his French translator, Ibsen wrote: "You are quite right when you say that the series which ends with the epilogue [*When We Dead Awaken*] really began with *The Master Builder*. However, I am reluctant to say more on this subject."[1] In a review of *When We Dead Awaken* in 1900, James Joyce noted what this final group of four plays had in common: "One cannot but observe in Ibsen's later work a tendency to get out of closed rooms. Since *Hedda Gabler* this tendency is most marked. The last act of *The Master Builder* and the last act of *John Gabriel Borkman* take place in the open air. But in this play [*When We Dead Awaken*] the three acts are *al fresco*."[2] Furthermore, in the other play in this group, *Little Eyolf*, two of the three acts are "*al fresco*." In fact, the four plays, as a sequence, show a distinct temporal and spatial progression that, given the unity Ibsen insisted on for the group (and, in another place, for the cycle as a whole—see p. 142), cannot be accidental. The sequence of last-act settings of the group reveals a distinct advance: temporally, from evening, to late evening, through night, to the dawn, as in the Act 3 sequence of *Peer Gynt*; and vertically, from Solness's tower to Rubek and Irene's mountain summit. As these last acts represent the final stage each play has reached, so the sequence of endings should prove important for our interpretation of Ibsen's art. The sequence can be set out as follows:

The Master Builder	*Little Eyolf*	*John Gabriel Borkman*	*When We Dead Awaken*
			Mountain peak
		Hilltop	
	"A Height" in the estate		
Tower			
			Dawn
Evening	Late evening	Night	before sunrise

1. *Letters of Henrik Ibsen*, trans. John Nilsen Laurvik and Mary Morison (New York: Duffield, 1908), 445.
2. James Joyce, "Ibsen's New Drama," *Fortnightly Review* 73 (1900).

The plays gradually reclaim the "metaphysical landscape" of *Peer Gynt*. This release from spatial confinement to outdoor spaces is matched by the greater scale of the characters' gestures and actions. While the main characters search more deeply into their inner dramas over which they have brooded for years, they also reclaim the natural world as the rightful arena for their actions. Solness reenacts an earlier act of cosmic defiance in the open air, against a sun-streaked sky; in *Little Eyolf* the whole landscape of earth, sea, sky, and stars seems involved in the characters' passionate confrontation with the mysterious power of death; John Gabriel Borkman ends his long self-immolation by climbing to a height and uttering a hymn to the surrounding mountain landscape; and Rubek and Irene, in *When We Dead Awaken*, passionately and fatally reunite, ascending to a mountain summit.

Two distinct groups of characters occupy these plays. One, usually more elderly, seems to have reached a condition of *aporia* (literally, "the impassable path"): what Ulfheim, in *When We Dead Awaken*, calls being "bergfast," that is, rock-trapped—a "sticking place" in which any forward movement, horizontally, seems impossible. Such movement is reserved only for a contrasting group, usually a younger generation, who escape the fatal dialectic of the elders and move on. The older generation, it seems, can advance only vertically in actions of suicidal self-affirmation. Even the non-elderly Allmers and Rita in *Little Eyolf*, who survive, remain fixed in the same place, their former life together now ended. George Benard Shaw's account of these last four plays, subtitled "Down Among the Dead Men," declares that Ibsen's world now "passes into the shadow of death, or rather into the splendor of its sunset glory."[3]

The plays open with the older generation locked in a spiritual impasse that is broken by the arrival of a startling figure, an unexpected visitor, who appears (usually from the past) as if summoned by unacknowledged promptings from within the unconscious depths of the protagonists. As James Joyce wrote of *The Master Builder*: "though we only see Solness during one night and up to the following evening, we have in reality watched with bated breath the whole course of his life up to the moment when Hilda Wangel enters his house."[4] Solness is trapped in a condition of self-tormenting guilt and fear of the younger generation. The opening image and words of the play emphasize sickness: Knut Brovik, "as if in distress, breathing heavily and with difficulty," exclaims, "No, I can't hold out much longer!" A doctor is in attendance on the household, and Solness suspects Aline and the doctor of watching for symptoms of his own sickness.

Between Solness and his human "helpers and servers" there is resentment and distrust amounting to paranoia, driving Solness to suppression of the younger generation. Between Solness and his wife, distrust is mingled with remorse and self-reproach on both sides. It is

3. George Bernard Shaw, *The Quintessence of Ibsenism* (1913; reprint, New York: Hill and Wang, 1957), 117–45.
4. Joyce, "Ibsen's New Drama."

into this stifling milieu that the younger generation, in the shape of
Hilde Wangel, enters, audaciously "knocking on the door," to prepare
Solness for his ambiguous destiny.

The Master Builder†

Characters

KNUT BROVIK
KAJA FOSLI
RAGNAR BROVIK
HALVARD SOLNESS
ALINE SOLNESS
DR. HERDAL
HILDA WANGEL
LADIES

The action takes place in the house and garden of master builder
Solness.

Act One

*A simply furnished workroom in master builder Solness's house.
Sliding doors in the left wall lead out to the hall. On the right is
a door leading to the inner rooms. In the rear wall, an open door
to the draftsmen's office. Downstage left, a desk with books, papers, and writing materials. Beyond the doors is a stove. In the
right-hand corner a sofa with a table and a couple of chairs. On
the table is a carafe of water and a glass. A smaller table with a
rocking chair and armchair in the foreground, right. Lighted
lamps, on the table in the draftsmen's office, on the corner table
and on the desk.*

*(In the draftsmen's office Knut Brovik and his son Ragnar are
sitting, occupied with blueprints and calculations. At the desk in
the workroom Kaja Fosli is standing, writing in the ledger. Knut
Brovik is an elderly, frail man with white hair and beard. He is
dressed in a threadbare but well-kept black coat. He wears
glasses and a white, somewhat discolored neckcloth. Ragnar
Brovik is about thirty, a fair-haired man with a slight stoop. Kaja
Fosli is a slightly built girl in her twenties, smartly dressed but
sickly in appearance. She wears a green eyeshade. All three work
for a while in silence.)*

† Translated by Brian Johnston.

KNUT BROVIK (*Suddenly rises from the table, as if in distress, breathing heavily and with difficulty, as he comes into the doorway.*) No, I can't hold out much longer!

KAJA (*Going to him.*) Is it really bad with you this evening, Uncle?

BROVIK I think it gets worse every day.

RAGNAR (*Has risen and approaches.*) You really should go home, Father. Try to get a little sleep.

BROVIK (*Impatiently.*) Go to bed, you mean? You'd have me smothered completely?

KAJA Well then, take a little walk.

RAGNAR Yes, do that. I'll come with you.

BROVIK (*Fiercely.*) I'm not leaving until he comes! This evening, I'll really have it out with— (*With suppressed anger.*) —with him—the chief.

KAJA (*Anxiously.*): Oh no, Uncle—don't do that yet!

RAGNAR Yes, better wait, Father!

BROVIK (*Breathing with difficulty.*) Hah—hah—! I don't have time to wait much longer.

KAJA (*Listening.*) Hush! I can hear him down on the stairs!
   (*All three sit and work again. A short silence.*)
   (*The master builder, Halvard Solness, comes in through the hall door. He is a somewhat elderly man, healthy and strong, with close-cut, curly hair, dark moustache and dark, thick eyebrows. He wears a grey-green, buttoned jacket, with turned-up collar and broad lapels. On his head he wears a soft, grey felt hat; under his arm are a couple of portfolios.*)

SOLNESS (*In the doorway, pointing at the draftsmen's room and whispering.*) Are they gone?

KAJA (*Softly, shaking her head.*) No. (*She takes off her eyeshade.*)
   (*Solness crosses the room, throws his hat on a chair, and places the portfolios on the table by the sofa, returning to the desk again. Kaja writes continuously but seems nervous and uneasy.*)

SOLNESS (*Aloud.*) What are you entering there, Miss Fosli?

KAJA (*Starting.*) Oh, only something that—

SOLNESS Let me see, Miss Fosli. (*Bending over her, he pretends to be looking at the ledger, and whispers.*) Kaja!

KAJA (*Softly, still writing.*) Yes?

SOLNESS Why do you always take off your eyeshade when I approach?

KAJA (*As before.*) Because I look so hideous with it on.

SOLNESS (*Smiling.*) And you don't want to be that, do you, Kaja?

KAJA (*Half-glancing up at him.*) Not for anything in the world. Not in your eyes.

SOLNESS (*Lightly stroking her hair.*) Poor, poor little Kaja—

KAJA Hush, they can hear you.
> (*Solness strolls over to the right of the room, turns, and pauses at the door of the draftsmen's office.*)

SOLNESS Has anyone been here asking after me?

RAGNAR (*Getting up.*) Yes, the young couple who want a villa built out at Løvstrand.

SOLNESS (*Growling.*) Oh, that pair! Well, they must wait. I haven't satisfied myself about the plans, yet.

RAGNAR (*Approaching somewhat hesitantly.*) They were very keen on getting the drawings soon.

SOLNESS (*As before.*) Yes, God help us, that's what they all want!

BROVIK (*Looking up.*) They said they're longing so much to move into their own house.

SOLNESS Of course, of course. Just what I'd expect! And so they're willing to take whatever they can get. Just so they get a—a living space. Some kind of den—but nothing you'd call a home. No thank you! Let them take themselves off to someone else. Tell them that, next time they turn up here.

BROVIK (*Pushing his spectacles up on his forehead, staring in amazement.*) To someone else? You'd let that commission go?

SOLNESS (*Impatiently.*) Yes, yes, devil take it! If it's always going to be like this. It's better than slaving away putting up shacks. (*Vehemently.*) I don't even know anything about these people.

BROVIK They're solid enough people. Ragnar knows them—he often visits the family. Thoroughly solid people.

SOLNESS Ah, solid—solid! As if that's what I mean! Good Lord, don't you understand me, either? (*Angrily.*) I'll have nothing to do with these strangers. Let them go to whomever they please, for all I care!

BROVIK (*Rising.*) You mean that seriously?

SOLNESS (*Sullenly.*) Yes, I do. For once, at least. (*He crosses the room.*)
> (*Brovik exchanges glances with Ragnar, who makes a warning gesture. Then he comes into the front room.*)

BROVIK May I speak a few words to you?

SOLNESS Yes. Go ahead.

BROVIK (*To Kaja.*) Go in there for a while, Kaja.

KAJA (*Uneasily.*) Oh, but Uncle—

BROVIK Do as I say, child. And close the door after you.
> (*Reluctantly, Kaja goes into the draftsmen's room, glancing anxiously and imploringly at Solness and closing the door.*)

BROVIK (*Lowering his voice somewhat.*) I don't want the poor children to find out just how bad I am.

SOLNESS Yes, you've been looking pretty sickly these last days.

BROVIK It will soon be all over with me. My strength is ebbing away—from one day to the next.

SOLNESS Sit down for a bit.

BROVIK Thanks—may I?

SOLNESS (*Drawing an armchair across.*) Here. Go ahead. Well?

BROVIK (*Has seated himself with some difficulty.*) Yes, well, this has got to do with Ragnar. It's what's weighing most on my mind. What's to become of him?

SOLNESS Your son? Naturally, he can stay here with me as long as he wants.

BROVIK But that's just what he doesn't want. He doesn't think he can—any longer.

SOLNESS Well, I'd say he's got quite a good situation here. But if he wants something more, I'd not be unwilling to—

BROVIK No, No! It's not that at all. (*Impatiently.*) Sometime he's got to be able to strike out on his own.

SOLNESS (*Without looking at him.*) You really think Ragnar has the talent for that?

BROVIK No, you see, that's what's so distressing. That I should begin to have doubts about the boy. Because you've never said so much as—as an encouraging word about him. But I must believe anything else is impossible—he must have the talent.

SOLNESS But he hasn't learned anything—not the basics. Apart from being able to draw.

BROVIK (*Looking at him with covert hatred, saying hoarsely.*) You hadn't learned much of the business, either, when you worked for me. Yet you made your way, well enough. (*Drawing breath heavily.*) Forced your way to the top. And kept me—and many others—from doing the same.

SOLNESS Yes—well that's how things turned out for me.

BROVIK Yes, you're right there. Everything gave way to you. But then you can't have the heart to let me go to my grave—without seeing what Ragnar's capable of. I so much want to see them married—before I pass on.

SOLNESS (*Sharply.*) Is that what she wants?

BROVIK Not Kaja so much. But Ragnar talks about it every day. (*Pleading.*) You must—you must help him get some work of his own now! I have to see something the boy has done, do you hear!

SOLNESS (*Irritably.*) But damn it, I can't just pull a commission for him down from the moon.

BROVIK He can get a fine commission right now. A big job.

SOLNESS (*Uneasy and startled.*) He can?

BROVIK If you'll give your consent.

SOLNESS What kind of job is it?

BROVIK (*Hesitantly.*) He can get to build the villa out at Løvstrand.

SOLNESS That! I'm building that myself!

BROVIK Ah, but you're not interested in it.

SOLNESS (*Flaring up.*) Not interested! I? Who dares to say that?

BROVIK You said so yourself, just now.

SOLNESS Oh, never mind what I—say. Can Ragnar get to build the villa?

BROVIK Yes. He knows the family. And then, just for the fun of it, he's made drawings, and estimates, and so on.

SOLNESS And these drawings, they're pleased with them—the people who'll be living in the house?

BROVIK Yes. So, if you'll just look at them and approve of them—

SOLNESS Then they'll let Ragnar build the house for them?

BROVIK They were immensely pleased with what he wanted to do. They thought it was something totally new, they said.

SOLNESS Aha! New. Not the old-fashioned stuff I'm used to turning out.

BROVIK They thought it was something different.

SOLNESS (*With suppressed bitterness.*) And so it was Ragnar that they came to see, when I was out!

BROVIK They came here to call on you. To ask if you'd be willing to step aside.

SOLNESS Step aside! I!

BROVIK In the event you found Ragnar's drawing—

SOLNESS I should step aside for your son!

BROVIK Step aside from the commission, they meant.

SOLNESS Oh, it all comes to the same thing. (*Laughs bitterly.*) So that's it! Halvard Solness—he's to start stepping aside now! To make room for the young. For the very youngest, perhaps. Simply make room. Room! Room!

BROVIK Good Lord, there's room here for more than just one man—

SOLNESS Oh, there's not such an abundance of room, either. But, whatever the case—I'm not stepping aside—I'll never consent to that. Never of my own will. Never in this world will I do that!

BROVIK (*Rising with difficulty.*) So must I pass from life without this consolation? Without happiness? With no faith or trust in Ragnar? Without getting to see a single work of his—is that what I must do?

SOLNESS (*Half-turning and muttering.*) Hm—don't ask me any more now.

BROVIK Yes, answer me! Am I to pass from life so utterly poor?

SOLNESS (*Seeming to struggle with himself; finally saying in a low but firm voice.*) You must pass from life as best you can.

BROVIK Then so be it. (*He goes across the room.*)

SOLNESS (*Following him, half in desperation.*) Because I can't do otherwise, don't you see? It's just the way I am! And I can't make myself any different.

BROVIK No, no, it seems you really can't. (*Staggers and pauses by the sofa table.*) May I have a glass of water?

SOLNESS By all means. (*Pours a glass and hands it to him.*)

BROVIK Thanks. (*Drinks and sets down the glass.*)

(*Solness goes up and opens the door to the draftsmen's office.*)

SOLNESS Ragnar, you must come and take your father home.

(*Ragnar rises quickly. He and Kaja come into the workroom.*)

RAGNAR What is it, Father?

BROVIK Give me your arm. Let's go now.

RAGNAR Very well. You put your things on, too, Kaja.

SOLNESS Miss Fosli must stay a while. Only for a moment. I have a letter for her to write.

BROVIK Good night. Sleep well—if you can.

SOLNESS Good night.

(*Brovik and Ragnar exit through the hallway door. Kaja goes to the desk. Solness stands with bowed head, to the right by the armchair.*)

KAJA (*Uncertainly.*) Is there a letter—?

SOLNESS (*Curtly.*) No, of course not. (*Looking sternly at her.*) Kaja!

KAJA (*Frightened, in a low voice.*) Yes.

SOLNESS (*Pointing commandingly to the floor.*) Come here! At once!

KAJA (*Hesitantly.*) Yes.

SOLNESS (*As before.*) Nearer!

KAJA (*Obeying.*) What do you want with me?

SOLNESS (*Looking at her for a while.*) Is it you I'm to thank for all this?

KAJA No, no, you mustn't think that!

SOLNESS But getting married—is that what you want now?

KAJA (*Softly.*) Ragnar and I have been engaged for four or five years, and so—

SOLNESS And so you think it's time there was an end of it. Isn't that so?

KAJA Ragnar and Uncle say I should. So I think I will have to give in.

SOLNESS (*More gently.*) Kaja, don't you care for Ragnar just a little, too?

KAJA I cared for Ragnar very much, once. Before I came here to you.

SOLNESS But now no longer? Not at all?

KAJA (*Passionately, clasping her hands toward him.*) Oh, you know very well there's only one person I care for now. And no one else in the whole world. I can never care for anyone else.

SOLNESS Yes, you say that. But you'll leave me just the same. Leave me alone here to take care of everything.

KAJA But couldn't I stay here with you, even if Ragnar—

SOLNESS (*Dismissively.*) No, no, that would never work. If Ragnar goes his own way and works for himself, then he'll have a need for you.

KAJA (*Wringing her hands.*) Oh, I can't imagine how I can part from you. It's totally impossible.

SOLNESS Then try to persuade Ragnar to get rid of these stupid ideas. Marry him as much as you please— (*Changing his tone.*) —that is, I mean, convince him to keep his good position here with me. Because then I can keep you, too, Kaja.

KAJA Oh, how wonderful that would be, if it could be arranged that way!

SOLNESS (*Clasps her head in his hands and whispers.*) Because I can't do without you, you understand? I must have you with me here every day.

KAJA (*In nervous rapture.*) Oh God! Oh God!

SOLNESS (*Kissing her hair.*) Kaja—Kaja!

KAJA (*Sinks down before him.*) Oh, how good you are to me. How inexpressibly good you are!

SOLNESS (*Vehemently.*) Get up! Get up before—I hear someone— (*He helps her get up. She staggers to the desk.*)
(*Mrs. Solness enters through the door to the right. She looks thin and careworn, with traces of an earlier beauty. Blonde ringlets. Dressed elegantly, entirely in black. She speaks somewhat slowly and plaintively.*)

MRS. SOLNESS (*In the doorway.*) Halvard!

SOLNESS (*Turning.*) Ah, is that you, dear—?

MRS. SOLNESS (*With a glance at Kaja.*) I'm afraid I've come at an inconvenient moment.

SOLNESS Not at all. Miss Fosli just has a short letter to write.

MRS. SOLNESS Yes, so I see.

SOLNESS What was it you wanted with me, Aline?

MRS. SOLNESS I only wanted to tell you that Doctor Herdal is sitting in the drawing room. Perhaps you could come in and see him, Halvard.

SOLNESS (*Looking mistrustfully at her.*) Hm, does the doctor particularly want to speak with me?

MRS. SOLNESS No, not particularly. He really came to see me. But he would like to say hello to you while he's here.

SOLNESS (*Laughs quietly.*) Yes, I can well believe it. Well, you must ask him to wait a little.

MRS. SOLNESS But you'll come into him soon?

SOLNESS Very likely. Later—later dear. In a little while.

MRS. SOLNESS (*After a glance at Kaja.*) Yes, don't forget to do that, Halvard. (*Retreating and closing the door behind her.*)

KAJA (*Softly.*) Oh God! Oh God!—I'm sure your wife thinks badly of me!

SOLNESS Oh, not in the least. At any rate, not more than usual. But it might be best if you left now, Kaja.

KAJA Yes, yes. I must leave now.

SOLNESS (*Firmly.*) And see about taking care of that other business for me. Do you hear!

KAJA Oh, if it were only up to me, then—

SOLNESS I *will* have it taken care of, I say! And tomorrow. No later!

KAJA (*Fearfully.*) And if there's nothing else for it, then I'll break it off with him.

SOLNESS (*Flaring.*) Break it off! Are you quite mad? You'd actually break it off?

KAJA (*Desperately.*) Yes, sooner that. For I must—I must stay here with you. I can't leave you. That's impossible—completely impossible.

SOLNESS (*Bursting out.*) But, damn it, it's Ragnar above all—it's precisely Ragnar that I—

KAJA (*Looking at him with terrified eyes.*) Is it mostly for Ragnar's sake that—that you—

SOLNESS (*Controlling himself.*) No, no, of course not! You don't understand me either. (*Gently and softly.*) Of course it's you I want to keep. You above all. But that's the very reason you must get Ragnar to keep his position here. There, there, run off home now.

KAJA Very well. Good night, then.

SOLNESS Good night. (*As she is leaving.*) Are Ragnar's drawings lying in there?

KAJA Yes, I didn't see him take them with him.

SOLNESS Well, go in there and find them for me. I might glance over them, after all.

KAJA (*Happily.*) Oh yes, *do* that, please!

SOLNESS For your sake, Kaja dear. So, let me have them at once, you hear?

(*Kaja hurries into the draftsmen's room, searches anxiously in the table drawer, finds the portfolio, and brings it with her.*)

KAJA Here are all the drawings.

SOLNESS Good. Set them down there on the table.

KAJA (*Putting down the portfolio.*) Good night, then. And think kindly of me.

SOLNESS Oh, I always do. Good night, my dear little Kaja. (*Glances to the right.*) Go, go now.

(*Mrs. Solness and Dr. Herdal enter through the door to the right. He is an elderly, stoutish man with a round, good-humored face, clean-shaven, with thin, light hair and gold spectacles.*)

MRS. SOLNESS (*Still in the doorway.*) Halvard, I can't keep the doctor waiting any longer.

SOLNESS Well, then come in.

MRS. SOLNESS (*To Kaja, who is turning down the lamp on the desk.*) All done with the letter, Miss Fosli?

KAJA (*Confused.*) The letter—?

SOLNESS Yes, it was a fairly short one.

MRS. SOLNESS It must have been very short.

SOLNESS You may go now, Miss Fosli. And be here in good time tomorrow morning.

KAJA I will, definitely. Good night, Mrs. Solness. (*She goes out through the hall door.*)

MRS. SOLNESS It was most convenient for you, Halvard, getting hold of that girl.

SOLNESS It certainly was. She's useful in all sorts of way.

MRS. SOLNESS So it would seem.

DR. HERDAL Clever at bookkeeping, too?

SOLNESS Well—of course she's had a good deal of practice these last two years. And then she's very pleasant and willing to do whatever she's asked.

MRS. SOLNESS Yes, that really must be a great comfort—

SOLNESS It is. Especially when one's not too used to that kind of thing.

MRS. SOLNESS (*Mildly reproachful.*) How can you say that, Halvard?

SOLNESS Ah, no, no, my dear Aline. Please forgive me.

MRS. SOLNESS There's no reason to. So, Doctor, you'll come back later and have a cup of tea with us?

DR. HERDAL As soon as I'm through with that house call, I'll be here.

MRS. SOLNESS Thank you. (*She goes out through the door on the right.*)

SOLNESS Are you in a hurry, Doctor?

DR. HERDAL Not in the least.

SOLNESS May I have a few words with you?

DR. HERDAL Yes, with pleasure.

SOLNESS Then let's sit down. (*He motions the doctor to take the rocking chair while he sits in the armchair. He looks probingly at him.*) Tell me, did you notice anything about Aline?

DR. HERDAL Just now, when she was in here, you mean?

SOLNESS Yes, in her attitude toward me. Did you notice anything?

DR. HERDAL (*Smiling.*) Well, it's hard not to notice that your wife—hm—

SOLNESS Well?

DR. HERDAL That your wife doesn't think too much of this Miss Fosli.

SOLNESS Is that all? I could see that for myself.

DR. HERDAL Which, after all, is hardly surprising.

SOLNESS What is?

DR. HERDAL That she doesn't exactly welcome your having another woman with you all day.

SOLNESS No, no, you, may be right there. And Aline, too. But as far as that's concerned, it can't be otherwise.

DR. HERDAL Couldn't you employ an office clerk?

SOLNESS And take the best that just happens to turn up first? No thanks, that won't do for me!

DR. HERDAL But suppose your wife—? Delicate as she is—if this situation should be too much for her?

SOLNESS It can't be any different—in fact I'd go so far as to say I must keep Kaja Fosli. I can't use anyone but her.

DR. HERDAL No one else?

SOLNESS (*Curtly.*) No, no one else.

DR. HERDAL (*Drawing his chair nearer.*) Listen to me now, my dear Mr. Solness. Would you let me put you a question in all confidence?

SOLNESS By all means.

DR. HERDAL Women, you see—in certain matters—have a devilishly keen intuition—

SOLNESS That they have. No doubt about it. But—

DR. HERDAL Well then, listen now. If your wife simply can't endure this Kaja Fosli—

SOLNESS Yes, what then?

DR. HERDAL Might she not have some—some slight grounds for these ill-feelings?

SOLNESS (*Looking at him and getting up.*) Aha!

DR. HERDAL Now don't take offense—but mightn't she?

SOLNESS (*Curtly and firmly.*) No.

DR. HERDAL No grounds whatsoever?

SOLNESS None, outside of her own suspicious imagination.

DR. HERDAL I understand you've known a good many women in your time.

SOLNESS I have, it's true.

DR. HERDAL And got on very well with some of them, too.

SOLNESS Oh yes, that too.

DR. HERDAL But with this Miss Fosli—? Nothing like that involved?

SOLNESS No, nothing at all—on my side.

DR. HERDAL But on hers, then?

SOLNESS I don't think you've the right to ask about that, Doctor.

DR. HERDAL It was your wife's intuition we were discussing.

SOLNESS So we were. And as far as that goes—. (*Lowers his voice.*) Aline's intuition, as you term it—in some ways it's been on the right track.

DR. HERDAL Well, there you see!

SOLNESS (*Sitting.*) Doctor Herdal—now I'm going to tell you a strange story—if you don't mind hearing it.

DR. HERDAL No. I like listening to strange stories.

SOLNESS Very well then. No doubt you remember I took Knut Brovik and his son into my employ—that time things went so badly for the old man.

DR. HERDAL I know something of the sort, yes.

SOLNESS Because actually you see, they're a very talented pair, those two. They have ability, each in his own way. But then the son decided to get engaged. Then, naturally, he wanted to get married—and start building for himself. That's how they all think, these young people.

DR. HERDAL (*Laughing.*) Yes, they have this unfortunate tendency to want to be together.

SOLNESS Yes. But that was of no use to me. I needed Ragnar myself, you see. And the old man, too. He's very clever at calculating stresses and cubic content and all that devilish detail work.

DR. HERDAL Yes, that's all part of it, I suppose.

SOLNESS It is. But Ragnar was set and determined to start on his own. There was no talking him out of it.

DR. HERDAL Yet he stayed with you all the same.

SOLNESS Yes, but just listen why. One day she—Kaja Fosli—came here on some errand. She'd never been here before. And when I came to see how completely infatuated with each other those two were, the thought occurred to me: If I could only get her here in the office, then maybe Ragnar would stay also.

DR. HERDAL That was only a reasonable conclusion.

SOLNESS Yes, but at the time I never breathed the slightest hint of any such thing. I just stood looking at her, and wishing so intently that I'd secured her here. I chatted to her a little in a friendly way, about this and that. And then she went on her way.

DR. HERDAL Well?

SOLNESS Well, the next day, late in the evening after old Brovik and Ragnar had gone home, she came to me here, again, acting as though we'd made a bargain with each other.

DR. HERDAL A bargain? About what?

SOLNESS Precisely the thing I'd stood here wishing. About which I had not uttered a single word.

DR. HERDAL That was most extraordinary.

SOLNESS Yes, wasn't it? And then she wanted to know what her duties here would be. And whether she should begin immediately the next morning. That sort of thing.

DR. HERDAL Don't you think she did that just to be close to her fiancé?

SOLNESS That's what I thought at first. But no, that wasn't it. She began to drift away from him the moment she came to me.

DR. HERDAL And drifted over to you?

SOLNESS Yes, entirely. I can tell she senses when I'm looking at her even when her back is turned. She quivers and trembles if I only come near her. What do you think of that?

DR. HERDAL Hm—I expect there's an explanation.

SOLNESS But what about the other thing? That she believed I'd told her what I'd only wished and willed—and in silence. Inwardly, to myself? What do you say to that? Can you explain something like that, Doctor Herdal?

DR. HERDAL No, I wouldn't try to.

SOLNESS I could have guessed that in advance. It's why I never cared to talk about it till now. But it's so damned inconvenient for me in the long run, you understand. I have to go about, day after day, pretending I—. And then it's so unfair to her, poor girl. (*Vehemently.*) But I can't do otherwise! If she leaves me— then Ragnar will go his own way, too.

DR. HERDAL And you've not told your wife anything of this business?

SOLNESS No.

DR. HERDAL Why on earth don't you?

SOLNESS (*Looks steadily at him and says in a low voice.*) Because I feel it's rather like—rather like a kind of salutary self-torture in letting Aline do me an injustice.

DR. HERDAL (*Shaking his head.*) I don't understand a single blessed word of this.

SOLNESS Yes, you see—it's a little like paying off a tiny part of a boundless, immeasurable debt—

DR. HERDAL To your wife?

SOLNESS Yes. And that always eases one's mind a little. One can breathe more freely for a while, you understand?

DR. HERDAL No, God help me, if I understand a word—

SOLNESS (*Breaking off and rising again.*) Yes, well—let's not talk about it any more. (*He saunters across the room, returns, and stands by the table. He smiles at the doctor.*) I guess you think you've drawn me out pretty effectively, eh Doctor?

DR. HERDAL (*Irritably.*) Drawn you out? Again, I haven't the slightest idea what you're getting at, Mr. Solness.

SOLNESS Now why not come clean and admit it. Because I've seen quite clearly what's going on.

DR. HERDAL What have you seen?

SOLNESS (*Quietly and slowly.*) That you go around here discreetly keeping an eye on me.

DR. HERDAL I do! Why on earth should I do such a thing?

SOLNESS Because you think that I—(*Flaring up.*) Well, what the hell—you believe the same thing about me that Aline does.

DR. HERDAL And what does she believe?

SOLNESS (*Recovering control.*) She's begun to believe that I am somehow—somehow—sick.

DR. HERDAL Sick! You! She's never breathed a single word about it to me. What's supposed to be wrong with you?

SOLNESS (*Leans over the back of the chair and whispers.*) She goes about thinking that I'm mad. That's what she thinks.

DR. HERDAL (*Getting up.*) But my dear Mr. Solness—!

SOLNESS Yes, upon my life—she does. That's how it is. And she's got you to think it too! Oh, I can assure you, Doctor, I see plainly enough you do. I'm not easily fooled, let me tell you.

DR. HERDAL (*Looking at him in amazement.*) Never, Mr. Solness—never has such a thought occurred to me.

SOLNESS (*With an incredulous smile.*) Oh yes? Hasn't it really?

DR. HERDAL No, never! Nor to your wife, either. I think I can swear to that.

SOLNESS Well, perhaps you'd better not do that. For in a way, you see, it could be she's got good grounds for thinking so.

DR. HERDAL Come now, I really must say—!

SOLNESS (*Interrupting with a wave of his hand.*) Yes, yes, my dear doctor—don't let's go on with this any longer. It's better we agree to differ. (*Changes to quiet amusement.*) But listen now, Doctor—hm—

DR. HERDAL Well?

SOLNESS Since you don't believe I'm—somehow—sick—or crazy—or mad—that sort of thing—

DR. HERDAL Well?

SOLNESS Then you must imagine I'm a very fortunate man.

DR. HERDAL Would I only be imagining?

SOLNESS (*Laughing.*) No, no, of course not! God forbid! Just

think—to be master builder Solness! Halvard Solness! Oh, I'm
thankful enough for that!

DR. HERDAL Yes, I really have to say, as far as I can gather, you've
had good fortune on your side to an incredible degree.

SOLNESS (*Suppressing a gloomy smile.*) So I have. Can't complain
about that.

DR. HERDAL First, that grim old bandits' castle burned down for
you. And that truly was a great piece of luck.

SOLNESS (*Seriously.*) It was Aline's family home that burned. Remember that.

DR. HERDAL Yes, for her it must have been a sad loss.

SOLNESS She's not been able to get over it to this day. Not in these
twelve–thirteen years.

DR. HERDAL What followed after must have been the worst blow for
her.

SOLNESS The one with the other.

DR. HERDAL But you—yourself—you soared up from those ashes.
Started out as a poor boy from a country village—and now you
stand the first man in your profession. Oh yes, Mr. Solness,
good fortune's on your side all right.

SOLNESS (*Glances warily at him.*) Yes, but that's precisely what I'm
so horribly afraid of.

DR. HERDAL Afraid of? That good fortune's been on your side?

SOLNESS Morning and night I'm racked with such fear—such fear.
Because at some time, you understand, change will have to
come.

DR. HERDAL Nonsense! Where will the change come from?

SOLNESS (*Firmly, with conviction.*) It will come from youth.

DR. HERDAL Puh! From youth! You're not laid on the shelf yet, I
should hope. Oh no, you're probably standing on firmer foundations than you've ever stood.

SOLNESS But change will come. I can sense it. I feel it approaching.
Someone or other is going to demand: Step aside for me! And
then all the others will storm in after, threatening and shouting: Make room! Make room! Make room! Ah yes, just you
watch, Doctor. Sometime youth will come here knocking at
the door—

DR. HERDAL (*Laughing.*) Well, good Lord, what if it does?

SOLNESS What if it does? Then it's all over with master builder Solness.

(*There is a knock on the door, left.*)

SOLNESS (*Starting.*) What's that? Did you hear anything?

DR. HERDAL Someone's knocking.

SOLNESS (*Loudly.*) Come in!

(*Hilda Wangel enters through the hallway door. She is of middle*

*height, supple, and of slim build. Somewhat suntanned. She is
dressed in touring clothes with her skirt hitched up for walking,
an open sailor's collar, and a small sailor's hat on her head. She
has a knapsack on her back, a plaid in a strap and a long alpen-
stock.*)

HILDA (*Going straight to Solness with sparkling happy eyes.*) Good
evening.

SOLNESS (*Looking uncertainly at her.*) Good evening—

HILDA (*Laughing.*) I almost believe you don't recognize me!

SOLNESS No, I have to admit that—just at the moment—

DR. HERDAL (*Approaching.*) But *I* recognize you, young lady—

HILDA (*Pleased.*) No, is it really you that—?

DR. HERDAL Quite right, it's me. (*To Solness.*) We met up at one of
the mountain lodges last summer. (*To Hilda.*) What became of
all the other ladies?

HILDA Oh, they headed westward.

DR. HERDAL They didn't much like all the racket we made in the
evenings.

HILDA No, they certainly didn't.

DR. HERDAL (*Wagging his finger.*) And it can't be denied, either, that
you did flirt with us a little.

HILDA Well, it was certainly better fun than sitting there knitting
socks with all those old biddies.

DR. HERDAL (*Laughing.*) I entirely agree with you there.

SOLNESS You came to town this evening?

HILDA Yes, I just got in.

DR. HERDAL All alone, Miss Wangel?

HILDA That's right!

SOLNESS Wangel? Your name's Wangel?

HILDA (*Looking in amused surprise at him.*) Yes, it most certainly is.

SOLNESS So maybe you're the daughter of the district doctor up at
Lysanger?

HILDA Yes, who else should I be the daughter of?

SOLNESS Oh, then we've met up there. That summer I built the
tower on the old church.

HILDA (*More gravely.*) Yes, that was the time.

SOLNESS Well, that was a long time ago.

HILDA (*Looking steadily at him.*) It was exactly ten years ago.

SOLNESS You could only have been a child at the time, I should
think.

HILDA (*Casually.*) About twelve–thirteen, at any rate.

DR. HERDAL Is this the first time you've been here in town, Miss
Wangel?

HILDA Yes, that's right.

SOLNESS So you probably don't know anyone here?

HILDA No one except you. Oh, and your wife.

SOLNESS So you know her, too?

HILDA Just slightly. We spent a few days together at the sanatorium.

SOLNESS Ah. Up there.

HILDA She said I really ought to call on her if I came here to town. (*Smiling.*) Not that she needed to.

SOLNESS And yet she's never spoken about it—

(*Hilda sets her stick down by the stove, removes the knapsack and lays it and the plaid on the sofa. Dr. Herdal attempts to help her. Solness stands and gazes at her.*)

HILDA (*Going over to him.*) So, I'd like to ask if I might stay the night here.

SOLNESS That can easily be arranged.

HILDA Because I've no other clothes than these I've got on. Oh, and a set of underclothes in the knapsack. But they need washing—they're really filthy.

SOLNESS That can be seen to easily enough. I'll just let my wife know—

DR. HERDAL Meanwhile, I'll go and call on my patient.

SOLNESS Yes, do that. And come back again later.

DR. HERDAL (*Playfully, with a glance at Hilda.*) Yes, you can count on that for sure! (*Laughing.*) You prophesied truly after all, Mr. Solness!

SOLNESS How do you mean?

DR. HERDAL Youth did come along and knock on your door.

SOLNESS (*Buoyantly.*) Yes, but in a different way completely.

DR. HERDAL That's true, indeed. No doubt about that! (*He leaves by the hall door. Solness opens the door on the right and calls into the room beyond.*)

SOLNESS Aline! Would you come in here, please? Here's a Miss Wangel, someone you know.

MRS. SOLNESS (*Appearing in the doorway.*) Who, do you say? (*Sees Hilda.*) Oh, is it *you*, Miss Wangel? (*Approaches and offers her hand.*) So you came to town after all!

SOLNESS Miss Wangel arrived just this moment. She wonders if she can stay overnight.

MRS. SOLNESS Here with us? Yes, certainly.

SOLNESS So she can get her things in order, you understand.

MRS. SOLNESS I will see to it as best I can. It's no more than one's duty. Your trunk's following after?

HILDA I *have* no trunk.

MRS. SOLNESS Well, it can all be managed, I expect. But now you'll have to make yourself at home with my husband for a while, until I get a room comfortable for you.

SOLNESS Can't we use one of the nurseries? They're standing there ready.

MRS. SOLNESS Oh yes. We've more than enough room there. (*To Hilda.*) Sit down and rest a little. (*She goes out, right.*)
(*Hilda, her hands behind her back, strolls round the room and looks at various things. Solness stands in front of the table, his hands similarly behind his back, following her with his eyes.*)

HILDA (*Stopping and looking at him.*) Do you have several nurseries, then?

SOLNESS We've three nurseries in the house.

HILDA That's a lot. Then you must have ever so many children.

SOLNESS No, we've no children. But now you can be the child, for a while.

HILDA For tonight, yes. I shan't cry. I'm going to see if I can't sleep like a stone.

SOLNESS Yes. You must be fearfully tired, I think.

HILDA Not at all! But just the same—. Because it's terribly delicious to lie like that and dream.

SOLNESS Do you often dream at night?

HILDA I do! Almost always.

SOLNESS What do you dream about most?

HILDA I'm not saying tonight. Another time—perhaps. (*She wanders about the room, stops by the desk, and turns over some of the books and papers.*)

SOLNESS (*Approaching.*) Is there something you're after?

HILDA No, just looking at these things here. (*Turning.*) But perhaps I shouldn't?

SOLNESS No, go ahead.

HILDA Is it *you* who writes in this big ledger?

SOLNESS No, it's the bookkeeper.

HILDA A woman?

SOLNESS (*Smiling.*) Yes, of course.

HILDA Someone you keep with you here?

SOLNESS Yes.

HILDA Is she married?

SOLNESS No, she's single.

HILDA I see.

SOLNESS But she'll soon be getting married.

HILDA That's a good thing for *her.*

SOLNESS But not such a good thing for *me.* For then I'll have no one to help me.

HILDA Can't you get someone else who'll do just as well?

SOLNESS Perhaps *you'd* like to stay here and write in the ledger.

HILDA (*Surveying him.*) So *that's* what you think! No thank you—

THE MASTER BUILDER

we're having none of that. (*She strolls around the room again, then sits in the rocking chair. Solness goes to the table. As before.*) Because there are other things that definitely need doing around here. (*Smiling at him.*) Wouldn't *you* agree, too?

SOLNESS Of course. First of all, you'll want to tour the shops and get yourself smartened up.

HILDA (*Cheerfully.*) No, I think I'll let that pass.

SOLNESS Really?

HILDA Yes, since you must know—I've run through all my money.

SOLNESS (*Laughing.*) No trunk and no money either!

HILDA Neither one nor the other. But hell—! What difference does it make?

SOLNESS You know, I really like you for that!

HILDA Only for that?

SOLNESS For that and for other things. (*Sits in the armchair.*) Is your father still living?

HILDA Yes, father's still living.

SOLNESS And now maybe you're thinking of studying here in town?

HILDA No, that hadn't occurred to me.

SOLNESS But you'll be staying here some time, I imagine?

HILDA That depends on how things turn out. (*She sits a while, rocking herself and looking at him, half gravely, half with a suppressed smile. Then she takes off her hat and sets it on the table in front of her.*) Master builder Solness?

SOLNESS Yes?

HILDA Are you very forgetful?

SOLNESS Forgetful? No, not as far as I know.

HILDA Then you don't want to talk to me at all about what happened up there?

SOLNESS (*Briefly surprised.*) Up at Lysanger? (*Casually.*) Well, there's not much to talk about, I would think.

HILDA (*Looking reproachfully at him.*) How can you sit there and say such a thing!

SOLNESS Well then, *you* tell *me* about it.

HILDA When the tower was finished, we had a great celebration in town.

SOLNESS Yes, I won't forget that day so easily.

HILDA (*Smiling.*) You won't? How very nice of you to say so!

SOLNESS Nice?

HILDA There was music in the churchyard. And many, many hundreds of people. We schoolgirls were all in white, and we all had flags.

SOLNESS Ah yes, the flags. I remember them well enough.

HILDA Then you climbed right up the scaffolding. Right to the very top, and you had a wreath with you, and you hung that wreath way up on the weather vane.

SOLNESS (*Curtly interrupting.*) I used to do that in those days. It's an old custom.

HILDA It was so wonderfully thrilling to stand below, looking up at you. Imagine, if he should fall. He, the master builder himself!

SOLNESS (*As if dismissively.*) Yes, yes, yes, that could well have happened. For one of those little devils in white—she carried on in such a way and screamed up at me—

HILDA (*Her eyes sparkling happily.*) "Hurrah for master builder Solness!" Yes.

SOLNESS —and waved and swung so with her flag I almost grew dizzy at the sight of it.

HILDA (*Quietly and gravely.*) That little devil, that was me.

SOLNESS (*Steadily fixing his eyes on her.*) I am sure of it now. It must have been you.

HILDA (*Once again lively.*) Because it was so fearfully glorious—and thrilling! I couldn't imagine there was a builder in the whole world who could build such a tremendously high tower. And then, that you could stand at the very top of it! As bright—as large as life! That you weren't in the least bit dizzy! It was *that* that was almost—so—dizzying to think about.

SOLNESS How can you be so sure that I wasn't—?

HILDA (*Rejecting this.*) What an idea! No! I knew it instinctively. Otherwise you couldn't have stood up there singing.

SOLNESS (*Looks in amazement at her.*) Singing? I *sang*?

HILDA You most certainly did.

SOLNESS (*Shaking his head.*) I've never sung a note in my life!

HILDA Well, you sang that time. It sounded like harps in the air.

SOLNESS (*Thoughfully.*) There's something uncanny in all this.

HILDA (*Looks at him for a moment, then says in a low voice.*) But it was then—afterward—that the real thing happened.

SOLNESS The real thing?

HILDA (*Sparkling and lively.*) Yes, surely I don't have to remind you about that?

SOLNESS Oh yes, remind me of that, too. Just a little.

HILDA Don't you remember how a great banquet was held for you at the club?

SOLNESS Yes, very well. That must have been the same afternoon. Because I left the next morning.

HILDA And after the club, you were invited to our house for the evening.

SOLNESS You are perfectly right, Miss Wangel. It's remarkable how well you've kept alive all these little details.

HILDA Little details! Now that's great! It was only a little detail, I suppose, that I was alone in the room when you arrived?

SOLNESS You were?

HILDA (*Without answering him.*) You didn't call me a little devil, then.

SOLNESS No, I don't suppose I did.

HILDA You said I was lovely in my white dress. That I looked just like a little princess.

SOLNESS I'm sure you did, Miss Wangel. I was feeling so light and so free that day.

HILDA Then you said that when I grew up I should be your princess.

SOLNESS (*Laughing a little.*) Well, well—did I say that too?

HILDA You did. And when I asked you how long I would have to wait, you said you'd come back again in ten years—like a troll—and carry me off. To Spain or somewhere like that. And you promised you'd buy me a kingdom.

SOLNESS (*As before.*) Well, after a good meal one doesn't usually count the pennies. But did I really say all this?

HILDA (*Laughing quietly.*) Yes. And you said, as well, what this kingdom would be called.

SOLNESS Well, then?

HILDA It would be called the kingdom of Orangia, you said.

SOLNESS Well, that's certainly an appetizing name.

HILDA No, I didn't like that at all. It seemed like you were wanting to make fun of me.

SOLNESS I'm sure that wasn't my intention.

HILDA No, I shouldn't think so! Considering what you did after that—

SOLNESS And what in all the world did I do after that?

HILDA No, that's really the limit if you've forgotten that as well. Something like that must always be remembered, I would have thought.

SOLNESS Well, just set me a little on the right track and then perhaps—Well?

HILDA (*Looks steadily at him.*) You held me and kissed me, master builder Solness.

SOLNESS (*Open-mouthed, he gets up from his chair.*) I did *that*?

HILDA Yes you did. You took me in your arms and bent me backwards, and kissed me. Many times.

SOLNESS No, but my dear Miss Wangel—

HILDA (*Rising.*) You're never going to deny it?

SOLNESS Yes, I most certainly do deny it!

HILDA (*Surveying him scornfully.*) Oh, indeed! (*She turns and goes slowly over to the stove where she remains standing motionless,*

*turned away from him and motionless, her hands behind her
back. A short silence.*)

SOLNESS (*Walking warily up behind her.*) Miss Wangel— (*Hilda is
silent, motionless.*) Don't stand there like a stone statue. All
this you've just said—it must be something you've dreamt.
(*Lays his hand upon her arm.*) Listen, now. (*Hilda makes an impatient movement with her arm. Solness as if struck by a sudden
thought.*) Or else—! Wait a moment! There's something deeper
beneath all this, you'll see! (*Hilda does not stir. Solness quietly
but forcefully.*) All this you say, I must have *thought*. I must
have *willed* it. Have *wished* it, *desired* it. And then—. Mightn't
that explain it? (*Hilda remains silent. Solness impatiently.*) Oh
yes, all right—damn it!—so I *did* do it as well.

HILDA (*Turns her head a little but without looking at him.*) Then
you admit it at last?

SOLNESS Yes—whatever you like.

HILDA That you held me in your arms?

SOLNESS Yes!

HILDA And bent me back?

SOLNESS Very far back.

HILDA And kissed me?

SOLNESS Yes, so I did.

HILDA Many times?

SOLNESS As many as you like.

HILDA (*Turning swiftly to face him. Her eyes have once again their
sparkling, happy expression.*) There, you see, I did pry it out of
you in the end!

SOLNESS (*With a faint smile.*) Yes, imagine my forgetting something
like that.

HILDA (*Again a little sulky, she retreats from him.*) Oh, I expect
you've kissed so many in your time.

SOLNESS No, you mustn't think that of me. (*Hilda sits in the armchair. Solness stands, leaning on the rocking chair. He looks intently at her.*) Miss Wangel?

HILDA Yes?

SOLNESS How was it, now? What happened next—between us two?

HILDA Nothing happened next. You know that perfectly well. Because just then the other guests arrived and then—ecch!

SOLNESS Ah, quite right! The others arrived. Imagine forgetting
that, too!

HILDA Oh, you haven't really forgotten anything. You're just a little
ashamed. One doesn't forget things like that, I'm sure.

SOLNESS One wouldn't suppose so.

HILDA (*Lively again, looking at him.*) Or maybe you've forgotten
what day it was?

SOLNESS What day—?

HILDA Yes, what day you hung the wreath on the tower. Well? Tell me now!

SOLNESS Hm—the exact day—I must confess I've forgotten. I only know it was ten years ago. Sometime in the fall.

HILDA (*Slowly nodding her head several times.*) It was ten years ago. The nineteenth of September.

SOLNESS Ah yes, it must have been about then. So you remember *that*, too! (*Stops.*) Just a moment—! Today's also the nineteenth of September.

HILDA Yes, that's right. The ten years are up. And you didn't come, as you'd promised me.

SOLNESS Promised you? Threatened, I guess you mean?

HILDA I didn't find it the least bit threatening.

SOLNESS Well, teased you, then.

HILDA Was *that* all you wanted? Just to tease me?

SOLNESS Well, fooling with you a bit, then. God knows, I don't remember. But it must have been something like that. For you were just a child at the time.

HILDA Oh, maybe not quite such a child, either. Not such an innocent as you think.

SOLNESS (*Looking at her searchingly.*) Did you truly and seriously think I'd come back for you?

HILDA (*Hiding a half-playful smile.*) Of course! That's what I expected of you.

SOLNESS That I'd come to your house and take you away with me?

HILDA Exactly like a troll, yes!

SOLNESS And make you a princess?

HILDA It's what you promised me.

SOLNESS And give you a kingdom as well?

HILDA (*Looking up at the ceiling.*) Why not? It didn't need to be an ordinary, real kingdom.

SOLNESS But something else just as good?

HILDA Yes, at least as good. (*Looks at him a moment.*) If you could build the highest church tower in the world, then surely you could find your way to producing some kind of kingdom or other—so it seemed to me.

SOLNESS (*Shaking his head.*) I really can't make you out, Miss Wangel.

HILDA You can't? I think it's all so simple.

SOLNESS No, I really can't make up my mind whether you actually mean everything you say, or whether you're sitting there having some fun—

HILDA (*Smiling.*) Teasing you, perhaps. I, too?

SOLNESS Yes, exactly. Teasing. Both of us. (*Looks at her.*) How long
    have you known I was married?

HILDA Oh, I've known all along. Why do you ask about that?

SOLNESS (*Lightly.*) No, no, it just occurred to me. (*Looking seriously
    at her and saying in a low voice.*) Why have you come?

HILDA Because I want my kingdom. The time's up.

SOLNESS (*Laughing involuntarily.*) You're an odd one, you are!

HILDA (*Gaily.*) Come up with my kingdom, master builder! (*Raps
    with her fingers.*) My kingdom on the table!

SOLNESS (*Pushing the rocking chair nearer and sitting down.*) Seri-
    ously speaking, why have you come? What do you really want
    to do here?

HILDA Well, to start with, I'd like to go round and look at all the
    things you've built.

SOLNESS That'll give you more than enough to go chasing after.

HILDA Yes, you've definitely built an awful lot.

SOLNESS So I have. Mostly these last years.

HILDA Many church towers, also? Tremendously high ones?

SOLNESS No, I don't build church towers anymore. Nor churches,
    either.

HILDA Then what *do* you build, now?

SOLNESS Homes for human beings.

HILDA (*Reflectively.*) Couldn't you arrange it so there's some kind
    of—of church tower over these homes as well?

SOLNESS (*Starting.*) What do you mean by that?

HILDA I mean—something that points—up into the free air. With a
    weather vane above at a great, dizzy height.

SOLNESS (*Pondering a little.*) How strange you should say that. It's
    what I've wanted to do most of all.

HILDA (*Impatiently.*) Then why on earth don't you do it?

SOLNESS (*Shaking his head.*) Because people don't want it.

HILDA Imagine—not wanting that!

SOLNESS (*More lightly.*) But now I'm building myself a new home.
    Opposite, over there.

HILDA For yourself?

SOLNESS Yes. It's almost finished. And that's got a tower.

HILDA A high tower?

SOLNESS Yes.

HILDA Very high?

SOLNESS People are bound to say, much too high. For a house, that
    is.

HILDA I'll be going out to look at that tower first thing in the morn-
    ing.

SOLNESS (*Sitting with his hand beneath his cheek, gazing at her.*)

Tell me, Miss Wangel, what is your name? Your first name, I mean?

HILDA My name's Hilda, of course.

SOLNESS (*As before.*) Hilda? I see.

HILDA Don't you remember *that*? You called me Hilda yourself. That day you—misbehaved yourself.

SOLNESS I did that, too?

HILDA But then you said "little Hilda." I didn't like that.

SOLNESS So you didn't like that, Miss Hilda?

HILDA No, not on an occasion like that. However, Princess Hilda—. I think that will do quite nicely.

SOLNESS Very well. Princess Hilda of—of—. What *was* that kingdom to be called?

HILDA Ecch! I don't want to hear about that stupid kingdom. I'm after a completely different one.

SOLNESS (*He leans back in his chair and looks directly at her.*) Isn't it strange—? The more I think about it now—it's as if for many long years I've gone around tormenting myself with—hm—

HILDA With what?

SOLNESS —Trying to track down something—some experience I thought I'd forgotten. But I could never discover a clue as to what it could be.

HILDA You should have tied a knot in your handkerchief, master builder.

SOLNESS Then I'd only have worried over what the knot could mean.

HILDA Ah, yes. There are trolls of that sort in the world, too.

SOLNESS (*Slowly gets up.*) It's inexpressibly good that you've come to me now.

HILDA (*With a searching look.*) *Is* it so good?

SOLNESS Because I've been so alone here. And feeling so completely helpless . . . (*Lowering his voice.*) I have to tell you— I've begun to be so afraid—so dreadfully afraid of the young.

HILDA (*Snorting.*) Pooh!—as if the young are anything to be afraid of!

SOLNESS They are—definitely! And because of that I've locked and barred myself in. (*Secretively.*) You'll see, youth will come here and thunder at the door. Smash their way in to me.

HILDA Then I think you should go open the door to the young.

SOLNESS Open the door?

HILDA Yes. So youth can find its way to you. In the friendliest way.

SOLNESS No, no, no! Youth, can't you see—it's retribution. It comes as the spearhead of change. As if under a new banner.

HILDA (*Rises, looking at him with a trembling of her lips.*) Can you use me in any way, master builder?

SOLNESS Yes, now I can, most certainly. Because you've come here too, as if under a new banner. It's youth against youth, then—

DR. HERDAL (*Enters through the hallway door.*) What, are you and Miss Wangel still here?

SOLNESS Yes. We two found so much to talk about.

HILDA Both old and new.

DR. HERDAL No, have you really?

HILDA And it's all been so amusing. For master builder Solness— he's got such an unbelievable memory. All the tiniest details he remembers in the blink of an eye.

(*Mrs. Solness enters through the door to the right.*)

MRS. SOLNESS There, Miss Wangel, now the room's all ready for you.

HILDA Oh, how kind you're being!

SOLNESS (*To his wife.*) The nursery?

MRS. SOLNESS Yes. The middle one. But first let's go in to supper.

SOLNESS (*Nodding to Hilda.*) Hilda will sleep in the nursery, then.

MRS. SOLNESS (*Looking at him.*) Hilda?

SOLNESS Yes, Miss Wangel's called Hilda. I knew her when she was a child.

MRS. SOLNESS No, did you really, Halvard? Well, shall we go? Supper is on the table.

(*She takes Dr. Herdal's arm and goes out with him to the right. Hilda meanwhile has been gathering her traveling things.*)

HILDA (*Swiftly and softly to Solness.*) Is it true what you said just now? Can you find a use for me?

SOLNESS (*Taking the things from her.*) You're the one I've most desperately needed.

HILDA (*Gazing at him with joyful, wondering eyes and clasping her hands.*) Oh, you great and beautiful world—

SOLNESS (*Eagerly.*) What—?

HILDA Then I have my kingdom.

SOLNESS (*Involuntarily.*) Hilda—!

HILDA (*Once more with a trembling of her lips.*) Almost—I was about to say.

(*She goes out to the right. Solness follows her.*)

Act Two

A pleasantly furnished, small drawing room in Solness's house. In the rear wall, a glass door leading out to the veranda and garden. The right-hand corner is cut by a large bay window with flower stands. A similarly cut-off corner to the left, with a papered, concealed door. On each side, an ordinary door. In the front, on the right, a console table with a large mirror over it. Flowers and plants richly displayed. In the front on the left a sofa with a table and chairs. Farther back, a bookcase. In the foreground of the room, in front of the bay window, a small table and two chairs. It is early morning.

Solness is sitting by the small table with Ragnar Brovik's portfolio before him. He is turning the drawings over and closely examining some of them. Mrs. Solness moves noiselessly about with a little watering can, watering the plants. She is dressed in black, as before. Her hat, cloak, and parasol lie on a chair by the mirror. Solness occasionally follows her with his eyes, unnoticed. Neither of them speaks. Kaja Fosli enters silently through the door to the left.

SOLNESS (*Turns his head and speaks in an apparently casual tone.*) Oh, is it you?

KAJA I just wanted to tell you I'm here.

SOLNESS Yes, yes, that's fine. Isn't Ragnar here, too?

KAJA No, not yet. He had to stay behind and wait for the doctor. But he'll be here soon to hear if—

SOLNESS How is the old man today?

KAJA It's bad. He asks you to excuse him, but he must keep to his bed today.

SOLNESS Of course. Let him do that by all means. But you go on to your work now.

KAJA Yes. (*Standing in the doorway.*) Will you be speaking to Ragnar when he comes in?

SOLNESS No—I've nothing special to say to him.

(*Kaja goes out again to the left. Solness continues to sit, turning over the drawings.*)

MRS. SOLNESS (*Over by the plants.*) I wonder if he isn't going to die now, he too.

SOLNESS (*Looking at her.*) He too? Who is the other?

MRS. SOLNESS (*Without answering.*) Yes, yes—old Brovik, he's going to die now, too, Halvard. You'll see that he will.

SOLNESS Aline dear, shouldn't you be taking a little walk?

MRS. SOLNESS Yes, I really suppose I should. (*She continues watering the flowers.*)

SOLNESS (*Bent over the drawings.*) Is she still asleep?

MRS. SOLNESS (*Looking at him.*) Is it Miss Wangel you're sitting there thinking about?

SOLNESS (*Casually.*) I just happened to call her to mind.

MRS. SOLNESS Miss Wangel's been up long since.

SOLNESS Oh, has she now?

MRS. SOLNESS When I went in there, she was busy sorting out her things. (*She goes to the mirror and slowly begins putting on her hat.*)

SOLNESS (*After a short silence.*) So we found a use for the nurseries after all, Aline.

MRS. SOLNESS Yes, so we did.

SOLNESS And I think that's better than all of them standing empty.

MRS. SOLNESS That emptiness is dreadful—you're right there.

SOLNESS (*Closes the portfolio and approaches her.*) Just you see, Aline, it's going to be better for us from now on. A lot pleasanter. Life will be easier. Especially for you.

MRS. SOLNESS (*Looking at him.*) From now on?

SOLNESS Yes, believe me, Aline—

MRS. SOLNESS Do you mean—because *she's* arrived here?

SOLNESS (*Restraining himself.*) I mean, of course—as soon as we've moved into the new house.

MRS. SOLNESS (*Taking her cloak.*) Do you really think so, Halvard? That it will be any better *there*?

SOLNESS I can't think otherwise. Don't you feel the same?

MRS. SOLNESS I feel absolutely nothing about the new house.

SOLNESS (*Discouraged.*) It really hurts me to hear you say that. It's mostly for your sake I've built it. (*He offers to help her with her cloak.*)

MRS. SOLNESS (*Evading him.*) The fact is you do far too much for my sake.

SOLNESS (*With some vehemence.*) No, no, don't talk like that, Aline. I can't bear hearing you say such things.

MRS. SOLNESS Then I won't say them, Halvard.

SOLNESS But I stand by what I say. You'll see, it's going to be splendid for you over there.

MRS. SOLNESS Oh God—splendid for me—!

SOLNESS (*Eagerly.*) It will! It will! You can be sure of that, Aline! Because, you see, there's so much to remind you of your own—

MRS. SOLNESS Of what had been Father's and Mother's. And that burned to the ground.

SOLNESS (*His voice subdued.*) Yes, yes, poor Aline. That was a terrible blow for you.

MRS. SOLNESS (*Breaking out in a lament.*) Build as much as you want, Halvard—you'll never build a true home again for *me*.

SOLNESS (*Crossing the room.*) Well, in God's name, let's not say any more about it then.

MRS. SOLNESS We hardly ever talk about it at all. Because you only push the subject away from you—

SOLNESS (*Stopping suddenly and looking at her.*) I do? Why should I do that? Push it from me?

MRS. SOLNESS Oh, I understand you so well, Halvard. You're so anxious to spare me. To make excuses for me. As much as you can.

SOLNESS (*With astonished eyes.*) You! Is it *you*—yourself—you're talking about, Aline?

MRS. SOLNESS Yes, only myself. Who else?

SOLNESS (*Involuntarily to himself.*) That too!

MRS. SOLNESS As for the old house, well, what happened was only what had to be. Once misfortune's let loose, then—

SOLNESS Yes, you're right there. "Misfortune will reign although we complain"—as the saying goes.

MRS. SOLNESS It's the horrible thing the fire brought after it—! *That's* the thing! That, that, that.

SOLNESS (*Vehemently.*) Don't even think about it, Aline!

MRS. SOLNESS But it's precisely what I have to think about. And finally speak about for once, too. Because I don't think I can bear it any longer. And then never to be able to forgive myself—!

SOLNESS (*Exclaiming.*) Yourself!

MRS. SOLNESS Yes, for I had duties on both sides. Both to you and to the little ones. I should have hardened myself. Not let the horror take hold of me. Nor grieved because my home was burned down. (*Wringing her hands.*) Oh, Halvard, if I had only had the strength!

SOLNESS (*Softly, moved, approaches her.*) Aline, you must promise me you will never think these thoughts again. Promise me that, at least.

MRS. SOLNESS Oh God—promises! Promises! One can promise anything—

SOLNESS (*Clenching his hands and crossing the room.*) Oh, how hopeless this is! Never a ray of the sun! Not so much as a gleam of light in this home!

MRS. SOLNESS This is no home, Halvard.

SOLNESS Ah, no, you may well say that. (*Heavily.*) And God knows, if you're not right after all—it won't be any better for us in the new house, either.

MRS. SOLNESS It can never be any better. Just as empty. Just as desolate. There, like here.

SOLNESS (*Vehemently.*) Then why in all the world have we built it? Can you tell me that?

MRS. SOLNESS No, you must answer that yourself.

SOLNESS (*Glances suspiciously at her.*) What do you mean by that, Aline?

MRS. SOLNESS What do I mean?

SOLNESS Yes, damn it—! You said it so strangely. As if there was a meaning hidden behind it.

MRS. SOLNESS No, I assure you—

SOLNESS (*Approaching nearer.*) Oh, many thanks! I know what I know. I can see and hear as well, Aline. You can count on that!

MRS. SOLNESS But what's all this about? What is it?

SOLNESS (*Confronting her.*) Don't you try to discover a secret, hidden meaning in the most innocent thing I say?

MRS. SOLNESS *I*, you say! *I* do that!

SOLNESS (*Laughs.*) Well, that's only reasonable, Aline. When you're dealing with a sick man in the house, then—

MRS. SOLNESS (*Anxiously.*) Sick? Are you *sick*, Halvard?

SOLNESS (*Bursting out.*) Half-mad, then! A crazy man! Whatever you want to call me.

MRS. SOLNESS (*Feeling for a chair and sitting down.*) God in heaven, Halvard—!

SOLNESS But you're wrong, both of you. Both you and your doctor. It's not like that with me. (*He paces up and down the room. Mrs. Solness anxiously follows him with her eyes. At last he goes up to her.*) In fact there's nothing wrong with me at all.

MRS. SOLNESS No, there isn't, is there? But what's troubling you then?

SOLNESS It's this—that many times I'm ready to sink under this terrible burden of debt—

SOLNESS Debt, you say! But you're not in debt to anyone, Halvard!

SOLNESS (*Quietly, with emotion.*) I owe a boundless debt to you—to you, Aline—to you.

MRS. SOLNESS (*Slowly rising.*) What's behind all this? It's better you tell me right now.

SOLNESS Nothing's behind it. I've never done you any wrong. Not knowingly, at any rate. And yet all the same—it's as if a crushing guilt was pressing and weighing down on me.

MRS. SOLNESS Guilt toward me?

SOLNESS To you most of all.

MRS. SOLNESS Then you are sick, after all, Halvard.

SOLNESS (*Heavily.*) Could well be. Or something of the sort. (*Looking toward the door to the right, which now opens.*) Ah! Now it grows lighter.

(*Hilda Wangel enters. She has made some changes in her dress, letting down the skirt.*)

HILDA Good morning, master builder!

SOLNESS (*Nodding.*) Slept well?

HILDA Wonderfully! Like in a cradle. Ah, I lay and stretched myself like—like a princess!

SOLNESS (*Smiling a little.*) Perfectly comfortable, then?

HILDA I should think so.

SOLNESS And dreamt as well, I suppose?

HILDA I did, yes. But that was awful.

SOLNESS How?

HILDA Because I dreamt that I was falling over a fearfully high, sheer precipice. Do you ever dream such things?

SOLNESS Oh yes—now and then—

HILDA It's so terribly thrilling—when you are falling and falling—

SOLNESS It feels like your blood's turning to ice.

HILDA Do you tuck your legs up under you while you're falling?

SOLNESS Yes, as high as ever I can.

HILDA That's what *I* do, too.

MRS. SOLNESS (*Taking her parasol.*) I must go into town now, Halvard. (*To Hilda.*) And I'll see if I can find one or two things that you might be needing.

HILDA (*Ready to clasp her arms round her neck.*) Oh you dear, lovely Mrs. Solness! It's really so kind of you! Terribly kind—

MRS. SOLNESS (*Preventing her and slipping free.*) Oh, not at all—far from it. It's merely my duty, so I'm glad to do it.

HILDA (*Resentfully, pouting.*) Actually, I really think I'm fit to tour the town myself—now that I've tidied up my outfit. Or perhaps you don't agree.

MRS. SOLNESS To speak frankly, I think people will stare at you.

HILDA Pooh! Is that all? That could be quite fun.

SOLNESS (*With suppressed bad humor.*) Yes, but then you see, people might get to thinking *you're* mad, too.

HILDA Mad too? Are there so many mad folk here in town, then?

SOLNESS (*Pointing to his forehead.*) Here you can see *one*, at least.

HILDA *You*—master builder!

MRS. SOLNESS Oh no, don't, my dear Halvard!

SOLNESS Haven't you noticed that, yet?

HILDA No, I really can't say I have. (*Reflects and then laughs slightly.*) Well, perhaps in just one thing, after all.

SOLNESS Do you hear that, Aline?

MRS. SOLNESS What's this one thing, Miss Wangel?

HILDA No, I'm not telling.

SOLNESS Go on, tell!

HILDA No, thank you. I'm not as mad as that!

MRS. SOLNESS When you and Miss Wangel are alone, she'll tell you all right, Halvard.

SOLNESS Oh yes—you think so?

MRS. SOLNESS Oh definitely. You've known her so well in the past. Ever since she was a child—so you say. (*She goes out through the door to the left.*)

HILDA (*Shortly after.*) Can't your wife get to like me?

SOLNESS You think you saw that in her?

HILDA Couldn't you see it yourself?

SOLNESS (*Evasively.*) Aline's become extremely shy of people these last years.

HILDA Has she really?

SOLNESS If only you could get to know her really well—. Because she's really so kind—and so good—so fine, deep down—

HILDA (*Impatiently.*) But if she's all that—what makes her come up with all this stuff about duty?

SOLNESS About duty?

HILDA Yes. She said she'd go out and buy something for me, because it was her *duty*. Oh, I can't stand that hideous, vicious word.

SOLNESS Why ever not?

HILDA I can't—for it sounds so cold and sharp and cutting. Duty—duty—duty. Don't you think so too? As if it's stabbing you?

SOLNESS Hm. I've not given it that much thought.

HILDA Well, it is! And if she's so nice—as you claim she is—why should she talk in that way?

SOLNESS But good Lord, what should she have said?

HILDA She could have said she'd do it because she liked me so much. Something like that, she might have said. Something truly warm and heartfelt, don't you see?

SOLNESS (*Looking at her.*) Is *that* how you want it?

HILDA Yes, like that. (*She crosses the room, stands by the bookcase, and looks at the books.*) You've a great many books.

SOLNESS I've collected quite a few.

HILDA And you read all these books?

SOLNESS I tried to, in the past—not any more, though. How about you?

HILDA No, never! Not any more. I no longer see what they all add up to.

SOLNESS It's exactly the same with me.

HILDA (*Wanders about a little, stops by the little table, opens the portfolio, and leafs through it.*) Have you drawn all these?

SOLNESS No, they're a young man's who helps me here.

HILDA Someone you've taught.

SOLNESS Oh yes, he's definitely learned something from me, too.

HILDA (*Sitting.*) He must be very clever, then? (*Glancing at the drawings.*) Isn't he?

SOLNESS Oh, not too bad. Though for what I need—

HILDA Oh yes! He must be fearfully clever.

SOLNESS You think you can see that from the drawings?

HILDA Puh! This stuff? But since he's been learning from you—

SOLNESS Well, for *that* matter—there are many here who've learnt from me. And haven't come to much, for all that.

HILDA (*Looks at him and shakes her head.*) Well, for the life of me, I can't understand how you can be so stupid.

SOLNESS Stupid? You think I'm so very stupid, then?

HILDA Yes, I really do! How you can let yourself go around teaching all these fellows, then—

SOLNESS (*Starting.*) Well, and why not?

HILDA (*Rises, half-serious, half-laughing.*) Ah, *no*, master builder! What's the use of that? Nobody but *you* should have the right to build. You should be the only one. Do it all yourself—alone. Now you know.

SOLNESS (*Involuntarily.*) Hilda—!

HILDA Well?

SOLNESS How on earth did you come by that idea?

HILDA You think it's such a crazy idea then?

SOLNESS No, it's not that. But now I must tell you something.

HILDA Well then?

SOLNESS I go around here—endlessly—in silence and solitude— brooding on that same idea.

HILDA Well, it seems to me that's only natural.

SOLNESS (*Looking somewhat searchingly at her.*) No doubt you've noticed it already?

HILDA No, I can't say I have.

SOLNESS But just before, when you said you thought I was—unbalanced.

HILDA I was thinking of something entirely different.

SOLNESS What, for example?

HILDA You'll have to figure it out for yourself, master builder.

SOLNESS (*Crossing the room.*) All right, all right, just as you like. (*Stands by the bay window.*) Come over here; I want to show you something.

HILDA (*Going over.*) What is it?

SOLNESS Do you see—over there in the garden—?

HILDA Yes?

SOLNESS (*Pointing.*) Just above the great quarry—?

HILDA That new house, you mean?

SOLNESS The one still being built, yes. Almost finished.

HILDA It's got a very high tower, I think.

SOLNESS The scaffolding's still up.

HILDA Is that your new house?

SOLNESS Yes.

HILDA The house you'll soon be moving into?

SOLNESS Yes.

HILDA (*Looks at him.*) Are there nurseries in *that* house, too?

SOLNESS Three. Just like here.

HILDA And no children?

SOLNESS Nor ever will be.

HILDA (*With a half-smile.*) So isn't it just as I said—?

SOLNESS That—?

HILDA That you are—in some way—a little mad after all.

SOLNESS Was that what you were thinking of?

HILDA Yes, of all those empty nurseries I slept in.

SOLNESS (*Lowers his voice.*) We *did* have children, Aline and I.

HILDA (*Looks intently at him.*) Did you—?

SOLNESS Two small boys. Both the same age.

HILDA Twins, then.

SOLNESS Yes, twins. It was eleven–twelve years ago.

HILDA (*Cautiously.*) And so both of them are—? You don't have the twins anymore?

SOLNESS (*With quiet emotion.*) We kept them barely three weeks. Hardly that, even. (*Bursts out.*) Oh, Hilda, how incredibly good for me that you've come! For now at last I've got someone I can talk to.

HILDA Can't you talk with—with *her*?

SOLNESS Not about this. Not in the way I want to and *must*. Nor about much else, either.

HILDA (*Subduedly.*) Was *this* all you meant, when you said you needed me?

SOLNESS That was mainly it. Yesterday, at least. Today I'm not so sure that's so. (*Breaking off.*) Come and let's sit down, Hilda. You sit here on the sofa—so that you're looking at the garden. (*Hilda sits in the corner of the sofa. Solness draws a chair close.*) Would you like to hear about it?

HILDA Yes, I'd like very much to sit and listen to you.

SOLNESS (*Sitting.*) *Then* I'll tell you all about it.

HILDA Now I'm looking both at the garden and you, master builder. So tell me now. Right away!

SOLNESS (*Pointing toward the bay window.*) Over there on the high ground—where you can also see the new house—

HILDA Yes?

SOLNESS It was there Aline and I lived in those first years. Because up there there used to be an old house that had belonged to her mother. We inherited it after her. With the whole of the great garden which came along with it.

HILDA Was there a tower on that house, as well?

SOLNESS Not a trace of such a thing. From the outside it was a huge, ugly, dark wooden crate. But snug and comfortable enough inside, just the same.

HILDA Did you tear down the old heap, then?

SOLNESS No. It burned down on us.

HILDA All of it?

SOLNESS Yes.

HILDA Was that a great misfortune for you?

SOLNESS Depends on how you look at it. As a builder, my career took off with that fire—

HILDA Well, but—?

SOLNESS We'd just had the two little boys at the time—

HILDA The poor little twins, yes.

SOLNESS They came into the world so sound and healthy. And they grew from day to day. You actually could see it.

HILDA Babies do grow so quickly in the first days.

SOLNESS It was the most beautiful sight you could imagine, to see Aline lying there with those two—. But then came the night of the fire—

HILDA (*Tensely.*) What happened! Tell me! Was anyone inside burned?

SOLNESS No, not that. Everyone was rescued from the house—

HILDA Well, but then what—?

SOLNESS The fright had shaken Aline tremendously. The fire alarm—the flight from the house—everything so confused— and on top of it all, the ice-cold night air—. For they had to be carried out just as they lay. She and the little ones.

HILDA And they couldn't survive that?

SOLNESS Oh, they survived all right. But Aline contracted a fever. And that affected her milk. But she would breastfeed them herself—she insisted on it. It was her duty, she said. And both our little boys, they— (*Clenching his hands.*) —they—oh!

HILDA They didn't get over that?

SOLNESS No, they didn't get over that. That's what took them from us.

HILDA It must have been dreadfully hard for you.

SOLNESS Hard enough for me. But tenfold harder for Aline. (*Clenching his hands in suppressed fury.*) Oh, that such things are allowed to happen in this world! (*Shortly and firmly.*) From the day I lost them I lost all desire for building churches.

HILDA Not even for the church tower you built in our town?

SOLNESS No, not for that. I know how happy and free I felt when the tower stood finished.

HILDA I know that, too.

SOLNESS And now I'll never build—anything like that again! Neither churches nor church towers.

HILDA (*Nodding slowly.*) Only houses people can live in.

SOLNESS Homes for human beings, Hilda.

HILDA But homes with high towers and spires.

SOLNESS If possible. (*Changes to a lighter tone.*) So, you see, as I said, that fire set me up—as a master builder, that is.

HILDA Why don't you call yourself an architect, like others do?

SOLNESS I never went through the training for it. What I know is mostly what I found out for myself.

HILDA All the same, you've done very well for yourself, master builder.

SOLNESS All from the fire, yes. I cut up almost the whole garden into lots for villas. And *there* I was able to build exactly as I wanted. And then things really took off for me.

HILDA (*Giving him a searching look.*) You must be a very happy man, the way things turned out for you.

SOLNESS (*Darkly.*) Happy? Do you say that too? Just like all the others.

HILDA Yes, I should think you must be. If you could just stop thinking about the two little children.

SOLNESS (*Slowly.*) Those two little children—they're not so easy to forget, Hilda.

HILDA (*Somewhat uncertainly.*) Do they still affect you so much? From such a long, long time back?

SOLNESS (*Looking steadily at her, without answering.*) A happy man, you said—

HILDA Well, but aren't you—in everything else?

SOLNESS (*Continuing to look at her.*) When I told you all that about the fire—hm—

HILDA Well?

SOLNESS Didn't one idea strike you as odd?

HILDA (*Pondering without result.*) No. What idea should that be?

SOLNESS (*With quiet emphasis.*) It was simply and solely because of that fire that I was given the chance to build homes for human beings. Comfortable, cozy, and bright homes, where the father and mother and a whole troop of children could live safely and cheerfully—aware of how happy a thing it is to be alive in this world. Above all, to belong to each other in both great things and small.

HILDA (*Warmly.*) Yes, but then isn't it a great joy to be able to create such beautiful homes?

SOLNESS The price, Hilda. The terrible price I had to pay to gain that chance.

HILDA Is that something you can never get over?

SOLNESS No. Because in order to build homes for others I've had to renounce—to renounce for all time—any chance of a home for myself. I mean a home for a troop of children. And for the father and mother, too.

HILDA (*Cautiously.*) But did you have to do that? For all time, you say?

SOLNESS (*Nodding slowly.*) It was the price for that luck people are always talking about. (*Breathes heavily.*) That luck, hm—. That luck—it wasn't to be got any cheaper, Hilda.

HILDA (*As before.*) Mightn't it turn out right after all?

SOLNESS Never in this world. Never. That also follows from the fire. And from Aline's sickness afterwards.

HILDA (*Looking at him with an inscrutable expression.*) Yet you still build yourself all these nurseries?

SOLNESS (*Seriously.*) Have you never noticed, Hilda, how the impossible—how it beckons and calls to you?

HILDA (*Reflecting.*) The impossible? (*Animatedly.*) Oh yes! Have *you* felt that too?

SOLNESS Yes, I have.

HILDA Then there's definitely—something of the troll in *you* also?

SOLNESS Why of the troll?

HILDA Well, what would you call it then?

SOLNESS (*Rising.*) Well, well, it could be so. (*Vehemently.*) But how can I help being a troll—when all the time this is how things go with me—in everything? In everything!

HILDA How do you mean?

SOLNESS (*Quietly, with inward emotion.*) Mark what I tell you, Hilda. Everything I've succeeded in creating, in shaping, building in beauty, security, and comfort—in grandeur, also—(*Clenching his hands.*) Oh, how terrible just to think—

HILDA What is so terrible?

SOLNESS That for all this I've got to atone. Pay for. Not with money, but with human happiness. And not with my own happiness alone, but with others', also. Yes, yes, don't you see, Hilda? That's the price my place as an artist has cost me—and others. And every single day I have to go about and watch how that price is paid for me once more. And again, and again, always yet again.

HILDA (*Rises and looks steadily at him.*) Now you're thinking—of *her.*

SOLNESS Yes. Mostly of Aline. For Aline—*she* had her vocation, too. Just as I had mine. (*His voice shaking.*) But that mission had to be stunted, shattered, smashed utterly to pieces—so that mine could win through to—to some kind of great victory. Yes, because you see Aline—she had a gift for building too.

HILDA She! For building?

SOLNESS (*Shaking his head.*) Not houses and towers and spires—the sort of things I work at—

HILDA Well, but what then?

SOLNESS (*Quietly, with emotion.*) For building up the souls of little children, Hilda. Building up children's souls so that they could stand perfectly poised, in noble, beautiful forms. So they could grow into upright human souls. That is what Aline had the gift for. And all of this—now lies there, unused and useless forever. Like the ruins after a fire.

HILDA Yes, but even if this were so—

SOLNESS It *is* so! It *is* so! I know it!

HILDA Well, but in any case, you are not responsible for that.

SOLNESS (*Fixes his eyes on her and nodding slowly.*) But, you see, just *that* is the great, the appalling question. *That* is the doubt that gnaws at me—both day and night.

HILDA That?

SOLNESS Yes. Suppose I *am* guilty. In a way, that is.

HILDA You! For the fire!

SOLNESS For all of it. For everything. And yet perhaps—I could be completely innocent after all.

HILDA (*Looks anxiously at him.*) Oh, master builder—if you can talk in that way, then you must be—sick after all.

SOLNESS Hm—I'll never be totally easy where *that's* concerned.
(*Ragnar Brovik cautiously opens the little door in the left-hand corner. Hilda crosses the room.*)

RAGNAR (*When he sees Hilda.*) Oh, excuse me, Mr. Solness. (*He starts to leave.*)

SOLNESS No, no, stay here. Let's get it over with.

RAGNAR Oh yes—if only we could.

SOLNESS Your father's getting no better, I hear.

RAGNAR Father's sinking fast now. And therefore I'm begging you—please write a few kind words on one of the drawings! Something father can read before he—

SOLNESS (*Vehemently.*) Don't talk to me any more about those drawings of yours.

RAGNAR Have you looked at them?

SOLNESS Yes—I have.

RAGNAR And they don't amount to anything? And *I* don't amount to anything either?

SOLNESS (*Evasively.*) Stay here with me, Ragnar. You can have anything you want. You can marry Kaja. Live carefree. Happily, no doubt, too. Only don't think of building on your own.

RAGNAR So, then—I must go home and tell my father what you say. For that's what I promised him. Is *that* what I'm to tell him—before he dies?

SOLNESS (*Agonized.*) Oh, tell him—tell him what you will from me. Best tell him nothing. (*Explosively.*) I *can't* act differently than I'm doing, Ragnar.

RAGNAR May I take the drawings with me?

SOLNESS Yes, take them—just take them! They're lying on the table.

RAGNAR (*Goes over to the table.*) Thanks.

HILDA (*Puts her hand on the portfolio.*) No, no. Leave them there.

SOLNESS Why?

HILDA Because *I* want to look at them, too.

SOLNESS But you've already— (*To Ragnar.*) Very well then, let them stay here.

RAGNAR As you wish.

SOLNESS And go home at once to your father.

RAGNAR Yes, I'd better do that.

SOLNESS (*As if in desperation.*) Ragnar—you mustn't ask me for what I can't give. Do you hear, Ragnar? You mustn't!

RAGNAR No, no. Excuse me— (*He bows and goes out through the corner door. Hilda goes over and sits on a chair by the mirror.*)

HILDA (*Looks angrily at Solness.*) That was absolutely hideous, what you just did.

SOLNESS You think so too?

HILDA Yes, it was hideously ugly. And hard and evil and cruel as well.

SOLNESS Oh, you don't understand my situation.

HILDA Just the same—. No, you shouldn't be like that, not *you.*

SOLNESS You said yourself just now that only I should be allowed to build.

HILDA *I* may say that. But you mustn't.

SOLNESS I most of all—after paying so dearly for my position.

HILDA Oh yes—with what you call family comforts and suchlike.

SOLNESS And all my peace of mind into the bargain.

HILDA (*Rising.*) Peace of mind! (*With feeling.*) Yes, yes, there you're right! Poor master builder—you really imagine that—

SOLNESS (*With a quiet chuckling laugh.*) Just sit down again, Hilda. Then you'll hear something amusing.

HILDA (*Excited, sitting.*) Well?

SOLNESS It sounds like such a ludicrous little thing; for you see, the whole business merely turns upon a crack in a chimney.

HILDA No more than that?

SOLNESS No, at least not to begin with. (*He draws a chair closer to Hilda and sits down.*)

HILDA (*Impatiently slapping her knee.*) Well, then, the crack in the chimney!

SOLNESS I'd noticed the split in the flue long, long before the fire.

Each time I went up into the attic I would look to see if it was still there.

HILDA And it *was*?

SOLNESS Yes. Because no one else knew about it.

HILDA And you didn't say anything.

SOLNESS No, I didn't.

HILDA And you never thought of repairing the flue, either?

SOLNESS Oh, I thought about it, but nothing more than that. Every time I'd get ready to start on it, it was exactly as if a hand reached out to stop me. Not today, I'd think—tomorrow. So nothing was done.

HILDA Yes, but why did you keep putting it off?

SOLNESS Because I was turning something over in my mind. (*Slowly and in a low voice.*) Through that little black hole in the chimney, perhaps I might win my way to success—as a master builder.

HILDA (*Looking straight in front of her.*) That must have been thrilling.

SOLNESS Irresistible, almost. Utterly irresistible. For at the time it all seemed so easy and straightforward. I wanted it to happen in winter. A little before midday. I would be out driving Aline in the sleigh. The people at home would have made huge fires in the stoves—.

HILDA Yes, because it would be fearfully cold that day?

SOLNESS Quite bitter, that's true. And they would want Aline to find it really snug and warm when she came home.

HILDA She feels the cold quite keenly, doesn't she?

SOLNESS She does. And so it was to be on our way home that we'd see the smoke.

HILDA Only the smoke?

SOLNESS First the smoke. But when we drove up to the garden gate, then the huge old wooden crate would be a blazing mass of flames. That's how I wanted it to be, you see.

HILDA Oh why, in God's name, couldn't it have happened that way!

SOLNESS Yes, you can well ask that, Hilda.

HILDA But listen now, master builder. Are you really so very sure the fire started from that little crack in the chimney?

SOLNESS No, on the contrary—I am convinced that the crack in the chimney had absolutely nothing to do with it.

HILDA What's that!

SOLNESS It's been made perfectly clear that the fire broke out in a clothes closet—in a completely different part of the house.

HILDA Then why on earth are you sitting here babbling away about a crack in the chimney?

SOLNESS May I go on talking a little more to you, Hilda?

HILDA Yes, if you would only talk sense, then—

SOLNESS I'll try to. (*He moves his chair closer.*)

HILDA So, go on then, master builder.

SOLNESS (*Confidentially.*) Don't you believe too, Hilda, that there exist certain, special, chosen people gifted with the ability and power of *craving* something, *desiring* something, *willing* something—so insistently and so—so inexorably—that it *must* come about in the end. Don't you believe that?

HILDA (*With an inscrutable expression in her eyes.*) If that's so, then one day we'll see—if *I* belong among the chosen.

SOLNESS It's not one's self alone that brings these things about. Oh no—the helpers and servers—they must be there too—if it's going to come about. But they never come of themselves. One must call for them persistently. Inwardly, you understand.

HILDA What are these helpers and servers?

SOLNESS Oh, we can talk about that some other time. For the present, let's keep to the matter of the fire.

HILDA Don't you think the fire would have happened anyway, without your wishing it?

SOLNESS If old Knut Brovik had owned the house, it would never in this world have burned down so conveniently for him. I'm convinced of that. Because he didn't know how to call upon the helpers nor upon the servers either. (*Rising in agitation.*) So you see, Hilda, I bear the guilt that both the little boys had to give up their lives. And don't I bear the guilt, also, that Aline never became all she could and should have been? And most longed to be?

HILDA Well, but if it was only these helpers and servers, then—

SOLNESS Who called for the helpers and servers? I did! And so they came and submitted to my will. (*In rising excitement.*) And *that's* what our good people call having luck on my side. But let me tell you what this luck feels like. It feels like a great patch of raw flesh here on my breast. And the helpers and servers go on flaying pieces of skin off other people to heal my wound. But the wound will not heal. Never—never! Ah, if you only knew how sometimes it gnaws and burns inside me.

HILDA (*Looks attentively at him.*) You *are* ill, master builder. Very ill, I'd almost say.

SOLNESS Say mad. For that's what you mean.

HILDA No, I don't believe there's anything wrong with your mind.

SOLNESS In *what* way, then? Out with it!

HILDA I wonder whether you didn't come into the world with a sickly conscience.

SOLNESS A sickly conscience. What, in the devil's name, is that?

HILDA I mean the conscience in you seems very frail. Somewhat delicate. Not made to seize things. Can't lift and bear much weight.

SOLNESS Hm. Then how should a conscience be, may I ask?

HILDA In you I'd like to see a conscience that was—well, that was thoroughly robust.

SOLNESS So? Robust? Well. Have you a robust conscience, perhaps?

HILDA Yes, I think I have. I've not noticed otherwise.

SOLNESS It hasn't been put to a really severe test, I'd imagine.

HILDA (*With a trembling of the lips.*) Oh, it was not so easy leaving Father, whom I'm so terribly fond of.

SOLNESS Oh come! When it's just for a month or two—

HILDA I'm never going home again.

SOLNESS Never? Why did you leave him, then?

HILDA (*Half-serious, half-playful.*) Aren't you forgetting again that the ten years are up?

SOLNESS Nonsense. Was something or other wrong at home? Well?

HILDA (*Completely serious.*) There was something inside me goading and urging me here. Tempting and drawing me here, too.

SOLNESS (*Eagerly.*) There it is! There it is! There's a troll alive in you as well. Just as in me. For it's the troll in one, you see— that calls to the powers outside us. And then we must submit—whether we want to or no.

HILDA I rather believe you are right, master builder.

SOLNESS (*Pacing the room.*) Oh, there are amazingly many devils in the world one doesn't see, Hilda.

HILDA Devils, too?

SOLNESS (*Stops.*) Good devils and bad devils. Light-haired devils and dark-haired. If only you could always know whether it was the light or the dark that had hold over you! (*Pacing and giving a short laugh.*) There'd be no problem, then!

HILDA (*Following him with her eyes.*) Or if one had a really full-blooded, vigorously healthy conscience. So that one dared what one wanted!

SOLNESS (*Standing by the console table.*) I think most people are as fearful as myself in that regard.

HILDA Perhaps that's so.

SOLNESS (*Leaning on the table.*) In the sagas—have you read any of these old sagas?

HILDA Oh yes! In the days when I used to read books.

SOLNESS In the sagas you learn about Vikings who sailed to distant lands and plundered and burned and killed men—

HILDA And captured women—

SOLNESS —and kept them captive—

HILDA —and brought them home in their ships—

SOLNESS —and behaved with them like the—like the worst of trolls.

HILDA (*Looks straight ahead with a half-concealed look.*) I think that must have been thrilling.

SOLNESS (*With a short, deep laugh.*) What, to carry off women?

HILDA To *be* carried off.

SOLNESS (*Looks briefly at her.*) Indeed.

HILDA (*As if breaking off the subject.*) But what were you going to say about those Vikings, master builder—?

SOLNESS Yes, now those fellows had your robust conscience all right. When they got back home they'd eat and drink and be as merry as children. As for the women—more often than not they'd not hear of leaving them. Can you understand that, Hilda?

HILDA I understand those women tremendously well.

SOLNESS Ah! Perhaps you'd do the same yourself?

HILDA Why not?

SOLNESS Live together—of your own free will—with a brute like that?

HILDA If it was a brute I'd really come to be fond of—

SOLNESS *Could* you become fond of someone like that?

HILDA Good Lord, you can't always help whom you're going to be fond of, that's for sure.

SOLNESS (*Looking thoughtfully at her.*) Ah no, it's the troll within that decides that.

HILDA (*Half-laughingly.*) And all those blessed devils you're so familiar with. Both the light-haired and the dark.

SOLNESS (*Warmly and quietly.*) Then I hope the devils choose kindly for you, Hilda.

HILDA They *have* chosen for me. Once and for all.

SOLNESS (*Looking intently at her.*) Hilda—you're like some wild bird of the forest.

HILDA In no way. I don't hide myself away in the bushes.

SOLNESS No, no. You are more like some bird of prey.

HILDA That's closer—maybe. (*Very fiercely.*) And why not a bird of prey! Why shouldn't I go hunting, too? Take the prey I want? If I really get my claws into it. Do what I want with it.

SOLNESS Hilda, do you know what you are?

HILDA Yes, I'm some strange kind of bird.

SOLNESS No. You are like the dawning day. When I look at you—it's like I was looking into the sunrise.

HILDA Tell me, master builder—are you sure that you've never called to me? Deep within yourself?

SOLNESS (*Quietly and slowly.*) I almost believe I must have done.

HILDA What do you want with me?

SOLNESS You are youth, Hilda.

HILDA (*Smiling.*) Youth, which you are so afraid of?

SOLNESS (*Nodding slowly.*) And yet which, deep within, I long for so painfully.
(*Hilda rises, goes over to the little table, and fetches Ragnar Brovik's portfolio.*)

HILDA (*Holding the portfolio to him.*) There's also the matter of these drawings—

SOLNESS (*Curtly, waving it aside.*) Put those things away! I've seen enough of them.

HILDA Yes, but you're going to write on them for him.

SOLNESS *Write* on them. Never in this world!

HILDA But now the poor old man's lying on his deathbed! Can't you grant some happiness to him and his son before they're parted? And perhaps he'll be able to build from them later.

SOLNESS Yes, that's precisely what he'd be able to do, that young upstart.

HILDA But good Lord, even so, can't you bring yourself to lie just a tiny little bit?

SOLNESS (*Furiously.*) Hilda—get away from me with that devil's drawings.

HILDA (*Drawing back the portfolio slightly.*) Now, now, now—don't bite me. You talk about trolls. But I think you're behaving like a troll yourself. (*Looking at him.*) Where do you keep your pen and ink?

SOLNESS I don't keep such stuff in here.

HILDA (*Goes to the door.*) But the girl out there must have them.

SOLNESS Stay where you are, Hilda! I ought to lie, you say. Oh yes, for his old father's sake, I could bring myself to do it. For I broke him once. Toppled him completely.

HILDA Him as well?

SOLNESS I needed room for myself. But this Ragnar—on no account must he be allowed to get ahead.

HILDA Poor boy, he's not very likely to. Not if he doesn't amount to much—

SOLNESS (*Approaches, looks at her and whispers.*) If Ragnar Brovik gets a start, he'll hurl me to the ground. Crush me—as I did his father.

HILDA *You!* He could do that?

SOLNESS Yes, you can be sure he can. He's part of the youth that stands ready to knock at my door. To put an end to master builder Solness.

HILDA (*Looking at him reproachfully.*) And yet you want to shut him out. Really, master builder!

SOLNESS It's cost me my heart's blood, this battle I've fought. And then I'm afraid the helpers and servers will no longer obey me.

HILDA Then you must make your way on your own. There's no other way.

SOLNESS It's hopeless, Hilda. My luck will turn. A little sooner, a little later. Retribution is bound to come.

HILDA (*Fearfully, holding her hand over her ears.*) Don't talk like that! Do you want to take away my life! Take away what's even more than my life!

SOLNESS And what is *that*!

HILDA To see you great. See you with a wreath in your hand. High, high up on a church tower. (*Calm again.*) Now, what about producing that pencil. For you do have a pencil on you?

SOLNESS (*Takes out his notebook.*) I've got one here.

HILDA (*Setting the portfolio on the sofa-table.*) Good. Now the two of us will sit down here, master builder. (*Solness sits by the table.*) And we'll write on the drawings. Something really nice and warm, that's what we'll write. For this awful Roar—or whatever he's called.

SOLNESS (*Writes some lines, turns his head and looks at her.*) Tell me one thing, Hilda.

HILDA Yes?

SOLNESS If you've been waiting for me all these ten years—

HILDA What then?

SOLNESS Why didn't you write to me? Then I could have written back to you.

HILDA (*Quickly.*) No, no, no! That was just what I didn't want.

SOLNESS Why not?

HILDA I was afraid then that the whole thing would fall apart—. But we were going to write on the drawings, master builder.

SOLNESS Yes, so we were.

HILDA (*Bends over and watches while he is writing.*) Very kind and heartfelt. Oh, how I hate this Roald—

SOLNESS (*Writing.*) Have you never really cared for anyone, Hilda?

HILDA (*Harshly.*) What did you say?

SOLNESS Whether you'd ever cared for anyone.

HILDA For anyone else, is that what you mean?

SOLNESS (*Looking up at her.*) For anyone else, yes. Haven't you ever? In all these ten years. Never?

HILDA Well, yes, once in a while. When I was really furious with you for not coming.

SOLNESS So you were interested in others, as well?

HILDA Very slightly, for a week or two. Good Lord, master builder, you know very well how these things are.

SOLNESS Hilda, what is it you've come here for?

HILDA Don't waste time talking. That poor old man might well be lying there dying all this time.

SOLNESS Answer me, Hilda. What is it you want of me?

HILDA I want my kingdom.

SOLNESS Hm. (*He gives a quick glance to the door on the left and continues to write on the drawings. Mrs. Solness enters at the same time. She has some packages with her.*)

MRS. SOLNESS I've brought you a few things here, Miss Wangel. The larger packages will be sent on later.

HILDA Oh, how very kind of you.

MRS. SOLNESS Only my simple duty. Nothing more.

SOLNESS (*Reading over what he has written.*) Aline!

MRS. SOLNESS Yes?

SOLNESS Did you notice whether she—whether the bookkeeper was out there?

MRS. SOLNESS Well, naturally *she* was there.

SOLNESS (*Putting the drawings in the portfolio.*) Hm—.

MRS. SOLNESS She was standing at the desk, as she always does—whenever *I* come into the room.

SOLNESS Then I'll give this to her now. And tell her that—

HILDA (*Taking the portfolio from him.*) Oh no, let me have that pleasure! (*She goes to the door, but turns.*) What's she called?

SOLNESS She's called Miss Fosli.

HILDA Ah, that sounds so cold. I meant her first name.

SOLNESS Kaja—I think.

HILDA (*Opens the door and calls.*) Kaja! Come in here. Hurry! The master builder wants to speak to you.

(*Kaja Fosli appears at the door.*)

KAJA (*Looking fearfully at him.*) Here I am—

HILDA (*Hands her the portfolio.*) Look, Kaja! You can take these now. Because the master builder's written on them.

KAJA Oh, at last!

SOLNESS Give them to the old man as quickly as you can.

KAJA I'll go home with them right away.

SOLNESS Yes, do that. And now Ragnar will be able to build.

KAJA Oh, may he come here and thank you for everything—?

SOLNESS (*Harshly.*) I don't want any thanks! Tell him that from me.

KAJA Yes, I will.

SOLNESS And tell him at the same time that from now on I've no more use for him. Nor for you either.

KAJA (*Softly and tremulously.*) Not for me either?

SOLNESS I've got other things to think about now. And to look after. And that's all for the best. Well, so go home with the drawings, Miss Fosli. At once, do you hear?

KAJA (*As before.*) Yes, Mr. Solness. (*She goes out.*)

MRS. SOLNESS God, what cunning eyes she has.

SOLNESS She! That poor little creature.

MRS. SOLNESS Oh—I can see what I see all right, Halvard. Are you really getting rid of them?

SOLNESS Yes.

MRS. SOLNESS Her too?

SOLNESS Wasn't that what you always wanted?

MRS. SOLNESS But that you can do without her—? Ah, but no doubt you've got someone in reserve, Halvard.

HILDA (*Playfully.*) Well, I'm not made for standing behind a desk.

SOLNESS Now, now—it will work out all right, Aline. Now all you have to think about is moving into our new home—as quickly as you can. This evening we'll hang the wreath— (*Turning to Hilda.*) —all the way to the top of the tower. What do you say to *that* Miss Wangel.

HILDA (*Looking at him with sparkling eyes.*) It will be fearfully splendid to see you high up there once again!

SOLNESS *Me!*

MRS. SOLNESS Oh God, Miss Wangel, don't even imagine such a thing! My husband—! When he gets so dizzy!

HILDA Dizzy! He's definitely not *that*!!

MRS. SOLNESS Ah, but he certainly is.

HILDA But I've seen him myself, right at the top of a high church tower.

MRS. SOLNESS Yes, I've heard people talk about that. But it is so completely impossible—

SOLNESS (*Vehemently.*) Impossible—impossible, yes! But I stood up there just the same!

MRS. SOLNESS No, how can you say that, Halvard. You can hardly bear to go out on the second-floor balcony here. You've always been like that.

SOLNESS You might see something different this evening.

MRS. SOLNESS (*Alarmed.*) No, no, no. With God's help I'll never see that. I'll write at once to the doctor. He'll put a stop to it.

SOLNESS But Aline—

MRS. SOLNESS Yes, because you really are ill, Halvard. It can't be anything else. Oh God—oh God. (*She goes hastily out to the right.*)

HILDA (*Looks searchingly at him.*) Is it true, or isn't it?

SOLNESS That I get dizzy?

HILDA That my master builder *dare* not—*can* not climb as high as he builds?

SOLNESS Is that the way you see it?

HILDA Yes.

SOLNESS I'm beginning to think there's scarcely a corner in me that's safe from you.

HILDA (*Looks toward the bay window.*) Up there then. All the way up.

SOLNESS (*Coming closer.*) In the topmost room in the tower—you could live there, Hilda. You could live like a princess.

HILDA (*Mysteriously, between earnest and jest.*) Yes, that's what you promised.

SOLNESS Did I, in fact?

HILDA Really, master builder! You said I was to be a princess. And that I'd get a kingdom from you. And so you took me and— Well!

SOLNESS (*Seriously.*) Are you quite sure this isn't some kind of dream—some fantasy—that has taken hold of you?

HILDA (*Scornfully.*) That perhaps you didn't do it?

SOLNESS I scarcely know myself—. (*More softly.*) But one thing I now know for certain—that I—

HILDA That you—Say it now!

SOLNESS That I *ought* to have done it.

HILDA (*In a joyful outburst.*) Never in this world could you be dizzy!

SOLNESS This evening we'll hang the wreath—Princess Hilda.

HILDA (*With a bitter expression.*) Over your new home, yes.

SOLNESS Over the new house. It will never be a home for me. (*He goes out through the garden door.*)

HILDA (*Looking straight ahead with a veiled expression and whispering to herself. One hears only:*)—fearfully thrilling—

Act Three

A large broad veranda belonging to Solness's house. Part of the house, with a door leading out to the veranda, can be seen to the left. Railings of the veranda to the right. Far back, on the narrow end of the veranda, a flight of steps leading down to the garden below. Large, ancient trees in the garden spread their branches over the veranda and toward the house. Far to the right, in between the trees, part of the new villa can be glimpsed, with scaffolding round the tower structure. In the background the garden is bounded by an old wooden fence. Outside the fence, a street with low, dilapidated cottages.

Evening sky with sunlit clouds. On the veranda a garden bench against the wall of the house and in front of the bench a long table. On the other side of the table an armchair and some stools. All the furniture is wickerwork. Mrs. Solness, wrapped in a large white shawl, sits resting in the armchair, gazing out to the right. Soon after, Hilda Wangel comes up the steps from the garden. She is dressed as before and is wearing her hat. In her bodice is a little bunch of wild flowers.

MRS. SOLNESS (*Turning her head a little.*) Have you been down to the garden, Miss Wangel?

HILDA Yes, I've been taking a look down there.

MRS. SOLNESS And found some flowers, I see.

HILDA Yes I have! There are plenty there in among the bushes.

MRS. SOLNESS Really, are there? Still? Well, I scarcely ever go down there.

HILDA (*Approaching.*) What's that! Don't you fly down to the garden every day?

MRS. SOLNESS (*With a wan smile.*) I don't "fly" anywhere. Not any more.

HILDA Well, but don't you go down every now and then and visit all the beautiful things there?

MRS. SOLNESS It's all become so strange to me. I'm almost afraid to look at it again.

HILDA Your own garden?

MRS. SOLNESS I don't feel it's *mine* anymore.

HILDA How can that be—?

MRS. SOLNESS No, no, it isn't. It isn't like it was in Mother's and Father's time. They've taken such a dreadful lot of the garden away, Miss Wangel. Just think—they've parceled it up—and built houses for strangers on it. People I don't know. Who can sit at their windows and look at me.

HILDA (*With a bright expression.*) Mrs. Solness?

MRS. SOLNESS Yes?

HILDA May I stay with you here a while?

MRS. SOLNESS Yes, certainly, if you want to.

HILDA (*Draws a stool to the armchair and sits.*) Ah, here you can really sit and sun yourself like a cat.

MRS. SOLNESS (*Lays her hand lightly on Hilda's neck.*) It's sweet of you to sit here with me. I thought you'd rather be with my husband.

HILDA What should I want with him?

MRS. SOLNESS To help him, I thought.

HILDA No thank you. In any case he isn't in. He's over there with his workmen but he looked so fierce that I didn't dare talk to him.

MRS. SOLNESS Oh, beneath all that he's really so mild and gentle.

HILDA He?

MRS. SOLNESS You don't really know him yet, Miss Wangel.

HILDA (*Looking warmly at her.*) Are you glad to be moving over to the new house?

MRS. SOLNESS I *ought* to be glad. For that's what Halvard wants—

HILDA Oh, not just for that, I would think.

MRS. SOLNESS Yes, yes, Miss Wangel. For it's only my duty, submitting to what he wants. But so often it is so hard to force oneself to obey.

HILDA Yes, *that* must be really hard to do.

MRS. SOLNESS Believe me, it is. When one's no better than I am.

HILDA When one's gone through so much unhappiness as you—

MRS. SOLNESS How do you know about that?

HILDA Your husband told me.

MRS. SOLNESS He so seldom speaks to me about these things. Yes, you can say I've gone through more than enough unhappiness in my life, Miss Wangel.

HILDA (*Looks sympathetically at her and nods slowly.*) Poor Mrs. Solness. First there was that fire—

MRS. SOLNESS (*With a sigh.*) Yes. Everything of mine burned.

HILDA And then came what was worse.

MRS. SOLNESS (*Looks inquiringly at her.*) Worse?

HILDA The worst of all.

MRS. SOLNESS What do you mean?

HILDA (*Softly.*) You lost your two small boys.

MRS. SOLNESS Oh yes, *that*. But that was something quite separate, you see. That was an act of Providence. And one can only submit before that. And be thankful, too.

HILDA Do you do that?

MRS. SOLNESS Not always, I'm afraid. I know very well it's my duty, but I *can't* do it all the same.

HILDA No, no, I would say that's only understandable.

MRS. SOLNESS And every now and then I must tell myself it was a righteous punishment upon me—

HILDA Why so?

MRS. SOLNESS Because I wasn't steadfast enough in misfortune.

HILDA But I don't understand—

MRS. SOLNESS Ah no, no, Miss Wangel—don't speak to me anymore about the two little boys. We should only be happy for them. Because they are so happy, so happy now. No, it is the small losses in life that cut to the heart. Losing things that others think of no importance.

HILDA (*Lays her arms on Mrs. Solness's knees and looks warmly up at her.*) Dear Mrs. Solness, tell me what kind of things they were.

MRS. SOLNESS Like I said, just small things. All the old portraits on the walls were burnt. And all the old silk dresses were burnt that had belonged to the family for generations and generations. And all of Mother's and Grandmother's lace—that was burnt also. And think, even the jewels! (*Sadly.*) And then all the dolls.

HILDA Dolls?

MRS. SOLNESS (*Choking with tears.*) I had nine lovely dolls.

HILDA And they burned also?

MRS. SOLNESS All of them. Oh, that was so hard, so hard for me.

HILDA Had you always hidden these dolls away—ever since you were little?

MRS. SOLNESS I didn't hide them. The dolls and I had always lived together.

HILDA After you'd grown up?

MRS. SOLNESS Yes, long after then.

HILDA After you were married, too?

MRS. SOLNESS Oh yes. So long as he didn't see it, then—. But then they were all burnt, poor things. No one thought of saving *them*. Oh, it's so sad to think about them now. Now, you mustn't laugh at me, Miss Wangel.

HILDA I'm not laughing in the least.

MRS. SOLNESS For in a certain way, there was life in them too. I carried them under my heart—just like little unborn children.
(*Dr. Herdal, his hat in his hand, comes out through the door and catches sight of Mrs. Solness and Hilda.*)

DR. HERDAL So, Mrs. Solness, you're sitting out here trying to catch a cold?

MRS. SOLNESS I find it so pleasant and warm today.

DR. HERDAL Well, well. But is there anything the matter? I got a note from you.

MRS. SOLNESS (*Getting up.*) Yes, there's something I must speak to you about.

DR. HERDAL Good. So let's go in. (*To Hilda.*) Still in your mountaineering outfit, Miss Wangel?

HILDA (*Gaily, rising.*) Oh yes! In full gear. But today I'm not inclined to risk breaking my neck. We two will just sit here below and look on, Doctor.

DR. HERDAL And what shall we be looking at?

MRS. SOLNESS (*Softly, terrified, to Hilda.*) Hush, hush, for God's sake! He's coming now! Just try to get him to give up that idea. And let's be friends, Miss Wangel, can't we?

HILDA (*Impulsively throws her arms round Mrs. Solness's neck.*) Oh, if only we could.

MRS. SOLNESS (*Gently freeing herself.*) Now, now, now! There, he's coming, Doctor! Let me have a word with you.

DR. HERDAL Is it to do with him?

MRS. SOLNESS Yes, definitely about him. Let's go inside. (*She and*

*the doctor go into the house. A moment later Solness comes up
the garden steps. Hilda's face takes on a serious expression.*)

SOLNESS (*Glances at the door of the house, which is being cautiously
closed from inside.*) Have you noticed, Hilda, that as soon as I
appear, she leaves?

HILDA I've noticed that as soon as you appear, you *make* her go.

SOLNESS Maybe so. But I can't help that. (*Looks attentively at her.*)
Are you feeling cold, Hilda? You look as if you are.

HILDA I've just now come up from a tomb.

SOLNESS What are you saying?

HILDA I feel the frost in my bones, master builder.

SOLNESS (*Slowly.*) I think I understand.

HILDA What brings you up here now?

SOLNESS I caught sight of you from over there.

HILDA But then you must have seen her too?

SOLNESS I knew she'd leave immediately I came.

HILDA Is it painful for you, that she always keeps out of your way?

SOLNESS In a way it's also something of a relief.

HILDA That she's not there before your eyes.

SOLNESS Yes.

HILDA Not always having to see how she suffers over the two little
boys?

SOLNESS Yes. That most of all.

(*Hilda walks across the veranda with her hands behind her back,
halts at the railing, and looks over the garden.*)

SOLNESS (*After a short pause.*) Were you talking with her for long?
(*Hilda stands motionless without answering.*) I asked was it
for long? (*Hilda continues as before.*) What were you talking
about? (*Hilda remains silent.*) Poor Aline. I suppose it was
about the little boys. (*A nervous shudder runs through her; she
nods quickly a couple of times.*) She'll never get over it. Never
in this world get over it. (*Approaching.*) Now you're standing
like a statue again. Just as you stood last night.

HILDA (*Turning and looking at him with large, serious eyes.*) I'm going away.

SOLNESS (*Sharply.*) Going away!

HILDA Yes.

SOLNESS But I won't let you!

HILDA What shall I do here now?

SOLNESS Just *be* here, Hilda!

HILDA (*Looks him up and down.*) Oh, thank you so much! You
know it wouldn't end there.

SOLNESS (*Recklessly.*) So much the better!

HILDA (*Vehemently.*) I can't do any harm against someone I *know.*
Can't take away what belongs to her.

SOLNESS Who said you should do that?

HILDA (*Continuing.*) A stranger, yes! For that's something quite different. Someone I had never set eyes on. But someone I've become close to—! Oh no, oh no. Ugh!

SOLNESS But I never suggested anything else!

HILDA Oh, master builder, you know only too well how it would turn out. And that's why I'm leaving.

SOLNESS And what's to become of me after you've gone? What will I have to live for then? Afterwards?

HILDA (*With the inscrutable look in her eyes.*) There's no problem where you're concerned. You have your duties toward her. Live for those duties.

SOLNESS Too late. These powers—these—these—

HILDA —devils—

SOLNESS Yes, devils! And the troll inside me also. They've drained all the life blood from her. (*Laughs desperately.*) They did it for the sake of my happiness and success! Yes, yes! (*Heavily.*) And I, living, am chained to the dead. (*In wild anguish.*) I—I, who *cannot* live life without joy!

HILDA (*Walks around the table and sits on the bench with her elbows on the table and her head supported by her hands. She sits a moment looking at him.*) What are you going to build next?

SOLNESS (*Shaking his head.*) I don't think I'll be building much more.

HILDA No more happy family homes for mothers and fathers—and the troops of children?

SOLNESS God knows if there'll be any use for such homes from now on.

HILDA Poor master builder! You, who've gone on here for ten years—giving your whole life—just for that alone!

SOLNESS Yes, you might well say that, Hilda.

HILDA (*With an outburst.*) Oh, I think it's really so stupid, so stupid, all of this!

SOLNESS All of what?

HILDA That one doesn't dare grasp one's own happiness. One's own life! And only because someone you know stands in your way.

SOLNESS Someone you have no right to push aside.

HILDA Who knows if in fact one really doesn't have that right? But all the same—Oh, if only one could sleep away the whole business! (*She lays her arms flat on the table and sinks the left side of her head on her hands, closing her eyes.*)

SOLNESS (*Turns the armchair around and sits at the table.*) Did you have a happy family home—up there with your father, Hilda?

HILDA (*Motionless, answering as if half asleep.*) A cage was all I had.

SOLNESS And you won't go back into it again?

HILDA (*As before.*) A forest bird will never choose a cage.

SOLNESS But would rather hunt in the free sky—

HILDA (*Still as before.*) The bird of prey loves hunting most—

SOLNESS (*Resting his eyes on her.*) If only one had the Viking spirit in life—

HILDA (*In an ordinary voice, opening her eyes but not moving.*) And what else? Say what it is!

SOLNESS A robust conscience.

HILDA (*Sits upright on the bench. Her eyes once again have their happy, sparkling expression. She nods to him.*) I know what you are going to build next time.

SOLNESS Then you know more than I do, Hilda.

HILDA Yes, these master builders, they're so stupid.

SOLNESS So what will it be?

HILDA (*Nodding again.*) The castle.

SOLNESS What castle?

HILDA My castle, of course.

SOLNESS Do you want a castle now?

HILDA Don't you owe me a kingdom, may I ask?

SOLNESS That's what I hear you tell me.

HILDA Well then! So you owe me this kingdom. And I would have thought a kingdom ought to have a castle.

SOLNESS (*More and more animatedly.*) Yes, that's usually the way.

HILDA Good. So build it for me. Right away!

SOLNESS (*Laughing.*) So it's got to be done this instant, too?

HILDA Yes, that's it! For now they've run out—those ten years. And I don't intend waiting any longer. Therefore—present the castle, master builder!

SOLNESS It's no light matter owing you anything, Hilda.

HILDA You should have thought of that before. Now it's too late. Therefore— (*Rapping on the table.*) —the castle on the table! It's *my* castle. I want it at once!

SOLNESS (*More seriously, leaning toward her, his arms on the table.*) How have you imagined this castle, Hilda?
(*Her expression changes, little by little. She seems to be gazing deep within herself.*)

HILDA (*Slowly.*) My castle shall stand high up. Very high it shall stand. And free on all sides. So that I can see far—far around.

SOLNESS And there will be a high tower?

HILDA A fearfully high tower. And right at the top of the tower there will be a balcony. And out on that balcony I'll be standing.

SOLNESS (*Involuntarily clutching his forehead.*) You could stand at such a dizzying height—

HILDA Yes, I can! I'll be standing right up there, gazing down on the others—those who build churches. And homes for mothers and fathers and troops of children. And you may also come up and gaze on them too.

SOLNESS (*In a low voice.*) Will the master builder be permitted to come up to the princess?

HILDA If the master builder wants to.

SOLNESS (*Quietly.*) Then I think the master builder will come.

HILDA (*Nodding.*) The master builder will come.

SOLNESS But never to build again—poor master builder.

HILDA (*Animatedly.*) Oh but yes! We two will do it together. And so we will build the loveliest, the absolutely loveliest thing in the whole world.

SOLNESS (*Tensely.*) Hilda, tell me what that is!

HILDA (*Looks smilingly at him, shakes her head slightly, purses her lips, and speaks as if to a child.*) Master builders, they're such stupid, such stupid people.

SOLNESS Yes, they're very stupid. But tell me what it is! That's the most beautiful thing in the world. And that we two will build together.

HILDA (*For a moment she is silent with an enigmatic expression in her eyes.*) Castles in the air.

SOLNESS Castles in the air?

HILDA (*Nodding.*) Yes, castles in the air. Do you know what it is—a castle in the air?

SOLNESS It's the most beautiful thing in the world, you say.

HILDA (*Rising impatiently and gestures somewhat scornfully with her hand.*) That's right, yes! Castles in the air—they're so easy to hide in. And easy to build, too. (*Looks at him scornfully.*) Especially for master builders who have a—a dizzy conscience.

SOLNESS (*Rising.*) From this day we will build together, Hilda.

HILDA (*With a half-doubting smile.*) Build a real castle in the air?

SOLNESS Yes. And on solid foundations.

(*Ragnar Brovik enters from the house. He carries a large wreath with flowers and silk ribbons.*)

HILDA The wreath! Oh, this will be fearfully splendid!

SOLNESS (*Surprised.*) You're bringing the wreath, Ragnar?

RAGNAR I promised the foreman I would.

SOLNESS (*Relieved.*) Ah, so your father's getting better?

RAGNAR No.

SOLNESS What I wrote—didn't that help him?

RAGNAR It came too late.

SOLNESS Too late?

RAGNAR When she brought it he was no longer conscious. He'd had a stroke.

SOLNESS Well, then go back home to him! Look after your father.

RAGNAR He doesn't need me anymore.

SOLNESS But you need to be with him.

RAGNAR *She's* sitting by his bed.

SOLNESS (*Somewhat uncertainly.*) Kaja?

RAGNAR (*With a dark look.*) That's right—Kaja, yes.

SOLNESS Go home, Ragnar. To both of them. Let me take the wreath.

RAGNAR (*Suppressing a smile.*) But you're never going to—?

SOLNESS I'm taking it down myself. (*Takes the wreath from him.*) So, you go home. I don't need you today.

RAGNAR I realize you won't be needing me after today. But today I'm staying.

SOLNESS Well, stay then—Since you're so determined to.

HILDA (*At the railing.*) Master builder—I'll be standing here and watching you.

SOLNESS Watching me!

HILDA It will be fearfully thrilling.

SOLNESS (*In a lower voice.*) We'll talk about that later, Hilda. (*He leaves, with the wreath, down the steps, and through the garden.*)

HILDA (*Looking after him; then she turns to Ragnar.*) I think you could have at least thanked him.

RAGNAR Thanked him? Should I have thanked him?

HILDA Yes, you should have—definitely!

RAGNAR More likely it's you I should have thanked.

HILDA How can you say that?

RAGNAR (*Not answering her.*) But just watch out, miss. You don't really know him yet.

HILDA (*Fiercely.*) Oh, I know him the best!

RAGNAR (*Laughing bitterly.*) Thank him, who's kept me down, year after year! Who made my father come to doubt me. Got me to doubt myself—And all just so he could—.

HILDA (*As if suspecting something.*) Just so he could—. Say it straight out!

RAGNAR So he could keep her with him.

HILDA (*With a movement toward him.*) The girl at the desk!

RAGNAR Yes.

HILDA (*Threatening, with clenched fists.*) That isn't true! You're lying about him!

RAGNAR I didn't want to believe it, either, before today—when she herself told me.

HILDA (*As if beside herself.*) What did she say! I want to know. Now, right away!

RAGNAR She said he'd taken possession of her mind—completely. All her thoughts are centered on him only. She says she can never be free of him—that she wants to stay here, where he is—

HILDA (*With flashing eyes.*) She'll never be allowed to!

RAGNAR (*Somewhat searchingly.*) Who won't allow her to?

HILDA (*Quickly.*) Nor him, either.

RAGNAR Oh no, now I understand it all very well. From now on she can only be—an inconvenience.

HILDA You don't understand anything—when you can talk like that! No, I'll tell you why he held on to her.

RAGNAR Why, then?

HILDA To keep hold of you.

RAGNAR He told you that?

HILDA No, but that's how it was. It has to be! (*Wildly.*) I *will*, I *will*, have it that way!

RAGNAR And the moment you came by—then he let her go.

HILDA It was you—you he let go. What use do you think he has for strange girls like her?

RAGNAR (*Reflectively.*) Then maybe he was afraid of me all this time?

HILDA Him! Afraid! Don't think so highly of yourself!

RAGNAR Oh, for a long time he must have realized that I amounted to something after all. In any case—afraid—that's just what he is, you see.

HILDA Him! Yes, just try to convince me!

RAGNAR In some ways he's afraid. He, the great master builder. Taking life's happiness from others—as he's done with my father and with me—no, he's not afraid of that. But just expect him to climb a pathetic bit of scaffolding—and he'll set about it as if praying to God he didn't have to.

HILDA You should have seen him as I once did—way up at a dizzying height.

RAGNAR You've seen that?

HILDA Yes, I certainly did. So proud and free he looked, standing and tying the wreath to the weather vane.

RAGNAR I know he dared do it once in his life. Once only. We've talked about it, we younger men. But no power on earth will get him to do it again.

HILDA Today he'll do it again.

RAGNAR (*Scornfully.*) If you can believe that—

HILDA We'll get to see it.

RAGNAR Neither of us will see that.

HILDA (*Fiercely, hysterically.*) I *will* see it. I *will* and *must* see it!

RAGNAR But he won't do it. He simply doesn't dare. Because that's his crippling weakness now—he, the great master builder.

(*Mrs. Solness comes from the house onto the veranda.*)

MRS. SOLNESS (*Looking about.*) Isn't he here? Where has he gone?

RAGNAR The master builder's down with the workmen.

HILDA He went with the wreath.

MRS. SOLNESS (*In terror.*) Went with the wreath! Oh, God, oh God! Brovik—you must go down to him. Try to get him up here!

RAGNAR Shall I say you want to speak to him?

MRS. SOLNESS Oh yes, dear, do that! No, no—don't say I want to! You can tell him that somebody's here. And that he must come straight away.

RAGNAR Very well. I'll do that, Mrs. Solness. (*He goes down the steps and out through the garden.*)

MRS. SOLNESS Oh, Miss Wangel, you just can't imagine how anxious I am on his account.

HILDA But is there anything here to be so frightened about?

MRS. SOLNESS Oh yes, you can be sure of that. Just think, if he takes all this seriously! If he should really try to climb that scaffolding.

HILDA (*Excitedly.*) You think he will?

MRS. SOLNESS I can never know what he might be up to. He could be planning anything.

HILDA Ah, you think maybe he's—a little—

MRS. SOLNESS I no longer know what to believe about him. The doctor's been telling me so many different things. And when I add it to all the other things I've heard him say— (*Dr. Herdal looks out through the door.*)

DR. HERDAL Will he soon be here?

MRS. SOLNESS Yes, I think so. In any case, I've sent a message to him.

DR. HERDAL (*Approaching.*) But I think you should go inside, Mrs. Solness.

MRS. SOLNESS No, no, I must stay here and wait for Halvard.

DR. HERDAL But some ladies have just arrived to see you—

MRS. SOLNESS Oh Lord, that too. And just at this moment.

DR. HERDAL And they're saying they absolutely must watch the ceremony.

MRS. SOLNESS Well, well, then I'd better go in to them after all. It is my duty, at least.

HILDA Couldn't you just ask the ladies to shift for themselves?

MRS. SOLNESS No, I couldn't possibly. Since they've come here, it's my duty to receive them. But you stay here a while and speak with him when he comes.

DR. HERDAL And try keeping him here, talking, as long as possible—

MRS. SOLNESS Yes, do that, Miss Wangel. Hold fast to him as much as you can.

HILDA Wouldn't it be better if you did that yourself?

MRS. SOLNESS Lord, yes—it's really my duty. But when you've duties in so many places—

DR. HERDAL (*Looking to the garden.*) Here he comes!

MRS. SOLNESS And to think I must go in now!

DR. HERDAL (*To Hilda.*) Say nothing about my being here.

HILDA I won't. I'll find plenty of other things to talk about to the master builder.

MRS. SOLNESS And hold fast to him. You can do it best, I think.
(*Mrs. Solness and Dr. Herdal go into the house. Hilda remains standing on the veranda. Solness comes up the steps from the garden.*)

SOLNESS I hear there's something someone wants me for.

HILDA Yes, it's me, master builder.

SOLNESS Ah, then it's you, Hilda. I was afraid it would be Aline or the doctor.

HILDA There's a lot you're afraid of, isn't there?

SOLNESS That's what you think?

HILDA Yes. People say that you're afraid of clambering about—like up on scaffolding.

SOLNESS Well, that's something all to itself.

HILDA But you're afraid of it—isn't that true?

SOLNESS Yes, I am.

HILDA Afraid of falling and killing yourself?

SOLNESS No, not of that.

HILDA Of what, then?

SOLNESS I'm afraid of retribution, Hilda.

HILDA Of retribution? (*Shaking her head.*) I don't understand.

SOLNESS Sit down and I'll tell you something.

HILDA Yes, do! Right away! (*She sits on a stool by the railing and looks expectantly at him.*)

SOLNESS (*Throws his hat on the table.*) You know that at first I started out by building churches.

HILDA (*Nods.*) Yes, I know that all right.

SOLNESS Because, you see, as a boy I came from a pious home in the country. Therefore I believed that building churches was the noblest vocation I could choose.

HILDA Yes, yes.

SOLNESS And I think I dare say I built those poor little country churches with such an ardent and honest spirit that—that—

HILDA That—? Yes—?

SOLNESS Well, that I believed He should have been pleased with me.

HILDA He? Which "he?"

SOLNESS He who was to have the churches. He whom they would serve in honor and glory.

HILDA I see. But are you so sure that—that He wasn't—pleased with you?

SOLNESS (*Scornfully.*) Pleased with me! How can you talk like that, Hilda? He who gave the troll in me permission to run riot as much as it wished. He who summoned them to the spot to serve me day and night—all these—these—

HILDA Devils—

SOLNESS Yes, both the one kind and the other. Oh no, I felt sure enough He wasn't pleased with me. (*Secretively.*) Actually, you see, that was why He let the old house burn down.

HILDA That was why?

SOLNESS Yes, don't you see? He wanted me to have the chance to be a master in my own realm—and build even greater churches to His glory. At first I didn't understand what He wanted. But then, all at once, it was clear to me.

HILDA When was that?

SOLNESS It was when I built the church tower up at Lysanger.

HILDA That's what I thought.

SOLNESS Because, you see, Hilda, up in that place where I was a stranger, I used to go around brooding and pondering to myself. And then I saw so clearly why He had taken my small children away from me. It was to make sure nothing else should occupy me. Nothing, like love or happiness, you understand. I was to be a master builder only. Nothing else. And so throughout my whole life I was to go on building for Him. (*Laughing.*) But that's not how it turned out.

HILDA What did you do, then?

SOLNESS First I searched into and tested myself—

HILDA And then—?

SOLNESS Then I did the impossible. I, just like Him.

HILDA The impossible!

SOLNESS I'd never before been able to climb high up—high and free. But that day I could.

HILDA (*Jumping up.*) Yes, yes, you could!

SOLNESS And when I stood right up there and hung the wreath over the weather vane, then I said to Him: Hear me, Almighty One! From this day on I, too, will be a free master builder. In my own realm. Just like you. I will never more build churches for you. Only homes for human beings.

HILDA (*With large sparkling eyes.*) That was the singing I heard in the air.

SOLNESS But He still got what He needed for His mill to grind.

HILDA What do you mean by that?

SOLNESS (*Looking dejectedly at her.*) This building homes for human beings—it's not worth a penny, Hilda.

HILDA You say that now?

SOLNESS Yes, because now I can see that human beings have no
use for these homes of theirs. Not for being happy in. And I
wouldn't have had use for such a home, either—if I'd owned
one. (*With a quiet, bitter laugh.*) So, that's the sum total as far,
as far back as I can see. Actually, nothing really built. And
nothing sacrificed to be able to build, either. Nothing, nothing,
all told.

HILDA Then you will never build anything new from now on?

SOLNESS (*Lively.*) Yes, now I'm going to begin.

HILDA What, then? What, then? Say it straight out!

SOLNESS The only thing I believe can create human happiness—
that's what I'll build, now.

HILDA (*Looking intently at him.*) Master builder, you mean our castles in the air?

SOLNESS Yes, castles in the air.

HILDA I'm afraid you'll get dizzy before we get halfway up.

SOLNESS Not if I go hand in hand with you, Hilda.

HILDA (*With a shade of suppressed resentment.*) Only with me?
Won't we have others with us?

SOLNESS What others do you mean?

HILDA Well, her—that Kaja at the desk. Poor thing, don't you want
her along, too?

SOLNESS Ah, so it was her that Aline sat here talking to you about.

HILDA Well, is it true or not?

SOLNESS (*Vehemently.*) I don't answer questions like that! You must
trust me totally and entirely.

HILDA For ten years I've trusted you so completely.

SOLNESS You must keep on trusting me.

HILDA Then let me see you up there—high and free!

SOLNESS (*Heavily.*) Oh, Hilda, I can't do that every day.

HILDA (*Passionately.*) I will see it! I will see it! (*Begging.*) Just once
more, master builder. Do the impossible again!

SOLNESS (*Looking deeply at her.*) If I did attempt it, Hilda, I'd stand
up there and talk to Him as I did last time.

HILDA (*With mounting excitement.*) What will you say to Him?

SOLNESS I will say: Hear me, Almighty One—you must now judge
me as you see fit. But from now on I will build only the most
beautiful thing in the world—

HILDA (*Enraptured.*) Yes—yes—yes.

SOLNESS —build it together with a princess that I love—

HILDA Yes, tell Him that! Tell Him that!

SOLNESS Yes. And then I'll say to Him: now I'm going down to hold her in my arms and kiss her—

HILDA Many times! Say that!

SOLNESS Many, many times, I'll tell Him.

HILDA And then—?

SOLNESS Then I'll swing my hat—and come down to earth—and do as I said.

HILDA (*With outstretched arms.*) Now I see you again as if there was singing in the air!

SOLNESS (*Looking at her with bowed head.*) How did you become what you are, Hilda?

HILDA How did you make me become what I am?

SOLNESS (*Brief and curt.*) The princess shall have her castle.

HILDA (*Jubilant, clapping her hands.*) Oh, master builder! My lovely, lovely castle. Our castle in the air.

SOLNESS On a solid foundation.

(*Out in the street many people have gathered and can be glimpsed fleetingly through the trees. Music from a brass band is heard from behind the new house. Mrs. Solness, with a fur stole around her neck, Dr. Herdal, with her white shawl over his arm, and several ladies come onto the veranda. Ragnar Brovik at the same time approaches from the garden.*)

MRS. SOLNESS (*To Ragnar.*) Is there going to be music, too?

RAGNAR Yes. It's the Builders Association. (*To Solness.*) The foreman asked me to tell you he's ready now to go up with the wreath.

SOLNESS (*Taking his hat.*) Good. I'll go down there myself.

MRS. SOLNESS (*Anxiously.*) What will you be doing down there, Halvard?

SOLNESS (*Curtly.*) I have to be down there with the men.

MRS. SOLNESS Yes, down below. Only down below.

SOLNESS It's what I usually do every time.

MRS. SOLNESS (*Calling after him from the railing.*) But please tell the man to be careful as he climbs up. Promise me that, Halvard!

DR. HERDAL (*To Mrs. Solness.*) You see, I was right. He's not thinking any more about that crazy business.

MRS. SOLNESS Oh, what a relief. Twice we've had men fall there, and both times they were killed. (*Turning to Hilda.*) Thank you, Miss Wangel, for taking hold of him like that. I know I couldn't have managed it.

DR. HERDAL (*Merrily.*) Yes, yes, Miss Wangel, you really know how to hold fast to a man when you want to!

(*Mrs. Solness and Dr. Herdal go over to the ladies who stand near the steps. Hilda remains standing at the railing. Ragnar goes over to her.*)

RAGNAR (*With suppressed laughter, speaking quietly.*) Miss Wangel, do you see all the young people down there in the street?

HILDA Yes.

RAGNAR They're my fellow students come to watch the master.

HILDA What will they be watching for?

RAGNAR They will watch him not dare to climb to the top of his own house.

HILDA Is that what the boys will be doing?

RAGNAR (*Harshly and scornfully.*) He's kept us down for so long. Now we'll be looking as he obligingly keeps himself down.

HILDA You'll not get to see that. Not today.

RAGNAR (*Smiling.*) So? How will we get to see him, then?

HILDA High—high up by the weather vane, that's where you'll see him.

RAGNAR (*Laughing.*) Him? You want me to believe that!

HILDA He intends to climb to the top—that's where you'll see him.

RAGNAR He *intends* to, yes—that I can believe. But he simply won't be able to. He'd be dizzy long, long before he got halfway up. He would have to crawl back down again on hands and knees.

DR. HERDAL (*Pointing.*) Look! There goes the foreman up the ladder.

MRS. SOLNESS And he's got to carry the wreath too. Oh, if only he'll be careful.

RAGNAR (*Crying out in surprise.*) But surely that's—

HILDA (*In an outburst of joy.*) It's the master builder himself!

MRS. SOLNESS (*Shrieking in terror.*) Yes, it's Halvard. Oh, dear God! Halvard! Halvard!

DR. HERDAL Hush. Don't call out to him.

MRS. SOLNESS (*Half-distracted.*) I must go to him! Get him to come down again!

DR. HERDAL (*Holding onto her.*) Don't anyone move. Not a sound!

HILDA (*Not moving, following Solness with her eyes.*) He's climbing and climbing. Always higher. Always higher. Look! Just look!

RAGNAR (*Breathless.*) Now he has to turn back. He can't do anything else!

HILDA Climbing and climbing. He's nearly there.

MRS. SOLNESS Oh, I'll die of fright. I can't bear to watch him.

DR. HERDAL Then don't look at him.

HILDA He's standing now on the highest plank. Right to the top!

DR. HERDAL Nobody say anything! You hear me!

HILDA (*With jubilant, quiet intensity.*) At last! At last! Now I see him great and free again!

RAGNAR (*Almost speechless.*) But all this is—

HILDA This is how I've seen him all these ten years. How strong he stands! Fearfully thrilling after all. Look at him! Now he's hanging the wreath on the spire!

RAGNAR All this I'm seeing here is completely impossible.

HILDA Yes, it's the impossible that he's doing now. (*With the inscrutable look in her eyes.*) Can you see anyone else up there with him?

RAGNAR There's no one else.

HILDA Yes, there's someone he's struggling with.

RAGNAR You're mistaken.

HILDA Can't you hear singing in the air, either?

RAGNAR It must be the wind in the treetops.

HILDA I hear a singing. A powerful singing. (*Crying out in joyful exultation.*) Look, look! Now he's waving his hat. Waving to us down here. Oh, wave back up to him there. For now, now it is fulfilled! (*Snatches the white shawl from the doctor, waves it, and cries out.*) Hurray for master builder Solness!

DR. HERDAL Stop! Stop! For God's sake!

(*The ladies on the veranda wave their handkerchiefs, and shouts of "Hurray" come from the street. Suddenly they stop and the crowd gives out a cry of horror. A human body, along with some planks and branches, can be glimpsed falling between the trees.*)

MRS. SOLNESS AND THE LADIES (*At the same time.*) He's falling! He's falling!

(*Mrs. Solness sways and sinks back fainting; the ladies catch her amid cries and confusion. The crowd in the street breaks down the fence and storms into the garden. Dr. Herdal also rushes down below. A short pause.*)

HILDA (*Staring fixedly upward and speaking as if petrified.*) My master builder.

RAGNAR (*Leans, trembling, against the railing.*) He must be crushed to bits. Killed on the spot.

ONE OF THE LADIES (*As Mrs. Solness is carried into the house.*) Run down to the doctor—

RAGNAR I can't move a foot.

ANOTHER LADY Call down to somebody, then!

RAGNAR (*Trying to call.*) How is he? Is he alive?

A VOICE (*In the garden.*) Master builder Solness is dead.

OTHER VOICES His whole head is crushed. He fell right into the quarry.

HILDA (*Turning to Ragnar and speaking quietly.*) I can no longer see him up there.

RAGNAR How horrible this is. So he couldn't do it after all.

HILDA (*As if in quiet, subdued triumph.*) But he went right to the top. And I heard harps in the air. (*Swings the shawl up overhead and cries out with wild intensity.*) My—my master builder!

END OF PLAY

BACKGROUNDS

Correspondence and Documents

Peer Gynt

To BJÖRNSTJERNE BJÖRNSON.[†]

Rome, *9th December* 1867.

DEAR BJÖRNSON,—What sort of infernal nonsense is it that comes between us at every turn? One might almost believe that the devil himself was casting his shadow between us. I had received your letter. In the man who writes as you write there, there is no guile. There are things which it is impossible to counterfeit. I, too, had written from a full and grateful heart, in answer. One cannot return thanks for being praised; but being understood—that makes one inexpressibly grateful. But now I can't send my letter. I have torn it to pieces. An hour ago I read Mr. Clemens Petersen's review in *Fœdrelandet*. If I am to answer your letter now, I must begin in another way; I must acknowledge the receipt of your esteemed communication of such and such a date with the enclosed criticism from a certain paper.[1]

If I were in Copenhagen, and some one there was as great a friend of mine as Clemens Petersen is of yours, I would have thrashed the life out of him before I would have permitted him to commit such an intentional crime against truth and justice. There is a lie involved in Clemens Petersen's article—not in what he says, but in what he refrains from saying. And he intentionally refrains from saying a great deal. You are quite at liberty to show him this letter. As surely as I know that he has a profound, ardent apprehension of what really makes this life worth living, so surely do I know that this article will come to burn and scathe his soul; for the lie in-

---

† From *Letters of Henrik Ibsen*, trans. John Nilsen Laurvik and Mary Morison (New York: Duffield, 1908), 144–50, 269–71, 333–35, 268–69.
1. The first edition of *Peer Gynt* was published in Copenhagen on the 14th of November 1867, and the second edition only a fortnight later. Björnson reviewed the book in a letter from Copenhagen to the *Norsk Folkeblad*. A week later it was reviewed in *Fœdrelandet* by Clemens Petersen. Petersen declared that the work is not "real poetry," because "in its transpositions from reality to art it neither completely fulfils the requirements of art nor those of reality." It is, in his opinion "full of fallacious ideas" and of "riddles which are insoluble because there is nothing in them at all." He assigns it to the domain of polemical journalism.

425

volved in keeping silence is as much a lie as the positive assertion. And on Clemens Petersen there rests a great responsibility, for God has entrusted him with a great task.

Do not believe that I am a blind, conceited fool! I can assure you that in my quiet moments I sound and probe and dissect my own inward parts—and where it hurts most, too.

My book *is* poetry; and if it is not, then it will be. The conception of poetry in our country, in Norway, shall be made to conform to the book. There is no stability in the world of ideas. The Scandinavians of this century are not Greeks. He says that the Strange Passenger is symbolic of terror. Supposing that I had been about to be executed, and that such an explanation would have saved my life, it would never have occurred to me. I never thought of such a thing. I stuck in the scene as a mere caprice. And tell me now, is Peer Gynt himself not a personality, complete and individual? *I* know that he is. And the mother, is she not? There are many things to be learned from Clemens Petersen, and I have learned much from him; but there is something that it might do him good to learn, and in which I, even though I cannot teach it to him, have the advantage of him—and that is what you in your letter call "loyalty." Yes, that is just the word! Not loyalty to a friend, a purpose, or the like, but to something infinitely higher.

However, I am glad of the injustice that has been done me. There has been something of the God-send, of the providential dispensation in it; for I feel that this anger is invigorating all my powers. If it is to be war, then let it be war! If I am no poet, then I have nothing to lose. I shall try my luck as a photographer. My contemporaries in the North I shall take in hand, one after the other, as I have already taken the nationalist language reformers.[2] I will not spare the child in the mother's womb, nor the thought or feeling that lies under the word of any living soul that deserves the honour of my notice.

Dear Björnson, you are a good, warm-hearted soul; you have given me more of what is great and fine than I can ever repay you; but there is something in your nature that may easily cause your good fortune—yes, that more than anything else—to be a curse to you. I have a right to tell you this; for I know that, underneath the crust of folly and frowardness, I have taken life very seriously. Do you know that I have entirely separated myself from my own parents, from my whole family, because a position of half-understanding was unendurable to me?

What I have written is somewhat incoherent, but, put together, it amounts to this: I will not be an antiquarian nor a geographer; I

2. In the figure "Huhu" in the Fourth Act of *Peer Gynt*, Ibsen aims at the "Maalstrævere," the would-be nationalisers of the Norwegian language.

will not cultivate my talent for the Monrad philosophy; in short, I will not follow good advice. But one thing I will do, even though the powers without and the powers within drive me to pull the roof down upon my head—I will always, so help me God, continue to be—Your faithfully and sincerely devoted,

HENRIK IBSEN.

10th December.—I have slept upon the above lines, and have now read them in cold blood. They are the expression of my mood of yesterday, but still they shall be sent.

I will now tell you, calmly and after due consideration, what will be the result of Mr. Clemens Petersen's article.

I have no intention of yielding, and Mr. Clemens Petersen cannot oust me; it is too late for that. He may possibly oblige me to withdraw from Denmark; but in that case I intend to change more than my publisher. Do not under-estimate my friends and my adherents in Norway. The party whose newspaper has opened its columns to calumnies about me, will be made to feel that I do not stand alone. When things go beyond a certain point, I know no consideration; and if I am only careful to do what I am quite capable of, namely, combine this relentlessness of mind with deliberateness in the choice of means, my enemies shall be made to feel that if I cannot build up, I am, at least, able to pull down.

This, however, concerns only the future. Now I will tell you something of present moment.

I am carrying on no correspondence with any one at home; nevertheless I can give you a piece of home intelligence. Do you know what they are saying just now in Norway, wherever Carl Ploug's paper is read? They are saying: "It is evident from Clemens Petersen's review that Björnson is in Copenhagen."

If you have reviewed *Peer Gynt* in the *Norsk Folkeblad*, they are saying: "Diplomatic, but not clever enough." Some will say it in all good faith; others from vindictiveness and resentment. The critics will divide into parties, for or against. You will see that I am right.

They will call Clemens Petersen's review a return for favours received. A man unknown to me wrote some articles in the *Morgenblad* lately, in which he unmercifully disparaged Mr. Petersen's literary work; I was favourably mentioned in them. These combinations will be recalled. I know the way the fellows reason.

Dear Björnson, do let us try to hold together. Our friends have often enough made life miserable for us, and the struggle more onerous than it need be.

You see, from the very fact that I write all this to you, that I harbour no suspicion of you in this matter. I neither am nor ever shall be on the side of my adherents when they are opposed to you. When the opposition is to your friends, that is another matter.

Mr. Petersen's article—to return to that again—will not do me any harm. The absentee has always a great advantage in the very fact of his being absent. But to write the article in such a style, was imprudent. In his review of *Brand*, he treated me with respect, and the public will not find anything in the intervening years which renders me deserving of contempt. The public will not permit Mr. Petersen to dispose of me as summarily as he has attempted to do. He ought to leave such attempts to those of his colleagues who live *by* their critical labours. Until now I believed that Mr. Petersen lived *for* his.

All I reproach you with is inaction. It was not kind of you to permit, through negligence, such an attempt to be made to place my literary reputation under the auctioneer's hammer in my absence.

There! I have written myself into a good temper again. Now do you abuse me like a pickpocket. I shall be glad if you find it necessary to do so in a long letter.

Accept in a friendly spirit a friendly greeting from us all. Do not show your wife this letter; but give her our best wishes for Christmas and New Year, and, most particularly, for the approaching third great event.—Yours,

HENRIK IBSEN.

To BJÖRNSTJERNE BJÖRNSON.

Rome, 28*th December* 1867.

DEAR BJÖRNSON,—Nothing in the wide world could have been more welcome than the greeting which your letter, received on Christmas morning, brought me.

The thought of the cargo of nonsense which I shipped to you in my last epistle had not left me at peace with myself for an hour in the interval. The worst that a man can do to himself is to do injustice to others. Thank you, noble-minded man that you are, for taking the matter as you have done. I could see nothing before me but dispeace and bitterness for a long time to come; and yet now it appears to me as only what might have been expected of you, that you should take it just as you did, and in no other way. I read your letter over and over again, every day, and read myself free from the tormenting thought that I have hurt you.

Do not understand what I said in my former letter to mean that my conception of what is essential in poetry is entirely different from Clemens Petersen's. On the contrary, I understand and am entirely in accord with him. But I contend that I have fulfilled the requirements. He says: No.

He writes of our over-reflective age, which makes the witches in

Macbeth symbolise something which takes place in Macbeth him-self; yet in the very same article he himself makes a distracted pas-senger on board a ship symbolise "terror"! Why, proceeding in this manner, I will undertake to turn your works and those of every other poet into allegories, from beginning to end. Take *Götz von Berlichingen*. Say that Götz himself represents the ferment of the idea of liberty in the nation, that the Emperor represents the idea of the state, etc. etc.; and what result do you arrive at? Why, that it is not poetry!

As for my "paroxysms," do not worry about them; there is nothing unhealthy in them, either one way or another. I shall very probably take your advice and write a comedy for the stage; the idea had been occupying my own mind. It is possible that we shall go to Northern Italy for the summer, but where we shall spend next win-ter I do not know. I only know that it will not be in Norway. Were I to go home now, one of two things would happen: I should either within a month make an enemy of every one there; or else I should sneak myself into favour again in all manner of disguises, and thus become a lie, both to myself and others.

Dear Björnson, are you really going back to the theatre again? There is work for you there, undoubtedly; but you have a task call-ing to you, much nearer at hand, in your authorship. If your taking up theatrical work meant merely a loss of time, meant merely that all the visions, moods, and imaginings of the poet were put aside, to make their appearance later, it would not matter so much. But such is not the case. Others come, but the intervening ones die unborn. For a poet, the toil of a theatre is equivalent to a daily fœticide. The civil laws make this a punishable crime; I do not know if God is more lenient. Think it over, dear Björnson! A man's gifts are not a property; they are a duty.[1]

No, go abroad, carissimo! Both because distance gives a wider range of vision, and because much more value is set upon the man who is out of sight. I am certain that the good people of Weimar were Gœthe's worst public.

* * *

To EDWARD GRIEG.

Dresden, *23rd January* 1874.

DEAR MR. GRIEG,—My object in writing to you is to ask if you would care to co-operate with me in a certain undertaking.

It is my intention to arrange *Peer Gynt*—of which the third edi-

1. In June 1867, Björnson had given up the managership of the Christiania Theatre; but before many months had passed, negotiations were being carried on with the view of his becoming "artistic director." They were unsuccessful; he would not accept the condi-tions offered. [Note that Edward is English for "Edvard"—*Editor*.]

tion is soon to appear—for performance on the stage. Will you compose the music which will be required? I will briefly indicate to you how I think of arranging the play.

The First Act is to be retained in full, with only a few abridgments of the dialogue. Peer Gynt's monologue on pages 23, 24, and 25, I wish to have treated either melodramatically, or in part as a recitative. The wedding-scene in the house (page 28) must, by means of a ballet, be made into something more than is in the book. For this purpose a special dance-melody will have to be composed, which is to be continued softly to the end of the Act.

In the Second Act, the musical treatment of the scene with the three Sæter girls, pages 57 to 60, must be left to the discretion of the composer—but there must be devilry in it! The monologue on pages 60–62 should, I think, be accompanied by chords, in melodramatic style, as also the scene between Peer and the Green-clad One, pages 63–66. There must also be some kind of accompaniment to the episodes in the Hall of the Old Man of the Dovrë; here, however, the speeches are to be considerably shortened. The scene with the Boyg, which is to be given in full, must also be accompanied by music; the Bird-Cries are to be sung; bell-ringing and psalm-singing are heard in the distance.

In the Third Act I need chords, but not many, for the scene between Peer, the Woman, and the Ugly Brat, pages 96–100; and I imagine that a soft accompaniment would be appropriate from the beginning of page 109 to the foot of page 112.

Almost the whole of the Fourth Act is to be omitted at the performance. In place of it I think there should be a great musical tone-picture, suggesting Peer Gynt's wandering all over the world; American, English, and French airs might occur as alternating and disappearing motives. The chorus of Anitra and the Girls, pages 144 and 145, is to be heard behind the curtain, in combination with the orchestra. During this music the curtain is raised, and there is seen, like a distant dream-picture, the scene described at the foot of page 164, in which Solveig, now a middle-aged woman, sits in the sunshine outside her house. After her song the curtain is again slowly lowered, the music continuing, but changing into a suggestion of the storm at sea with which the Fifth Act opens.

This Fifth Act, which at the performance will be called the Fourth Act or the Epilogue, must be considerably shortened. A musical accompaniment is needed from pages 195 to 199. The scenes on the capsized boat and in the churchyard are omitted. On page 221 Solveig sings, and the music continues, accompanying Peer Gynt's speeches, and changing into that required for the choruses, pages 222–225. The scenes with the Button-Moulder and the Old Man of the Dovrë are to be shortened. On page 254, the people on

their way to church sing on the forest path; bell-ringing and distant
psalm-singing are suggested in the music played during what follows. Then Solveig's song ends the play; and whilst the curtain is
falling, the psalm-singing is heard again, nearer and stronger.

These are my ideas. Will you let me know if you are willing to undertake the task? If I receive a favourable answer from you, I shall
at once write to the Management of the Christiania Theatre, sending along with my letter the revised and abridged text, to make
sure, before we go any further, that our play will be performed. I intend to ask 400 specie-dollars for it, to be divided equally between
us. I am certain that we may also count upon the play being produced in Copenhagen and Stockholm. But I shall be obliged by
your keeping the matter secret at present. Please reply as soon as
possible.—Yours most sincerely,

HENRIK IBSEN.

P.S.—My address here in Dresden is: Wettiner-Strasse, 22, 2.
Etage.[1]

To LUDWIG PASSARGE.

Munich, 16th June 1880.

DEAR SIR,—Permit me to reply briefly to your esteemed letter of
the 4th inst.

I am very glad to learn that you have found a first-class publisher
for your translation of *Peer Gynt*. But, with every desire to oblige, I
am not in a position to give explanations of the many allusions in
the book which may be unintelligible to German readers; for it is
impossible for me, as a foreigner, to judge what needs explanation
and what does not. For the same reason I consider that it would be
useless for me to apply to Dietrichson or any other Norwegian. I
believe that no one can judge better in this matter than yourself;
and if there is any particular point on which you feel uncertain, it
should be easy for you to obtain information during your approaching visit to Norway. But it is my impression that you know as much
of matters Norwegian as any native.

Neither is it possible for me to give you an account of the circumstances which led to the production of *Peer Gynt*. To make the
matter intelligible, I should have to write a whole book, and for that
the time has not yet come. Everything that I have written has the
closest possible connection with what I have lived through, even if
it has not been my own personal experience; in every new poem or

---

1. *Peer Gynt*, with Grieg's music, was performed at the Christiania Theatre for the first
time on the 24th of February 1876. The abridgment was carried out, in some respects,
on a different plan from that proposed by Ibsen.

play I have aimed at my own spiritual emancipation and purification—for a man shares the responsibility and the guilt of the society to which he belongs. Hence I once wrote the following dedicatory lines in a copy of one of my books:

> At *leve* er krig med trolde
> i hjertets og hjernens hvælv;
> at *digte*—det er at holde
> dommedag over sig selv.[1]

It is only natural that you do not know the word "pusselanker," for it does not belong to the written language at all; it means "little legs or feet," and is only used by mothers and nurses in talking to small children.

The meaning of the verses about which you ask is this: *Peer Gynt* claims as a title of admission to hell that he has been a slave-dealer. To this "the lean one" replies that there are many who have done worse things, who have, for instance, trafficked in wills and souls, and yet, from the fact that they have done it in a "twaddling way," that is to say, without demoniacal earnestness, have not qualified themselves for hell, but only for the "casting-ladle."

This short answer is all I am able to give you at present. Wishing you a pleasant journey to Norway, and hoping that you will remember me to any of my friends and acquaintances whom you may happen to meet there,—I remain, Yours respectfully and sincerely,

HENRIK IBSEN.

To EDMUND GOSSE.

Dresden, 15*th January* 1874.

*   *   *

I am greatly obliged to you for your kind review of my new drama.[1] There is only one remark in it about which I must say a word or two. You are of opinion that the drama ought to have been written in verse, and that it would have gained by this. Here I must differ from you. The play is, as you must have observed, conceived in the most realistic style; the illusion I wished to produce was that of reality. I wished to produce the impression on the reader that what he was reading was something that had really happened. If I had employed verse, I should have counteracted my own intention and prevented the accomplishment of the task I had set myself. The many ordinary, insignificant characters whom I have intention-

---

1. To *live*—is to war with fiends / That infest the brain and the heart; / To *write*—is to summon one's self / And play the judge's part.
1. Ibsen writes to Edmund Gosse explaining why he abandoned verse drama for prose. Gosse had reviewed Ibsen's *Emperor and Galilean* in 1873 and had regretted it was not written in verse [*Editor*].

ally introduced into the play would have become indistinct, and indistinguishable from one another, if I had allowed all of them to speak in one and the same rhythmical measure. We are no longer living in the days of Shakespeare. Among sculptors there is already talk of painting statues in the natural colours. Much can be said both for and against this. I have no desire to see the Venus of Milo painted, but I would rather see the head of a negro executed in black than in white marble. Speaking generally, the style must conform to the degree of ideality which pervades the representation. My new drama is no tragedy in the ancient acceptation; what I desired to depict were human beings, and therefore I would not let them talk the "language of the Gods."

I have a great deal more to say to you, both about this and other things; but I am always hoping for an opportunity of doing it by word of mouth. I shall, therefore, stop for to-day. Thanking you again most heartily, I remain—Yours very sincerely,

HENRIK IBSEN.

A Doll House

The Alternative German Ending†

Under strong pressure, and very reluctantly, Ibsen wrote an alternative ending for the German theatre. Both Maurice in Hamburg and Laube in Vienna pressed for a 'conciliatory' ending, as also did Frau Hedwig Niemann-Raabe who was to play Nora on tour. In the end, Ibsen himself provided the following additional dialogue:

NORA. . . . dass unser Zusammenleben eine Ehe werden könnte. Leb' wohl. [*Will gehen.*]

HELMER. Nun denn gehe! [*Fasst sie am Arm.*] Aber erst sollst Du Deine Kinder zum letzten Mal sehen!

NORA. Lass mich los! Ich will sie nicht sehen! Ich kann es nicht!

HELMER [*zieht sie gegen die Thür links*]. Du sollst sie sehen! [*Öffnet die Thür und sagt leise.*] Siehst Du; dort schlafen sie sorglos und ruhig. Morgen, wenn sie erwachen und rufen nach ihrer Mutter, dann sind sie—mutterlos.

NORA [*bebend*]. Mutterlos. . . !

HELMER. Wie Du es gewesen bist.

NORA. Mutterlos! [*Kämpft innerlich, lässt die Reisetasche fallen und sagt.*] O, ich versündige mich gegen mich selbst, aber ich kann sie nicht verlassen. [*Sinkt halb nieder vor der Thür.*]

† *The Oxford Ibsen*, trans. and ed. James W. McFarlane et al. (New York: Oxford University Press, 1960–77), 5:287–88.

HELMER [*freudig, aber leise*]. Nora!

[*Der Vorhang fällt.*]

NORA. . . . Where we could make a real marriage out of our lives together. Goodbye. [*Begins to go.*]

HELMER. Go then! [*Seizes her arm.*] But first you shall see your children for the last time!

NORA. Let me go! I will not see them! I cannot!

HELMER [*draws her over to the door, left*]. You shall see them. [*Opens the door and says softly.*] Look, there they are asleep, peaceful and carefree. Tomorrow, when they wake up and call for their mother, they will be—motherless.

NORA [*trembling*]. Motherless. . . !

HELMER. As you once were.

NORA. Motherless! [*Struggles with herself, lets her travelling bag fall, and says.*] Oh, this is a sin against myself, but I cannot leave them. [*Half sinks down by the door.*]

HELMER [*joyfully, but softly*]. Nora!

[*The curtain falls.*]

For an insight into what eventually persuaded Ibsen to commit this 'barbaric outrage'—as he himself called it—see his letters to a Copenhagen newspaper of 17 Feb. 1880, to Heinrich Laube of 18 Feb. 1880, and to Moritz Prozor of 23 Jan. 1891 * * *

To the "NATIONALTIDENDE."†

Munich, 17*th February* 1880.

To the EDITOR.

SIR,—In No. 1360 of your esteemed paper I have read a letter from Flensburg, in which it is stated that *A Doll's House* (in German *Nora*) has been acted there, and that the conclusion of the play has been changed—the alteration having been made, it is asserted, by my orders. This last statement is untrue. Immediately after the publication of *Nora*, I received from my translator, Mr. Wilhelm Lange, of Berlin, who is also my business manager as far as the North German theatres are concerned, the information that he had reason to fear that an "adaptation" of the play, giving it a different ending, was about to be published, and that this would probably be chosen in preference to the original by several of the North German theatres.

In order to prevent such a possibility, I sent to him, for use in case of absolute necessity, a draft of an altered last scene, according to which Nora does not leave the house, but is forcibly led by

† From *Letters of Henrik Ibsen*, trans. John Nilsen Laurvik and Mary Morison (New York: Duffield, 1908), 325–27, 436–37.

Helmer to the door of the children's bedroom; a short dialogue takes place, Nora sinks down at the door, and the curtain falls.

This change I myself, in the letter to my translator, stigmatise as "barbaric violence" done to the play. Those who make use of the altered scene do so entirely against my wish. But I trust that it will not be used at very many German theatres.

As long as no literary convention exists between Germany and the Scandinavian countries, we Scandinavian authors enjoy no protection from the law here, just as the German authors enjoy none with us. Our dramatic works are, therefore, in Germany exposed to acts of violence at the hands of translators, theatrical directors, stage-managers, and actors at the smaller theatres. When my works are threatened, I prefer, taught by experience, to commit the act of violence myself, instead of leaving them to be treated and "adapted" by less careful and less skilful hands.—Yours respectfully,

HENRIK IBSEN.

To HEINRICH LAUBE.[1]

Munich, 18*th February* 1880.

HONOURED SIR,—It was a great pleasure to me to learn that my latest play, *A Doll's House*, is to be acted at the "Wiener Stadttheater" under your widely renowned management.

You are of opinion that the play, on account of its ending, does not properly come under the category of "Schauspiel"; but, dear Sir, do you really attach much value to categories? I, for my part, believe that the dramatic categories are elastic, and that they must accommodate themselves to the literary facts—not *vice versâ*. This much is certain, that the play with its present ending has had an almost unprecedented success in Stockholm, Christiania, and Copenhagen.

The alternative altered ending I have prepared, not because I thought it was required, but simply at the request of a North German manager and of an actress who is going on tour in North Germany as "Nora." I herewith send you a copy of the altered scene, on reading which you will, I hope, acknowledge that the effect of the piece can only be weakened by employing it. I trust that you will decide to produce the play in its original form. With the assurance of my highest esteem, believe me, honoured Sir,—Yours respectfully,

HENRIK IBSEN.

1. Heinrich Laube (1806–1884), one of the best known authors belonging to the school known as Young Germany, was Director of the Burgtheatre in Vienna from 1849 to 1867. He afterwards founded and managed the "Wiener Stadttheater." He powerfully influenced the German stage in the direction of a more faithful representation of human nature.

To MORITZ PROZOR.

Munich, 23rd *January* 1891.

DEAR COUNT PROZOR,—Mr. Luigi Capuana has, I regret to see, given you a great deal of trouble by his proposal to alter the last scene of *A Doll's House* for performance in the Italian theatres.

I do not for a moment doubt that the alteration you suggest would be distinctly preferable to that which Mr. Capuana proposes. But the fact is that I cannot possibly directly authorise any change whatever in the ending of the drama. I may almost say that it was for the sake of the last scene that the whole play was written.

And, besides, I believe that Mr. Capuana is mistaken in fearing that the Italian public would not be able to understand or approve of my work if it were put on the stage in its original form. The experiment ought, at any rate, to be tried. If it turns out a failure, then let Mr. Capuana, on his own responsibility, employ your adaptation of the closing scene; for I cannot formally authorise, or approve of, such a proceeding.

I wrote to Mr. Capuana yesterday, briefly expressing my views on the subject; and I hope that he will disregard his misgivings until he has proved by experience that they are well founded.[1]

At the time when *A Doll's House* was quite new, I was obliged to give my consent to an alteration of the last scene for Frau Hedwig Niemann-Raabe, who was to play the part of Nora in Berlin. At that time I had no choice. I was entirely unprotected by copyright law in Germany, and could, consequently, prevent nothing. Besides, the play in its original, uncorrupted form, was accessible to the German public in a German edition which was already printed and published. With its altered ending it had only a short run. In its unchanged form it is still being played.

The enclosed letter from Mr. Antoine I have answered, thanking him for his intention to produce *The Wild Duck*, and urging him to make use of your translation. Of course I cannot tell what he will decide. But as the Théâtre Libre is really of the nature of a private society, it is probably not possible to procure a legal injunction. There are, besides, reasons which would render the taking of such a step inadvisable, even if possible. However, I leave the decision of this question entirely to you, assured that you will act in the best way possible.

With my very respectful regards to Countess Prozor, and with cordial thanks to yourself for all the favour and kindness shown me, I remain—Your sincere and obliged,

HENRIK IBSEN.

1. Luigi Capuana (born 1839), an Italian novelist and dramatic critic, translated *A Doll's House* into Italian. It was the famous actress Eleonora Duse, who wished him to alter the last scene of the play; but she finally accepted and acted it in the original form.

*Speech at the Banquet of the Norwegian League
for Women's Rights†*

Christiania, May 26, 1898

[A month after the official birthday celebrations were over, Ibsen and his wife were invited to a banquet in his honor given by the leading Norwegian feminist society.]

I am not a member of the Women's Rights League. Whatever I have written has been without any conscious thought of making propaganda. I have been more the poet and less the social philosopher than people generally seem inclined to believe. I thank you for the toast, but must disclaim the honor of having consciously worked for the women's rights movement. I am not even quite clear as to just what this women's rights movement really is. To me it has seemed a problem of mankind in general. And if you read my books carefully you will understand this. True enough, it is desirable to solve the woman problem, along with all the others; but that has not been the whole purpose. My task has been the *description of humanity*. To be sure, whenever such a description is felt to be reasonably true, the reader will read his own feelings and sentiments into the work of the poet. These are then attributed to the poet; but incorrectly so. Every reader remolds the work beautifully and neatly, each according to his own personality. Not only those who write but also those who read are poets. They are collaborators. They are often more poetical than the poet himself.

With these reservations, let me thank you for the toast you have given me. I do indeed recognize that women have an important task to perform in the particular directions this club is working along. I will express my thanks by proposing a toast to the League for Women's Rights, wishing it progress and success.

The task always before my mind has been to advance our country and to give our people a higher standard. To achieve this, two factors are important. It is for the *mothers*, by strenuous and sustained labor, to awaken a conscious feeling of *culture* and *discipline*. This feeling must be awakened before it will be possible to lift the people to a higher plane. It is the women who shall solve the human problem. As mothers they shall solve it. And only in that capacity can they solve it. Here lies a great task for woman. My thanks! And success to the League for Women's Rights!

† From *Ibsen: Letters and Speeches*, ed. Evert Sprinchorn (New York: Hill and Wang, 1964), 337–38. Reprinted by permission of Farrar, Straus and Giroux.

The Wild Duck

To FREDERIK HEGEL.†

Gossensass, *2nd September* 1884.

DEAR MR. HEGEL,—Along with this letter I send you the manuscript of my new play, *The Wild Duck*. For the last four months I have worked at it every day; and it is not without a certain feeling of regret that I part from it. Long, daily association with the persons in this play has endeared them to me, in spite of their manifold failings; and I am not without hope that they may find good and kind friends among the great reading public, and more particularly among the actor tribe—to whom they offer rôles which will well repay the trouble spent on them. The study and representation of these characters will not be an easy task; therefore it is desirable that the book should be offered to the theatres as early as possible in the season; I shall send the letters, which you will be good enough to despatch along with the different copies.

In some ways this new play occupies a position by itself among my dramatic works; in its method it differs in several respects from my former ones. But I shall say no more on this subject at present. I hope that my critics will discover the points alluded to; they will, at any rate, find several things to squabble about and several things to interpret. I also think that *The Wild Duck* may very probably entice some of our young dramatists into new paths; and this I consider a result to be desired.

*   *   *

To HANS SCHRØDER‡

Rome, *14th November* 1884

[*The Wild Duck* was published on November 11 in a first printing of 8,000 copies and proved so popular that a second printing appeared on December 1. The major Scandinavian theaters staged the play during the 1884–85 season, the Bergen theater opening first on January 9, and the Christiania Theater only two days later. The unusual demands that the play made of the actors prompted Schrøder, the head of the Christiania Theater, to write the author for advice.]

DEAR MR. SCHRØDER, On my return here last night I found your telegram; as a reply to which allow me to note the following.

---

† From *Letters of Henrik Ibsen*, trans. John Nilsen Laurvik and Mary Morison (New York: Duffield, 1908), 383–84.

‡ From *Ibsen: Letters and Speeches*, ed. Evert Sprinchorn (New York: Hill and Wang, 1964), 241–43. Reprinted by permission of Farrar, Straus and Giroux.

I myself have no desire to cast my new play, nor could I very readily assume that responsibility, since several members of the company are unknown to me, and, in regard to others, I have no way of knowing their development except through newspaper reviews, which very often do not give a reliable picture.

However, I have supposed that Hjalmar will be played by Reimers. This part must definitely not be rendered with any touch of parody nor with the faintest suggestion that the actor is aware that there is anything funny about his remarks. He has a warm and sympathetic voice, as Relling says, and that should be maintained above all else. His sentimentality is genuine, his melancholy charming in its way—not a bit of affectation. Confidentially, I would like to call your attention to Kristofer Janson who, frankly, can be charming when he's talking the worse nonsense. This is a hint for the actor in question.

Gina, I think, could be acted well by Mrs. Wolf. But where can we get a Hedvig? I do not know. And Mrs. Sørby? She is supposed to be attractive, witty, and not at all vulgar. Could Miss Reimers solve the problem? Or can Mrs. Gundersen? Gregers is the most difficult character in the play as far as acting is concerned. Sometimes I think Hammer could do it, or perhaps Bjørn B. Old Ekdal can be given either to Brun or to Klausen; Relling perhaps to Selmer. I would prefer to get rid of Isachsen, because he always carries on like a strange actor and not like an ordinary man; but he might perhaps make something out of Molvik's few lines. The two servants must not be neglected. Pettersen could perhaps be given to Bucher, and Jensen to Abelstad, if he is not needed as one of the gentlemen at the dinner party. The guests! Simple supernumeraries cannot be used of course without destroying the whole act. And what about the merchant Werle? There is Gundersen, of course. But I do not know if he is capable of evoking what I want and in the way I want it evoked.

In both the ensemble acting and in the stage setting, this play demands truth to nature and a touch of reality in every respect. The lighting too, has its significance; it differs from act to act and is calculated to correspond to the basic mood that characterizes each of the five acts. . . .

To AUGUST LINDBERG

Rome, 22nd November 1884

[More than the other Scandinavian directors, Lindberg appreciated the theatrical richness of The Wild Duck. After reading it, he said, "I get dizzy thinking about it. Such great opportunities for us actors! Never before have we been faced with such possibilities." To the playwright he wrote, "With Doctor Ibsen's newest play we have entered virgin territory where we have to make our way with pick and shovel. The people in the play are completely new, and where would we get by relying on old theatrical clichés?" Preparing to put the play into rehearsal immediately, he wrote to Ibsen about some details of the staging and got the following reply.]

DEAR MR. LINDBERG: In reply to your inquiry I hasten to inform you that *The Wild Duck*, just like all my other plays, is arranged from the point of view of the audience and not from that of the actor. I arrange everything as I visualize it while writing it down.

When Hedvig has shot herself, she should be placed on the couch in such a way that her feet are downstage, so that her right hand holding the pistol can hang down. When she is carried out through the kitchen door, I have imagined Hjalmar holding her under her arms and Gina carrying her feet.

I lay much stress in this play on the lighting. I have wanted it to correspond to the basic mood prevailing in each of the five acts.

I am especially delighted to learn that you yourself are likely to take a part in the play. . . .

Hedda Gabler

To MORITZ PROZOR.†

Munich, *4th December* 1890.

DEAR COUNT PROZOR,—I at once reply briefly to the letter which I have just had the pleasure of receiving from you.

The title of the play is *Hedda Gabler*. My intention in giving it this name was to indicate that Hedda as a personality is to be regarded rather as her father's daughter than as her husband's wife.

It was not really my desire to deal in this play with so-called problems. What I principally wanted to do was to depict human beings, human emotions, and human destinies, upon a groundwork of certain of the social conditions and principles of the present day. When you have read the whole, my fundamental idea will be clearer to you than I can make it by entering into further explanations.

Before these lines reach you, you will probably have received forty-eight pages more from Copenhagen. And a few days later, the last sixty-four pages, together with the title-page and the list of characters, will come to hand.

† From *Letters of Henrik Ibsen*, trans. John Nilsen Laurvik and Mary Morison (New York: Duffield, 1908), 435–36.

Please present my respectful compliments to Countess Prozor,
and believe me to be—Yours most sincerely and gratefully,

HENRIK IBSEN.

To HANS SCHRØDER†

Munich, 27th December 1890

[Schrøder was still head of the Christiania Theater.]

. . . Hedda should undoubtedly be played by Miss Bru[u]n, whom
I trust will take pains to express the demonical basis of the character. I saw Mrs. Heiberg five years ago at the Bergen theater and
at that time I received a very strong impression of her natural
talents. But both for the sake of my play and herself I feel it would
be desirable that she not be assigned to a task that she could not,
at the present time, handle satisfactorily in several essential
areas. . . .

To KRISTINA STEEN

Munich, 14th January 1891

[Kristina Steen was an actress at the Christiania Theater.]

DEAR MISS STEEN: You have been good enough to send my wife a
letter, which on one particular point concerns me and therefore I
personally have wished to answer briefly.

Mrs. Wolf wishes to be released from playing the maid, Berte, in
my new play and feels that this part could be handled by any other
actress at the theater.

She is mistaken. There is no one else up there who could play
Berte in the way I want to have her represented. Mrs. Wolf is the
only one who can do it. But apparently she has not taken the trouble to read the play through attentively. Otherwise it seems to me
that she would have understood this herself.

Jørgen Tesman, his old aunts, and the faithful servant Berte together form a picture of complete unity. They think alike, they
share the same memories and have the same outlook on life. To
Hedda they appear like a strange and hostile power, aimed at her
very being. In a performance of the play the harmony that exists between them must be conveyed. And this could happen if Mrs. Wolf
takes the part. But only if she does.

Out of regard for Mrs. Wolf's good judgment I cannot seriously
believe that she considers it beneath her dignity as an artist to por-

† From *Ibsen: Letters and Speeches*, ed. Evert Sprinchorn (New York: Hill and Wang,
1964), 298–300. Reprinted by permission of Farrar, Straus and Giroux.

tray a maid. After all, I have not considered it beneath my dignity to *create* this good-natured, simple, oldish person.

Here in Munich this unassuming individual is represented by one of the foremost actresses of the Court Theater. And she embraces her task with love and interest. For besides being an actress, she is also an artist. I mean, she does not pride herself on "acting parts" but in creating real people from these fictitious roles.

An Enemy of the People is now being performed at the Burgtheater in Vienna. Among the many subordinate characters of the fourth act, there is a drunkard with only a few lines to say. This character, who disappears in the play, is portrayed by the great Gabillon,[1] well known throughout Europe. . . .

Autobiographical

Sketch of Childhood†

"At the time when, a number of years ago, the streets of my native town of Skien were named,—or perhaps rechristened,—the honor was done me of giving to one of them my name. At least report has said so, and I have been told of it by trustworthy travellers. According to their accounts, this street runs from the market-place down to the sea, or 'muddringen.'[1]

"But if this description be accurate, I cannot imagine why the street has come to bear my name, for in it I was neither born nor did I ever live. On the contrary, I was born in a court near the market-place,—Stockmann's Court, it was then called. This court faces the church, with its high steps and its noteworthy tower. At the right of the church stood the town pillory, and at the left the town-hall, with the lockup and the madhouse. The fourth side of the market-place was occupied by the common and the Latin schools. The church stood in a clear space in the middle.

"This prospect made up, then, the first view of the world that was offered to my sight. It was all architectural; there was nothing green, no open country landscape. But the air above this four-cornered enclosure of wood and stone was filled, the whole day long, with the subdued roar of the Langefos, the Klosterfos, and the many other falls, and through this sound there pierced, from morning till night, something that resem-

1. Ibsen neglected to mention, or perhaps did not know, that Ludvig Gabillon made a career of playing "bit" parts. In forty-two years he played 320 roles.
† This autobiographical sketch of his childhood was written by Ibsen for Henrik Jæger's *Henrik Ibsen, A Critical Biography*, trans. William Morton Payne (1888; reprint Chicago: A. C. McClurg, 1901), 18–24.
1. The word may perhaps be translated "mud-flats"—TR.

bled the cry of women in keen distress, now rising to a shriek, now subdued to a moan. It was the sound of the hundreds of saws, that were at work by the falls. When I read of the guillotine afterwards, I always had to think of these saws.

"The church was naturally the most imposing building of the town. At the time when, one Christmas eve near the close of the last century, Skien was set on fire through the carelessness of a servant-maid, the church which then stood there burned with the rest. The servant-maid was, as might easily happen, put to death. But the town, rebuilt with straight and broad streets upon the slopes and in the hollows where it lies, gained thereby a new church, of which the inhabitants boasted with a certain pride that it was built of yellow Dutch clapboards, that it was the work of an architect from Copenhagen, and that it was exactly like the Kongsberg church. I was not able at that time fully to appreciate these advantages, but my mind was deeply impressed by a white, stout, and heavy-limbed angel, with a bowl in his hand, on week-days suspended high up under the roof, but on Sundays, when children were to be baptized, lowered gently into our midst.

"Even more than by the white angel in the church, my thoughts were occupied by the black poodle who lived at the top of the tower, where the watchman called out the hours of the night. It had glowing red eyes, but was not often seen; in fact, it appeared, as far as I know, upon one occasion only. It was a New Year's night, and the watchman had just called 'One' from the window in the front of the tower. Just then the black poodle came up the tower steps behind him, stood for a moment, and glared at him with the fiery eyes,—that was all, but the watchman at once fell head foremost out of the tower-window down into the market-place, where he was seen lying dead next morning by all the pious folk who went to the early New Year's service. Since that night no watchman has ever called out 'One' from *that* window in the tower of Skien church.

"This incident of the watchman and the poodle occurred long before my time, and I have since heard of such things having happened in various other Norwegian churches, in the days of old. But the tower-window in question has stood prominently in my memory since I was a child, because from it I got my first deep and lasting impression. For my nurse took me up into the tower one day, and let me sit right in the open window, held from behind, of course, by her stout arms. I remember distinctly how it struck me to see the crowns of the people's hats; I looked down into our own rooms, saw the window-frames and curtains, saw my mother standing at one of the windows; I could even see over the roof of the house into the yard, where our brown horse stood tied near the barn-door and was whisking his tail. I remember that on the side of the barn there hung a bright tin pail. Then there was a running about, and a beckoning from our front door, and the nurse pulled me hastily in, and hurried downstairs with me. I do not remember the rest, but I was often told afterwards that my mother had caught sight of me up in the tower-window, that she had shrieked, had fainted,—as was common enough then,—and, having got hold of me again, had wept, and kissed and caressed me. As a boy, I never after that crossed the market-place without looking up to the tower-window. I felt that the window especially concerned me and the church poodle.

"I have preserved but one other recollection from those early years. Among the gifts at my christening there was a big silver coin bearing the image of a man's head. The man had a high forehead, a large hooked nose, and a projecting under lip; furthermore, his neck was bare, which I thought singular. The nurse told me that the man on the coin was 'King Fredrik Rex.' Upon one occasion I took to rolling the coin on the floor, and, as an unfortunate consequence, it rolled into a crack. I believe that my parents saw an evil omen in this, since it was a christening gift. The floor was torn up, and thorough and deep search was made, but King Fredrik Rex never again saw the light of day. For a long time afterwards I looked upon myself as a grave criminal, and whenever Peter Tysker, the town policeman, came out of the town hall and across to our front door, I ran as hurriedly as I could into the nursery, and hid under the bed.

"We did not live long in the court by the market-place. My father bought a bigger house, into which we moved when I was about four years old. My new home was on a corner, a little farther up town, just at the foot of the 'Hundevad' hill, named after an old German-speaking doctor, whose imposing wife drove a 'glass coach,' that was transformed into a sleigh for winter. There were many large rooms in this house, both up and down stairs, and we lived a very sociable life there. But we boys were not much within doors. The market-place, where the two biggest schools were situated, was the natural meeting-place and field of battle for the village youth. Rector Oern, an old and lovable man, ruled in the Latin school at that time; in the common school there was Iver Flasrud, the beadle, also an imposing old fellow, who filled the post of village barber as well. The boys of these two schools had a good many warmly contested battles around the church, but as I belonged to neither, I was generally present as a mere onlooker. For the rest, I was not much given to fighting as a boy. I was much more attracted by the pillory, already mentioned, and by the town hall, with its gloomy mysteries. The pillory was a reddish-brown post, of about a man's height; on top there was a big

round knob, that had been black at one time; it now looked
like an inviting and benevolent human face, a little awry. From
the front of the post hung an iron chain, and from this an open
bow, which always seemed to me like two small arms, ready to
grasp my neck with the greatest of pleasure. It had not been
used for many years, but I remember well that it stood there all
the time that I lived in Skien. Whether or not it is still there, I
do not know.

"And then there was the town hall. Like the church, it had
high steps. Underneath there were dungeon cells, with grated
windows looking into the market-place. Within the bars I have
seen many pale and sinister faces. One room in the basement
of the town hall was called the madhouse, and was really,
strange as it now seems to me, at one time used for the confinement of the insane. This room had a grated window like
the others, but inside the grating the whole opening was filled
by a heavy iron plate, perforated with small round holes, so
that it looked like a colander. Furthermore, this cell was said
to have served for the confinement of a criminal named Bran-
deis, much talked of at the time and afterwards branded. It
was also inhabited, I believe, by a life-convict, who had escaped, was recaptured, and flogged out on the Li market-
ground. Of this latter, eye-witnesses related that he danced
when he was led to the place of punishment, but had to be
drawn back to the lockup in a cart.

"In my boyhood Skien was a lively and sociable town, entirely
different from what it was afterwards to become. Many highly-
gifted, prominent, and respected families then dwelt, both in
the town itself, and on great farms in the neighborhood. These
families were mutually bound together by relationships, more
or less near, and balls, daytime companies, and musical assem-
blies followed one upon another in close succession, both summer and winter. Also many travellers came to town, and, there
being then no inns, the visitors stopped with friends and relatives. We nearly always had visiting strangers in our spacious
place, and especially at Christmas and fair time our rooms were
full, and open house the rule from morning till evening. The
Skien Fair came off in February, and it was a happy time for us
boys. We began to save up our skillings six months beforehand
for the jugglers, and rope-dancers, and circus-riders, and for
the purchase of honey-cakes in the fair booths. I do not know if
this fair did much for trade; I think of it as of a great popular
festival, lasting the whole week through.

"In those years not much account was made of the 17th of
May[2] in Skien. A few young men shot with pop-guns out on

2. May 17, 1814, the date of adoption of the Norwegian constitution.

Blege Hill, or burned fireworks; that was about all. I have an idea that this reserve in our otherwise demonstrative towns-people was due to consideration for a certain highly-esteemed gentleman, who had a country-seat in the neighborhood, and whose head was respected for various reasons.

"But it was all the merrier on St. John's eve.[3] This was not celebrated by all the people together, but the boys and the grown-up people grouped themselves into five, six, or more companies, each of which worked to collect the material for its own bonfire. From as early as Whitsuntide we used to go in crowds around the wharves and shops to beg tar-barrels. In this matter a peculiar custom had reigned from time immemorial. Whatever we could not get freely given us was stolen, without either owner or police ever thinking to complain of this sort of violence. A company could thus by degrees collect a whole stack of empty tar-barrels. We had the same time-honored right to old barges. Whenever we found them ashore, if we could succeed in getting one quietly away, and well concealing it, we thereby acquired the right of possession, or, at least, our claims were not contested. The day before St. John's eve the barge was borne in triumph through the streets to the place of the bonfire. A fiddler sat up in the barge. I have often witnessed and taken part in such processions."

What Ibsen has thus told us is sufficient to give an idea of the sort of impressions which his youth received. The sad and the heavy preponderate. The solemnity of the church, the cheerlessness of the lockup, the severity of the pillory, the terror of the madhouse,—these were impressions which were certainly capable of casting a shadow over the joyousness of youth, awakening seriousness and an early habit of thought, even when we take account of the opposing influences of Fair diversions and St. John's eve bonfires.

To MAGDALENE THORESEN.†

Rome, *3rd December* 1865.

MY DEAR MOTHER-IN-LAW,[1]—It has been my intention for long to write to you—for I can do it now. Until now I have never been quite myself in my relations with you, neither in personal intercourse nor in correspondence. My real thoughts and feelings always got ex-

---

3. Midsummer eve, June 23.
† From *Letters of Henrik Ibsen*, trans. John Nilsen Laurvik and Mary Morison (New York: Duffield, 1908), 90–94, 80–82, 204–05, 207–10, 217–19, 256–58, 322–23, 446–47.
1. Fru Magdalene Thoresen, the authoress, who became a widow just before Ibsen's marriage with her step-daughter, had settled in Copenhagen in 1861. She wrote there under her own name; her previous works had been published anonymously. *The Story of Signe* came out in 1864, and was very soon translated into Swedish, German, English, and Dutch. She took her subjects from Norwegian peasant life; and it was her ambition,

pressed wrongly; and, as I felt this, I shut myself in. But a time abroad such as I am now having makes many changes in a man, and in my case they have been for the better.

I am not going to tell you of my adventures and the sights I have seen; I could not do it satisfactorily; nor is it this that is of real importance. The eventful and significant thing for me has been that I have got far enough away from home to see the hollowness of all the lies that parade themselves in our so-called public life, and the despicability of that canting spirit that is glibly eloquent in talk about "a great cause," but has neither will nor ability nor feeling of duty when a great deed is called for. How often we hear good people in Norway talk with the heartiest self-satisfaction about Norwegian discretion, which is really nothing more than a lukewarmness of blood that makes the respectable souls incapable of committing a grand piece of folly. It is a well-drilled troop; that cannot be denied. The uniformity is in its way exemplary; step and time are the same for all. It is very different here, I can tell you! The man who has managed to retain and bring here with him a certain amount of human feeling, becomes keenly conscious that there is something better worth having than a clever head, and that is a whole soul. I know of mothers away up in Piedmont, women of Genoa, Novara, Alessandria, who took their boys of fourteen from school to send them with Garibaldi on his daring expedition to Palermo;[2] and, remember, it was not a case of saving their country then, but of realising an idea. How many of the members of our Storthing will do the same, I wonder, when the Russians enter Finmark? With us the impossible begins as soon as the demand exceeds what is expected of us every day of our lives.

My journey down here was by no means a pleasure-trip, I assure you. I was in Berlin when the triumphal entry took place. I saw the rabble spit into the mouths of the cannon from Dybböl, and to me it seemed an omen that history will one day spit in the face of Sweden and Norway because of their behaviour then.[3] Here, in Rome, I found all kinds of spiritual depravity among the Scandinavians. What will you think when I tell you that even Danish men and women sat among the Germans in the chapel of the Prussian Embassy on Sundays while the war was going on, and listened devoutly to the Prussian clergyman praying for the success of the Prussian

though she was of Danish birth, to be regarded as a *Norwegian* writer. In 1866 she went to live in Christiana; but after a hard struggle there for four years, was obliged, from financial considerations, to return to Denmark. In Copenhagen in the Sixties she was, we learn from reliable sources, still unable to appreciate Ibsen's gifts.

2. Giuseppe Garibaldi, Italian patriot and leader of the Risorgimento, liberated Sicily and Naples with only a thousand volunteers in 1860 [*Editor*].

3. In 1864 Austria and Prussia invaded Denmark, which was forced to cede Schlesvig, Holstein, and Lavenberg to the conquerers. Ibsen was indignant at the failure of the other Scandinavian nations to come to Denmark's aid [*Editor*].

arms in the just war against their enemy. But I assure you I have stormed and raged and put things into a little better order; for I am afraid of nothing here; at home I was afraid, when I stood in that clammy crowd and felt its wicked smile behind me. What tempts you to go to Norway? In Denmark there is so much that is good and beautiful even now. My little boy shall never, with my consent, belong to a people whose aim it is to become Englishmen rather than human beings. It often seems to me hopeless to work at a time like the present. Unless the spiritual life of the people has an endless future before it, it does not really matter whether the time granted is one year or a hundred. And my idea of Norway and Sweden is this—we have not the will to make the sacrifice when the time comes. We have nothing to rally around—no great sorrow, such as Denmark has; because our people lack the elevation of soul which is a condition of being able to sorrow. The downfall of the *state* would be regarded by our countrymen as the worst thing that could happen; but the downfall of a *state* cannot be a reason for sorrow; and the significance of the downfall of the nation they would not feel. Denmark will not perish as a nation; for as long as a people can sorrow, so long will that people live. I do not understand any one saying that Denmark is in a worse position than our other two countries. You may believe me when I say that this is not the case.

Have you not written anything lately? No poems? It seems to me you should be able to do so now. That most beautiful work, "The Story of Signe," we have here; when we meet again, I can talk to you about it. Until now there has always seemed to be a barrier between us. And this was undoubtedly what you meant when you said, at parting, that things would become different and better. I understood you so far even then; but you may be sure that I appreciate you now as you deserve, and have always deserved. But I had to get away from the beastliness up there before I could begin to be purified. I could never lead a consistent spiritual life there; I was one man in my work and another outside of it—and for that very reason my work failed in consistency too. I am aware that my present standpoint is in all probability only a transitory one, but I do feel solid ground under my feet. I have written a long dramatic poem this summer, which will be published by Hegel at Christmas-time. A copy will be sent you at once; do write to me when you have read it, and tell me exactly what you think of it. In the enclosed letter I ask Clemens Petersen[4] to review it, and to do so promptly; the Norwegian reviewers are inefficient.

* * *

4. Clemens Petersen, born 1834, was the chief Danish literary critic of the day. From 1857 to 1868 he wrote in *Fædrelandet*. In 1864, Hostrup the poet wrote of him that he was "one of the doctrinary æsthetes who do great injustice with their ready-made standards"; a remark the truth of which Ibsen proved when *Peer Gynt* appeared. [See p. 425.]

Of Rome it is impossible to write; one may describe it, but one always fails to convey what is best, what is unique about it. I work a great deal and stay in-doors. Susanna and Sigurd[5] roam about the city in all directions—now among the ruins, now in the museums and galleries. Everything here is stupendous; but an indescribable peace rests over it all. No politics, no commercial spirit, no militarism, give a one-sided character to the population; they are undoubtedly people who cannot do much and do not know much, but they are indescribably beautiful, and sound, and calm. I wish you could spend some time here.

Sigurd can read now: he reads legends and fairy-tales every day; but if you could send us a small Bible history with any one coming this way, I believe you would be doing a genuine good deed.

* * *

Farewell!—Yours most sincerely,

HENRIK IBSEN.

To BJÖRNSTJERNE BJÖRNSON

Rome, *28th January* 1865.

DEAR BJÖRNSON,—I am very anxious and troubled. About the middle of last month I wrote acknowledging and thanking you for the cheque for 100 specie-dollars (£22, 10s.) enclosed in your letter of the 4th of October. At the same time I took advantage of your kind suggestion in that letter, that I should let you know when I needed more money, to inform you that I should be penniless towards the end of the month. In fact, my money gave out before that; for my monthly outlay comes to 40 scudi,[1] and I had been obliged to borrow, to defray my expenses from the 1st of October until the arrival of the remittance on the 16th of October.

To this last letter of mine I have received no answer; and although I can imagine many reasons for delay on your part, such as your having been away from Christiania, or your having had difficulty in procuring the money, etc. etc., I am inclined to the belief that my letter has not reached you. In spite of my being kept in such suspense I am really glad if this is the case; for I must confess to you (supposing you not to have seen it) that the letter was written in an unamiable, bitter, and possibly too hopeless spirit, in so far as regards the affairs and the outlook of our country. I have regretted pouring out all that bitterness to you, instead of giving you bright descriptions of all the splendour here, which you have put me in a position to be ennobled and uplifted by. But I cannot keep myself from dwelling with sadness on the situation at home; nor was

5. Ibsen's wife and son [*Editor*].
1. Equivalent to about £8, 10s [about $500 today—*Editor*].

I able to do so during my whole journey. If I had stayed longer in Berlin, where I saw the triumphal entrance in April, with the howling rabble tumbling about among the trophies from Dybböl,[2] riding on the gun-carriages and spitting into the cannon—the cannon that received no help and yet went on shooting until they burst—I do not know how much of my reason I should have retained.

When you write, be sure to tell me what you think of the condition of our affairs? What direction are they likely to take? And what do you believe our leaders can accomplish with the present generation? It will be a comfort to me to hear. I know that you have hope and confidence, but I should like to know their basis. The possibility of our complete ruin often seems inconceivable to me, too. A state may be annihilated, but not a nation. Poland is not really a nation; it is a state. The aristocracy have their interests, the citizens theirs, and the peasants theirs—all independent of, or even antagonistic to, each other. And Poland has no literature, art, or science with any special mission for the world's advancement. If Poland is made Russian, the Polish people will cease to exist; but we Scandinavians, even if we were deprived of our apparent independence, even if our countries were conquered and our states disintegrated, should still survive as a nation. The Jews were both a state and a nation; the Jewish state is destroyed, but the nation still lives. What is best in us will, I believe, live thus—provided our national spirit has life enough to thrive in and on misfortune. But this is the great and decisive question. Oh, for faith and confidence; But now a truce to politics for to-day.

The beauty of the antique sculpture becomes more and more evident to me, as you predicted in your letter that it would. The perception of it comes in flashes, but such an occasional flash casts its light over vast areas. Do you remember "The Tragic Muse," which stands in the room outside of the rotunda in the Vatican? No statue that I have yet seen in Italy has taught me so much as this. I verily believe that it has revealed to me what Greek tragedy was. That indescribably great, noble, calm joy in the expression of the face, that richly wreathed head which has something supernaturally exuberant and bacchantic about it, those eyes, that look inward and yet through and far beyond the outward object they are fixed on,—such was Greek tragedy. The statue of Demosthenes in the Lateran, the faun in the Villa Borghese, and the faun (Praxiteles') in the Vatican (Bracchio Nuovo), have also given me a deep insight into Greek life and character, and have, moreover, helped me to understand what the imperishable element in beauty really is. Would that I could

2. The capture of Dybböl (German, Düppel) from the Danes was the most decisive event in the war of 1864.

bring this understanding to bear upon my own work. I had not seen Michael Angelo's "Moses" in San Pietro in Vincoli when I last wrote to you, but I had read about it, and constructed in my own mind something to which the reality did not quite come up; however, I have only seen it once.

How glorious nature is down here! Both in form and colour there is an indescribable harmony. I often lie for half a day among the tombs on the Via Latina, or on the old Appian Way; and I do not think this idling can be called waste of time. The Baths of Caracalla have also a special attraction for me.

* * *

To GEORGE BRANDES.[1]

Dresden, 20th December 1870.

* * *

At last they have taken Rome away from us human beings, and given it to the politicians. Where shall we take refuge now? Rome was the one sanctuary in Europe; the only place that enjoyed true liberty—freedom from the political liberty-tyranny. I do not think I shall visit it again after what has happened. All that is delightful—the unconsciousness, the dirt—will now disappear; for every statesman that makes his appearance there, an artist will be ruined. And then the glorious aspiration after liberty—that is at an end now. Yes—I must confess that the only thing I love about liberty is the struggle for it; I care nothing for the possession of it.

One morning, some time ago, my new work became strikingly clear to me; and in the over-welling joy of the moment I wrote you a letter. It was not sent; for the mood did not last long; and when it was over, the letter was useless.

The great events of the day occupy my thoughts much at present. The old, illusory France has collapsed; and as soon as the new, real Prussia does the same, we shall be with one bound in a new age. How ideas will then come tumbling about our ears! And it is high time they did. Up till now we have been living on nothing but the crumbs from the revolutionary table of last century, a food out of which all nutriment has long been chewed. The old terms require to have a new meaning infused into them. Liberty, equality, and fraternity are no longer the things they were in the days of the late-lamented guillotine. This is what the politicians will not understand; and therefore I hate them. They want only their own special revolutions—revolutions in externals, in politics, etc. But all this is

1. Brandes was at this time ill in Rome. [Note that "George" is a mistranslation of "Georg"—Editor.]

mere trifling. What is all-important is the revolution of the spirit of man; and in this you will be one of those who lead. But the first thing to do is to get rid of your fever.—Your devoted friend,

HENRIK IBSEN.

To GEORGE BRANDES.

Dresden, *17th February* 1871.

DEAR BRANDES,—I suspected that my long silence would make you angry; but I confidently trust that our relations are such that they will stand the strain. In fact, I have a decided feeling that a brisk correspondence would be a much more dangerous thing. Once we have actually met, many things will assume another aspect; much will be cleared up on both sides. Until then I really run the danger of exhibiting myself to you, by means of my casual remarks, in quite a wrong light. You philosophers can reason black into white—and I have no desire to allow myself to be reduced, per correspondence, to a stone or a cock—even with the possibility in view of being restored, after an oral explanation, to the rank of a human being.[1] In your previous letter, you ironically admire my undisturbed mental equilibrium under the present conditions. There we have the stone! And now in your last friendly (?) note, you make me out a hater of liberty. The cock! The fact is that my mind is calm because I regard France's present misfortune as the greatest good fortune that could befall her. As to liberty, I take it that our dispute is a mere dispute about words. I shall never agree to making liberty synonymous with political liberty. What you call liberty, I call liberties; and what I call the struggle for liberty is nothing but the constant, living assimilation of the idea of freedom. He who possesses liberty otherwise than as a thing to be striven for, possesses it dead and soulless; for the idea of liberty has undoubtedly this characteristic, that it develops steadily during its assimilation. So that a man who stops in the midst of the struggle and says: "Now I have it"—thereby shows that he has lost it. It is, however, exactly this dead maintenance of a certain given standpoint of liberty that is characteristic of the communities which go by the name of states—and this it is that I have called worthless.

Yes, to be sure, it is a benefit to possess the franchise, the right of self-taxation, etc., but for whom is it a benefit? For the citizen, not for the individual. Now there is absolutely no reasonable necessity for the individual to be a citizen. On the contrary—the state is the curse of the individual. With what is the strength of Prussia as a state bought? With the merging of the individual in the political

---

1. The philosophical "reduction to a stone or a cock" is to be found in Holberg's comedy, *Erasmus Montanus*.

and geographical concept. The waiter makes the best soldier. Now, turn to the Jewish nation, the nobility of the human race. How has it preserved itself—isolated, poetical—despite all the barbarity from without? Because it had no state to burden it. Had the Jewish nation remained in Palestine, it would long since have been ruined in the process of construction, like all the other nations. The state must be abolished! In that revolution I will take part. Undermine the idea of the state; make willingness and spiritual kinship the only essentials in the case of a union—and you have the beginning of a liberty that is of some value. The changing of forms of government is mere toying with degrees—a little more or a little less—folly, the whole of it.

Yes, dear friend, the great thing is not to allow one's self to be frightened by the venerableness of the institution. The state has its root in Time: it will have its culmination in Time. Greater things than it will fall; all religion will fall. Neither the conceptions of morality nor those of art are eternal. To how much are we really obliged to pin our faith? Who will vouch for it that two and two do not make five up in Jupiter?

These suggestions I cannot and will not enlarge upon in writing. My best thanks for your poem! It is not the last you will write; for the (poet's) calling proclaims itself in every line. That you overestimate me, I set down to the account of our friendship; and I thank you. Keep me ever so in your thoughts; I shall not fail you![2]

And now get strong again; and come to Dresden on two sound legs! That leg business—did you not feel as if there was a nemesis in it? You were once so furious with another philosopher because he stood on *two* legs. Thank God that you did not have to demonstrate the possibility of a philosopher's being able to do with *one*. I take it for granted that all danger is past, otherwise I should most certainly not jest on the subject.

I have as yet received only the First Part of *Criticisms and Portraits* from Hegel; but even if I had received the whole, I should have confined myself to thanking you heartily for the book.[3] I am an exceedingly poor critic. Concerning certain works I am unable to express myself; and what my general conception of you, as a complete personality, is, you already know.

I have been occupied almost night and day since Christmas, preparing for the publication of my collected poems. It has been an accursed business, having to go over all the many points of view which I had long ago done with. However, taken together, they

2. From the hospital in Rome, on the night between the 9th and 10th of January 1871, Brandes had send his poem, "To Henrik Ibsen," as an answer to the concluding words of Ibsen's letter of the 20th of December 1870.
3. Part First of Brandes's book, *Criticisms and Portraits*, was published in February 1870; Part Second, in April of the same year.

make something like a whole; and I am very anxious to hear what you will say about the book.

The thousand and one things which your letter might give occasion for writing about, I shall at present leave untouched. I must first learn if I may expect to see you here soon. Then we shall discuss both "Bishop Arius and the Seven Electors"; you shall see that it is not for nothing I have lived two years in the vicinity of Gert Westphaler's native land.[4]

Sincerest wishes for restored health and all that is good, from— Yours most sincerely,

HENRIK IBSEN.

P.S.—As soon as I come into possession of a fairly respectable photograph of myself, I will send you one; meanwhile accept the enclosed. I hope you will send one in return.

To GEORGE BRANDES.

Dresden, 24th September 1871.

DEAR BRANDES,—It is always with a strangely mixed feeling that I read your letters. They are more like poems than letters. What you write comes to me like a cry of distress from one who has been left the sole survivor in some great tract where all other life is extinct. And I cannot but rejoice, and thank you, that you direct this cry to me. But then, again, I become most anxious, when I ask myself: "To what will such a mood lead?" And I have nothing to comfort myself with but the hope that it is only a transition. You seem to me to be passing through the same crisis which I passed through in the days when I began to write *Brand*; and I am certain that you, too, will find the remedy which drives whatever is the cause of the disease out of the body. Energetic productivity is a capital specific.

What I chiefly desire for you is a genuine, full-blooded egoism, which shall force you for a time to regard what concerns you yourself as the only thing of any consequence, and everything else as non-existent. Now don't take this wish as an evidence of something brutal in my nature! There is no way in which you can benefit society more than by coining the metal you have in yourself. I have never really had any very firm belief in solidarity; in fact, I have only accepted it as a kind of traditional dogma. If one had the courage to throw it overboard altogether, it is possible that one would be rid of the ballast which weighs down one's personality most heavily.—There are actually moments when the whole history

---

4. "Arius and the Seven Electors" were among the stock subjects of conversation of Gert Westphaler, the hero of the comedy of Holberg, to which he gives his name.

of the world appears to me like one great shipwreck, and the only important thing seems to be to save one's self.

From special reforms I expect nothing. The whole race is on the wrong track; that is the trouble. Or is there really anything tenable in the present situation—with its unattainable ideals, etc.? The whole succession of human generations remind me of a young shoemaker who has forsaken his last and gone on the stage. We have made a fiasco both in the heroic and the lover rôles. The only parts in which we have shown a little talent, are the naïvely comic; but with our more highly developed self-consciousness we shall no longer be fitted even for that. I do not believe that things are better in other countries than in our own; the masses, both at home and abroad, are without all understanding of higher things.

And so I ought to raise a banner, ought I? Alas, dear friend! that would be much the same kind of performance as Louis Napoleon's landing at Boulogne with an eagle on his head. Later, when the hour of his destiny struck, he needed no eagle. In the course of my occupation with *Julian*,[1] I have in a way become a fatalist; and yet this play will be a kind of banner. Do not fear, however, any underlying purpose; I study the characters, the conflicting plans, the *history*, and do not concern myself with the *moral* of the whole— always assuming that by the moral of history you do not mean its philosophy; for that *that* will clearly shine forth, as the final verdict on the struggle and the victory, is a matter of course. But all this can only be made intelligible by practical application.

Your last letter on this subject did not cause me any uneasiness— in the first place, because I was prepared for such misgivings on your part; in the second, because I am not handling the subject in the way you assume.

I have received your book; and all I can say is that I never tire of reading it.

It is incomprehensible to me, my dear, good Brandes, that you can be despondent—you whose spiritual calling is unmistakable in a degree vouchsafed to few. What is the use of being despondent? Have you any right to be so? But do not think that I do not understand you perfectly.

Oblige me by forwarding enclosed visiting cards to Dr. Fr. Knudtzon, Amalie Street; and should you happen to meet him, remember me to him; I have in many ways a very high opinion of him—and I may add that he has an enthusiastic and unbounded admiration for you.

And now, in conclusion, accept my best thanks for your visit to

---

1. The hero of Ibsen's world-historical tragedy, *Emperor and Galilean* (1873 [*Editor*]).

Dresden; those were festive hours for me. Best wishes for health, courage, happiness—everything good!—Yours most sincerely,

HENRIK IBSEN.

To GEORGE BRANDES.

Dresden, 30th April 1873.

DEAR BRANDES,—You certainly have good cause to complain of my negligence in letter-writing; but the fact is that my pen has scarcely been out of my hand since we saw each other last, except whilst I have eaten and slept. This must serve as my excuse.

My best thanks for the books. I have read *Ladislaus Bolski* with great interest, although I must say that the description you gave me of the contents of the book made even more impression upon me than the reading of the book itself.[1]

But now as to Stuart Mill's book![2] I do not know whether I ought to express my opinion on a subject in which I am not an expert. Yet, when I remember that there are authors who write on philosophy without knowing Hegel, or without even a general knowledge of German scholarship, many things seem to me permissible. I must honestly confess that I cannot in the least conceive of any advancement or any future in the Stuart Mill direction. I cannot understand your taking the trouble to translate this work, the sage-like philistinism of which suggests Cicero and Seneca. I am convinced that you could have written a ten times better book yourself in half of the time the translation must have taken you. I also believe that you do Stuart Mill gross injustice when you doubt the truth of his assertion that he got all his ideas from his wife.

You once remarked, when we were talking on the subject, that whereas German philosophy set itself the task of defining the meaning of things, English philosophy concerned itself with showing the laws of things. This remark made me desirous of reading something of what the English philosophers have written; but it does not seem to me that Stuart Mill has accomplished what, according to you, was his task. "Things" are surely not all kinds of fortuitous occurrences. A great deal of acumen may be contained in such a work; but if this is science, then *The Ethics of Christianity*[3] is also a scientific work.

I dare not enter into this subject further in writing; but some day, in conversation, I hope to defend my opinion.

I am looking forward with great pleasure to your book on the

---

1. The book here referred to is a Danish translation of Victor Cherbuliez's *L'aventure de Ladislas Bolski*, published in 1872, with a preface by George Brandes.
2. Brandes published, in 1872, a translation of John Stuart Mill's *Utilitarianism*.
3. *Den christelige Ethik*, a work by H. L. Martensen, a Danish bishop.

German Romantic School,[4] and with no less to meeting you again. But where are we to meet? I cannot possibly go to Munich this summer. Can you not travel *via* Dresden? About the middle of June I go to Vienna, to remain there until the end of July. If you can arrange your plans to fit in with this, I trust you will do so.

Our mutual friend, Adolf Strodtmann, has taken my poem, "The Signals of the North," amiss. In the preface to his book he called it a "Hohngedicht" (poem of scorn) directed against Germany. I wrote to him on the subject; but as he chose to remark, in his answer to my letter, that he had not imagined I wished them to remain ignorant in Germany of what I wrote in the Danish papers, I have had nothing further to say to him. Of course I have nothing against their knowing in Germany what I write in Denmark; but what I must protest against is the false interpretation of what I write. The poem is scornful, that is true; but it is not directed against Germany. There is too much in our own countries deserving of scorn and derision for me to go out of my way to deride the Germans. Now, no more to-day on the subject of Strodtmann's book, though I shall have a good deal to say to you about it when we meet.

Come soon! I look forward with joy to having you here in spite of all our differences of opinion. At all events, let me hear from you. I promise you to be more punctual in answering, since I have now much more time at my disposal.

With kindest regards from my wife and myself,—Yours ever,

HENRIK IBSEN.

To JOHN PAULSEN.

Amalfi, 20*th September* 1879.

*   *   *

But, dear Mr. Paulsen, is it of advantage for your training and development generally to remain so long in Paris? I cannot believe that it is. French literature you can study just as well elsewhere; and many other studies which are imperative, if you are to make your way in the profession you have chosen, can be pursued with much more advantage in Germany. You ought to go to Munich, and work hard there for a whole year, or even two—attending lectures at the University according to a fixed, well-considered plan. Nothing contributes so much to mature a man's mind as acquiring a thorough knowledge of some one subject. History would be the most suitable subject for you. You ought to make a thorough study of the history of civilisation, of the history of literature, and of the history of art; and there are particularly good professors in Munich

---

4. *The Romantic School in Germany*, vol. ii. of "Main Currents in Nineteenth Century Literature."

in these branches. An extensive knowledge of history is indispensable to an author; without it he is not in a position to understand the conditions of his own age, or to judge men, their motives and actions, except in the most incomplete and superficial manner.

Now, think over this, and if you can, come to Munich this winter. With kindest regards from all of us,—I remain, Yours very sincerely,

HENRIK IBSEN.[1]

To GEORGE BRANDES.

Christiania, 11th October 1896.

DEAR BRANDES,—I herewith briefly answer your questions.

1. I declare, on my honour and conscience, that I have never in my life, neither in my youth nor at any later period, read a single book of George Sand's. I once began to read *Consuelo* in a translation, but stopped immediately, as the story seemed to me to be the production of an amateur philosopher, not of a poet. But I read only a few pages, so that I may be mistaken in my judgment of it.

2. The above makes an answer to this question unnecessary.

3. To Alexandre Dumas I owe nothing, as regards dramatic form—except that I have learned from his plays to avoid several very awkward faults and blunders, of which he is not infrequently guilty.

My best thanks to you for taking the trouble to correct these French illusions![1]—Yours ever,

HENRIK IBSEN.

To GEORGE BRANDES.

Christiania, 3rd June 1897.

*   *   *

When I write of our meeting, I am not making use of an empty phrase. Can you guess what I am dreaming about, and planning, and picturing to myself as something delightful? The making a home for myself near the Sound, between Copenhagen and Elsinore, on some free, open spot, whence I can see all the sea-going ships starting on and returning from their long voyages. That I cannot do here. Here all the sounds are closed, in every acceptation of the word—and all the channels of intelligence are blocked. Oh, dear Brandes, it is not without its consequences that a man lives for twenty-seven years in the wider, emancipated and emancipating

1. Paulsen went to Munich in October 1879.
1. In an article on the new influences from Scandinavian literature, Jules Lemaître had maintained that Ibsen's ideas were all already to be found in George Sand's early novels and in the plays of Alexandre Dumas. Brandes protested in an article in *Cosmopolis* (January 1897), entitled "Henrik Ibsen en France."

spiritual conditions of the great world. Up here, by the fjords, is my native land. But—but—but! Where am I to find my home-land?

In my loneliness here I am employing myself in planning something new of the nature of a drama. But I have no distinct idea yet what it will be.

Now, in the first place, see that you get well again, and that with as little trouble as possible. And then, let us meet in the new home, with the Sound lying open before us.—Yours devotedly and faithfully,

HENRIK IBSEN.

To the Reader†

Christiania, March 1898

[As part of Ibsen's seventieth-birthday celebration, the first *volumes* of his collected works were published simultaneously in German and Danish editions in March, 1898. For the Danish edition Ibsen wrote a special prefatory note, which was later included in the German edition.]

When my publisher was kind enough to suggest the publication of a collected edition of my works in chronological order, I realized immediately the great advantages this would offer for a better understanding of my plays.

Simultaneously with the production of my works another generation of readers has grown up, and I have often noticed with regret that their knowledge of my more recent works was considerably more detailed than of my earlier ones. Consequently these readers lack an awareness of the mutual connections between the plays, and I attribute a not insignificant part of the strange, imperfect, and misleading interpretations that my later works have been subjected to in so many quarters to this lack of awareness.

Only by grasping and comprehending my entire production as a continuous and coherent whole will the reader be able to receive the precise impression I sought to convey in the individual parts of it.

I therefore appeal to the reader that he not put any play aside, and not skip anything, but that he absorb the plays—by reading himself into them and by experiencing them intimately—in the order in which I wrote them.

† From *Ibsen: Letters and Speeches*, ed. Evert Sprinchorn (New York: Hill and Wang, 1964), 330. Reprinted by permission of Farrar, Straus and Giroux.

CRITICISM

Peer Gynt

W. H. AUDEN

Genius and Apostle†

No genius has an in order that: *the Apostle has absolutely and para-
doxically an* in order that.

SØREN KIERKEGAARD

I

In such theoretical discussions concerning the nature of drama as I
have read, it has always seemed to me that insufficient attention
was paid to the nature of the actor. What distinguishes a drama
from both a game and a rite is that, in a game, the players play
themselves and, in a rite, though the participants may *represent*
somebody else, a god, for instance, they do not have to *imitate* him,
any more than an ambassador to a foreign country has to imitate
the sovereign whom he represents. Further, in both a game and a
rite, the actions are real actions, or at least, real to the participants—goals are scored, the bull is killed, the bread and wine are
transubstantiated—but, in a drama, all actions are mock actions—
the actor who plays Banquo is not really murdered, the singer who
plays Don Giovanni may himself be a henpecked husband.

No other human activity seems as completely gratuitous as "acting"; games are gratuitous acts, but it can be argued that they have
a utile value—they develop the muscles or sharpen the wits of
those who play them—but what conceivable purpose could one human being have for imitating another?

The fact that dramatic action is mock action and mimetic art completely gratuitous makes the dramatic picture of human life a peculiar one. In real life, we exist as bodies, social individuals and unique
persons simultaneously, so that there can be no human deed or act of
personal choice which is without an element of human behavior,

---

† From *"The Dyer's Hand" and Other Essays* (New York: Random House, 1962), 433–55.
Reprinted by permission of Random House, Inc., and Faber & Faber. Page references in
brackets are to this Norton Critical Edition.

what we do from necessity, either the necessities of our physical nature or the habits of our socially acquired "second nature." But on the stage, the kind of human life we see is a life of pure deeds from which every trace of behavior has been eliminated. Consequently, any human activity which cannot be imagined without its element of necessity, cannot be represented on the stage. Actors, for example, can toy with cucumber sandwiches, but they cannot eat a hearty meal because a hearty meal cannot be imagined taking less than three quarters of an hour to consume. Dramatists have been known to expect an actor to write a letter on stage, but it always looks ridiculous; on stage a letter can be read aloud but not written in silence. Nor can an actor do any serious piece of work, for real work cannot be imagined apart from the real time it takes. Only deeds can be divorced from real time. Thus, a man might write in his diary, "I began or I finished work at 9:15," but he would never write "I worked at 9:15"; (as a court witness he might say, "I was working at 9:15"); on the other hand, he might very well write, "At 9:15 I proposed to Julia and she accepted me" because, although his words of proposal and hers of acceptance must have taken a certain length of time to utter, this is irrelevant to the dramatic significance of the event.

Since human life, as the stage can present it, is, firstly, a life of pure action and, secondly, a public life—the actors play to an audience, not to themselves—the characters best-suited to drama are men and women who by fate or choice lead a public existence and whose deeds are of public concern. Worldly ambition, for example, is a more dramatic motive than sexual passion, because worldly ambition can only be realized in public, while sexual passion unless, like that of Antony and Cleopatra, it has political consequences, affects only a handful of persons. Unfortunately for the modern dramatist, during the past century and a half the public realm has been less and less of a realm where human deeds are done, and more and more a realm of mere human behavior. The contemporary dramatist has lost his natural subject.

This process was already far advanced in the nineteenth century and dramatists, like Ibsen, who took their art seriously, were beginning to look for new kinds of heroes. The romantic movement had brought to public notice a new kind of hero, the artist-genius. The public interest taken in figures like Victor Hugo, Dickens and Wagner would have been unthinkable two centuries earlier.

It was inevitable that, sooner or later, a dramatist would ask himself if the artist-genius could be substituted for the traditional man-of-action as a dramatic hero. A sensible dramatist, however, would immediately realize that a direct treatment would be bound to fail. An artist is not a doer of deeds but a maker of things, a worker, and work cannot be represented on stage because it ceases to be work if the time it takes is foreshortened, so that what makes an artist of interest, his art—aside from which he is not an artist but simply a man—will have to take place off stage. Secondly, the audience will have to be convinced that the figure they are told is a genius really is one, not somebody without any talent who says he is a genius. If he is a poet, for example, the poetry of his which the audience hear must be of the first order. But, even if the dramatist is himself a great poet, the only kind of poetry he can write is his own; he cannot make up a special kind of poetry for his hero, unlike his own yet equally great. Lastly, while deeds and character are identical, works and character are not; the relation between who an artist is as a person and what he makes is too vague to discuss. To say that Lesbia's treatment of Catullus and his love for her were the cause of his poetry is a very different thing from saying that Macbeth's ambition and the prophecies of the witches were the cause of Banquo's murder. Had both their characters been different, the poems would, no doubt, have been different, but their characters do not explain why Catullus wrote the actual poems he did, and not an infinite number of others which he might equally well have written but did not.

In order to become an artist, a man must be endowed with an exceptional talent for fabrication or expression, but what makes it possible for him to exercise this talent and for his public to appreciate it is the capacity of all human beings to imagine anything which is the case as being otherwise; every man, for example, can imagine committing a murder or laying down his life for a friend's without actually doing so. Is there, one can picture Ibsen asking himself, perhaps subconsciously, any figure traditionally associated with the stage who could be made to stand for this imaginative faculty? Yes, there is: the actor. Keats' famous description of the poet applies even more accurately to the actor.

> As to the poetic character itself, it is not itself: it has no self—it is everything and nothing. The Sun, the Moon, the sea, and men and women who are creatures of impulse, are poetical and have about them an unchangeable attribute—the poet has none: no identity.

Throughout *Peer Gynt*, one question keeps being asked and answered in various ways, namely, *Who am I? What is my real self?* For the animals, the question does not arise.

> What innocence is in the life of beasts.
> They perform the behest of their great creator.
> They are themselves.

The nearest human approximation to this animal selfhood is the "second nature" a man acquires through heredity and social custom.

> My father thieves,
> His son must steal.
> My father received,
> And so must I.
> We must bear our lot,
> And be ourselves.

So, too, with the drowning cook who gets as far in the Lord's Prayer as *Give us this day our daily bread* and then sinks.

> Amen, lad.
> You were yourself to the end.

Next comes the social "idiot" in the Greek sense, the individual whose life is as conditioned by one personal overriding interest as the conventional individual's is by social habit. In the first act Peer sees a young peasant cutting off a finger in order to escape conscription; Peer is fascinated and shocked:

> The thought perhaps—the wish to will,
> That I can understand, but really
> To do the deed. Ah me, that beats me.

In the last act he hears a funeral sermon about the same peasant in which the parson says:

> He was a bad citizen, no doubt,
> For Church and State alike, a sterile tree—
> But up there on the rocky mountain side
> Where his work lay, *there* I say he was great
> Because he was himself.

Neither of these human ways of being oneself, however, satisfy Peer. He tells his mother he means to be a King and Emperor, but there is only one kind of empire which nobody else can threaten or conquer, the empire of one's own consciousness, or, as Peer defines it:

> The Gyntian Self—An army that,
> Of wishes, appetites, desires!
> The Gyntian Self—It is a sea
> Of fancies, claims, and aspirations.

But the Peer we see on stage has no appetites or desires in the ordinary sense; he plays at having them. Ibsen solves the problem of presenting a poet dramatically by showing us a man who treats nearly everything he does as a role, whether it be dealing in slaves and idols or being an Eastern Prophet. A poet in real life would have written a drama about slave trading, then another drama about a prophet but, on the stage, play acting stands for making.

The kinship of the poet to the dreamer on the one hand and the madman on the other and his difference from them both is shown by Peer's experiences, first in the kingdom of the trolls and then in the asylum. The kingdom of dreams is ruled by wish or desire; the dreaming ego sees as being the case whatever the self desires to be the case. The ego, that is to say, is the helpless victim of the self; it cannot say, "I'm dreaming." In madness it is the self which is the helpless victim of the ego: a madman says, "I am Napoleon," and his self cannot tell him, "You're a liar." (One of the great difficulties in translating *Peer Gynt* is, I understand, that Norwegian has two words, one for the I *which is conscious* and another for the self *of which it is conscious*, where English has only one. *Myself* can mean either.)

Both the dreamer and the madman are in earnest; neither is capable of play acting. The dreamer is like the moviegoer who writes abusive letters to the actor he has seen playing a villain; the madman is like the actor who believes the same thing about himself, namely, that he is identical with his role.

But the poet pretends for fun; he asserts his freedom by lying— that is to say, by creating worlds which he *knows* are imaginary. When the troll king offers to turn Peer into a real troll by a little eye operation, Peer indignantly refuses. He is perfectly willing, he says, to swear that a cow is a beautiful maiden, but to be reduced to a condition in which he could not tell one from the other—that he will never submit to.

The difference between trolls and men, says the king, is that the Troll Motto is *To Thyself Be Enough*, while the Human Motto is *To Thyself Be True*. The Button-Moulder and the Lean One both have something to say about the latter.

> To be oneself is: to slay oneself.
> But on you that answer is doubtless lost;
> And therefore we'll say: to stand forth everywhere
> With Master's intention displayed like a sign-board. [132]

> Remember, in two ways a man can be
> Himself—there's a right and wrong side to the jacket.
> You know they have lately discovered in Paris
> A way to take portraits by help of the sun.
> One can either produce a straightforward picture,
> Or else what is known as a negative one.
> In the latter the lights and the shades are reversed. [136]

But suppose there is such a thing as a poetic vocation or, in terms of Ibsen's play, a theatrical vocation; how do their words apply? If a

man can be called to be an actor, then the only way he can be
"true" to himself is by "acting," that is to say, pretending to be what
he is not. The dreamer and the madman are "enough" to themselves because they are unaware that anything exists except their
own desires and hallucinations; the poet is "enough" to himself in
the sense that, while knowing that others exist, as a poet he does
without them. Outside Norway, Peer has no serious relations with
others, male or female. On the subject of friendship, Ibsen once
wrote to Georg Brandes:

> Friends are a costly luxury, and when one invests one's capital
> in a mission in life, one cannot afford to have friends. The ex-
> pensiveness of friendship does not lie in what one does for
> one's friends, but in what, out of regard for them, one leaves
> undone. This means the crushing of many an intellectual
> germ.

But every poet is also a human being, distinguishable from what he
makes, and through Peer's relations to Ase and Solveig, Ibsen is trying to show us, I believe, what kind of person is likely to become a
poet—assuming, of course, that he has the necessary talent. According to Ibsen, the predisposing factors in childhood are, first, an
isolation from the social group—owing to his father's drunkenness
and spendthrift habits, he is looked down on by the neighbors—
and second, a playmate who stimulates and shares his imaginative
life—a role played by his mother.

> Ay, you must know that my husband, he drank,
> Wasted and trampled our gear under foot.
> And meanwhile at home there sat Peerkin and I—
> The best we could do was to try to forget. . . .
> Some take to brandy, and others to lies;
> And we—why, we took to fairy-tales. [32]

It is not too fanciful, I believe, to think of laboring as a neuter activity, doing as masculine, and making as feminine. All fabrication
is an imitation of motherhood and, whenever we have information
about the childhood of an artist, it reveals a closer bond with his
mother than with his father: in a poet's development, the phrase
The milk of the Word is not a mere figure of speech.

   In their games together, it is the son who takes the initiative and
the mother who seems the younger, adoring child. Ase dies and be-
queaths to Solveig, the young virgin, the role of being Peer's Muse.
If the play were a straight realistic drama, Peer's treatment of
Solveig would bear the obvious psychoanalytic explanation—
namely, that he suffers from a mother-fixation which forbids any serious sexual relation: he cannot love any women with whom he
sleeps. But the play is a parable and, parabolically, the mother-child

relationship has, I believe, another significance: it stands for the kind of love that is unaffected by time and remains unchanged by any act of the partners. Many poets, it would seem, do their best work when they are "in love," but the psychological condition of being "in love" is incompatible with a sustained historical relationship like marriage. The poet's Muse must either be dead like Dante's Beatrice, or far away like Peer's Solveig, or keep on being reincarnated in one lady after another. Ase's devotion gives Peer his initial courage to be a poet and live without an identity of his own, Solveig gives him the courage to continue to the end. When at the end of the play he asks her, "Where is the real Peer?"—the human being as distinct from his poetic function—she answers, "In my faith, in my hope, in my love." This is an echo of his own belief. Ibsen leaves in doubt the question whether this faith is justified or not. It may be that, after all, the poet must pay for his vocation by ending in the casting-ladle. But Peer has so far been lucky: "He had women behind him."

The insoluble difficulty about the artist as a dramatic character is that, since his relations with others are either momentary or timeless, he makes any coherent plot impossible. *Peer Gynt* is a fascinating play, but one cannot say its structure is satisfying. Practically the whole of the drama (and nearly all of the best scenes) is a Prologue and an Epilogue: the Prologue shows us how a boy comes to be destined for the vocation of poet rather than a career as a statesman or an engineer, the Epilogue shows us the moral and psychological crisis for a poet in old age when death faces him and he must account for his life. Only in the Fourth Act are we shown, so to speak, the adult poet at work, and in this act the number of scenes and the number of characters introduced are purely arbitrary. Ibsen uses the act as an opportunity to make satirical comments on various aspects of Norwegian life, but Peer himself is only accidentally related to the satire.

II

Two years before *Peer Gynt*, Ibsen wrote *Brand*. Both were composed in Italy, and Ibsen said of them:

> May I not like Christoff in Jacob von Tyboe, point to Brand and Peer Gynt and say—See, the wine cup has done this.

The heroes of these two plays are related to each other by being each other's opposite. To Peer the Devil is a dangerous viper who tempts man to do the irretrievable; to Brand the Devil is Compromise.

Brand is a priest. Ibsen once said that he might equally well have made him a sculptor or a politician, but this is not true. In Rome Ibsen had met and been deeply impressed by a young Norwegian theological student and Kierkegaard enthusiast, Christopher Brunn. At the time Ibsen was very angry with his fellow countrymen for having refused to come to the aid of Denmark when Germany attacked her and annexed Schleswig-Holstein. Brunn had actually fought as a volunteer in the Danish army and he asked Ibsen why, if he had felt as strongly as he professed, he had not done likewise. Ibsen made the answer one would expect—a poet has other tasks to perform—but it is clear that the question made him very uncomfortable and *Brand* was a product of his discomfort.

Whether he had read it for himself or heard of it from Brunn, it seems evident that Ibsen must have been aware of Kierkegaard's essay on the difference between a genius and an apostle. In *Peer Gynt* he deals with the first; in *Brand*, which he wrote first, with the second.

*   *   *

A Doll House

BERNARD SHAW

A Doll's House Again†

A DOLL'S HOUSE. By Henrik Ibsen. Globe Theatre, 10 May 1897.
[15 *May* 1897]

At last I am beginning to understand anti-Ibsenism. It must be that
I am growing old and weak and sentimental and foolish; for I cannot stand up to reality as I did once. Eight years ago, when Mr
Charrington, with A Doll's House, struck the decisive blow for Ibsen—perhaps the only one that has really got home in England as
yet—I rejoiced in it, and watched the ruin and havoc it made
among the idols and temples of the idealists as a young war corre-
spondent watches the bombardment of the unhealthy quarters of a
city. But now I understand better what it means to the unhappy
wretches who can conceive no other life as possible to them except
the Doll's House life. The master of the Doll's House may endure
and even admire himself as long as he is called King Arthur and
prodigiously flattered; but to paint a Torvald Helmer for him, and
leave his conscience and his ever-gnawing secret diffidence to whisper "Thou art the man" when he has perhaps outlived all chance of
being any other sort of man, must be bitter and dreadful to him. Dr
Rank, too, with his rickets and his scrofula, no longer an example,
like Herod, of the wrath of God, or a curiosity to be stared at as vil-
lagers stare at a sheep with two heads, but a matter-of-fact completion of the typical picture of family life by one of the inevitable
congenital invalids, or drunkards, or lunatics whose teeth are set on
edge because their fathers have eaten sour grapes: this also is a
horror against which an agony of protest may well be excused.

It will be remarked that I no longer dwell on the awakening of the
woman, which was once the central point of the controversy as it is
the central point of the drama. Why should I? The play solves that
problem just as it is being solved in real life. The woman's eyes are

† From *Our Theatres in the Nineties* (London: Constable, 1932), 3:129–134. Reprinted by
permission of The Society of Authors, on behalf of the Bernard Shaw Estate.

471

opened; and instantly her doll's dress is thrown off and her husband left staring at her, helpless, bound thenceforth either to do without her (an alternative which makes short work of his fancied independence) or else treat her as a human being like himself, fully recognizing that he is not a creature of one superior species, Man, living with a creature of another and inferior species, Woman, but that Mankind is male and female, like other kinds, and that the inequality of the sexes is literally a cock and bull story, certain to end in such unbearable humiliation as that which our suburban King Arthurs suffer at the hands of Ibsen. The ending of the play is not on the face of it particularly tragic: the alleged "note of interrogation" is a sentimental fancy; for it is clear that Helmer is brought to his senses, and that Nora's departure is no clap-trap "Farewell for ever," but a journey in search of self-respect and apprenticeship to life. Yet there is an underlying solemnity caused by a fact that the popular instinct has divined: to wit, that Nora's revolt is the end of a chapter of human history. The slam of the door behind her is more momentous than the cannon of Waterloo or Sedan, because when she comes back, it will not be to the old home; for when the patriarch no longer rules, and the "breadwinner" acknowledges his dependence, there is an end of the old order; and an institution upon which so much human affection and suffering have been lavished, and about which so much experience of the holiest right and bitterest wrong has gathered, cannot fall without moving even its destroyers, much more those who believe that its extirpation is a mortal wound to society. This moment of awe and remorse in A Doll's House was at first lightened by the mere Women's Rights question. Now that this no longer distracts us, we feel the full weight of the unsolved destiny of our Helmers, our Krogstads, our Ranks and our Rank ancestors, whom we cannot, like the Heavenly Twin, dispose of by breaking their noses and saying, "Take that, you father of a speckled toad."

It may be, however, that this difference between the impression made by the famous performance in 1889 and the present revival is due partly to artistic conditions. On Monday last Mr Courtenay Thorpe accomplished the remarkable feat of playing Helmer in the afternoon and the Ghost in Hamlet in the evening, and doing both better than we have seen them done before. Mr Waring, our original Helmer, realized the importance of this most unflattering part, and sacrificed himself to play it. But he could not bring himself to confess to it wholly. He played it critically, and realized it by a process of intentional self-stultification. The resultant performance, excellently convincing up to fully nineteen-twentieths, was, as regards the remaining twentieth obviously a piece of acting in which a line was drawn, as a matter of self-respect, between Mr Waring and Mr Helmer. Nevertheless, it was badly missed when

Mr Charrington tried the part later on and achieved a record as the very worst Helmer in the world through sheer incompatibility of temperament. But Mr Courtenay Thorpe obliterates both records. He plays Helmer with passion. It is the first time we have seen this done; and the effect is overwhelming. We no longer study an object lesson in lord-of-creationism, appealing to our sociological interest only. We see a fellow-creature blindly wrecking his happiness and losing his "love life," and are touched dramatically. There were slips and blunders, it is true. Mr Courtenay Thorpe did not know his dialogue thoroughly; and when the words did not come unsought he said anything that came into his head (stark nonsense sometimes) sooner than go out of his part to look for them. And he succumbed to the temptation to utter the two or three most fatuously conceited of Helmer's utterances as "points," thereby destroying the naturalness that could alone make them really credible and effective. But it did not matter: the success was beyond being undone by trifles. Ibsen has in this case repeated his old feat of making an actor's reputation.

Miss Achurch's Nora is an old story by this time; and I leave its celebration to the young critics who saw it on Monday for the first time. It still seems to me to place her far ahead of any living English actress of her generation in this class of work—the only class, let me add, which now presents any difficulty to actresses who bring some personal charm to the aid of quite commonplace attainments. Here and there we have had some bits of new-fashioned work on the stage—for instance, Mrs Kendal's extraordinarily fine and finished performance in The Greatest of These, and Miss Winifred Emery's last serious feat of acting in The Benefit of the Doubt. These shew that Miss Achurch's monopoly is not one of executive skill, but of the modernity of culture, the mental power and quickness of vision to recognize the enormous value of the opportunity she has seized. In the eight years since 1889 she has gained in strength and art; and her performance is more powerful, more surely gripped, and more expertly carried out than it used to be; but it has losses to shew as well as gains. In the old days Nora's first scene with Krogstad had a wonderful *naïveté*: her youthfully unsympathetic contempt for him, her certainty that his effort to make a serious business of the forgery was mere vulgarity, her utter repudiation of the notion that there could be any comparison between his case and hers, were expressed to perfection. And in the first half of the renowned final scene the chill "clearness and certainty" of the disillusion, the quite new tone of intellectual seriousness, announcing by its freshness and coolness a complete change in her as she calls her husband to account with her eyes wide open for the first time: all this, so vitally necessary to the novel truth of the scene and the convincing effect of the statement that she no longer loves him, came with lifegiving naturalness. But these two scenes have now become unmistakeably stale to Miss Achurch. In the Krogstad one she plays as if the danger of penal servitude were the whole point of it; and she agonizes over the cool opening of the explanation with Helmer with all the conventional pangs of parting in full play from the first. This ages her Nora perceptibly. Physically she is youthful enough: Helmer's "squirrel" still dances blithely, sings unmercifully, and wears reckless garments at which the modish occupants of the stalls stare in scandal and consternation (and which, by the way, are impossible for a snobbish bank manager's wife). But Miss Achurch can no longer content herself with a girl's allowance of passion and sympathy. She fills the cup and drains it; and consequently, though Nora has all her old vitality and originality, and more than her old hold on the audience, she is less girlish and more sophisticated with the passions of the stage than she was at the Novelty when she first captivated us.

Mr Charrington's Rank, always an admirable performance, is now better than ever. But it is also sterner and harder to bear. He has very perceptibly increased the horror of the part by a few touches which bring and keep his despair and doom more vividly before the audience; and he no longer softens his final exit by the sentimental business of snatching Nora's handkerchief.

The effect of a performance of the Doll's House with the three most important parts very well played, and the economy of the mounting—which involves a disembowelled sofa—got over by intelligent stage management and a little judicious hiring and borrowing, is almost painfully strong. It is mitigated by the earnest but mistaken efforts of Mr Charles Fulton and Miss Vane Featherstone as Krogstad and Mrs Linden. Mr Fulton, invaluable at the Adelphi, struggles with his part like a blacksmith mending a watch; and the style of play which makes Miss Vane Featherstone so useful and attractive in the unrealistic drama produces, in a realistic part, exactly the effect that might have been expected. The flattering notion, still current in the profession, that anybody can play Ibsen, is hardly bearing the test of experience. Happily, the elements of strength in the performance triumph over all drawbacks. If The Wild Duck next week is as good as A Doll's House, the Independent Theatre (for which, as a small shareholder, I have a certain partiality) will have done very well.

*   *   *

ROLF FJELDE

Introduction to *A Doll House*†

Much—perhaps too much—has been written about the historic influence of *A Doll House* (1879) on the course of Western drama. Making its entrance when the theater was overrun with pseudo-Shakespearean costume pageants and well-carpentered French melodramas, it swept across the serious stages of Europe and America like a cleansing wind from the north. Appealing at first only to the few, often scheduled for special matinees labeled "Not for Children" to keep out the queues of mothers with pinafored daughters, its understated and revolutionary simplicity eventually carried the day in a thousand imitations by several hundred diversely derivative Ibsens, nearly all of whom lacked the transforming deeper purpose of their model. That purpose, his contemporary partisans were sure, was, through an exploratory operation on one complacent, middle-class home, to lay bare the anatomy of a marriage where the wife was no more than a legal infant and her husband's virtual slave.

Certainly, at the time the play was written, Ibsen had strong opinions on the subject of women's rights. In February 1879, when his proposal to the Scandinavian Club in Rome that its female members be granted equal voting rights was narrowly defeated, he made a blistering attack on the male majority, daring them to assert that women were in any way inferior to men in culture, intelligence, knowledge or artistic talent. Nineteen years later, however, in a talk before the Norwegian League for Women's Rights, he took the opportunity to place the matter in the larger context of the artist's freedom and the evolution of the race in general, stating in part: "I am not a member of the Women's Rights League. Whatever I have written has been without any thought of making propaganda. I have been more the poet and less the social philosopher than people generally seem inclined to believe. . . . My task has been the *description of humanity.*"[1]

As Ibsen's retrospective emphasis insists, details throughout *A Doll House* release their richer meanings only when freed from the compulsions of propaganda. Early in Act One, for example, when Nora displays her Christmas purchases—a sword for Ivor, a horse and trumpet for Bob, a doll and doll's bed for Emmy—feminists

† From *Henrik Ibsen: The Complete Major Prose Plays*, trans. and ed. Rolf Fjelde (New York: Farrar, Straus and Giroux, 1978), 120–22. Reprinted by permission of Farrar, Straus and Giroux.
1. See p. 435 in this volume [*Editor*].

might choose to focus on the convention-bound assignment of sex roles. Quite rightly so, for the playwright had merely claimed to be less, rather than not at all, the social philosopher. But since by Ibsen's definition to be a poet is most of all to see, we are meant to perceive more comprehensively in this the pattern of a self-fulfilling prophecy: Nora, the doll-child of her father, the doll-wife of her husband, unthinkingly transmitting her doll-identity to her own daughter. And by that generalizing of implication which *is* poetry, this small pattern implies a system, a certain authoritarian set of mind elaborated into a whole culture. Torvald, being a determinist, believes such patterns cannot, must not be broken. ("It's deep in your blood. Yes, these things are hereditary, Nora.") What Nora learns traumatically, through the sudden crisis of the action, is that if the alternative is an intolerable situation ("I've lived by doing tricks for you, Torvald"), then patterns—even those wherein we live and move and have our being—can and must be broken.

Thus, by poetic inference, we are shown that people whose lives are prose and whose actions will never be history, people who may have long been patronized and casually discounted, can pick themselves up out of comfortable humiliation and, by so doing, find unsuspected resources, a whole other personality even, within themselves. Aiming for such universality of reference, Ibsen titled his play *Et dukkehjem—A Doll House*, without the possessive *'s*. Torvald in his way is as humanly undeveloped, as much a doll, as Nora. It is the entire house (*hjem*, home) which is on trial, the total complex of relationships, including husband, wife, children, servants, upstairs and downstairs, that is tested by the visitors that come and go, embodying aspects of the inescapable reality outside. No character is superfluous in the design, nor negligible in performance.

For with this play, the second in the cycle, Ibsen's mature artistic method, his style of metaphoric realism, comes into its own, subsuming the well-made machinery evident in *Pillars of Society*. In that work, plot had, to some degree, manipulated character; from this point on, character, setting and idea generate plot. Through three consecutive acts the unchanging walls of the Helmers' apartment take on the figurative quality of a prison (only *Hedda Gabler* is as hermetically cut off from the outdoors and the natural world), and the sense of confinement works silently, increasingly, on both Nora and the audience to prepare the emotional logic of the final doorslam. Likewise Ibsen's dedication to realism, the meticulous care with which he built his characters stroke by stroke until, in his words, he had penetrated to the last wrinkle of their souls, is the outward correlative of another kind of caring. Since *A Doll House*, modern drama has delivered far more brutal, and brutalized, shocks to its audiences than a wife walking out on a husband and three

small children. The fact that Ibsen's play can still grip, stir and unsettle stems not so much from what happens as from the depth of
understanding from which its significance was artistically realized
and projected.

SANDRA SAARI

Female Become Human: Nora Transformed†

A little over a hundred years ago, in October 1878, the Norwegian
playwright Henrik Ibsen sat in Rome, sketching some ideas for
what he called 'the modern-day tragedy'. Those notes ran like this:

> There are two kinds of moral law, two kinds of conscience, one
> in the man and a completely other one in the woman. They do
> not understand one another; but the woman is judged in prac-
> tical life according to the man's law, as if she were not a
> woman but a man.[1]

Ibsen was contemplating a play in which the central character would
be a woman. This was his first attempt at creating a modern-day
female protagonist; her dilemma would issue from the disparity
between her innate sense of right and her society's laws. This idea
might have led to a modern-day Antigone, one in whom the sense of
duty was grounded in a specifically feminine conscience. However,
Ibsen's further notes indicate that this contemplated female protagonist would not have the requisite purposive vision to be a heroic
figure:

> The wife in the play finally doesn't know which way to turn in
> regard to what is right or wrong; innate feelings on the one
> hand and belief in authority on the other bring about a com-
> plete confusion.

Ibsen's notes continue to outline the conflict between two kinds of
moral law and conscience, between the feminine, with love as its
highest value, and the masculine, with its social and legal moor-
ings. The conflict leads to depression and loss of faith on the part
of the female. The notes conclude grimly: 'desperation, struggle,
and destruction'.

Although Ibsen wrote nearly an entire draft based on this idea of

---

† From *Contemporary Approaches to Ibsen*, ed. Bjørn Hemmer and Vigdis Ystad (Oslo:
Norwegian University Press, 1988), 6:41–55. Copyright © Universitetsforlaget, Oslo
1988. Reprinted by permission of the publisher. Page references in brackets are to this
Norton Critical Edition.
1. This and subsequent translations of Ibsen are mine, from Henrik Ibsen, *Samlede Verker,
Hundreårsutgave*, Vols. VIII and XV. The exception is 'Anitra's Song' from *Peer Gynt*.

a feminine soul destroyed by a masculine world, it turns out that he never did end up completing that play. During his eleven months of writing in Italy, something happened. The vision Ibsen had recorded so clearly in his notes and had worked out so carefully in much of his Draft became radically transformed. Rejecting the concept of two mutually unintelligible kinds of conscience segregated by gender, Ibsen ultimately embraced an entirely different fundamental premise. Retaining a female protagonist, he created a play based on the premise that, though they traditionally inhabit different realms of the social and legal world, males and females demonstrate no essential difference in their spiritual makeup. We cannot know precisely what caused this change; we do know it occurred in Italy. And we can trace the immediate effects, because they are recorded in the play that Ibsen ended up writing, the fair copy of which he mailed from Amalfi in September, 1879. The play is, of course, *A Doll House*.

What I propose to do is to trace in detail the major changes from the Draft to the Final Copy of *A Doll House*, to show by means of those trajectories of alteration Ibsen's revised perception of the nature of the masculine and the feminine, in order to demonstrate the radical transformation of Nora from female to human being.[2] I will conclude with one or two remarks about the relation of this fundamental change to Ibsen's residence in Italy.

Visually, the most striking change from the Draft to the Final Copy occurs in the dance scene that marks the climax of Act 2. Krogstad's blackmail letter revealing Nora's secret loan and forgery is in the mailbox. To prevent Torvald from reading it, Nora distracts him. In the Draft she sings a song, then dances a shawl dance; in the Final Copy she dances the tarantella. In both the scene serves the plot function of postponing the crisis. However, in terms of characterizing the relationship between Torvald and Nora, the scenes differ dramatically.

In the Draft, as Torvald heads toward the mailbox, Nora strikes familiar chords on the piano. Beguiled by the promised recital, Torvald equips himself and Rank with 'genuine Turkish cigarettes', then sits back to bask in Nora's rendition of homage to male magnificence—her singing Anitra's song from *Peer Gynt*. This song from Act 4 celebrates Peer as the holy Prophet himself. Sung by Anitra, a dancing slave girl, it begins:

> His steed is like milk, the purest white,
> That streams in the rivers of Paradise.

2. Though the characters are variously named in stages of the Draft, for the sake of simplicity I will use throughout the names from the Final Copy.

Bend your knee! Cover your face!
His eyes are stars, tender and bright.
No child of clay can endure
The rays of their heavenly fire.[3] [79]

The text elaborates this visionary appearance of the male whose brilliance so bedazzles the mere female mortal that her eye is incapable of beholding it. Like the stars, like the sun in whose wake is the night, the Prophet comes to enlighten and to fulfil. Singing this, Nora gives explicit voice to the theme of the male as lord and master of the universe, whose wisdom and dominion are absolute and to whom the female owes grateful and adoring devotion. Torvald's offering Turkish cigarettes and Rank's remark about Nora's singing, 'Turkish, but lovely, isn't it?', reinforce the comparison between a magnificent pasha's lordly relationship to a slave girl and Torvald's relationship to Nora.

Nora then dances with shawls. Torvald the connoisseur remarks to Rank, 'How lovely she is, Rank. Look at the delicate bending of her neck. What grace in her movements, and she is unaware of it.' Torvald takes aesthetic pride in this beauty of his, displaying Nora as his art object. Nora's lack of self-awareness, and thereby lack of self-possession, serves to increase his pleasure by increasing his definitive ownership. Underscoring this exhibition's being solely for male apprehension and appreciation, Nora comes over and, like a good little child, asks, 'Did you enjoy it?' 'Was it pretty?' Anitra's song and shawl dance in the Draft reinforce in verbal and visual terms the characterization of the relationship between husband and wife. Torvald is the all-knowing, adult authority figure, Nora the unself-possessed and adoring child.

As opposed to dancing attendance upon Torvald, in the Final Copy Nora does not sing and dance graceful obeisance. She dances the tarantella, a dance of her own self-expression whose increasingly wild execution displeases Torvald mightily. Far from beguiling Torvald by celebrating a hierarchical male-female relationship, the tarantella incenses Torvald by its abandon and deviation from his careful teachings. The folklore about the tarantella dance links it with the spider's poisonous bite, as either a cure or a consequence. Similarly in the play, the dance is the visual bodying forth of the fear of impending death that Nora cannot confide to anyone, but that she tries to stave off. The tarantella also serves as the first point in the play where Nora does not heed, at least in some superficial way, Torvald's commands. Unable to exert any direct control over her, he finally commands Rank to stop in order to force Nora

---

3. Rolf Fjelde's translation, Henrik Ibsen, *Peer Gynt*, 2nd edn. (Minneapolis: Univ. of Minnesota Press, 1980), p. 116.

to stop. With absolute bafflement he says, 'I would have never believed it. You have forgotten everything I taught you.' Exactly the opposite of reinforcing their hierarchical relationship, the tarantella is the visual embodiment of Nora's response to a reality that lies completely outside Torvald's tutelage.

While the substitution of the tarantella at the end of Act 2 alters to its diametric opposite the image of the husband-wife relationship, the off-stage introduction of the tarantella in Act 3 alters by a dramatic addition the characterization of Torvald. Of the two major changes in Torvald's characterization between the Draft and the Final Copy, the most vivid is the one linked to the tarantella: the addition of Torvald's sensuality.

The Draft of the first half of Act 3 differs markedly from the Final Copy. The party is a children's party, to which Nora has gone for the children's sake. Nora enters in an evening dress, having left the party early and alone. Torvald comes to bring her back to the party, inquiring why she left without even saying good-bye. Nora says she will return to fetch the children, that she can't stay long, but that Torvald should stay to dance. Later Nora and the nursemaid return with the children. Torvald arrives later, and, still having a couple hours' work to do before he goes to bed, encourages Nora not to sit up too long, but to get some rest.

In the Final Copy, Torvald displays none of this calm, self-controlled rationality that would lead him to do a few more hours' work. He initiated the departure from what is now an adult party, a mascarade ball, having pulled the reluctant Nora away as soon as she had danced the tarantella. Making impatient small-talk with Mrs. Linde, he says his reason for leaving was to enhance the artistic effect: '. . . she was a success; she was a tremendous success. Should I let her stay after that? To weaken the effect? No, thank you; I took my lovely little Capri girl, capricious little Capri girl, I should say—by the arm; a swift turn around the room; a bow to all sides, and—as they say in the novels—the beautiful vision vanished. A finish should always be effective, Mrs. Linde' [192]. Among other means, Torvald's attempt to represent himself as a man motivated by an exacting aesthetic sensibility is belied by the pulp novel cliché that informs his description.

But when Nora and Torvald are alone, another motive, at whose base lies something quite other than aesthetic demands, emerges. Approaching her, Torvald says, 'Hm,—it *is* grand to be back home by oneself again; to be completely alone with you.—Oh, you enchantingly lovely young woman!' **Nora:** 'Don't look at me like that, Torvald!' **Torvald:** 'Shouldn't I look at my most treasured possession? At all the magnificence that is mine, mine alone, mine wholly and completely.' Nora retreats to the other side of the table, saying,

'You must not talk to me that way tonight.' Torvald follows her, interpreting her commands as coyness: 'You still have the tarantella in your blood, I see. And that makes you even more seductive' [193–94]. After describing his fantasy of possessing in secret the young, innocent Nora, with 'that marvelous bend of the nape of her neck', Torvald presses to his conclusion: 'The whole evening I have yearned for nothing other than you. When I saw you chasing and luring in the tarantella,—my blood was boiling; I couldn't stand it any longer;—that was why I took you down here with me so early—' In the Final Copy, Torvald is far from maintaining the connoisseur's cool, aesthetic distance from which he can invite his friend to appreciate 'the delicate bend of her neck'. Here, Torvald's desired conclusion has a good deal more urgency than one could reasonably ascribe to strictly aesthetic urgings.

The significant point is that Ibsen is here depicting a male character, for the first time since Peer Gynt, frankly and openly motivated by sensuality. Rather than being reported as some past, dark secret, as in the case of Karsten Bernick in *Pillars of Society*, Torvald's champagne-heightened and tarantella-induced sexual promptings are represented on stage. And though Torvald's need to fantasize about a child-bride as his exclusive possession to bed underscores the serious failing of their male-dominated, hierarchical relationship, nevertheless his sensuality itself is not linked to any type of moral disapproval or social disgrace. It is represented as a perfectly normal male motivation.

Peer Gynt, the first play Ibsen fully conceived during his first residence in Italy, represented on stage male sensuality as a dominant motivation. However, the judgment by the mother, the community, and the play's very conclusion, about Peer's being thus motivated is repeatedly negative. It is only with his second residence in Italy that Ibsen represents sensuality as an acceptable aspect of male motivation in *A Doll House*. In the subsequent play also written in Italy, *Ghosts*, Ibsen traces as a major action the hard-won realization by the protagonist that her negative judgments about her dead husband's sensuality are wrong. But it is in *A Doll House* that Ibsen links the representation of male sensuality explicitly to Italy—with the tarantella dance. The description of Nora's off-stage dance as involving 'chasing and luring' and seductive refusal, identifies the mascarade ball version of the tarantella as the boldly flirtatious couples' dance whose effect is to release Torvald's sensuality.

The other major change in Torvald's characterization is the subtraction of any elements that might legitimize Torvald's claim to superiority. In the Draft, Torvald had obtained his new job at the bank by crusading against the present corrupt system in a pamphlet, in a series of newspaper articles, and in a pointed speech at the last general meeting. With the appointment, he sees his life's mission as increasing the public confidence in the bank by making a clean sweep, getting rid of unreliable employees such as Krogstad. In taking a public risk in pursuit of ethical goals, Torvald has a measure of heroic stature. In the Final Copy, all such heroic elements have disappeared. Torvald is an ordinary man who has received his new appointment by working hard and by only taking legal cases that would be certain to cast a favorable light on his reputation. He is not motivated by abstract ethical goals; his dismissal of Krogstad has nothing to do with eliminating untrustworthy employees. Krogstad's use of the familiar form of address is an intolerable embarrassment to Torvald, who seeks to maintain an immaculate public image.

Further, in the Draft a Pygmalian motif—the male as artist-creator, the female as art object-creation—articulates a position of superiority. Among Torvald's many reassurances, towards the end of Act 3, that he has forgiven Nora and still loves her, is this: 'Oh, aren't you precisely doubly dear to me now, after this? Aren't you now doubly mine, mine, wholly and entirely mine, my creation?' This Pygmalian motif was first implied with Anitra's song. After the song, Peer had gone on to play the Prophet, promising to create in Anitra enough soul to get her into Paradise, this goldly infusion of soul to occur in exchange for her ample physical favors being visited upon Peer. The motif is repeated with Torvald's proud demonstration to Rank of Nora's artistic beauty. And it is reinforced by Nora's catalogue of Torvald's insistence on her reciting monologues from plays they had seen and her dressing up in picturesque costumes. Nora gives a final echo to this motif when she tells Torvald that he forfeited her love 'when I could no longer look up to you as the lofty and superior one'.

In the Final Copy, the Pygmalian motif has disappeared. Nora is not Torvald's creation, she is simply his property. Torvald now says that when a husband has forgiven his wife, 'she has become, in sort of a double sense, his possession; he has brought her into the world anew; she is in a way both his wife and his child as well' [200]. The egotism of proprietorship replaces any potential claim to ethical or aesthetic superiority. This trajectory of Torvald's descent into mundane egotism is nowhere so clearly evidenced as in his ecstatic response upon Krogstad's return of the forged document. In the Draft Torvald says, 'Nora, you're saved'; in the Final Copy, 'Nora, I'm saved!' [199].

The two major alterations in the characterization of Torvald diminish his motivation by abstract reason and by aesthetic and ethical convictions, and add his motivation by sensuality. The result of these changes is a Torvald who responds to human rather than heroic promptings.

Notwithstanding that Ibsen makes radical alterations in the scenic shift with Anitra's dance of obeisance substituted by the tarantella's inner drive for life, and in the character shift with Torvald's aestheticism become sensuality, his public crusading become private fastidiousness, his role as creator become that of possessor; nevertheless Ibsen's most thorough-going and profound conceptual transformation from the original notes and Draft to the Final Copy is manifested in the shift of Nora's fundamental essence from female to human. In the Final Copy, Nora is 'first and foremost a human being'; her actions, thoughts, and ideals are *not* gender-specific.

Of the three major changes in the characterization of Nora, the most obvious is the elimination of her hysterical 'female' behavior. In the Draft, Act 2 is replete with Nora's increasingly distraught behavior as she is caught between Krogstad's blackmail threat if he is not reemployed and Torvald's refusal to reinstate Krogstad. Not knowing where to turn, she appeals to a higher power for a miracle: 'Oh God, oh God, do something to change Torvald's mind, so he won't provoke that horrible man. Oh God, oh God, I have *three little children*. Oh, do it for my little children's sake.' Her behavior displays a desperate distraction at the thought of her husband's learning the truth. She goes out to get some fresh air; within seconds she comes back, saying that she couldn't stand to stay out, that she had been overcome with such anxiety. Repeatedly she starts off to see the children, then stops in mid-step. She tells Rank about being so horribly full of anxiety as to be in complete confusion. With suicide in mind, she frantically denies thoughts of not being with her husband and becomes terror-stricken at the thought of not seeing her children grow up. She listens at the door, desperately trying to hear what Torvald and Rank are saying about her. Act 2 culminates with Nora keeping Torvald from the mailbox by threatening to jump out of the window. On the basis of this irrational, hysterical behavior, Torvald and Rank conclude, not surprisingly, that Nora is mentally ill. All the overt symptoms are there in the Draft. They are all eliminated in the Final Copy.

The second major change in the characterization of Nora is the addition of rational purpose to her childish behavior towards Torvald. Although the frequency of her wide-eyed, simple-minded behavior increases from the Draft, in the Final Copy these incidents are deliberately childish in order to conceal or to ingratiate. From the outset, Nora's lark-twittering, squirrel-frisking, carefree behavior is rendered less monolithic in the Final Copy by the addition of the concealed macaroons. In the Draft, Torvald chides Nora for frittering away even the money she earned at copy work. In the Final Copy, he patronizingly teases her about the cat having destroyed her efforts at surprise Christmas decorations; that in actuality she had been doing paid copy work is a depth he doesn't perceive. Nora, on the other hand, perceives very clearly in the Final Copy the depth of Torvald's male egotism and acts to safeguard it. Early in Act 1, she explains to Mrs. Linde why he hasn't been told of the loan: 'Torvald with his manly pride—how embarrassing and humiliating it would be for him to know that he owed something to me. It would entirely disrupt the relationship between us; our lovely, happy home would no longer be what it is now' [156]. In the Draft, like a child hiding something certain to anger the parent, Nora had concealed the loan because Torvald is so strict about such things and more than anything else in the world hates to be in debt'. Understanding, in the Final Copy, that he needs to feel completely in power, Nora employs deliberately childish behavior to wheedle Torvald, on-stage, into giving Mrs. Linde a job at the bank. In the Draft, she had 'pestered him' off-stage. Her feigned incapacity to conceive a mascarade costume adds yet another display of helplessness, which again she assumes to maneuver Torvald into a good mood, the better to entreat him on Krogstad's behalf.

That Nora in the Final Copy is fully aware of her practised self-effacement is evident in the exchange about Torvald's solution of the Neapolitan fisher-girl costume:

> TORVALD Yes, wasn't it a pretty good idea on my part?
> NORA Marvelous! But wasn't I also good to give in to you?
> TORVALD (*taking her under the chin*) Good—because you give in to your husband? There, there, you crazy little thing, I know perfectly well you didn't mean it like that. [174]

In spy-story terms, Nora has nearly 'blown her cover'. She is so desperately anxious to ingratiate herself with Torvald, in order to make him receptive to her renewed pleading for Krogstad, that she inadvertently lets slip a clue to her own inner identity. Because it is so discontinuous with his understanding, Torvald discounts the clue as meaningless. But it corresponds perfectly to the self-awareness Nora has already revealed to Mrs. Linde: that someday Nora might tell Torvald her big secret, that she borrowed money and thereby saved his life, someday, 'many years from now, when I am no longer as pretty as now. Don't laugh at that! I mean, naturally, when Torvald no longer feels as good about me as now; when he no longer gets pleasure from my dancing for him and my dressing up and reciting. Then it might be good to have something in reserve' [156]. Though naturally she would not like to think that the day of Torvald's lessening interest would ever come, nevertheless she takes comfort in having the 'insurance' of a heroic deed with which to counteract such an eventuality. Given her capacity to measure present actions against future outcomes, Nora is obviously not to be confused with 'the elfin girl dancing in the moonlight' that she tells Torvald, in the Final Copy, she will play for him. Far from the irrational, hysterical Nora of the Draft, the purposive Nora of the Final Copy deliberately adopts a childish and self-effacing posture towards Torvald in order to achieve her goals. The depth of Nora's revised character reveals a discerning and rational adult.

The third, and by far the most significant, change in Nora's characterization involves the identification of her thoughts and ideals as human rather than feminine. Whereas in the Draft Nora had a specifically feminine conscience, in the Final Copy the makeup of Nora's conscience is in its essence the same as that of the male characters. This change is brought about primarily by additions and alterations to the secondary male characters.

In the Final Copy, Nora's suicidal thoughts are the result of human, not feminine, desperation. Ibsen inserts a lengthy dialogue that explicitly establishes, not merely the similarity, but the actual identity, of Krogstad's and Nora's desperate thoughts.

> KROGSTAD —Therefore, if you are coming up with one or another wild resolution—
> NORA So I am.
> KROGSTAD —if you are thinking of running away from hearth and home—
> NORA So I am!
> KROGSTAD —or you are thinking of that which is worse—
> NORA How did you know that?
> KROGSTAD —then give up such thoughts.
> NORA How did you know that I am thinking of *that*?
> KROGSTAD Most of us think of *that*, at first. I thought of that too; but, Lord knows, I didn't have the courage—
> NORA (*flatly*) I don't either. [182–83]

In the Draft, Krogstad's suicide thoughts were dispatched in a single contemptuous speech: 'Bah, your life, your life. I also thought it was a matter of life and death when it caught up with me—but you can see for yourself that I lived through it.' The lengthy, point-by-point comparison of sympathetic dialogue in the Final Copy intertwines the male and female thoughts into a double-stranded chord of interwoven human despair. Though they are fierce antagonists, Nora and Krogstad reach a momentary communion on the basis of their common human experience.

Nora's ideas of love and death are likewise not characteristic of

gender. Ibsen's radical alteration of Rank's function in the play—
from being Torvald's confidant in the Draft, to being Nora's closest
friend in the Final Copy—serves to establish Nora's conception of
these fundamental issues as a human conception. Whereas in Act 2
of the Draft, Nora is filled with revulsion and leaves within seconds
of hearing about Rank's impending death, in the Final Copy Nora,
not Torvald, is the comforter to whom Rank confides his imminent
doom. In Act 3 of the Draft, Nora is the mute onlooker while Torvald and Rank discuss Rank's dying. In the Final Copy, the uncomprehending Torvald impatiently waits to be alone with Nora, while
Rank and Nora talk of laboratory tests and mascarades. Torvald's
patronizing remarks, 'Just look; little Nora talking about scientific
investigations!' and 'You little frivolous thing,—are you really thinking about the next one [mascarade] already!' [195], demonstrate
with dramatic irony his lack of awareness of the approaching death
of his boyhood friend. That these remarks are completely disre-
garded by Nora and Rank serves to underscore in the strongest
possible manner their sustained empathetic reverie on the human
confrontation of personal death. Rank's revised function as Nora's
'closest and truest friend' allows her thoughts and comprehension
of death to be portrayed as fully human.

Facing death is but one of the understandings of human experience shared by Rank and Nora. The other, more important in terms
of the play, is love. In terms of the shift in Nora's characterization
between the Draft and the Final Copy, this is Rank's most critical
specific function in establishing Nora as a human being. In the
Draft, Nora's concept of losing one's life for love is consigned to females and fantasy. Rank discounts as mere words Nora's idea that
Torvald, in his love for her, might not withstand losing her: '. . . in
most cases, something being the death of someone is in reality only
a figure of speech, at least as far as men are concerned.' When
Nora declares that she must perish, because otherwise Torvald will,
Krogstad brusquely responds, 'I don't believe in novels', thereby as-
signing her idea to a fictional world. Nor does Torvald say anything
in the Draft that would indicate that he ascribes to such a concept.
Nora's conception of love as the ideal for which one would lose
one's life is not a view of the real world from the male perspective
in the Draft.

In the Final Copy, love as the highest ideal is ascribed to by
males as well. Torvald verbally embraces this ideal several times,
the most memorable recital of which occurs in Act 3: 'Oh, Nora my
beloved wife; I feel I can't hold you close enough. You know,
Nora,—many times I've wished that an impending danger would
threaten you, so that I could risk life and limb and all, all, for your
sake' [197]. Such an explicit statement gives Nora the resolution to

have him read Krogstad's blackmail letter. Moments later, however, Torvald's actions reveal that this was sheer rhetoric, that preservation of public image is by far the higher value for him, and that, when he is at risk, such lofty sentiments are mere empty, foolish phrases.

It is Rank who provides the confirmation that Nora's conception of love is not simply a construct of the feminine mind, but is to be taken seriously as a human ideal. In the Final Copy of Act 2, Torvald cuts off Nora's entreaties for Krogstad's reinstatement with the reassurance that whatever happens, he, Torvald, 'is man enough to take everything on himself' [176]. Nora, horrified, interprets this as Torvald's willingness, out of love, to sacrifice his career and reputation to save her. Though earlier she had been entertaining thoughts of running away to avoid poisoning her children, she now sees that she must at all costs prevent Torvald's self-sacrifice. She is galvanized to action. Far from hysterical, she conceives of a rational solution to Krogstad's blackmail: she will pay off the loan and thus retrieve the forged note.

Despite his announcement of imminent death, Nora approaches her friend Rank with the intention of asking for the money that would prevent Torvald's self-sacrifice:

> NORA You know how wonderfully, how indescribably much Torvald loves me; never for a moment would he hesitate to give his life for my sake.
> RANK (*bending toward her*) Nora,—do you think that he is the only one—?
> NORA (*with a faint start*) Who—?
> RANK —who would gladly give up his life for your sake. [180]

Since moments later Rank states explicitly that he loves Nora, it is not to avoid that overt statement that Ibsen has Rank repeat Nora's phrase. By reiterating, 'who would gladly give up his life for your sake', Rank gives witness to love as an ideal for which a male is prepared to give his life. In the Final Copy, Nora's highest value is not a mere figure of speech in the male world. Ideal love is a shared, supremely valued concept of the human conscience for Nora and Rank.

By her actions, Nora immediately testifies to the strength of this ideal of love. Interrupted by Rank's profession of love, Nora abandons her intention to ask him for the money, despite his repeated requests to be allowed to do her a favor. She tells Krogstad that she has no solution for obtaining the money that she 'chooses to make use of' [182]. She finds instead the courage to choose suicide.

In his first notes for the play, Ibsen conceived of the conflict leading to complete confusion and finally to destruction. In the Final Copy, the conflict leads to Nora's clear, rational perception of reality and consequently to her rejection of the child-wife role. When the miracle doesn't happen, Nora is no longer willing to base her actions toward Torvald on the ideal of love. From the beginning of the play, Nora perceives that Torvald has faults such as egotism and jealousy, but, understanding that 'miracles don't happen every day', she discounts these faults as being superficial, not essential. There is good reason for her to interpret them thus. Torvald describes himself as having great inner strength in a crisis, and he explicitly espouses love as his highest value.

In the Draft, Nora says Torvald forfeited her love when she saw that he wasn't better than she was. In the Final Copy, she says he forfeited her love when the miracle didn't happen. 'The miracle', the approach of which Nora had already announced to an uncomprehending Mrs. Linde in Act 2, has the ring of unrealistic fantasy. But it is, in fact, a further development in the Final Copy, of Nora's ability to see things in a rational and ordered manner. What she means by 'miracle' is: an action in the real world that confirms beyond all doubt her belief that their marriage is based on the shared ideal of love, in particular, that Torvald loves her, as she loves him, above all else, above even life itself. When the miracle doesn't happen, when what happens is instead a disconfirmation of her belief, then she relinquishes her belief.

The disconfirmation is unarguable. Upon receiving Krogstad's first letter, revealing the forgery and blackmail, Torvald responds with unmistakable self-centeredness. He dismisses Nora's protestations of having done it because 'I have loved you above all else in the world', as mere 'idiotic alibis'. He berates Nora as 'a hypocrite, a liar, and, even worse, a criminal' [198], the social offense being for him the worst. He blames her father for her lack of proper upbringing, and her, for destroying all his own happiness, after all he has done for her. And it virtually goes without saying that he capitulates immediately to the blackmail and focusses all his concern on how to preserve appearances in the eyes of the world. There is never the slightest hint of any self-sacrifice to protect Nora. At Torvald's core is more of the petty egotism whose manifestations Nora had inaccurately interpreted as merely superficial.

But it is not this evidence Nora cites in describing what makes Torvald a stranger to her. He is someone with whom she is no longer able to associate herself because of his hypocrisy. 'After your terror was over', she says, 'and when all danger was past, then for you, it was as though nothing at all had happened. I was, precisely as before, your little songbird, your doll, about whom you had to be twice as protective from now on' [204]. If Torvald can complacently return to their former relationship, if his actions don't strike him as highly anomalous in view of his professed ideals, then all along his professed ideals were a form of hypocrisy, were mere superficial rhetoric and not the description of his essential self that Nora had taken them to be. If that which would make them equal in essence—the mutuality of ideal love—doesn't inform the husband-wife relationship, then the form—male-dominated, hierarchical—in fact turns out to be the essence of the marriage. If Torvald's first duty isn't to her, then Nora's first duty is to herself.

At the end of Act 2, Nora had 'danced herself free', to use Daniel Haakonsen's felicitous phrase,[4] in response to a reality that didn't conform to Torvald's instruction. At the end of Act 3, Nora has rationally thought herself into freedom from Torvald's interpretation of reality. She then sets out to define reality for herself.

Some time after the first time he had lived in Rome, Ibsen wrote what he considered to be his *tour de force*, *Emperor and Galilean*, in which he depicted the pagan world and the Christian world in historical conflict. When he came to live in Rome in 1878, he intended to depict the masculine conscience and the feminine conscience in a modern conflict. While in Amalfi, at some point in composing the Draft of the second part of Act 3, Ibsen must have begun to perceive that his fundamental premise of two radically different gender-specific natures was flawed. The last part of Act 3 bears a close resemblance to the Final Copy in its basic conception of Torvald and Nora. When, in the Draft, he penned Nora's words, 'I believe that I am first and foremost human', Ibsen had virtually arrived at his final conception. In revising, he had only to make her declaration even more explicit: 'I believe that I am first and foremost a human being, just the same as you are' [203].

I am guessing that what Ibsen finally saw in Amalfi—that he couldn't see in Germany, whose cultural patterns were similar to Norway's, and that he couldn't see in Rome, where his involvement with the Scandinavian circle kept familiar patterns before his eyes—was that Italian behavior was sharply defined along gender lines as well, but that the definition was notably different. Noticing that, he could have inferred that if gender behavior can differ so markedly by society, then much of what appears to be innate in gender behavior is actually a social construct. That could have led to the fundamental perception upon which he predicated the Final Copy of *A Doll House* and his subsequent plays: that the essential definition of a person is humanness, not gender, and that what cause things to appear otherwise are social constructs.

Nearly nineteen years after his completion of *A Doll House*, Ib-

4. *Henrik Ibsen: mennesket og kunstneren* (Oslo: Aschehoug, 1981), p. 191.

sen was invited to address the Norwegian League for Women's Rights. In what has often been taken as a disingenuous statement, he said that he hadn't deliberately been working for the woman's cause, that he wasn't even completely clear what the woman's cause really was. 'To me', he asserted, 'it has seemed to be a human being cause.' And he went on to describe his own work: 'My task has been the portrayal of human beings' [437]. Seen in the light of our investigation today, Ibsen's statement is a simple and accurate reflection of the fundamental alteration of perception he underwent in Italy when writing A Doll House.

The Wild Duck

J. S. WELHAVEN

Søfuglen (The Sea Bird)†

En Vildand svømmer stille
ved Øens høie Kyst;
de klare Bølger spille
omkring dens rene Bryst.

A wild duck floats serenely
along the steep isle coast;
the limpid waves are playing
about its pristine breast.

En Jæger gaar og bøier
sig i den steile Ur,
og skyder saa for Løier
det smukke Kreatur.

A hunter comes and crouches
against the rocky steep,
and just for sport shoots
the beautiful creature.

Og Fuglen kan ei drage
til Redens lune Skjød,
og Fuglen vil ei klage
Sin Smerte og sin Nød.

And the bird cannot find home
to the comfort of the nest,
and the bird will not bemoan
Its grief and its distress.

Og derfor taus den dukker
dybt i den mørke Fjord,
og Bølgen kold sig lukker,
og sletter ud dens Spor.

And so it plunges silent
deep in the murky fjord,
the cold wave on it closes,
and wipes out all trace thereof.

I Søens dybe Grunde
gror Tangen bred og frisk;
derunder vil den blunde,—
der bor den stumme Fisk.

Deep in the water's bottom
the sea weed flourishes;
there below it will slumber,—
there dwells the silent fish.

---

† From J. S. Welhaven, *Samlede Skrifter*, trans. Dounia B. Christiani (København: Gyldendalske Boghandel, 1867), 3:55. This 1839 poem by J. S. Welhaven, whom Ibsen admired, may have prompted the central metaphor of *The Wild Duck*.

RAINER MARIA RILKE

Letter to Clara Rilke†

29 RUE CASSETTE, PARIS VIe.
29 May 1906

* * *

* * * But the most remarkable part of this very long day was the evening. We saw Ibsen's *Wild Duck* at the Antoine. Excellently rehearsed, with a great deal of care and shaping—marvellous. Of course, by reason of certain differences in temperament, details were distorted, crooked, misunderstood. But the poetry! Thanks to the fact that the two female characters (Hjalmar Ekdal's wife and the fourteen-year-old Gina) were simple, without French frippery, all its splendour came from the inside and almost to the surface. There was something great, deep, essential. Last Judgement. A finality. And suddenly the hour was there when Ibsen's majesty deigned to look at me for the first time. A new poet, whom we shall approach by many roads now that I know one of them. And again someone who is misunderstood in the midst of fame. Someone quite different from what one hears. And another experience: the unprecedented laughter of the French public (albeit very low in the pit) at the softest, tenderest, most painful places where even the stirring of a finger would have hurt. Laughter—there! And once more I understood Malte Laurids Brigge and his northernness and his downfall in Paris. How he saw and felt and suffered it. * * *

MICHAEL GOLDMAN

Style as Vision: *The Wild Duck*, Child Abuse, and History‡

III

Produced in 1884, five years after *A Doll's House* had catapulted Ibsen into European recognition, *The Wild Duck* left many in its audience confused. Perhaps no play in the past two centuries had

† From *Selected Letters 1902–1926*, trans. R. F. C. Hull (London: Quartet Books, 1988), 93–96.
‡ From *Ibsen: The Dramaturgy of Fear* (New York: Columbia University Press, 1999), 78–91. Reprinted by permission of Columbia University Press. Page references in brackets are to this Norton Critical Edition.

so disconcertingly mixed comedy with painful emotional content. Equally disconcerting was the way it directed much of its mockery at a figure who seemed to embody Ibsen's own presumed zeal for social reform. Gregers Werle, the rebellious son of a rich business-man, attaches himself to the family of his old friend, Hjalmar Ek-dal, urging them to follow a program of honesty and truth in all things, especially their own relationships. Gregers's bungling efforts to persuade the vain and self-dramatizing Hjalmar to follow his "summons to the ideal" would seem comical except that they lead to the suicide of Hjalmar's beloved, if carelessly exploited daughter, Hedvig. Bewildered by Gregers's insistence that she sacrifice her pet wild duck to prove her love for her father, the fourteen year old turns the pistol on herself.

The Wild Duck abounds with references to sight and seeing. We are frequently reminded that the Ekdal family's living room, where most of the action takes place, doubles as a photographic studio. The reference to photography has seemed to many to suggest the superior accuracy of realism, and Ibsen did at one point refer to himself as a photographer but the emphasis is much less on the re-ality of what is seen than on distortions of the visual process. Hed-vig Ekdal may have inherited her weak eyes from Gregers's father, for old Werle was her mother's lover, but it is Hjalmar who endan-gers her sight by allowing her to take over his work retouching pho-tographs. As in his earlier plays, Ibsen makes the movement of the plot feel initially like a movement to enlightenment, but, even more deeply than in *Ghosts*, the enlightenment, when it appears, proves ambiguous. * * * In *The Wild Duck* it is not clear whether any-thing has been discovered at all. A child is destroyed, and the com-peting "insights" offered at the play's end are no less fictive and distorted than the confused symbolic identifications that have driven her to suicide.

The method of the play becomes clear if we try to express its ac-tion in terms of a spine. It will be recalled that a spine, as we have defined it, is a single infinitive phrase, the more concrete the better, which describes with equal accuracy the dominant motivation or "through-line" of each of a play's major characters. To my mind, the most concrete infinitive phrase that can be accurately applied to all the characters in *The Wild Duck* is *to make the picture come out right*—to adjust reality so that it "looks good," as when one re-touches a photograph.

Though its hero is a photographer, we never actually see anyone take a picture in *The Wild Duck*. Instead we witness a few brief, cranky discussions of the business side of photography, one mo-mentary evocation of the social ambiguity of the photographer's position (Is Hjalmar being patronized at Werle's dinner?) and a single encounter with a photographic subject—significantly, the customers are invisible and are being assured by his wife, Gina, that they will receive their pictures soon, which stresses the gap between taking and making the picture. Above all, however, we see the work that seems to fill the gap, the work of retouching. So photography in the play is largely a matter of making the picture come out right, the way the customer wants or the photographer deems beautiful. That is the effort, the recurrent action, that the play's characters have in common, often with a quite literal visual component.

Hjalmar's occupation as a retoucher clearly extends to all the narratives by which he constructs and justifies his life. In the second act we see him telling the story of the dinner we have witnessed, so that what seemed painfully embarrassing in the first act now appears in a favorable light. His daughter and wife cooperate in this; indeed they work always to soothe him, to make him look good, to allow him a vision of himself as breadwinner, scientific genius, self-sacrificing father. Both Hjalmar and his father are given to grandiloquent, literary phrases that lend their lives an aura of romance and heroism. Gregers accuses his own father of trying to compose a false picture ("Tableau of father with son" [222]) but is equally guilty of trying to make a picture come out right in his portrait of Hjalmar as a man of unusual moral qualities. The sardonic Dr. Relling, with his theory of the "life-lie," claims to see a similar process of self-delusion at work universally, but even this theory allows Relling to retouch some unflattering features of his own existence.

There is an unusual amount of repairing, rearranging, and tidying up in the play. It begins, for example, with servants straightening up Werle's den for the party. We see Gina and Hedvig cleaning up their living quarters on several occasions (including at the end of act 2, where the sleeping Ekdal is carried off to bed), and the offstage mess she has to set to rights in Gregers's room is vividly described. To this may be added Hjalmar's careful piecing together of the document he has torn apart.

One important version of making the picture come out right is the composition of little playlets designed to reinforce some illusion a character wants to cherish. Gregers persuades Hedvig to kill the wild duck in order to convince her father that she loves him, and after the offstage shot rings out in act 5, Gregers and Gina join forces to convince Hjalmar of this scenario. But perhaps the most elaborate and pointed example of the process occurs immediately afterward, when Hedvig is brought in dead.

Here Ibsen gave careful thought to the composition of his own stage picture, as his direction suggests:

HJALMAR, GINA, *and* GREGERS *drag* HEDVIG *into the studio; her right hand hangs down and her fingers curve tightly around the pistol.* [284–85][1]

This arresting visual focus serves mainly to sharpen our awareness of the various interpretive operations directed *at* it, each to some degree self-serving, each an attempt to make the picture we are observing make the "right" kind of sense.

Hjalmar's first effort, not surprisingly, stresses his own importance: the child died out of love for him. But this presents him in too cruel a light, so he quickly shifts the emphasis to himself as the victim of a cruel god:

> And I drove her from me like an animal! And she crept terrified into the loft and died out of love for me! (*Sobbing*) Never to make it right again! Never to let her know—! (*Clenching his fists and crying to heaven*) Oh, you up there—if you *do* exist. Why have you done this to me?

Gina offers a simple religious explanation in terms of guilt:

> We just didn't deserve to keep her, I guess.

Molvik, who is drunk, turns to a theological cliché:

> The child isn't dead; she sleepeth.

They next turn from figurative to literal vision, from the moral to the visual aspects of the picture. Hjalmar offers a poetic impression:

> There she lies, so stiff and still.

Relling tries physically to change the effect:

> (*Trying to remove the pistol*) She holds it so tight, so tight.

Gina reasonably objects to this piece of retouching:

> No, no, Relling, don't break her fingers. Let the gun be.

We may remember how Hjalmar has irritably tried to touch up Gina's speech by getting her to call it a "pistol." Now Hjalmar and Gina bend their attentions to displaying the body in what they consider an appropriate manner:

> HJALMAR She should have it with her.
> GINA Yes, let her. But the child shouldn't lie displayed out here. She ought to go into her own little room, she should. Give me a hand, Hjalmar. [285–86]

And they carry her off to another setting, as they carried off old Ekdal at the end of act 2, leaving Molvik, Relling, and Gregers to con-

1. See also *The Oxford Ibsen*, vol. 5 (1961), p. 440.

tinue the battle over how to view her death. (From the point of view of accuracy and self-deception in seeing, it is interesting that during the scene with Hedvig's body, two of the characters on stage are drunk and two others are suffering from a hangover. Everyone in this scene is having difficulty trying to see straight.)

Broken up into its components like this, the threnos over Hedvig's body seems to highlight the savagely comic aspect of Ibsen's art, but the lament is poignant, too, and the pain, the tragic weight, derives from what underlies Ibsen's interest in *seeing* in this play.

In *The Wild Duck*, seeing is not so much a question of what is to be seen but of what is behind the eyes, of whose eyes one sees with:

> You've seen me with your mother's eyes. . . . But you should remember that those eyes were—clouded at times. [222]

As this speech of old Werle's suggests, "making the picture come out right" is not only a matter of hypocrisy or convenient self-deception. It rises from the cloudiest springs of human disposition, from our most crippling needs and passions. "Seeing" as a determinative activity, as a crucial component of agency, is subtextual—buried and alienated in its origins, doing its fatal work in secret. Just as the play, for all its humor, is not simply comic, so the drive to retouch is located by Ibsen not simply in the human comedy of saving appearances or in the relatively conscious motors of self-interest but in deep and deeply deformed sources of imagination and desire. A child is at the center of *The Wild Duck* because the adult efforts at retouching that shape its action are all linked to the volatile and distorted psychic life we bring with us from childhood.

We come to understand this in part through the childhood histories of certain characters—Hedvig, Gregers, Hjalmar—and we feel it through the powerful subtextual currents Ibsen requires of his actors, but we also experience it in our own visual efforts with the stage picture—notably with its most spectacular feature. For there is a major element in the stage set that is constantly changing its appearance, constantly distracting and teasing us with altering contours and valences. Huge, complex, partially obscured, located at the back of the stage where it cannot help being noticed but cannot fully be observed, the garret where the duck is housed in an artificial forest literally upstages the photographer's studio. It is at once ludicrous and romantically evocative.

What is usually forgotten in discussions of the stage set in *The Wild Duck* is the way it engages the audience, the way it arouses our own not always fully conscious activity as spectators. In this case, it is an activity particularly concerned with the effort to see. We do not simply *respond* to the loft room (as we do, say, to the fjord scene glimpsed at the back of the *Ghosts* set); we try to look at it. There are things there we cannot quite see but wish to see, even when we are supposed to be looking somewhere else. It is the most complex and subtle stage set ever devised, certainly without parallel in theatrical history at the time Ibsen created it. He suggests its complexity—its dynamic engagement with the audience—in the stage directions:

> *The doorway opens on an extensive, irregular loft room with many nooks and corners, and two separate chimney shafts ascending through it. Clear moonlight streams through skylights into certain parts of the large room; others lie in deep shadow.* [234]
> *Morning sunlight shines through the skylights. A few doves fly back and forth; others perch, cooing, on the rafters. Chickens cackle now and then from back in the loft.* [241]

Not only does the loft look different at different times of day—a feature it shares with the set as a whole, and on which Ibsen insisted in his discussions with the original producers[2]—but it keeps us looking and noticing. We see it in at least four different lights. It invites curiosity, theatrical wonder, mixed feelings. The irregularity, the nooks and corners, the moonlight and shadow evoke romantic associations but also an effort to peer into what is not clearly seen—in part because it is not clearly lit, in part because it is at the back, beyond our clearest view, in part because of the way the characters describe it. The birds and animals moving around in it (or even simply asleep, as we are told they are when we first see the loft) are both an attraction and distraction. We will look for them, strain to see them, glance away to follow their flight or movement even when something is going on in the foreground, some necessary question of the play on which we should be focusing. We forget what we should remember and remember what we wish to forget. It is a process something like thinking over one's personal history or trying to recover a dream—the uncertain, groping attempt to separate fantasy from memory.

The play of light and dark and of animal life off in the background, as we strain to see it, makes it mysterious, fascinating, "a world of its own" as Hedvig calls it. Yet at the same time the loft is associated with a sense of delusion, self-deception, failure, pathetic limitation. We are watching not bears in a forest but rabbits in an urban attic, a piece of ingenious yet amateur carpentry, filled with the cackling of chickens as well as the cooing of doves, a source of embarrassment as well as interest for Hjalmar and Gregers, something which, like all live animals in the theater, both heightens and

2. See his letters to H. Schroeder and August Lindberg, ibid.

threatens the illusion, an effect that reminds us simultaneously of theater-as-magic and theater-as-contraption.

Hedvig finds it a mysterious and wonderful world, and thus it is associated with the rich, volatile imagination of a sensitive adolescent on the threshold of sexual maturity. But it is also something her father has made, and though, as such, it is an escape from his responsibilities (we see him tinkering with it when he should be retouching photographs), at the same time it shows Hjalmar at his best, the little boy who loves constructing toylike mechanisms. And our involuntary engagement as spectators in this huge contraption implicates us in his escapism. Indeed why should we call it involuntary, since we have come to the theater, the place of such "realism" and ingenuity, of our own free will?

The attic, then, combines the shabbiness and deceit of theater with its transfiguring power. It operates as a kind of reminder of the mental life we bring with us from childhood—the imaginative background which, poisoned and enfeebled as it may be, continues to affect us through our adult life. One process that seems everywhere figured in *The Wild Duck*, that seems central to Ibsen's view of life and that perhaps becomes clear to him for the first time as he writes this play, is that of people coming up injured from the depths of childhood.

The primary examples of this process are, of course, Hedvig, Gregers, and Hjalmar, and part of the play's originality lies in the way it shows the two adults drawing on their own childhood injuries to damage the child fatally. To show us this—to make this kind of process visible for the first time onstage—Ibsen made new demands on his actors. We have already seen the kind of subtextual contact on which the pivotal scenes between Gregers and Hedvig depend.

We must not forget that, like Hedvig, Gregers is also an abused child. As Ibsen says in his work notes for the play, Gregers "experiences the child's first and deepest sorrows—sorrows of family— everyday anguish of family life." Hedvig was the name of Ibsen's sister, the one member of his family to whom he felt close. And he has given to Hedvig many details from his own childhood experience, especially of the fantasy world into which he withdrew. In *The Wild Duck* she pores over the very books that fascinated Ibsen as a child. But in the play Ibsen has made her brother—made himself, that is—into a stepbrother, a twisted and vengeful character, responsible for a suicide which, like little Eyolf's a decade later, punishes a self-absorbed, sensual parent.

In the end Hedvig is particularly vulnerable because she has been brutally and inexplicably rebuffed by her father. To win back his love, she is ready to accept Gregers's suggestion that she kill the duck; the sacrifice of something so precious to her will convince Hjalmar that she loves him. Just before she fires the shot, she overhears Hjalmar say, "If I asked her then: Hedvig, are you willing to give up life for me? (*Laughs derisively*) Yes, thanks—you'd hear all right what answer I'd get!" [283] At that moment she kills herself. So Hedvig's death is the result of her father's selfish mixture of affection and indifference, of the intimacy Gregers establishes and then manipulates, of the sexual secrets and suspicions that circulate through her household.

But there is also a social dimension to her victimization. Exploited like many child laborers, she endangers her eyes (and thus becomes more isolated) so that Hjalmar may live in relative leisure. His sudden anger at her is heightened by his suspicion that he in turn has been exploited by the wealthy Werle. Indeed the fantasy world of the garret is a compensation for the Ekdals' descent in class, which has closed the forests to them and locked them in a shabby urban life. Gregers, moreover, sees himself as a social reformer (he began his career distributing pamphlets to his father's employees), but his projects become increasingly identified with the bitterness he has carried with him since childhood and with his fatal, unseeing assault on Hedvig's imagination.

With Gregers, as with all the characters, one gets the sense of two juxtaposed modes of action: the relatively conscious effort to adjust the picture—to reform, meddle, tidy up, arrange, and interpret life; and a more unconscious, as it were subtextual, stumbling or groping in the depths. There is a strong premonitory image of the second kind of action early in the play, at the end of act 1:

> GREGERS Look—your gentleman friends are playing blindman's buff with Mrs. Sørby. . . . (*Laughter and joking from the company, which moves into view in the inner room*). [223]

The image is not only memorable; over the course of the play it operates in a kind of time-delayed subterranean manner, its meanings shifting and looming, quite literally in the background. Physically it occupies the stage space that will become the garret room in the succeeding acts. The space has remained brightly lit and largely unoccupied for most of act 1, which now closes on the arresting picture of a dozen well-dressed, well-fed adults groping about blindly in a child's game in this large light-filled area. The audience, at this point, may tentatively assign the image a rather superficial satirical, socially "progressive" meaning, easy mockery of the local plutocrats. This might well be the way Gregers would see it, and we tend to see things with his eyes at this moment in the play. But the image carries more power than that. The light-filled room initiates a suggestion that will be heightened by both the duck and the garret and by what we come to share of the characters' lives. It will remain in the audience's memory, half-forgotten, perhaps disconcertingly remembered, and as we struggle with what are now its half-lit nooks and crannies, the memory of that brightly lit pantomime of blindness is likely to seem more poignant and prophetic. For if it is true that we all come up injured from the depths of childhood, we also retain something of childhood's magic—something of its wildness, expansiveness, mystery, authenticity, though in wounded or tainted form. Life for all of us is a blindman's buff, a child's game now played by clumsy grown-ups whose groping mocks and mimes the lonely bewilderments of childhood. And that is both the comedy and the pity of it.

Coming up from childhood we enter history—and *The Wild Duck*, with its class conflicts, reform pamphlets, new inventions, and Darwinian imagery, is full of references to historical process and the forces that drive it. In Gregers and Hedvig, ambiguously linked figures of reformer and victim, we see a tormented image of social action which will be increasingly explored in the plays that follow. * * *

Hedda Gabler

HENRY JAMES

On the Occasion of *Hedda Gabler* (1891)†

Whether or no Henrik Ibsen be a master of his art, he has had a fortune that, in the English-speaking world, falls not always even to the masters—the fortune not only of finding himself the theme of many pens and tongues, but the rarer privilege and honour of acting as a sort of register of the critical atmosphere, a barometer of the intellectual weather. Interesting or not in himself (the word on this point varies from the fullest affirmation to the richest denial), he has sounded in our literary life a singularly interesting hour. At any rate he himself constitutes an episode, an event, if the sign of

† From *The Scenic Art, Notes on Acting & the Drama: 1872–1901* ed. Allan Wade (New Brunswick, N.J.: Rutgers University Press, 1948), 243–60. Copyright © 1948 by the trustees of Rutgers College in New Jersey. Reprinted by permission of Rutgers University Press.

"Henrik Ibsen: On the Occasion of Hedda Gabler" appeared in the New Review, June, 1891, and was reprinted as the first part of the essay "Henrik Ibsen" in *Essays in London and Elsewhere*, 1893. The date at which Henry James made the discovery of Ibsen may be gathered from an unpublished letter to Edmund Gosse of January 29, 1889, in which he says: "I have perused your very interesting account of Ibsen, as I always peruse you when I find you. You must tell me more about I. That is not in this case female-American for me." A little later in the year came the first impact of Ibsen on the London stage (for two earlier attempts at adaptation had made no mark) with the appearance of Janet Achurch as Nora in *A Doll's House* at the Novelty Theatre on June 7. If Henry James was in London during that month it seems certain that his interest in Ibsen would have taken him to see the performance, which indeed made a considerable stir. Possibly he may also have attended a morning performance,

ten days later, of *The Pillars of Society* at the Opera Comique in which Elizabeth Robins played the part of Martha. It is, at any rate, certain that he accompanied Geneviève Ward to see a revival of the *Doll's House* at Terry's Theatre on January 27, 1891, in which Elizabeth Robins was playing Mrs. Linden. The next month, on February 28, *Rosmersholm* was played at the Vaudeville, with Florence Farr as Rebecca, and on March 13 the Independent Theatre, to which James was a subscriber, gave its celebrated performance of *Ghosts* in defiance of the Lord Chamberlain's veto. Finally, on April 20, came the production of *Hedda Gabler* by Elizabeth Robins and Marion Lea which formed the "occasion" of Henry James's essay. He wrote it, he says, six weeks after the production, so that it would have been finished by the end of May, and it was promptly published in the *New Review*, at that time still edited by Archibald Grove [*Allan Wade's note*].

such action be to have left appearances other than you found them. He has cleared up the air we breathe and set a copy to our renouncement; has made many things wonderfully plain and quite mapped out the prospect. Whenever such service is rendered, the attentive spirit is the gainer; these are its moments of amplest exercise. Illusions are sweet to the dreamer, but not so to the observer, who has a horror of a fool's paradise. Henrik Ibsen will have led him inexorably into the rougher road. Such recording and illuminating agents are precious; they tell us where we are in the thickening fog of life, and we feel for them much of the grateful respect excited in us at sea, in dim weather, by the exhibition of the mysterious instrument with which the captain takes an observation. We have held *Ghosts*, or *Rosmersholm*, or *Hedda Gabler* in our hand, and *they* have been our little instrument—they have enabled us to emulate the wary mariner; the consequence of which is that we know at least on what shores we may ground or in what ports we may anchor. The author of these strange works has in short performed a function which was doubtless no part of his purpose. This was to tell us about his own people; yet what has primarily happened is that he has brought about an exhibition of ours.

It is a truly remarkable show, for as to where *nous en sommes*, as the phrase goes, in the art of criticism and the movement of curiosity, as to our accumulations of experience and our pliancy of intelligence, our maturity of judgement and our distinction of tone, our quick perception of quality and (peculiar glory of our race) our fine feeling for shades, he has been the means of our acquiring the most copious information. Whether or no we may say that as a sequel to this we know Dr. Ibsen better, we may at least say that we know more about ourselves. We glow with the sense of how we may definitely look to each other to take things, and that is an immense boon, representing in advance a wonderful economy of time, a saving of useless effort and vain appeal. The great clarifying fact has been that, with *Hedda Gabler* and *Ghosts* and all the rest, we have stood in an exceptionally agitated way in the presence of the work of art, and have gained thereby a peculiarly acute consciousness of how we tend to consider it. It has been interesting to perceive that we consider the work of art with passion, with something approaching to fury. Under its influence we sweep the whole keyboard of emotion, from frantic enjoyment to ineffable disgust. Resentment and reprobation happen to have been indeed in the case before us the notes most frequently sounded; but this is obviously an accident, not impairing the value of the illustration, the essence of which is that our critical temper remains exactly the *naïf* critical temper, the temper of the spectators in the gallery of the theatre who howl at the villain of the play.

It has been the degree in general, of the agitation that has been remarkable in the case before us, as may conveniently be gathered from a glance at the invaluable catalogue of denouncements drawn up by Mr. William Archer after perusal of the articles lately dedicated by the principal London journals to a couple of representations of Ibsen; that, if I mistake not, of *Ghosts* and that of *Rosmersholm*. This catalogue is a precious document, one of those things that the attentive spirit would not willingly let die. It is a thing, at any rate, to be kept long under one's hand, as a mine of suggestion and reference; for it illuminates, in this matter of the study of Ibsen, the second characteristic of our emotion (the first as I have mentioned, being its peculiar intensity): the fact that that emotion is conspicuously and exclusively moral, one of those cries of outraged purity which have so often and so pathetically resounded through the Anglo-Saxon world.

We have studied our author, it must be admitted, under difficulties, for it is impossible to read him without perceiving that merely book in hand we but half know him—he addresses himself so substantially to representation. This quickens immensely our consideration for him, since in proportion as we become conscious that he has mastered an exceedingly difficult form are we naturally reluctant, in honour, to judge him unaccompanied by its advantages, by the benefit of his full intention. Considering how much Ibsen has been talked about in England and America, he has been lamentably little seen and heard. Until *Hedda Gabler* was produced in London six weeks ago, there had been but one attempt to represent its predecessors that had consisted of more than a single performance. This circumstance has given a real importance to the undertaking of the two courageous young actresses who have brought the most recent of the author's productions to the light and who have promptly found themselves justified in their talent as well as in their energy. It was a proof of Ibsen's force that he had made us chatter about him so profusely without the aid of the theatre; but it was even more a blessing to have the aid at last. The stage is to the prose drama (and Ibsen's later manner is the very prose of prose) what the tune is to the song or the concrete case to the general law. It immediately becomes apparent that he needs the test to show his strength and the frame to show his picture. An extraordinary process of vivification takes place; the conditions seem essentially enlarged. Those of the stage in general strike us for the most part as small enough, so that the game played in them is often not more inspiring than a successful sack-race. But Ibsen reminds us that if they do not in themselves confer life they can at least receive it when the infusion is artfully attempted. Yet how much of it they were doomed to receive from *Hedda Gabler* was not to be divined till we had seen *Hedda Gabler* in the frame. The play, on perusal, left one comparatively muddled and mystified, fascinated, but—in one's intellectual sympathy—snubbed. Acted, it leads that sympathy over the straightest of roads with all the exhilaration of a superior pace. Much more, I confess, one doesn't get from it; but an hour of refreshing exercise is a reward in itself. The sense of being moved by a scientific hand as one sits in one's stall has not been spoiled for us by satiety.

Hedda Gabler then, in the frame, is exceedingly vivid and curious, and a part of its interest is in the way it lights up in general the talent of the author. It is doubtless not the most complete of Ibsen's plays, for it owes less to its subject than to its form; but it makes good his title to the possession of a real method, and in thus putting him before us as a master it exhibits at the same time his irritating, his bewildering incongruities. He is nothing, as a literary personality, if not positive; yet there are moments when his great gift seems made up of negatives, or at any rate when the total seems a contradiction of each of the parts. I premise of course that we hear him through a medium not his own, and I remember that translation is a shameless falsification of colour. Translation, however, is probably not wholly responsible for three appearances inherent in all his prose work, as we possess it, though in slightly differing degrees, and yet quite unavailing to destroy in it the expression of life; I mean of course the absence of humour, the absence of free imagination, and the absence of style. The absence of style, both in the usual and in the larger sense of the word, is extraordinary, and all the more mystifying that its place is not usurped, as it frequently is in such cases, by vulgarity. Ibsen is massively common and "middle-class," but neither his spirit nor his manner is small. He is never trivial and never cheap, but he is in nothing more curious than in owing to a single source such distinction as he retains. His people are of inexpressive race; they give us essentially the *bourgeois* impression; even when they are furiously nervous and, like Hedda, more than sufficiently fastidious, we recognise that they live, with their remarkable creator, in a world in which selection has no great range. This is perhaps one reason why they none of them, neither the creator nor the creatures, appear to feel much impulse to *play* with the things of life. This impulse, when it breaks out, is humour, and in the scenic genius it usually breaks out in one place or another. We get the feeling, in Ibsen's plays, that such whims are too ultimate, too much a matter of luxury and leisure for the stage of feeling at which his characters have arrived. They are all too busy learning to live—humour will come in later, when they know how. A certain angular irony they frequently manifest, and some of his portraits are strongly satirical, like that, to give only two instances, of Tesman, in *Hedda Gabler* (a play indeed suffused with irrepressible irony), or that of Hialmar Ekdal, in *The Wild Duck*. But it is the ridicule without the smile, the dance without the music, a sort of sarcasm that is nearer to tears than to laughter. There is nothing very droll in the world, I think, to Dr. Ibsen; and nothing is more interesting than to see how he makes up his world without a joke. Innumerable are the victories of talent, and art is a legerdemain.

It is always difficult to give an example of an absent quality, and, if the romantic is even less present in Ibsen than the comic, this is best proved by the fact that everything seems to us inveterately observed. Nothing is more puzzling to the readers of his later work than the reminder that he is the great dramatic poet of his country, or that the author of *The Pillars of Society* is also the author of *Brand* and *Peer Gynt*, compositions which, we are assured, testify to an audacious imagination and abound in complicated fantasy. In his satiric studies of contemporary life, the impression that is strongest with us is that the picture is infinitely *noted*, that all the patience of the constructive pessimist is in his love of the detail of character and of conduct, in his way of accumulating the touches that illustrate them. His recurrent ugliness of surface, as it were, is a sort of proof of his fidelity to the real, in a spare, strenuous, democratic community; just as the same peculiarity is one of the sources of his charmless fascination—a touching vision of strong forces struggling with a poverty, a bare provinciality, of life. I call the fascination of Ibsen charmless (for those who feel it at all), because he holds us without bribing us; he squeezes the attention till he almost hurts it, yet with never a conciliatory stroke. He has as little as possible to say to our taste; even his large, strong form takes no account of that, gratifying it without concessions. It is the oddity of the mixture that makes him so individual—his perfect practice of a difficult and delicate art, combined with such aesthetic density. Even in such a piece as *The Lady from the Sea* (much the weakest, to my sense, of the whole series), in which he comes nearer than in others—unless indeed it be in *Hedda Gabler*—to playing with an idea from the simple instinct of sport, nothing could be less picturesque than the general effect, with every inherent incentive to have made it picturesque. The idea might have sprung from the fancy of Hawthorne, but the atmosphere is the hard light of Ibsen. One feels that the subject should have been tinted and distanced; but, in fact, one has to make an atmosphere as one reads, and one winces considerably under "Doctor Wangel" and the pert daughters.

For readers without curiosity as to their author's point of view (and it is doubtless not a crime not to have it, though I think it is a misfortune, an open window the less), there is too much of "Doctor Wangel" in Ibsen altogether—using the good gentleman's name for what it generally represents or connotes. It represents the ugly interior on which his curtain inexorably rises and which, to be honest, I like for the queer associations it has taught us to respect: the hideous carpet and wall-paper and curtains (one may answer for them), the conspicuous stove, the lonely centre-table, the "lamps with green shades," as in the sumptuous first act of *The Wild Duck*, the pervasive air of small interests and standards, the sign of limited local life. It represents the very clothes, the inferior fashions, of the figures that move before us, and the shape of their hats and the tone of their conversation and the nature of their diet. But the oddest thing happens in connection with this effect—the oddest extension of sympathy or relaxation of prejudice. What happens is that we feel that whereas, if Ibsen were weak or stupid or vulgar, this parochial or suburban stamp would only be a stick to beat him with, it acts, as the case stands, and in the light of his singular masculinity, as a sort of substitute—a little clumsy, if you like—for charm. In a word, it becomes touching, so that practically the *blasé* critical mind enjoys it as a refinement. What occurs is very analogous to what occurs in our appreciation of the dramatist's remarkable art, his admirable talent for producing an intensity of interest by means incorruptibly quiet, by that almost demure preservation of the appearance of the usual in which we see him juggle with difficulty and danger and which constitutes, as it were, his only coquetry. There are people who are indifferent to these mild prodigies; there are others for whom they will always remain the most charming privilege of art.

Hedda Gabler is doubtless as suburban as any of its companions; which is indeed a fortunate circumstance, inasmuch as if it were less so we should be deprived of a singularly complete instance of a phenomenon difficult to express, but which may perhaps be described as the operation of talent without glamour. There is notoriously no glamour over the suburbs, and yet nothing could be more vivid than Dr. Ibsen's account of the incalculable young woman into whom Miss Robins so artistically projects herself. To "like" the play, as we phrase it, is doubtless therefore to give one of the fullest examples of our constitutional inability to control our affections. Several of the spectators who have liked it most will probably admit even that, with themselves, this sentiment has preceded a complete comprehension. They would perhaps have liked it better if they had understood it better—as to this they are not sure; but they at any rate liked it well enough. Well enough for what? the question may of course always be in such a case. To be absorbed, assuredly, which is the highest tribute we can pay to any picture of life, and a higher one than most pictures attempted succeed in making us pay. Ibsen is various, and *Hedda Gabler* is probably an ironical pleasantry, the artistic exercise of a mind saturated with the vision of human infirmities; saturated, above all, with a sense of the infinitude, for all its mortal savour, of *character*, finding that an endless romance and a perpetual challenge. Can there have been at the source of such a production a mere refinement of conscious power, an enjoyment of difficulty and a preconceived victory over it? We are free to imagine that in this case Dr. Ibsen chose one of the last subjects that an expert might have been expected to choose, for the harmless pleasure of feeling and of showing that he was in possession of a method that could make up for its deficiencies.

The demonstration is complete and triumphant, but it does not conceal from us—on the contrary—that his drama is essentially that supposedly undramatic thing, the picture not of an action but of a condition. It is the portrait of a nature, the story of what Paul Bourget would call an *état d' âme*, and of a state of nerves as well as of soul, a state of temper, of health, of chagrin, of despair. *Hedda Gabler* is, in short, the study of an exasperated woman; and it may certainly be declared that the subject was not in advance, as a theme for scenic treatment, to be pronounced promising. There could in fact, however, be no more suggestive illustration of the folly of quarrelling with an artist over his subject. Ibsen has had only to take hold of this one in earnest to make it, against every presumption, live with an intensity of life. One can doubtless imagine other ways, but it is enough to say of this one that, put to the test, it imposes its particular spectacle. Something might have been gained, entailing perhaps a loss in another direction, by tracing the preliminary stages, showing the steps in Mrs. Tesman's history which led to the spasm, as it were, on which the curtain rises and of which the breathless duration—ending in death—is the period of the piece. But a play is above everything a work of selection, and Ibsen, with his curious and beautiful passion for the unity of time (carried in him to a point which almost always implies also that of place), condemns himself to admirable rigours. We receive Hedda ripe for her catastrophe, and if we ask for antecedents and explanations we must simply find them in her character. Her motives are just her passions. What the four acts show us is these motives and that character—complicated, strange, irreconcilable, infernal—playing themselves out. We know too little why she married Tesman, we see too little why she ruins Lövborg; but we recognise that she is infinitely perverse, and Heaven knows that, as the drama mostly goes, the crevices we are called upon to stop are singularly few. That Mrs. Tesman is a perfectly ill-regulated person is a matter of course, and there are doubtless spectators who would fain ask whether it would not have been better to represent in her stead a person totally different. The answer to this sagacious question seems to me to be simply that no one can possibly tell. There are many things in the world that are past finding out, and one of them is whether the subject of a work had not better have been another subject. We shall always do well to leave that matter to the author (*he* may have some secret for solving the riddle); so terrible would his revenge easily become if we were to accept a responsibility for his theme.

The distinguished thing is the firm hand that weaves the web, the deep and ingenious use made of the material. What material, indeed, the dissentient spirit may exclaim, and what "use," worthy of the sacred name, is to be made of a wicked, diseased, disagreeable woman? That is just what Ibsen attempts to gauge, and from the moment such an attempt is resolute the case ceases to be so simple. The "use" of Hedda Gabler is that she acts on others and that even her most disagreeable qualities have the privilege, thoroughly undeserved doubtless, but equally irresistible, of becoming a part of the history of others. And then one isn't so sure she is wicked, and by no means sure (especially when she is represented by an actress who makes the point ambiguous) that she is disagreeable. She is various and sinuous and graceful, complicated and natural; she suffers, she struggles, she is human, and by that fact exposed to a dozen interpretations, to the importunity of our suspense. Wrought with admirable closeness is the whole tissue of relations between the five people whom the author sets in motion and on whose behalf he asks of us so few concessions. That is for the most part the accomplished thing in Ibsen, the thing that converts his provincialism into artistic urbanity. He puts *us* to no expense worth speaking of—he takes all the expense himself. I mean that he thinks out our entertainment for us and shapes it of thinkable things, the passions, the idiosyncrasies, the cupidities and jealousies, the strivings and struggles, the joys and sufferings of men. The spectator's situation is different enough when what is given him is the mere dead rattle of the surface of life, into which *he* has to inject the element of thought, the "human interest." Ibsen kneads the soul of man like a paste, and often with a rude and indelicate hand to which the soul of man objects. Such a production as *The Pillars of Society*, with its large, dense complexity of moral cross-references and its admirable definiteness as a picture of motive and temperament (the whole canvas charged, as it were, with moral colour), such a production asks the average moral man to see too many things at once. It will never help Ibsen with the multitude that the multitude shall feel that the more they look the more intentions they shall see, for of such seeing of many intentions the multitude is but scantily desirous. It keeps indeed a positively alarmed and jealous watch in that direction; it smugly insists that intentions shall be rigidly limited.

This sufficiently answers the artless question of whether it may be hoped for the author of *The Pillars of Society* that he shall acquire popularity in this country. In what country under heaven might it have been hoped for him, or for the particular community, that he *should* acquire popularity? Is he in point of fact so established and cherished in the Norwegian theatre? Do his countrymen understand him and clamour for him and love him, or do they content themselves—a very different affair—with being proud of him when aliens abuse him? The rumour reaches us that *Hedda Gabler* has found no favour at Copenhagen, where we are compelled to infer that the play had not the happy interpretation it enjoys in London. It would doubtless have been in danger here if tact and sympathy had not interposed. We hear that it has had reverses in Germany, where of late years Ibsen has been the fashion; but, indeed, all these are matters of an order as to which we should have been grateful for more information from those who have had lately had the care of introducing the formidable dramatist to the English and American public. He excites, for example, in each case, all sorts of curiosity and conjecture as to the quality and capacity of the theatre to which, originally, such a large order was addressed: we are full of unanswered questions about the audience and the school.

What, however, has most of all come out in our timid and desultory experiments is that the author of *The Pillars of Society*, and of *The Doll's House*, of *Ghosts*, of *The Wild Duck*, of *Hedda Gabler*, is destined to be adored by the "profession." Even in his comfortless borrowed habit he will remain intensely dear to the actor and the actress. He cuts them out work to which the artistic nature in them joyously responds—work difficult and interesting, full of stuff and opportunity. The opportunity that he gives them is almost always to do the deep and delicate thing—the sort of chance that, in proportion as they are intelligent, they are most on the look out for. He asks them to paint with a fine brush; for the subject that he gives them is ever our plastic humanity. This will surely preserve him (leaving out the question of serious competition) after our little flurry is over. It was what made the recent representation of *Hedda Gabler* so singularly interesting and refreshing. It is what gives importance to the inquiry as to how his call for "subtlety" in his interpreters has been met in his own country. It was impossible the other day not to be conscious of a certain envy (as of a case of artistic happiness) of the representatives of the mismated Tesmans and their companions—so completely, as the phrase is, were they "in" it and under the charm of what they had to do. In fact the series of Ibsen's "social dramas" is a dazzling array of parts. Nora Helmer will be undertaken again and again—of a morning, no doubt, as supposedly, though oddly, the more "earnest" hour—by young artists justly infatuated. The temptation is still greater to women than to men, as we feel in thinking, further, of the Rebecca of *Rosmersholm*, of Lona Hessel and Martha Bernick in the shapely *Pillars*, of the passionate mother and the insolent maid in the extraordinarily compact and vivid *Ghosts*—absurd and fascinating work; of Mrs. Linden, so quietly tragic, so tremulously real, in *The Doll's House*, and of that irresistibly touching image, so untainted with cheap pathos, Hedvig Ekdal, the little girl with failing eyes, in *The Wild Duck*, who pores over her story-book in the paltry photographic studio of her intensely humbugging father. Such a figure as this very Hialmar Ekdal, however, the seedy, selfish—subtly selfish and self-deceptive—photographer, in whom nothing is active but the tongue, testifies for the strong masculine side of the list. If *The League of Youth* is more nearly a complete comedy than any other of Ibsen's prose works, the comedian who should attempt to render Stensgard in that play would have a real portrait to reproduce. But the examples are numerous: Bernick and Rosmer, Oswald and Manders (Ibsen's compunctious "pastors" are admirable), Gregers Werle, the transcendent meddler in *The Wild Duck*, Rörlund, the prudish rector in the *Pillars*, Stockmann and the Burgomaster in *The Enemy of the People*, all stand, humanly and pictorially, on their feet.

This it is that brings us back to the author's great quality, the quality that makes him so interesting in spite of his limitations, so rich in spite of his lapses—his habit of dealing essentially with the individual caught in the fact. Sometimes, no doubt, he leans too far on that side, loses sight too much of the type-quality and gives his spectators free play to say that even caught in the fact his individuals are mad. We are not at all sure, for instance, of the type-quality in Hedda. Sometimes he makes so queer a mistake as to treat a pretty motive, like that of *The Lady from the Sea*, in a poor and prosaic way. He exposes himself with complacent, with irritating indifference to the objector as well as to the scoffer, he makes his "heredity" too short and his consequences too long, he deals with a homely and unaesthetic society, he harps on the string of conduct, and he actually talks of stockings and legs, in addition to other improprieties. He is not pleasant enough nor light enough nor casual enough; he is too far from Piccadilly and our glorious standards. Therefore his cause may be said to be lost; we shall never take him to our hearts. It was never to have been expected, indeed, that we should, for in literature religions usually grow their own gods, and *our* heaven—as every one can see—is already crowded. But for those who care in general for the form that he has practised he will always remain one of the talents that have understood it best and extracted most from it, have effected most neatly the ticklish trans-fusion of life. If we possessed the unattainable, an eclectic, artistic, disinterested theatre, to which we might look for alternation and variety, it would simply be a point of honour in such a temple to sacrifice sometimes to Henrik Ibsen.

The Master Builder

HENRY JAMES

On the Occasion of *The Master Builder* (1893)

In spite of its having been announced in many quarters that Ibsen would never do, we are still to have another chance, which may very well not be the last, of judging the question for ourselves. Not only has the battered Norseman had, in the evening of his career, the energy to fling yet again into the arena one of those bones of contention of which he has in an unequalled degree the secret of possessing himself, but practised London hands have been able to catch the mystic missile in its passage and are flourishing it, as they have flourished others, before our eyes.[1] In addition to an opportunity of reading the play I have had the pleasure of seeing a rehearsal of the performance—so that I already feel something of responsibility of that inward strife which is an inevitable heritage of all inquiring contact with the master. It is perhaps a consequence of this irremediable fever that one should recklessly court the further responsibility attached to uttering an impression into which the premature may partly enter. But it is impossible, in any encounter with Ibsen, to resist the influence of at least the one kind of interest that he exerts at the very outset, and to which at the present hour it may well be a point of honour promptly to confess one's subjection. This immediate kind is the general interest we owe to the refreshing circumstances that he at any rate gives us the sense of life, and the practical effect of which is ever to work a more or less irritating spell. The other kind is the interest of the particular production, a varying quantity and an agreeable source

---

1. In the *Pall Mall Gazette* the article continued at this point: "The English version of *Bygmester Solness* lately prepared by Mr. Edmund Gosse and Mr. William Archer and now, under the title of *The Master-Builder*, about to appear as a volume, is, on Monday afternoon next and on the following afternoons, to be presented at the Trafalgar Square Theatre by a company of which Mr. Herbert Waring, Miss Elizabeth Robins, and Miss Louise Moodie are the principal members."

   This paragraph was omitted when the article was reprinted in *Essays in London*.

of suspense—a happy occasion in short for that play of intelligence, that acuteness of response, whether in assent or in protest, which it is the privilege of the clinging theatre-goer to look forward to as a result of the ingenious dramatist's appeal, but his sad predicament for the most part to miss yet another and another chance to achieve. With Ibsen (and that is the exceptional joy, the bribe to rapid submission) we can always count upon the chance. Our languid pulses quicken as we begin to note the particular direction taken by the attack on a curiosity inhabiting, by way of a change, the neglected region of the brain.

In *The Master Builder* this emotion is not only kindled very early in the piece—it avails itself to the full of the right that Ibsen always so liberally concedes it of being still lively after the piece is over. His independence, his perversity, his intensity, his vividness, the hard compulsion of his strangely inscrutable art, are present in full measure, together with that quality which comes almost uppermost when it is a question of seeing him on the stage, his peculiar blessedness to actors. *Their* reasons for liking him it would not be easy to overstate; and surely, if the public should ever completely renounce him, players enamoured of their art will still be found ready to interpret him for that art's sake to empty benches. No dramatist of our time has had more the secret, and has kept it better, of making their work interesting to them. The subtlety with which he puts them into relation to it eludes analysis, but operates none the less strongly as an incitement. Does it reside mainly in the way he takes hold of their imagination, or in some special affinity with their technical sense; in what he gives them or in what he leaves it to them to give; in the touches by which the moral nature of the character opens out a vista for them; or in the simple fact of connection with such a vivified whole? These are questions at any rate that Mr. Herbert Waring, Miss Robins, Miss Moodie, enviable with their several problems, doubtless freely ask themselves, or even each other, while the interest and the mystery of *The Master Builder* fold them more and more closely in. What is incontestable is the excitement, the amusement, the inspiration of dealing with material so solid and so fresh. The very difficulty of it makes a common cause, as the growing ripeness of preparation makes a common enthusiasm.

I shall not attempt to express the subject of the play more largely than to say that its three acts deal again, as Ibsen is so apt to deal, with the supremely critical hour in the life of an individual, in the history of a soul. The individual is in this case not a Hedda, nor a Nora, nor a Mrs. Alving, nor a Lady from the Sea, but a prosperous architect of Christiania, who, on reaching a robust maturity, encounters his fate all in the opening of a door. This fate—infinitely strange and terrible, as we know before the curtain falls—is foreshadowed in Miss Elizabeth Robins, who, however, in passing the threshold, lets in a great deal more than herself, represents a heroine conceived, as to her effect on the action, with that shameless originality which Ibsen's contemners call wanton and his admirers call fascinating. Hilda Wangel, a young woman whom the author may well be trusted to have made more mystifying than her curiously charmless name would suggest, is only the indirect form, the animated clock-face, as it were, of Halvard Solness's destiny; but the action, in spite of obscurities and ironies, takes its course by steps none the less irresistible. The mingled reality and symbolism of it all give us an Ibsen within an Ibsen. His subject is always, like the subjects of all first-rate men, primarily an idea; but in this case the idea is as difficult to catch as its presence is impossible to overlook. The whole thing throbs and flushes with it, and yet smiles and mocks at us through it as if in conscious supersubtlety. The action at any rate is superficially simple, more single and confined than that of most of Ibsen's other plays; practically, as it defines itself and rises to a height, it leaves the strange, doomed Solness, and the even stranger apparition of the joyous and importunate girl (the one all memories and hauntings and bondages, the other all health and curiosity and youthful insolence), face to face on unprecedented terms—terms, however, I hasten to add, that by no means prevent the play from being one to which a young lady, as they say in Paris, may properly take her mother. Of all Ibsen's heroines Hilda is indeed perhaps at once the most characteristic of the author and the most void of offence to the "general." If she has notes that recall Hedda, she is a Hedda dangerous precisely because she is *not* yet *blasée*—a Hedda stimulating, fully beneficent in intention; in short "reversed," as I believe the author defined her to his interpreters. From her encounter with Halvard Solness many remarkable things arise, but most of all perhaps the spectator's sense of the opportunity offered by the two rare parts; and in particular of the fruitful occasion (for Solness from beginning to end holds the stage), seized by Mr. Herbert Waring, who has evidently recognised one of those hours that actors sometimes wait long years for—the hour that reveals a talent to itself as well as to its friends and that makes a reputation take a bound. Whatever, besides refreshing them, *The Master Builder* does for Ibsen with London playgoers, it will render the service that the curious little Norwegian repertory has almost always rendered the performers, even to the subsidiary figures, even to the touching Kaia, the touching Ragnar, the inevitable Dr. Herdal, and the wasted wife of Solness, so carefully composed by Miss Moodie.

"Henrik Ibsen: On the Occasion of The Master Builder" appeared, under the title "Ibsen's New Play," in the Pall Mall Gazette, February 17, 1893, and was reprinted as the second part of the essay "Henrik Ibsen" in Essays in London and Elsewhere, 1893.

The whole story of Miss Robins's heroic adventure in Ibsen production and of the devoted interest in it mani-

fested by Henry James may be read in her volume Theatre and Friendship, 1932. It was, no doubt, with the intention of stimulating public interest that James wrote his article, which appeared three days before the first performance of the play. Miss Robins has reprinted it in her book in its original form, which included a short paragraph afterwards omitted.

BRIAN JOHNSTON

Plot and Story in *The Master Builder*†

In Ibsen's plays the major characters arrive onstage with stories from the past that threaten to open up an endless profusion of arbitrary detail. However, instead of following the 'real life' tendency to disperse into endless anecdotal detail, the stories are channeled into tight retrospective plots, where the arbitrary events of the stories reveal the structure of necessity, design, even nemesis. (The classic model for this procedure is Sophokles' *Oedipus tyrannos*.) The *plot's* transformation of the details of the *story* is the essence of Ibsen's dramaturgy—a process similar to that of the kaleidoscope in which scattered colored fragments, when the toy is manipulated, reveal symmetrical patterns. Through theatric devices—the sequence and shaping of the onstage actions—the Ibsen plot subjects the story material to an insistent aesthetic restructuring. This process is not "an imitation of everyday life" but a restoration of its disfigured condition.

There is a parallel between the Ibsen plot's re-creation of the material of the stories, and the revolution in the world of painting in Ibsen's time. Realist painters, like Edouard Manet and the Impressionists, chose as their subjects the most everyday aspects of the contemporary scene. But they translated the objects of the scene into the "non-photographic" requirements of the Impressionist aesthetic. As a consequence, they were derided for ineptitude in recreating an everyday reality familiar to the average viewer—a charge

† This essay is original to this Norton Critical Edition.

also made against Ibsen's plot-driven plays when compared with more strictly naturalistic playwriting.

The Impressionists' insistence on the aesthetic integrity of the new artistic method was at first baffling. For these painters, everyday reality as traditionally represented was not a "truth" they sought to replicate; on the contrary, everyday reality needed to be radically reorganized into aesthetic truth, by an often alienating perspective upon modern life. The "reality" of the artwork was not some model outside the canvas but the problematic composition on the canvas, translating the object into a painterly artifact. This has been the evolving program of the most significant modernist art—including drama. "If contemporary life was to be represented with its banality, ugliness and mediocrity undistorted, then the aesthetic interest had to be shifted from the objects represented to the means of representation."[1]

The Ibsen *plots*, similarly, are deliberately alienating perspectives brought to bear upon the arbitrary, everyday subject matter of the *stories*. The meaning of an Ibsen play is its *dialectic*: the unceasing activity of the plot at work transfiguring the material of the story from the opening moments to the ambiguous, open-ended close. As with Aeschylus' vision, the originary act in the past that set off the tragic sequence can only be speculatively pondered, and the end of the play cannot achieve a final closure. The play has taken up only a section of an endless dialectical sequence. The logic imposed on the story by the plot is an opening up, not a closing off, of perspectives. The goal of the action, therefore, is not, as in a whodunit or "thesis-play," a tidy explanation of a mystery or problem. Instead, the goal is the *adequacy* of response of both protagonists and audience to the scale and complexity of the human condition unveiled.

The plot-controlled sequence of events enacted by the performers *is* the subject of the play. The extraordinarily symmetrical and repetitive plot structure of *The Master Builder*, for example, is intended to be an *insistent aesthetic presence* throughout a performance. The intention of the Ibsen plot was never the faithful imitation of everyday reality but the subversion of its claim to truth, which runs counter to a current theater punditry on the role of plots in plays. As Michael Goldman observes:

> There is a tendency . . . to see the plot as an expedient, a way of delivering other, more important materials. From this point of view, the aim of the plot is to get out of the way with as little distortion of reality as possible. Any pressure the plot imposes is likely to seem a limitation on Ibsen's artistry.[2]

1. Charles Rosen and Henri Zerner, *Romanticism and Realism: The Mythology of Nineteenth Century Art* (New York: Norton, 1984), 149–50.
2. Michael Goldman, *Ibsen, The Dramaturgy of Fear* (New York: Columbia University Press, 1999), 39.

The predominance of the naturalistic aesthetic in the United States in particular, in which an emphasis upon a particular phase of Stanislavskian teaching made low-keyed "facsimile" performance an ideal of acting (exacerbated by cinema and television dramas with their relative indifference to dramatic structure), has encouraged an inability to understand the function of dramatic plotting. Michael Goldman reminds us of the aesthetics of Ibsen's plot strategies:

> The neat interlinking of incident and information from the past that Ibsen developed . . . may too easily be misread as a kind of novelistic narration. . . . In performance, however, an Ibsen play strikes us not as a retrospective description of past events but as an unfolding succession of conflicts. Its dialogue constitutes a series of mini-crises that force bits and pieces of the past, with their attendant fears and desires, to be discovered, suffered, defined by the actor/character in the present. The emphasis is on the rendering of spontaneous choice in continually emergent situations.[3]

This deliberate violation of our everyday experience directs the audience through the details of the story to the play's archetypal and metaphoric supertext.[4] Rather than imitating nineteenth-century Norway, Ibsen is *reinventing* it on his stage as a space where extraordinary powers can manifest themselves. As his son, Sigurd Ibsen, wrote: "Art gives liberty of action to forces and possibilities to which life does not grant the chance of coming into their rights."[5] Merely to imitate everyday reality would be to take a debased version of our natural and spiritual inheritance as authentic. To recover what has been lost and disfigured, the true artist must, like the Impressionists, create a counter-discourse to the world's false discourse, must "negate the negation." We need to see that this is to the credit of Ibsen's play, as the strict selectivity of a Manet is more impressive than the meticulous abundance of anecdotal detail of the conventional salon painters.

In *The Master Builder* the implications of the story could beget a series of novels: the childhoods of Halvard and Aline; their marriage; his career; the defeat and subjugation of Old Brovik and of other rivals Solness "hammered to the ground"; the birth and brief life of the twins; the fire; Aline's disastrous reaction and later death-in-life; the love of Ragnar and Kaja; her mysterious visit to

3. Ibid., 61.
4. By "supertext" I mean the historical, cultural, and archetypal patterns of memories, ideas, images, and conflicts built into our culture and invoked or implied by the story-plot dialectic.
5. Sigurd Ibsen, *Human Quintessence* (1911; reprint, Freeport, N.Y.: Books for Libraries Press, 1972), 92.

Solness and later enthrallment; Solness's visit to Lysanger; his climbing the tower and meeting with Hilde Wangel; her home life; his increasingly tyrannous repression of the younger generation; the Henry Jamesian situation of Solness's and Aline's mutually watchful but delusive perceptions of each other with which they torment themselves. However, the *plot* of the play, like a kaleidoscope, will gather these diffuse fragments of the *story* into a meaningful pattern.

The main arc of the play is from Solness's tortuous and fearful confinement and retreat from decisive action in the opening scenes to his heroic self-affirmation at the close. The plot's three acts *visually* enact liberation from confinement and brooding obsession through a sequence of progressively expanding light and space. This visual emancipation of the *scene* is accompanied by an increasing liberation of metaphoric vistas in the *dialogue*. In Act One, the scene is an artificially lit, windowless workroom; in Act Two, a drawing room with large bay windows and flooding light; in Act Three it is open air, a verandah, the scene bathed in the light of a sunset. This visual expansion is repeated in the dialogue and action of the play. The emancipation of the scene from windowless interior to increasing light and space simultaneously opens more vistas of the past for resurrection and confrontation. Halvard Solness's awakening consciousness, under the prompting of Hilde Wangel, haltingly but gradually abandons its debilitating legacy of guilt and fear of retribution to create a version of the past that, though it may or may not be what "actually happened," is what "ought to" have happened because it re-creates the past more adequately to the heart's desire.

The plot procedure seems bewilderingly cavalier with regard to the actual facts of the story. Solness and Hilde, interchanging roles of guru and disciple, transform the past through creative memory into something more adequate to the needs of the spirit. Solness (*sol* = sun) once encountered Hilde Wangel ten years ago to the day (September 19) at Lysanger (*lys* = light) and now is challenged by her to repeat his defiance of the "Creator" and ascend (and fall) at the autumnal equinox. The elaborate metaphoric and symbolic detail and patterning in the play involves increasing light and space; a verbal imagery of churches, houses, castles in the air, a fire in winter, dead twins, helpers and servers (both visible and invisible), the collision of youth and maturity, harps in the air, a challenge to the "Creator," and so on. These odd details of the text are "worked" for metaphoric and archetypal more than for factual value. They are there to build up the overall metaphor of the play, not as a proliferation of facts drawn from a real world outside the plot. *The Master Builder* asks the audience to collaborate in the project of its protagonists, Solness and Hilda, to bring their desired fiction into being, as reality, the emblem of which is the unfinished house with its scaffolding to be climbed, glimpsed only in the last act.

A struggle takes place to establish the dominant language of the play. By means of the plot, the metaphoric language of Solness and Hilde gradually wins out against the other languages that threaten it: Aline's fatalism, Dr. Herdal's pragmatism, or Ragnar Brovik's cynicism. Remarkably, the play repeats the same action in each of its three acts, each act beginning with Solness's despairing self-recriminations in which the past seems to overwhelm and defeat him and each ending with his exultant affirmation of overcoming this past, like the sun breaking free of clouds. As the same story is repeated in each act, it accumulates more and more of both the negative and positive "material" from the past.

The effect of this remarkable sequence of repetitions is that an incrementally "positive" past of Solness (the Lysanger ascent, challenge to the "Creator," and alliance with the "princess") is seen to struggle with an incrementally increasing "negative" past. The positive element represents Solness's visionary and subversive aspirations; the negative, the legacy of devastation these aspirations have brought about. This spiritual battle is transposed, in Hilde's imagination, into the image of Solness struggling with the Creator at the top of the tower, accompanied by the sound of harps. The effect on the audience is of experiencing the terms of the play's *story* by means of the *plot*, escaping the constraining versions of the events represented by Dr. Herdal, Aline, and Ragnar, and taking up the more liberating, visionary terms affirmed by Solness and Hilde. All "official" versions of the past, in which we are indoctrinated since childhood, are themselves manufactured from questionable sources, motives, limitations, and prejudices—history, we know, is written by the victors. Solness and Hilde only choose a more satisfactory fiction of the past than most of us are persuaded to settle for.

Hilde brings to Solness a startling story that, after at first protesting, he begins *creatively* to "recollect" and then to link to his own selectively remembered past of guilty triumph and transgression against Aline. Whether Solness acted as Hilde recounts is deliberately kept ambiguous, but the play will show him accepting and developing the subversively audacious dimensions of her version of the story until it becomes a reality that he acknowledges as his own. Until Hilde's arrival, Solness was crushed by the self-punitive and penitential version of his past. Hilde displaces this negative past by reviving and reactivating the positive Faustian challenge of the Lysanger ascent.

From one perspective, Solness destroys himself through a delusional acceptance of Hilde's re-vision of past events. From an alternative perspective, he liberates himself by letting the metaphoric or mythopoetic dimensions of her version work on him. The two continually interchange the roles of guru and disciple, each seeking to grasp the concept the other is intuiting. The decisive moment of this ambiguous action is at the conclusion of Act Two:

> HILDA (*Looks searchingly at him.*) Is it true, or isn't it?
> SOLNESS That I get dizzy?
> HILDA That my master builder *dare* not—*can* not climb as high as he builds?
> SOLNESS Is that the way you see it?
> HILDA Yes.
> SOLNESS I'm beginning to feel there's scarcely a corner in me that's safe from you.
> HILDA (*Looks toward the bay window.*) Up there then. All the way up.
> SOLNESS (*Coming closer.*) In the topmost room in the tower— you could live there, Hilda. You could live like a princess.
> HILDA (*Mysteriously, between earnest and jest.*) Yes, that's what you promised.
> SOLNESS Did I, in fact?
> HILDA Really master builder! You said I was to be a princess. And that I'd get a kingdom from you. And so you took me and—Well!
> SOLNESS (*Seriously.*) Are you quite sure this isn't some kind of dream—some fantasy—that's taken hold of you?
> HILDA (*Scornfully.*) That perhaps you didn't do it?
> SOLNESS I scarcely know myself—. (*More softly.*) But one thing I know for certain—that I—
> HILDA That you—Say it now!
> SOLNESS That I *ought* to have done it.

The scene concludes with Solness's promise to hang the wreath over his new home: to establish a very ambiguously recovered past as a reality for the future. In the alien modern and bourgeois setting, Hilda and Solness are validating a semi-mythic fable: of Solness's Lysanger ascent, the towered castle with its princess, the singing in the air, the passionate embrace. The audience finds itself colluding in the lovers' audacious version of the story, their mutual affirmation of its reality, which will undergo fabulous elaborations in the following act. We cannot know if any of this recollected past actually happened and the skeptical critic may demur at the mythopoetic elaborations of the story Hilda and Solness perform. We witness Solness taking Hilda's story, accepting its fabulous dimensions, and asserting its ideal truth—"I *ought* to have done it." Less important than whether or not the events actually happened in the past, however, is that their validation is happening *now*. The plot of the play *is* the protagonists working upon and re-creating the story. The final scene of the play, of Solness's ascent of the tower, his challenge to the Creator, watched by Hilde and the crowd of spectators, is not only a recollection, but a *re-enactment* of the most subversive elements of their version of the past action, the Lysanger ascent. In a bold re-enactment of time and space, Solness and Hilde, in Solness's garden, re-create the action at Lysanger where Hilde, in the churchyard, waved to Solness ascending his last church tower.

Above
Tower

Hilde (from mountains) At beginning of the play	Solness (above) At Lysanger and end of the play
Solness (below Windowless workroom At beginning of the play	Hilde (below) Among spectators At Lysanger and the end of the play

Below
Churchyard/Garden

The play's *plot*—the action on stage watched by the audience—subordinates the negative past of Solness's *story* of guilt, retribution, and defeat and replaces it with a positive alternative. Solness and Hilde confront the past and free it from the constrictions of conventional reality. This duplicates the action of Ibsen writing the play. In the struggle for the play's dominant language, the plot's metaphoric and archetypal ambition strains against the tyranny of factual history and realistic plausibility. Like an architect's project that threatens to exceed the resources of the available technology, the play challenges the limitations of the realist convention Ibsen himself for so long has been establishing for the modern theater. Like the new house with the tower and the scaffolding, the play, too, is a project in the process of being completed while the theater audience watches its author's hazardous ascent.

The Master Builder's audacious bid to transcend its own realist method is encapsulated in the play's final staged action, seen by Hilda: the tower ascent, and the struggle of Solness with the Creator—a smaller-scaled re-enactment of the fabulous Lysanger ascent. Wonder and terror are generated in the onlookers by the somewhat banal act of a middle-aged architect with vertigo climb-

ing a scaffolding. Hilde and the skeptical and resentful Ragnar duel
to establish the appropriate language for the event:

> HILDA (*With jubilant, quiet intensity.*) At last! At last! Now I see
> him great and free again!
>
> RAGNAR (*Almost speechless.*) But all this is—
>
> HILDA This is how I've seen him all these ten years. How strong
> he stands! Fearfully thrilling, after all. Look at him! Now
> he's hanging the wreath on the spire!
>
> RAGNAR All this I'm seeing here is completely impossible.
>
> HILDA Yes, it's the impossible, now that he's doing. (*With the
> inscrutable look in her eyes.*) Can you see anyone else up
> there with him?
>
> RAGNAR There's no one else.
>
> HILDA Yes, there's someone he's struggling with.
>
> RAGNAR You're mistaken.
>
> HILDA Can't you hear singing in the air, either?
>
> RAGNAR It must be the wind in the treetops.
>
> HILDA I hear a singing. A powerful singing. (*Crying out in joyful
> exultation.*) Look, look! Now he's waving his hat. Waving to
> us down here. Oh, wave back up to him there. For now, now
> it is fulfilled! (*Snatches the white shawl from the doctor,
> waves it, and cries out.*) Hurray for master builder Solness!
>
> DR. HERDAL Stop! Stop! For God's sake! [421]

The ambition to find expression for desires that have liberated
themselves from the tyranny of factual realism opens the dialogue
of the final moments to such evocative imagery as "castles in the
air" a "kingdom" with its "princess," a battle with the Creator, and a
"great singing in the air"—which have visual stage counterparts in
the sun-streaked sky, the ascending Solness, above, and, below, the
gathered crowd of alarmed or rapt observers, the accompanying
music. Against the triumph claimed by Hilda is counterpointed the
skeptical voice of Ragnar and Dr. Herdal's alarmed warning as
Hilda *re-enacts* her past Lyanger action of waving the white object
(this time Aline's shawl) that signaled her act of worship and dangerous discipleship. Solness falls and is killed, which would seem to
validate Ragnar and Herdal's view, but Hilda's refusal to accept this
as defeat—"But he went right to the top. And I heard harps in the
air!"—challenges their reading of the event. Her cry, "For now, now
it is fulfilled," is, as one critic has noted, "made to echo Christ's last
words on the Cross,"[6] wresting victory from defeat.

The visual symbolism of this scene insists that Solness's death-
fall is at the least a contested outcome. Focusing on the *story*, it is

6. Inga-Stina Ewbank, "Ibsen's Dramatic Language as a Link Between His Realism and
His Symbolism," in *Contemporary Approaches to Ibsen* (Oslo: Universitetsforlaget,
1966), 104.

possible to see the play as a cautionary tale for middle-aged men on the dangers of succumbing to youthful sirens. However, to attend to the *plot* of the play—the repeated pattern in the dialogue of gathering both the negative and the positive past and affirming the latter; its scenic evolution, act by act, from tormented confinement to outside the confines of the house and its unhappy history—makes a negative reading contradict what the play is *doing*.

The plot engaged with the past story, combated and gradually discarded the negative content paralyzing Solness's creativity, and allowed alternative affirmative energies to emerge. What was arbitrary, debilitating, and self-tormenting in the past told by the *story* is replayed as liberating new possibility by the transforming dynamic of the *plot*. A debilitating version of the past is set aside and replaced by one that reasserts the human spirit's amoral, Faustian ambition for transcendence. The play began with the chaotic and arbitrary details of a conscience-stricken past of uncreative self-reproach; the plot imposes a startling new coherence upon these details and launches them on a dangerous trajectory.

History is always, ultimately, about the present, because our present consciousness is the only medium in which the past can exist. It is totally dependent on how the present conceives it, what it intends to make of it for good or ill; how it uses the past for its own projects. Until it is challenged, the past can constrain and tyrannize over us. The redemption of the past is the subversive lesson Nietzsche's Zarathustra claimed to have given to humanity:

> I taught them to work on the future and redeem with their creation all that *has* been. To redeem what is past in man and to recreate all "it was" until the will says "Thus I willed it! Thus I shall will it!"—this I call redemption and this alone I taught them to call redemption.[7]

Such a moment of redemption of the past is signaled as emerging at the moment when Solness, in response to Hilde's "Say it now!" exclaims, "I *ought* to have done it."

An Ibsen play always "tells a good story" within its "realistic" dimensions; but the plots contain strategies that encompass the larger metaphoric dimensions of all major drama. In *The Master Builder*, Ibsen opens up the realist aesthetic to perspectives once claimed only by the most ambitious poetic drama. These perspectives include the diurnal and seasonal rhythm of the sun's rising and setting; the biological and cultural contest between the generations, old and young, where the old leader of the herd must give way to the new; the wasteland theme of atrophied energies where,

7. Friedrich Nietzsche, *Collected Works*, ed. Oscar Levy (1909–11; reprint, New York: Russell and Russell, 1964), 11:34.

in a reversal of the Sleeping Beauty legend, the "princess" enters the enchanted realm, frees the imprisoned young lovers (Ragnar and Kaja), perhaps restoring fertility to the childless "kingdom," while releasing the hero from his torment to take his leave, splendidly, like a superb setting of the sun. A story of plausible modern reality becomes the site where a metaphysical drama also takes place. The goal of this enterprise, of discovering metaphysical possibility within the seemingly intractable mundanity of modern experience, has been attempted since by others in the modern theater,[8] but never with more difficulty and audacity than by Ibsen in his Realist Cycle.

8. By T. S. Eliot, for example, in his modern verse dramas.

General Themes

EINAR HAUGEN

Poetry in the Round†

My poem's like the heather-covered slope
That rises steadily above the peasant's farm.
Behind the slope—if you are standing free—
You gaze upon a ring of snow-clad peaks.
My lute is tuned to play a muted song;
But deeper strings lend color to the chords.
Within the poem thus a poem is concealed;
And he who fathoms this will understand the song.

Ibsen, *The Epic Brand*, st. 9[1]

In a moment of unusual candor, when he was angered by critic Clemens Petersen's claim that *Peer Gynt* was not poetry, Ibsen wrote to Bjørnson: "My work *is* poetry; and if it is not, it shall become so. The concept of poetry in our country, in Norway, shall come to conform with this book."[2] His prediction, which must have seemed rash to Bjørnson, has been fulfilled. It has increasingly been recognized, not only for *Peer Gynt* and not only in Norway, that he *was* a poet, not only in verse but also in prose. This development sustains his own judgment, as expressed to the Women's League on his seventieth birthday: "I have been more a poet, less a social philosopher, than people generally seem inclined to think."[3] These two statements show him battling on two fronts, in defense first of his verse, then of his prose as poetry. It was hard for his con-

---

† From *Ibsen's Drama: Author to Audience* (Minneapolis: University of Minnesota Press, 1979), 95–109. Copyright © University of Minnesota Press. Reprinted by permission of the publisher. Page references in brackets are to this Norton Critical Edition.
1. Henrik Ibsen, *Samlede Verker* [*Hundreårsutgaven*], ed. Francis Bull, Halvdan Koht, Didrik Arup Seip, 21 vols. (Oslo: Gyldendal, 1928–58)—hereafter *HU*—5.367; trans. based on Henrik Ibsen, *The Oxford Ibsen*, ed. James Walter McFarlane, 8 vols. (London: Oxford University Press, 1960–77)—hereafter *OI*—3.38. See discussion of the epic *Brand* by McFarlane in *OI* 3.4–12; this was the incomplete draft of a narrative poem, which Ibsen abandoned in favor of the drama.
2. Letter to Bjørnson, 9 Dec. 1867 (*HU* 16.198; Henrik Ibsen, *Letters and Speeches*, ed. Evert Sprinchorn (New York: MacGibbon and Kee, 1965)—hereafter *LS*—67; *OI* 3.488).
3. Speech to Norsk Kvindesagsforening (Norwegian League for Women's Rights), 26 May 1898 (*HU* 15.417; Sprinchorn, *LS*, 337; *OI* 5.456).

temporaries, and for many of his critics down to the present, to recognize a poetic genre that was neither lyrical nor epic but essentially dramatic. Francis Fergusson called it "theatrical poetry," a
"hidden poetry, masquerading as reporting; it is a 'poetry of the theater' (in M. Cocteau's phrase) and not a poetry of words."[4]

In this chapter I shall focus on the formal qualities of Ibsen's
message that give it validity as poetry. Especially in his "social"
plays Ibsen is often thought of as unpoetical, because he was echoing the "flat" speech of everyday conversation. Here we must first
discount the distortions of translators who failed to reproduce the
nuances of his language, either because they were unaware of them
or because it was not possible to reproduce them in English. We
have seen that Ibsen's language is often ambiguous, carrying in addition to its surface meaning some deeper sense. According to
William Empson, ambiguity is one of the weapons in the armory of
poets, without being in itself poetic.[5] Ambiguity is inherent in all
natural language, which is the despair of scientists, who strive to be
precise (by definitions, formulas, mathematical logic); but it offers
the poet an opportunity to make his or her language richer and
more suggestive of a variety of meanings.

In the special Ibsen genre I have here called "dramatic poetry," he
has to give form not merely or primarily to the words spoken but to
the dramatic structure as a whole. His "cryptogram" has to be
wrapped in a form that will convey his message without apparent
distortion. In verse, with its severe requirements of rhyme and
rhythm, this is obviously true, but in prose it is less easily perceived.
It is not too much to describe Ibsen's prose dialogue as a masterpiece of poetic cryptography, as hard to write and as astonishing in
its perfection as anything he wrote in verse. The topics may fade and
the ideas age, but the poetry remains, as modern critics have increasingly been willing to recognize. Even when the paint on his
statues cracks and peels, the grace of his sculpture remains.

Ibsen, being also a literary critic, was quite clear and even insis-
tent on the importance of form in poetry. In a poem of his youth,
"In the Picture Gallery" (1859), he made a major critical statement:
"The *form* it is that makes my verses poems!"

> Do not forget that in the realms of art
> It is the *form* alone that ranks;
> If you would judge the singer's scales,
> Attend to *how* he sings, not *what*.[6]

4. Francis Fergusson, *The Idea of a Theater* (Garden City, N.Y.: Doubleday, 1953; orig. pub. 1949), 160.
5. William Empson, *Seven Types of Ambiguity* (New York: New Directions, n.d.; orig. pub. London: Chatto and Windus, 1930).
6. *HU* 14.243.

RHYME AS FORM

In Ibsen's youth, verse was the prime language of dramatic literature, all in good romantic fashion. From the Greeks and the French to Shakespeare and Goethe and on to their Danish epigones Oehlenschläger and Heiberg, the grand tradition called for serious plays, especially tragedies, to be written in verse. *Catiline* was, not surprisingly, written in verse greatly reminiscent of such predecessors as the Norwegians Wergeland and Welhaven. Ibsen's earliest preserved verse is from 1847, and with it the nineteen-year-old amazed his companions in Grimstad. He brought this talent to perfection in *Brand* and *Peer Gynt*, but it does not carry over well in translation, especially since rhyme is in disrepute in the modern lyric. But rhyme is the lifeblood of Ibsen's verse, giving shape and dignity to his serious passages and a light touch to his humor (as in Thomas Hood, W. S. Gilbert, or Ogden Nash).

The year 1859 was a turning point for Ibsen in his technical skill as a rhymester, as in so much else.[7] He then initiated the so-called Ibsen strophe, a nine-line, alternately three- and four-beat stanza, usually rhymed a b a b c d c c d, known from "On the Heights" and his popular narrative poem "Terje Vigen." In the succeeding years he wrote three of his most interesting dramas entirely in rhymed verse: *Love's Comedy* (1862), *Brand* (1866), and *Peer Gynt* (1867). These are not in strophes, but in sharply chiseled lines, often run-on, with the rhymes intertwined. He used a mixture of masculine and feminine rhymes, with a sprinkling of trisyllabics, as in *Peer Gynt*'s *vandene, strandene, vikende, skrikende* (which are the despair of translators). In *Brand* he spiced the satire of the mayor by letting him rhyme such absurdities as *pesthus, arresthus, festhus* ("pest house," "arrest house," "fest house," i.e., hospital, jail, and banquet hall, to be built under one roof to make a "community center").[8] In *Love's Comedy* an iambic five-beat line is used throughout, except in the interspersed songs. *Brand* is written in a four-beat line, some two-thirds iambic, the more elevated passages trochaic.[9] In *Peer Gynt* the rhymes and rhythms run riot. Nearly every scene has a different line length or rhythm, iambic or trochaic, three-beat or four-beat, with the rhymes intertwined and often witty.

Translation problems also bar recognition of his lyric poems, which are restricted in form and theme but are often intensely moving. In 1871 he was prevailed upon to publish his one collection (*Digte*), but only after a severe prunning and rewriting which

7. Leif Mæhle, *Ibsens rimteknikk, Småskrifter* no. 27, ed. F. Bull (Oslo: Malling, 1955), 42.
8. *HU* 5.277–78; *OI* 3.169.
9. Åse Hiorth Lervik, *Ibsens verskunst i Brand* (Oslo: Universitetsforlaget, 1969), 41.

left a mere fifty-five poems. Nine were added in later editions, and one can now read every scrap in the centennial works of 1928. The best of them are pungent and epigrammatic, often expressing the poet's inmost feelings more directly than the plays. The theme may be ironic, as in "Building Plans," or bitter, as in "The Eider Duck," and it may be openly autobiographical, as in "The Miner." A few longish poems, like his "Balloon Letter" or "A Letter in Rhyme," are versified essays on the state of the world, and others in narrative form are miniature dramas. The one concession to popular taste is his much beloved and declaimed "Terje Vigen," an episode from the British blockade of Denmark-Norway during the Napoleonic wars. As Koht emphasized, personal and patriotic themes are here effectively blended, the personal being Ibsen's struggle with and victory over himself in 1861.[1] A number of poems are purely lyrical and were found worthy of being set to music by Edvard Grieg, e.g., "A Swan," "With a Water Lily," "Gone," "Margaret's Cradle Song," "Solveig's Song," and the like.[2]

Having achieved mastery in versification, Ibsen proceeded in the early 1870s to abandon it totally. As noted earlier, this represented a real sacrifice for him. A decade later, having mastered the art of prose, he rejected a request from actress Lucie Wolf for a verse prologue: "I myself have scarcely written a single verse in the last 7–8 years, having exclusively cultivated the far more difficult art of composing in a plain, truthful, realistic language." His reasons were that the verse form, he thought, would not in the immediate future be used in the drama. Art forms, he suggested, were like the prehistoric animals (e.g., the dinosaurs) that had died out when their time was past. "A tragedy in iambic pentameter is even now as rare a creature as the dodo bird, a few specimens of which still live on an African island."[3]

As late as 1871 he could still define the importance of verse and his need for it in his "Rhymed Letter to Fru Heiberg":

> Prose is suited to ideas,
>   Verse to visions.
> Joy of spirit, woes of spirit,
> Sorrow like the snows of winter,
>   Anger flashing—
> Fullest life I freest give
>   In bonds of verse.[4]

1. Halvdan Koht, *Life of Ibsen*, trans. Einar Haugen and A. E. Santaniello (New York: Blom, 1971), 132.
2. Opus 25, "Six Songs," is all by Ibsen; information from Arvid Vollsnes (personal communication).
3. Letter, 25 May 1883 (*HU* 17.511; Sprinchorn, *LS*, 218).
4. *HU* 14.425; cf. Michael Meyer, *Ibsen, A Biography* (New York: Doubleday, 1971), 433.

This poem would prove to be one of the last he wrote. Six years earlier he had supported Clemens Petersen's opinion that "versified form with a symbolic background is my most natural medium."[5] But in 1874 he turned a deaf ear to Edmund Gosse's disappointment that *Emperor and Galilean* was not written in verse, "My new play is no tragedy in the old style; what I wanted to portray was people, and precisely for that reason I did not allow them to speak in 'the tongue of the gods.' "[6]

He had, of course, written prose in such plays as *St. John's Night*, *Lady Inger*, and *The Vikings at Helgeland*, but in a mannered, historical style. There is much living dialogue in *The Pretenders*, in spite of its thirteenth-century setting. Not until he wrote *The League of Youth* (1869) did he wrestle with the problem of creating believable contemporary dialogue. Few would be so naive as to think that this is the same as a real-life tape-recorded conversation, which is usually repetitious, only mildly structured, full of false starts and self-corrections, interruptions and changes of topics. Except to those who participate in conversations, they are usually boring and undramatic. Credible dialogue has to incorporate some of these features, but it must also further the action of the play and keep the audience awake.

THE NUANCES OF NORWEGIAN

At this point we may digress to say a few words about the spoken Norwegian of Ibsen's day. Within his social class a standard speech had evolved, which differed only in minor detail from city to city. This "cultivated" speech was not only a prestigious class marker but for people like Ibsen an entirely natural idiom. The anomaly was that although it differed profoundly from the corresponding cultivated Danish, it was identically spelled. In the course of their four centuries of political union, the citizens of Denmark and Norway had developed a common written language, which rendered both Danish and Norwegian speech in a very imperfect way. In 1814 this form of writing was called "Danish" in Denmark and "Norwegian" in Norway, but the growing nationalism of Norwegians soon began to identify it as "Danish." Agitation sprang up on behalf of developing a purely Norwegian written language, which would correspond to Norwegian speech and reflect Norwegian identity. Reforms began already in Ibsen's lifetime, but only after his death were sweeping changes instituted (1907–38) which made his spelling quaintly obsolete. Since 1960 his works have been reissued in a contemporary orthography

5. Letter to Clemens Petersen, 4 Dec. 1865 (*HU* 16.122).
6. Letter to Edmund Gosse, 15 Jan. 1874 (*HU* 17.123; Sprinchorn, *LS*, 145).

that again makes it possible for younger people to read him with ease.[7]

From the almost pure Danish writing of his first plays Ibsen moved step by step toward the Norwegian speech that was natural to him. During his romantic period he adopted many words peculiar to Norwegian rural life, especially in plays with a rural setting like *Peer Gynt*.[8] In principle, he was committed to a gradual Norwegianization, which effectively suffused his romantic plays with a richly poetic quality. "I have myself adopted words from the country dialects, if they are understandable and can enhance the esthetic effect. In this way I contribute to the enrichment and development of our language." But he sharply rejected the efforts of some reformers to replace his language with one based on the dialects: "I will not assist in the liquidation of the literature I myself have helped to develop."[9] In *Peer Gynt* the comic figure of Huhu is Ibsen's gibe at those who wish to restore "the language of the orangutangs," i.e., the Old Norwegian language. Ibsen agreed with the linguistic adviser at the Christiania Norwegian Theater, Knud Knudsen, that the language change should be an evolution, not a revolution.

Part of his problem in writing believable dialogue was that in a framework of Danish spelling and grammar he had to give the effect of bourgeois Norwegian speech. Within this norm he could vary from a formal to an informal style, the formal drawing on Danish, the informal on Norwegian. In his letters and articles the style is generally formal; in the plays formal style is limited to public orations and to the speech of persons characterized as bookish or pompous. Ibsen enjoyed lampooning the pomposity of politicians and officials by using a flowery, rhetorical style, which could be dangerously reminiscent of Bjørnson's oratory. In *The League of Youth* Stensgaard harangues the multitude, "I have observed talents glinting and glittering deep down among the people. I have also observed the spirit of corruption that weighs oppressively upon these talents and keeps them in subjection."[1] The words are hollow and amusingly pompous, particularly when one realizes that Stensgaard is really talking about his own "talents."

The ability to characterize his persons by small, but telling features of their style may not be considered a major poetic triumph. But the employment of appropriate registers of speech is one of the

---

7. On the Norwegian language problem see Einar Haugen, *Language Conflict and Language Planning: The Case of Modern Norwegian* (Cambridge, Mass.: Harvard University Press, 1966), esp. 54–61.
8. For details see Trygve Knudsen, "Phases of Style and Language in the Works of Henrik Ibsen," *Scandinavica* 2 (1963), 1–20.
9. *HU* 15.434 (statement made in 1899).
1. *HU* 6.370; *OI* 4.35.

important formal features of dramatic dialogue. They are a problem for every translator in exactly the same way as rhymes in verse, as noted by Popperwell when commenting on McFarlane's translations in the *Oxford Ibsen*.[2] As a formal feature they do not reproduce reality, in the way phonetic writing might, but they stimulate the imagination to visualize the character and give the play an added dimension. Meyer rightly calls this feature "one of Ibsen's supreme strengths, and one of his main contributions to the technique of prose dramas."[3]

The prose plays from *Pillars* to *Enemy* are rich with examples of sharply characterized speech styles. Ibsen refers to the problem of style several times, e.g., in connection with a performance of *Enemy* in 1882, when he writes that journalist Billing must be sure to speak "East Norwegian."[4] This can only mean that his accent should reinforce the image he gives of himself as a man of the people. There is little evidence of this in the printed text, except for his frequent reliance on profanity. The only other character in the play who swears freely is Dr. Stockmann himself, whose surprise and anger at the opposition is picturesquely profane.[5]

Ibsen even anticipated the current interest in differences between male and female speech styles. He asked a casual visitor in Munich, "Have you ever noticed how in conversation a woman usually ends a remark with a word of two or three syllables, a man with a monosyllable?"[6] Linguist Alf Sommerfelt noted some of the differences in the dialogue of Ibsen's men and women: Hedda Gabler and Hilde Wangel are addicted to the word *deilig* "lovely" and generally prefer the form *isj* to *œsj* for "ugh, ick" (the same feature in Gregers Werle no doubt suggests a certain effeminacy, perhaps a part of his mother fixation).[7] Ibsen remarked to his Boswell, John Paulsen, "There are a thousand finesses in dramatic art. Have you ever thought of the fact that the lines in a play should have a different cast according to whether they are spoken in the morning or in the evening?"[8] In a letter to a prospective French translator of *The Wild Duck*, he wrote that it "presents very special problems in that one must be very closely familiar with the Norwegian language to be able to understand how thoroughly every single character in

2. In *Scandinavica* 2 (1963), 52–56.
3. Meyer, *Ibsen*, 433.
4. Letter to Schröder, 14 Dec. 1882 (in Ibsen, *Brevveksling med Christiania Theater, 1878–1899*, ed. Øyvind Anker (Oslo: Theaterhistorisk Selskap, 1965), *Skrifter* no. 6, 25–31.
5. E.g., Billing in *OI* 6.64, Stockmann in *OI* 6.119, 121; Henrik Ibsen, *Ibsen: The Complete Major Prose Plays*, trans. Rolf Fjelde (New York: Farrar Strauss and Giroux/New American Library, 1978)—hereafter MPP—325, 379, 381.
6. Kristian Gløersen, "Henrik Ibsen: minder fra mit samvær med ham i utlandet." *Kringsjaa* (Christiania) 1906, 343–44.
7. Alf Sommerfelt, *Sproget som samfundsorgan* (Oslo: Stenersen, 1935), 21.
8. John Paulsen, *Samliv med Ibsen* (Copenhagen and Christiania: Gyldendal, 1906), 168.

the play has his or her particular individual mode of expression, by means of which the degree of cultivation of that person is marked. For instance, when Gina speaks, one must at once be able to hear that she has never learned grammar and that she has issued from the lower classes. And so on in different ways for all the other characters."[9]

DIALOGUE AS FORM

As mentioned, natural dialogue tends to be interrupted and unfinished. In *The Lady from the Sea* Arnholm discovers on a return visit to the Wangel home that his former pupil Bolette has grown into a marriageable young woman. He follows her with his eyes and starts to say, "She's really a lovely—," but covers his embarrassment by starting over, "They're really lovely girls these children who have grown up now—." Later Ellida speaks to him about their onetime affair, "At that time Wangel was still—at that time the girls' mother was still alive."[1] The interruption allows her to avoid saying "still married" and suggests to the audience that she is troubled by her position as a second wife. When Edmund Gosse reviewed the English performance of *Hedda Gabler* in 1891, the form of dialogue in it was so novel that he did not quite know what to make of "this unceasing display of hissing conversational fireworks, fragments of sentences without verbs, clauses that come to nothing, adverbial exclamations and cryptic interrogations." He did admit that "on the stage, no doubt, this rigid broken utterance will give an extraordinary sense of reality."[2]

A sense of reality is of course not reality but part of the poetic illusion. So are the many *verbal echoes* in the dialogue, which can be compared to the use of musical motifs in the work of Wagner, a contemporary of Ibsen's. In *Pillars of Society* the word "society" is firmly planted in the opening scene and gets repeated in virtually every scene after that; no one can remain in doubt of what the play is about. But this key word is not without its poetic function. Each person who uses it has his own interpretation of it, and this ambiguity illuminates the thinking of the characters. When Krap asks foreman Aune why he agitates, his reply (in the original) is, "Det gør jeg for at støtte samfundet," literally "I do it in order to support the society." His words strike the keynote of the play by alluding directly to its title, *Samfundets Støtter*, literally "Supports of Society." The verb *støtte* "support" associates directly with the noun *støtte*, which can mean any kind of supporter, including pillars. The English title per-

9. Letter to Victor Barrucand, 6 Mar. 1891 (*HU* 18.288; Sprinchorn, *LS*, 301).
1. *HU* 11.62, 66; trans. from *OI* 7.38; Fjelde, *MPP*, 602, 605.
2. Edmund Gosse, *Fortnightly Review*, 1 Jan. 1891.

mits no such play on words, since *pillar* cannot be a verb. But it turns out that Aune is not talking about "society" in a wider sense, only the Workingman's Society which he heads. Krap misunderstands and quotes Bernick as having called Aune's agitation "samfundsopløsende," i.e., destructive of society, antisocial. To this, Aune quite properly replies that "my society is not Mr. Bernick's society," and Krap counters by telling him off: "Your obligation is to the society known as Mr. Bernick's firm, for that is what we all live on."[3] In four speeches the word *samfunn* has been used in as many meanings, illuminating the contrasting interpretations of worker and employer, and setting the stage for a wider interpretation that will go beyond the selfish interests of either. In addition, this Norwegian word suggests "communion," as in "the communion of saints." Such verbal associations and playful echoes are mostly lost in translation.

Other key words that echo through the play and stay in the minds of the spectators are "the spirit of truth and freedom" enunciated by Lona Hessel, Nora's "miracle of miracles," Osvald's "joy of life," Dr. Stockmann's "damned compact majority." When reviewing *A Doll's House* on its appearance in 1879, a perceptive Norwegian critic, Erik Vullum, noted the absence of traditional imagery in the text, concluding that Ibsen "no longer needs to resort to any graphic aid to natural dialogue."[4] For us the important point is that the whole play is a dramatic metaphor, as proclaimed in its title, *Et Dukkehjem*. In spite of the English translations, this title does not mean a house for dolls, which in Norwegian is *dukkehus*, or *dukkestue*. Before Ibsen, *et dukkehjem* was a small, cozy, neat home; his play gave it the pejorative meaning. Nora is a doll only in a metaphorical sense, having been spoiled by her father and now by her husband. Her home is therefore not a home for adults but a playhouse. When William Archer saw it performed for the first time, he wrote, "The play is not a mere realistic drama, but a poem, and its poetry should be emphasized to give it full effect."[5] In 1971, two decades after his prosaic rewriting of *An Enemy of the People*, Arthur Miller wrote that he now saw the play "rather as a poem, a symbolic demand for a new stage of human evolution."[6]

THE POETRY OF PROSE

If this can be validly maintained for the "social" plays, as I believe it can, it grows increasingly true as we move into the world of *The*

3. *HU* 8.34; *OI* 5.24; Fjelde, *MPP*, 16.
4. Erik Vullum, review of *Et Dukkehjem* in *Dagbladet*, 6 and 13 Dec. 1879; here from Meyer, *Ibsen*, 455.
5. Letter from William to Charles Archer, printed in "Ibseniana," *Edda* 31 (1931), 455–56; *OI* 5.457.
6. Letter, Repertory Theater Recording of Miller's adaptation of *An Enemy of the People*, 1971.

Wild Duck and the plays that follow. We have seen how the play is built around a deadly metaphor that takes root in Gregers Werle's diseased brain. He, too, suffers from a "sickly conscience," which Relling unfeelingly diagnoses as "integrity fever," or "rectitudinitis," as we might also translate Ibsen's matchless *retskaffenhedsfeber*. Nordau suggests that it is one of Ibsen's many versions of "original sin."[7] Gregers, as the Christian he is, believes in the value of confession, followed by forgiveness. But Gina refuses to confess and Hjalmar refuses to forgive. Gregers imposes the demand of Christian sacrifice on little Hedvig, as if Hjalmar were a god to be appeased. The author balances the absurdly comic rhetoric of Hjalmar against the absurdly tragic rhetoric of Gregers: both of them have a "mission" in life. Hedvig's death is itself a poem of love, a young girl's love for an unworthy father, who blindly allows her to be crushed between the harsh demands of the ideal and the real.

Poetic mood grows ever more prominent in the following plays. Both Rosmer and Rebecca are deeply poetic figures. Rosmer brings with him the delicate fragrance of an old, decaying tradition, Rebecca the passion of the bewitching North. "It swept over me like a storm at sea. Like one of those storms we sometimes get in the winter up North. It takes hold of you—and carries you off with it, you see—for as long as it lasts. It never occurs to you to resist."[8] The play opens and closes on a poetic folklore motif—the white horse that warns the folk of Rosmersholm that a death will occur. At crucial turns of the action comes Brendel, bohemian and would-be poet, whose every speech is in a comic-poetic mode: "The ecstasies I've relished in my time, John! The mysterious beatitude of creation—or, again, its equivalent—the plaudits, the acclaim, the celebrity, the laurel crowns—all these I've gathered in my grateful hands, trembling with joy."[9] The conversation of Rosmer and Rebecca as they go hand in hand to the millrace is as ceremonial and ritualistic as a church service:

> ROSMER The husband shall go with his wife, as the wife with her husband.
> REBECCA But first tell me this: is it you who go with me or I with you?
> ROSMER That is something we shall never fathom.
> REBECCA Yet I would so much like to know it.
> ROSMER We two go with one another, Rebecca. I with you and you with me.
> REBECCA I almost think that is so.
> ROSMER For now we two are one.[1]

7. Max Nordau, *Degeneration* (New York: Appleton, 1895), 358.
8. *HU* 10.426; trans. from *OI* 6.369; Fjelde, *MPP*, 573.
9. *HU* 10.363; *OI* 6.310; trans. from Fjelde, *MPP*, 514.
1. *HU* 10.438; *OI* 6.380; Fjelde, *MPP*, 584.

The title of *The Lady from the Sea* in the original is *Fruen fra havet*, a lightly rewritten form of *havfruen*, "the mermaid." Mermaids, being both fabled and female, are poetic by definition. The theme of fascination with danger is also an old poetic motif. Here it is worked out in several forms, from the not-so-childish games that Hilde plays with the tubercular artist Lyngstrand (it's so "thrilling"!) to the very real fixation of Ellida on the strange seaman with the fish eyes, her "merman" who would lure her back into the sea. As the moment of choice is upon her, the text grows lyrical:

> WANGEL (quietly and sadly). I see it so well, Ellida. Inch by inch you're slipping away from me. This hunger for the boundless, the infinite—the unattainable—will finally drive your mind out completely into darkness.
> ELLIDA Oh, yes, yes—I feel it—like black, soundless wings hanging over me![2]

In *Hedda Gabler* one of the main figures, Løvborg, is another bohemian, a scholar so imaginative and unorthodox that he chooses to speculate about the future. His secret love, Hedda, is more fascinated than fond of him. In her spiritual confinement he represents to her the dream of beauty that she covets and that she misses in her own life. She spins a web of poetry around him in the hope that he will live out her dream for her. Her "vine leaves in the hair" is a classical motif, as we have seen, and it stands at the other end of the spectrum from General Gabler's pistols, which are cold, hard, and modern. These two images define her character and suggest better than anything else the extremes between which she swings.

While working on *The Master Builder*, Ibsen wrote one of the rare poems of his later years, a sad little ditty about an elderly couple whose home has burned and who now are searching in the ashes for a jewel they lost:

> But even if they find, these burned-out folk,
> The precious, unconsumed treasure—
> *She* will never again find her faith,
> Nor *he* the happiness that burned.[3]

In the play the theme of the home that burned is at the root of Solness's and his wife's deep frustration in marriage, a symbol of the love that has burned out between them. Solness is weighed down by guilt and fears the retribution that is coming. To his doctor he says: "The turn is coming. I can sense it. I feel it getting closer. Someone or other is going to demand: Make way for me! And then

2. *HU* 11.153; *OI* 7.120; trans. from Fjelde, *MPP*, 685.
3. *HU* 14.463; *OI* 7.521.

all the others will come storming after, threatening and screaming: Make way, make way, make way! Yes, just you watch doctor. One of these days youth will come here, knocking on the door—"[372][4] This rhythmic, dramatically exalted speech is typical of the later plays.

The fact that youth does indeed knock on the door immediately after Solness has predicted it is so highly coincidental and so pat that no truly realistic play could tolerate it. But there is poetic justice and humor in the shape that youth takes—not the young rivals that Solness is thinking of but a radiant, trustful young woman, Hilde Wangel. She comes to claim the "kingdom" Solness had promised her ten years earlier. Both phrase and idea are poetic, arising as they do out of the world of fairy tale, and the fact that the episode may never have occurred only adds to its mystic charm. Ironically, she *is* the one who eventually destroys him by insisting that he live up to her ideal of him. The verbal dance that these two perform, the lonely artist and the lovely girl, is sheer dramatic poetry. We spoke earlier of the symbolism of the tower and its meaning. Let us now look at its poetic value. Solness served the ideal by building churches, the real by building homes; in old age he clumsily tried to fuse them by building a home with a spire. But he foresees that it will bring him no happiness, for he himself remains outside these structures, alienated from God, isolated from people. With Hilde he dreams of a new synthesis, again a mythic symbol, the "castle in the air," in which no one can live. So, when he succeeds in climbing the tower, he has to fall, as did Icarus when his wings melted, because death is the inflexible limit to man's earthly aspirations.

The Master Builder calls to mind, as we noted earlier, the Tower of Babel. But it also suggests another well-known folklore theme: the builder who is promised some great reward if he can finish a church. Ultimately, he is frustrated by forces beyond his reach, just as Solness finds that he is unable to complete the church of his own life. He calls on forces beyond reality, his "helpers and servers," who have served him well until the end, when they finally desert him. In his youth Ibsen wrote: "Since the subject matter of myth is timeless, its validity in time can never be so limited as to disqualify an author from laying another stone upon that mythical foundation."[5] In this play he added another stone to the builder's legend by making it into a metaphor for human striving and, by implication, for his own.

Ibsen's last three plays are built in much the same way, with allusions to mythical-poetic themes, in dialogues that are charged with

4. *HU* 12.51–52; *OI* 7.375; Fjelde, *MPP*, 800.
5. *Manden*, 23 Mar. 1851 (*HU* 15.45).

poetic feeling, expressed in symbolic objects or phrases that stir the imagination.

In *Little Eyolf* the Rat Wife is a modern Pied Piper of Hamelin, eerily peering about for anything in the house that is "gnawing." We discover soon enough that there are plenty of "gnawing" things in the house, above all Allmers's relationship with his wife, Rita. They are alienated from each other and from their son, Eyolf, who is left to be lured "into the depths" by the fascinating Rat Wife, just as Hedvig was lured by Gregers. Allmers is a dreamer, another of Ibsen's unproductive poets, who longs for "the solitude up among the mountain peaks and on the great desolate open spaces."[6] These characters are all surrounded by magnetic fields of mystic fascination that draw them together and then push them apart as they approach one another.

John Gabriel Borkman is Ibsen's last and most majestic picture of financial failure, a monumental projection of his father's fate. In a setting of "faded splendor," John Gabriel is living out his aged alienation, mystically brooding over the possibilities for human happiness that he has dreamed of providing by his enterprise. The woman he had rejected for money and career tells him, "The Bible speaks of a mysterious sin for which there is no forgiveness. I have never understood before what that could be. Now I do understand. The great sin for which there is no forgiveness is to murder love in a human soul."[7] Like Hilde Wangel and Ibsen himself, he is looking for his "kingdom." He reaches the heights of poetic prose as he develops the myth of the hidden treasure that is found and then vanishes as it is about to be extracted: "But I'll whisper to you here in the silence of the night. I love you, lying there unconscious in the depths and the darkness! I love you, you riches straining to be born—with all your shining aura of power and glory. I love you, love you, love you."[8] John Gabriel's vision becomes a religious rite, studded with words from biblical terminology.

This is equally true of Ibsen's epilogue, *When We Dead Awaken*, which he at first thought of calling *Resurrection*. From the solidly realistic starting point in the small talk of Rubek and Maja on their return to Norway from the south, the play quickly takes off into the world of poetry. Even their talk is subtly mannered, in short, alternate thrusts that draw them out; the young wife is so bored that she can "hear the stillness." Emotional relief enters in the shape of a strange white-clad woman, who proves to be Rubek's old model Irene, and a faunlike huntsman who will function as the "he-man" Maja has missed in her marriage. Irene's conviction that she is

6. *HU* 12.203; trans. from *OI* 8.50; Fjelde, *MPP*, 879.
7. *HU* 13.86; trans. from *OI* 8.197.
8. *HU* 13.124; *OI* 8.231; trans. from Fjelde, *MPP*, 1021.

dead, murdered by Rubek's rejection of her love, is reinforced by her shroudlike dress and the contrasting blackness of the nun that attends her. The dialogues are misty, poetic conversations around the theme of art and life, specifically the artist's exploitation of life and happiness as material for art. Rubek has begun to lose faith in the value of his art: "All the talk about the artist's high calling and the artist's mission, and so on, began to strike me as basically empty and hollow and meaningless."[9] In its place he would like to put what he calls "life," but now it is too late. The only life he can experience is death on the heights, in the avalanche, which now becomes the final shroud. The play is built around the theme of resurrection, which is symbolized by his statue, as well as Irene's aphorism, "When we dead awaken, we discover that we have never lived."[1]

So Ibsen ends in poetry, where he had begun fifty years earlier. The prose of his last plays is better poetry than the verse of his first. Although he shifted from verse to prose in mid-career, he never stopped writing poetry. But it was a poetry to suit the modern theater. Even at its most prosaic, his dialogue has a form that gives it dramatic shape. The elements in this form of poetry are the play of dialogue, the balancing of characters, the use of verbal echoes and keywords, and the invention of symbols to give centrality to the plays. There is always underlying patterning in these plays, which becomes apparent to the naked eye only with careful analysis but which can still be felt by reader and spectator as a pervasive quality.

The characters form constellations that we recognize as figures on the firmament of Ibsen's mythology. This is an archetypal pattern of men and women who are trying to harmonize the oppositions of life and finding it not merely difficult but ultimately impossible. They are looking for a harmony that will not be a compromise, and they strive for it even though (or because) it is impossible and will lead to their destruction. The verbal echoes sometimes are no more than mannerisms of speech, which on a realistic plane serve to identify certain characters and make them memorable. But they are also dramatically significant by giving poetic shape and continuity to the plays. Then there are the symbols, which are elements in Ibsen's code, as we saw, but which are also poetic in themselves: Brand's ice church, Gerd's hawk, Peer's madhouse in Cairo, Bernick's rotten ships, Nora's desperate tarantella, Alving's flaming orphanage, Stockmann's poisoned baths, Hedvig's wild duck, Rosmer's white horse, Ellida's eerie seaman, Hedda's fatal pistol, Solness's dizzying tower, Eyolf's floating crutch, Borkman's veins of gold, and Rubek's tainted Resurrection. These

9. *HU* 13.251; *OI* 8.270; trans. from Fjelde, *MPP*, 1063.
1. *HU* 13.271; *OI* 8.285; Fjelde, *MPP*, 1080.

central symbols are only a few of the many Ibsen created. Together, the features described comprise a poetic statement about the glory and the frustration of being human.

They also tell us, when compared with Ibsen's explicit statements, something of his theory of art and his view of life. Having tried in his early years to combine artistic creation with social participation, he found his true calling in the creative life and virtually isolated himself from physical contact with the human race. After having supported (if a bit reluctantly) the ideal causes of his day—nationalism, Scandinavianism, internationalism, feminism, even socialism—he withdrew. Brandes wrote that "Ibsen became himself by becoming a solitary . . ." His poetry, he said, is that of "loneliness, portraying the lonely need, the lonely strife, and the lonely protest."[2] He became the "esthete" on the "heights," who defined the act of poetic creation as essentially "to see," believing that "life and its phenomena are best viewed by a writer at a distance, in both time and space."[3] By remaining uncommitted, he could capitalize on his divided self, enabling him to take the topics of the times, project them on the stage, give them an underlying significance, and make a poetic statement that could reach the hearts of women and men, and not only in his own time.

Ibsen's poetic quality is best summed up in the words written almost a half-century ago by the great English novelist E. M. Forster: "Ibsen was a poet at forty. . . . He was a poet at sixty also. . . . Not only was he born a poet—he died one, and as soon as we try to understand him instead of asking him to teach us, the point becomes clearer."[4]

READINGS AND REFERENCES

Ibsen's use of the Norwegian language has been explored by several linguists: see, for example, Johan Storm, "Ibsen og det norske Sprog," in *Henrik Ibsen: Festskrift*, ed. Gerhard Gran (Bergen, 1898), 147–205; Didrik Arup Seip, "Ibsens retskrivning og sprogform," in Henrik Ibsen, *Samlede verker* [*Hundreårsutgaven*], ed. Francis Bull, Halvdan Koht, and Didrik Arup Seip (Oslo: Gyldendal, 1928), 1.16–24, and "Henrik Ibsen og språket," in his *Studier i norsk språkhistorie* (Oslo: Aschehoug, 1934), 228–36 (originally published in 1928); Trygve Knudsen, "Phases of Style and Language in the Works of Henrik Ibsen," *Scandinavica* 2 (1963), 1–20.

2. Georg Brandes, review of Ibsen's poem, *Illustreret Tidende* (Copenhagen), 22 Oct. 1871; here from Meyer, *Ibsen*, 348–49.
3. Kristian Gløersen, *Kringsjaa*, 347; cit. in Meyer, *Ibsen*, 517.
4. E. M. Forster, "Ibsen the Romantic," in *Abinger Harvest* (London: Arnold, 1936), 82; reprinted in Fjelde, *Ibsen*, 174–78, and in Henrik Ibsen, *A Critical Anthology*, ed. James W. McFarlane (London: Penguin, 1970), 231–36.

On Ibsen as poet, one can now read John Northam, *Ibsen: A Critical Study* (Cambridge: University Press, 1973), who flatly states (p. 1) that "all of his books, early or late, in verse or in modern prose, are a form of poetry" and who goes on to demonstrate this for six plays. His views have been challenged by Ronald Gray, who contends that the claim is built on a misunderstanding of the Norwegian word *digte* (like German *dichten*). Gray's book *Ibsen—a Dissenting View: A Study of the Last Twelve Plays* (Cambridge: University Press, 1977) argues from a more traditional view of the meaning of "poetry." It may be regarded as a healthy antidote or reaction, but it represents a point of view that I believe cannot be sustained on the evidence.

Inga-Stina Ewbank illuminates the poetry of Ibsen's prose in her "Ibsen and 'the far more difficult art' of prose" (*Contemporary Approaches to Ibsen 2*, ed. Daniel Haakonsen [Oslo: Universitetsforlaget, 1971], 60–83). She speaks (on p. 76) of the fact that in *Rosmersholm* "the whole verbal tissue of the play has a peculiar density and ambiguity about it," which fulfills the ideal of the greatest dramatic poetry by suggesting "complexities of character which are beyond the scope of the most exacting discursive analysis" (quoting John Bayley).

JENNETTE LEE

Ibsen's Symbolism Defined†

The decade from 1867 to 1877 marks a dead centre in Ibsen's work. Except for the "Emperor and Galilean," which was the mere elaboration of a sketch made in Rome some years before, and which bears no relation, either in content or in interest, to the time in which it was written—except for this play he produced no artwork from the writing of "The Young Men's League," begun in 1868, to the presentation of "Pillars of Society" in 1877. Up to this period he had produced, from the time he was twenty years old, an almost regular succession of dramatic works of highly romantic character; after this period, from 1877 to 1899, he produced every other year a play of the most realistic nature—each play belonging to the same order, and the whole differing in every regard from the work of his earlier period. They make in all a dozen plays that may prove to be the most significant work, artistically, of the nineteenth century. Certainly the nineteenth century has no parallel to offer to

† From *The Ibsen Secret: A Key to the Prose Dramas of Henrik Ibsen* (New York: G. P. Putnam's Sons, 1907), 45–58.

the change of ideal that they mark. At the age of fifty, after thirty
years of writing and thinking. Ibsen began his lifework anew. Tolstoi, it is true, changed from artist to reformer in his old age, and
Wagner, after middle life, composed *Parsifal* and the *Niebelungen
Ring*, the greatest operas of musical history; but Tolstoi only struck,
in each successive work, a little more loudly the note of the reformer, a little less clearly the note of the artist, till the voice of the
artist was lost; and Wagner but brought to perfection in Parsifal the
motives that shaped the Flying Dutchman and Tannhäuser and
Lohengrin. Neither Tolstoi nor Wagner changed his ideal.

But Ibsen faced squarely about. He forswore the gods of his
youth and waited ten years for the dawning of a new hierarchy. He
had worked twenty years, now he waited ten, and again he wrought
twenty. That is the sum of his life-work, fitting itself, approximately,
into decades for the pleasure of the curious. The work of the first
twenty years is of the most ultra-romantic character. All literature
would have to be searched to find a companion piece for *Peer Gynt*
in its romantic emphasis. The plays of this earlier period—which
are romantic and poetic and highly artistic—deal, for the most part,
with the past. The plays of the second period—which are realistic
and written in prose—deal entirely with the present. Thus a change
of artistic ideal that is generally accomplished only by generations
has taken place in the life and soul of one man. Ibsen's realistic
work is even more perfect and finished than his romantic. It is as if,
when a young man, he had engaged in literature through mere
overflow of spirit, a kind of Viking energy that must expend itself—
in historical romance, in Norse fancy, in finished phrase, and
hurried, tumbling rhymes and lines—work so spontaneous and intricate and finished that it has taxed translators to the utmost to
give a conception of its free, bubbling nature and exact perfection
of form. Then there came a pause. The man seems to have stayed
his hand, considering—"Why should I fashion these romantic trifles, playthings of art? The men and women of my own time, society, life as it is,—these are what fascinate the mind and elude it."
He planned a new play, *The Young Men's League*. It should be in
prose, and it should treat of Norwegian society of the present day.
He sets forth his ideal in a letter written to Mr. Edmund Gosse:[1]

> There is one point which I must discuss with you. You think
> my new drama ought to be written in verse, and that it will
> gain an advantage if it is. Here I must simply contradict you;
> for the piece is, as you will find, developed in the most realis-
> tic way possible. The illusion I wish to produce is that of truth

1. Ibsen, in this extract, is referring to *Emperor* and *Galilean* (1873), not to *The League of
Youth* (1869). [*Editor*]

itself; I want to produce upon the reader the impression that what he is reading is actually taking place before him. If I were to use verse, I should by so doing be stultifying my own intention and the object which I placed before me. The variety of every-day and unimportant characters which I have intentionally introduced into the piece would be effaced and blended into one another if I had allowed them all to converse in a rhythmic movement. . . . —My new drama is not indeed a tragedy in the old-world signification of the word, but what I have tried to depict in it is human beings, and for that very reason I have not allowed them to talk the language of the gods!

The Young Men's League has, in itself, no interest. It is prosaic, hard, and unconvincing. Biographically it has the greatest interest. In it Ibsen had tried and failed. Then he waited. Ten years earlier he had made a similar attempt at prose form in *Love's Comedy*, a satiric drama treating of modern society. Failing to satisfy himself— failing in realism, that is—he had turned the whole bodily into verse, sometimes line for line and sometimes with free hand. He had recognised that prose is the form suited to treatment of modern life, and prose he could not handle; therefore he returned to verse. But now, ten years later, a change had come over him. He would not return to the old form and he could not go on. Therefore he waited.

He was intensely interested in the life and problems of his own time. They fascinated and eluded him. He must treat these, or nothing. But he was, first and foremost, an artist—more artist than reformer. He would never write a second *Young Men's League*.

Slowly, it may be, out of the years of waiting, or in a flash, the secret of his later art form came to him. Surrounded in his Dresden retreat by the noblest art-work of the past, and by the *Music of the Future*, with its richness of harmony and melody and dramatic motive, he groped his way to a new dramatic form such as no playwright had ever dreamed. Art-form he must have. He would write of the people of his own time; therefore he must write in prose. And prose as a dramatic art-form was unknown. He must hew it out of the rock of his own being. In 1877 he produced *Pillars of Society*. His form was found. He has never varied from it. He has only perfected and developed it.

The new form was symbolism.

Literature, as the record of universal experience, has gradually acquired certain symbols that have become conventionalised—a kind of stage property of poets and artists and common people. The lily is a symbol of purity, the eagle of strength, red of passion, and gray of peace. These are symbols that carry their meaning in the mere naming of them. They serve their use most perfectly when the symbolic quality is most revealed. Rossetti's work is full of conventional symbolism—mystery and charm and unreality. We walk among his poems as in a garden where perfume and shape and colour haunt the senses with curious, hidden meaning. One may not pluck a flower, or touch it, lest the dream be broken.

Of this conventional symbolism Ibsen's work has no trace. His work gives, first and foremost, a sense of intense reality—of actuality even. It is not till later that a hidden intent is guessed, and when this intention is traced to its source, the symbols discovered are original. Each of them—the pistol, the tarantelle, the wild duck, the white horses, the rotten ship—reveals perfectly that for which it stands. They originate in Ibsen's imagination, and serve his purpose because they are the concrete images of his thought.

The symbolism of character—if it may be so called—in which a character stands for a universal type,—Othello for jealousy and Macbeth for ambition—is found in the work of Ibsen's earlier period. In his first play, *Catilina*, for example, the two women, Aurelia and Furia, embody two abstract principles in the life of Catiline, one drawing out all that is tender and gentle, the other inciting him to wild deeds. Jaeger calls attention to them as prototypes of Ibsen's later women. Symbolism of this more obvious character will be found both in Ibsen's earlier and later plays, as in all dramatic work. But symbolism of this sort, if it may be called symbolism at all, differs from the conventional order in that it attains its highest excellence when the symbolic quality is submerged and the reality appears to occupy the stage alone. Othello is not embodied jealousy, but a jealous man; Rita Allmers is not the embodiment of physical beauty and wealth, but a living woman who charms the senses.

It is not, however, types of this sort that are referred to when Ibsen's symbols are mentioned, but, as I have tried to point out in *A Doll's House* and *Hedda Gabler*, symbols that stand, first, for a character of the play; and second, as has not yet been shown, for the meaning of the play as a whole. An object or event is used as a central theme or motive of the play. Toward this symbol the ostensible action of the play moves, and from it, it recedes. This object or event—as the tarantelle—also stands for the character of the play, whose soul is the stage of the real action of the play; and thus the symbol stands, at last, for the play itself.

It was the discovery of this artistic device that enabled Ibsen to go on with the prose drama. "On the whole," he had written earlier to Mr. Gosse, "my feeling is that literary form ought to be in relation to the amount of ideality which is spread over the representation." This he had at last achieved. His prose dramas preserve the sense of reality. They "produce upon the reader the impression that what he is reading is actually taking place before him." But they convey at the same time a sense of art, of removal, a picture set in its frame, a touch of the higher reality that is called truth, a meaning underlying and refining the whole. This sense of art is produced by the use of symbol. It reserves itself, is not puffed up, thinketh not of itself more highly than it ought; but all the time it is there, constant, pervasive, convincing—persuading the spectator that that which he looks upon is life itself and that, more than life, it is truth.

RAINER MARIA RILKE

From The Notebooks of Malte Laurids Brigge†

There I sat before your books, obstinate man, trying to understand them as the others do, who don't leave you in one piece but chip off their little portion and go away satisfied. For I still didn't understand fame, that public demolition of someone who is in the process of becoming, whose building-site the mob breaks into, knocking down his stones.

Young man anywhere, in whom something is welling up that makes you shiver, be grateful that no one knows you. And if those who think you are worthless contradict you, and if those whom you call your friends abandon you, and if they want to destroy you because of your precious ideas: what is this obvious danger, which concentrates you inside yourself, compared with the cunning enmity of fame, later, which makes you innocuous by scattering you all around?

Don't ask anyone to speak about you, not even contemptuously. And when time passes and you notice that your name is circulating among men, don't take this more seriously than anything else you might find in their mouths. Think rather that it has become cheapened, and throw it away. Take another name, *any* other, so that God can call you in the night. And hide it from everyone.

Loneliest of men, holding aloof from them all, how quickly they have caught up with you because of your fame. A little while ago they were against you body and soul; and now they treat you as their equal. And they pull your words around with them in the cages of their presumption, and exhibit them in the streets, and tease them a little, from a safe distance. All your terrifying wild beasts.

---

† From *The Selected Poetry of Rainer Maria Rilke*, ed. and trans. Stephen Mitchell (New York: Vintage, 1989), 101–03. Copyright © 1982 by Stephen Mitchell. Reprinted by permission of Random House, Inc.

When I first read you, these words broke loose and fell upon me in my wilderness, in all their desperation. As desperate as you yourself became in the end, you whose course is drawn incorrectly on every chart. Like a crack it crosses the heavens, this hopeless hyperbola of your path, which curves toward us only once, then recedes again in terror. What did you care if a woman stayed or left, if this man was seized by vertigo and that one by madness, if the dead were alive and the living seemed dead: what did you care? It was all so natural for you; you passed through it the way someone might walk through a vestibule, and didn't stop. But you lingered, bent over, where our life boils and precipitates and changes color: inside. Farther in than anyone has ever been; a door had sprung open before you, and now you were among the alembics in the firelight. In there, where, mistrustful, you wouldn't take anyone with you, in there you sat and discerned transitions. And there, since your blood drove you not to form or to speak, but to reveal, there you made the enormous decision to so magnify these tiny events, which you yourself first perceived only in test tubes, that they would be seen by thousands of people, immense before them all. Your theater came into being. You couldn't wait until this life almost without spatial reality, this life which had been condensed by the weight of the centuries into a few small drops, could be discovered by the other arts: until it could gradually be made visible to a few connoisseurs who, little by little, acquire insight and finally demand to see these august rumors confirmed in the parable of the scene opened in front of them. You couldn't wait for that; you were there, and everything that is barely measurable—an emotion that rises by half a degree, the angle of deflection, read off from up close, of a will burdened by an almost infinitesimal weight, the slight cloudiness in a drop of longing, and that barely perceptible color-change in an atom of confidence—all this you had to determine and record. For it is in such reactions that life existed, *our* life, which had slipped into us, had drawn back inside us so deeply that it was hardly possible even to make conjectures about it any more.

Because you were a revealer, a timelessly tragic poet, you had to transform this capillary action all at once into the most convincing gestures, into the most available forms. So you began that unprecedented act of violence in your work, which, more and more impatiently, desperately, sought equivalents in the visible world for what you had seen inside. There was a rabbit there, an attic, a room where someone was pacing back and forth; there was a clatter of glass in a nearby bedroom, a fire outside the windows; there was the sun. There was a church, and a rock-strewn valley that was like a church. But this wasn't enough: finally towers had to come in and whole mountain-ranges; and the avalanches that bury landscapes spilled onto a stage overwhelmed with what is tangible, for the sake of what cannot be grasped. Then you could do no more. The two ends, which you had bent together until they touched, sprang apart; your demented strength escaped from the flexible wand, and your work was as if it had never existed.

If this hadn't happened, who could understand why in the end you refused to go away from the window, obstinate as you always were? You wanted to see the people passing by; for the thought had occurred to you that someday you might make something out of them, if you decided to begin.

E. M. FORSTER

Ibsen the Romantic†

'My book *is* poetry, and if it is not poetry, then it will be.'
—Ibsen to Björnson.

Ibsen was a poet during the earlier part of his life. He began as a lyricist, and his first plays are either in verse or are inspired by an imaginative contemplation of the past. When he was about forty, a change occurred, the importance of which has been differently estimated. Certain critics, both friendly and hostile, regard it as a fundamental change. They argue that with *The League of Youth* the real or realistic Ibsen begins to emerge, the singer dies, the social castigator is born, the scene clarifies and darkens, and ideas come to the front which do not necessarily contradict previous ideas, but which are given a prominence that entirely alters the dramatic emphasis. We pass from the epic to the domestic. Peer Gynt becomes Hialmar Ekdal, and Brand as Gregers Werle tears the spectacles of illusion from his eyes, and they work out their tragedy not among forests and fjords, but in a photographic studio opening into a sort of aviary. The aviary contains a few dead Christmas trees, also a water trough, some rabbits but no bears, one wild duck and that a damaged one. We could not be further from romance, the critics say, and turn, if we are friendly, to the character drawing, the technique, and the moral and social issues; if they are hostile, to the squalor. 'Somewhere in the course of the battle of his life Ibsen had a lyric Pegasus killed under him,' writes Brandes. 'Novel and per-

† From *Abinger Harvest* (London: Edward Arnold, 1940), 81–86. Copyright © 1936 and renewed 1964 by Edward M. Forster. Reprinted by permission of Harcourt, Inc., The Provost and Scholars of King's College, Cambridge, and The Society of Authors as the Literary Representative of the E. M. Forster Estate.

ilous nonsense,' wrote the *Daily Telegraph*. The critics agree in thinking that the poetry, if ever there was any, has gone.

Has it gone? Can the habits of forty years be set aside? Of twenty years—yes; most people are romantic at twenty, owing to lack of experience. As they grow older life offers various alternatives, such as worldliness or philosophy or the sense of humour, and they usually accept one of these. If, in spite of more solid temptations, they still cling to poetry, it is because a deep preference has to be satisfied. Ibsen was a poet at forty because he had that preference. He was a poet at sixty also. His continued interest in avalanches, water, trees, fire, mines, high places, travelling, was not accidental. Not only was he born a poet—he died one, and as soon as we try to understand him instead of asking him to teach us, the point becomes clearer.

He is, of course, not easy to understand. Two obstacles may be noted. In the first place although he is not a teacher he has the air of being one, there is something in his method that implies a message, though the message really rested on passing irritabilities, and not on any permanent view of conduct or the universe. In the second place, he further throws us off the scent by taking a harsh or a depressing view of human relationships. As a rule, if a writer has a romantic temperament, he will find human relationships beautiful. His characters may hate one another or be unhappy together, but they will generate nobility or charm, they will never be squalid, whatever their other defects. And the crux in Ibsen is that, though he had the romantic temperament, he found personal intercourse sordid. Sooner or later his characters draw their little knives, they rip up the present and the past, and the closer their intimacy the better their opportunities for exchanging pain. Oswald Alving knows how to hurt his mother, Rosmer his mistress, and married couples are even more favourably placed. The Helmers, the Tesmans, the Wangels, Solnesses, Allmers, Borkmans, Rubeks—what a procession, equally incapable of comradeship and ecstasy! If they were heroic or happy once, it was before the curtain rose, and only survives as decay. And if they attain reconciliation, like the Rentheim sisters, the curtain has to fall. Their intercourse is worse then unfriendly, it is petty; moral ugliness trespasses into the æsthetic. And when a play is full of such characters and evolves round their fortunes, how can it possibly be a romantic play? Poetry might perhaps be achieved if Ibsen's indignation was of the straight-hitting sort, like Dante's. But for all its sincerity there is something automatic about it, he reminds us too often of father at the breakfast table after a bad night, sensitive to the defects of society as revealed by a chance glance at the newspaper, and apt to blame all parties for them indiscriminately. Now it is the position of women that upsets father, now the lies people tell, now their inability to lie, now the drains, now the newspaper itself, which he crumples up, but his helpers and servers have to retrieve it, for bad as are all political parties he must really see who got in at Rosmersholm. Seldom can a great genius have had so large a dose of domestic irritability. He was cross with his enemies and friends, with theatre-managers, professors, and students, and so cross with his country-men for not volunteering to help the Danes in 1864 that he had to go to Italy to say so. He might have volunteered in person—he was in the prime of life at the time—but this did not occur to him, he preferred instead to write a scathing little satire about a Norwegian mother whose son was safe at the front. And it is (if one may adopt the phrase) precisely the volunteer spirit that is absent from his conception of human relationships. He put everything into them except the strength of his arm.

'Not a great writer . . . almost great, but marred by this lack of generosity.' How readily the phrases rise to the lips! How false they are! For this nagging quality, this habitual bitterness—they are essential in his greatness, because they beckon to the poetry in him, and carry it with them under the ground. Underground. Into the depths of the sea, the depths of the sea. Had he been of heroic build and turned to the light and the sun, his gifts would have evaporated. But he was—thank heaven—subterranean, he loved narrow passages and darkness, and his later plays have a romantic intensity which not only rivals the romantic expansion of their predecessors, but is absolutely unique in literature. The trees in old Ekdal's aviary are as numerous as a forest because they are countless, the water in the chickens' trough includes all the waves on which the Vikings could sail. To his impassioned vision dead and damaged things, however contemptible socially, dwell for ever in the land of romance, and this is the secret of his so-called symbolism: a connection is found between objects that lead different types of existence; they reinforce one another and each lives more intensely than before. Consequently his stage throbs with a mysteriousness for which no obvious preparation has been made, with beckonings, tremblings, sudden compressions of the air, and his characters as they wrangle among the oval tables and stoves are watched by an unseen power which slips between their words.

A weaker dramatist who had this peculiar gift would try to get his effect by patches of fine writing, but with Ibsen as with Beethoven the beauty comes not from the tunes, but from the way they are used and are worked into the joints of the action. *The Master Builder* contains superb examples of this. The plot unfolds logically, the diction is flat and austere, the scene is a villa close to which another villa is being erected, the chief characters are an elderly couple and a young woman who is determined to get a thrill out of her visit, even if it entails breaking her host's neck. Hilda is a minx, and though her restlessness is not as vulgar as Hedda Gabler's it is quite as pernicious and lacks the saving gesture of suicide. That is one side of Hilda. But on the other side she touches Gerd and the Rat Wife and the Button Moulder, she is a lure and an assessor, she comes from the non-human and asks for her kingdom and for castles in the air that shall rest on solid masonry, and from the moment she knocks at the door poetry filters into the play. Solness, when he listened to her, was neither a dead man nor an old fool. No prose memorial can be raised to him, and consequently Ibsen himself can say nothing when he falls from the scaffolding, and Bernard Shaw does not know that there is anything to say. But Hilda hears harps and voices in the air, and though her own voice may be that of a sadistic schoolgirl the sound has nevertheless gone out into the dramatist's universe, the avalanches in *Brand* and *When We Dead Awaken* echo it, so does the metal in John Gabriel Borkman's mine. And it has all been done so competently. The symbolism never holds up the action, because it is part of the action, and because Ibsen was a poet, to whom creation and craftsmanship were one. It is the same with the white horse in *Rosmersholm*, the fire of life in *Ghosts*, the gnawing pains in *Little Eyolf*, the sea in *The Lady from the Sea*, where Hilda's own stepmother voices more openly than usual the malaise that connects the forces of nature and the fortunes of men. Everything rings true and echoes far because it is in the exact place which its surroundings require.

The source of Ibsen's poetry is indefinable; presumably it comes from the same place as his view of human nature, otherwise they would not harmonize as they do in his art. The vehicle in which poetry reached him—that can easily be defined; it was, of course, the scenery of western and south-western Norway. At some date previous to his Italian journey he must have had experiences of passionate intensity among the mountains, comparable to the early experiences of Wordsworth in the English lakes. All his life they kept returning to him, clothed in streams, trees, precipices, and hallowing his characters while they recriminated. In *Brand* and *Peer Gynt* they filled the stage; subsequently they shrank and concentrated; in the two last plays they again fill the stage and hasten the catastrophes by a shroud of snow. To compare Ibsen with Wordsworth is to scandalize the faithful in either camp, yet they had one important point in common: they were both of them haunted until the end of their lives by the romantic possibilities of scenery. Wordsworth fell into the residential fallacy; he continued to look at his gods direct, and to pin with decreasing success his precepts to the flanks of Helvellyn. Ibsen, wiser and greater, sank and smashed the Dovrëfjeld in the depths of the sea, the depths of the sea. He knew that he should find it again. Neither his satire nor his character drawing dwelt as deep; neither the problems he found in human conduct nor the tentative solutions he propounded lay at the roots of his extraordinary heart. There, in that strange gnarled region, a primæval romanticism lurked, frozen or twisted or exuding slime, there was the nest of the great Boyg. The Great Boyg did not strive, did not die, lay beneath good and evil, did not say one thing more than another:

> Forward or back, and it's just as far;
> Out or in, and it's just as strait.

What do the words mean, and, apart from their meaning, are they meant to be right? And if right, are the prayers of Solveig, which silence them for a moment, wrong? It is proper that we should ask such questions as these when focussing on the moral and social aspect of his work, and they have been brilliantly asked and answered by Bernard Shaw. But as soon as we shift the focus the questions go dim, the reformer becomes a dramatist, we shift again and the dramatist becomes a lyric poet, listening from first to last for the movements of the trolls. Ibsen is at bottom Peer Gynt. Side whiskers and all, he is a boy bewitched:

> The boy has been sitting on his mother's lap.
> They two have been playing all the life-day long.

And though the brow that bends over him can scarcely be described as maternal, it will assuredly preserve him from the melting ladle as long as books are read or plays seen.

[1928]

HUGH KENNER

Joyce and Ibsen's Naturalism†

Joyce is commonly admired for a sort of raw realism which unresolved theological preoccupations have unfortunately rendered somewhat defective. Harry Levin treats *Ulysses* as a shotgun wedding between naturalism and symbolism; Wyndham Lewis, less inhibited by academic usage, calls its heaping-up of thousands of concrete stupidities "a record diarrhoea." It would be easy to multiply instances of the assumption that Joyce took seriously the sort of *tranche-de-vie* reproduction of externals sanctioned by the French

† From *Sewanee Review* 49.1 (Winter 1951): 75–96. Copyright © 1951 by the University of the South. Reprinted by permission of the editor.

realists of the Nineteenth Century and by the cult of Ibsen at the beginning of the Twentieth. The intemperance with which the young Joyce championed Ibsen at Dublin, and his palpable imitation of Ibsenian methods in *Exiles*, have contributed to this misunderstanding; the Joyce legend has been thoroughly mixed up with the Ibsen legend, apparently with Joyce's overt endorsement.

It is not difficult to cast serious doubt on the bucolic simplification of Joyce as realist *manqué*; this involves getting Ibsen, and Joyce's relations with Ibsen, into some sort of rational perspective, a problem complicated by the absence of any critically respectable book on Ibsen in English. Such being the case, it is useful to start by indicating (though a proper demonstration must wait) what sort of respect for naturalistic conventions *Ulysses* in fact represents.

> What did the first drawer unlocked contain?
> A Vere Foster's handwriting copybook, property of Milly (Millicent) Bloom, certain pages of which bore diagram drawings marked *Papli*, which showed a large globular head with 5 hairs erect, 2 eyes in profile, the trunk full front with 3 large buttons, 1 triangular foot: 2 fading photographs of Queen Alexandra of England and of Maud Branscombe, actress and professional beauty: a Yuletide card, bearing on it a pictorial representation of a parasitic plant, the legend, *Mizpah*, the date Xmas 1892, the name of the senders, from Mr. and Mrs. M. Comerford, the versicle: *May this Yuletide bring to thee, Joy and peace and welcome glee:* . . .[1]

and so on for fifty lines. It is not likely to be disputed that the function of such a passage (it is representative of the 73-page *Ithaca* episode) is comic: it parodies not only Bloom's foolishly meticulous interest in the matter in which his spirit is immersed, but in its insane superabundance the methods of naturalism proper. From beginning to end *Ulysses* parodies the naturalistic novel with genial ferocity. Nor does this parody proceed from an irrelevant temperamental whim of Joyce's. He regards the naturalistic superstition as a social product coming within his diagnostician's provenance as much as any other freak of popular culture: a Bloomian product, by Blooms for Blooms. There are several indications that Bloom would like to write the sort of book many readers imagine *Ulysses* to be: a fact which should not be altogether comforting for such readers:

> Time I used to try jotting down my cuff what she said dressing. Dislike dressing together. Nicked myself shaving. Biting her nether lip, hooking the placket of her skirt. Timing her. 9.15. Did Roberts pay you yet? 9.20. What had Gretta Conroy on? 9.23. What possessed me to buy this comb? 9.24. I'm

1. James Joyce, *Ulysses* (New York: The Modern Library, 1934), p. 705.

swelled after that cabbage. A speck of dust on the patent leather of her boot.

Such systematic false notes as the enumeration of the hairs in Milly's drawing have persuaded almost no one that a vigorous comic consciousness is everywhere present. At most, they have been taken as humorless lapses of taste. The Ibsen legend is of the same kind. William Archer makes scandalized noises at what he conceives to be the radical lapse of *When We Dead Awaken*:

> . . . He sacrificed the surface reality to the underlying meaning. Take, for instance, the history of Rubek's statue and its development into a group. In actual sculpture this development is a grotesque impossibility. In conceiving it we are deserting the domain of reality, and plunging into some fourth dimension where the properties of matter are other than those we know. . . . Here, . . . without any suggestion of the supernatural, we are confronted with the wholly impossible, the inconceivable. . . . So great is the chasm between *John Gabriel Borkman* and *When We Dead Awaken* that one could almost suppose his mental breakdown to have preceded instead of following the writing of the latter play.[2]

The analogies of What is the Exact Age of Hamlet? and How Many Children Had Lady Macbeth? will occur to the reader. It is difficult to imagine the author of *Finnegans Wake* being impressed by Archer's notions of the probable in art; and we have seen the author of *Ulysses* concealing his grin. Insofar as dramaturgy à la William Archer is the basis for Ibsen's reputation (and his reputation so based is only beginning to be shaken) Joyce was never an Ibsenite at all.

This much by way of quelling the temptation to explain Joyce's interest in Ibsen by way of "naturalism." Ibsen represented for Joyce, first and foremost, a remarkable prototype of the successful provincial artist—one who might offer not only a paradigm of personal integrity but a set of strategies for dealing with a starved milieu and a half-baked culture. This sort of example was not to be found at the cliché-Ibsenite levels of the realistic setting and the socially unmentionable subject. Joyce must be granted sufficient acuteness to have realized that the sort of greatness he sensed in the Norwegian dramatist was incompatible with a habitual use of barren Archerese. That is why, at the age of seventeen or so, he taught himself Dano-Norwegian. Rehabilitating Ibsen, Miss M. C. Bradbrook writes: "Ibsen's prose is dramatic, which means that in balance, movement, and rhythm it is adapted for speaking; and it is literature, which means that it is built on the natural virtues of the

2. Introduction to *When We Dead Awaken*. Ibsen, *Works*, New York, 1917, vol. 11, pp. 357–358.

tongue and upon Ibsen's personal idiom as he fashioned it for his needs. His writing can be understood only in terms of the Norse, with its clear, pungent but concrete vocabulary, its strong, live metaphors ("we felt our hearts *beat strongly towards* him"), its lack of reverberations or overtones."[3]

It is possible to see, without becoming involved in a far-reaching revaluation of Ibsen, that Joyce by reading him in the original could find a writer congenial to his own preoccupations with setting language significantly in action. If Ibsen wrote no *Anna Livia Plurabelle* (and Joyce, it should be remembered, was writing *English* in the densest sections of *Finnegans Wake*, exploiting to the full a sophisticated and hybrid tongue), he did do whatever a strong sensibility and tentacular roots to a vigorous popular culture could do with a sinewy if barren language: so much so that Miss Bradbrook's quotations are a satisfactory index of linguistic life, even when we come to the Norse with the help of a translation and by way of its affinities with German and Anglo-Saxon. It is, for instance, illuminating to be told apropos of a key phrase in *Rosmersholm* that "*Kinsmen* in Norwegian are *skyldfolk*, those who share a common guilt": a typical example of thematic immersion in language that defies translation. Ibsen (like Dante and Joyce, though this is not to imply equations of value) wrote in a language whose relations with popular culture were still uneasy and just becoming consolidated. Writes Miss Bradbrook, "A multiplicity of dialects were spoken in the countryside; the official language, Dano-Norwegian, had only just come into use as a spoken tongue. Ibsen was of the first generation who naturally wrote and spoke in this form." Ibsen's biographer Koht offers a still more suggestive phrase: "For the older Norwegian writers the Danish language had been much more purely a book language than it was for the new generation." That English was a book-language explains much of the vacuity of the Anglo-Irish poets from Moore and Mangan to early Yeats. It abetted the *Zeitgeist*'s drift toward private worlds. Yeats became a great poet when with Pound's help he related his use of English to the spoken idiom; as Joyce, encouraged by Ibsen and Ben Jonson, had never from the beginning failed to do. Joyce's advantage in dealing with a language that was still in process of becoming fused with an already vigorous cultural sensibility (the analogy of Shakespeare's relations with the Elizabethan word-hunger is suggestive) underlies the range and zest of his vocabulary and grammar, and the sureness with which he could spot and parody cliché. It is possible that Ibsen's ability to disentangle moral realities from pious formulae is related to the analogous freedom of his new idiom from common-

3. M. C. Bradbrook, *Ibsen the Norwegian* (Hamden, Conn., 1966), p. 24.

places. Only when thought is carried on in living language can the intellect be maintained at the tips of the senses.

Joyce's unwillingness to flirt with Yeats, Lady Gregory, and the Gaelic League was probably stiffened by the example of Ibsen's experience. Ibsen in his early years had been involved in a similar campaign for a national drama and a purely Norwegian language. Imbued with a Yeatsian resolve to recall to the people "the rich imagery of the distant past" and "the forgotten tales of childhood," he wrote one popular success and a series of failures. With *Brand* he dropped the ballad-themes and came to terms with himself; and the fall of 1866 found him removing the ultra-Norwegian words for a new edition of *Love's Comedy*. He had wasted fifteen years.

The 18-year-old Joyce's essay on *Ibsen's New Drama* indicates the importance he attached to Ibsen's personal integrity. The key phrases of the opening paean, "Seldom, if at all, has he condescended to join battle with his enemies. It would appear as if the storm of fierce debate rarely broke in upon his wonderful calm. The conflicting voices have not influenced his work in the very smallest degree," are readily assimilated with the portrait of the dramatic artist, "refined out of existence, aloof, paring his fingernails." The extent to which Ibsen offered a personal example should not be underrated, and his biography—disgust with Norway, exile, early poems, middle monuments of construction and solidity accompanied by *succèss de scandale*, later symbolic experiments, denounced by fellow-travelers as madness—this career, excepting his ultimate return to homeland fame, resembles Joyce's in the most striking way; and a recent writer on Ibsen whom one need not suppose has given Joyce a thought remarks on the striking parallel between Dano-Norse and Anglo-Irish relations. This was the sector of Ibsen's appeal which the young Joyce found it easiest to focus. The letter he sent Ibsen in 1901 speaks of "what, as it seemed to me, was your highest excellence— your lofty impersonal power," with only a glance at what were later to become less kinetic and more nourishing preoccupations, "your satire, your technique and orchestral harmony." The letter goes on:

> I did not tell them (i.e. the Dubliners) what bound me closest to you. I did not say how much I could discern dimly of your life was my pride to see, how your battles inspired me— not the obvious material battles but those that were fought and won behind your forehead, how your wilful resolution to wrest the secret from life gave me heart and how in your resolute indifference to public canons of art, friends, and shibboleths you walked in the light of your inward heroism.

This, of course, is Stephen Dedalus talking; the decisive reorientation that was to make possible *Dubliners* and all the later achievement was still nearly five years off. For this reason one should be chary of supposing that Joyce in 1901 had said all there is to say about the importance his mature self attached to Ibsen. A Joyce who was merely Ibsen would be merely provincial; the Norwegian at his best does not belie the clumsy iconoclasm with which his disciples have been associated. The man who roared at a review of *Peer Gynt*, "My book *is* poetry, and if it is not, it shall be. The conception of poetry shall in our land, in Norway, come to adapt itself to the book"; who at sixteen told his sister that his ambition was to attain the utmost perfection of greatness and clarity and after that to die; and who insisted with the vehemence of uneasiness that he did not write only for the immediate future but for all eternity, could not help being on his weakest as well as on his strongest side congenial to the lustful arrogance of Stephen Dedalus, and could not have mustered the ironic detachment from his own weakness to have written more than a caricature of *Ulysses*. The uncompromising meddling of the Brand-like Gregers Werle in *The Wild Duck* invites no sympathy whatever, while Brand invites too much of the wrong kind, and is perfunctorily extinguished in a closing scene which neither Ibsen nor any commentator has satisfactorily related to the rest of the drama. On the Dedalian idealist Ibsen blows with alternate vehemence hot and cold; much of the teasing interest of the generic problem-play derives simply from an inability to digest and detach himself from his passions.

Joyce had done this digesting by 1905; the casting off of the devil represented by Dedalus is one of his major themes, and led him on to those vast explorations of the possibility of metaphysical self-sufficiency of which *Exiles* is a firm preliminary statement. Now the relation of Ibsen's earliest poems to his latest plays (which Miss Bradbrook[4] has done a great service to emphasize) indicates how Ibsen, even in his "realistic" middle period, was obsessed with a similar theme, the theme of the unfulfillable vocation, what may be generalized as the moral paradox of the human condition. It is toward a definition of this theme that the sordid particularities in which he deals become numinous symbols: the crippling inherited disease, the rotten ship, the captive wild duck. A personal conflict centering around the particular example of the artist's vocation (Ibsen left Norway for much the same reasons that drove Joyce from Ireland) and particularized in many modes in some highly relevant poems and in over a dozen plays is what gives Ibsen's work thematic coherence. This cannot be too much insisted upon. One would have thought from the claims made by his disciples that he conceived himself primarily as a reformer of the middle class. Yet however he

---

4. *Ibsen the Norwegian*, pp. 26–35.

might throw his weight about in practical politics, he always denied that, for example, *A Doll's House* was circumscribed by the feminist movement, or had any frame of reference less wide than "humanity."

Nor was Joyce ever deceived on this point. In a portion of the *Stephen Hero* manuscript that can hardly date later than 1904, the following exchange occurs:

> —Ah, if he were to examine even the basest things, said the President with a suggestion of tolerance in store, it would be different if he were to examine and then show men the way to purify themselves.
> —That is for the Salvationists, said Stephen.
> —Do you mean. . . .
> —I mean that Ibsen's account of modern society is as genuinely ironical as Newman's account of English Protestant morality and belief.
> —That may be, said the President appeased by the conjunction.
> —And as free from any missionary intention.
> The President was silent.[5]

On an earlier page is an even more unequivocal ascription of poetic rather than rhetorical virtues: a conventional Ibsenite says to Stephen,

> —That is not the teaching of Ibsen.
> —Teaching! cried Stephen.
> —The moral of *Ghosts* is just the opposite of what you say.
> —Bah! You regard the play as a scientific document.
> —*Ghosts* teaches self-repression. . . .
> —You have connected Ibsen and Eno's fruit salt forever in my mind, said Stephen.

The essential conflicts which are realized and elaborated in the early plays appear half-swallowed in the early poems, which in turn bear a striking relation to the final "symbolic" plays. One of them, *Et Vers*, clearly places the origin of art in experimental conflict:

> To live is to war with the troll
> In the caverns of heart and of skull.
> To write poetry—that is to hold
> Doom-session upon the soul.[6]

Joyce was saved from the Romantic disease, the uncritical obtrusion of the bleeding heart, by a Jesuit education that preserved communications with pre-Romantic ethics and rhetoric. Ibsen's in-

---

5. James Joyce, *Stephen Hero* (London: Jonathan Cape; New York: New Directions, 1944), p. 92.
6. Miss Bradbrook's translation (op. cit., p. 16). It is incidentally convenient to be able to show that Joyce knew this poem (and inferentially, the rest of Ibsen's) in the Norse. The

sistence on doom-session rather than out-pouring has a slighter pedigree reaching merely to Hegel. The Danish poet and critic Johan Ludvig Heiberg, who introduced Hegel to Scandinavia and became the intellectual dictator and aesthetic teacher of Ibsen's generation, had proclaimed as his first aesthetic law that "the poet, instead of yielding himself to his inspiration, should through the power of the intellect make himself its master." With the help of Hegel, he had also "shown that the desire for freedom was of necessity a revolt against restraint, that it was born in strife and could live only in strife,"[7] setting the witchword "freedom" in a dramatic context that on the one hand redeemed from a doctrinaire Shavianism Ibsen's handling of controversial topics, and on the other hand betrayed him all too easily to a doctrinaire misreading. Here, of course, Joyce's Aristotelian heritage saved him. For Stephen Dedalus conflict is the negation of order: he is at best and at worst a contemplative.

On Hegel and Heiberg may be blamed Ibsen's lifelong inability to assess the validity of the artist's role; he worried whether the very writing of *Brand* had not constituted an evasion of the strenuous action it advocated, a worry which he cast in Kierkegaardian terms. It was through this Hegelian stage-door that Ibsen stepped into an indefensible but roughly practicable role of Byronic scorn. The contradiction inherent in that role constituted his lifelong theme.

The poem *On the Vidda* (1859–60; aetat. 32) establishes most clearly the themes of which *When We Dead Awaken* (which had special relevance for Joyce) was the final exploration. The young hero of the poem lies on the heather upland thinking of his betrothed and wishing her path may be difficult so that he can smooth it. His wish is granted more terribly than he can foresee: when she at length comes to wed another man he has not only tired of her, but has lost all taste for the level of practical action represented by her existence in the valley. He has been visited by a strange hunter "with cold eyes like mountain lakes" who has called him to a life of strenuous contemplation, and induced him to stay in the mountains all summer. An impulse to see his mother and his sweetheart has been frustrated by the snow-choked passes of winter; and the first stage of his transformation into an artist has been the recognition that the life of the valley is no longer for him.

account on page 199 of *Finnegans Wake*, of HCE "hunger-striking all alone and holding doomsdag over hunselv" alludes to the last two lines, which read in Norwegian, "At digte—det er at holde / dommedag over sig selv." Ibsen the Norwegian has many analogues with HCE the Scandinavian invader, who supersedes Finnegan at Dublin in the same way that Joyce's Gargantuan novels supersede easygoing popular art, and who undergoes a nightlong introspection looking forward to the (unwritten) epilogue *When We Dead Awaken*.

7. Halvdan Koht, *Life of Ibsen*, trans. McMahon and Larsen (New York: W. W. Norton, 1931), vol. I, pp. 60–61.

When his mother's cottage burns, "the hunter coolly points out the beauty of the fire and advises on the best way to get the view. Then he disappears and leaves the son with his blood freezing and burning, yet acknowledging after all, in spite of himself, the beauty of the scene." In the last section, watching the bridal procession of his beloved and another man wind through the trees, "he discovers that he has grieved himself free at last. *Cantat vacuus*. He curves his hand to get the perspective right . . . self-steeled he looks on at joy from above life's snowline. The Strange Hunter reappears and tells him he is now free. . . ." The young man's final speech strikes the now-congenial Dedalus pose:

> Now I am steel-set: I follow the call
> To the height's clear radiance and glow.
> My lowland life is lived out: and high
> On the *vidda* are God and Liberty—
> Whilst wretches live fumbling below.[8]

The author of *The Holy Office* (1904) appears to have taken several gestures from this poem:

> So distantly I turn to view
> The shamblings of that motley crew,
> Those souls that hate the strength that mine has
> Steeled in the school of old Aquinas.
> Where they have crouched and crawled and prayed
> I stand, the self-doomed, unafraid,
> Unfellowed, friendless, and alone,
> Indifferent as the herring-bone,
> Firm as the mountain ridges where
> I flash my antlers in the air.

The interest of *The Holy Office* lies partly in its date: it indicates how, even after the scrupulously ironic and intensely felt writing of *Dubliners* was under way, the Dedalus pose remained as a habit behind which Joyce's rhetorical energy could most readily be mobilized. It bears all the marks of extremely rapid writing (a distinction, it must be insisted, not only from *Finnegans Wake* but from the simplest phrases of the *Portrait* and *Dubliners*); and its relations to violent feelings to which Joyce did not mind attaching public importance is implicit in the fact that he had it printed and mailed to all the victims mentioned in the text. When in the *Portrait* or in *Ulysses* Stephen Dedalus is shown behaving with comparable centrifugal irrelevance, careful writing and scrupulous irony invariably set him in semi-comic contrast with a wide frame of reference. The

8. This translation, like the substance of the outline above, is taken from Miss Bradbrook (p. 33).

aesthete becomes himself an aesthetic object. No one doubts that Joyce knew Dedalus from the inside; it should be equally clear that the writer who "placed" him from the outside exhibits a habitual wisdom inaccessible to Dedalus himself. Joyce is not Stephen. Yet it is evident that Stephen is for his creator something more than comic; there is tragic intensity in the spectacle of the aesthete's mask becoming fused to his flesh. And this tragic necessity, which energized the scornful violence of such a production as *The Holy Office*—the necessity, for a provincial artist deprived of any respectable tradition,[9] of becoming the enemy of his society in ways incompatible with the human necessity of remaining in touch with human wisdom—corresponds to Ibsen's generic theme of the impossible vocation. Neither Joyce nor Ibsen should be said to have succumbed to this necessity, though both experienced it insofar as it was necessary. Both made art of its central antithesis: dramatized it.

The necessity for a central portion of the contemporary artist's soul being turned toward enmity for his society, and the corollary necessity of the artist's being either on the one hand an anarchic aesthete (like Dedalus or the unhappy hero of *On the Vidda*) who sacrifices all human ties to his art, or on the other hand, if not a split man, at least a man both partly of his community and partly at cross-purposes with it (like Joyce or Ibsen)—this necessity, a reflex of the disproportionate burden laid on the artist by failure of the community, makes obvious contact at several points with the cultural history of the last two centuries. In fact, the forces that pushed the Byronic aristocrat into an anti-social role of destructive action and the Shelleyan Blithe Spirit into emasculate thrill-seeking; that drove the former forward and upward into sub-human scientific activities (so that the pedigree of the tycoon and of the sleuth reaches back through Huxley and Darwin to Byron and beyond) and that drove the latter downward and outward into complacent garrulity (so that from Shelley through Tennyson to Edgar Guest the line of descent and diffusion is clear): these dichotomizing forces reach back through the Cartesian dualism of the Seventeenth Century to the breakup of mediaeval order in the Fifteenth. The split artist reflects the split man of the split community: as martyr to that split, he is like Shem the Penman "honor bound to his own cruelfiction." His plight is therefore of more than professional significance; which is the reason for the universal contemporary validity of the myth which Ibsen and Joyce (Joyce more explicitly) construct on the plight of the provincial artist. (Of

9. Cf. Joyce in *The Day of the Rabblement*, 1901: ". . . The Irish Literary Theatre must now be considered the property of the rabblement of the most belated race in Europe. . . . A nation which never advanced so far as a miracle play affords no literary model to the artist. . . ."

course the feeble novelist writes autobiography because he has no other interests; *he* is not here in question except as a symptom.) It is no accident that Kierkegaard's "crisis theology" (a tragically barren rationalization of the plight of the sensitive in a cultural vacuum) stands behind Ibsen and Kafka alike; or that Kafka occupies for the earnest elite of today the symbolic position a previous generation had accorded to Ibsen. In Kafka the theme of the impossible vocation gets the fullest possible statement: whatever his intentions may have been, to leave his novels unfinished was the most appropriate denouement he could have contrived.

There is, then, no paradox in saying that a deeply-rooted personal conflict, which certain early productions (notably *On the Vidda* and the play *Love's Comedy*) had explicitly stated as an artist-myth, provides the underlying tension for the ironically-detailed social documentation on which Ibsen's reputation has come to be based. (In the same way, *The Holy Office* implies *Dubliners*). *Brand* marks a transition from the personal to the public statement of this tension; Ibsen by that time (1866, aetat. 38: the age by which Joyce had nearly finished *Ulysses*) was at least conceptually uneasy about the naïve heroics of *On the Vidda*. Brand as clergyman (a more general statement of the artist as communal scapegoat) makes, like the young man on the vidda, one ruthless personal sacrifice after another in a spirit of self-conscious humility of which the better-nourished wisdom of T. S. Eliot has provided in *Murder in the Cathedral* a more complex and less ambiguous statement.[1] Having demanded the supreme sacrifice of his mother, his child, his wife, and his congregation, he winds up both among the mountain-peaks of his ambition and in the Ice-Church appropriate to his nature; when finally, renouncing pride and calling on the God of Love, he melts the ice, he and his troll-lover are engulfed in the ruins.

The extent to which Ibsen's intellectual life was conducted in jejune slogans (which must strike any reader of Koht's biography, and which no amount of allowance for the naïveté of the biographer can do much to cancel) not only underlies the Byronic indigestibility of *Brand* but makes clear how serviceable a document it could be to the supple and ironic sensibility of a Joyce intent on portraying a Stephen. The five chapters of *A Portrait of the Artist as a Young*

1. Compare with the speeches of Eliot's Fourth Tempter the following:
     It is not martyrdom to toss
     In anguish on the deadly cross:
     But to have *will'd* to perish so.
     To *will* it through each bodily throe,
     To will it with still-tortured mind.
     This, only this, redeems mankind.
     —*Brand* III; in *Works*, vol. III, p. 114

Man constitute a rewriting of the five acts of *Brand* with infinitely greater local sensitivity and within a richly nourished milieu of classical ethics. It is from Brand that many of the most humorlessly arrogant gestures of Stephen Dedalus are derived: his behavior at his mother's deathbed, his rejection of the Christianity of the clergy, his romantic positives expressed in terms of "the spell of arms and voices" and of "exultant and terrible youth," corresponding to Ibsen's "flashing eye" and his dawn above the ice-fields. If the similarities are obvious, so are the differences. Many can be enumerated; but more important are the ones that can only be illustrated, and of which only the reader's sensibility can furnish ultimate proof: differences that reflect the civilized heritage of sensibility available to the Dubliner. If Ireland was "the afterthought of Europe," it was still European; it is partly the impossibility of a revolt against the bourgeois frontier ethics of Norway becoming enfleshed in anything more concrete than stern intentions that makes *Brand*, for the English reader, so stiff and bony. Here a letter of Ibsen's to Georg Brandes (1871) provides useful evidence:

> Undermine the idea of the State, set up voluntary choice and spiritual kinship as the only determining factors for union—that is the beginning of a freedom that is worth something. Yes, my dear friend, it is imperative not to let one's self be frightened by its venerable vested rights. The State has its roots in time, it will culminate in time. Greater things than this will fall; all religions will fall. Neither moral principles nor artistic forms have any eternity ahead of them. How much are we at bottom obliged to hold fast to? Who can guarantee that two and two are not five on Jupiter?[2]

Denial of the rational and political nature of man could scarcely go further; it is startling to learn that Ibsen was accustomed to using his question about two and two as a serious argument. This envacuumed skeletal righteousness deprived of all social, political, or theological context sharply contradistinguishes itself from the sense of collective wisdom that secures Wordsworth (who denied its intellectual roots) a dignified place in the English tradition, and that for the fifty generations running from Cicero through St. Augustine to Erasmus had nourished a complex communal ideal of which Wordsworth merely furnishes the death-mask. Ibsen shatters the mask; it is by anguish rather than by consistency that his dramas are saved from ethical anarchy. The reader should have no difficulty seeing that Stephen Dedalus at his most iconoclastic prizes a fidelity to existent being much closer to the pragmatic Ibsen as a

2. Koht, vol. II, p. 84.

practicing dramatist (post-*Brand*) than to Ibsen's avowed anarchic idealism.

> —The modern spirit is vivisective. Vivisection itself is the most modern process one can conceive. The ancient spirit accepted phenomena with a bad grace. The ancient method investigated law with the lantern of justice, morality with the lantern of revelation, art with the lantern of tradition. But all these lanterns have magical properties: they transform and disfigure. The modern method examines its territory by the light of day. Italy has added a science to civilization by putting out the lantern of justice and considering the criminal in production and in action. All modern political and religious criticism dispenses with presumptive States, and presumptive Redeemers and Churches. It examines the entire community in action and reconstructs the spectacle of redemption.[3]

This was written before 1906; and while the mature Joyce would not have defined Stephen's position in quite that way as a naïve modern-vs.-ancient dualism, yet to dispense with a priori presumptive States is very different from Ibsen's a priori positivism. Indeed, Stephen, in the spirit of the author of *Ulysses*, goes on to distinguish Aristotle from the dialectical Aristotelians:

> — . . . I do not think he is the special patron of those who proclaim the usefulness of the stationary march. . . . The toy life which the Jesuits permit these docile young men to live is what I call a stationary march. The marionette life which the Jesuit himself lives as a dispenser of illumination and rectitude is another variety of the stationary march. And yet both these classes of puppets think that Aristotle has apologized for them before the eyes of the world.

The Stephen who could emancipate Aristotle from the claims of the stationary marchers is on the way to becoming the author of *Ulysses* and *Finnegans Wake*. Stephen Hero is in fact very nearly the young James Joyce. He talks a great deal of sense of which the later and better-known book contains no hint. The Stephen of *A Portrait of the Artist as a Young Man* has been carefully recast, with the aid of *Brand*, as an anarchic aesthete, destined in the company of Buck Mulligan (a variation on Peer Gynt) to come to comprehensive grief in *Ulysses*, beneath the eyes of an author who "examines the entire community in action and reconstructs the spectacle of redemption."

It is clear that the relation of Brand to his author is highly peculiar. *Brand*, as T. S. Eliot has said of *Hamlet* in a phrase which is

---

3. *Stephen Hero*, p. 186.

fast becoming a critical cliché, is "full of some stuff that the writer could not drag to light, contemplate, or manipulate into art." Eliot goes on, "The supposed identity of Hamlet with his author is genuine to this point: that Hamlet's bafflement at the absence of an objective equivalent to his feelings is the prolongation of the bafflement of his creator in the face of his artistic problem." It is so: for Hamlet read Brand. Ibsen in the utter absence of a tradition couldn't even decide whether writing were worth while.[4] A valid perception of the distinction between artist and dilettante was elevated through Kierkegaard's categorical absolutism into an Either-Or conflict which energized all his plays, yet prevented him from achieving a plenary resolution of the conflicts of any of them. The surplus emotional energy thus left lying was absorbed by the generic irony of his "naturalist" convention: his passion for documentation in the prose plays prevents the emotion from becoming rhetorical, and the emotion saves the documentation from being trivial. It was Ibsen's triumph to have achieved in the problem-play an adequate personal form, as it was Joyce's to control through the manipulation of myths an even more complex personal tension, between the artist as contemporary rebel, and the man as inheritor of a massive structure of civilization. Neither Ibsen nor Joyce can be blamed for the botches of interpreters and imitators.

The plays on which Ibsen's reputation is chiefly based, from *Pillars of Society* to *The Master Builder*, depend on a number of thematic conventions and assumptions that have been from the beginning largely obscured by a complexly-motivated cloud of unknowing. The completely irrelevant valuations to which Ibsen has thus been subjected present an instructive likeness to the legend that since the first stir and rumor of *Ulysses* has enshrouded the achievement of Joyce. The "naturalist" red herring has already been mentioned. It arose in England partly from the barrenness of the Archer translations (a barrenness the product of doctrine more than illiteracy), but much more from the sequence of what we may describe as "inevitable accidents" by which Ibsen's reputation fell into the hands of muscular missionaries whose type is Bernard Shaw, and who combined utter insensitivity to the complex rhetorical modes of traditional art with a naïve determination to pull the theater, with its obvious facilities for the imitation of superficies, out of the hands of irresponsible popular entertainment and into

4. Cf. Koht, vol. II, p. 27: "Recently, while writing *Brand*, he had felt as if he were taking part in strife and action, and there had been a sense of jubilation within him. . . . Now, afterwards, it seemed to him that he had merely evaded the struggle and the call to action; it appeared to him, as he wrote in a letter, that *Brand* was 'wholly and thoroughly an aesthetic work without a trace of anything else.' " It should be remembered that "aesthetic" was, in the Kierkegaardian system, pejorative.

the purlieu of the social reformer. The contemporary attempt to make the cinema an "art" form via the documentary is similar in intention. Shaw's *Quintessence of Ibsenism* is a representative document of this preconception; Archer's *The Old Drama and the New* rewrites European dramatic history in its light in an attempt to provide the problem-play, by Darwinian strategies, with a pedigree.

Of even greater importance in establishing conventional attitudes to Ibsen was the "unpleasant subject," the socially-unmentionable theme: the most celebrated example is the hereditary insanity in *Ghosts*. So thoroughly did the very defense-mechanism he was concerned to analyse frustrate Ibsen's intention, that champion and detractor alike have failed to notice that he was employing mental unbalance of venereal origin as a relevant metaphor for original sin. His biographer notes that Oswald and his illness were for a long time regarded as the center of *Ghosts*, and doctors discussed whether the case was rightly diagnosed: an attitude which the present decade has not really outgrown. Koht further shows (vol. II, p. 166) by a consideration of early drafts that it was the mother's sin rather than the father's lust that Ibsen meant the disease to transmit: and the mother's sin had a spiritual rather than a physical connection with the disease.

A couplet in *Brand*, "Blood of the children must be spilt / To atone for parents' guilt," points to the religious orientation of one of Ibsen's constant preoccupations; that his characters, like his audience, were aware of such principles only when they presented themselves in terms of corporeal pathology is one of the perceptions controlling the organization of *Ghosts*; a good example of his ironic use of naturalist conventions. The scrupulous documentation of externals masking psychological and supernatural realities to which, until the catastrophe, the protagonists are indifferent, is an elaborate aesthetic imitation of the condition of a whole society. In Joyce a similar technique transcends social preoccupations to make the ironic and unsuspected presence of supernatural significance in natural facts an image of the entire condition of man. In these terms it is easy to see that Joyce and Ibsen employed "unmentionable" themes not as Shavian Ibsenites thought with the purpose of promoting "open discussion," but because of the dramatic significance that could be extracted from the social and psychological mechanisms that insured their going unmentioned. The irony directed toward audiences and protagonists who imagine because of their grasp on external phenomena, that they are in strict control of the business of living while remaining frantically oblivious to the kinds of meaning concealed by the vaunted profusion of data, is clearly related to the resolve of the artist to pursue intelligibility at the expense of exclusion from the crowd; it is one more example of the thematic bearings of the artist-myth discussed above. Ibsen's conception of the entire drama as a presentation of dawning moral illumination, a colossal catastrophe motivated by the nemesis entrained by hidden sins, has obvious affinities with, for example, the tragedy of Oedipus that underlies *Finnegans Wake*, and that was Aristotle's showpiece of *anagnoesis* combined with *peripeteia*. The naturalist technique is plainly functional to this conception: it projects the dramatically essential unawareness of the protagonists.

It ought to be said that for the mature artist the use of the "naturalist" convention will invariably involve and permit an irony of this kind, because of the insistent indication, beneath the superficially thorough documentation, of what is being left out. Joyce and Ibsen display this irony on inspection, though it will scarcely carry its full weight to the reader unable to realize their implications, in the charged handling of language, of what a very different convention, like the Shakespearean, would permit. Mr. Eliot's experiments with modern diction convey the ironic judgment (it cannot be called simply a sneer at the speakers) in a similar though simpler way:

> People with money from heaven knows where—
> > Dividends from aeroplane shares.
> They bathe all day and they dance all night
> In the absolute *minimum* of clothes.

This reflection of supercultivated gossip is framed and "placed" by a superimposed rhythm (that of the dance-tune and of *Sweeney Agonistes*) belonging to what the speakers innocently imagine to be a very different world. And it follows, in its context, a sudden shift from the charged intensity of:

> O Sun, that was once so warm, O Light that was taken
> > for granted
>
> When I was young and strong, and sun and light
> > unsought for
> And the night unfeared and the day expected
> And clocks could be trusted, tomorrow assured
> And time would not stop in the dark!

It is a subtlety of this kind (not, by Eliot's best standards, really very subtle; but he was writing for a contemporary theater audience) that a critic like Cyril Connolly, in preferring *Sweeney Agonistes* to the rest of Eliot's output because it reflects the way people really talk, has palpably missed. Because Joyce employs this critical principle from his first published pages to his last, it is fatal for the Joycean to miss it; though it is perhaps no accident that Mr. Connolly on *Ulysses* ("Narcissus with his pool before him") sounds exactly like all the other commentators.

There was then, despite what we are told by historians of the naturalistic novel, no simple formula for the meaning of Ibsen for Joyce. It was a relation of affinity and of differentiation, of example and of caution, an interpenetration neither definitive enough to be accounted "influence," nor sufficiently alien to be disowned. Ibsen was both a catalyst and a heresiarch: a warning. He understood as did no one else in his time the burden of the dead past and the wastefulness of any attempt to give it spurious life: his "I think we are sailing with a corpse in the cargo!" is in the mode of Stephen Dedalus' apprehension of the nightmare of history from which H. C. Earwicker strains to awake. But he had never known, and could not know in the frontier vacuum of the fiords, the traditions of the European community, of richly-nourished life; and the lonely starvation of his ideal of free personal affinity in no context but that of intermingling wills inspired Joyce with a fascination which generated *Exiles* and a civilized repulsion that found its objective correlative when Leopold Bloom felt "the apathy of the stars."

GEORGE STEINER

From The Death of Tragedy†

* * *

With Ibsen, the history of drama begins anew. This alone makes of him the most important playwright after Shakespeare and Racine. The modern theatre can be dated from *Pillars of Society* (1877). But like most great artists, Ibsen worked from within the available conventions. The four plays of his early maturity—*Pillars of Society*, *A Doll's House*, *Ghosts*, and *An Enemy of the People*—are marvels of construction in the prevailing manner of the late nineteenth-century drawing-room play. The joints are as closely fitted as in the domestic melodramas of Augier and Dumas. What is revolutionary is the orientation of such shopworn devices as the hidden past, the purloined letter, or the deathbed disclosure toward social problems of urgent seriousness. The elements of melodrama are made responsible to a deliberate, intellectual purpose. These are the plays in which Ibsen is the dramatist Shaw tried to make of him: the pedagogue and the reformer. No theatre has ever had behind it a stronger impulse of will and explicit social philosophy.

† From *The Death of Tragedy* (New York: Alfred A. Knopf, 1961), 290–98. Reprinted by permission of Georges Borchardt, Inc., and Faber & Faber.

But these tracts, enduring as they may prove to be by virtue of their theatrical vigour, are not tragedies. In tragedy, there are no temporal remedies. The point cannot be stressed too often. Tragedy speaks not of secular dilemmas which may be resolved by rational innovation, but of the unaltering bias toward inhumanity and destruction in the drift of the world. But in these plays of Ibsen's radical period, such is not the issue. There are specific remedies to the disasters which befall the characters, and it is Ibsen's purpose to make us see these remedies and bring them about. *A Doll's House* and *Ghosts* are founded on the belief that society can move toward a sane, adult conception of sexual life and that woman can and must be raised to the dignity of man. *Pillars of Society* and *An Enemy of the People* are denunciations of the hypocrisies and oppressions concealed behind the mask of middle-class gentility. They tell us of the way in which money interests poison the springs of emotional life and intellectual integrity. They cry out for explicit radicalism and reform. As Shaw rightly says: "No more tragedy for the sake of tears." Indeed, no tragedy at all, but dramatic rhetoric summoning us to action in the conviction that truth of conduct can be defined and that it will liberate society.

These programmatic aims extend into Ibsen's middle period. But with *The Wild Duck* (1884), the dramatic form deepens. The limitations of the well-made play and its deliberate flatness of perspective began crowding in on Ibsen. While retaining the prose form and outward conventions of realism, he went back to the lyric voice and allegoric means of his early experimental plays, *Brand* and *Peer Gynt*. With the toy forest and imaginary hunt of old Ekdal in *The Wild Duck*, drama returns to a use of effective myth and symbolic action which had disappeared from the theatre since the late plays of Shakespeare. In *Rosmersholm*, *The Lady from the Sea*, and *Hedda Gabler*, Ibsen succeeded in doing what every major playwright had attempted after the end of the seventeenth century and what even Goethe and Wagner had not wholly accomplished: he created a new mythology and the theatrical conventions with which to express it. That is the foremost achievement of Ibsen's genius, and it is, as yet, not fully understood.

As we have seen, the decline of tragedy is inseparably related to the decline of the organic world view and of its attendant context of mythological, symbolic, and ritual reference. It was on this context that Greek drama was founded, and the Elizabethans were still able to give it imaginative adherence. This ordered and stylized vision of life, with its bent toward allegory and emblematic action, was already in decline at the time of Racine. But by strenuous observance of neo-classic conventions, Racine succeeded in giving to the old mythology, now emptied of belief, the vitality of living form. His was a brilliant rear-guard action. But after Racine the ancient habits of awareness and immediate recognition which gave to tragic drama its frame of reference were no longer prevalent. Ibsen, therefore, faced a real vacuum. He had to create for his plays a context of ideological meaning (an effective mythology), and he had to devise the symbols and theatrical conventions whereby to communicate his meaning to an audience corrupted by the easy virtues of the realistic stage. He was in the position of a writer who invents a new language and must then teach it to his readers.

Being a consummate fighter, Ibsen turned his deprivations to advantage. He made the precariousness of modern beliefs and the absence of an imaginative world order his starting point. Man moves naked in a world bereft of explanatory or conciliating myth. Ibsen's dramas presuppose the withdrawal of God from human affairs, and that withdrawal has left the door open to cold gusts blowing in from a malevolent though inanimate creation. But the most dangerous assaults upon reason and life come not from without, as they do in Greek and Elizabethan tragedy. They arise in the unstable soul. Ibsen proceeds from the modern awareness that there is rivalry and unbalance in the individual psyche. The ghosts that haunt his characters are not the palpable heralds of damnation whom we find in *Hamlet* and *Macbeth*. They are forces of disruption that have broken loose from the core of the spirit. Or, more precisely, they are cancers growing in the soul. In Ibsen's vocabulary, the most deadly of these cancers is "idealism," the mask of hypocrisy and self-deception with which men seek to guard against the realities of social and personal life. When "ideals" seize upon an Ibsen character, they drive him to psychological and material ruin as the Weird Sisters drive Macbeth. Once the mask has grown close to the skin, it can be removed only at suicidal cost. When Rosmer and Rebecca West have attained the ability to confront life, they are on the verge of death. When the mask no longer shields her against the light, Hedda Gabler kills herself.

To articulate this vision of a God-abandoned world and of man's splintered and vulnerable consciousness, Ibsen contrived an astounding series of symbols and figurative gestures. Like most creators of a coherent mythology, moreover, he determined early on his objective incarnations. The meanings assumed by the sea, the fjord, the avalanches, and the spectral bird in *Brand* carry over to Ibsen's very last play, *When We Dead Awaken*. The new church in *Brand* brings on the moment of disaster, as does the new steeple in *The Master Builder*. The white stallion of Peer Gynt foreshadows the ghost-chargers at Rosmersholm. From the start, Ibsen uses certain material objects to concentrate symbolic values (the wild duck, General Gabler's pistols, the flagpole standing in front of the house in *The Lady from the Sea*). And it is the association of an explicit, responsible image of life with the material setting and objects best able to denote and dramatize this image that is the source of Ibsen's power. It allows him to organize his plays into shapes of action richer and more expressive than any the theatre had known since Shakespeare. Consider the stress of dramatic feeling and the complexity of meaning conveyed by the tarantella which Nora dances in *A Doll's House*; by Hedda Gabler's proposal to crown Lövborg with vine leaves; or by the venture into high narrow places that occurs in *Rosmersholm*, *The Master Builder*, and *When We Dead Awaken*. Each is in itself a coherent episode in the play, yet it is at the same time a symbolic act which argues a specific vision of life. Ibsen arrived at this vision, and he devised the stylistic and theatrical means that give it dramatic life. This is his rare achievement.

Ibsen's late plays represent the kind of inward motion that we find also in the late plays of Shakespeare. *Cymbeline*, *The Winter's Tale*, and *The Tempest* retain the conventions of Jacobean tragicomedy. But these conventions act as signposts pointing toward interior meanings. The storms, the music, the allegoric masques have implications which belong less to the common imaginative repertoire than they do to a most private understanding of the world. The current theatrical forms are a mere scaffold to the inner shape. That is exactly the case in *The Master Builder*, *Little Eyolf*, *John Gabriel Borkman*, and *When We Dead Awaken*. These dramas give an appearance of belonging to the realistic tradition and of observing the conventions of the three-walled stage. But, in fact, this is not so. The setting is thinned out so as to become bleakly transparent, and it leads into a strange landscape appropriate to Ibsen's mythology of death and resurrection.

It is in these four plays—and they are among the summits of drama—that Ibsen comes nearest tragedy. But it is tragedy of a peculiar, limited order. These are fables of the dead, set in a cold purgatory. Halvard Solness is dead long before he ascends the tower of his new villa. Allmers and Rita are dead to each other in the suffocation of their marriage. Borkman is an enraged ghost pacing up and down in a coffin that has the semblance of a house. In *When We Dead Awaken*, the purgatorial theme is explicit. In the mad egotism of his art, Rubeck has trampled on the quick of life. He has destroyed Irene by refusing to treat her as a living being. But in such destruction there is always a part of suicide, and the great sculptor—the shaper of life—has withered to a grotesque shadow. Yet there remains a chance of miracle; in sharing mortal danger, the dead may awaken. And so Rubeck and Irene press on, up the storm-swept mountain.

There are in these fierce parables occasional resonances from classic and Shakespearean tragedy. We do, I think, experience a related sense of tragic form when Agamemnon strides across the purple carpet and Solness mounts to his tower. But the focus is utterly different. Ibsen starts where earlier tragedies end, and his plots are epilogues to previous disaster. Suppose Shakespeare had written a play showing Macbeth and Lady Macbeth living out their black lives in exile after they had been defeated by their avenging enemies. We might then have the angle of vision that we find in *John Gabriel Borkman*. These are dramas of afterlife, engaging vivid shadows such as animate the lower regions of the *Purgatorio*. But even in these late works, there is a purpose which goes beyond tragedy. Ibsen is telling us that one need not live in premature burial. He is reading the lesson of meaningful life. The Allmers and the Rubecks of the world can waken from their living death if they establish among themselves relations of honesty and sacrifice. There is a way out, even if it leads up to the glaciers. There is no such way for Agamemnon or Hamlet or Phèdre. In the gloom of the late Ibsen the core of militant hope is intact.

Why is it that this magnificent body of drama has not exercised a greater or more liberating influence on the modern theatre? Such playwrights as Arthur Miller stand toward Ibsen rather as Dryden stood toward Shakespeare. They have observed the technical means of the Ibsen play and adopted some of its conventions and defining gestures. But the rich and complex critique of life implicit in Ibsen, and the transparency of his realistic settings to the light of symbolism, are absent. Where Ibsen has been influential, as in the case of Shaw, it is the programmatic plays that have counted, not the harrowing dramas of his maturity. Why should this be? In part, the answer is that Ibsen did his work too well. Many of the hypocrisies that he strove against have loosened their grip on the mind. Many of the spectres of middle-class oppression have been exorcized. The triumph of the reformer has obscured the greatness of the poet. In part, there is the barrier of language. Those who read Norwegian tell one that Ibsen's mature prose is as tightly wrought in cadence and inner poise as is good verse. As in poetry, moreover, the force and direction of meaning often hinge on the particular inflections and array of sounds. These resist translation. And so there is in the versions of Ibsen's plays available to most readers a prosaic flatness entirely inappropriate to the symbolic design and lyricism of the late dramas. In short, that which translates best in Ibsen is perhaps the least notable. Thus we do not yet have the Ibsen playhouse for which Shaw pleaded at the turn of the century.

*   *   *

G. WILSON KNIGHT

From Henrik Ibsen†

Conclusion

Ibsen's work is in the central line of western drama. In compact-
ness of form and the use of crisis it is Greek; its retrospective technique recalls the *Oedipus Tyrannus* and its insight into female
instinct Euripides. There are also correspondences to Shakespeare.
Both start with fairy-lore and history and move through problem-
plays and tragedies to dramas of mystic intimation. Much of Ibsen
is covered by the social and cosmic implications of *Timon of
Athens*; and *The Master Builder* and *When We Dead Awaken* look
back on Ibsen's progress as *The Tempest* looks back on Shakespeare's. There are, naturally, differences. In so clearly posing and
facing the central conflict of Renaissance culture *Emperor and
Galilean* is, though only in its emphasis, new: what Ibsen adds to
the tradition is generally nearer clarification than reversal.

The most important link between Shakespeare and Ibsen is Byron,
whom Ibsen admired. "His works," he wrote to Frederik Gjertsen from
Dresden on 21 March 1872, "would be of great assistance in freeing
our aesthetics from many moral prejudices. . . . It is acknowledged
here that German literature required Byron's assistance to enable it to
reach its present standpoint; and I maintain that we need him to free
us from ours."[1] Byron's dramas use Shakespearian material with a
more intellectual pointing. In their ethical transvaluations, their blend
of revolution and aristocracy, their will to advance joined to sense of a
ghostly and ruling past (as at *Manfred*, III. iv. 40); in their modern oc-
cultism; in all this they render explicit what was in Shakespeare implicit and look ahead to Ibsen's yet more deliberated expositions.[2]

The plays following *Emperor and Galilean* are peculiarly purpose-
ful. Though Ibsen's subtlety of human delineation may too readily
be forgotten while we are concentrating on his more universal statements,[3] there is really no final distinction. Edmund Gosse quotes
William Archer's record of a conversation with Ibsen in 1887:

> It seems that the *idea* of a piece generally presents itself before
> the characters and incidents, though, when I put this to him

† From *Henrik Ibsen* (New York: Grove Press, 1962), 107–17. Copyright © 1962 by
  G. Wilson Knight. Reprinted by permission of Grove/Atlantic, Inc.
1. *The Correspondence of Henrik Ibsen*, tr. and ed. Mary Morison (1905), 229.
2. See my article, "Shakespeare and Byron's Plays," *Shakespeare-Fahrbuch* (1959).
3. The subtlety of Ibsen's characterisation is elaborately handled by Hermann J. Weigand,
   in *The Modern Ibsen* (1925).

flatly, he denied it. It seems to follow, however, from his saying that there is a certain stage in the incubation of a play when it might as easily turn into an essay as into a drama. He has to incarnate the ideas, as it were, in character and incident, before the actual work of creation can be said to have fairly begun.[4]

Complications, we are told, arose during composition, and the completed creation did not necessarily resemble the first intention. We may say that Ibsen shows us human personalities playing out their destinies according to certain prevailing and recurring laws, but that these are laws of their own being and the providential plan.

We are inevitably drawn to interpretation in terms of "themes." Throughout we have an emphasis on vocation, on the instinctive will, forcing the persons to self-realisation: Hamlet's "To be or not to be" might serve as a text for Ibsen's life-work.[5] Paganism is balanced against Christianity, clerics, except for Brand, cutting poor figures, and doctors being repositories of good sense. Women here assume a frightening stature. Unlike the violent heroines of Greek and Renaissance drama, Ibsen's strong women possess not only strength but also authority: men often seem mere wax for their moulding. We have two primary female types: the strong, whether dark or light, and the softer and more sweet-natured, the latter normally of lower dramatic status, despite instances of formulated approval, than the former. Unhappy marriages are normal, and in general both sexual and Christian love bend before the compulsion to self-realisation. Self-realisation may involve incorporation of the Dionysian, and after *Emperor and Galilean* Ibsen dramatises attempts at such an incorporation in contemporary terms. The main antagonists to be faced and fought are convention, hypocrisy, sexual passion, marriages of expedience, a corrupt press, and vested interests; and, hardest of all, the past, either of society or of oneself, which may involve guilt and hamper freedom. Dramas of diagnosis and detonation are made from a retrospective technique unwinding fold on fold to reveal the living contours of situation and character and force an honest conclusion.

Among Ibsen's positive values are his strong women; his dream of a new nobility; maternal love, as in *Peer Gynt*; youth's romantic love-vision and youth as students, in *Love's Comedy*; youth wronged by its elders, or carrying seraphic intimations, as in Eyolf's eyes, Asta and Hilda Wangel; art, provided that it be surpassed; and, above all, genius, whose destiny it will be to surpass art, strive for a

4. Edmund Gosse, *Ibsen* (1907), 252.
5. See my essay, "Hamlet Reconsidered," in *The Wheel of Fire*, enlarged edn., 1949.

wholeness including love, touch the occult, and challenge death. Spiritualism interpenetrates Ibsen's sense of human destiny. Of humour there is, comparatively, little. *Love's Comedy* has it, and *Peer Gynt* preeminently, and the Bishop's death in *The Pretenders*. Julian, Hialmar, Dr Stockmann and Foldal are humorously diagnosed. Ibsen could have written great comedy had he wished to, but he chose a different path. His highest value we may perhaps define as the bisexual integration from which the plays are composed. Ibsen is as much in his women as in his men and *Hedda Gabler* an emotional autobiography.

In an Ibsen drama the most trivial remarks, stage-directions or actions may have significant overtones.[6] Weather and seasons are carefully designated and exactly used. Birds, especially birds of prey such as the falcon, or hawk, and eagle, and in contrast gentler breeds, are active symbols; and flowers. The major powers of sea, mountains and sun, which were likewise Byron's favourites, almost constitute a mythology, a grand symbolic trinity, the recurring fires representing the satanic. The impressions are conveyed for the most part visually. There is less reliance on aural impressions, the most important being ships' sirens, Borkman's footsteps, and the Dionysian art, music; especially dance-music, fierce or sombre.

These highly intellectualised dramas labour to define the super-rational powers and establish contact between them and human life. This contact may be explosive.

Morality as we know it is questioned; but in his ratification of dark energies Ibsen is only rendering explicit what has for long been implicit in our dramatic tradition. Tragedy, as Nietzsche explains, is born of courage; it is a record less of failures than of adventures and aspirations. That is why in Shakespeare we find a mysterious upthrust, in both protagonist and dramatic action, subtly countering the appearances of failure; and it is precisely this unmoral counter-force that makes Shakespearian tragedy so health-giving. In such tragedies we are made subtly aware of an appeal beyond morality and an achievement beyond life. In descent from Shakespeare's, Byron's plays work out a number of ethical transvaluations, and Ibsen carries the process further. Cain was given a case by Byron and at the heart of Ibsen's dramatic statement he and Judas are accorded respect as implements of the world-will. Such dramatic persons, among whom Hedda Gabler constitutes an extreme example, demand our respect as bearers of energies as yet unassimilated and undirected. Ibsen's dramas and Nietzsche's semi-dramatic *Thus Spake Zarathustra*, with its dominant symbols of sun and mountains, strive in similar fashion for a

6. These are excellently treated by John Northam, in *Ibsen's Dramatic Method* (1953).

new ratification of implanted energies to heal man's at present fractured being and blaze a path for some higher righteousness as yet insusceptible of any but such poetic definitions as Browning attempted in *The Statue and the Bust*. Whatever this new "righteousness" may be, the first signature of its authority will be its surpassing of morality in that particular sense of the "conventional" which the word both etymologically and imaginatively implies. The process is analogous to that described in *Peer Gynt* whereby strong sins are as negative plates serving to print off great virtues. If this were not so, our involvement in great drama might be dangerous.

It is easy to see why a more exact definition is impossible, since what Ibsen and Nietzsche are working for is the ratification of powers already active, consciously or unconsciously, in man; and what will finally come of it is not our business. That is God's business. In both *Brand* and *Peer Gynt* we were told that man's task is to realise God's *already implanted design*. A difficulty was certainly admitted; the design has to be glimpsed intuitively, if we are to collaborate (*Peer Gynt*, v. ix.); in both Nietzsche and Ibsen the critical and moral faculties are present, though they act as constituents and not dictatorially. Guidance can only come through the subtle interrelations and counterpointing of drama or some dramatic equivalent, wherein we simultaneously recognise ourselves and submit the imagination to a sovereign impact.

To speak psychologically, we may suggest that our most repellent fantasies, the troll-world of *Peer Gynt* where, as in *Macbeth*, fair and foul change places, must be accepted and assimilated by the man who truly wills himself. It was the troll in Solness that called and was answered by the "helpers and servers," and the seraphic Hilda was, like Gerd, in part troll. One of the darkest of all problems is this strange relation born by the obscene to spiritual perception.[7]

Conventional morality is almost entirely a technique for living, but our problems are further complicated when we recognise that Ibsen's dramatic thought is equally, or more, at home with dying. In *The Lady from the Sea* and *Little Eyolf* death is dramatised as a magnetic and fascinating power, and Ibsen is the great dramatist of mortal defiance. Death may, variously, be escape, expiation, martyrdom, or quest, but it is freely engaged and dramatically honoured. Ibsen much prefers life through death to death in life.

Dramatic suicides have an honourable ancestry. In Shakespeare Cassius' dagger may prove that circumstance cannot be "retentive to the strength of spirit" (*Julius Caesar*, I. iii. 95), and Cleopatra knows that it is great "to do that thing that ends all other deeds"

---

7. See my article, "Lawrence, Joyce and Powys," in *Essays in Criticism* XI. iv (Oct. 1961).

(*Antony and Cleopatra*, v. ii. 5); and so does Byron's Sardanapalus. Edgar in *King Lear* (v. ii. II) counsels instead a philosophy of "ripeness." For Hamlet "self-slaughter" may be a sin, but suicide-thoughts are central in his soliloquy on being, and elsewhere he finds greatness in the warring of Fortinbras precisely because of its free-hearted death-daring (*Hamlet*, I. ii. 131; III. i. 56–88; IV. iv. 47–65). The thoughts of the war-woman Hiördis and the general's daughter Hedda Gabler impel them to a willed dying. Brand, Solness, Borkman, Rubek and Irene fall in spiritual fight. Ibsen admired the warrior valuations, as did his son Sigurd after him.[8] Only through a death-friendly wisdom shall we respond to his dramatic conclusions.

Of this wisdom other poets offer us glimpses, as when Keats, in "Why did I laugh tonight!" writes:

> Verse, Fame and Beauty are intense indeed,
> But Death intenser—Death is Life's high meed.

In their *Goethe and Faust*,[9] F. Melian Stawell and G. Lowes Dickinson quote Goethe's lines from *The Singer's Book*:

> Tell no man, tell wise men only,
>   For the world might count it madness,
> Him I praise who thirsts for fire,
>   Thirsts for death, and dies in gladness.

Again:

> Die and grow! Until thou hearest
>   What that word can say,
> The world is dark and thou a wanderer
>   Who has lost his way.

The thought has an element in common with Christianity, and we may recall the authoritative statement in *Peer Gynt* that "to be oneself is to slay oneself" (v. ix. 252) and that what Julian most admired in his Christian opponents was their capacity for martyrdom. Nothing less than a complete self-realisation contents Ibsen and if this is not apparently attainable in normal terms, he must, in Goethe's phrase, make, or let, his people "die" to "grow." Ibsen is writing, to use Coleridge's description of his friend in the lines *To William Wordsworth*, "from the dread watch-tower of man's absolute self."

He had the advantage of nineteenth-century spiritualism, in which the occult traditions of western drama were being newly

8. See Halvdan Koht, *Life of Ibsen*, tr. R. L. McMahon and H. A. Larsen (1931), I. 184–5, and Sigurd Ibsen, *Menneskelig Kvintessens*, tr. M. H. Janson as *Human Quintessence*, London 1913, 282–9.
9. 1928; 56–7.

clarified.[1] Spiritualism is of central importance in *Emperor and Galilean* and *Little Eyolf*, and yet in those no suicide, direct or indirect, crowns the action. The most certain assurance, we are told, does not make suicide any easier; and conversely the act of suicide draws on resources of will and courage that are independent of belief. This, to Ibsen, is the crux. Nothing to him is ultimately valid that does not exist in the realms of will and deed. The positive quality in death must accordingly be projected, almost *incarnated*, through flesh-and-blood people who dare, of free choice and with no guidance, this appalling step; and we are invited to link our subjective experience to theirs. Sometimes the dramatist may, in more objective terms, garland the deed with happy associations; so that we, as audience, receive a dual benefit, simultaneously experiencing risk and recognising triumph. Though *The Master Builder* and *When We Dead Awaken* do not actually dramatise an after-life, everything possible is done through a highly-powered impressionism to show their heroes' death as an extension of living: we feel that Solness, Rubek, and Irene *have to pass on*.

Christianity rejects suicide, and so does Spiritualism, explaining that it solves nothing and contravenes law; and Ibsen's emphasis on creative dying might be regarded as dangerous. Yet, as we have seen, the moral judgment does not cover the dramatic problem. Dramatically we participate in a willed union with death regarded less as self-destruction than as self-assertion. Our subjective identification with the act somehow arouses a cosmic trust which endures within us as accounts of life beyond death, however authentic, cannot; and the experience may be re-expressed by us very differently. Like so many of the darker elements in drama, these adventures probably act more as an inoculation against actual violence than as an encouragement to it. They are as explosions, or flares, igniting spiritual perception; and most of them are associated closely with love. Moreover, as we saw in our analyses of *The Lady from the Sea* and *Little Eyolf*, the greater our respect to the occult and cosmic powers the nearer we shall draw to the perfect balance for which Julian looked, and the less necessity will there be for any violent conclusion; and there is a lesson here, today, for the whole of mankind.

However, death comes sooner or later to all of us, and meanwhile we may derive strength from watching Ibsen's heroes challenge it. Death does not, in Ibsen, involve "overthrow." Hiördis expected enthronement beyond death and led the ride to Valhalla; Hedvig died

---

1. In *The Lamp and the Lute* (1929), 17–18, Bonamy Dobrée well observes that Ibsen's "helpers and servers" in *The Master Builder* are as realistically felt as Judge Brack. Ibsen approved—perhaps unwisely—of a performance in which Solness used the gestures of a hypnotist (Koht, II. 302).

in the place of her dreams. At her end Rebecca assumes, like Cleopatra in her last robes, the symbolic white shawl; and Hedda's deed is honoured. The sense of death as dawn observed in *Catiline* and *Love's Comedy* is central to our understanding of Ibsen. *Love conditions it* and Agnes in *Brand* is its perfect voice. Ibsen's most *warmly*-realised scene is Peer's driving of his mother to "Soria-Moria Castle" in *Peer Gynt*; sunrise and dawn are key-impressions in *The Master Builder* and *When We Dead Awaken*; and even *Ghosts*, the lowest circle of his *Inferno*, was lit by the splendour.

Ibsen and Nietzsche stand close together, though Ibsen has a spirit-knowledge not explicit in Nietzsche, and *Thus Spake Zarathustra* a sweetness lacking in Ibsen. We today find both rather difficult. Christianity we think we understand, and can place, and we are at home with a rational agnosticism and with sexual passion. But what can we make of these astringent yet volcanic idealisms claiming to outspace, though they need not deny, both Christianity and rationalism, and preferring Dionysus to Aphrodite? What we have in effect done is to use them, or at least all those tendencies they represent, without full acknowledgment and understanding. Ibsen's two main emphases, which might be called the Nietzscheian and the spiritualistic, assert the two most vital soul-impulses of our century, which have for long been steadily if quietly influencing respectively our psychology and our religion, and are still active in creation of our future. To that future Ibsen points us; his is a drama of a new kind, of which Byron's was a forerunner. Like Byron, he was a regular reader of the Bible.[2] He is a prophetic dramatist, striving for the union of love and power; or, put differently, for the advent of Christ *as* power.

Ibsen may be trusted. Drama speaks through human impulse and human action; everything in it is tested and has to convince, and convince a grouped audience, immediately. It has accordingly an authenticity beyond the peregrinations of doctrine, and to its supreme exponents we must bring a high degree of respect. Here is Ibsen's statement, made at a banquet in Stockholm in 1887:

> I belive that an epoch is about to dawn when our political and social concepts will cease to exist in their present forms, and that the two will grow together into a single whole which will embody, for the present, the conditions making for the happiness of mankind. I believe that poetry, philosophy and religion will be fused into a new category and a new vital force, of the nature of which we, of the present generation, can obviously have no adequate notion.
>
> I have been charged on various occasions with being a pes-

2. Edmund Gosse, *Ibsen*, 241.

simist. And that is what I am, in so far as I do not believe in the absoluteness of human ideals. But I am at the same time an optimist in so far as I believe fully and steadfastly in the ability of ideals to propagate and to develop. Particularly and specifically do I believe that the ideals of our age, in passing away, are tending toward that which in my drama *Emperor and Galilean* I have tentatively called The Third Empire.[3]

That comparatively cold statement must be enriched by our remembrance of the dramas: of the persistent will towards a greater stature in man, at once personal and communal; of Falk's "I stamp no copper happiness as gold" and Brand's "In death I see not overthrow"; of the power-quest on earth and love for the dawn-flower beyond; of the many intimations of some newly royal life-way, and death-way, beyond the serried ranges of human endeavour outreaching to the kingdom and the power and the glory.

RICK DAVIS

The Smiling Ibsen: Comedy and Romance in Three Plays of the Prose Cycle†

Play with me, for a moment, a word-association game. The category for today? Masters of Modern Drama. The list? Strindberg: violent, misogynistic, strange. Chekhov: somber, static, melancholy, "indirect." Ibsen: grim, gloomy, cold, critical. All three: somehow good for you, like a dose of cultural castor oil.

The frustrating thing about such reactions, familiar to anyone who has proposed these writers for production by a theater, or taught them in a classroom, is that they each contain a germ of truth. Why have these attractive but reductive shorthand analyses become so widely accepted? Because we—and this "we" includes theater professionals along with scholars, critics, and teachers of drama—have often unthinkingly passed along a series of received opinions that by now have become critical signposts, pointing the quickest way to an appreciation of these plays. Everyone likes to have a shorthand tag to attach to complex ideas, to help organize our mental filing system.

My modest proposal here is to suggest a partial revision of *one* misconception about *one* writer—that cold and gloomy fellow—by making the perhaps surprising assertion that Ibsen, like Homer, Sophocles, and Shakespeare (the company he keeps in the Dead

---

3. As quoted by Hermann J. Weigand, *The Modern Ibsen*, 213.
† This essay is original to this Norton Critical Edition.

Writer Pantheon and Social Club), had within him a consistent command of a full range of comic, satiric, and romantic voices.

In every play of Ibsen's prose cycle, the magisterial twelve-play entity comprising *Pillars of Society* (1877) through *When We Dead Awaken* (1899) with which he closed his fifty-year career as playwright and cultural revolutionary, at least a hint of the smile appears. These hints take the form not only of wit and humor, which are external manifestations of the comic vision, but also consistent glimpses of a more profound attitude toward comedy, satire, or romance, located typically in a secondary character or a structural motif. By romance I don't mean just the typical "grim Norwegian boy meets sad Norwegian girl" story. Literary romance, after all, has more to do with the idea of the quest, of loss and restoration, separation and reunion, as in Shakespeare and Dante, Euripides and Goethe.

Recognizing the comic spirit in these twelve plays might be useful if only because the prose cycle is principally responsible for Ibsen's monolithic reputation. The poet of *Peer Gynt* and *Love's Comedy* (an unfortunately neglected early work of great charm and sophistication) can easily be credited with possession of a comic voice. But these verse masterpieces are less widely known (especially in production), leaving the last twelve plays to paint the formidable portrait of the "scold of the North." My goal is not to make him any less formidable, but to suggest that, like all the greatest dramatists, Ibsen found room for a constructive coexistence of the tragic and the comic worldview.

This notion of Ibsen as grim, gloomy, cold, critical, and unpleasantly good for you has not only prevented him from being produced more often, but it has influenced those who do present him. Actors, responding to the intuitive impulses that their training has cultivated, may tend to distrust and censor those impulses when they reveal a comic moment. Actorial censorship may stem from several sources: a too-reverential attitude toward the mistaken idea of Ibsen as—to use John Gassner's word—an "evangelist," or the common notion that there is a properly grave tonality for Ibsen, as with equal injustice there is, or was, supposed to be a "Chekhovian" mood or tone.

Directors may fear critical invective if they acknowledge the comedy in Ibsen by letting it play itself, as it will surely do; so they sometimes actively work against it, smoothing out the wrinkles in the dramatic fabric that constitute the source of much of Ibsen's comedy. Writers of criticism and program notes, always eager to point out something significant, fail to realize that seriousness of purpose does not require solemnity of tone, either on their own part or Ibsen's. And so it follows that audiences and readers, necessarily responsive to the work of the above, have developed a conditioned set of aesthetic reflexes that, far from being tools for appreciation, are in fact handicaps to an open and unencumbered viewing of the work.

The roadblocks to the liberation of Ibsen's *vis comica* are being challenged today with increasing frequency and success, yet they persist in two major categories of misconception. First of these is the "high church" Ibsen, the evangelist; the second, all too common, might be called the curator's Ibsen, the museum classic who is an honored predecessor to today's more "vital" and "relevant" theater.

Of the two views, the former is probably preferable, but it has its dangers, just as bardolatry had (and has) a deadening effect on Shakespeare interpretation and production. The benefit is clear: assuming genius in a writer, we become more fully responsible to the work. We charge ourselves to understand that what may look like flaws or lapses in fact are necessary components in the dramatic whole.

For example: If not dismissed as Scribean or melodramatic fossils, Ibsen's so-called creaky plots can stand revealed as brilliant self-commenting structures, gloriously artificial and as fully in command of the theatrical metaphor as Shakespeare's. The drop of Krogstad's letter in the mail slot in *A Doll House*, the famous knock at the door by the impudent young Hilda Wangel in *The Master Builder* just after Solness has expressed his fear that "youth will soon come knocking on my door"—these locate Ibsen's art in the same metatheatrical ballpark as "I hold the world but as the world, Gratiano—a stage, where every man must play a part, and mine a sad one." Playwrights love to call attention to their medium. The exuberance of Shakespeare's theater allows him to speak of it overtly, calling out loud for his muse of fire; Ibsen's more realistic form requires that the revealed artifice be one of structure and incident, not self-conscious language.

But the danger is that the seriousness of our belief can cast a deadly pall of solemnity over the entire work. If one of Ibsen's "alarming coincidences" turns out to elicit laughter in performance, should we run from that or embrace it? If we accept it as conscious craft and not sloppy playwriting, should we try to cover it up, or let it sing out? Very often the preconceived notion of Ibsenian tone wins out, and the moment is played with an embarrassed understatement, hoping that the audience won't somehow suspend their suspension of disbelief—a highly suspect activity in the first place that Dr. Johnson effectively destroyed in his Preface to Shakespeare as long ago as 1765.

In a suitably unsolemn frame of mind, then, we can turn our attention to *A Doll House*, a cultural castor-oil play if there ever was one, and try to see beneath the surface of domestic demolition anything of the comic, satiric, or romantic spirit that I'm claiming for Ibsen's artistic method. Ibsen was attacked and supported by all manner of advocates on the left and right, but late in his career, in 1898, he gave a speech in Norway—to the Norwegian Society for Women's Rights—that contained this famous passage: "Whatever I have written has been without any conscious thought of making propaganda. I have been more the poet and less the social philosopher than people seem generally inclined to believe. . . . My task has been the description of humanity."

Interpretation of *A Doll House* in recent times has tended to concentrate on the question of whether Nora's story is a feminist document. In that same speech, Ibsen perhaps somewhat impolitely denied any ideological connection to his hosts and benefactors that day: "I must disclaim the honor of having consciously worked for women's rights. I am not even quite sure what women's rights really are. To me it has been a question of human rights."

Of course, the place of *A Doll House* in the feminist struggle, regardless of its author's perhaps false modesty, cannot be disputed. But emphasizing the social utility of a text doesn't necessarily encourage the most comprehensive reading—or theatrical production—of a play. You often end up leaving those details unconsidered that don't fit the *schema*. In *The Tempest*, Prospero can be made an imperialist villain, but at the expense of the fifth act. In the case of *A Doll House*, this has led to a general devaluing of all the stories in the play except that of Nora, who is a legitimate culture hero, but who is not the only subject of Ibsen's attention. If Nora's action—leaving husband and children to embark on a quest for the discovery of a satisfactory self—stands (as I think it does) as a metaphor for all humanity's need to confront the unknown, the void, in full knowledge of one's total ignorance—then Torvald's remaining behind, trapped in the narrow world of his devising, stands equally powerfully for those of us hanging back in the caves, afraid in equal measure of the darkness and the light. It is his failure of spiritual imagination—his inability to recognize Nora's invocation of the "most wonderful thing of all," the self-transformation that could make their lives together into a real marriage—that creates whatever tragic feeling the play creates. Nora's leaving is a personal and societal necessity—you feel the pressure, especially now, of all of Western culture pushing her out the door. But Torvald's *staying* manifests the essence of the tragic situation: a human being caught up, in his ignorance, at a crossroads where every turn he takes is wrong.

These actions, much discussed in the critical literature and so powerful in the theater when well performed, create the serious core of meaning that has made the play a classic. But let us turn our attention to the matter at hand to see if part of the work's genius, part of its lasting vitality, can be found in its employment of the devices and tonalities of comedy and romance.

Throughout the play's three acts, Ibsen sounds the comic note, often in close juxtaposition with the most serious of scenes. The play begins in a deliciously light vein, in a holiday mood—it is Christmas Eve after all—with Nora and Torvald playing games in a spirit of obvious affection. The animal names (lark, songbird, squirrel) and the more fanciful appellations (my little sweet-tooth, and the invention of a new bird species, the spendthrift) certainly have been noticed as examples of how Torvald treats Nora like a child; but note how willingly, how consciously, and to what spectacularly successful effect she plays along with this game. Her mastery of Torvald (allowing her to win every early encounter in the play, from the ingestion of several forbidden macaroons to the garnering of a substantial amount of money from the normally tightfisted banker) is so total that I believe we can laugh with, not at, the comedy of that first scene. Those macaroons allow for comic chewing and hiding bits in the best "I Love Lucy" tradition. The human transactions established in their first encounters—which are full of lies, half-lies, platitudes, and hypocrisies on both sides, all delivered so charmingly so as to disguise their true foundation—serve as paradigm for the larger underlying seismic fault that will bring down the doll house in the third act.

The character of Dr. Rank—whose dramatic function is often puzzled over—supplies a coloration of humane, urbane, sophisticated, and rueful wit, especially in the sensually charged "silk-stockings" scene, when Nora is considering asking him to help her out of her difficulties with a sum of money, and in the ultimate metaphysical jest, well-remarked by both Rank and Nora, of his unearned demise. Rank allows us to see the dead hand of the past—with all its metaphorical freight—at work in the present and looks forward to Ibsen's next play, *Ghosts*, in which that theme is a primary obsession. Yet Rank is able, except for a couple of self-pitying moments of morbidity, to sustain a witty tone throughout—quite clearly the creation of a playwright with more than one side of human nature at his command.

Perhaps Ibsen's boldest employment of simple humor comes in the last act, just before the grand moment that changed Western drama forever, the imperative heard 'round the world, when Nora says, "Torvald, sit down—we have a lot to talk about." Prior to that temblor, Torvald and Nora have returned from the party upstairs; Nora has danced her tarantella to great acclaim, though Torvald claims to have found the performance, in his words, a "little too naturalistic." Now Torvald, flushed with champagne and lust for his wife, has his intentions frustrated twice by unexpected visitors. Kristine Linde is waiting for them when they return from the party, and Torvald can't contain his irritation. He finally sends her off with a comic demonstration of the comparative elegance of needle-point and knitting. He cannot know that in three or four minutes his world is about to change forever, and whether we remember or not, we laugh at the absurdity of his gesture. This is bold playwriting.

Structurally, too, there is a layer of comedy in the play. The Krogstad/Kristine action re-creates one of the classic motifs in comedy and romance: reunification. Notice how Ibsen allows for both a comic and a tragic ending in Act III by bringing the long-sundered Kristine and Krogstad together in a scene that swells to a romantic climax with Krogstad—the erstwhile "villain" of the piece—proclaiming that he's never felt such happiness. Kristine, freed by widowhood from a long and loveless marriage, and Krogstad, clawing his way back to social respectability after a life marked by struggles and desperate schemes, even uses the imagery of a shipwreck—one of the basic plot devices of literary romance, remembering *The Tempest* and *Pericles*—to describe their over-whelming loss and the possibility that they just might save each other. When these two, reunited, leave the room (and the play), that romantic tonality is removed—after Ibsen reminds us that it is possible in the world—and the stage is clear for the tragic action that follows.

The term "tragic" can be understood in several ways—I mentioned a moment ago that Torvald's ending fulfills one sense of the tragic in his inability to discover a correct choice to make—but it's not really the idea of the tragic that we perhaps somewhat vaguely associated with the classical tradition (grand downfall of titanic figures, unutterable sadness, devastation visited upon kingdoms, and so on), but in those posited by Albert Cook in his 1948 study of genre theory, *The Dark Voyage and the Golden Mean*, in which Cook roughly separates comedy and tragedy into the worlds of the "probable" and the "wonderful." In comedy, the probable, rational, social modes of thinking tend to dominate, while tragedy concerns itself with the wonderful, the ideal, the transcendent.

Kristine and Krogstad's union satisfies the notion of the "probable": it is an accommodation to reality, a solution to a mutual social problem. It is also, to put it another way, a happy ending. Both of them get something that they desperately need—each other, and the security of a partner on the life raft as they paddle away from the shipwreck of their past lives toward a new shore.

Nora and Torvald's ending is not happy, but it is "wonderful." The search for an individuated self upon which Nora embarks, the quest for self-knowledge and a personal, felt, "owned" understanding of the world, her need to transcend the ethical and intellectual strictures of her world—all these stand, in Cook's scheme of things, for the world of tragedy, the world of "the wonderful."

As Brian Johnston has pointed out, it is no accident that Nora uses that word at least nine times throughout the play, in triplet form at key moments in each of the three acts, to describe her situation. In the first act, "the wonderful" simply refers to the material world, the world of money and clothes and Christmas presents. In the second act, "the wonderful" has taken on an eerie meaning, wrapped up in a complex of notions about Torvald's willingness to take the blame for Nora's action, and Nora's intention to stave that off by taking her own life—a kind of impossible Wagnerian or Viking romance of mutual self-sacrifice. In the third act, in its key iteration, the "wonderful" becomes, finally, "the most wonderful thing of all"—the as-yet inarticulate process by which Nora and Torvald's union would transform itself from a mere "living together" to a "marriage." How that is to be accomplished is left a provocatively open question.

In any case, the Torvald/Nora ending is in direct opposition, both in action and tone, to the Kristine/Krogstad resolution. Cook suggests (though without reference to Ibsen) that the most satisfying and sophisticated kind of work of art is one in which the probable and the wonderful, the comic and tragic, are brought together, as in certain romances such as *The Tempest*. Here, in *A Doll House*, Ibsen presents them side by side for the sake of clear comparison, and because of his relentlessly dialectical cast of mind at this point in his prose cycle; they will be united impressively in the great "romances" of his later career such as *The Master Builder* and *When We Dead Awaken*.

All of this serves to suggest that even in plays as designedly serious as *A Doll House*, there is not only wit and humor—it's all right to laugh out loud at this play, even in the third act—but a more profound comic structure that coexists significantly and fruitfully alongside the tragic structure that is too often given predominance if not exclusive priority.

The Wild Duck—one of Ibsen's most hauntingly and authentically moving plays on a purely emotional level—also is infused with the spirit of comedy and satire. From the very beginning (the "feather duster scene" drawn from the already-hoary expositional conventions of mid-century), to the party with its gallery of guests named only by type—"A Fat Man, a Bald-Headed Man, a Near-

Sighted Man"—Ibsen sets up an edgy, satiric tone in the first act against which the rest of the action will resonate. As the play progresses, its systematic undercutting of both Hjalmar Ekdal's futile dreams and Gregers Werle's championing of the banner of the ideal play out in tonalities ranging from gentle absurdity (Ekdal's invention) to biting, almost savage wit (Relling's invective).

Even the physical world of this play is darkly, disorientingly comic—it pushes its characters into accommodations with their essential selves that they might perhaps wish to avoid, and it creates existential obstacles for others. One minor but telling example emerges in Ibsen's floor plans for the play's two settings—the sumptuous sitting-room of the Werle household and the spacious but simple upstairs apartment of the Ekdal family—the plans of which, as Rolf Fjelde notes, are "curiously congruent." The placement of doors and the offstage rooms onto which they open controls, of course, a certain amount of stage movement. But to one character in particular, Old Ekdal, the environment bears almost a personal relation. In both settings, the world as structured by Ibsen keeps Old Ekdal on the periphery. He enters upstage center in the Werle sitting room, and his destination is the office door downstage left; his traffic pattern coupled with the circumstances of the scene logically keep him almost hugging the walls. In the Ekdal apartment, he enters from the hallway upstage left, pops his head in the attic up center, goes into his room up right, then comes out of his room and moves directly to the kitchen, the door to which is on the same wall as the door to his room; he then returns to his room, all within about a minute and a half of stage time. In both environments, Ibsen keeps Old Ekdal comically scuttling around on the edges of things, a reflection in stage movement of his position in the world's affairs and of his importance to the play's main action: a central character rendered peripheral by the world of the stage he inhabits. There is, I think, a deeply witty sensibility at work here. We have seen it operating in structural and characterological terms, and now it extends itself even to the design of the scenery.

Hedda Gabler offers perhaps the clearest example of the high-comedy mode that Ibsen created in his last twelve prose plays. Various critics have likened the style of the play to Restoration comedy, with its gallery of typed characters and its actions and behaviors rooted squarely in the ferocious pursuit of those two greatest earthly goods, sex and money. The characters are full of comic excess—Eilert Løvborg is a kind of Restoration rake-turned-Puritan, libidinous and drunken in his past and future lives, piously reformed for the first two acts of the play, but always in danger of slipping. He is at first too sober and later too drunk, a classic example of comic exaggeration. George Tesman, historian and collector of domestic craftwork of medieval Brabant, is the comic pedant, forever intending to write a great work of history but whose real job in life is collecting and ordering the work of others. Ibsen gives him a delicious speech pattern that mocks the image of scholarly demeanor, Tesman's famous "eh?" or "huh?" or "what?" that ends a good percentage of his utterances. Judge Brack is another kind of rake, a dangerous one, whose lust is linked with considerable worldly power. Yet Hedda at first enjoys his company as a relief from the grim world of her husband, and their scenes are laced with the kind of sexual double and triple meanings that would have pleased William Wycherley.

Ibsen refines the formula somewhat, of course, lest he be accused of frivolity. The struggle within *Hedda Gabler* is played out on no smaller a stage than the struggle between the pagan and Christian worldviews. Hedda and Løvborg, brilliant world-historical scholar, represent a frustrated and thwarted glimpse back to an image of classical antiquity—Hedda wants to imagine Eilert with "vine leaves in his hair, fiery and bold." conqueror of his inner demons, master of the alcohol addiction that had plagued him, champion sensualist and intellect to redeem them both from the stultifying values of the conventionally Christian world inhabited by her husband, the timid archivist Tesman and his circle. The humor of the play, which exists side by side with its tragic quality, comes about as the result of this clash of worlds. Hedda is so desperately uncomfortable in her directionless middle-class life that she deliberately mocks and offends everyone within it. Seeing the fine new hat that Tesman's maiden aunt Julie bought to come visiting lying on a chair, she pretends to think it belongs to Berta, the maid, and tells Tesman and Julie that they'll have to fire dear old Berta because she can't keep leaving her old things lying around on the furniture. She mocks her childhood friend, Thea Elvsted, calling her by the wrong name, threatening only half in jest to burn her hair off, and filling her full of dangerous ideas about Løvborg, whose life Thea had managed to straighten out—or at least reclaim in part from the call of the pagan wild.

One of Hedda's last actions in the play, before the gunshot that ends her life, is to mimic, with deadly satiric accuracy, everyone else in the drawing room that she is soon to recognize cannot contain her. Moving from Thea to Tesman, who are laboring in the dull heat of archival passion over Løvborg's old notes in an attempt to reconstruct his lost masterpiece, to Judge Brack, the boor who has been trying to maneuver her into a position where his sexual blackmail rules the roost, she adopts their language and tone, asking each in turn a question. The inadequacy—or rather, the utter predictability within a hypocritically conventional world—of their answers help drive her into the inner room where the pistol awaits her. But the dramaturgical point is that, in a good production of the play, the audience is laughing up until about thirty seconds before that startling gunshot. And they may legitimately laugh a moment or two later, when Judge Brack utters his now-famous understatement in response to seeing Hedda's sprawled body: "But, Good God—people just don't act that way." Ibsen has us trapped in diametrically opposed emotional states, which is characteristically just where he wants us.

And so it continues, in play after play of this twelve-play masterwork. The rueful laugh, the pointed satire, the unexpected discontinuity, the sudden eruption of sunlight, the tentative movement toward reconciliation: these are the tools of the dramatic genius, employed to full value in a mammoth undertaking that is fundamentally serious, not monolithically solemn. These tonalities open us up to a more complex, nuanced, and fully human world as artfully composed by a writer whose reputation for importance of serious purpose has sometimes overshadowed his own avowed task, "the description of humanity." For Ibsen, as for the greatest dramatic poets, that means humanity in full, in the round, often in trouble, but never completely dispossessed of the spirit of the smile.

JOAN TEMPLETON

Genre, Representation, and the Politics of Dramatic Form: Ibsen's Realism†

The Case Against Ibsen's Realism

It is an axiom of current theatre criticism and production that realism is a dead, and, in some cases, despised form. Writing in *The New York Times* a few months ago, Richard Schechner declared: "The plays of Ibsen and Chekhov, which once were up to date in themes, behavior, costume and language, are now period works."[1] There are two reasons for this, Schechner explained: the first is that the "substance of realist drama" no longer exists, for "very little living these days exists as extended spans of conversation in the

† From *Proceedings: IX International Ibsen Conference, Bergen 5–10 June 2000*, ed. Pål Bjørby and Asbjørn Aarseth (Bergen: Alvheim and Eide, 2001), 49–64. Reprinted by permission of Alvheim and Eide Akademisk Forlag. Page references to this Norton Critical Edition appear in brackets following the author's original citations.
1. "Already Working the Classics of Modern Realism," *The New York Times* (February 13, 2000), "Arts and Leisure" 7.

home," and the second is that the realist style has been made obsolete by the "new media": film, of course, or the camera, "the collage that is television," and, more recently, digitized computer graphics, in general, the "hypertext mentality" (18). Because of the death of realism, Schechner goes on to say, revisionist directors of classic realist texts are free to use them in any way they choose, as "raw material" for "the construction of new, highly original theater pieces" (7).

A recent example of such an effort is last season's production of *Gengangere* [*Ghosts*] at the Volksbühne in Berlin, whose artistic director, Frank Castorf, has, to quote Marvin Carlson, "built a reputation on productions of classic works that are frequently outrageous even by German standards."[2] In Carlson's review of the production, he describes how the director, Sebastian Hartmann, pushes the characters

> beyond caricature into grotesque parody. Is Regina flirting with Pastor Manders in the first scene? In Berlin, as she tries to take the umbrella he is holding in front of him, she rapidly opens and closes it in a gesture that we suddenly realize is one of simulated masturbation. Is Osvald attracted to Regina? In Berlin, he masturbates behind a chair while she strikes erotic poses on the dining room table. Is Regina angry at Mrs. Alving for the way she has been treated? In Berlin, she bursts in dressed as a terrorist and guns down . . . Mrs. Alving (Carlson 1999: 5).

The first two emendations we can politely call "glosses," or, less politely, a melodramatic "dumbing down" of Ibsen's text; in the first case, the director adds an overtly sexual gesture, and in the second, a sexual act. Ibsen, appropriately sexed up, is now our contemporary. The third change—the transformation of Regina into a political terrorist gunning down her oppressor Mrs. Alving—is of a different sort. Reflecting a long program note by Jacques Derrida discussing the "ghosts" of capitalism, the director's making of Regina into a revolutionary attacking the representative of the system that oppresses her directly contradicts Ibsen's action; leaving Mrs. Alving behind, Regina chases after Manders and Engstrand to join the system and reap its spoils. My criticism that, in the first two instances, the director has cheapened Ibsen's text, and, in the second, that he has contradicted it, would be regarded as irrelevant at the Volksbühne; where, as Carlson points out,

> lack of balance, inconsistency, and a tendency toward caricature are none of them grounds for complaint . . . ; indeed all

2. *Ghosts* on Two Continents and Two Cultures at 20th-Century's End," *Ibsen News and Comment* 19 (1999) 4.

are assiduously cultivated. . . . Here there is no problem of
slipping into melodrama; melodrama is one of the best strategies, along with farce, and indeed every sort of extreme expression (4–5).

The subtleties of Ibsen's nuanced realism are jettisoned in the service of shock tactics. The descent of realism has its roots in Brecht,
who has become a Bible not only for theories of drama, but for
much of post-modern literary theory. In the first full account of his
anti-illusionist theatre, "The Modern Theatre Is The Epic Theater,"
Brecht fashioned his now famous double columns. Whereas the
Aristotelian, or "dramatic" theatre "implicates the spectator in a
stage situation, wears down his capacity for action," the epic theatre "turns the spectator into an observer, arouses his capacity for
action."[3] In the dramatic theatre, "the human being is taken for
granted [and] he is unalterable," while in the epic theatre, "the human being is the object of the inquiry, he is alterable and able to alter" (Brecht 37). In both types of theatre, form mirrors content: the
dramatic theatre is based on "plot," in which "one scene makes another," with "linear development" and with its "eyes on the finish,"
whereas the epic theatre is based on "narrative," in which "each
scene [exists] for itself," the development is "in curves," and with
its "eyes on the course" (37).

As Raymond Williams and others have pointed out, Brecht's account of Aristotelian theatre would have surprised Aristotle; what
Brecht was "really referring to," writes Williams, "was naturalist
theatre, and what he was concerned with was the problem of empathy."[4] Brecht claimed that the realist-naturalist theatre of the
19th century, which he called the bourgeois theatre, had no lasting significance: "Works by Ibsen and Strindberg remain important
historical documents, but they no longer move anybody. A modern
spectator can't learn anything from them" ("Interview With An
Exile," Brecht 66). For Brecht, part of Ibsen's and Strindberg's
unimportance lies in their interest in the "individual psyche,"
which in Brecht's Marxist view is "utterly uninteresting" because
the human being is only "the tool [of the capitalist production
process] and not the guiding hand" (67), but an equally important
part of their insignificance lies in their illusionist form. First, it is
out of date: the world has so changed, Brecht writes in 1929, that
"Even to dramatize a simple newspaper report one needs something
much more than the dramatic technique of a Hebbel or an Ibsen.
. . . It is impossible to explain a present-day character by features or
a present-day action by motives that would have been adequate in

---

3. *Brecht on Theatre*, ed. and trans. John Willett (New York: Hill, 1964) 37.
4. *Politics and Letters: Interviews with New Left Review* (London: NLB, 1979) 217.

our fathers' time" ("On Form and Subject-Matter," Brecht 30). Secondly, "engendering of illusion" claims to show the world as it is, pretending "not to be theatre" but to be the world as it is, thus arousing the audience's empathy rather than its critical judgment ("The Street Scene," Brecht 122). While the dramatic theatre's spectator says "Yes, I have felt like that too—Just like me—It's only natural—It'll never change," the epic theatre's spectator says "I'd never have thought it—That's not the way—That's extraordinary, hardly believable—It's got to stop" ("Theatre for Pleasure or Theatre for Instruction," Brecht 71).

Realism was dealt another blow by post-structuralism. For Barthes, who was influenced by Brecht, and who championed his theatre in France,[5] the honest sign, whether word or symbol, draws attention to its condition as sign, not substance. Since all signs are arbitrary, signs that try to appear "natural" are suspect, and ultimately both ideological and authoritarian. And the literary style that is the most ideological and authoritarian is realism, which in concealing the constructed nature of its language is attempting to pass itself off as the "natural" language. Unlike symbolism, which openly distorts surface reality into subjective shapes, realism inherently presents itself as a translucent window on to reality; in giving us the illusion that we are perceiving reality without its intervention, it is philosophically false because we can only define what is "real" by imposing structures of signification on experience.[6] In his famous tour de force, S/Z, Barthes puts his theory into practice. Through his violent taking apart of Balzac's realistic novella *Sarrasine*, in a practice that later became known as deconstruction, Barthes claims to show that the text unknowingly includes the opposite of what it is seeking to communicate and thus questions the very assumptions that rule it. The representational value of Balzac's and all other realists' signs is thus called into question. In an opposition that draws on Brecht's distinction between the bourgeois theatre, in which the spectator is confronted with a given world not subject to change, and his own epic theatre, in which the spectator is challenged to complete in the real world the play he has witnessed, Barthes distinguishes between texts that are *lisible*—those which are to be merely read by the reader—and those that are *scriptible*—those which the reader can write. The texts of classic realism, Barthes maintains, are *lisible* texts that are complicit accomplices to the reigning political, social and cultural ideology of their time, and are now therefore irrelevant. What is needed are *scriptible* texts, whose readers, like Brecht's

5. Barthes' *Critical Essays* (1964) includes a laudatory essay on Brecht.
6. My summary of Barthes' post-structuralist phase owes a great deal to Terry Eagleton's useful paraphrase of it in *Literary Theory* (London: Methuen, 1976) 118.

spectators at the epic theatre, can respond to by remaking them.[7]

Barthes' notion of the hidden ideology of the literary text was complemented by the work of Althusser, most notably in the celebrated essay "Ideology and Ideological State Apparatuses." Literature, Althusser argues, in an entirely Brechtian mode, along with "the Arts, sports, etc." [sic] belongs to "the cultural Ideological State Apparatuses" that, in presenting their subjects as "always already" what they are, represses them into subjectivity and prevents questioning. Althusser does not explain *how* literature is repressive, and spends, in fact, very little time on the "cultural State apparatuses"—his main targets are the "ideological State apparatuses," e.g., the French educational system, the family, the law, the political party system—but his essay, which Terry Eagleton has called "perhaps the key text in the theory of ideology for our time,"[8] has had an immense influence on post-modern literary theory.

The inherent conservatism of the realist text is now an accepted tenet of post-modern literary theory. In *Criticism and Meaning*, a primer of the movement, Catherine Belsey writes that

> realism can never surprise us. . . . The experience of reading a realist text is ultimately reassuring, however harrowing the events of the story, because the world evoked in the fiction, its patterns of cause and effect, of social relationships and moral values, largely confirm the patterns of the world we seem to know.[9]

Drawing on Althusser, Belsey argues that even in drama, in which the author "is apparently absent from the self-contained fictional work on the page," in fact,

> the author is present as a shadowy authority and as source of the fiction, and the author's presence is substantiated by the name on the cover of the programme: . . . 'a new play by Ibsen'. . . . And at the same time . . . the *form* of the classic realist text acts in conjunction with the expressive theory and with ideology by interpellating the reader as subject. The reader is invited to perceive and judge the 'truth' of the text, the coherent, non-contradictory interpretation of the world as it is perceived by an author whose antonomy is the source and evidence of the truth of the interpretation (68–69).

Borrowing the term *declarative* from the French post-structuralist critic Benveniste, Belsey distinguishes between realism, which she ar-

---

7. The next, perhaps inevitable, step in Barthes' development was *The Pleasure of the Text* (1970), in which all ideology and all meaning have become inherently terroristic, and "writing" is the only uncolonized domain in which human beings can be free.
8. *Ideology*, ed. Eagleton (London: Longman, 1994) 87.
9. (London: Methuen, 1980) 51.

gues is a "declarative" mode, "imparting 'knowledge' to a reader whose position is therefore stabilized," and the "interrogative" text, which

> disrupts the unity of the reader by discouraging identification with a unified subject. . . . The position of the 'author' inscribed in the text, if it can be located at all, is seen as questioning or as literally contradictory . . . [and it] does literally invite the reader to produce answers to the questions it implicitly or explicitly raises (91).

The "consistently interrogative writer who comes most readily to mind is, of course, Brecht" (94).[1] Another influence on the demise of theatrical realism, especially in the United States, comes from performance theory, whose anti-establishment stance is strongly influenced by Brecht, Althusser, and the post-structuralists. Performance, Elin Diamond explains, defines itself

> in opposition to theatre structures and conventions. . . . [Theatre] was charged with obeisance to the playwright's authority, with actors disciplined to the referential task of representing fictional entities. In this narrative, spectators are similarly disciplined, duped into identifying with the psychological problems of individual egos and ensnared in a unique temporal-spatial world whose suspense, reversals, and deferrals they can more or less comfortably decode. Performance, on the other hand, has been honored [sic] with dismantling textual authority, illusionism, and the canonical actor.[2]

While all dramatic authors' texts, i.e., plays, are part of what performance theorists refer to as "the verbal tradition,"[3] realist drama is particularly spurned, in the words of Richard Schechner, because "realism is no longer real, it is just another theatrical style" ("Already Reworking the Classics" 7).

Illogicalities and Critical Problems: Illusionism and Representation

The first thing to point out here is that theatrical realism never claimed to be real, for theatre of whatever sort is illusion. In his

---

1. Belsey claims that "in arguing that the interrogative text enlists the reader in contradiction while classic realism does its best to efface contradiction, I do not mean to suggest that the interrogative text is therefore 'good' and classic realism ideologically misleading, and therefore 'bad.' But if we are not simply to subject ourselves (in every sense) to ideology, we need a new way of approaching classic realism" (103). This disclaimer strikes me as disingenuous at best, coming as it does after page after page of criticism of the closed world of realism; it is curious that it never occurs to Belsey that nonrealist texts might also subject "ourselves (in every sense)" to ideology.
2. "Introduction," *Performance and Cultural Politics*, ed. Diamond (London: Routledge, 1996) 3.
3. See Marvin Carlson, *Performance: A Critical Introduction* (London: Routledge, 1996) 117.

book on the phenomenology of the theatre, *Great Reckonings in Little Rooms*, Bert States serves up Dr. Johnson on this matter: "The truth is that the spectators are always in their senses, and know, from the first act to the last, that the stage is only a stage, and that the players are only players. They come to hear a certain number of lines recited with just gesture and elegant modulation."[4]

What might seem more worthy of debate is the claim made by realism's detractors that it claims to "represent" reality. The idea that literature reflects or mirrors life is, of course, both intensely old—as old as Aristotle's "imitation"—and intensely problematic, especially, as Terry Eagleton points out, "in its cruder formulations," which suggest "a passive, mechanistic relationship between literature and society, as though the work, like a mirror or photographic plate, merely inertly registered what was happening 'out there'."[5] Even in Marxist literary criticism, which has always used reflectionism as a major tenet in arguing against formalism, theorists have been careful to guard against the simplistic notion that art directly mirrors life. Trotsky claimed that art "is a deflection, a changing and a transformation of reality, in accordance with the peculiar laws of art" (*Marxism and Literary Criticism* 50), and Lukács, whose version of reflectionism Eagleton terms "clearly the most reputable [Marxist] form of the reflectionist theory," wrote that great art gives us "a more profound and comprehensive reflection of objective reality than is given in appearance" (50). Brecht himself wrote in the "Short Organum" that "If art reflects life, it does so with special mirrors" (Brecht 204).

It would seem evident, in fact, to all but the most naive of viewers that the dramatist, like all artists, does not posit his work as a mirror of life. Logically speaking, the argument in itself is a good example of a false assumption. But for the sake of the argument, let us entertain the assumption and claim that Ibsen believed himself to be copying "reality." Let us use *Hedda Gabler*, the zenith of the playwright's realist method, as our example: Ibsen, believing that he had experienced the "real" Hedda, the "real" Tesman, the "real" Tante Julie, then determined to give to the world his own mirror of it. This account, which makes Ibsen into a kind of mad Neo-Platonist, is clearly absurd; objectors to my scenario, however, will point out that it is not Ibsen who is being accused of engaging in such a practice, but his text; in imitating reality, it is passing itself off as reality. Quite apart from the issue of whether a fictional text can undertake a critical practice, in this case, representing itself as something, what needs to be said is that imitating a thing is not the same thing as claiming to be the thing. In logical terms, the post-

4. (Berkeley: University of California Press, 1985) 9.
5. *Marxism and Literary Criticism* (London: Methuen, 1976) 49.

structuralists have confused *mimesis* with *existensias*, representing with being.

The Brechtian notion that a non-illusionist text like the epic theatre is more interrogative because its mode is not realistic, assumes, *ipso facto*, that one dramatic mode is less false than another. Logically, this cannot be so. In his highly influential *Speech Acts*, the philosopher of language John Searle distingishes between "normal real world talk" and what he calls "parasitic forms of discourse such as fiction, play-acting, etc."[6] In real world talk, one cannot refer to Sherlock Holmes because he does not exist. But if one shifts to the "fictional, play acting, let's pretend mode of discourse," Sherlock Holmes indeed exists. However, "the fact that there is such a character as Sherlock Holmes does not commit us to the view that he exists in some supra-sensible *world or that he has a special mode of existence*") 79; italics mine). Searle points out that within the fictional world, there are no "changes in the *meanings* of words or other linguistic elements in fictional discourse. . . . it is essential to realize that even in 'The Little Red Riding Hood,' *red* means red. The conventions of fiction don't change the meanings of words or other linguistic elements" (79).

In *Expression and Meaning*, Searle expands his distinction between fictional and non-fictional worlds. While a non-fictional speech act must commit itself to fulfilling certain quite specific "semantic and pragmatic rules," e.g., it must believe in "the truth of the expressed proposition"[7] and must be in a position to provide evidence for this truth, none of the rules for non-fictional discourse apply to fictional speech acts, and, in fact, are irrelevant to them, for the writer of the fictional world is pretending to represent a state of affairs that does not exist and has never existed. Of course, fictional worlds contain references to real places, real persons, and real events—Searle mentions Russia and the Napoleonic wars in *War and Peace*, and London and Baker Street in *The Adventures of Sherlock Holmes*, and one could, of course, add countless others, e.g., The Thirty Years War in *Mother Courage and her Children*, Ibsen's parodies of the Norwegian language reformers in *Peer Gynt*, but these references do not de-fictionalize the fiction.

It follows from this that if all fictional worlds are pure fiction, then none can be less fictional than another. We can say, using aesthetic or political or whatever other criteria please us, that some fictional worlds are better or more interesting than others, but we cannot say that one fictional world is more real than another.

It follows that the conventions of fictional worlds are equally fic-

6. *Speech Acts: An Essay in the Philosophy of Language* (Cambridge: Cambridge University Press, 1969) 78.
7. (Cambridge: Cambridge University press, 1973) 62–63.

tional. In his discussion of dramatic conventions in *Drama from Ibsen to Brecht*, Raymond Williams discusses how the dramatic soliloquy fell out of fashion; the complaint was that it was "artificial," or "not true to life," or even "undramatic"; yet, Williams writes, "it is surely as natural and as 'true to life,' when one is on a stage before a thousand people, to address them, as to pretend to carry on as if they were not there."[8] Similarly, devices of that much maligned form, the intrigue drama, are not, in themselves, any more or less real, or more or less worthy, than any other theatrical conventions.

> Many of them, indeed, go back to the recognition scenes and the catastrophes based on misunderstanding in Greek tragedy [*Oedipus the King* is the most famous example]. They are again extensively used in Renaissance drama; the most famous scene of the passing of the poisoned cup device is, after all, in *Hamlet*, and Shakespeare and his contemporaries repeatedly used fatal documents and falsely compromising objects, as well as identifying talismans and birthmarks (Williams 1968: 27).

The argument that these conventions are out of date is a false one. "Life was no more like that then than now; the critical case cannot be made in those terms" (27). The 19th-century intrigue drama is an inferior genre not because of its conventions, but because these conventions had become the *raison d'être* for its existence. It was nothing but convention. One post-structuralist critic of the drama, Elin Diamond, explains, "Realism disgusted Brecht . . . because it dissimulates its conventions."[9] But all conventions are "simulated" because none is real. The illusionist conventions of the realistic theatre, like conventions of all other theatrical modes, mean nothing in themselves.

Realism and Reform

In arguing that the realistic theatre was ideologically conservative, Brecht deliberately and, I would argue, disingenuously ignored the reformist nature of much of realist drama to strengthen the originality and importance of his own epic theatre. After all, social and political reform, including class consciousness, was from the beginning an important component of realistic drama, which had its roots in the revolutionary impulses of 18th-century domestic tragedy.[1] It is a commonplace that Ibsen earned the status of the

8. (London: Chatto, 1968) 14.
9. *Unmasking Mimesis* (London: Routledge, 1997) 50.
1. The German cultural critic, Arnold Hauser, in his monumental *The Social History of Art* (1952), gives us in his essay "The Origins of Domestic Drama" what Eric Bentley has called "the key, or at least a key, to modern drama as a whole" (*The Theory of the Modern Stage*, ed. Bentley [London: Penguin, 1968] 401). Tracing the 19th-century realist drama to its roots in the bourgeois tragedy of Lessing and Lillo, Hauser describes how

founder of modern drama by doing two things simultaneously: inventing the realistic prose play and making the theatre a forum for debate. The origins of modern European drama, according to an authoritative study of modernism, lie in "the compulsive attention the eighties and the nineties gave to the problematic and the contemporary" and "the restless exploration of the resources of prose as a dramatic medium. Both things point unwaveringly back to Ibsen."[2] Eric Bentley summarizes succinctly: "Calling attention to the rotten bottoms of ships, the subjection of Victorian wives, the ravages of syphilis, and the corruption of municipal politics and journalism, [Ibsen] made himself the father of the reformist drama of the end of the century" (*The Playwright as Thinker*, 92).

But Ibsen's true reformism was not as a writer of "problem plays" but as a writer in the revolutionary spirit of Brandes and his "Inaugural Lecture" of 1871 (in the series that later became the great *Main Currents in 19th-Century Literature*). In this seminal essay, Brandes did not call merely for literature to put "problems" to debate, but to do so in the context of nothing less than a general revolution in thinking. "For it is not so much our laws that need changing," he wrote, "as it is our whole conception of society. The younger generation must plough it up and replant it before a new literature can bloom and flourish."[3] Brandes' notion had an enormous influence on Ibsen's work; when he first read it, he wrote to Brandes, it even kept him from sleeping. Beginning with *Samfundets Støtter*, and until the end of the century, "Ibsenism" was synonymous with modernism because Ibsen was the most fearless debunker of the idols of Western culture during a time when, as Peter Gay has it, "ideas, relationships unchanged since time out of mind were vulnerable to attack and open to amendment."[4] Ibsen wrote to Brandes: "What will be the outcome of this mortal combat between two epochs, I do not know. But anything is better than the existing state of affairs."[5] This is a very Brechtian declaration.

Although Brecht's anti-Ibsen stance was influenced by Marx and Engels' dismissal of Ibsen as petit-bourgeois, his anti-realist stance

these 18th-century precursors of realism and naturalism challenged the reigning social and political hierarchies; nothing describes the new moral outlook better, Hauser remarks, than Lessing's words in *Nathan the Wise*: "Kein Mensch muss müssen" (*The Theory of the Modern Stage*, 424). One of the stock figures of the bourgeois drama is "the rebel against bourgeois morality and way of life, the scoffer at bourgeois conventions and philistine narrowmindedness," who embodies the "gradual alienation of modern literature from the middle classes . . . [from the 18th-century drama] through the 'Storm and Stress' right up to Ibsen and Shaw" (419).

2. Malcolm Bradbury and James McFarlane, eds., *Modernism: A Guide to European Literature, 1890–1930* (1976; London: Penguin, 1971) 400.
3. Trans. Evert Sprinchorn, *The Theory of the Modern Stage*, ed. Eric Bentley (London: Penguin, 1968) 425, 430.
4. *The Education of the Senses* (New York: Oxford University Press, 1984) 172.
5. *Henrik Ibsen: Letters and Speeches*, trans. Evert Sprinchorn (New York: Hill, 1964) 123.

puts him in direct confrontation with the Marxist critical tradition, which considered realism to be the most propitious form for revolutionary art. In "The Sociology of Modern Drama," George Lukács writes that modern drama "is the first [drama] to grow out of conscious class confrontation; the first with the set intention of expressing the patterns of thought and emotion, as well as the relations with other classes."[6] That Lukács continued to champion realism throughout his life as the most vital form of reformist literature led to Brecht's famous chastisement of him as wanting to bring literature back into the 19th century.[7] In denouncing realism, Brecht was breaking both with Lukács, whose Marxism is closely allied to the tradition of liberal humanism, and, relatedly, with Trotsky, who in his *Literature and Revolution* argued that Socialist art must be "realist," but in no narrow sense, for realism is inherently neither revolutionary nor reactionary. Lenin had a decided preference for realist art, above all Tolstoy, whose reactionary Christianity, Lenin argued, did not prevent him from achieving great art. And Engels, in the two famous letters he wrote to novelists who had asked him for comment on their works, notes that overt political argument is unnecessary in fiction because realist writing itself will necessarily dramatize the forces of social life. This conception was later developed into the theory of "objective partisanship," i.e., an author is already partisan if he portrays reality objectively. The most famous example of this in Marxist literary criticism is Marx and Engels' championing of Balzac, who, they argued, understood the significance of his own historical period despite his Catholic and legitimist beliefs. Engels commented that Balzac's "satire is never keener, his irony never more bitter, than when he sets in motion the very men and women with whom he sympathizes most deeply— the nobles" (Eagleton, *Marxism and Literary Criticism* 48). Engels was, in fact, deconstructing Balzac *avant la lettre*.

Anti-realist to the end, Brecht continued to insist that realism was a dead form. Even in the compromise of the "Short Organum," in which he changed course to announce that the end of drama was pleasure as well as instruction and to embrace Aristotle's dictum that the plot was the soul of drama, Brecht continued to castigate "the stage's inaccurate representations of our social life, including those classed as so-called Naturalism" (Brecht 179). To read plays like *Gengangere* and *Die Weber*, one needs the "deadweight of old habits . . . although there the social structure, in the shape of a 'setting,' presents itself as more open to question" (190).

6. "The Sociology of Modern Drama," trans. Lee Baxandall, *The Theory of the Modern Stage*, 430.
7. See H. Arvon, *Marxist Aesthetics* (Ithaca: Cornell University Press, 1970), for a thorough account of this controversy.

In taking this stance against realism and against Ibsen, Brecht was implying that realism should and could have been other than what it was, which, ironically enough, is an impossibility in Marxist theory because history, including the laws of artistic production, proceeds in inevitable, determined stages. There can be no such thing as "before its time."

Post-Realism in Ibsen's Realism: The Character Figure

I want to suggest that Ibsen's realism is less realistic or illusionist than is commonly believed. I am not speaking here of the "poet in the theatre" or the much commented on symbols—the ghosts, the white horses, the vine-leaves, the wild duck—all that has been thoroughly examined. After the seminal work of John Northam, we have now come far enough in Ibsen studies to accept as a given that Ibsen's realism is highly and powerfully symbolic. I want briefly to discuss two post-realist aspects of the prose plays, first, the character-figure, and second, the fourth-wall bourgeois parlor.

In the late plays, a certain kind of character appears who is both the psychologically developed character we associate with realism, sometimes termed "three-dimensional," and at the same time a figure in the symbolic design of the action. The first of these is Ulrik Brendel of *Rosmersholm*, who is barely credible as a character. Appearing out of nowhere in act one, speaking in sententious abstractions, with tag-lines from various languages, suddenly reappearing in act four to give Rebecca riddling instructions for her self-immolation, Brendel's function is to provide a parody of Rosmer's ambitions; his absurd, failed mission is a burlesque of Rosmer's own, and his instructions to Rebecca are a parody of what Rosmer will shortly ask her to do. Brendel's characterhood is both grotesque and realistic. In the play that followed *Rosmersholm*, *Fruen fra Havet*, the protagonist, while more psychologically developed than Brendel, is also a figure, a mermaid in Ibsen's version of the old folk motif of the mermaid's struggle to acclimatize to land. Ibsen insists throughout that Ellida's strangeness makes her essentially different from the other characters: she is "so erratic—so elusive . . . Ellida's one of the sea people."[8] The Stranger, even more than Ellida, also belongs to two planes of reality; he is both a figure in a parable, the Merman to whom the Mermaid is drawn, and an ordinary sailor walking into the back garden wearing a Scotch cap. Ibsen is merging two sorts of representation at the same time. In *Bygmester Solness*, only one character exists on two planes of reality, the victorious antagonist Hilde Wangel, the weird

8. *The Complete Major Prose Plays*, trans. Rolf Fjelde (New York: New American Library, 1978) 656.

girl with macabre tastes of *Fruen fra Havet* who now arrives "grown up" knocking on Solness' door. Solness, for all his mad theories of "helpers and servers," never exits the realistic plane, whereas the demanding, compassionate, and, it has been argued, neurotic and even psychotic Hilde is both person and summoned spirit, not in the sense of a "symbol" of Solness' longings, but as the embodiment of them. She is both a realistic character and an expressionist figure, and the power of the play, which comes close to being Hilde's power, comes in her partaking of these two kinds of representation.

The character-figure who is most figure and least character in Ibsen's prose plays is the Rottejumfruen, the traveling free-lance exterminator of *Lille Eyolf*. She is far less Frøken Varg (Miss Wolf) than a fantastic creature of folklore; "maybe it's really true that she's a werewolf at night," says Eyolf (873). The Rat Wife, a "Munch-like amalgam of woman as goddess and crone," in Errol Durbach's apt phrase,[9] exists in her fantastic form on the same plane as the witches in *Macbeth*. Like Shakespeare's female creatures, the Rat Wife inhabits "an anarchic, richly ambiguous zone both in and out of official society" and, again like the weird sisters, she represents that which "must be exiled and repressed as dangerous."[1] As the witches taunt and tease Macbeth in word play, the Rat Wife taunts and teases the Allmers: "If your graces notice anything here that nibbles and gnaws—and creeps and crawls—then you just call on me" (878). The Rat Wife as exterminator of the "little beauties" (877)—the "rats and all the little rat babies" (875)—embodies Rita's wish to get rid of the "little heartbreaker" (877), Eyolf, the crippled obstacle to the gratification of her desire. The Rat Wife makes a mockery of Rita's smiling welcome to the hated sister-in-law, rival Asta, the second "Eyolf" Rita would be rid of as well, and of Allmers' self-sacrificing plans for his son, whom he has neglected in favor of his magnum opus. The Rat Wife is the paid underling, servicing the masters to get rid of what they prefer not to face. She anticipates the Samsa family's maid in Kafka's expressionist novella *Die Verwandlung*, who "takes care of" the insect-son and gleefully removes his annoying and dessicated corpse while the family goes shopping.

In *Når Vi Døde Vågner*, Irene, like Hilde in Solness, is both a real woman who has returned to claim what is hers, and a figure, a summoned spirit, who arrives from the realm of the dead to invade the living dead. And much of the power of the play, like that of *Solness*, depends on the woman's dual modes of representation. And fi-

---

9. *'Ibsen the Romantic': Analogues of Paradise in the Later Plays* (Athens: The University of Georgia Press, 1982) 110–11.

1. These phrases are Terry Eagleton's in his brilliant little book *William Shakespeare* (London: Blackwell, 1986) 2–3.

nally, in the character of the Diakonissen, Irene's *Doppelgänger*, we have a pure figure, the presence both of Irene's dead self and her destiny, gliding through the play like a sinister shadow, re-appearing at the last to pronounce the benediction over Irene and Rubek: "Pax Vobiscum."

The character-figures in these late plays infuse the realistic mode with a kind of quickening. They are uncanny presences, disturbing and undermining the world they inhabit, reminding us that surface reality is not what it seems to be. They are also immensely theatrical, heightening the action and widening the illusionist stage.

The Fourth-Wall Bourgeois Parlor

I want to focus on what is normally regarded as the quintessence of Ibsen's illusionist realism, the bourgeois parlor, equipped with what Bert States has rightly termed the "most concrete manifestation of theatrical realism": actual furniture (*Great Reckonings* 25). Henry James, appalled and fascinated, describes Ibsen's famous setting: "the hideous carpet and wall-paper and curtains (one may answer for them), the conspicuous stove, the lonely centre-table, the 'lamps with green shades' ".[2] Let us consider a brief catalog of some of Ibsen's important parlors: the Helmers' comfortable, "tastefully" furnished living room, with its armchairs and sofa, rocking chair, engravings, etagère with china figures, bookcase "with richly bound books" (125) [146–47]; Mrs. Alving's "large garden room," with its sofa and sewing table, round table and chairs, books, magazines (203); Werle's "richly and comfortably furnished study," with bookcases and upholstered furniture, issuing into a "large, fashionable room, brightly lit by lamps and candlelabra" (393); the "spacious, old-fashioned and comfortable" living room at Rosmersholm (497), with its sofa and table, armchairs, plant stand, ancestral portraits; the Tesmans' "large, attractively furnished drawing room," with its sofas and armchairs, tables, tabourets, footstool, piano, etagères with terra cotta and majolica ornaments, thick carpets, heavy curtains, vases filled with flowers (695) [209]; the Solness' living room, "attractively furnished," with a sofa, table and chairs, bookcase, console table; the Allmers' "attractive, elegantly decorated garden room, filled with furniture, flowers and plants" (867) [290], sofa, throw rugs, table with armchairs; Mrs. Borkman's living room, "furnished in old-fashioned, faded elegance" (943), with its horsehair sofa, armchair, heavy curtains; Borkman's quarters, the former grand salon with its walls "covered with old tapestries, depicting hunting scenes, shepherds and shepherdesses, in faded, mottled

2. "On the Occasion of *Hedda Gabler*," *Ibsen: The Critical Heritage*, ed. Michael Egan (London: Routledge, 1972) 239.

colors," a large, carved oak desk, sofa, piano, chairs and table in "austere Empire style" (967).

Brecht would have it that the function of these "settings" is to show something of "the social structure" of the world being dramatized ("The Short Organum," Brecht 190). But the parlors' function lies far less in what they show us than in what they don't. For Ibsen's subject is what is unshowable, indeed, unmentionable in the bourgeois parlor: the disavowed, the disallowed, the rebellious, the anarchic. What is all this proliferation of objects and furniture for—if not to exclude difference, deny contingency, fill up void? Messiness, dysfunction, unhappiness, or indeed happiness—neither the problems, nor the misery, nor, perhaps most of all, the joy of life—none of this is allowed in the bourgeois parlor, which only has room, so to speak, for its furniture. Nora's crime, Captain Alving's and Løvborg's dissipations, Oswald's sickness, Beata's and Rebecca's passions, Elida's longings, Hedda's desperation, Solness' despair, Rita's fury, Borkman's megalomania cannot be accommodated here.

In opposition to the bourgeois parlor, a synecdoche for the bourgeois home, Ibsen places alternate, offstage geographies. The first challenge to the hegemony of the bourgeois home is a very large place—the "America" of Samfundets Støtter, where people are "not so respectable and moral," but more "natural" (53) than those in the Bernick parlor, where schoolmaster Rørlund lectures to ladies as they sew on "white things" to distribute to the "morally disabled" people who don't belong there (38); the second alternate place, that of Et Dukkehjem, is even larger—the wide world itself, to which the newly born woman exits out of the confinement of her diminuitive, toy habitat. In Gengangere, it is Paris, of course, where the sun shines and the joy of life reigns, that is the alternate place to Norway, but there is also an alternate place nearer home, "Captain Alving's home," Engstrand's clever nomenclature for his sailors' entertainment center, the sort of place Captain Alving preferred to his parlor at Rosenvold. In Rosmersholm, the alternate to the old, stately manor of the "foremost family of the country" (509), whose menfolk have served Norway for generations, is wild, unsettled Finnmark, where the current mistress of Rosmersholm broke the supreme taboo, incest; in Fruen fra Havet, it is the great sea, for which Ellida feels an "overpowering homesickness" that draws her away from Wangel's home. In Hedda Gabler, it is Hedda's inner room, which the defiant protagonist makes into a place of outrageous defiance against the denizens of the larger parlor; in Bygmester Solness, it is Hilde's immaterial "castles in the air," which answer Solness' longing to abandon dreary domestic architecture, including that of his own home, and his sickly wife, indeed, his desire to abandon the world altogether. In *John Gabriel Borkman*, the alternate place is underneath the earth, in the mines, where Borkman, free of the constraints of bourgeois morality, can unleash the power of the gleaming gold. It is when Borkman moves out of the confines of the Rentheim villa into the "expansive landscape, with fjords and high, distant mountain ranges towering one after another" (1036) that he can locate his underground kingdom. And finally, in *Når Vi Døde Vågner*, the "villa" and the "great big town house" (1066) are left behind forever for the forests and the "wild mountain, gashed with fissures," where "sheer precipices" plunge and "snow-mantled peaks rise" (1081), the place where one discovers that down below, one has never lived.

Under the force of the alternate worlds, all the tastefully furnished living rooms and attractive, elegantly decorated garden rooms with their actual furniture vanish like so much bric-a-brac. All that is solid melts into air. Ibsen's realism, Brecht to the contrary, is not "period," for the period is what is in motion. The bourgeois parlor is less a setting than a sign—of a vanishing order under siege from alternate worlds. Ibsen's missing fourth wall does not frame a hegemonic, static world that was and is "already always there," but rather a highly charged world that is constantly straining against itself, not in a state of being, but of becoming. Ibsen's realism posits sign against sign—Ibsen, our post-modernist brother.

Henrik Ibsen: A Chronology

1828	Henrik Ibsen is born March 20 in Skien, Norway. Leo Tolstoy born in Russia.
1830–31	G. W. F. Hegel delivers his lectures on "The Philosophy of History."
1832–33	The Ibsen family moves to a more expensive property in Skien.
1835	Financial problems compel the Ibsen family to move to a smaller house outside town.
1836	Ibsen's father, Knud Ibsen, is declared bankrupt. Ibsen leaves home, at age fourteen, to earn his living as an apothecary's apprentice in the seacoast town of Grimstad. Except for one brief visit, he never returns to his hometown.
1846	Ibsen fathers an illegitimate son with a housemaid ten years his senior. Despite his own straitened circumstances, Ibsen contributes to the support of this son for the next fifteen years.
1848	Ibsen writes verses in support of revolutions throughout Europe. The revolutions are ultimately suppressed. Karl Marx and Friedrich Engels publish *Manifesto of the Communist Party*.
1848–49	Ibsen writes his first play, the verse tragedy *Catiline*.
1849	Charles Dickens's *David Copperfield* published. August Strindberg born in Sweden.
1850	*Catiline* published. Ibsen leaves Grimstad for Christiania (Oslo) to cram for university entrance examinations. Fails in Greek and mathematics. Writes a second play, *The Warriors Barrow* (*Kjaempehøjen*), which will be the first play by Ibsen to be staged.
1851	Various journalistic activities. Edits a student paper. In November, Ibsen is engaged as playwright-in-residence at the new Norwegian Theater in Bergen. Herman Melville's *Moby-Dick* published.
1852	Studies the theater in Copenhagen and Dresden. Alexandre Dumas publishes his play *La Dame aux Camélias*.

1853   Ibsen's *Midsummer Eve* (*Sancthansnatten*) is performed
              at Bergen's Norwegian Theater January 2. Herbert
              Spencer coins the term *evolution*.

1854   *The Warrior's Barrow* performed at Bergen January 2 in
              a revised form.

1855   *Lady Inger of Østraat* performed at Bergen January 2.
              This is Ibsen's first attempt at a full-length tragedy.
              Ibsen reads a paper on Shakespeare and his influence
              on Scandinavian literature to a Bergen literary society.
              Walt Whitman publishes *Leaves of Grass*. Danish
              philosopher Søren Kierkegaard dies.

1856   *The Feast at Solhoug* successfully performed at Bergen,
              January 2. Performed at the Christiania Theater,
              March 13. Ibsen meets Susannah Thoresen, his future
              wife.

1857   *Olaf Liliekrans* performed at Bergen January 2. Ibsen
              takes up new post of artistic director of the Norwegian
              Theater in Christiania. Charles Baudelaire publishes
              Les Fleurs du mal.

1858   Ibsen marries Susannah Thoresen on June 18. *The
              Vikings at Helgeland* performed at the Norwegian The-
              ater in Christiania. Gustave Flaubert's *Madame Bovary*
              published. Apparition of the Virgin Mary reputed to
              have appeared to Bernadette Soubirous at Lourdes,
              France.

1859   Ibsen writes the poems "On the Heights" (Paa Vid-
              derne) and "In the Picture Gallery." Ibsen's son Sigurd
              is born December 23. Charles Darwin publishes *The
              Origin of Species*, which is quickly translated into the
              Scandinavian languages and is avidly discussed.
              Charles Dickens's *A Tale of Two Cities* published. John
              Stuart Mill writes *Essay on Liberty*.

1860   Unification of Italy by Garibaldi and Victor Emmanuel.
              Anton Chekhov born in Russia.

1861   Ibsen writes "Terje Vigen," his most popular poem. Out-
              break of American Civil War.

1862   The Norwegian Theater in Christiania goes bankrupt,
              and Ibsen loses his job. He will have no regular income
              for the next two years. He travels extensively in Norway
              on a university grant, gathering folk songs and legends.
              Ibsen writes *Love's Comedy*, his first major play, pub-
              lished in a supplement to a journal. The play is harshly
              attacked as "an offence against human decency" and
              becomes the object of much critical abuse. The Chris-
              tiania Theater dares not produce the play.

1863   Becomes literary adviser to the Christiania Theater and publishes *The Pretenders*, a major historical tragedy. Ibsen receives another university grant to travel and collect folk songs. He is also awarded a travel grant by the government. Édouard Manet's exhibition at Martinet Gallery, Paris. Edvard Much, Norwegian painter, born. Constantin Stanislavsky, Russian theatrical producer, born. Schleswig incorporated into Denmark.

1864   *The Pretenders* performed at the Christiania Theater. Ibsen begins his long self-exile from Norway, which will continue until 1891. He settles in Rome with his family. Dano-Prussian war. Denmark cedes Schleswig, Holstein, and Lavenberg to Austria and Prussia. Ibsen comments bitterly on this event.

1866   *Brand* is published and creates a sensation in Scandinavia. Fyodor Dostoevsky's *Crime and Punishment* published.

1867   *Peer Gynt* published, less favorably received than *Brand*, but later to become Ibsen's most popular work. Karl Marx's *Das Kapital* published. Émile Zola writes *Thérèse Raquin*, the first naturalist novel. Garibaldi defeated in his third march on Rome and taken prisoner by French and papal forces. Ibsen, in Rome, comments favorably on Garibaldi's followers, comparing their heroism with the pusillanimity of the Scandinavians over the Dano-Prussian war.

1868   After staying in Florence, Bologna, and Venice, Ibsen settles briefly in Munich and permanently in Dresden.

1869   *The League of Youth* published. Ibsen's mother dies. Ibsen travels widely in Egypt, Nubia, and the Red Sea area and is invited by the Khedive of Egypt as Norwegian representative at the opening of the Suez Canal. Ibsen also begins his lifelong intellectual friendship with the young Danish critic, Georg Brandes, although Brandes had written unfavorably about *Brand*. Brandes would later come under attack from the arbiters of Danish cultural life for his own onslaughts on religious orthodoxy. He, too, would go into exile to become one of the major modern literary critics. Wyoming, U.S.A., establishes women's suffrage. John Stuart Mill writes *On the Subjection of Women*.

1870   The Franco-Prussian War begins July 19. France declares war on Prussia and is defeated. Napoleon III capitulates at Sedan. Revolt in Paris and proclamation of the Third Republic. Heinrich Schliemann begins excavations at Troy. Charles Dickens dies.

1871   Election of socialists to the Paris Commune, upon which troops led by General Thiers, on behalf of the French bourgeoisie, massacred over 25,000 Communards—men, women, and children—in one week. Thousands more were later executed or deported to tropical penal colonies. Ibsen comments on these events to Georg Brandes. Georg Brandes's inaugural lecture of the series that will become his monumental six-volume *Main Currents of Nineteenth Century Literature*. Ibsen declared that the inaugural lecture "disturbed my sleep. No more dangerous book could fall into the hands of a pregnant writer. It is one of those works which place a yawning gap between yesterday and today" (Letter, April 4, 1872).

1872   Works on *Emperor and Galilean*, ten-act "world historic drama" describing the collision between the Christians and Emperor Julian's attempt to restore Hellenic paganism to the Roman Empire. Friedrich Nietzsche's *The Birth of Tragedy*.

1873   *Emperor and Galilean* published. Ibsen insisted to the end of his life that this was his major work. Serves as a judge for the International Art Exhibition in Vienna.

1874   First Impressionist exhibition in Paris. On a visit to Norway, Ibsen is honored by students with a torchlight procession.

1875   Leo Tolstoy's *Anna Karenina* published. Hans Christian Andersen dies.

1876   First performance of *Peer Gynt*, with Edvard Grieg's music, at the Christiania Theater. *The Vikings at Helgeland* performed to acclaim at the Court Theater in Munich; King Ludwig, Richard Wagner's patron, congratulates Ibsen. The Duke of Saxe-Meiningen produces *The Pretenders*. Ibsen is a guest of the duke, who decorates him with the Ernestine Order. The opening of Bayreuth for the first complete performance of Richard Wagner's cycle, *Der Ring des Nibelungen*; Ibsen is living in Munich, close to Bayreuth.

1877   *Pillars of Society* published, inaugurating Ibsen's twelve-play Realist Cycle. The play is performed at the Royal Theater in Copenhagen. Russo-Turkish War breaks out. Ibsen's father dies.

1879   Publishes *A Doll House*. Premiere at the Royal Theater in Copenhagen.

1880   Fyodor Dostoevsky's *The Brothers Karamazov* and Émile Zola's *Nana* published. Rodin sculpts *The Thinker*.

1881   Publication of *Ghosts* creates a major scandal. In Scandinavia bookshops return copies of the play to the publisher. It does not sell out for ten years. No established theater in Scandinavia would perform the play. Fyodor Dostoevsky dies.

1882   *An Enemy of the People* published. World premiere of *Ghosts*, in Norwegian, takes place in Chicago before an audience of Scandinavian immigrants. This production toured other American cities, including Minneapolis. No notices of the production are recorded. James Joyce born.

1883   First European performance of *Ghosts*, by August Lindberg, who was to direct and act in other Ibsen plays. Friedrich Nietzsche writes *Also Sprach Zarathustra*. Bjørnstjerne Bjørnson's *Beyond Human Endurance* published.

1884   *The Wild Duck* published. Herbert Spencer writes *Man versus the State*.

1885   First performance of *The Wild Duck* in Bergen and Stockholm. June 14 speech by Ibsen to the workingmen of Trondhjem.

1886   *Rosmersholm* published. The Duke of Saxe-Meiningen invites Ibsen to a performance of *Ghosts* by the Meiningen Players. In London a reading of *A Doll House* is given by the daughter of Karl Marx, Eleanor Marx-Aveling, with William Morris's daughter, May, and Bernard Shaw. Nietzsche writes *Beyond Good and Evil*.

1887   *Rosmersholm* staged by the Bergen Theater. August Strindberg writes *The Father*. André Antoine establishes the Théâtre Libre, the first of the minority theaters to take up the cause of Ibsen's dramas.

1888   *The Lady from the Sea* published.

1889   Otto Brahm and Paul Schlenter open the Freie Bühne (Independent Theater) in Berlin in order to evade censorship and perform *Ghosts*. In Paris, the opening of the Eiffel Tower.

1890   *Hedda Gabler* published. Antoine produces *Ghosts* at the Théâtre Libre. The production is called "a thunderbolt in French theatrical history" by Lugné Poë, who will later stage Ibsen's plays in a nonrealistic style. Oscar Wilde's *The Picture of Dorian Gray* published.

1891   J. T. Grein opens the Independent Theater in London, on March 13, with *Ghosts*, giving rise to the greatest controversy in British theatrical history. The Lord Chamberlain bans the play from public performance.

The ban will stay in effect until 1914. Premiere of *Hedda Gabler* at the Munich Residenz-Theater. Ibsen is feted in Vienna and Budapest. In July, Ibsen leaves Munich to settle in Norway. Bernard Shaw's *The Quintessence of Ibsenism* published.

1892   *The Master Builder* published. Ibsen's son, Sigurd, marries Bjørnstjerne Bjørnson's daughter, Bergliot. Oscar Wilde's *Lady Windermere's Fan* published. Wilde's *Salomé* is banned from public performance. Bernard Shaw's first play, *Widowers' Houses*, performed by the Independent Theater. Gerhart Hauptmann's *The Weavers* published. Maurice Maeterlinck publishes *Pelléas et Mélisande*.

1894   *Little Eyolf* published. Shaw's *Arms and the Man* published.

1896   *John Gabriel Borkman* published.

1897   Edmond Rostand's *Cyrano de Bergerac* published.

1899   *When We Dead Awaken* published in London, then in Scandinavia and Germany. Also published that year are H. G. Wells' *When the Sleeper Wakes*, Leo Tolstoy's *Resurrection*, and Oscar Wilde's *The Importance of Being Earnest*. National Theater opened in Christiania. Ibsen attends the opening.

1900   Sigmund Freud publishes *The Interpretation of Dreams*. Friedrich Nietzsche dies. James Joyce writes an enthusiastic review of *When We Dead Awaken*.

1901   Ibsen suffers his first stroke and has to stop writing. Queen Victoria dies, succeeded by her son, Edward VII. Strindberg writes *The Dance of Death*.

1902   Anton Chekhov publishes *The Three Sisters*. Émile Zola dies.

1903   Ibsen suffers a second stroke. He is now unable to write or walk. Shaw writes *Man and Superman*.

1904   Chekhov writes *The Cherry Orchard*. Chekhov dies. Sigmund Freud publishes *The Psychopathology of Everyday Life*.

1905   Norwegian Parliament votes to separate from Sweden.

1906   Prince Charles of Denmark elected King Haakon VII of Norway. Ibsen dies on May 23 and is buried as a national and international figure. Samuel Beckett born. Richard Mansfield stars in first professional production in the United States of *Peer Gynt*.

Selected Bibliography

EDITIONS

Ibsen, Henrik. *Samledeverker, hundreårsutgave*. Ed. Halvdan Koht, Francis Bull, and Didrik Arup Seip. 21 vols. Oslo: Gyldendal, 1928–57.
Breve fra Henrik Ibsen. Ed. Halvdan Koht and Julius Elias. 2 vols. København og Kristiania: Gyldendalske Boghandel Nordisk Forlag, 1904.

TRANSLATIONS IN ENGLISH

The Collected Works of Henrik Ibsen. Ed. William Archer. 13 vols. New York: Scribner, 1917.
The Complete Major Prose Plays. Trans. and ed. Rolf Fjelde. New York: Farrar, Strauss and Giroux, 1978.
Ibsen: Letters and Speeches. Ed. Evert Sprinchorn. New York: Hill and Wang, 1964.
Ibsen, Volume I: Four Major Plays. Trans. Rick Davis and Brian Johnston. Lyme, N.H.: Smith and Kraus, 1995.
Ibsen, Volume II: Four Plays. Trans. Brian Johnston. Lyme, N.H.: Smith and Kraus, 1996.
Ibsen, Volume III: Four Plays. Trans. Brian Johnston with Rick Davis. Lyme, N.H.: Smith and Kraus, 1998.
The Oxford Ibsen. Tranl and ed. James W. McFarlane, et al. 8 vols. New York: Oxford UP, 1960–77. (Includes drafts, working notes, commentaries, correspondence, etc.)

BIOGRAPHIES

Ibsen, Bergliot. *The Three Ibsens, Memories of Henrik Ibsen, Suzannah Ibsen and Sigurd Ibsen*. Trans. Gerik Schjelderup. New York: American-Scandinavian Foundation, 1952; London: Hutchinson, 1951.
Jæger, Henrik. *Henrik Ibsen: A Critical Biography*. 2nd ed. Trans. William Morton Payne. Chicago: A. C. McClurg, 1901.
Jæger, Henrik. *The Life of Ibsen*. Trans. Clara Bell, with the verse done into English by Edmund Gosse. London, 1890.
Koht, Halvdan. *Life of Ibsen*. New edition. Trans. and ed. Einar Haugen and A. E. Santiello. New York: Benjamin Blom, 1971.
Meyer, Michael. *Ibsen, A Biography*. Garden City, N.Y.: Doubleday, 1971.

CRITICISM

• indicates works excerpted in this Norton Critical Edition.

Abrams, M. H. *Natural Supernaturalism: Tradition and Revolution in Nineteenth Century Literature*. New York: W. W. Norton, 1971.
Andreas-Salomé, Lou. *Ibsen's Heroines*. Ed. and trans. with an introduction by Siegfried Mandel. Redding, Conn.: Black Swan Books, 1985.
Antoine, André. *Mes Souvenirs sur le Théâ-Libre*. Paris, 1921. *Memories of the Théâtre-Libre*. Trans. Marvin A. Carlson. Ed. H. D. Albright. Coral Gables, Fla.: U of Miami Press, 1964.
Archer, William. *The Old Drama and the New*. London: Heinemann, 1923.

——. *Playmaking*. New York: Dover Publications, 1960.

Arup, Jens. "Narrative and Symbol in Ibsen." In *Discussions of Henrik Ibsen*. Ed. James Walter McFarlane. Boston: D. C. Heath, 1962.

• Auden, W. H. *"The Dyer's Hand" and other Essays*. New York: Random House, 1962.

Bentley, Eric. *In Search of Theater*. New York: Alfred A. Knopf, 1953.

——. *The Life of the Drama*. New York: Athaneum, 1967.

Beyer, Edvard. *Ibsen: The Man and His Work*. Trans. Marie Wells. New York: Taplinger, 1980.

Boyesen, Hjalmar Hjorth. *A Commentary on the Works of Henrik Ibsen*. London, 1894.

——. *The Playwright as Thinker*. New York: Harcourt, Brace, 1946. Rev. ed. San Diego, Calif.: Harcourt, Brace, Jovanovich, 1987.

Bradbrook, M. C. *Ibsen the Norwegian: A Revaluation*. London: Chatto and Windus, 1966.

Brandes, Georg. *Henrik Ibsen, A Critical Study*. 1899. Reprint, New York: Benjamin Blom, 1964.

——. *Main Currents in Nineteenth Century Literature*. 5 vols. New York: Boni and Liveright, 1923.

Brustein, Robert. *The Theatre of Revolt*. Boston: Little Brown, 1964.

Burke, Kenneth. *A Grammar of Motives*. Berkeley: U of California P, 1945.

Carlson, Marvin. *Theories of Drama*. Ithaca, N.Y.: Cornell UP, 1984.

Clurman, Harold. *Ibsen*. New York: Macmillan, 1977.

Downs, Brian W. *Ibsen, the Intellectual Background*. New York: Cambridge UP, 1948.

Durbach, Errol. *"Ibsen the Romantic": Analogues of Paradise in the Later Plays*. Athens: U of Georgia P, 1982.

——, ed. *Ibsen and the Theatre: Essays in Celebration of the 150th Anniversary of Henrik Ibsen's Birth*. London: Macmillan, 1980.

Edwards, Herbert. "Henry James and Ibsen." In *American Literature* 54, no. 2 (May 1952): 208–23.

Egan, Michael. *Ibsen, The Critical Heritage*. Boston: Routledge and Kegan Paul, 1972.

Ewbank, Inga-Stina. "Ibsen's Dramatic Language." In *Contemporary Approaches to Ibsen*. Oslo: Universitetsforlaget, 1966.

Fjelde, Rolf, ed. *Ibsen, A Collection of Critical Essays*. Englewood Cliffs, N.J.: Prentice Hall, 1965.

Flores, Angel, ed. *Ibsen: Four Essays*. New York: Critics Group, 1937. (Essays by Engels, Mehring, Plekhanov, Lunacharsky.)

• Forster, E. M. *Abinger Harvest*. London: Edward Arnold, 1940.

• Goldman, Michael. *Ibsen: The Dramaturgy of Fear*. New York: Columbia UP, 1999.

Goldmann, Emma. *The Social Significance of Modern Drama*. New York: Applause Books, 1987.

Gray, Ronald. *Ibsen: A Dissenting View*. London: Cambridge UP, 1977.

Grene, David. *Reality and the Heroic Pattern: Last Plays of Ibsen, Shakespeare, and Sophocles*. Chicago: U of Chicago P, 1967.

• Haugen, Einar. *Ibsen's Drama: Author to Audience*. Minneapolis: U of Minnesota P, 1979.

Heiberg, Hans. *Ibsen: A Portrait of the Artist*. Trans. John Tate. Coral Gables: U of Miami P, 1969.

Holtan, Orley I. *Mythic Patterns in Ibsen's Last Plays*. Minneapolis: U of Minnesota P, 1970.

Hornby, Richard. *Patterns in Ibsen's Middle Plays*. Lewisburg, Penn.: Bucknell UP, 1981.

Hurt, James. *Catiline's Dream: An Essay on Ibsen's Plays*. Urbana: U of Illinois P, 1972.

• James, Henry. *The Scenic Art*. New Brunswick, N.J.: Rutgers UP, 1948.

Johnston, Brian. *The Ibsen Cycle*. Rev. ed. University Park: Pennsylvania State UP, 1992.

——. *Text and Supertext in Ibsen's Drama*. University Park: Pennsylvania State UP, 1989.

——. *To the Third Empire: Ibsen's Early Drama*. Minneapolis: U of Minnesota P, 1980.

Jorgenson, Theodore. *Henrik Ibsen: A Study in Art and Personality*. Northfield, Minn.: St. Olaf College P, 1945.

Joyce, James. "Ibsen's New Drama." *Fortnightly Review* 73 (1900).

• Kenner, Hugh. "Joyce and Ibsen's Naturalism." In *Critical Essays on Henrik Ibsen*. Ed. Charles R. Lyons. Boston: G. K. Hall, 1987. 53–66.

• Knight, G. Wilson. *Henrik Ibsen*. Edinburgh: Oliver and Boyd; New York: Grove, 1962.

Kott, Jan. *The Theater of Essence*. Evanston, Ill.: Northwestern UP, 1984.

• Lee, Jennette. *The Ibsen Secret: A Key to the Prose Dramas of Henrik Ibsen*. 1907. Reprint, Honolulu, Hawaii: UP of the Pacific, 2001.

Lyons, Charles R. *Henrik Ibsen: The Divided Consciousness*. Carbondale: Southern Illinois P, 1972.

Lyons, Charles R., ed. *Critical Essays on Henrik Ibsen*. Boston: G. K. Hall, 1987.

McFarlane, James W. *Ibsen and the Temper of Norwegian Literature*. New York: Oxford UP, 1960.

——. *Ibsen and Meaning*. Norwich, U.K.: Norvik P, 1989.

————, ed. *The Cambridge Companion to Ibsen*. Cambridge: Cambridge UP, 1994.

————, ed. *Henrik Ibsen: A Critical Anthology*. Harmondsworth: Penguin Books, 1970.

Marinelli, Donald. *Henrik Ibsen's Ghosts: A Dramaturgical Sourcebook*. Pittsburgh: Carnegie Mellon UP, 1997.

Marker, Frederick J., and Christopher Innes, eds. *Modernism in European Drama: Ibsen, Strindberg, Pirandello, Beckett*. Toronto: U of Toronto P, 1998.

Northam, John. *Ibsen: A Critical Study*. Cambridge: Cambridge UP, 1973.

————. *Ibsen's Dramatic Method: A Study of the Prose Dramas*. London: Faber and Faber, 1953.

Pearce, John C. "Hegelian Ideas in Three Tragedies by Ibsen." *Scandinavian Studies* 34 (1962): 245–57.

Postlewait, Thomas, ed. *William Archer on Ibsen*. Westport, Conn.: Greenwood P, 1984.

• Rilke, Rainer Maria. *Selected Letters, 1902–1926*. London: Quartet Books, 1988.

• ————. *The Selected Poetry of Rainer Maria Rilke*. Ed. and trans. Stephen Mitchell. New

Robins, Elizabeth. *Ibsen and the Actress*. 1928. Reprint, New York: Haskell House, 1973.

Rosen, Charles, and Henri Zerner. *Romanticism and Realism: The Mythology of Nineteenth-Century Art*. New York: W. W. Norton, 1984.

• Saari, Sandra. "Female Become Human: Nora Transformed." In *Contemporary Approaches to Ibsen*. Vol. 6. Ed. Bjørn Hemmer and Vigdis Ystad. Oslo: Norwegian UP, 1988. 41–55.

Selenik, Laurence, ed. *National Theatres in Northern and Eastern Europe*. Cambridge: Cambridge UP, 1991.

• Shaw, George Bernard. *Our Theatres in the Nineties*. 3 vols. London: Constable, 1932.

————. *The Quintessence of Ibsenism: Now Completed to the Death of Ibsen*. 1913. Reprint, New York: Hill and Wang, 1957.

• Steiner, George. *The Death of Tragedy*. New York: Oxford UP, 1980.

• Templeton, Joan. "Genre, Representation, and the Politics of Dramatic Form: Ibsen's Realism." In *Proceedings: IX International Ibsen Conference, Bergen 5–10 June 2000*. Ed. Pål Bjørby and Asbjørn Aarseth. Bergen: Alvheim and Eide, 2001. 49–64.

Tennant, P. F. D. *Ibsen's Dramatic Technique*. London: Cambridge UP, 1948.

Theoharis, Theoharis C. *Ibsen's Drama: Right Action and Tragic Joy*. New York: St. Martin's P, 1996.

Valency, Maurice. *The Flower and the Castle: Introduction to Modern Drama*. New York: Macmillan, 1963.

Weigand, Hermann J. *The Modern Ibsen: A Reconsideration*. 1925. Reprint, New York: 1960.

Williams, Raymond. *Drama: From Ibsen to Eliot*. London: Chatto and Windus, 1961.

Zucker, A. E. *Ibsen, the Master Builder*. London, 1929.

IBSEN ON THE INTERNET

The World Wide Web is an ideal medium to share new ideas, collaborate and engage in discussion. This is especially true for the study of Ibsen, whose scholars and enthusiasts are spread across the world. At present there are a number of Web sites that offer a wealth of resources and information. Though many sites only touch on Ibsen briefly they often include contemporary observations, showing how Ibsen's work transcends age and cultural bounds. There are several sites which are solely devoted to the study of Ibsen, and there is an opportunity for even more growth.

Some of the more noteworthy sites include:

www.ibsen.net
The official Web site of the National Ibsen Committee of Norway. Available in multiple languages, ibsen.net is a content-rich multidisciplinary portal to the world of Ibsen.

www.hf.uio.no/ibsensenteret/
Web site of the University of Oslo's Ibsen Centre. The Ibsen Centre aims to strengthen and coordinate Ibsen research in Norway and abroad. Its Web site shows the results and direction of its ambitious research projects.

www.ibsensociety.liu.edu
Official Web site of the Ibsen Society of America. The ISA is an open organization set up to foster a deeper understanding of Ibsen's work through lectures, readings, performances, conferences, and publications.

**www.museumsnett.no/alias/HJEMMESIDE/munchmuseet/munch_ibsen/english/
eindex1.htm**
The Munch Museum's Internet exhibition *From Stage to Canvas.* A presentation of Edvard
Munch's drawings, paintings, and stagesets of Ibsen's plays, illustrating thematic connections between the plays and Munch's work.

www.ibsenvoyages.com
The official Web site of Brian Johnston. Ibsen Voyages contains critical analyses of the in-
dividual plays and offers an account of the Realist Cycle (from *Pillars of Society* to *When
We Dead Awaken*) as a single dramatic structure.

For a more complete and up-to-date list of interesting Web sites dedicated to the study of
Ibsen, visit Ibsen Voyages' link page located at: www.ibsenvoyages.com/links